Java Challenges

100+ Proven Tasks that Will Prepare You for Anything

Michael Inden

Apress®

Java Challenges: 100+ Proven Tasks that Will Prepare You for Anything

Michael Inden
Zurich, Switzerland

ISBN-13 (pbk): 978-1-4842-7394-4   ISBN-13 (electronic): 978-1-4842-7395-1
https://doi.org/10.1007/978-1-4842-7395-1

Managing Director, Apress Media LLC: Welmoed Spahr
Acquisitions Editor: Steve Anglin
Development Editor: Matthew Moodie
Coordinating Editor: Mark Powers
Copyeditor: Mary Behr

Cover designed by eStudioCalamar

Cover image by Michael Inden

Distributed to the book trade worldwide by Apress Media, LLC, 1 New York Plaza, New York, NY 10004, U.S.A. Phone 1-800-SPRINGER, fax (201) 348-4505, e-mail orders-ny@springer-sbm.com, or visit www.springeronline.com. Apress Media, LLC is a California LLC and the sole member (owner) is Springer Science + Business Media Finance Inc (SSBM Finance Inc). SSBM Finance Inc is a **Delaware** corporation.

For information on translations, please e-mail booktranslations@springernature.com; for reprint, paperback, or audio rights, please e-mail bookpermissions@springernature.com.

Apress titles may be purchased in bulk for academic, corporate, or promotional use. eBook versions and licenses are also available for most titles. For more information, reference our Print and eBook Bulk Sales web page at www.apress.com/bulk-sales.

Any source code or other supplementary material referenced by the author in this book is available to readers on GitHub via the book's product page, located at www.apress.com/9781484273944. For more detailed information, please visit www.apress.com/source-code.

Printed on acid-free paper

Table of Contents

TABLE OF CONTENTS

About the Author

Michael Inden is an Oracle-certified Java developer with over 20 years of professional experience designing complex software systems for international companies. He has worked in various roles such as SW developer, SW architect, consultant, team leader, CTO, head of academy, and trainer. Currently, he is working as a freelancer.

His special interests are creating high-quality applications with ergonomic GUIs, developing and solving programming puzzles, and coaching. He likes to pass on his knowledge and has led various courses and talks, both internally and externally, as well as at conferences such as JAX/W-JAX, JAX London, and Oracle Code One.

He is also an author of technical books. His German books, *Der Weg zum Java-Profi*, *Java Challenge*, and *Python Challenge*, and others, are all published by dpunkt.verlag.

About the Technical Reviewer

Jeff Friesen is a freelance teacher and software developer with an emphasis on Java. In addition to authoring *Java I/O, NIO and NIO.2* (Apress), and *Java Threads and the Concurrency Utilities* (Apress), Jeff has written numerous articles on Java and other technologies (such as Android) for JavaWorld (`JavaWorld.com`), informIT (`InformIT.com`), `Java.net`, SitePoint (`SitePoint.com`), and other web sites. Jeff can be contacted via his web site at `JavaJeff.ca` or via his LinkedIn profile (`www.linkedin.com/in/javajeff`).

Preface

First of all, thank you for choosing this book. Here you will find a wide range of practice exercises on a broad mix of topics that will improve your knowledge in an entertaining way. It can also help prepare you for job interviews and will certainly help improve your problem-solving skills.

Practice Makes Perfect

We all know the saying "practice makes perfect." Day-to-day life involves a lot of practice, and serious training and exercising is undertaken for specific disciplines— such as sports, music, or art. But the serious case or competition is rare. Oddly enough, this is often significantly different for us software developers. We actually spend almost all of our time implementing and tend to rarely spend time practicing and learning, sometimes not at all. Why is that?

Presumably, this is due to the time pressure that usually dominates and the fact that there is not much suitable exercise material available—even if there are textbooks on algorithms as well as books on coding. But, often they are either too theoretical or too source code-focused and contain too little explanation of the solutions. This book aims to change that.

Why This Book?

So how did I come to tackle this book project (originally written in German)? There are several reasons. On the one hand, I was asked again and again by mail or personally by participants in my workshops, if there was a tutorial book as a supplement to my book *Der Weg zum Java-Profi* [Ind20a]. That's how the first idea came about.

What really triggered the whole thing was that a recruiter from Google approached me quite by surprise with a job request. As preparation for the upcoming job interviews and to refresh my knowledge, I started to search for suitable reading material and developed some exercises for myself. In the process, I discovered the great, but also partly quite challenging, book *Cracking the coding interview* by Gayle Laakmann McDowell [McD16], which inspired me further.

A few months after publishing the German version of this book, I translated and finished this English version due to the support of the people at Apress.

Who Is This Book Aimed At?

This book is explicitly not intended for programming novices but is aimed for readers who already have basic or even good knowledge of Java and want to deepen it with exercises. By solving small programming exercises, you will expand your knowledge about Java, algorithms, and sound OO design in an entertaining way.

The following target groups are addresses in particular:

- **High school and college students**: First of all, this book is meant for pupils with an interest in computer science as well as for students of computer science, who already know Java quite well as a language and now want to deepen their knowledge by doing exercises.

- **Teachers and lecturers**: Of course, teachers and lecturers may also benefit from this book and its large number of exercises of varying difficulty, either as a stimulus for their own teaching or as a template for exercises or exams.

- **Hobby programmers and young professionals**: In addition, the book is aimed at dedicated hobby programmers but also young professionals who like to program with Java and want to develop themselves further. Furthermore, solving the tasks helps prepare for potential questions in job interviews.

- **Experienced software developers and architects**: Finally, the book is intended for experienced software developers and architects who want to supplement or refresh their knowledge to be able to assist their junior colleagues more effectively and are looking for some inspiration and fresh ideas to do so. In addition, various exercises can also be used in job interviews, with the convenience of having the sample solutions directly at hand for comparison. But also for the old hands there should be one or two aha experiences in finding solutions and for algorithms and data structures.

In general, I use the masculine form to keep the text easier to read. Of course, I include all female readers, and I am pleased about them.

What Does This Book Teach?

A wide-spread mix of exercises on different topics is provided by this book. Some- times some puzzles may not be of direct practical importance, but indirectly, because they improve your creativity and your ability to find solutions.

In addition to exercises and documented solutions, each topic covered in the book starts with a short introduction. By this, even those readers who may not have built up a lot of know-how in specific areas benefit. You can then use the introductions to get to grips with the exercises up to about the medium level of difficulty. In each subject area, there are always a few easier exercises to get you started. With a little practice, you should also be able to tackle more difficult problems. Occasionally there are some really challenging problems, which experts can try their hand at, or those who want to become experts.

Practical Tips and Advice

This book is packed with various practical tips. They include interesting background information. Besides, pitfalls are pointed out.

HINT: TIP FROM THE TRENCHES

In boxes formatted like this you will find some tips worth knowing and additional hints to the actual text later in the book.

Difficulty Level at a Glance

A well-balanced, appealing exercise book needs a large number of tasks of different levels of difficulty, which offer you as a reader the possibility to improve your knowledge step by step. Although I assume a good understanding of Java, the solutions never require deep knowledge of a specific topic or special language features.

To keep the level of difficulty obvious and straightforward, I have used the star categorization known from other areas, whose meaning in this context is explained in more detail in the following table.

Stars (Meaning)	Estimation	Duration
★☆☆☆☆ (very easy)	These tasks should be solvable in a few minutes with simple Java knowledge.	< 15 min
★★☆☆☆ (easy)	The tasks require a little bit of thinking, but then they are directly solvable.	< 30 min
★★★☆☆ (medium)	The tasks are well manageable, but need some thinking, a little bit of strategy, and sometimes a look at different constraints.	~ 30 – 45 min
★★★★☆ (difficult)	Proven problem-solving strategies, good knowledge of data structures, and Java knowledge are required for the solution.	~ 45 – 90 min
★★★★★ (very difficult)	The tasks are really tricky and difficult to solve. These are candidates only after the other tasks do not cause you difficulties anymore.	> 60 min

These are only estimations from my side and rather rough classifications. Please keep in mind that the difficulty perceived by each individual also depends very much on their background and level of knowledge. I have seen colleagues have a hard time with tasks that I considered quite easy. But I also know the opposite: While others seem to solve a task easily, you are in despair yourself because the penny just won't drop. Sometimes a break with a coffee or a short walk helps.

Do not get demotivated! Everyone struggles with some task at some time or another.

NOTE: POSSIBLE ALTERNATIVES TO THE SAMPLE SOLUTIONS

Please note that for problems there are almost always some variants, which might be even more catchy for you. Therefore I will present interesting alternatives to the (sample) solution from time to time as food for thought.

Structure of This Book

Now that you have a rough picture of the contents of this book, I will introduce the topics of each chapter briefly. As already indicated, the exercises are grouped thematically. In this context, the six chapters after the introduction build the basis, and the subsequent three chapters deal with more advanced topics.

- **Chapter 1—Introduction:** This chapter describes the basic structure of the following chapters with the *Introduction*, *Tasks*, and *Solutions* sections. Additionally, it provides a framework for the unit tests that are often used to prove that the solutions are working. Finally, I give some hints for trying out the examples and solutions.

- **Chapter 2—Mathematical Problems** The second chapter is dedicated to mathematical operations as well as tasks about prime numbers and the Roman numeral system. Besides, I present a few ideas for number games.

- **Chapter 3—Recursion:** Recursion is an important basic building block concerning the definition of algorithms. This chapter provides a short introduction, and the various exercises should help you understand recursion.

- **Chapter 4—Strings:** Strings are known to be sequences of characters that offer a variety of methods. A solid understanding is of elementary importance since almost no program can operate without strings. Therefore you will get to know the processing of strings through various exercises.

- **Chapter 5—Arrays:** Along with strings, arrays are also basic building blocks in programming. Arrays are—as you know—simple data structures for storing values, but without too much convenience. In practice, it is therefore often recommended to use the data structures of the Collections framework. Chapter 7 discusses them in detail.

- **Chapter 6—Date Processing:** With Java 8 the JDK was extended by some functionality for date processing. Every Java developer should be familiar with this. The exercises will give you a good introduction to the topic, so that the transfer into practice should be easy.

- **Chapter 7—Basic Data Structures: Lists, Sets, and Maps:** In the Collections framework, lists, sets, and maps as key-value mappings are implemented by various container classes. For everyday programming, a solid understanding and fluent use are of great advantage, which is offered by this chapter's exercises.

- **Chapter 8—Recursion Advanced:** Chapter 3 covered the topic of recursion in an introductory manner. This chapter reveals some more advanced aspects of recursion. You start with the optimization technique called memoization. After that, you look at backtracking as a problem-solving strategy, which is based on trial and error. Just trying out possible solutions may help in keeping various algorithms fairly understandable and elegant.

- **Chapter 9—Binary Trees:** Tree structures play an important role in computer science theory as well as in practice. In many application contexts, trees can be used profitably. This is the case, for example, for the administration of a file system, the representation of a project with subprojects, and a task or a book with chapters, subchapters, and sections.

- **Chapter 10—Searching and Sorting:** Searching and sorting are two elementary topics in computer science in the area of algorithms and data structures. The Collections framework implements both of them and thus takes a lot of effort away from you. However, it is also worth taking a look behind the scenes, for example, at different sorting methods and their specific strengths and weaknesses.

- **Chapter 11—Conclusion and Supplementary Literature:** In this chapter, I summarize the book and give an outlook on supplementary literature. To expand your skills, besides the training in programming, it is recommended to study other books. A selection of helpful titles closes the main part of this book.

- **Appendix A—Quick Start for JShell:** In this book, various examples are explored directly on the console. The main reason is that Java supports since version 9 an interactive command line application named JShell as REPL (Read Evaluate Print Loop), which I will briefly introduce in this appendix.

- **Appendix B—Short Introduction to JUnit 5:** Unit tests have proven to be useful for testing smaller program modules. With JUnit 5, this is especially useful when formulating test cases for multiple input combinations. Many of the solutions created in this book are tested with unit tests. So, this appendix provides an introduction to the topic.

- **Appendix C—Quick Start for O-notation:** In this book, I sometimes estimate the running time behavior and classify the complexity of algorithms. This appendix presents essentials about it.

Conventions and Executable Programs
Character Sets Used

Throughout the text, the following conventions are applied concerning font: Normal text appears in the present font. Important text passages are marked *italic* or ***italic and bold***. Sourcecode listings are written in the font `Courier` to clarify that this text is a part of a Java program. Also, classes, methods, constants, and passing parameters are displayed in this font.

Abbreviations Used

In the book, I use the abbreviations shown in the table below. Other abbreviations are listed in parentheses in the running text after their first definition and subsequently used as needed.

Abbreviation	Meaning
API	Application Programming Interface
ASCII	American Standard Code for Information Interchange
(G)UI	(Graphical) User Interface
IDE	Integrated Development Environment
JDK	Java Development Kit
JLS	Java Language Specification
JRE	Java Runtime Environment
JSR	Java Specification Request
JVM	Java Virtual Machine

Java Version(s) Used

Almost all examples were developed and tested with Java 11 LTS (Long Term Support) and Java 16—some even with the latest Java 17 LTS. The newer Java versions bring some helpful syntax changes and API extensions, which are, however, not of importance for the solution of the tasks—except for some special tasks (e. g. to `switch` which requires more modern Java).

Classes Used from the JDK

If classes from the JDK are referenced for the first time in the text, their fully qualified name including the package structure is printed. For the class `String` this would be, for instance, `java.lang.String`. This facilitates a search in the JDK. In the subsequent text, this specification is omitted for better readability, and only the class name is stated. Besides, to save space in the listings, `import` statements are rarely shown in the listings.

Method calls described in the text usually contain the type information of the parameters passed, such as `substring(int, int)`. If the arguments are not critical in a context, their specification is omitted for better readability, or they are replaced by the abbreviation ....

Downloads, Source Code, and Executables

The source code of the examples is available on the website

https://github.com/Apress/java-challenges

for download and is integrated into an Eclipse project. Because this is a hands-on book, some of the programs are executable using Gradle tasks. Their name is given in small capitals, such as LOCALEEXAMPLE—alternatively, of course, execution in the IDE or as a unit test is possible.

Alternatively, you can execute and test many code snippets in the JShell. To guarantee this, already developed methods are sometimes shown again in a suitable place.

Rework after project import   After the initial import, the external libraries' dependencies need to be updated in the Eclipse project with the command `gradle cleanEclipse eclipse`.

Acknowledgements (English Book)

First of all, I am very grateful to all the people mentioned below in the acknowledgments section of the German version of this book. Making this English version was more than a dream and realizing it was possible due to the effort of Steve Anglin of Apress. He organized a lot to finalize the contract and all the nitty-gritty details around publishing rights. Additionally, Mark Powers was a great help in offering information on the process and many other things around finalizing the manuscript. Guys, my warm thanks go to you.

Acknowledgements (German Book)

Writing a technical book is a beautiful but laborious and tedious task. You can hardly do it on your own. Therefore I would like to thank all those who have directly or indirectly contributed to the book's emergence. In particular, I benefited from a strong team of proofreaders during the preparation of the manuscript. It is helpful to learn from different perspectives and experiences.

First of all, I would like to thank Michael Kulla, who is well known as a trainer for Java SE and Java EE, for his multiple, thorough reviews of many chapters, the well-founded comments, and the great effort. I am also very grateful to Prof. Dr. Dominik Gruntz for a multitude of suggestions for improvements. Besides, I received one or the other helpful suggestions from Jean-Claude Brantschen, Prof. Dr. Carsten Kern, and Christian Heitzmann. Once again, Ralph Willenborg has also read this book very carefully and found several typing errors. Many thanks for that!

Thanks also go to the team at dpunkt.verlag (Dr. Michael Barabas, Martin Wohlrab, Anja Weimer, and Birgit Bäuerlein) for the great cooperation. Also, I would like to thank Torsten Horn for his sound professional help and Ursula Zimpfer for her eagle eyes in copy editing.

Finally, I would like to thank my wife, Lilija, for her understanding and support, especially for several nudges to get on the bike and go for a ride instead of just working on the book.

Suggestions and Criticism

Although great care has been taken and the text was proofread several times, misunderstandable formulations or even errors can unfortunately not be completely excluded. If any of these should be noticeable to you, please do not hesitate to let me know. I am also happy to receive suggestions or ideas for improvement. Please contact me by mail at:

michael_inden@hotmail.com

Zurich, August 2021
Michael Inden

CHAPTER 1

Introduction

Welcome to this workbook! Before you get started, I want to outline briefly what you can expect when reading it.

This book covers a broad range of practice-relevant topics, represented by exercises of different levels of difficulty. The exercises are (for the most part) independent of each other and can be solved in any order, depending on your mood or interest.

Besides the exercises, you will find the corresponding answers, including a short description of the algorithm used for the solution and the actual source code, which is commented on at essential points.

1.1 Structure of the Chapters

Each chapter shares the same structure, so you will quickly find your way around.

1.1.1 Introduction

Each chapter begins with an introduction to the topic to enable readers who may not yet be familiar with the subject area or get you in the right mood for the tasks that follow.

1.1.2 Exercises

The introduction is succeeded by a bunch of exercises and the following structure:

- **Task**: Each exercise first will have an assignment. In this, the desired functionality to be realized is described in a few sentences. Often a method signature is already included as a clue to the solution.

- **Examples**: Supplementary examples are almost always given for clarification with inputs and expected results. For some quite simple tasks, which mainly serve to get to know an API, examples are sometimes omitted.

1

© Michael Inden 2022
M. Inden, *Java Challenges*, https://doi.org/10.1007/978-1-4842-7395-1_1

Often, different value assignments of input parameter(s), as well as the expected result, are shown in a table, for example, as follows:

Input A1	Input B	Result
[1, 2, 4, 7, 8]	[2, 3, 7, 9]	[2, 7]

The following notation styles apply to the specifications:

- "AB" represents textual specifications

- true/false stands for Boolean values

- 123 represent numeric values

- [value1, value2, ...] represents collections like sets or lists, but also arrays

- { key1 : value1, key2 : value2, ... } describes maps

1.1.3 Solutions

The solutions follow the structure described below.

- **Task definition and examples**: First, I repeat the task description again so that you don't have to constantly flip back and forth between tasks and solutions. Instead the description of solutions is self-contained.

- **Algorithm**: A description of the chosen algorithm follows. For didactics, I consciously sometimes present an erroneous way or a not-that-optimal solution to then uncover pitfalls and iteratively come to an improvement. In fact, one or the other brute force solution is sometimes even usable but offers optimization potentials. Exemplarily, I will present then and when corresponding, sometimes astonishingly simple, but often very effective improvements.

- **Examination**: Some of the tasks are quite easy or only serve to get used for syntax or API functionality. For this, it often seems sufficient to execute a few calls directly in the JShell. That's why I don't use unit tests for this. The same applies if a graphical presentation of a solution is better (e.g., displaying a Sudoku board) and if the corresponding unit test would probably be more difficult to understand.

However, the more complicated the algorithms become, the more sources of errors exist, for instance, wrong index values, an accidental or omitted negation, or an overlooked edge case. For this reason, it makes sense to check functionality with the help of unit tests—in this book, for reasons of space, this is only accomplished for important inputs. The companion resources then contain over 90 unit tests with roughly 750 test cases—a pretty good start. Nevertheless, in practice, the network of unit tests and test cases should be even more voluminous if possible.

1.2 Basic Structure of the Eclipse Project

The included Eclipse project closely follows the structure of the book. It offers a separate package for each relevant chapter (those with exercises) such as ch02_math or ch08_recursion_advanced. I deviate exceptionally from the naming convention for packages because I consider the underscores, in this case, a readable notation.

Some of the source code snippets from the respective introductions are located in a subpackage named intro. The provided (sample) solutions are collected in their own subpackages named solutions and the classes are named according to the task as follows: Ex<No>_<taskdescription>.java.

The entire project follows the Maven standard directory structure. Thus, you will find the sources under src/main/java and the tests under src/test/java.

Sources – src/main/java: Figure 1-1 shows an outline for Chapter 2:

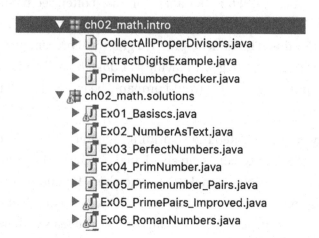

Figure 1-1. An outline for Chapter 2

Test classes – src/test/java: Figure 1-2 shows some associated tests:

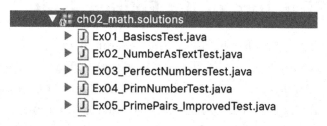

Figure 1-2. Associated tests

Utility classes   All the handy utility methods developed in the respective chapters are included in the provided Eclipse project in the form of utility classes. For example, in Chapter 5 you implement some useful methods, including swap() and find() (all described in section 5.1.1). They are then combined into a class named ArrayUtils, which is stored in its own subpackage, util—for the chapter on arrays this is in the subpackage ch05_arrays.util. The same applies to other chapters and topics.

1.3 Basic Framework for Unit Tests

To not exceed the scope of the book, the illustrated unit tests only show the test methods but not the test class and the imports. To provide you with a basic framework into which you can insert the test methods and as a starting point for your own experiments, a typical test class is as follows:

```java
import static org.junit.jupiter.api.Assertions.assertEquals;
import static org.junit.jupiter.api.Assertions.assertTrue;

import java.time.LocalDate;

import org.junit.jupiter.api.Test;
import org.junit.jupiter.params.ParameterizedTest;
import org.junit.jupiter.params.provider.CsvSource;
import org.junit.jupiter.params.provider.ValueSource;
import org.junit.jupiter.params.provider.MethodSource;

public class SomeUnitTests
{
    @ParameterizedTest(name = "value at pos {index} ==> {0} should be perfect")
    @ValueSource(ints = { 6, 28, 496, 8128 } )
    void testIsPerfectNumberSimple(int value)
    {
        assertTrue(Ex03_PerfectNumbers.isPerfectNumberSimple(value));
    }

    @ParameterizedTest
    @CsvSource({"2017-01-01, 2018-01-01, 53", "2019-01-01, 2019-02-07, 5"})
    void testAllSundaysBetween(LocalDate start, LocalDate end, int expected)
    {
        var result = Ex09_CountSundaysExample.allSundaysBetween(start, end);

        assertEquals(expected, result.count());
    }

    @ParameterizedTest(name = "calcPrimes({0}) = {1}")
    @MethodSource("argumentProvider")
    void testCalcPrimesBelow(int n, List<Integer> expected)
```

```
{
    List<Integer> result = Ex04_PrimNumber.calcPrimesBelow(n);

    assertEquals(expected, result);
}

// if parameters are lists of values => Stream<Arguments>
static Stream<Arguments> argumentProvider()
{
    return Stream.of(Arguments.of(2, List.of(2)),
                     Arguments.of(3, List.of(2, 3)),
                     Arguments.of(10, List.of(2, 3, 5, 7)),
                     Arguments.of(15, List.of(2, 3, 5, 7, 11, 13)));
}
}
```

In addition to the imports and the extensively used parameterized tests that allow testing multiple combinations of values in a simple way, the provision of test inputs via @CsvSource and @MethodSource in combination with a Stream<Arguments> is shown here. For details, please see Appendix B.

1.4 Note on Programming Style

From time to time, during discussions, the question came up if certain things should be made more compact. This is why I would like to mention in advance something about the programming style used in this book.

1.4.1 Thoughts on Source Code Compactness

The most important things for me when programming and especially for the implementations in this book are easy comprehensibility and a clear structure. This leads to simplified maintainability and changeability. Therefore, the shown implementations are programmed as understandable as possible and avoid, for example, the ?-operator for more complex expressions. Of course it is acceptable for simple things like (x < y) ? x : y. Following these rules, not every construct is maximally compact, but as a result, it is understandable. I like to favor this aspect in this book. In practice, it is often easier to live with this than with bad maintainability but more compact programming.

1.4.2 Example 1

Let's have a look at a small example for clarification. First, examine the readable, easy-to-understand variant for inverting the contents of a string, which also shows very nicely the two important elements of recursive termination and descent:

```java
static String reverseString(final String input)
{
    // recursive termination
    if (input.length() <= 1)
        return input;

    final char firstChar = input.charAt(0);
    final String remaining = input.substring(1);

    // recursive descent
    return reverseString(remaining) + firstChar;
}
```

The following much more compact variant does not offer these advantages:

```java
static String reverseStringShort(final String input)
{
    return input.length() <= 1 ? input :
            reverseStringShort(input.substring(1)) + input.charAt(0);
}
```

Think briefly about which of the two methods you feel safe making a subsequent change to. And what if you want to add unit tests? How do you find suitable value sets and checks?

Keep in mind that the upper variant is automatically converted by the JVM to something similar to the lower variant either already during the compilation (conversion into bytecode) or later during the execution and optimization—just with the advantage of better readability during programming.

1.4.3 Example 2

Let me bring in another example to illustrate my point. Concerning the following method, countSubstrings(), which counts the number of occurrences of one string in another and for the two inputs "helloha" and "ha," it returns the result 2.

First, you implement this reasonably straightforwardly as follows:

```java
static int countSubstrings(final String input, final String valueToFind)
{
    // recursive termination
    if (input.length() < valueToFind.length())
        return 0;

    int count;
    String remaining;

    // does the text start with the search string?
    if (input.startsWith(valueToFind))
    {
        // match: continue the search for the found
        // term after the occurrence
        remaining = input.substring(valueToFind.length());
        count = 1;
    }
    else
    {
        // remove first character and search again
        remaining = input.substring(1);
        count = 0;
    }

    // recursive descent
    return countSubstrings(remaining, valueToFind) + count;
}
```

Let's take a look at how you could try to realize this compactly:

```
static int countSubstringsShort(final String input,
                                final String valueToFind)
{
    return input.length() < valueToFind.length() ? 0 :
           (input.startsWith(valueToFind) ? 1 : 0) +
           countSubstringsShort(input.substring(1), valueToFind);
}
```

Would you prefer to change this method or the one shown before?

By the way, the lower one still contains a subtle functional deviation! For the inputs of "XXXX" and "XX" the first variant always *consumes* the characters and finds two occurrences. The lower, however, moves only one character at a time and thus finds three occurrences.

Further, integrating the previously realized functionality of advancing by the whole search string into the second variant will lead to more obscure source code. On the other hand, you can easily shift by only one character by simply adjusting the upper `substring(valueToFind.length())` call and then even pull this functionality out of the `if`.

1.4.4 Thoughts on `final` and `var`

Normally I prefer to mark immutable variables as `final`. In this book, I omit this from time to time, especially in unit tests, to keep them as short as possible. Another reason is that the JShell does not support the `final` keyword everywhere, but fortunately in the important places, namely for parameters and local variables.

Local Variable Type Inference (`var`)   Since Java 10, the so-called Local Variable Type Inference is available, better known as `var`. This allows omitting the explicit type specification on the left side of a variable definition provided that the compiler can determine the concrete type for a local variable from the definition on the right side of the assignment:

```
var name = "Peter";                // var => String
var chars = name.toCharArray();    // var => char[]

var mike = new Person("Mike", 47); // var => Person
var hash = mike.hashCode();        // var => int
```

Especially in the context of generic containers the Local Variable Type Inference shows its advantages:

```
// var => ArrayList<String>
var names = new ArrayList<String>();
names.add("Tim");
names.add("Tom");
names.add("Jerry");

// var => Map<String, Long>
var personAgeMapping = Map.of("Tim", 47L, "Tom", 12L,
                              "Michael", 47L, "Max", 25L);
```

Convention: var if more readable   As long as comprehensibility does not suffer, I will use var in appropriate places to keep the source code shorter and clearer. However, if a type specification is of greater importance for comprehension, I prefer the concrete type and avoid var—but the boundaries are fuzzy.

Convention: final or var   One more note: While it is possible to combine final and var I don't favor this approach stylistically and use either one or the other.

1.4.5 Notes on Method Visibility

You may wonder why the presented methods are often not marked as public. Methods presented in this book are normally shown without visibility modifiers, because they are mainly called in the package and context where they are defined. Thus they can be invoked without problems for the accompanying unit tests and may be used for experiments in the JShell. Sometimes I extract some auxiliary methods from the implementation of the exercises for better structure and readability. These are then usually private, to express this circumstance accordingly.

In fact, I combine the most important utility methods in dedicated utility classes where for other packages they are of course public and static to allow access.

1.4.6 Block Comments in Listings

Please note that there are various block comments in listings, which serve as orientation and for better understanding. It's advisable to use such comments with caution and preferable to extract individual source code sections to methods in practice. For the book's examples, these comments serve, however, as reference points because the introduced or presented facts are probably still new and unfamiliar to you as a reader.

```java
// create process
final String command = "sleep 60s";
final String commandWin = "cmd timeout 60";
final Process sleeper = Runtime.getRuntime().exec(command);
//    ...

// Process => ProcessHandle
final ProcessHandle sleeperHandle = ProcessHandle.of(sleeper.pid()).
                                orElseThrow(IllegalStateException::new);
//    ...
```

1.4.7 Thoughts on Formatting

The formatting used in the listings deviates slightly from the coding conventions of Oracle.[1] I align myself to those of Scott Ambler,[2] who suggests in particular (opening) parentheses on separate lines each. For this purpose, I created a special format called Michaelis_CodeFormat. This is integrated into the project download.

1.5 Trying Out the Examples and Solutions

Basically, I prefer to use as comprehensible constructs as possible instead of fancy syntax or API features of special Java versions. If not explicitly mentioned in the text, the examples and solutions should work even with the previous LTS version Java 11. However, in a few exceptions, I use syntax extensions from modern and current Java 17 LTS because they make daily programming life much easier and more pleasant.

---

[1] www.oracle.com/java/technologies/javase/codeconventions-contents.html
[2] www.ambysoft.com/essays/javaCodingStandards.html

Special features for Java 17 previews   Due to the short interval of six months between the Java releases, some features are presented to the developer community as previews. If you are to use them, certain parameters have to be set in the IDEs and build tools. This is necessary both with compiling and for execution, approximately as in the following example:

```
java --enable-preview -cp build/libs/Java17Examples.jar \
    java17.SwitchExamples
```

I provide more details about Java 14 in my book *Java – die Neuerungen in Version 9 bis 14: Modularisierung, Syntax- und API-Erweiterungen* [Ind20b].

Trying with JShell, Eclipse, and as a JUnit test   In many cases, you can copy the source code snippets shown into JShell and execute them. Alternatively, you will find all relevant sources in the Eclipse project that comes with the book. The programs can be started by a main() method or—if available— by corresponding unit tests.

1.6 Let's Go: Discovering Java Challenge

So, now it is enough of the preface, and you are probably already excited about the first challenges through the exercises. Therefore, I hope you will enjoy this book and gain some new insights while solving the exercises and experimenting with the algorithms.

If you need a refresher on JUnit, JShell, or O-notation, you might want to take a look at the appendices first.

PART I

Fundamentals

CHAPTER 2

Mathematical Problems

In this chapter, you will learn some basics about a few mathematical operations, including prime numbers and the Roman numeral system. Additionally, I present a couple of ideas for number games. With this knowledge, you should be well prepared for a multitude of exercises.

2.1 Introduction

2.1.1 Short Introduction to Division and Modulo

Besides multiplication and division, the modulo operation (%) is also used quite frequently. It is intended to determine the remainder of a division. Let's illustrate this as follows for integers where division remainders fall under the table:

$$(\mathbf{5} * 7 + 3) / 7 = 38 / 7 = 5$$
$$(5 * 7 + \mathbf{3}) \% 7 = 38 \% 7 = 3$$

Even with these few operations, you can solve various tasks. Please recall the following things for actions on (integer) numbers:

- n % 10—Determines the remainder of a division by 10 and thus the last digit.

- n / 10—Obviously divides by the value 10 and thus allows to truncate the last digit.

© Michael Inden 2022
M. Inden, *Java Challenges*, https://doi.org/10.1007/978-1-4842-7395-1_2

Extraction of digits   To extract the digits of a number, you combine modulo and division as long as the remaining value is greater than 0:

```
void extractDigits(final int startValue)
{
    int remainingValue = startValue;
    while (remainingValue > 0)
    {
        final int digit = remainingValue % 10;
        System.out.print(digit + " ");

        remainingValue = remainingValue / 10;
    }
    System.out.println();
}
```

Call this method once to understand its way of working—please note that the digits are output in reverse order:

```
jshell> extractDigits(123)
3 2 1
```

Determining the number of digits   Instead of extracting individual digits, you can also use a repeated division to determine the number of digits in a decimal number by simply dividing by 10 until there is no remainder left:

```
int countDigits(final int number)
{
    int count = 0;

    int remainingValue = number;
    while (remainingValue > 0)
    {
        remainingValue = remainingValue / 10;
        count++;
    }

    return count;
}
```

2.1.2 Short Introduction to Divider

In the following, you examine how to determine all real divisors of a number (i.e., those without the number itself). The algorithm is quite simple: You go through all numbers up to half of the value (all higher values cannot be integer divisors because 2 is already a divisor) and check if they divide the given number without a remainder. If this is the case, then this number is a divisor and included in a result list. You implement the whole thing as follows:

```java
List<Integer> findProperDivisors(final int value)
{
    final List<Integer> divisors = new ArrayList<>();

    for (int i = 1; i <= value / 2; i++)
    {
        if (value % i == 0)
        {
            divisors.add(i);
        }
    }

    return divisors;
}
```

Call this method once to understand its operation and confirm it to be working fine based on the output conforming to expectations:

```
jshell> findProperDivisors(6)
$2 ==> [1, 2, 3]

jshell> findProperDivisors(24)
$3 ==> [1, 2, 3, 4, 6, 8, 12]

jshell> findProperDivisors(7)
$4 ==> [1]
```

2.1.3 Short Introduction to Prime Numbers

A prime number is a natural number that is greater than 1 and is exclusively divisible by itself and by 1. There are two quite understandable algorithms for checking whether a given number is prime or for calculating primes up to a given maximum value.

17

Brute force algorithm for prime numbers   Whether a number is a prime number or not can be determined as follows: You look for the number to be checked starting from 2 up to at most half of the number, whether the current number is a divisor of the original number.[1] In that case, it's not a prime. Otherwise, it needs to be checked further. In Java, this can be written as follows:

```java
boolean isPrime(final int potentiallyPrime)
{
    // check for all relevant numbers if they represent a divisor
    for (int i = 2; i <= potentiallyPrime / 2; i++)
    {
        if (potentiallyPrime % i == 0)
            return false;
    }
    return true;
}
```

To try it out, run the method in a loop and determine all prime numbers up to the value 25. The program outputs demonstrate that the functionality works correctly.

```
jshell> var primes = new ArrayList<>()
primes ==> []

jshell> for (int i = 2; i < 25; i++)
   ...> {
   ...>        if (isPrime(i))
   ...>            primes.add(i);
   ...> }

jshell> System.out.println("Primes < 25: " + primes)
Primes < 25: [2, 3, 5, 7, 11, 13, 17, 19, 23]
```

Optimization: Sieve of Eratosthenes   Another algorithm for determining prime numbers up to a given maximum value is called the *Sieve of Eratosthenes*. It dates back to the Greek mathematician with the same name.

---

[1] As an optimization, you actually only have to calculate up to the root. I briefly discuss this in the *Possible optimizations* practical tip.

The whole thing works as follows: Initially, all numbers starting at the value 2 up to the given maximum value are written down, for example:

$$2, 3, 4, 5, 6, 7, 8, 9, 10, 11, 12, 13, 14, 15$$

All numbers are initially considered as potential candidates for prime numbers. Now the numbers that cannot be prime numbers are eliminated step by step. The smallest unmarked number is taken, in this case, the number 2, which corresponds to the first prime number. Now all multiples of it are eliminated (in the example 4, 6, 8, 10, 12, 14):

$$2, 3, \cancel{4}, 5, \cancel{6}, 7, \cancel{8}, 9, \cancel{10}, 11, \cancel{12}, 13, \cancel{14}, 15$$

Further, you continue with the number 3, which is the second prime number. Now again, the multiples are eliminated. They are the numbers 6, 9, 12, 15:

$$2, 3, \cancel{4}, 5, \cancel{6}, 7, \cancel{8}, \cancel{9}, \cancel{10}, 11, \cancel{12}, 13, \cancel{14}, \cancel{15}$$

The next unmarked number and thus a prime number is 5. The procedure is repeated as long as there are still unmarked numbers after the current prime number.

$$2, 3, \cancel{4}, 5, \cancel{6}, 7, \cancel{8}, \cancel{9}, \cancel{10}, 11, \cancel{12}, 13, \cancel{14}, \cancel{15}$$

This leads to the following result for all prime numbers smaller than 15:

$$2, 3, 5, 7, 11, 13$$

Check this algorithm with the following values:

Limit	Result
15	[2, 3, 5, 7, 11, 13]
25	[2, 3, 5, 7, 11, 13, 17, 19, 23]
50	[2, 3, 5, 7, 11, 13, 17, 19, 23, 29, 31, 37, 41, 43, 47]

HINT: POSSIBLE OPTIMIZATIONS

As you can see, numbers are often crossed out several times. If you are mathematically a little more experienced, you can prove that at least one prime factor of a composite number must always be smaller equal to the root of the number itself. The reason is that if x is a divisor greater than $sqrt(n)$, then it holds that $p = n/x$ is smaller than $sqrt(n)$ and thus this value has already been tried. Thus you can optimize the multiples' elimination. Firstly, you can start the elimination with the square of the prime number since all smaller multiples are already eliminated. Secondly, the calculation has to be done only up to the root of the upper limit.

2.1.4 Roman Numbers

The Roman numeral system works with special letters and combinations of them to represent numbers. The following basic mapping is applicable:[2]

Roman Number	I	V	X	L	C	D	M
Value	1	5	10	50	100	500	1000

The corresponding value is usually calculated by adding the values of the individual digits from left to right. Normally (see the following rules), the largest number is on the left, and the smallest number is on the right, for example, XVI for the value 16.

2.1.5 Rules

Roman numerals are composed according to certain rules:

- **Addition rule:** Same digits next to each other are added, for example XXX = 30. Likewise, this applies to smaller digits after larger ones, so XII = 12.

- **Repetition rule:** No more than three identical digits may follow each other. According to rule 1, you could write the number 4 as IIII, which this rule 2 forbids. This is where the subtraction rule comes into play.

---

[2] Interestingly the value 0 does not exist in Roman numerals.

- **Subtraction rule:** If a smaller number symbol appears in front of a larger one, the corresponding value is subtracted. Let's look again at the 4: This can be represented as subtraction $5 - 1$. This is expressed as IV in the Roman numeral system. The following rules apply to the subtraction:

  - I precedes only V and X.

  - X precedes only L and C.

  - C precedes only D and M.

2.1.6 Examples

For better understanding and clarification of the above rules, let's look at some notations of Roman numerals and their corresponding values:

$$
\begin{aligned}
VII &= 5 + 1 + 1 & &= 7 \\
MDCLXVI &= 1000 + 500 + 100 + 50 + 10 + 5 + 1 &= 1666 \\
MMXVIII &= 1000 + 1000 + 10 + 5 + 1 + 1 + 1 &= 2018 \\
MMXIX &= 1000 + 1000 + 10 - 1 + 10 &= 2019
\end{aligned}
$$

2.1.7 Noteworthy

The Arabic numerals common in our modern world rely on the decimal system. The digits' position determines their value. Thus, 7 can be the number itself, but it can also represent 70 or 700. However, in the Roman numeral system, the V always stands for a 5, regardless of the position.

Because of that particular structure of Roman numerals, many math operations are complex; even a simple addition may cause a bigger or sometimes even a complete change of the number. This becomes very obvious for the numbers 2018 and 2019 or for the addition III + II = V. Even worse: Significantly more complex is a multiplication or division. There are speculations that this was one of the factors why the Roman Empire collapsed.

NOTE: LARGER NUMBERS

There are special notations for representing larger Roman numerals (in the range of ten thousand and above) because no four or more Ms are allowed to follow each other. This has no relevance for the tasks of this book. If interested, the reader may consult the Internet or other sources.

2.1.8 Number Games

In this section, you'll look at a few special number constellations:

- Perfect numbers

- Armstrong numbers

- Checksums

In many of the algorithms used below, you subdivide numbers into their digits to be able to perform corresponding number games.

2.1.9 Perfect Numbers

By definition, a number is called a *perfect number* if its value is equal to the sum of its real divisors (i.e., excluding itself). This may sound a bit strange, but it is quite simple. Let's consider the number 6 as an example. It possesses as real divisors the numbers 1, 2, and 3. Interestingly, it now holds

$$1 + 2 + 3 = 6$$

Let's look at another counterpart: the number 20, which has the real divisors 1, 2, 4, 5, and 10, but their sum is 22 and not 20:

$$1 + 2 + 4 + 5 + 10 = 22$$

2.1.10 Armstrong Numbers

In the following, you will examine so-called Armstrong numbers. These are numbers whose individual digits are first exponentiated by the number of digits in the number and then added together. If this sum then corresponds to the original number's value, it is called an Armstrong number. To keep things a little simpler, let's look at the special case of three-digit numbers. To be an Armstrong number, the following equation must be satisfied with this number:

$$x*100 + y*10 + z = x^3 + y^3 + z^3$$

The digits of the number are modeled as x, y, and z and are all in the range from 0 to 9. Let's consider two examples for which this formula is satisfied:

$$153 = 1*100 + 5*10 + 3 = 1^3 + 5^3 + 3^3 = 1 + 125 + 27 = 153$$
$$371 = 3*100 + 7*10 + 1 = 3^3 + 7^3 + 1^3 = 27 + 343 + 1 = 371$$

Variation As a modification it is also quite interesting for which digits or numbers of the following equation are fulfilled:

$$x*100 + y*10 + z = x^1 + y^2 + z^3$$

or

$$x*100 + y*10 + z = x^3 + y^2 + z^1$$

For the first equation, there are the following solutions:

$$[135, 175, 518, 598]$$

For the second equation, there is no solution for x, y, and z in the range up to 100. If you like, you can verify this yourself when implementing the bonus part of task 9—or look at the solutions.

2.1.11 Algorithm for a Simple Checksum

A checksum is coded into various numbers so that it is easy to prove validity. This applies, for example, to credit card numbers and to data transfers via special protocols.

Let's assume that a checksum had to be calculated for a number with four digits (hereafter modeled as a to d). Then you can perform the following calculation based on the position:

$$abcd \Rightarrow (a*1 + b*2 + c*3 + d*4)\%10$$

Once again, I will illustrate the calculation with examples:

Input	Position calculation	Value	Checksum
1111	1 * 1 + 1 * 2 + 1 * 3 + 1 * 4	1 + 2 + 3 + 4 = 10	10 % 10 = 0
1234	1 * 1 + 2 * 2 + 3 * 3 + 4 * 4	1 + 4 + 9 + 16 = 30	30 % 10 = 0
4321	4 * 1 + 3 * 2 + 2 * 3 + 1 * 4	4 + 6 + 6 + 4 = 20	20 % 10 = 0
7271	7 * 1 + 2 * 2 + 7 * 3 + 1 * 4	7 + 4 + 21 + 4 = 36	36 % 10 = 6
0815	0 * 1 + 8 * 2 + 1 * 3 + 5 * 4	0 + 16 + 3 + 20 = 39	39 % 10 = 9
5180	5 * 1 + 1 * 2 + 8 * 3 + 0 * 4	5 + 2 + 24 + 0 = 31	31 % 10 = 1

2.2 Exercises

2.2.1 Exercise 1: Basic Arithmetic (★☆☆☆☆)

Exercise 1a: Basic Arithmetic Operations (★☆☆☆☆)

Write method int calc(int, int) that multiplies two variables, m and n of type int, then divides the product by two, and outputs the remainder with respect to division by 7.

Examples

m	n	m * n	m * n / 2	Result ((n * m / 2) % 7)
6	7	42	21	0
3	4	12	6	6
5	5	25	12	5

As a short reminder here: With an integer division, the remainder is truncated. Therefore 25/2 results in the value 12.

Exercise 1b: Statistics (★★☆☆☆)

Find the number as well as the sum of natural numbers, which are divisible by 2 or 7 up to a given maximum value (exclusive) and output it to the console. Write method void calcSumAndCountAllNumbersDivBy_2_Or_7(int). Extend it so that it returns the two values instead of performing the console output.

Examples

Maximum	Divisible by 2	Divisible by 7	Result Count	Sum
3	2	-/-	1	2
8	2, 4, 6	7	4	19
15	2, 4, 6, 8, 10, 12, 14	7, 14	8	63

Exercise 1c: Even or Odd Number (★☆☆☆☆)

Create the methods boolean isEven(n) and boolean isOdd(n) that will check if the passed integer is even or odd, respectively.

2.2.2 Exercise 2: Number as Text (★★☆☆☆)

Write method String numberAsText(int) which, for a given positive number, converts the respective digits into corresponding text.

Start with the following fragment for the last digit of a number:

```
static String numberAsText(final int n)
{
    final int remainder = n % 10;
    String valueAsText = "";

    if (remainder == 0)
        valueAsText = "ZERO";
    if (remainder == 1)
        valueAsText = "ONE";
```

```
    // ...

    return valueAsText;
}
```

Examples

Input	Result
7	"SEVEN"
42	"FOUR TWO"
24680	"TWO FOUR SIX EIGHT ZERO"
13579	"ONE THREE FIVE SEVEN NINE"

2.2.3 Exercise 3: Perfect Numbers (★★☆☆☆)

By definition, a natural number is called a *perfect number* if its value is equal to the sum of its real divisors. This is true, for example, for the numbers 6 and 28:

$$1 + 2 + 3 = 6$$

$$1 + 2 + 4 + 7 + 14 = 28$$

Write method `List<Integer> calcPerfectNumbers(int)` that calculates the perfect numbers up to a maximum value, say 10,000.

Examples

Input	Result
1000	[6, 28, 496]
10000	[6, 28, 496, 8128]

2.2.4 Exercise 4: Prime Numbers (★★☆☆☆)

Write method `List<Integer> calcPrimesUpTo(int)` to compute all prime numbers up to a given value. As a reminder, a prime number is a natural number greater than 1 and exclusively divisible by itself and by 1. To compute a prime number, the so-called Sieve of Eratosthenes was described before.

Examples

Check your algorithm with the following values:

Input	Result
15	[2, 3, 5, 7, 11, 13]
25	[2, 3, 5, 7, 11, 13, 17, 19, 23]
50	[2, 3, 5, 7, 11, 13, 17, 19, 23, 29, 31, 37, 41, 43, 47]

2.2.5 Exercise 5: Prime Number Pairs (★★☆☆☆)

Compute all pairs of prime numbers with a distance of 2 (twin), 4 (cousin), and 6 (sexy) up to an upper bound for n. For twins then the following is true:

$$isPrime(n) \,\&\&\, isPrime(n+2)$$

Examples

The following results are expected for limit 50:

Type	Result
Twin	3=5, 5=7, 11=13, 17=19, 29=31, 41=43
Cousin	3=7, 7=11, 13=17, 19=23, 37=41, 43=47
Sexy	5=11, 7=13, 11=17, 13=19, 17=23, 23=29, 31=37, 37=43, 41=47, 47=53

2.2.6 Exercise 6: Checksum (★★☆☆☆)

Create method int calcChecksum(String) that performs the following position-based calculation for the checksum of a number of any length given as a string, with the n digits modeled as z_1 to z_n:

$$z_1 z_2 z_3 \ldots z_n \Rightarrow \left(1 * z_1 + 2 * z_2 + 3 * z_3 + \ldots + n * z_n\right) \% 10$$

Examples

Input	Sum	Result
"11111"	$1 + 2 + 3 + 4 + 5 = 15$	15 % 10 = 5
"87654321"	$8 + 14 + 18 + 20 + 20 + 18 + 14 + 8 = 120$	120 % 10 = 0

2.2.7 Exercise 7: Roman Numbers (★★★★☆)

Exercise 7a: Roman Numbers → Decimal Numbers (★★★☆☆)

Write method int fromRomanNumber(String) that computes the corresponding decimal number from a textually valid Roman number.[3]

Exercise 7b: Decimal Numbers → Roman Numbers (★★★★☆)

Write method String toRomanNumber(int) that converts a decimal number to a (valid) Roman number.

---

[3] For syntactically invalid Roman numbers, such as IXD, an incorrect result, here 489, can be computed—by subtraction rule twice in a row: $0 - 1 - 10 + 500$.

2.2.11 Exercise 11: Related Numbers (★★☆☆☆)

Two numbers n_1 and n_2 are called friends if the sum of their divisors is equal to the other number:

$$sum(divisors(n_1)) = n_2$$

$$sum(divisors(n_2)) = n_1$$

Write method `Map<Integer, Integer> calcFriends(int)` to compute all friends numbers up to a passed maximum value.

Examples

Input	Divisors
$\sum(divisors(220)) = 284$	div(220) = 1, 2, 4, 5, 10, 11, 20, 22, 44, 55, 110
$\sum(divisors(284)) = 220$	div(284) = 1, 2, 4, 71, 142
$\sum(divisors(1184)) = 1210$	div(1184) = 1, 2, 4, 8, 16, 32, 37, 74, 148, 296, 592
$\sum(divisors(1210)) = 1184$	div(1210) = 1, 2, 5, 10, 11, 22, 55, 110, 121, 242, 605

2.2.12 Exercise 12: Prime Factorization (★★★☆☆)

Any natural number greater than 1 can be represented as a multiplication of primes— remember the fact that 2 is also a prime. Write method `List<Integer> calcPrimeFactors(int)` that returns a list of prime numbers whose multiplication yields the desired number.

Examples

Input	Prime factors	Result
8	2 * 2 * 2	[2, 2, 2]
14	2 * 7	[2, 7]
42	2 * 3 * 7	[2, 3, 7]
1155	3 * 5 * 7 * 11	[3, 5, 7, 11]
2222	2 * 11 * 101	[2, 11, 101]

2.3 Solutions

2.3.1 Solution 1: Basic Arithmetic (★☆☆☆☆)

Solution 1a: Basic Arithmetic Operations (★☆☆☆☆)

Write method int calc(int, int) that multiplies two variables, *m* and *n* of type int, then divides the product by two, and outputs the remainder with respect to division by 7.

Examples

m	n	m * n	m * n / 2	Result ((n * m / 2) % 7)
6	7	42	21	0
3	4	12	6	6
5	5	25	12	5

As a short reminder here: With an integer division, the remainder is truncated. Therefore 25/2 results in the value 12.

Algorithm   The implementation directly follows the mathematical operations:

```
public int calc(final int m, final int n)
{
    return (m * n / 2) % 7;
}
```

Solution 1b: Statistics (★★☆☆☆)

Find the number as well as the sum of natural numbers, which are divisible by 2 or 7 up to a given maximum value (exclusive) and output it to the console. Write method void calcSumAndCountAllNumbersDivBy_2_Or_7(int). Extend it so that it returns the two values instead of performing the console output.

Examples

Input	Result
7	"SEVEN"
42	"FOUR TWO"
24680	"TWO FOUR SIX EIGHT ZERO"
13579	"ONE THREE FIVE SEVEN NINE"

Algorithm   Always compute the remainder (i.e., the last digit), print it out, and then divide by ten. Repeat this until no remainder exists anymore. Note that the digit's representation has to be appended to the text's front since the last digit is always extracted. Otherwise, the digits would appear in the wrong order.

```java
static String numberAsText(final int n)
{
    String value = "";
    int remainingValue = n;

    while (remainingValue > 0)
    {
        String remainderAsText = digitAsText(remainingValue % 10);
        value = remainderAsText + " " + value;

        remainingValue /= 10;
    }
    return value.trim();
}
```

You implement the mapping from digit to text with a lookup map as follows:

```java
static Map<Integer, String> valueToTextMap =
        Map.of(0, "ZERO", 1, "ONE", 2, "TWO", 3, "THREE", 4, "FOUR",
               5, "FIVE", 6, "SIX", 7, "SEVEN", 8, "EIGHT", 9, "NINE");

static String digitAsText(final int n)
{
    return valueToTextMap.get(n % 10);
}
```

HINT: NOTES ON STRING CONCATENATIONS

Keep in mind that the concatenation using + on strings may not be as performant. However, this only matters for huge numbers of calls. Here it should be unimportant, and the + is often easier to read.

Verification

For testing, use a parameterized test that can be formulated elegantly using JUnit 5:

```
@ParameterizedTest
@CsvSource({"7, SEVEN", "42, FOUR TWO", "7271, SEVEN TWO SEVEN ONE",
            "24680, TWO FOUR SIX EIGHT ZERO",
            "13579, ONE THREE FIVE SEVEN NINE"})
void numberAsText(int number, String expected)
{
    String result = Ex02_NumberAsText.numberAsText(number);

    assertEquals(expected, result);
}
```

2.3.3 Solution 3: Perfect Numbers (★★☆☆☆)

By definition, a natural number is called a *perfect number* if its value is equal to the sum of its real divisors. This is true, for example, for the numbers 6 and 28:

$$1 + 2 + 3 = 6$$

$$1 + 2 + 4 + 7 + 14 = 28$$

Write method List<Integer> calcPerfectNumbers(int) that calculates the perfect numbers up to a maximum value, say 10,000.

Examples

Input	Result
1000	[6, 28, 496]
10000	[6, 28, 496, 8128]

Algorithm   The simplest variant is to check all numbers from 2 to half of the desired maximum value to see if they represent the original number's divisor. In that case, the sum of the divisors is increased by exactly that value. The sum starts with the value 1 because this is invariably a valid divisor. Finally, you only have to compare the determined sum with the actual number.

```
static boolean isPerfectNumberSimple(final int number)
{
    // always divisible by 1
    int sumOfMultipliers = 1;

    for (int i = 2; i <= number / 2; i++)
    {
        if (number % i == 0)
            sumOfMultipliers += i;
    }

    return sumOfMultipliers == number;
}
```

Based on this, the actual method is straightforward to implement:

```
static List<Integer> calcPerfectNumbers(final int maxExclusive)
{
    final List<Integer> results = new ArrayList<>();

    for (int i = 2; i < maxExclusive; i++)
    {
        if (isPerfectNumberSimple(i))
            results.add(i);
    }

    return results;
}
```

Verification

For testing, you use the following inputs, which show the correct operation for dedicated numbers:

```
@ParameterizedTest(name = "{0} should be perfect")
@ValueSource(ints = { 6, 28, 496, 8128 })
void isPerfectNumberSimple(int value)
{
    boolean result = Ex03_PerfectNumbers.isPerfectNumberSimple(value);

    assertTrue(result);
}
```

Now you have tested the basic building block of the examination. However, you should still make sure that no other values than perfect numbers are supplied, and in fact, only these—for the testing. Thus the first four perfect numbers are namely the numbers 6, 28, 496, and 8128.

```
@ParameterizedTest(name = "calcPerfectNumbers({0}) = {1}")
@MethodSource("maxAndPerfectNumbers")
void calcPerfectNumbers(int maxExclusive, List<Integer> expected)
{
    List<Integer> result = Ex03_PerfectNumbers.calcPerfectNumbers(maxExclusive);

    assertEquals(expected, result);
}

private static Stream<Arguments> maxAndPerfectNumbers()
{
    return Stream.of(Arguments.of(1000, List.of(6, 28, 496)),
                     Arguments.of(10000, List.of(6, 28, 496, 8128)));
}
```

Implementation Optimization

Based on the findProperDivisors(int) method already presented in the introductory section of this chapter that finds all true divisors, you can simplify the check as follows:

```java
static boolean isPerfectNumberBasedOnProperDivisors(final int number)
{
    final List<Integer> divisors = findProperDivisors(number);

    return sum(divisors) == number;
}
```

You still need a helper method for summing up the elements of a list. The easiest way to solve this is to use the Stream API as follows:

```java
static int sum(final List<Integer> values)
{
    return values.stream().mapToInt(n -> n).sum();
}
```

2.3.4 Solution 4: Prime Numbers (★★☆☆☆)

Write method List<Integer> calcPrimesUpTo(int) to compute all prime numbers up to a given value. As a reminder, a prime number is a natural number greater than 1 and exclusively divisible by itself and by 1. To compute a prime number, the so-called Sieve of Eratosthenes was described before.

Examples

Check your algorithm with the following values:

Input	Result
15	[2, 3, 5, 7, 11, 13]
25	[2, 3, 5, 7, 11, 13, 17, 19, 23]
50	[2, 3, 5, 7, 11, 13, 17, 19, 23, 29, 31, 37, 41, 43, 47]

Algorithm   The algorithm follows the Sieve of Eratosthenes. At first an array of booleans is created and initialized with `true` since all numbers are considered potential prime numbers. Mentally, this is analogous to initially writing down the numbers 2, 3, 4, ... up to a given maximum value, like

$$2, 3, 4, 5, 6, 7, 8, 9, 10, 11, 12, 13, 14, 15$$

Now, starting at the value 2, the *sieving* is started. Because the number 2 is not crossed out, it is included in the list of prime numbers. Afterwards every multiple of it is crossed out, because they can't be prime numbers:

$$2, 3, \cancel{4}, 5, \cancel{6}, 7, \cancel{8}, 9, \cancel{10}, 11, \cancel{12}, 13, \cancel{14}, 15$$

Iteratively you look for the next not-eliminated number. In this case it is 3, which is the second prime number. Once again, all multiples of this number are eliminated:

$$2, 3, \cancel{4}, 5, \cancel{6}, 7, \cancel{8}, \cancel{9}, \cancel{10}, 11, \cancel{12}, 13, \cancel{14}, \cancel{15}$$

This procedure is repeated until half of the maximum value is reached. This prime number calculation is implemented in Java as follows:

```java
static List<Integer> calcPrimesUpTo(final int maxValue)
{
    // initially mark all values as potential prime number
    final boolean[] isPotentiallyPrime = new boolean[maxValue+1];
    Arrays.fill(isPotentiallyPrime, true);

    // run through all numbers starting at 2, optimization only up to half
    for (int i = 2; i <= maxValue / 2; i++)
    {
        if (isPotentiallyPrime[i])
            eraseMultiplesOfCurrent(isPotentiallyPrime, i);
    }

    return buildPrimesList(isPotentiallyPrime);
}
```

The functionality of crossing out or erasing the multiples is extracted to the following helper method eraseMultiplesOfCurrent(). As a trick, you use on the one hand the step size of *i* and on the other hand that the first multiple is determined by adding the start value. For first attempts, the commented console output can be helpful:

```java
private static void eraseMultiplesOfCurrent(final boolean[] values,
                                            final int i)
{
    for (int n = i + i; n < values.length; n = n + i)
    {
        values[n] = false;
        // System.out.println("Eliminating " + n);
    }
}
```

Finally, you need to reconstruct a list of numbers from the boolean[] as follows:

```java
private static List<Integer> buildPrimesList(final boolean[]
            isPotentiallyPrime)
{
    final List<Integer> primes = new ArrayList<>();
    for (int i = 2; i < isPotentiallyPrime.length; i++)
    {
        if (isPotentiallyPrime[i])
            primes.add(i);
    }
    return primes;
}
```

Verification

For testing, you use the following inputs that show the correct operation. To provide a list of results, you rely on `Stream<Arguments>`:

```
@ParameterizedTest(name = "calcPrimes({0}) = {1}")
@MethodSource("argumentProvider")
void calcPrimesUpTo(int n, List<Integer> expected)
{
    List<Integer> result = Ex04_PrimeNumber.calcPrimesUpTo(n);

    assertEquals(expected, result);
}

static Stream<Arguments> argumentProvider()
{
    return Stream.of(Arguments.of(2, List.of(2)),
                     Arguments.of(3, List.of(2, 3)),
                     Arguments.of(10, List.of(2, 3, 5, 7)),
                     Arguments.of(15, List.of(2, 3, 5, 7, 11, 13)),
                     Arguments.of(25, List.of(2, 3, 5, 7, 11, 13,
                                              17, 19, 23)),
                     Arguments.of(50, List.of(2, 3, 5, 7, 11, 13,
                                              17, 19, 23, 29, 31,
                                              37, 41, 43, 47)));
}
```

2.3.5 Solution 5: Prime Number Pairs (★★☆☆☆)

Compute all pairs of prime numbers with a distance of 2 (twin), 4 (cousin), and 6 (sexy) up to an upper bound for n. For twins then the following is true:

$$isPrime(n) \ \&\& \ isPrime(n + 2)$$

Examples

The following results are expected for limit 50:

Type	Result
twin	3=5, 5=7, 11=13, 17=19, 29=31, 41=43
cousin	3=7, 7=11, 13=17, 19=23, 37=41, 43=47
sexy	5=11, 7=13, 11=17, 13=19, 17=23, 23=29, 31=37, 37=43, 41=47, 47=53

Algorithm   As a first step, you need to define the conditions for pairs. This can be done explicitly via if statements or more elegantly by the definition of suitable predicates. For all numbers starting at 2 up to a desired upper limit, you have to check whether the number itself and the corresponding other number added by 2, 4, or 6 are prime numbers. For this purpose you can call a method isPrime(int), which in turn uses the previously written method for determining the prime numbers. For more details on prime twins, see. https://en.wikipedia.org/wiki/Twin_prime.

```java
public static void main(final String[] args)
{
    final Predicate<Integer> isTwinPair = n -> isPrime(n) && isPrime(n + 2);
    final Predicate<Integer> isCousinPair = n -> isPrime(n) && isPrime(n + 4);
    final Predicate<Integer> isSexyPair = n -> isPrime(n) && isPrime(n + 6);

    final Map<Integer, Integer> twinPairs = new TreeMap<>();
    final Map<Integer, Integer> cousinPairs = new TreeMap<>();
    final Map<Integer, Integer> sexyPairs = new TreeMap<>();

    for (int i = 1; i < 50; i++)
    {
        if (isTwinPair.test(i))
            twinPairs.put(i, i+2);

        if (isCousinPair.test(i))
            cousinPairs.put(i, i+4);
```

```
        if (isSexyPair.test(i))
            sexyPairs.put(i, i+6);
    }

    System.out.println("Twins: " + twinPairs);
    System.out.println("Cousins: " + cousinPairs);
    System.out.println("Sexy: " + sexyPairs);
}

private static boolean isPrime(int n)
{
    // non-optimal call
    return Ex04_PrimeNumber.calcPrimesUpTo(n).contains(n);
}
```

The realization shown here uses already implemented functionality—which is preferable in principle—but has two drawbacks in this case:

1. Every time all prime numbers are computed again up to the given maximum value. This can be optimized by performing the computation only once and caching the results appropriately.

2. At the moment, the checks are still all interwoven. It is clearer to use a validation function that checks only one condition and returns only one result.

Optimization of the Implementation

Vulnerability 1: Repeated calls   First, you should compute the primes up to the maximum value only once. In this case, you need to raise the limit by 6 so that you can map all pairs correctly:

```
public static void calcPrimePairs(final int maxValue)
{
    final List<Integer> primes = Ex04_PrimeNumber.calcPrimesUpTo(maxValue + 6);

    final Predicate<Integer> isTwinPair = n -> isPrime(primes, n) &&
                                               isPrime(primes, n + 2);
```

```
    final Predicate<Integer> isCousinPair = n -> isPrime(primes, n) &&
                                        isPrime(primes, n + 4);
    final Predicate<Integer> isSexyPair = n -> isPrime(primes, n) &&
                                        isPrime(primes, n + 6);

    final Map<Integer, Integer> twinPairs = new TreeMap<>();
    final Map<Integer, Integer> cousinPairs = new TreeMap<>();
    final Map<Integer, Integer> sexyPairs = new TreeMap<>();

    for (int i = 1; i < maxValue; i++)
    {
        if (isTwinPair.test(i))
            twinPairs.put(i, i + 2);

        if (isCousinPair.test(i))
            cousinPairs.put(i, i + 4);

        if (isSexyPair.test(i))
            sexyPairs.put(i, i + 6);
    }

    System.out.println("Twins: " + twinPairs);
    System.out.println("Cousins: " + cousinPairs);
    System.out.println("Sexy: " + sexyPairs);
}
```

Computing the prime numbers is performed once at the beginning of the method. Thus you achieve a significant performance improvement.

Finally, you move the check for a prime number to the following method:

```
static boolean isPrime(final List<Integer> primes, final int n)
{
    return primes.contains(n);
}
```

Vulnerability 2: Unclear program structure   Your goal is to write more general-purpose methods. You have already created the basic building blocks. However, the determination of the pairs should be moved to method calcPairs(). This way, you can write it more clearly and understandably as follows:

```java
public static void calcPrimePairsImproved(final int maxValue)
{
    final Map<Integer, Integer> twinPairs = calcPairs(maxValue, 2);
    final Map<Integer, Integer> cousinsPairs = calcPairs(maxValue, 4);
    final Map<Integer, Integer> sexyPairs = calcPairs(maxValue, 6);

    System.out.println("Twins: " + twinPairs);
    System.out.println("Cousins: " + cousinsPairs);
    System.out.println("Sexy: " + sexyPairs);
}

static Map<Integer, Integer> calcPairs(final int maxValue, final int distance)
{
    final List<Integer> primes =
                        Ex04_PrimeNumber.calcPrimesUpTo(maxValue + distance);

    final Map<Integer, Integer> resultPairs = new TreeMap<>();
    for (int n = 1; n < maxValue; n++)
    {
        if (isPrime(primes, n) && isPrime(primes, n + distance))
        {
            resultPairs.put(n, n + distance);
        }
    }
    return resultPairs;
}
```

This conversion also lays the foundation to be able to test the whole thing with unit tests.

Verification

If you call the method with the maximum value of 50, you get this result:

```
Twins: {3=5, 5=7, 11=13, 17=19, 29=31, 41=43}
Cousins: {3=7, 7=11, 13=17, 19=23, 37=41, 43=47}
Sexy: {5=11, 7=13, 11=17, 13=19, 17=23, 23=29, 31=37, 37=43, 41=47, 47=53}
```

Now let's create another unit test with one test method per special case:

```java
int maxValue = 50;

@ParameterizedTest(name = "primepairs({0}, {1}) = {2}")
@MethodSource("distanceAndExpectd")
void calcPairs(int distance, String info,
            Map<Integer, Integer> expected)
{
    var result = Ex05_PrimePairs_Improved.calcPairs(maxValue, distance);

    assertEquals(expected, result);
}

private static Stream<Arguments> distanceAndExpectd()
{
    return Stream.of(Arguments.of(2, "twin",
                            Map.of(3, 5, 5, 7, 11, 13, 17,
                                19, 29, 31, 41, 43)),
                    Arguments.of(4, "cousin",
                            Map.of(3, 7, 7, 11, 13, 17,
                                19, 23, 37, 41, 43, 47)),
                    Arguments.of(6, "sexy",
                            Map.of(5, 11, 7, 13, 11, 17, 13,
                                19, 17, 23, 23, 29, 31, 37,
                                37, 43, 41, 47, 47, 53)));
}
```

2.3.6 Solution 6: Checksum (★★☆☆☆)

Create method int calcChecksum(String) that performs the following position-based calculation for the checksum of a number of any length given as a string, with the n digits modeled as z_1 to z_n:

$$z_1 z_2 z_3 \ldots z_n \Rightarrow \left(1 * z_1 + 2 * z_2 + 3 * z_3 + \ldots + n * z_n\right) \% 10$$

Examples

Input	Sum	Result
"11111"	1 + 2 + 3 + 4 + 5 = 15	15 % 10 = 5
"87654321"	8 + 14 + 18 + 20 + 20 + 18 + 14 + 8 = 120	120 % 10 = 0

Algorithm   Traverse all digits from the front to the last position, extract the digit at the given position, and multiply its numerical value by the current position. Add this to the sum. Finally, the modulo operation maps the sum to a digit:

```java
static int calcChecksum(final String input)
{
    int crc = 0;
    for (int i = 0; i < input.length(); i++)
    {
        final char currentChar = input.charAt(i);

        if (Character.isDigit(currentChar))
        {
            final int pos = i + 1;
            final int value = (currentChar - '0') * pos;

            crc += value;
        }
        else
            throw new IllegalArgumentException("illegal char: " + currentChar);
    }

    return crc % 10;
}
```

Verification   For testing, use the following inputs, which show the correct operation:

```
@ParameterizedTest(name="checksum({0}) = {1}")
@CsvSource({ "11111, 5", "22222, 0", "111111, 1",
"12345678, 4", "87654321, 0" })
void testCalcChecksum(String input, int expected)
{
    final int result = Ex10_CheckSumCalculator.calcChecksum(input);

    assertEquals(expected, result);
}
```

2.3.7 Solution 7: Roman Numbers (★★★★☆)

Solution 7a: Roman Numbers → Decimal Numbers (★★★☆☆)

Write method int fromRomanNumber(String) that computes the corresponding decimal number from a textually valid Roman number.[5]

Examples

Arabic	Roman
17	"XVII"
444	"CDXLIV"
1971	"MCMLXXI"
2020	"MMXX"

Algorithm   You must pay particular attention to the addition rule described in section 2.1.1: The relevant value is normally obtained by adding the individual digits' values from left to right whenever a larger character precedes a smaller one. However, if a smaller number character precedes a larger one, the corresponding value is subtracted.

---

[5] For syntactically invalid Roman numbers, such as IXD, an incorrect result, here 489, can be computed—by subtraction rule twice in a row: $0 - 1 - 10 + 500$.

With this knowledge, you traverse the characters from right to left and look up the relevant value in a lookup map. To decide between addition or subtraction, you remember the last relevant character.

```java
static int fromRomanNumber(final String romanNumber)
{
    int value = 0;
    int lastDigitValue = 0;

    for (int i = romanNumber.length() - 1; i >= 0; i-)
    {
        final char romanDigit = romanNumber.charAt(i);
        final int digitValue = valueMap.getOrDefault(romanDigit, 0);

        final boolean addMode = digitValue >= lastDigitValue;
        if (addMode)
        {
            value += digitValue;
            lastDigitValue = digitValue;
        }
        else
            value -= digitValue;
    }
    return value;
}

static Map<Character, Integer> valueMap =
                    Map.of('I', 1, 'V', 5, 'X', 10, 'L', 50,
                           'C', 100, 'D', 500, 'M', 1000);
```

Solution 7b: Decimal Numbers → Roman Numbers (★★★★☆)

Write method String toRomanNumber(int) that converts a decimal number to a (valid) Roman number.

Algorithm   When converting a decimal number to a Roman numeral, you again use a map. You sort this in descending order so that the largest value (i.e., 1000) is at the beginning. The current number value is divided by this factor. This yields the number of required repetitions of this value. Now the remainder is determined by modulo. The procedure is repeated until all values are checked, and the remainder is greater than 0. In the following, the procedure is shown exemplarily for the number 7:

```
7 => 7 / 1000 => 0 => 0 x 'M'
        ...
        7 / 5 = 1 => 1 x 'V'
        7 % 5 = 2
        2 / 1 = 2 => 2 x 'I'
        2 % 1 = 0
    => 'VII'
```

The procedure is implemented in Java as follows:

```java
static String toRomanNumber(final int value)
{
    String result = "";
    int remainder = value;

    // descending order
    final Comparator<Integer> reversed = Comparator.reverseOrder();
    final Map<Integer, String> sortedIntToRomanDigit = new
    TreeMap<>(reversed);
    sortedIntToRomanDigit.putAll(intToRomanDigitMap);

    // start with largest value
    var it = sortedIntToRomanDigit.entrySet().iterator();
    while (it.hasNext() && remainder > 0)
    {
        final Map.Entry<Integer, String> entry = it.next();

        final int multiplier = entry.getKey();
        final char romanDigit = entry.getValue();

        final int times = remainder / multiplier;
        remainder = remainder % multiplier;

        result += repeatCharSequence(romanDigit, times);
    }
    return result;
}
```

```
static Map<Integer, String> intToRomanDigitMap =
                     Map.of(1, "I", 5, "V", 10, "X", 50, "L",
                         100, "C", 500, "D", 1000, "M");
```

However, the conversion is not yet 100% correct because it does not respect the rule of three. Instead, it repeats the digits four times.

To fix this, you can implement special treatments, which are only hinted at in the following:

```
final int multiplier = entry.getKey();
final char romanDigit = entry.getValue();

if (remainder >= 900 && romanDigit == 'D')
{
    result += "CM";
    remainder -= 900;
}
// ...
else if (remainder >= 4 && romanDigit == 'I')
{
    result += "IV";
    remainder -= 4;
}
else
{
    final int times = remainder / multiplier;
    remainder = remainder % multiplier;
    result += repeatCharSequence(romanDigit, times);
}
```

This becomes confusing quickly. The insertion of further lookup values for special cases is more elegantly. However, you no longer call the of() methods because they are defined only up to 10 parameter pairs.

```
static Map<Integer, String> intToRomanDigitMap = new TreeMap<>()
{{
    put(1, "I");
    put(4, "IV");
```

```
        put(5, "V");
        put(9, "IX");
        put(10, "X");
        put(40, "XL");
        put(50, "L");
        put(90, "XC");
        put(100, "C");
        put(400, "CD");
        put(500, "D");
        put(900, "CM");
        put(1000, "M");
}};
```

HINT: REPEATING CHARACTER SEQUENCES

To repeat character sequences, you can use the `String.repeat()` method since Java 11. For older Java versions, this helper method is suitable:

```
static String repeatCharSequence(final String value, final int times)
{
    final StringBuilder result = new StringBuilder();
    for (int i = 0; i < times; i++)
        result.append(value);

    return result.toString();
}
```

Verification

Let's start the unit test with different values that show the correct conversion, especially including the four values of 17, 444, 1971, and 2020 from the example:

```
@ParameterizedTest(name = "fromRomanNumber(''{1}'') => {0}")
@CsvSource({ "1, I", "2, II", "3, III", "4, IV", "5, V", "7, VII", "9, IX",
            "17, XVII", "40, XL", "90, XC", "400, CD", "444, CDXLIV", "500, D",
            "900, CM", "1000, M", "1666, MDCLXVI", "1971, MCMLXXI",
            "2018, MMXVIII", "2019, MMXIX", "2020, MMXX", "3000, MMM"})
```

```
void fromRomanNumber(int arabicNumber, String romanNumber)
{
    int result = Ex06_RomanNumbers.fromRomanNumber(romanNumber);

    assertEquals(arabicNumber, result);
}
```

Now let's take a look at how the testing of the reverse direction is accomplished:

```
@ParameterizedTest(name = "toRomanNumber(''{0}'') => {1}")
@CsvSource({ "1, I", "2, II", "3, III", "4, IV", "5, V", "7, VII", "9, IX",
            "17, XVII", "40, XL", "90, XC", "400, CD", "444, CDXLIV", "500, D",
            "900, CM", "1000, M", "1666, MDCLXVI", "1971, MCMLXXI",
            "2018, MMXVIII", "2019, MMXIX", "2020, MMXX", "3000, MMM"})
void toRomanNumber(int arabicNumber, String romanNumber)
{
    String result = Ex06_RomanNumbers.toRomanNumber(arabicNumber);

    assertEquals(romanNumber, result);
}
```

You encounter a duplication of the specifications in @CsvSource here because it's considered a bidirectional mapping. To avoid duplication, you could also import the values from a file:

```
@ParameterizedTest(name = "toRomanNumber(''{0}'') => {1}")
@CsvFileSource(resources = "arabicroman.csv", numLinesToSkip = 1)
void toRomanNumber(int arabicNumber, String romanNumber)
{
    String result = Ex06_RomanNumbers.toRomanNumber(arabicNumber);

    assertEquals(romanNumber, result);
}
```

The CSV file will look like the following:

```
arabic,roman 1, I
2, II
3, III
```

4, IV
5, V
7, VII
9, IX
17, XVII
40, XL
90, XC
...

2.3.8 Solution 8: Combinatorics (★★☆☆☆)
Solution 8a: Computation of $a^2 + b^2 = c^2$

Compute all combinations of the values a, b, and c (each starting from 1 and less than 100) for which the following formula holds:

$$a^2 + b^2 = c^2$$

Algorithm   The brute force solution uses three nested loops and then checks if the above formula is satisfied. For squaring, simple multiplication provides better readability than the use of Math.pow() implied in the comment:

```
// brute force, three nested loops
for (int a = 1; a < 100; a++)
{
    for (int b = 1; b < 100; b++)
    {
        for (int c = 1; c < 100; c++)
        {
            if (a * a + b * b == c * c)
            // if ((Math.pow(a, 2)) + Math.pow(b, 2) == Math.pow(c, 2))
            {
                System.out.println("a = " + a + " / b = " + b + " / c = " + c);
            }
        }
    }
}
```

Bonus: Reduce the Running Time of $O(n^3)$ to $O(n^2)$ (★★★☆☆)

You see three nested loops in the upper solution, resulting in a running time of $O(n^3)$. Now let's reduce this to $O(n^2)$. To achieve this, apply the following transformation (resolving to c):

$$c = \sqrt{a*a + b*b}$$

Based on this transformation or resolution of the equation to c, the square root is calculated, and then the formula is verified. Additionally, you have to ensure that c is below 100.

```java
public void solveQuadratic()
{
    for (int a = 1; a < 100; a++)
    {
        for (int b = 1; b < 100; b++)
        {
            final int c = (int) Math.sqrt(a * a + b * b);
            if (c < 100 && a * a + b * b == c * c)
            {
                System.out.println("a = " + a + " / b = " + b + " / c = " + c);
            }
        }
    }
}
```

Verification

For testing, you call the solveQuadratic() method and perform the computation for some values:

```
jshell> solveQuadratic()
a = 3 / b = 4 / c = 5
a = 4 / b = 3 / c = 5
a = 5 / b = 12 / c = 13
a = 6 / b = 8 / c = 10
a = 7 / b = 24 / c = 25
```

```
a = 8  / b = 6  / c = 10
a = 8  / b = 15 / c = 17
a = 9  / b = 12 / c = 15
a = 9  / b = 40 / c = 41
a = 10 / b = 24 / c = 26
a = 11 / b = 60 / c = 61
a = 12 / b = 5  / c = 13
a = 12 / b = 9  / c = 15
a = 12 / b = 16 / c = 20
a = 12 / b = 35 / c = 37
...
```

NOTE: WHY DOES THE COMPUTATION WORK AT ALL?

Looking only briefly at the conversion, one might wonder why the computation does not yield a successful comparison for all values. In fact, this would be the case purely mathematically, since you are deriving c from a and b. However, you also use a cast to an int:

```
final int c = (int) Math.sqrt(a * a + b * b);
if (c < 100 && a * a + b * b == c * c)
{
    System.out.println("a = " + a + " / b = " + b + " / c = " + c);
}
```

As a result, the decimal digits are truncated. This, in turn, leads to the comparison being successful only for certain values.

Solution 8b: Computation of $a^2 + b^2 = c^2 + d^2$

Compute all combinations of the values a, b, c, and d (each starting from 1 and less than 100) for which the following formula holds:

$$a^2 + b^2 = c^2 + d^2$$

Algorithm   Analogous to the previous part of the exercise, the brute force solution is to use four nested loops and then check whether the above formula is satisfied. Again, simple multiplication is more readable than using `Math.pow()`:

```java
public void solveCubicEquationSimple()
{
    // brute force, four nested loops
    for (int a = 1; a < 100; a++)
    {
        for (int b = 1; b < 100; b++)
        {
            for (int c = 1; c < 100; c++)
            {
                for (int d = 1; d < 100; d++)
                {
                    if (a * a + b * b == c * c + d * d)
                    {
                        System.out.println("a = " + a + " / b = " + b +
                                          " / c = " + c + " / d = " + d);
                    }
                }
            }
        }
    }
}
```

Bonus: Reduce the Running Time of $O(n^4)$ to $O(n^3)$ (★★★☆☆)

As can easily be seen, the solution uses four nested loops, resulting in a running time of $O(n^4)$. Now you want to reduce this to $O(n^3)$. For that purpose, you use transformations. First, you separate to d and then you resolve to d:

$$d * d = a * a + b * b - c * c \implies d = \sqrt{a * a + b * b - c * c}$$

Based on this transformation or resolution of the equation to d, you can compute the square root and then validate the formula. Additionally, you have to ensure that the value is not negative and the resulting d is below 100.

```java
private static void solveCubicEquation()
{
    for (int a = 1; a < 100; a++)
    {
        for (int b = 1; b < 100; b++)
        {
            for (int c = 1; c < 100; c++)
            {
                final int value = a * a + b * b - c * c;
                if (value > 0)
                {
                    final int d = (int) Math.sqrt(value);

                    if (d < 100 && a * a + b * b == c * c + d * d)
                    {
                        System.out.println("a = " + a + " / b = " + b +
                                        " / c = " + c + " / d = " + d);
                    }
                }
            }
        }
    }
}
```

Verification

For testing, you use a method call and check some of the values:

```
jshell> solveCubicEquation()
a = 1 / b = 1 / c = 1 / d = 1
a = 1 / b = 2 / c = 1 / d = 2
a = 1 / b = 2 / c = 2 / d = 1
a = 1 / b = 3 / c = 1 / d = 3
a = 1 / b = 3 / c = 3 / d = 1
...
```

2.3.9 Solution 9: Armstrong Numbers (★★☆☆☆)

This exercise deals with three-digit Armstrong numbers. By definition, these are numbers for whose digits x, y, and z from 1 to 9 satisfy the following equation:

$$x*100+y*10+z = x^3 + y^3 + z^3$$

Write method `List<Integer> calcArmstrongNumbers()` to compute all Armstrong numbers for x, y, and z (each < 10).

Examples

$$153 = 1*100+5*10+3 = 1^3 + 5^3 + 3^3 = 1+125+27 = 153$$
$$371 = 3*100+7*10+1 = 3^3 + 7^3 + 1^3 = 27+343+1 = 371$$

Algorithm   Iterate through all combinations of three-digit numbers using three nested loops. The numeric value is calculated based on the position using the formula $x*100+ y*10 + z$. Also, compute the third power for each digit, sum them, and check if the sum matches the number.

```
static List<Integer> calcArmstrongNumbers()
{
    final List<Integer> results = new ArrayList<>();

    for (int x = 1; x < 10; x++)
    {
        for (int y = 1; y < 10; y++)
        {
            for (int z = 1; z < 10; z++)
            {
                final int numericValue = x * 100 + y * 10 + z;
                final int cubicValue = (int) (Math.pow(x, 3) +
                                              Math.pow(y, 3) +
                                              Math.pow(z, 3));

                if (numericValue == cubicValue)
                    results.add(numericValue);
            }
```

```
        }
    }
    return results;
}
```

NOTE: WHY DON'T THE LOOPS START AT 0?

Although you could also use the value 0, this is unusual for the first position and is frequently used to indicate octal numbers, which is why you do not use it here.

Verification

To test, you call the above method and examine whether the two combinations of values given as examples are included in the result list:

```
@Test
public void calcArmstrongNumbers()
{
    final List<Integer> result = Ex09_SpecialNumbers.calcArmstrongNumbers();

    assertEquals(List.of(153, 371), result);
}
```

Bonus (★★★☆☆)

Find a generic version with lambdas and then try the following three formulas:

$$x*100+y*10+z = x^3+y^3+z^3$$
$$x*100+y*10+z = x^1+y^2+z^3$$
$$x*100+y*10+z = x^3+y^2+z^1$$

Algorithm   Instead of the concrete computation, you add a call via a Functional Interface CubicFunction for computation:

```java
static List<Integer> calcNumbers(final CubicFunction func)
{
    final List<Integer> results = new ArrayList<>();

    for (int x = 1; x < 10; x++)
    {
        for (int y = 1; y < 10; y++)
        {
            for (int z = 1; z < 10; z++)
            {
                final int numericValue = x * 100 + y * 10 + z;
                final int cubicValue = func.calc(x, y, z);

                if (numericValue == cubicValue)
                    results.add(numericValue);
            }
        }
    }
    return results;
}
```

You now define a suitable functional interface in order to abstract the computations:

```java
@FunctionalInterface
interface CubicFunction
{
    int calc(int x, int y, int z);
}
```

Thus, the computation can be expressed as a lambda:

```java
CubicFunction special = (x, y, z) -> (int) (Math.pow(x, 3) +
                                            Math.pow(y, 3) +
                                            Math.pow(z, 3));
```

Based on this more general solution, you can now easily try other variants of computation rules without much effort:

```
CubicFunction special2 = (x, y, z) -> (int) (Math.pow(x, 1) +
                                             Math.pow(y, 2) +
                                             Math.pow(z, 3));
```

Likewise, you finally define the following:

```
CubicFunction special3 = (x, y, z) -> (int) (Math.pow(x, 3) +
                                             Math.pow(y, 2) +
                                             Math.pow(z, 1));
```

Verification

For testing, you invoke the above method with different computation rules and look for that of Armstrong numbers whether the two combinations of values given as examples are included in the result list:

```
jshell> CubicFunction special = (x, y, z) -> (int) (Math.pow(x, 3) +
   ...>                                             Math.pow(y, 3) +
   ...>                                             Math.pow(z, 3));
   ...> List<Integer> calcSpecialNumbers = calcNumbers(special);
calcSpecialNumbers ==> [153, 371]

jshell> CubicFunction special2 = (x, y, z) -> (int) (Math.pow(x, 1) +
   ...>                                              Math.pow(y, 2) +
   ...>                                              Math.pow(z, 3));
   ...> List<Integer> specialNumbers2 = calcNumbers(special2);
specialNumbers2 ==> [135, 175, 518, 598]

jshell> CubicFunction special3 = (x, y, z) -> (int) (Math.pow(x, 3) +
   ...>                                              Math.pow(y, 2) +
   ...>                                              Math.pow(z, 1));
jshell> List<Integer> specialNumbers3 = calcNumbers(special3)
specialNumbers3 ==> []
```

2.3.10 Solution 10: Max Change Calculator (★★★★☆)

Suppose you have a collection of coins of different values. Write method `calcMaxPossibl eChange(values)` that determines, for positive integers, what amounts can be *seamlessly* generated with it starting from the value 1. The maximum value should be returned as a result.

Examples

Input	Possible values	Maximum
1	1	1
1, 1	1, 2	2
1, 5	1	1
1, 2, 4	1, 2, 3, 4, 5, 6, 7	7
1, 2, 3, 7	1, 2, 3, 4, 5, 6, 7, 8, 9, 10, 11, 12, 13	13
1, 1, 1, 1, 5, 10, 20, 50	1, 2, 3, 4, 5, 6, ... , 30, ... , 39	39

Algorithm You could try solving this exercise by computing a mapping to all permutations of the sum of the numbers—but this gets complex fast. Let's consider another approach.

Input	Possible values	Maximum
1, 2, 3, 7	1, 2, 3, 4, 5, 6, 7, 8, 9, 10, 11, 12, 13	13
1, 2, 3, 8	1, 2, 3, 4, 5, 6, => _ <= , 8, 9, 10, 11, 12, 13, 14	6

If you take a look at the two examples, you may recognize for the cases 1, 2, 3, 7 and 1, 2, 3, 8 the clue to simplify the calculation decisively. Instead of always calculating all permutations and then checking for a gap in the number line, here indicated by an underscore (_), it is possible to start at the first number, always add the numbers to the previous sum, and repeat this iteratively until *nextNumber* > *sum* + 1 becomes true.

Let's apply this to Java. First, sort the input values. Start with the assumption that there is nothing to change initially, so *maxPossibleChange* = 0. Now check the following condition for each value. If *currentValue* > *maxPossibleChange* + 1 holds, then it is impossible to change. Otherwise, add the current value to *maxPossibleChange*. Repeat this until all values are processed or until the termination condition is met. This leads to the following implementation:

```java
static int calcMaxPossibleChange(final List<Integer> values)
{
    // wrapping necessary if input values are generated by List.of()
    final List<Integer> sortedNumbers = new ArrayList<>(values);
    sortedNumbers.sort(Integer::compareTo);

    int maxPossibleChange = 0;

    for (int currentValue : sortedNumbers)
    {
        if (currentValue > maxPossibleChange + 1)
            break;

        maxPossibleChange += currentValue;
    }

    return maxPossibleChange;
}
```

Verification

For testing, you use the following inputs, which show the correct operation:

```java
@ParameterizedTest(name = "calcMaxPossibleChange({0}) = {1}")
@MethodSource("inputsAndMaxChange")
void calcMaxPossibleChange(List<Integer> values, int expected)
{
    int result = Ex11_MaxChangeCalculator.calcMaxPossibleChange(values);

    assertEquals(expected, result);
}

private static Stream<Arguments> inputsAndMaxChange()
{
    return Stream.of(Arguments.of(List.of(1), 1),
                     Arguments.of(List.of(1,1), 2),
```

```
            Arguments.of(List.of(1, 5), 1),
            Arguments.of(List.of(1, 2, 4), 7),
            Arguments.of(List.of(1, 2, 3, 7), 13),
            Arguments.of(List.of(1, 2, 3, 8), 6),
            Arguments.of(List.of(1, 1, 1, 1, 5, 10, 20, 50), 39));
}
```

2.3.11 Solution 11: Related Numbers (★★☆☆☆)

Two numbers n_1 and n_2 are called friends if the sum of their divisors is equal to the other number:

$$sum(divisors(n_1)) = n_2$$

$$sum(divisors(n_2)) = n_1$$

Write method `Map<Integer, Integer> calcFriends(int)` to compute all friends numbers up to a passed maximum value.

Examples

Input	Divisors
$\sum(divisors(220)) = 284$	div(220) = 1, 2, 4, 5, 10, 11, 20, 22, 44, 55, 110
$\sum(divisors(284)) = 220$	div(284) = 1, 2, 4, 71, 142
$\sum(divisors(1184)) = 1210$	div(1184) = 1, 2, 4, 8, 16, 32, 37, 74, 148, 296, 592
$\sum(divisors(1210)) = 1184$	div(1210) = 1, 2, 5, 10, 11, 22, 55, 110, 121, 242, 605

Algorithm   It is easy to check whether two numbers are friends by determining for each number its divisors and its sum. Now the divisors can be determined from this sum and then added together. If this second sum is equal to the original number, then the numbers are friends.

```java
static Map<Integer, Integer> calcFriends(final int max)
{
    final Map<Integer, Integer> friends = new TreeMap<>();

    for (int number= 2; number < max; number++)
    {
        final List<Integer> divisors1 = findProperDivisors(number);
        final int sumDiv1 = sum(divisors1);

        final List<Integer> divisors2 = findProperDivisors(sumDiv1);
        final int sumDiv2 = sum(divisors2);

        if (number == sumDiv2 && sumDiv1 != sumDiv2)
        {
            friends.put(number, sumDiv1);
        }
    }

    return friends;
}

static int sum(final List<Integer> values)
{
    return values.stream().mapToInt(n -> n).sum();
}
```

The results are sorted by TreeMap<K,V>. For implementation, you also invoke the findProperDivisors() method already presented in the introduction to find all true divisors. Likewise, you use the Stream API for summation and not a custom implementation with a loop over all elements. Once again, you see the benefit of breaking down software into smaller, self-contained functionalities.

Verification

For testing, you use the following inputs, which show the correct operation. In this case, Stream<Arguments> is used again, providing both the maximum value and a map with the two numbers:

```
@ParameterizedTest(name = "calcFriends({0}) = {1}")
@MethodSource("upperBoundAndExpectedFriends")
void calcFriends(int maxValue, Map<Integer, Integer> expected)
{
    Map<Integer, Integer> result = Ex12_BefreundeteZahlen.
    calcFriends(maxValue);

    assertEquals(expected, result);
}

private static Stream<Arguments> upperBoundAndExpectedFriends()
{
    return Stream.of(Arguments.of(250, Map.of(220, 284)),
                    Arguments.of(300, Map.of(220, 284,
                                                284, 220)),
                    Arguments.of(2_000, Map.of(220, 284,
                                                284, 220,
                                                1184, 1210,
                                                1210,1184)));
}
```

2.3.12 Solution 12: Prime Factorization (★★★☆☆)

Any natural number greater than 1 can be represented as a multiplication of primes. Remember the fact that 2 is also a prime. Write method List<Integer> calcPrimeFactors(int) that returns a list of prime numbers whose multiplication yields the desired number.

Examples

Input	Prime factors	Result
8	2 * 2 * 2	[2, 2, 2]
14	2 * 7	[2, 7]
42	2 * 3 * 7	[2, 3, 7]
1155	3 * 5 * 7 * 11	[3, 5, 7, 11]
2222	2 * 11 * 101	[2, 11, 101]

Algorithm   Start by dividing the number by 2 as long as the number is even and greater than 2. Then, at some point, you reach an odd number. If this is 1, you are done (see the case for the number 8). Otherwise, you check if the odd number is a prime number and collect it. In this case, you are done (for example, above for the number 14). If not, you have to split the odd number further. Let's take 50 as an example. First, you divide by 2 so 25 remains, which is not a prime number. For this, you check for all prime numbers if they represent a divisor. You continue this procedure until you reach the number 1, which means that all divisors have been collected. For more info, see for example https://en.wikipedia.org/wiki/Integer_factorization.

```
static List<Integer> calcPrimeFactors(final int n)
{
    final List<Integer> allPrimes = Ex04_PrimeNumber.calcPrimesUpTo(n);
    final List<Integer> primeFactors = new ArrayList<>();

    int remainingValue = n;

    // as long as even, divide by 2 again and again
    while (remainingValue % 2 == 0 && remainingValue >= 2)
    {
        remainingValue = remainingValue / 2;
        primeFactors.add(2);
    }
```

```
    // check remainder for prime
    if (isPrime(allPrimes, remainingValue))
    {
        primeFactors.add(remainingValue);
    }
    else
    {
        // remainder is not a prime number, further check
        while (remainingValue > 1)
        {
            for (final Integer currentPrime : allPrimes)
            {
                if (remainingValue % currentPrime == 0)
                {
                    remainingValue = remainingValue / currentPrime;
                    primeFactors.add(currentPrime);
                    // start again from the beginning, because every divisor
                    // may occur more than once
                    break;
                }
            }
        }
    }

    return primeFactors;
}

static boolean isPrime(final List<Integer> allPrimes, final int n)
{
    return allPrimes.contains(n);
}
```

Optimized algorithm   If you look at the algorithm just developed, you might be bothered by all the special treatments. With a little thought, you may conclude that you don't need to check number 2 separately since it is also a prime number. Thus, this is covered by the while loop. Instead of the break for repeated checking of the same number, this can be expressed in a more stylistically pleasing way with a while loop. With these preliminary considerations, you arrive at the following implementation:

```
static List<Integer> calcPrimeFactorsOptimized(final int n)
{
    final List<Integer> allPrimes = calcPrimesUpTo(n);
    final List<Integer> primeFactors = new ArrayList<>();

    int remainingValue = n;
    while (remainingValue > 1)
    {
        for (final Integer currentPrime : allPrimes)
        {
            while (remainingValue % currentPrime == 0)
            {
                remainingValue = remainingValue / currentPrime;
                primeFactors.add(currentPrime);
            }
        }
    }
    return primeFactors;
}
```

Verification

For testing, you use the following inputs, which show the correct operation:

```
@ParameterizedTest(name = "calcPrimeFactors({0}) = {1}")
@MethodSource("valueAndPrimeFactors")
void calcPrimeFactors(int value, List<Integer> expected)
{
    var result = Ex13_PrimeFactors.calcPrimeFactors(value);

    assertEquals(expected, result);
}
```

```java
@ParameterizedTest(name = "calcPrimeFactorsOptimized({0}) = {1}")
@MethodSource("valueAndPrimeFactors")
void calcPrimeFactorsOpt(final int value, final List<Integer> expected)
{
    var result = Ex13_PrimeFactors.calcPrimeFactorsOptimized(value);

    assertEquals(expected, result);
}

private static Stream<Arguments> valueAndPrimeFactors()
{
    return Stream.of(Arguments.of(8, List.of(2, 2, 2)),
                     Arguments.of(14, List.of(2, 7)),
                     Arguments.of(42, List.of(2, 3, 7)),
                     Arguments.of(1155, List.of(3, 5, 7, 11)),
                     Arguments.of(2222, List.of(2, 11, 101)));
}
```

CHAPTER 3

Recursion

In nature and mathematics, you can find the topic ***self-similarity*** or recurring structures, such as snowflakes or fractals and Julia sets, which are interesting graphical formations. In this context, one speaks of ***recursion***, meaning that things repeat or resemble each other. Related to methods, this means that they call themselves. Important thereby is a termination condition in the form of special input values, which leads to the end of the self-calls.

3.1 Introduction

Various computations can be described very well as recursive functions. The goal is to break down a more complex task into several simpler subtasks.

3.1.1 Mathematical Examples

Below you will take a look at the computation of the factorial, summation, and Fibonacci numbers, three introductory examples for recursive definitions.

Example 1: Factorial

Mathematically, the ***factorial*** for positive number n is defined as the product (i.e., the multiplication) of all natural numbers from 1 to n, inclusive. For notation, the exclamation mark is placed after the corresponding number. For example, 5! stands for the factorial of the number 5:

$$5! = 5 * 4 * 3 * 2 * 1 = 120$$

This can be generalized as follows:

$$n! = n * (n - 1) * (n - 2) * ... * 2 * 1$$

© Michael Inden 2022
M. Inden, *Java Challenges*, https://doi.org/10.1007/978-1-4842-7395-1_3

Based on this, the recursive definition is derived:

$$n! = \begin{cases} 1, & n = 0, n = 1 \\ n \cdot (n-1)!, & \forall n > 1 \end{cases}$$

Here, the inverted A ($\forall$) denotes *for all*.

For the first n you get the following value progression:

n	1	2	3	4	5	6	7	8
n!	1	2	6	24	120	720	5040	40320

Calculation of the factorial in Java   Let's take a quick look at how the recursive calculation formula of the factorial can be transferred into a method of the same kind:

```java
public static int factorial(final int n)
{
    if (n < 0)
        throw new IllegalArgumentException("n must be >= 0");

    // recursive termination
    if (n == 0 || n == 1)
        return 1;

    // recursive descent
    return n * factorial(n - 1);
}
```

Let's clarify what this recursive definition generates in terms of calls. See Figure 3-1.

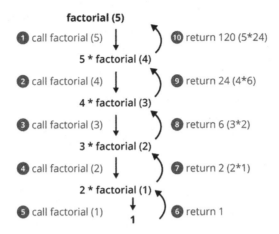

Figure 3-1. *Recursive calls to factorial(5)*

Example 2: Calculation of the Sum of Numbers Up to *n*

Mathematically, the *sum* for number *n* is defined as the addition of all natural numbers from 1 ascending up to and including *n*:

$$\sum_{1}^{n} i = n + n - 1 + n - 2 + \ldots + 2 + 1$$

This can be defined recursively as follows:

$$\sum_{1}^{n} i = \begin{cases} 1, & n = 1 \\ n + \sum_{1}^{n-1} i, & \forall n > 1 \end{cases}$$

For the first *n*, you get the following value progression:

n	1	2	3	4	5	6	7	8
sum(n)	1	3	6	10	15	21	28	36

Calculation of the sum in Java   Again, you convert the recursive calculation formula of the summation into a recursive method:

```java
public static int sum(final int n)
{
    if (n <= 0)
        throw new IllegalArgumentException("n must be >= 1");

    // recursive termination
    if (n == 1)
        return 1;

    // recursive descent
    return n + sum(n - 1);
}
```

ATTENTION: LIMITED CALL DEPTH

Please keep in mind that for summation, self-calls always happen. Therefore it is only possible to pass a value around 10.000 – 20.000. Larger values will cause a StackOverflowError. For other recursive methods similar restrictions apply regarding the number of self-calls.

Example 3: Fibonacci Numbers

The *Fibonacci numbers* are also excellent for recursive definition, although the formula is already a tiny bit more complex:

$$fib(n) = \begin{cases} 1, & n = 1 \\ 1, & n = 2 \\ fib(n-1) + fib(n-2), & \forall n > 2 \end{cases}$$

For the first n you get the following value progression:

n	1	2	3	4	5	6	7	8
fib(n)	1	1	2	3	5	8	13	21

If the calculation formula is visualized graphically, it quickly becomes obvious how wide the tree of self-calls potentially spans. For a larger n, the call tree would be much more expansive, as indicated by the dashed arrows in Figure 3-2.

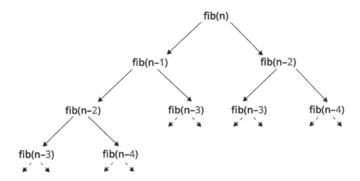

Figure 3-2. *Fibonacci recursive*

Even with this exemplary invocation, it is evident that various calls are made several times, for example for *fib*(n − 4) and *fib*(n − 2), but especially three times for *fib*(n − 3). This very quickly leads to costly and tedious computations. You will learn how to optimize this later in section 8.1.

HINT: DIFFERENT DEFINITION WITH ZERO AS START VALUE

It should furthermore be noted that there is a variation that starts at the value of 0. Then *fib*(0) = 0 and *fib*(1) = 1 are the base values and afterwards you get *fib*(n) = *fib*(n − 1) + *fib*(n − 2) according to the recursive definition. This produces the same sequence of numbers as the definition above, only with the value for 0 added.

3.1.2 Algorithmic Examples

In the introduction, you looked at mathematical examples. But recursion is also very well suited for algorithmic tasks. For example, it is possible to check for an array whether the values stored form a palindrome. A palindrome is a word that reads the same from the front and the back, such as OTTO or ABBA. Here it is meant that the elements match pairwise from the front and the back. This applies for example to a int[] with the following values: { 1, 2, 3, 2, 1 }.

Example 1: Palindrome – Recursive Variant

You can easily test for palindrome property recursively. You'll look at this as a program after I briefly describe the algorithm.

Algorithm   If the array has the length 0 or 1, then it is a palindrome by definition. If the length is two and greater, you must check the outer left and outer right elements for a match. After that, a copy of the array is created, shortened by one position at the front and one at the back. Further checking is then performed on the remaining part of the array, as shown here:

```java
static boolean isPalindromeSimpleRecursive(final int[] values)
{
    // recursive termination
    if (values.length <= 1)
        return true;

    int left = 0;
    int right = values.length - 1;

    if (values[left] == values[right])
    {
        // attention: copyOfRange() is exclusive end
        final int[] remainder = Arrays.copyOfRange(values, left + 1, right);

        // recursive descent
        return isPalindromeSimpleRecursive(remainder);
    }

    return false;
}
```

However, the described and implemented approach leads to many copies and extractions of subarrays. It is affordable to avoid this effort by keeping the idea but modifying the algorithm minimally by using a trick.

Optimized algorithm   Rather than using copies, you still use the original array. You include two position markers, left and right, which initially span the entire array. Now you check if the left and right values referenced by these positions match. If this is the case, the position markers are moved inward by one position on both sides, and the whole procedure is called recursively. This is repeated until the left position pointer reaches or skips the right one.

The implementation changes as follows:

```
static boolean isPalindromeRecursive(final int[] values)
{
    return isPalindromeRecursive(values, 0, values.length - 1);
}

static boolean isPalindromeRecursive(final int[] values,
                                     final int left, final int right)
{
    // recursive termination
    if (left >= right)
        return true;

    if (values[left] == values[right])
    {
        // recursive descent
        return isPalindromeRecursive(values, left + 1, right - 1);
    }

    return false;
}
```

Perhaps you wonder why I don't write the process more compactly and even using less return statements. My main concern in presenting algorithms is comprehensibility. Multiple returns are really only a problem if the method is very long and confusing.

HINT: AUXILIARY METHODS FOR FACILITATING RECURSION

The idea of position pointers in arrays or strings is a common tool used in solutions to recursion for optimization and avoidance of, say, array copying. To prevent the whole thing becoming inconvenient for callers, it is a good idea to have a high-level method calling a helper method that has additional parameters. This allows you to include certain information in the recursive descent. In this example, these are the left and right limits, so that potentially costly copying can be eliminated. Many subsequent examples will take advantage of the general idea.

Example 1: Palindrome – Iterative Variant

Although a recursive definition of an algorithm is sometimes quite elegant, the recursive descent produces self-calls. This potentially produces quite a bit of overhead. Conveniently, any recursive algorithm can be converted into an iterative one. Let's look at this for the palindrome calculation. You use two position pointers for the iterative conversion—instead of the recursive descent, you use a `while` loop. This terminates when all elements have been checked or if a mismatch has been detected before.

```java
private static boolean isPalindromeIter(int[] values)
{
    int left = 0;
    int right = values.length - 1;
    boolean sameValue = true;

    while (left < right && sameValue)
    {
        sameValue = values[left] == values[right];

        left++;
        right--;
    }

    return sameValue;
}
```

Again, a note on compactness: This method could be written as follows, omitting the auxiliary variable:

```java
static boolean isPalindromeIterativeCompact(final int[] values)
{
    int left = 0;
    int right = values.length - 1;

    while (left < right && values[left] == values[right])
    {
        left++;
        right--;
    }
}
```

```
    // left >= right || values[left] != values[right]
    return left >= right;
}
```

The return value is determined by the condition implied by the comment, if *left* >= *right* holds, then values is not a palindrome. With this variant, however, you have to think much more about the return—again, I prefer understandability and maintainability over brevity or performance.

Example 2: Fractal as an Example

As mentioned in the beginning, recursion allows you to create graphics as well. In the following, a graphically simple variant is displayed, which is based on the subdivisions of a ruler:

```
-
==
-
===
-
==
-
```

In fact, with the help of Java 11 on-board methods (repeat(n)), this can be easily implemented recursively as follows, where recursive descent occurs twice:

```java
static void fractalGenerator(final int n)
{
    if (n < 1)
        return;

    if (n == 1)
        System.out.println("-");
    else
    {
        fractalGenerator(n - 1);
        System.out.println("=".repeat(n));
        fractalGenerator(n - 1);
    }
}
```

If Java 11 and thus the method repeat() is not available, you simply write auxiliary method repeatCharSequence() (see section 2.3.7).

When using more complex drawing functions instead of ASCII characters, recursion offers the way to create interesting and appealing shapes, such as the snowflake embedded in a Swing application in Figure 3-3.

Figure 3-3. *Recursive graphic with drawSnowflake()*

This stylized representation of a snowflake can be implemented as follows:

```java
public static void drawSnowflake(final Graphics graphics,
                                 final int startX, final int startY,
                                 final int length, final int depth)
{
    for (int degree = 0; degree < 360; degree += 60)
    {
        final double rad = degree * Math.PI / 180;
        final int endX = (int) (startX + Math.cos(rad) * length);
        final int endY = (int) (startY + Math.sin(rad) * length);

        graphics.drawLine(startX, startY, endX, endY);
```

```
    // recursive descent
    if (depth > 0)
    {
        drawSnowflake(graphics, endX, endY, length / 4, depth - 1);
    }
    }
}
```

3.1.3 Steps When Multiplying the Digits of a Number

To conclude the algorithmic examples, I would like to clarify the individual steps and self-calls once more. As an artificial example, let's use the multiplication of the digits of a number, also called *cross product*, for example for the value $257 \Rightarrow 2 * 5 * 7 = 10 * 7 = 70$. Using modulo, the extraction of the individual digits and their multiplication can be implemented quite simply as follows:

```
static int multiplyAllDigits(final int value)
{
    final int remainder = value / 10;
    final int digitValue = value % 10;

    System.out.printf("multiplyAllDigits: %-10d | remainder: %d,
                      digit: %d%n", value, remainder, digitValue);

    if (remainder > 0)
    {
        final int result = multiplyAllDigits(remainder);

        System.out.printf("-> %d * %d = %d%n",
                          digitValue, result, digitValue * result);
        return digitValue * result;
    }
    else
    {
        System.out.println("-> " + value);
        return value;
    }
}
```

Let's look at the outputs for the two numbers 1234 and 257:

```
jshell> multiplyAllDigits(1234)
multiplyAllDigits: 1234      | remainder: 123, digit: 4
multiplyAllDigits: 123       | remainder: 12, digit: 3
multiplyAllDigits: 12        | remainder: 1, digit: 2
multiplyAllDigits: 1         | remainder: 0, digit: 1
-> 1
-> 2 * 1 = 2
-> 3 * 2 = 6
-> 4 * 6 = 24
$2 ==> 24

jshell> multiplyAllDigits(257)
multiplyAllDigits: 257       | remainder: 25, digit: 7
multiplyAllDigits: 25        | remainder: 2, digit: 5
multiplyAllDigits: 2         | remainder: 0, digit: 2
-> 2
-> 5 * 2 = 10
-> 7 * 10 = 70
$3 ==> 70
```

It is clearly visible how the recursive calls happen with a continuously shorter sequence of numbers. Finally, the result is constructed or calculated based on the last digit in the other direction.

3.1.4 Typical Problems

Recursion often allows you to formulate and implement the solution of problems in an understandable way. However, there are two things to keep in mind, which I discuss below.

Endless Calls and StackOverflowError

A detail worth knowing is that the self-calls lead to them being stored temporarily on the stack. For each method call, a so-called stack frame containing information about the called method and its parameters is stored on the stack. The stack is, however, limited in its size. Thus only a finite number of nested method calls can take place—usually, however, far over 10,000. This was already discussed briefly in a practical tip.

A huge number of recursive calls can result in a `StackOverflowError`. Sometimes the problem occurs because there is no termination condition in the recursion or the condition is formulated incorrectly:

```
// attention: deliberately wrong for demonstration
static void infiniteRecursion(final String value)
{
    infiniteRecursion(value);
}

static int factorialNoAbortion(final int number)
{
    return number * factorialNoAbortion(number - 1);
}
```

Sometimes the call is also just wrong, simply because no decreased value is passed:

```
// deliberately wrong for demonstration
static int factorialWrongCall(final int n)
{
    if (n == 0)
        return 1;
    if (n == 1)
        return 1;

    return n * factorialWrongCall(n);
}
```

You may still recognize a direct endless self-call fairly well. But this becomes more difficult with an increasing number of lines. With some experience and practice in recursion, even the missing termination condition in the method `factorialNoAbortion()` may still be quite recognizable. But, in the method `factorialWrongCall()` this is not so easy to determine. Here you must know more accurately what was intended.

You should take away two things from the examples:

1. **Termination condition**: A recursive method must always include at least one termination condition. But even if defined correctly, it is possible that, for example, the disallowed negative value range is not checked. For `factorial(int)` a call with a negative value would then lead to a `StackOverflowError`.

2. **Complexity reduction**: A recursive method must always subdivide the original problem into one or more smaller subproblems. Sometimes, this is already accomplished by reducing the value of a parameter by 1.

Unexpected Parameter Values

A rather nasty error, because easily made and difficult to spot, can occur in method calls, especially recursive ones, when you want to increment or decrement parameter values by one. Out of habit, you may be tempted to use post-increment or decrement (++ or --), as in the following example for the recursive (slightly clumsy) calculation of the length of a string, where the parameter `count` should contain the current length:

```java
static int calcLengthParameterValues(final String value, int count)
{
    if (value.length() == 0)
        return count;

    System.out.println("Count: " + count);
    final String remaining = value.substring(1);

    return calcLengthParameterValues(remaining, count++);
}
```

When viewing the outputs for the call

```java
final int length = calcLengthParameterValues("ABC", 0);
System.out.println("length: " + length);
```

you are probably surprised because instead of the value being increased by 1, it remains the same:

```
Count: 0
Count: 0
Count: 0
length: 0
```

In this example, only the shortening of the input will terminate the recursion.

Interestingly, the mistake in thinking can be detected faster, if you follow the good programming tradition and declares parameters as final. This way, the compiler directly produces an error message and notes that the variable is not mutable. Thereupon you might rather get the idea to choose the expression count + 1 instead of passing the variable. With this knowledge, the correction is easy:

```
static int calcLengthParameterValues(final String value, final int count)
{
    if (value.length() == 0)
        return count;

    System.out.println("Count: " + count);
    final String remaining = value.substring(1);
    return calcLengthParameterValues(remaining, count + 1);
}
```

More serious effects   The good habit of defining parameters as final can mitigate the problems presented. Nevertheless, say you omitted the final in the recursive palindrome check already presented and had also somewhat carelessly used ++ resp. --:

```
static boolean isPalindromeRecursive(int[] values, int left, int right)
{
    // recursive termination
    if (left >= right)
        return true;

    if (values[left] == values[right])
    {
```

```
    // recursive descent
    return isPalindromeRecursive(values, left++, right--);
}
    return false;
}
```

The effects are even worse than in the previous example, which at least terminates but returns a wrong value. With this palindrome check, you get a StackOverflowError after some time instead.

3.2 Exercises

3.2.1 Exercise 1: Fibonacci (★★☆☆☆)

Exercise 1a: Fibonacci Recursive (★☆☆☆☆)

Write method long fibRec(int) that recursively computes Fibonacci numbers based on the following definition:

$$fib(n) = \begin{cases} 1, & n = 1 \\ 1, & n = 2 \\ fib(n-1) + fib(n-2), & \forall n > 2 \end{cases}$$

Example For example, check the implementation with the following value progression:

n	1	2	3	4	5	6	7	8
fib(n)	1	1	2	3	5	8	13	21

Exercise 1b: Fibonacci Iterative (★★☆☆☆)

The recursive calculation of Fibonacci numbers is not efficient, and the running time increases enormously from about the 40th – 50th Fibonacci number. Write an iterative version for the calculation. What do you have to consider for the 1000th Fibonacci number?

3.2.2 Exercise 2: Process Digits (★★☆☆☆)

Exercise 2a: Count Digits (★★☆☆☆)

Write recursive method int countDigits(int) that finds the number of digits in a positive natural number. I discussed how to extract digits in Chapter 2, section 2.1.

Examples

Input	Number of digits	Cross sum
1234	4	1 + 2 + 3 + 4 = 10
1234567	7	1 + 2 + 3 + 4 + 5 + 6 + 7 = 28

Exercise 2b: Cross Sum (★★☆☆☆)

Calculate the sum of the digits of a number recursively. Write recursive method int calcSumOfDigits(int) for this purpose.

3.2.3 Exercise 3: GCD (★★☆☆☆)

Exercise 3a: GCD Recursive (★☆☆☆☆)

Write method int gcd(int, int) that computes the greatest common divisor (GCD)[1]. GCD can be expressed mathematically recursively as follows for two natural numbers a and b:

$$gcd(a,b) = \begin{cases} a, & b = 0 \\ gcd(b, a\%b), & b \neq 0 \end{cases}$$

---

[1] Colloquially, this is the largest natural number by which two integers can be divided without a remainder

Examples

Input 1	Input 2	Result
42	7	7
42	28	14
42	14	14

Exercise 3b: GCD Iterative (★★☆☆☆)

Create an iterative version for the GCD calculation.

Exercise 3c: LCM (★☆☆☆☆)

Write method int lcm(int, int) that computes the least common multiplier (LCM). For two natural numbers *a* and *b*, you can calculate this based on the GCD using the following formula:

$$lcm(a, b) = a * b / gcd(a, b);$$

Examples

Input 1	Input 2	Result
2	7	14
7	14	14
42	14	42

3.2.4 Exercise 4: Reverse String (★★☆☆☆)

Write recursive method String reverseString(String) that flips the letters of the input text passed in.

Examples

Input	Result
"A"	"A"
"ABC"	"CBA"
"abcdefghi"	"ihgfedcba"

3.2.5 Exercise 5: Array Sum (★★☆☆☆)

Write method int sum(int[]) that recursively computes the sum of the values of the given array.

Examples

Input	Result
[1, 2, 3]	6
[1, 2, 3, -7]	-1

3.2.6 Exercise 6: Array Min (★★☆☆☆)

Write method int min(int[]) that uses recursion to find the minimum of the values of the passed array. For an empty array, the value Integer.MAX_VALUE should be returned.

Examples

Input	Result
[7, 2, 1, 9, 7, 1]	1
[11, 2, 33, 44, 55, 6, 7]	2
[1, 2, 3, -7]	-7

3.2.7 Exercise 7: Conversions (★★☆☆☆)

Exercise 7a: Binary (★★☆☆☆)

Write method `String toBinary(int)` that recursively converts the given positive integer into a textual binary representation.

Examples

Input	Result
5	"101"
7	"111"
22	"10110"
42	"101010"
256	"100000000"

Exercise 7b: Octal and Hexadecimal Numbers (★★☆☆☆)

Write conversions to octal and hexadecimal numbers by implementing the corresponding methods `String toOctal(int)` and `String toHex(int)`.

Examples

Input	Method	Result
7	Octal	"7"
8	Octal	"10"
42	Octal	"52"
15	Hexadecimal	"F"
77	Hexadecimal	"4D"

3.2.8 Exercise 8: Exponential Function (★★☆☆☆)

Exercise 8a: Power of Two (★★☆☆☆)

Write recursive method `boolean isPowerOf2(int)` that evaluates the given positive integer to see if it is a power of two.

Examples

Input	Result
2	true
10	false
16	true

Exercise 8b: Exponentiation Recursive (★★☆☆☆)

Write recursive method `long powerOf(int, int)` that exponentiates the given positive integer with the positive number specified as the second parameter. For example, the call `powerOf(4, 2)` should return the square of 4, so compute $4^2 = 16$.

Exercise 8c: Exponentiation Iterative (★★☆☆☆)

Write an iterative version of this exponentiation functionality.

Examples

Input base	Input exponent	Result
2	2	4
2	8	256
4	4	256

3.2.9 Exercise 9: Pascal's Triangle (★★☆☆☆)

Write method void printPascal(int) that prints Pascal's triangle. For the value 5, the following output should be generated:

```
[1]
[1, 1]
[1, 2, 1]
[1, 3, 3, 1]
[1, 4, 6, 4, 1]
```

Starting with the third line, each subsequent line is calculated based on the previous one with the help of an addition, as shown in the last line of the following definition. For each line, these values are flanked by a 1 at the front and at the back. Since this is a two-dimensional structure, the recursive definition is a little more complex:

$$pascal(row, col) = \begin{cases} 1, & row = 1 \text{ and } col = 1 \text{ (top)} \\ 1, & \forall row \in \{1, n\} \text{ and } col = 1 \\ 1, & \forall row \in \{1, n\} \text{ and } col = row \\ pascal(row-1, col) + \\ pascal(row-1, col-1), & \text{otherwise (based on predecessors)} \end{cases}$$

Tip   You can find background information and an in-depth explanation here: https://en.wikipedia.org/wiki/Pascal's_triangle.

3.2.10 Exercise 10: Number Palindromes (★★★★☆)

A palindrome is a word that reads the same from the front and the back. We can extend this definition to the digits of a number. Write recursive method boolean isNumberPalindrome(int), but without resorting to functionalities from the class String.

Examples

Input	Result
7	true
13	false
171	true
47742	false

3.2.11 Exercise 11: Permutations (★★★☆☆)

Calculate all permutations of a sequence of letters given as a string; this means
all possible combinations of these letters. Implement this calculation in method
Set<String> calcPermutations(String). Consider also the case of duplicate letters.

Examples

Input	Result
"A"	"A"
"AA"	"AA"
"AB"	"AB", "BA"
"ABC"	"ABC, "BAC", "ACB", "CAB", "CBA", "BCA"
"AAC"	"AAC", "ACA", "CAA"

3.2.12 Exercise 12: Count Substrings (★★☆☆☆)

Write method int countSubstrings(String, String) that counts all occurrences of
the given substring. Thereby, when a pattern is found, it should be *consumed*, (i. e., it
should not be available for hits again). This is shown in the following table as the last
case.

Examples

Input	Search term	Result
"xhixhix"	"x"	3
"xhixhix"	"hi"	2
"mic"	"mic"	1
"haha"	"ho"	0
"xxxxyz"	"xx"	2

3.2.13 Exercise 13: Ruler (★★☆☆☆)

In the introduction, I showed how to draw a simple shape of a ruler as well as a stylized snowflake (see Figure 3-3) using recursion. In this exercise, you want to imitate an English-style ruler. This involves dividing an area of one inch into 1/2 and 1/4, and 1/8. In doing so, the length of the strokes decreases by one each time.

Example   The output should look somewhat like the following:

```
---- 0
-
--
-
---
-
--
-
---- 1
-
--
-
---
-
--
-
---- 2
```

3.3 Solutions

3.3.1 Solution 1: Fibonacci (★★☆☆☆)

Solution 1a: Fibonacci Recursive (★☆☆☆☆)

Write method long fibRec(int) that recursively computes Fibonacci numbers based on the following definition:

$$fib(n) = \begin{cases} 1, & n=1 \\ 1, & n=2 \\ fib(n-1) + fib(n-2), & \forall n > 2 \end{cases}$$

Example   For example, check the implementation with the following value progression:

n	1	2	3	4	5	6	7	8
fib(n)	1	1	2	3	5	8	13	21

Algorithm   Its implementation in Java is exactly derived from the mathematical definition:

```java
static long fibRec(final int n)
{
    if (n <= 0)
        throw new IllegalArgumentException("n must be >= 1");

    // recursive termination
    if (n == 1 || n == 2)
        return 1;

    // recursive descent
    return fibRec(n - 1) + fibRec(n - 2);
}
```

Solution 1b: Fibonacci Iterative (★★☆☆☆)

The recursive calculation of Fibonacci numbers is not efficient, and the running time increases enormously from about the 40th – 50th Fibonacci number. Write an iterative version for the calculation. What do you have to consider for the 1000th Fibonacci number?

Algorithm   Similarly to the recursive version, the iterative implementation checks at first the input for validity and then for the special cases for the invocation with the values 1 or 2. After that, you use two helper variables and a loop that runs from 2 to n. You then calculate the corresponding Fibonacci number from the sum of the two helper variables. After that, the two helper variables are assigned appropriately. This results in the following implementation:

```java
static long fibIterative(final int n)
{
    if (n <= 0)
        throw new IllegalArgumentException("n must be >= 1");

    if (n==1 || n == 2)
        return 1;

    long fibN_2 = 1;
    long fibN_1 = 1;

    for (int count = 2; count < n; count++)
    {
        long fibN = fibN_1 + fibN_2;

        // move forward by one
        fibN_2 = fibN_1;
        fibN_1 = fibN;
    }

    return fibN;
}
```

Fibonacci for larger numbers   For example, if you want to compute the 1000th Fibonacci number, the value range of a long is far from sufficient. As a fix, the computation must be performed using the BigInteger class.

Verification

For testing, you use the following inputs, which show correct functioning:

```
@ParameterizedTest(name = "fibRec({0}) = {1}")
@CsvSource({ "1, 1", "2, 1", "3, 2", "4, 3", "5, 5", "6, 8", "7, 13", "8, 21" })
void fibRec(int n, long expectedFibN)
{
    long result1 = Ex01_Fibonacci.fibRec(n);

    assertEquals(expectedFibN, result1);
}

@ParameterizedTest(name = "fibIterative({0}) =  {1}")
@CsvSource({ "1, 1", "2, 1", "3, 2", "4, 3", "5, 5", "6, 8", "7, 13", "8, 21" })
void fibIterative(int n, long expectedFibN)
{
    long result = Ex01_Fibonacci.fibIterative(n);

    assertEquals(expectedFibN, result);
}
```

3.3.2 Solution 2: Process Digits (★★☆☆☆)

Solution 2a: Count Digits (★★☆☆☆)

Write recursive method int countDigits(int) that finds the number of digits in a positive natural number. I discussed how to extract digits in Chapter 2, section 2.1.

Examples

Input	Number of digits	Cross sum
1234	4	1 + 2 + 3 + 4 = 10
1234567	7	1 + 2 + 3 + 4 + 5 + 6 + 7 = 28

Algorithm   If the number is less than 10, then return the value 1 because this corresponds to a digit. Otherwise, calculate the remaining value by dividing the number by 10. This invokes the counting method recursively as follows:

```java
static int countDigits(final int value)
{
    if (value < 0)
        throw new IllegalArgumentException("value must be >= 0");

    // recursive termination
    if (value < 10)
        return 1;

    final int remainder = value / 10;

    // recursive descent
    return countDigits(remainder) + 1;
}
```

Solution 2b: Cross Sum (★★☆☆☆)

Calculate the sum of the digits of a number recursively. Write recursive method int calcSumOfDigits(int) for this purpose.

Algorithm   Based on the solution for the first subtask, you only vary the returned value for the digit as well as the addition and the self-call as follows:

```java
static int calcSumOfDigits(final int value)
{
    if (value < 0)
        throw new IllegalArgumentException("value must be >= 0");

    // recursive termination
    if (value < 10)
        return value;

    final int remainder = value / 10;
    final int lastDigit = value % 10;
```

```
    // recursive descent
    return calcSumOfDigits(remainder) + lastDigit;
}
```

Verification

For testing, you use the following inputs, which show the correct operation:

```
@ParameterizedTest(name = "countDigits({0}) = {1}")
@CsvSource({ "1234, 4", "1234567, 7" })
void countDigits(int number, int expected)
{
    long result = Ex02_CalcDigits.countDigits(number);

    assertEquals(expected, result);
}

@ParameterizedTest(name = "calcSumOfDigits({0}) = {1}")
@CsvSource({ "1234, 10", "1234567, 28" })
void calcSumOfDigits(int number, int expected)
{
    long result = Ex02_CalcDigits.calcSumOfDigits(number);

    assertEquals(expected, result);
}
```

3.3.3 Solution 3: GCD (★★☆☆☆)

Solution 3a: GCD Recursive (★☆☆☆☆)

Write method int gcd(int, int) that computes the greatest common divisor (GCD)[2]. GCD can be expressed mathematically recursively as follows for two natural numbers a and b:

$$gcd(a,b) = \begin{cases} a, & b = 0 \\ gcd(b, a\%b), & b \neq 0 \end{cases}$$

---

[2] Colloquially, this is the largest natural number by which two integers can be divided without a remainder.

103

Examples

Input 1	Input 2	Result
42	7	7
42	28	14
42	14	14

Algorithm   The calculation of the greatest common divisor can be coded in Java fairly directly from the mathematical definition:

```java
static int gcd(final int a, final int b)
{
    // recursive termination
    if (b == 0)
        return a;

    // recursive descent
    return gcd(b, a % b);
}
```

Solution 3b: GCD Iterative (★★☆☆☆)

Create an iterative version for the GCD calculation.

Algorithm   The self-call is transformed into a loop that is executed until the condition of the recursive termination is met. The trick is to reassign the variables as specified by the recursive definition:

```java
static int gcdIterative(int a, int b)
{
    while (b != 0)
    {
        final int remainder = a % b;

        a = b;
        b = remainder;
    }
```

```
    // here applies b == 0
    return a;
}
```

Verification

For testing, you use the following inputs, which show the correct operation:

```
@ParameterizedTest(name = "gcd({0}, {1}) = {2}")
@CsvSource({ "42, 7, 7", "42, 28, 14", "42, 14, 14" })
void gcd(int a, int b, int expected)
{
    int result = Ex03_GCD.gcd(a, b);

    assertEquals(expected, result);
}

@ParameterizedTest(name = "gcdIterative({0}, {1}) = {2}")
@CsvSource({ "42, 7, 7", "42, 28, 14", "42, 14, 14" })
void gcdIterative(int a, int b, int expected)
{
    int result = Ex03_GCD.gcdIterative(a, b);

    assertEquals(expected, result);
}
```

Solution 3c: LCM (★☆☆☆☆)

Write method int lcm(int, int) that computes the least common multiplier (LCM). For two natural numbers *a* and *b*, you can calculate this based on the GCD using the following formula:

$$lcm(a, b) = a * b / gcd(a, b);$$

Examples

Input 1	Input 2	Result
2	7	14
7	14	14
42	14	42

Algorithm   The calculation of the least common multiplier can also directly implemented from the mathematical definition, as long as you have already completed the functionality for the GCD:

```
static int lcm(final int a, final int b)
{
    return a * b / gcd(a, b);
}
```

Verification

For testing, use the following inputs, which show the correct operation:

```
@ParameterizedTest(name = "lcm({0}, {1}) = {2}")
@CsvSource({ "2, 7, 14", "7, 14, 14", "42, 14, 42" })
void lcm(int a, int b, int expected)
{
    int result = Ex03_GCD.lcm(a, b);

    assertEquals(expected, result);
}
```

3.3.4 Solution 4: Reverse String (★★☆☆☆)

Write recursive method `String reverseString(String)` that flips the letters of the input text passed in.

Examples

Input	Result
"A"	"A"
"ABC"	"CBA"
"abcdefghi"	"ihgfedcba"

Algorithm   Extract the first character until you have a string of length 1 and then concatenate the whole in reverse order:

```java
static String reverseString(final String input)
{
    // recursive termination
    if (input.length() <= 1)
        return input;

    final char firstChar = input.charAt(0);
    final String remaining = input.substring(1);

    // recursive descent
    return reverseString(remaining) + firstChar;
}
```

Verification

For testing, use the following inputs, which show the correct operation:

```java
@ParameterizedTest(name = "reverseString({0}) => {1}")
@CsvSource({ "A, A", "ABC, CBA", "abcdefghi, ihgfedcba" })
void reverseString(String input, String expected)
{
    String result = Ex04_ReverseString.reverseString(input);

    assertEquals(expected, result);
}
```

3.3.5 Solution 5: Array Sum (★★☆☆☆)

Write method int sum(int[]) that recursively computes the sum of the values of the given array.

Examples

Input	Result
[1, 2, 3]	6
[1, 2, 3, -7]	-1

Algorithm Compute the partial sum with the recursive definition as long as

$$sum(values(0)) \;=\; values[0]$$
$$sum(values(0 \ldots n)) \;=\; values[0] + sum(values(1 \ldots n))$$

until only a single element is left. As mentioned in the introduction, a helper method is useful, containing the actual processing and logic. Here the current value in the array is added to the recursively determined result:

```
static int sum(final int[] values)
{
    return sum(values, 0);
}

static int sum(final int[] values, final int pos)
{
    // recursive termination
    if (pos >= values.length)
        return 0;
```

```
int value = values[pos];

// recursive descent
return value + sum(values, pos + 1);
}
```

Alternatively, it is also possible to let the pos counter run from length − 1 to 0, so the recursion reverses to the following:

$$sum(values(0 \dots n)) = sum(values(0 \dots n-1)) + values[n]$$

This will be implemented as follows with the method sumTail(int[], int):

```
static int sumTail(final int[] values, final int pos)
{
    if (pos < 0)
        return 0;

    int value = values[pos];

    // recursive descent
    return sumTail(values, pos - 1) + value;
}
```

Verification

For testing, use the annotation @MethodSource and the reference to the method valuesAndResult() to serve up desired inputs and results:

```
@ParameterizedTest(name="sum({0}) = {1}")
@MethodSource("valuesAndResult")
void sum(int[] values, int expected)
{
    int result = Ex05_ArraySum.sum(values);

    assertEquals(expected, result);
}
```

Besides the previously used annotation @CsvSource, @MethodSource is another way to pass data to a test case. This becomes necessary because you can't use @CsvSource to provide int[], which is what you need here. For this purpose, it is possible to use a Stream<Arguments>:

```
private static Stream<Arguments> valuesAndResult()
{
    return Stream.of(Arguments.of(new int[] { 1 }, 1),
                    Arguments.of(new int[] { 1, 2, 3 }, 6),
                    Arguments.of(new int[] { 1, 2, 3, -7 }, -1));
}
```

3.3.6 Solution 6: Array Min (★★☆☆☆)

Write method int min(int[]) that uses recursion to find the minimum of the values of the passed array. For an empty array, the value Integer.MAX_VALUE should be returned.

Examples

Input	Result
[7, 2, 1, 9, 7, 1]	1
[11, 2, 33, 44, 55, 6, 7]	2
[1, 2, 3, -7]	-7

Algorithm   Inspect the array starting from the first element and compare it to a minimum initially set to Integer.MAX_VALUE. If the current element is smaller, it becomes the new minimum. Repeat this process for the array shortened by one position until the position is at the end of the array.

```
static int min(final int[] values)
{
    return min(values, 0, Integer.MAX_VALUE);
}
```

```java
static int min(final int[] values, final int pos, int currentMin)
{
    // recursive termination
    if (pos >= values.length)
        return currentMin;

    final int current = values[pos];
    if (current < currentMin)
        currentMin = current;

    // recursive descent
    return min(values, pos + 1, currentMin);
}
```

Verification

For testing, use the following inputs, which show the correct operation:

```java
@ParameterizedTest(name="min({0}) = {1}")
@MethodSource("valuesAndMinimum")
void min(int[] input, int expected)
{
    int result = Ex06_ArrayMin.min(input);

    assertEquals(expected, result);
}

private static Stream<Arguments> valuesAndMinimum()
{
    return Stream.of(Arguments.of(new int[] { 7, 2, 1, 9, 7, 1 }, 1),
                     Arguments.of(new int[] { 11, 2, 33, 44, 55, 6, 7 }, 2),
                     Arguments.of(new int[] { 1, 2, 3, -7 }, -7),
                     Arguments.of(new int[] { }, Integer.MAX_VALUE));
}
```

3.3.7 Solution 7: Conversions (★★☆☆☆)

Solution 7a: Binary (★★☆☆☆)

Write method String toBinary(int) that recursively converts the given positive integer into a textual binary representation.

Examples

Input	Result
5	"101"
7	"111"
22	"10110"
42	"101010"
256	"100000000"

Algorithm   The conversion is based on the already known extraction of the last digit and the determination of remainder, as introduced in section 2.1. To convert a decimal number into a binary number, you check whether the number passed can be represented by a single digit in the binary system (i.e., whether it is smaller than 2). Otherwise, the last digit is extracted first using the modulo operator and then the remainder. For this, you call the method recursively and then concatenate the string representation of the last digit. This results in the following sequence for the value 22:

Invocation	Sequence	Result
toBinary(22)	toBinary(22/2) + valueOf(22%2) => toBinary(11) + "0"	"10110"
toBinary(11)	toBinary(11/2) + valueOf(11%2) => toBinary(5) + "1"	"1011"
toBinary(5)	toBinary(5/2) + valueOf(5%2) => toBinary(2) + "1"	"101"
toBinary(2)	toBinary(2/2) + valueOf(2%2) => toBinary(1) + "0"	"10"
toBinary(1)	valueOf(1) => "1"	"1"

Now let's implement the whole thing in Java as follows:

```java
static String toBinary(final int n)
{
    if (n < 0)
        throw new IllegalArgumentException("n must be >= 0");

    // recursive termination: check for digit in binary system
    if (n <= 1)
        return String.valueOf(n);

    final int lastDigit = n % 2;
    final int remainder = n / 2;

    // recursive descent
    return toBinary(remainder) + lastDigit;
}
```

Solution 7b: Octal and Hexadecimal Numbers (★★☆☆☆)

Write conversions to octal and hexadecimal numbers by implementing the corresponding methods String toOctal(int) and String toHex(int).

Examples

Input	Method	Result
7	octal	"7"
8	octal	"10"
42	octal	"52"
15	hexadecimal	"F"
77	hexadecimal	"4D"

Algorithm   The algorithm remains basically the same. You check whether the number passed can be represented by a single digit of the desired number system, so smaller than 8 (octal) or 16 (hexadecimal). Otherwise, you first extract the last digit using a modulo operation and also the remainder. For the remainder, this method is called recursively, and then the string representation of the last digit is concatenated.

```java
public String toOctal(final int n)
{
    if (n < 0)
        throw new IllegalArgumentException("n must be >= 0");

    // recursive termination: check for digit in octal system
    if (n < 8)
        return String.valueOf(n);

    final int lastDigit = n % 8;
    final int remainder = n / 8;

    // recursive descent
    return toOctal(remainder) + String.valueOf(lastDigit);
}

public String toHex(final int n)
{
    if (n < 0)
        throw new IllegalArgumentException("n must be >= 0");

    // recursive termination: check for digit in hexadecimal system
    if (n <= 15)
        return asHexDigit(n);

    final int lastDigit = n % 16;
    final int remainder = n / 16;

    // recursive descent
    return toHex(remainder) + asHexDigit(lastDigit);
}

// easier handling of hexadecimal conversion
static String asHexDigit(final int n)
{
    if (n < 0)
        throw new IllegalArgumentException("n must be >= 0");

    if (n < 9)
        return String.valueOf(n);
```

```
    if (n <= 15)
        return Character.toString(n - 10 + 'A');

    throw new IllegalArgumentException("value not in range 0 - 15, " +
                                        "but is: " + n);
}
```

HINT: POSSIBLE OPTIMIZATIONS

Although the implementation shown for converting a single hexadecimal digit to a string is fairly straightforward, there is an amazingly elegant alternative that is also easy to read and understand. It validates a number against a given set of characters using charAt(int):

```
static String asHexDigit(final int n)
{
    if (n < 0)
        throw new IllegalArgumentException("n must be >= 0");

    if (n <= 15)
    {
        final char hexdigit = "0123456789ABCDEF".charAt(n);
        return String.valueOf(hexdigit);
    }

    throw new IllegalArgumentException("value not in range 0 - 15, " +
                                        "but is: " + n);
}
```

Converting in the opposite direction from a character to a number can be achieved using Character.getNumericvalue(char). You will learn about this in section 4.1.3.

Verification

For testing, use the following inputs, which show the correct operation:

```
@ParameterizedTest(name = "toBinary({0}) => {1}")
@CsvSource({ "5, 101", "7, 111", "22, 10110", "42, 101010", "256, 100000000" })
void toBinary(int value, String expected)
```

```
{
    String result = Ex07_NumberConversions.toBinary(value);

    assertEquals(expected, result);
}

@ParameterizedTest(name = "toOctal({0}) => {1}")
@CsvSource({ "42, 52", "7, 7", "8, 10" })
void toOctal(int value, String expected)
{
    String result = Ex07_NumberConversions.toOctal(value);

    assertEquals(expected, result);
}

@ParameterizedTest(name = "toHex({0}) => {1}")
@CsvSource({ "77, 4D", "15, F", "16, 10" })
void toHex(int value, String expected)
{
    String result = Ex07_NumberConversions.toHex(value);

    assertEquals(expected, result);
}
```

3.3.8 Solution 8: Exponential Function (★★☆☆☆)

Solution 8a: Power of Two (★★☆☆☆)

Write recursive method boolean isPowerOf2(int) that evaluates the given positive integer to see if it is a power of two.

Examples

Input	Result
2	true
10	false
16	true

Algorithm   If the given number is smaller than the value 2, only the value 1 corresponds to a power, namely the 0th (i.e., 2^0). Now you have to check if it is an odd number. If this is the case, it is impossible for it to be a multiple and therefore not a power of 2. If the number is even, then check recursively with the number divided by 2:

```
static boolean isPowerOf2(final int n)
{
    // recursive termination
    if (n < 2)
        return n == 1;

    if (n % 2 != 0)
        return false;

    // recursive descent
    return isPowerOf2(n / 2);
}
```

For the initial check, you use a little trick with `return n==1`, which has the following effect:

$$n < 0: \quad \text{false} \quad \text{(negative number, so never the value 1)}$$
$$n = 0: \quad \text{false} \quad (0 \neq 1)$$
$$n = 1: \quad \text{true} \quad (1 = 1)$$

Let's take a look at a short version of the implementation. To my mind, the upper one is more comprehensible. Moreover, again in the first version, the recursive termination and the descent are much clearer:

```
static boolean isPowerOf2Short(final int n)
{
    return n == 1 || n > 0 && n % 2 == 0 && isPowerOf2Short(n / 2);
}
```

Solution 8b: Exponentiation Recursive (★★☆☆☆)

Write recursive method `long powerOf(int, int)` that exponentiates the given positive integer with the positive number specified as the second parameter. For example, the call `powerOf(4, 2)` should return the square of 4, so compute $4^2 = 16$.

Algorithm   Now, invoke the method recursively and multiply the number by the result of the self-call until the exponent reaches 0 or 1. Furthermore, you have to reduce the exponent by 1 with each call.

```
static long powerOf(int value, int exponent)
{
    if (exponent < 0)
        throw new IllegalArgumentException("exponent must be >= 0");

    // recursive termination
    if (exponent == 0)
        return 1;

    if (exponent == 1)
        return value;

    // recursive descent
    return value * powerOf(value, exponent - 1);
}
```

This alternative has a cost of *O(n)*. But it is quite easy to optimize this and reduce it to *O(log(n))*.

Optimized algorithm   For optimization, you use the trick of squaring the value and thereby halving the exponent. This leaves only the special treatment of an odd exponent, which requires another multiplication. To avoid an overflow of the value range, you have to change the type of the value from int to long:

```
static long powerOfOptimized(final long value, final int exponent)
{
    if (exponent < 0)
        throw new IllegalArgumentException("exponent must be >= 0");

    // recursive termination
    if (exponent == 0)
        return 1;

    if (exponent == 1)
        return value;
```

```
// recursive descent
final long result = powerOfOptimized(value * value, exponent / 2);
if (exponent % 2 == 1)
    return value * result;

return result;
}
```

Solution 8c: Exponentiation Iterative (★★☆☆☆)

Write an iterative version of this exponentiation functionality.

Examples

Input base	Input exponent	Result
2	2	4
2	8	256
4	4	256

Algorithm   As with the recursive version, you probably start with the two checks. Besides, the self-call has to be converted into a loop, and the number has to be multiplied with the previous intermediate result. Furthermore, in each pass, the exponent has to be reduced. However, a sharp look quickly shows that the two initial checks are already covered by the general case and therefore are no longer included in the listing.

```
long powerOfIterative(int value, int exponent)
{
    long result = 1;
    while (exponent > 0)
    {
        result *= value;
        exponent--;
    }

    return result;
}
```

Verification

For testing, use the following inputs, which show the correct operation:

```
@ParameterizedTest(name = "isPowerOf2({0}) => {1}")
@CsvSource({ "2, true", "3, false", "4, true", "10, false", "16, true" })
void isPowerOf2(int number, boolean expected)
{
    boolean result = Ex08_Exponentation.isPowerOf2(number);

    assertEquals(expected, result);
}

@ParameterizedTest(name = "powerOf({0}) => {1}")
@CsvSource({ "2, 2, 4", "4, 2, 16", "16, 2, 256", "4, 4, 256", "2, 8, 256" })
void powerOf(int number, int exponent, long expected)
{
    long result = Ex08_Exponentation.powerOf(number, exponent);

    assertEquals(expected, result);
}

@ParameterizedTest(name = "powerOfIterative({0}) => {1}")
@CsvSource({ "2, 2, 4", "4, 2, 16", "16, 2, 256", "4, 4, 256", "2, 8, 256" })
void powerOfIterative(int number, int exponent, long expected)
{
    long result = Ex08_Exponentation.powerOfIterative(number, exponent);

    assertEquals(expected, result);
}
```

3.3.9 Solution 9: Pascal's Triangle (★★☆☆☆)

Write method void printPascal(int) that prints Pascal's triangle. For the value 5, the following output should be generated:

```
[1]
[1, 1]
[1, 2, 1]
[1, 3, 3, 1]
[1, 4, 6, 4, 1]
```

Starting with the third line, each subsequent line is calculated based on the previous one with the help of an addition, as shown in the last line of the following definition. For each line, these values are flanked by a 1 at the front and at the back. Since this is a two-dimensional structure, the recursive definition is a little more complex.

$$pascal(row, col) = \begin{cases} 1, & row = 1 \text{ and } col = 1 \text{ (top)} \\ 1, & \forall row \in \{1, n\} \text{ and } col = 1 \\ 1, & \forall row \in \{1, n\} \text{ and } col = row \\ pascal(row - 1, col) + \\ pascal(row - 1, col - 1), & \text{otherwise (based on predecessors)} \end{cases}$$

Tip   You can find background information and an in-depth explanation here: https://en.wikipedia.org/wiki/Pascal's_triangle.

Algorithm   You implement the recursive definition as method as follows:

```java
static int calcPascal(final int row, final int col)
{
    // recursive termination: top
    if (col == 1 && row == 1)
        return 1;

    // recursive termination: borders
    if (col == 1 || col == row)
        return 1;

    // recursive descent
    return calcPascal(row - 1, col) + calcPascal(row - 1, col - 1);
}
```

Actually, there is no need for a separate termination condition for the top. Nevertheless, this is shown here for the sake of better comprehension—but of course, that is a matter of taste.

To calculate Pascal's triangle, the previous method must now be invoked for each position in the triangle using two nested loops covering all rows and columns:

```java
static void printPascal(final int n)
{
    for (int row = 1; row <= n; row++)
    {
        for (int col = 1; col <= row; col++)
            System.out.print(calcPascal(row, col));

        System.out.println();
    }
}
```

For testing, use the following inputs, which show the correct operation:

```
jshell> printPascal(4) [1]
[1, 1]
[1, 2, 1]
[1, 3, 3, 1]
```

Optimized algorithm   The pure recursive definition results in quite a lot of computations. It becomes easier to understand, easier to comprehend, and more performant if you work line by line.

The starting point is the first line, which contains only the value 1. For all other values, you have to call the method itself n times and then use the helper method List<Integer> calcLine(List<Integer>) to compute the new line. But to avoid mixing the computation and the console output, you add a parameter that is capable of performing actions, such as logging intermediate steps to the console:

```java
static List<Integer> calcPascal(final int n,
                                final Consumer<List<Integer>> action)
{
    // recursive termination
```

```
    if (n == 1)
    {
        action.accept(List.of(1));
        return List.of(1);
    }
    else
    {
        // recursive descent
        final List<Integer> previousLineValues = calcPascal(n - 1, action);

        final List<Integer> newLine = calcLine(previousLineValues);

        action.accept(newLine);
        return newLine;
    }
}
```

There is a bit more complexity in the helper method calcLine(List<Integer>) for calculating the values of the new line based on the previous one. It is important to keep in mind that the previous line contains at least two values and that you do not sum up to the last element, but only to the second last element:

```
static List<Integer> calcLine(final List<Integer> previousLine)
{
    final List<Integer> currentLine = new ArrayList<>();
    currentLine.add(1);

    for (int i = 0; i < previousLine.size() - 1; i++)
    {
        // value is calculated based on the two values of the predecessor line
        final int newValue = previousLine.get(i) + previousLine.get(i + 1);
        currentLine.add(newValue);
    }

    currentLine.add(1);
    return currentLine;
}
```

Verification

For testing, use the following call, which shows the correct operation:

```
jshell> calcPascal(7, System.out::println) [1]
[1, 1]
[1, 2, 1]
[1, 3, 3, 1]
[1, 4, 6, 4, 1]
[1, 5, 10, 10, 5, 1]
[1, 6, 15, 20, 15, 6, 1]
```

You can then check something more formal with a unit test:

```java
@ParameterizedTest(name = "calcPascal({0}) = {1}")
@MethodSource("valuesAndResults")
void calcPascal(int n, List<Integer> expected)
{
    final Consumer<List<Integer>> NOOP = whatever -> { };
    List<Integer> result = Ex09_PascalTriangle.calcPascal(n, NOOP);

    assertEquals(expected, result);
}

private static Stream<Arguments> valuesAndResults()
{
    return Stream.of(Arguments.of(1, List.of(1)),
                     Arguments.of(2, List.of(1,1)),
                     Arguments.of(3, List.of(1,2,1)),
                     Arguments.of(4, List.of(1,3,3,1)),
                     Arguments.of(5, List.of(1,4,6,4,1)));
}
```

3.3.10 Solution 10: Number Palindromes (★★★★☆)

A palindrome is a word that reads the same from the front and the back. You can extend this definition to the digits of a number. Write recursive method boolean isNumberPalindrome(int), but without resorting to functionalities from the class String.

Examples

Input	Result
7	true
13	false
171	true
47742	false

Algorithm   Because of the restriction demanded in the exercise, it is not possible to compare character by character. However, the operations modulo and division are suitable, which you have already used for similar tasks. You use both to separate and compare the left and right numbers.

Let's approach the solution with examples:

```
# of Digits   Value    Calculation
-----------------------------------------------------------------
1 digit                => special case, is always palindrome

2 digits      11       divisor = 10
< 100                      1 % 10 = 1
                          11 / 10 = 1        palindrome
              13
                           3 % 10 = 3
                          13 / 10 = 1      X

3 digits      171      divisor = 100
< 1000                     1 % 10 = 1
                         171 / 100 = 1
                       remainder: 7 (171 / 10 = 17 % 10 = 7) => check
                                 recursively

4 digits      4774     divisor = 1000
< 10000                    4 % 10 = 4
                        4774 / 1000 = 4    ok
                       remainder: 77 (4774 / 10 = 477 % 100 = 77) =>
                                 check recursively
```

The right and left digits of a digit have to be extracted. If these match, the new value is determined by first dividing by 10 (cutting off the last digit) and then using the modulo operator with the appropriately selected amount of digits to determine the remainder (i.e., cutting off the front number). In particular, you have to figure out the length of the number as a power of ten to get the correct divisor.

```java
static boolean isNumberPalindrome(final int number)
{
    if (number < 10)
        return true;

    final int factor = MathUtils.calcPowOfTen(number);
    final int divisor = (int)Math.pow(10, factor);

    if (number < divisor * 10)
    {
        final int leftNumber = number / divisor;
        final int rightNumber = number % 10;

        final int remainingNumber = (number / 10) % (divisor / 10);
        return leftNumber == rightNumber && isNumberPalindrome(
        remainingNumber);
    }

    return false;
}
```

In the following, the calculation of the power of ten, as well as the counting of digits, are shown as helper methods, which resides in the utility class MathUtils:

```java
static int calcPowOfTen(final int number)
{
    return countDigits(number) - 1;
}

static int countDigits(int number)
{
    int count = 0;
```

```
    while (number > 0)
    {
        number = number / 10;
        count++;
    }

    return count;
}
```

The solution shown is by no means optimal since the factors have to be determined constantly. Furthermore, the entire procedure is still quite difficult to understand from the source code, even though helper methods have already been extracted.

Optimized algorithm   As an optimization, you implement the following version: Always separate the last digit, divide by 10, and call the method with the new values. Beforehand, compute the new value from the current value and the last digit by multiplying the current value by 10 and appending the last digit. If it is a palindrome, then the original value corresponds to the calculated value. The recursive termination occurs when either no more digits exist or only one single digit exists. The trick is that you rebuild the number from the back and finally compare it with the original value. In contrast to the other recursive helper methods presented so far, you need two buffers here, one for the current value and one for the remaining value:

```
static boolean isNumberPalindromeRec(final int number)
{
    return isNumberPalindromeRec(number, 0, number);
}

static boolean isNumberPalindromeRec(final int origNumber,
                                     final int currentValue,
                                     final int remainingValue)
{
    // recursive termination
    if (origNumber == currentValue)
        return true;

    // recursive termination
    if (remainingValue < 1)
        return false;
```

```
final int lastDigit = remainingValue % 10;
final int newCurrent = currentValue * 10 + lastDigit;
final int newRemaining = remainingValue / 10;

System.out.println(String.format("lastDigit: %,4d, " +
                    "newCurrent: %,4d, newRemaining: %,4d",
                    lastDigit, newCurrent, newRemaining));

// recursive descent
return isNumberPalindromeRec(origNumber, newCurrent, newRemaining);
}
```

The calls for the value 121 can be illustrated as follows:

```
isNumberPalindromeRec(121, 0, 121) =>
lastDigit:   1, newCurrent:   1, newRemaining:  12
isNumberPalindromeRec(121, 1, 12) =>
lastDigit:   2, newCurrent:  12, newRemaining:   1
isNumberPalindromeRec(121, 12, 1) =>
lastDigit:   1, newCurrent: 121, newRemaining:   0
isNumberPalindromeRec(121, 121, 0)
true
```

Certainly it is of interest to see how the entire procedure works for a number, for example 123, which is not a palindrome:

```
isNumberPalindromeRec(123, 0, 123) =>
lastDigit:   3, newCurrent:   3, newRemaining:  12
isNumberPalindromeRec(123, 3, 12) =>
lastDigit:   2, newCurrent:  32, newRemaining:   1
isNumberPalindromeRec(123, 32, 1) =>
lastDigit:   1, newCurrent: 321, newRemaining:   0
isNumberPalindromeRec(123, 321, 0)
false
```

Verification

For testing, use the following inputs, which show the correct operation:

```
@ParameterizedTest(name = "isNumberPalindrome({0}) => {1}")
@CsvSource({ "7, true", "13, false", "171, true", "47742, false",
            "123321, true", "1234554321, true" })
void isNumberPalindrome(int number, boolean expected)
{
    boolean result = Ex11_NumberPalindrome.isNumberPalindrome(number);

    assertEquals(expected, result);
}
```

3.3.11 Solution 11: Permutations (★★★☆☆)

Calculate all permutations of a sequence of letters given as a string; this means all possible combinations of these letters. Implement this calculation in method Set<String> calcPermutations(String). Consider also the case of duplicate letters.

Examples

Input	Result
"A"	"A"
"AA"	"AA"
"AB"	"AB", "BA"
"ABC"	"ABC, "ACB", "BAC", "BCA", "CAB", "CBA"
"AAC"	"AAC", "ACA", "CAA"

Algorithm   The best way to compute all permutations for a given string is to take a look at the recursive definition and then implement it:

$$A \Rightarrow perm(A) \qquad\qquad\qquad\qquad\qquad = A$$

$$AA \Rightarrow A + perm(A) \cup A + perm(A) \qquad\qquad = AA \cup AA = AA$$

$$AB \Rightarrow A + perm(B) \cup B + perm(A) \qquad\qquad = AB \cup BA$$

$$ABC \Rightarrow A + perm(BC) \cup B + perm(AC) \cup C + perm(AB) \quad = ABC \cup ACB \cup \ldots$$

You recognize that for a single character, the permutations consist of the character itself. For multiple characters, the permutations are computed by finding the permutations of the remaining string without the character and by later combining them back with the character appropriately—more on this later. The original problem is reduced from a string of length n to n problems for strings of length $n - 1$. Thus, for the string ABC, you obtain the solution illustrated in Figure 3-4.

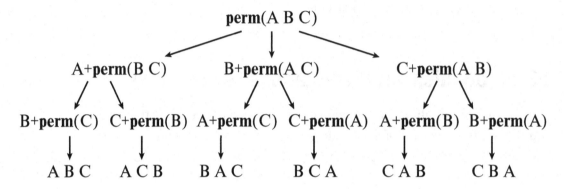

Figure 3-4. *Computation of the permutations of ABC*

With this knowledge in mind, the implementation will become much easier, and you transform the following steps into Java:

- Select and extract the ith character.

- Build the remaining string and calculate the permutations for it.

- Put the whole thing together again This is implemented as follows:

```java
static Set<String> calcPermutations(final String input)
{
    // recursive termination
    if (input.isEmpty() || input.length() == 1)
        return Set.of(input);

    final Set<String> combinations = new HashSet<>();
    for (int i = 0; i < input.length(); i++)
    {
        // extract i-th character as new first character
        final String newFirst = "" + input.charAt(i);
```

```
    // rest without i-th character
    final String newInput = input.substring(0, i) + input.substring(i + 1);

    // recursive descent
    final Set<String> permutations = calcPermutations(newInput);

    // adding the extracted character to all partial solutions
    for (final String perm : permutations)
    {
        combinations.add(newFirst + perm);
    }
    }
    return combinations;
}
```

This implementation leads to the creation of quite a lot of instances of strings and sets as intermediate buffers. How can this be improved?

Optimized algorithm   The drawbacks mentioned above are negligible for a short string. However, the longer the string gets, creating all the temporary objects and performing the string actions become more noticeable. IIow can this be avoided?

Here you revisit the ideas you've already seen in other solutions. Instead of assembling the strings each, you can cleverly pass them as parameters. One of them defines the remaining string, and the other one the currently already calculated prefix.

```
static Set<String> calcPermutationsMiniOpt(final String input)
{
    return calcPermutationsMiniOptImpl(input, "");
}
static Set<String> calcPermutationsMiniOptImpl(final String remaining,
                                               final String prefix)
{
    if (remaining.length() == 0)
        return Set.of(prefix);

    final Set<String> candidates = new HashSet<>();
```

```
for (int i = 0; i < remaining.length(); i++)
{
    final String newPrefix = prefix + remaining.charAt(i);
    final String newRemaining = remaining.substring(0, i) +
                                remaining.substring(i + 1);

    candidates.addAll(calcPermutationsMiniOptImpl(newRemaining, newPrefix));
}

return candidates;
}
```

Let me comment a bit on the optimization. While calling the method
calcPermutations("abcdefghij") with my iMac (i7 4 Ghz) takes about 7 to 8 seconds,
calcPermutationsMiniOpt("abcdefghij") finishes after only about 4 seconds. This is
due to the very large number of calls, for which smaller optimizations may be worthwhile.

However, if you only add one additional character, the overhead grows enormously
to around 111 seconds and for the optimized version to around 85 seconds. Such
increases in running time are, of course, absolutely undesirable. After reading Chapter 8
covering more advanced recursion techniques, you may want to look again at the
computation of the permutations to attempt an improvement with the help of
memoization. However, this will be at the expense of the required memory.

Verification

For testing, use the following inputs, which show the correct operation:

```
@ParameterizedTest(name = "calcPermutations({0}) = {1}")
@MethodSource("inputAndPermutations")
void calcPermutations(String input, Set<String> expected)
{
    Set<String> result = Ex12_Permutations.calcPermutations(input);

    assertEquals(expected, result);
}
```

```
private static Stream<Arguments> inputAndPermutations()
{
    return Stream.of(Arguments.of("A", Set.of("A")),
                    Arguments.of("AA", Set.of("AA")),
                    Arguments.of("AB", Set.of("AB", "BA")),
                    Arguments.of("ABC", Set.of("ABC", "BAC", "ACB",
                                            "CAB", "CBA", "BCA")),
                    Arguments.of("AAC", Set.of("AAC", "ACA", "CAA")));
}
```

3.3.12 Solution 12: Count Substrings (★★☆☆☆)

Write method int countSubstrings(String, String) that counts all occurrences of the given substring. Thereby, when a pattern is found, it should be *consumed* (i. e., it should not be available for hits again). This is shown in the following table as the last case.

Examples

Input	Search term	Result
"xhixhix"	"x"	3
"xhixhix"	"hi"	2
"mic"	"mic"	1
"haha"	"ho"	0
"xxxxyz"	"xx"	2

Algorithm   First of all, checked whether the first characters from the source text and the search string match. If this is the case, the number is increased, and the search continues. If there is no match, then the source text is shortened by the first character. The process is continued recursively as previously described. The termination criterion is that the length of the given input is smaller than that of the search text.

```java
static int countSubstrings(final String input, final String valueToFind)
{
    // recursive termination
    if (input.length() < valueToFind.length())
        return 0;

    final int count;
    final String remaining;

    // does the text start with the search string?
    if (input.startsWith(valueToFind))
    {
        // hit: continue the search for the found
        // term after the occurrence
        remaining = input.substring(valueToFind.length());
        count = 1;
    }
    else
    {
        // remove first character and search again
        remaining = input.substring(1);
        count = 0;
    }

    // recursive descent
    return countSubstrings(remaining, valueToFind) + count;
}
```

HINT: POSSIBLE VARIATION

You could imagine that a small modification of the requirements would now be to find all potential substrings rather than continuing to search behind them after finding a substring. Interestingly, this simplifies the implementation:

```java
static int countSubstringV2(final String input, final String valueToFind)
{
    if (input.length() < valueToFind.length())
        return 0;
```

```
    int count = 0;
    if (input.startsWith(valueToFind))
        count = 1;

    // remove first character and search again
    final String remaining = input.substring(1);

    return countSubstringV2(remaining, valueToFind) + count;
}
```

Optimized Algorithm   In the original algorithm, calls to substring() keep creating new strings. For short input values, this is not that dramatic. But if you assume a very long text, this may already be unfavorable.

Well, what might an optimization look like? You still traverse the input from left to right. But instead of shortening the input, it is more feasible to use a position pointer left. This causes the following adjustments:

1. Since the text does not get shorter, you now have to subtract the value of left from the original length.

2. You have used startsWith() to compare for a match. Conveniently there is a variant that allows providing an offset.

3. If there is a match, you have to move the position pointer by the number of characters in the search pattern; otherwise by one position.

This results in the following implementation:

```
static int countSubstringOpt(final String input, final String valueToFind)
{
    return countSubstringOpt(input, valueToFind, 0);
}

static int countSubstringOpt(final String input, final String valueToFind,
                             int left)
{
    if (input.length() - left < valueToFind.length())
        return 0;
```

```java
    int count = 0;
    if (input.startsWith(valueToFind, left))
    {
        left += valueToFind.length();
        count = 1;
    }
    else
    {
        // überspringe Zeichen und suche erneut
        left++;
    }

    return countSubstringOpt(input, valueToFind, left) + count;
}
```

Verification

The following inputs show the correct operation for the three variants:

```java
@ParameterizedTest(name = "countSubstring({0}) = {1}")
@CsvSource({ "xhixhix, x, 3", "xhixhix, hi, 2", "mic, mic, 1",
            "haha, ho, 0", "xxxxyz, xx, 2", "xxxx, xx, 2",
            "xx-xxx-xxxx-xxxxx-xxxxxx, xx, 9",
            "xx-xxx-xxxx-xxxxx-xxxxxx, xxx, 5"})
void countSubstring(String input, String searchFor, int expected)
{
    int result = Ex12_CountSubstrings.countSubstring(input, searchFor);

    assertEquals(expected, result);
}

@ParameterizedTest(name = "countSubstringV2({0}) = {1}")
@CsvSource({ "xhixhix, x, 3", "xhixhix, hi, 2", "mic, mic, 1",
            "haha, ho, 0", "xxxxyz, xx, 3", "xxxx, xx, 3",
            "xx-xxx-xxxx-xxxxx-xxxxxx, xx, 15",
            "xx-xxx-xxxx-xxxxx-xxxxxx, xxx, 10"})
```

```
void countSubstringV2(String input, String searchFor, int expected)
{
    int result = Ex12_CountSubstrings.countSubstringV2(input, searchFor);

    assertEquals(expected, result);
}

@ParameterizedTest(name = "countSubstringOpt({0}) = {1}")
@CsvSource({ "xhixhix, x, 3", "xhixhix, hi, 2", "mic, mic, 1",
            "haha, ho, 0", "xxxxyz, xx, 2", "xxxx, xx, 2",
            "xx-xxx-xxxx-xxxxx-xxxxxx, xx, 9",
            "xx-xxx-xxxx-xxxxx-xxxxxx, xxx, 5"})
void countSubstringOpt(String input, String searchFor, int expected)
{
    int result = Ex12_CountSubstrings.countSubstringOpt(input, searchFor, 0);

    assertEquals(expected, result);
}
```

In the first and last test case the same information is used in @CsvSource. It's also be possible to place them in a file and reference them as follows:

```
@ParameterizedTest(name="countSubstringOpt({0}) = {1}" )
@CsvFileSource(resources = "countsubstringinputs.csv", numLinesToSkip = 1)
void countSubstringOpt2(String input, String searchFor, int expected)
{
    int result = Ex12_CountSubstrings.countSubstringOpt(input, searchFor, 0);

    assertEquals(expected, result);
}
```

The CSV file will look like the following:

```
# input,searchFor,expected
xhixhix,x,3
xhixhix,hi,2
mic,mic,1
...
```

3.3.13 Solution 13: Ruler (★★☆☆☆)

In the introduction, I showed how to draw a simple shape of a ruler as well as a stylized snowflake (see Figure 3-3) using recursion. In this exercise, you want to imitate an English-style ruler. This involves dividing an area of one inch into 1/2 and 1/4 and 1/8. In doing so, the length of the stroke decreases by one each time.

Examples   The output should look somewhat like the following:

```
---- 0
-
--
-
---
-
--
-
---- 1
-
--
-
---
-
--
-
---- 2
```

Algorithm   The drawing of the full inch markers is done in a loop. The intermediate lines are generated in method `drawInterval()`. This, in turn, takes advantage of the recursive nature of the distribution of lines. A shorter line is drawn around each slightly longer centerline. This is repeated as long as the line length is greater than or equal to 1.

```
static void drawRuler(final int majorTickCount, final int maxLength)
{
    drawLine(maxLength, "0");

    for (int i = 1; i <= majorTickCount; i++)
    {
        drawInterval(maxLength - 1);
        drawLine(maxLength, "" + i);
    }
}
```

Finally, you need two helper methods for drawing an interval and a line of the specified length, including an optional marker (for the full inch numbers). You use the Java 11 functionality repeat() from the class String for this:

```
static void drawInterval(final int centerLength)
{
    if (centerLength > 0)
    {
        drawInterval(centerLength - 1);
        drawLine(centerLength, "");
        drawInterval(centerLength - 1);
    }
}

static void drawLine(final int count, final String label)
{
    System.out.println("-".repeat(count) + " " + label);
}
```

Verification

For testing, call the drawRuler() method as follows:

```
jshell> drawRuler(3, 4)
---- 0
-
--
-
---
```

CHAPTER 3 RECURSION

-
- -
-
- - - - 1
-
- -
-
- - -
-
- -
-
- - - - 2
-
- -
-
- - -
-
- -
-
- - - - 3

CHAPTER 4

Strings

Strings are character sequences that offer a variety of methods. In this chapter, you will learn about this topic and practice through various exercises.

4.1 Introduction

For processing strings there are the classes `String`, `StringBuffer,` and `StringBuilder`. All three satisfy the interface `java.lang.CharSequence`.

4.1.1 The Interface CharSequence

The read-only interface `CharSequence` mainly provides indexed access to single characters of type `char` as well as to character sequences, which in turn are of type `CharSequence`. The following methods, in particular, are declared for this purpose:

```java
public interface CharSequence
{
    public char charAt(int index);
    public int length();
    public CharSequence subSequence(int start, int end);
    public String toString();
}
```

The interface `CharSequence` thus makes it possible to process strings in an indexed manner without having concrete knowledge about the specific type. This allows interfaces to be kept more general.

© Michael Inden 2022
M. Inden, *Java Challenges*, https://doi.org/10.1007/978-1-4842-7395-1_4

ATTENTION: THINGS TO KNOW ABOUT THE INTERFACE CHARSEQUENCE

The interface CharSequence makes no assertions about the behavior of equals(Object) and hashCode(). Thus the result of comparing two CharSequence instances by equals(Object) is undefined. For example, if both instances are of type String, the result will be true if the textual contents are the same. However, a CharSequence instance could also be of type StringBuffer. A comparison of the types String and StringBuffer always yields false. However, since Java 11, CharSequence.compare(CharSequence, CharSequence) is useful to compare two CharSequences textually.

4.1.2 The Class String

The class java.lang.String represents character sequences which, up to Java 8, consisted of Unicode characters and stored their contents as an array of char. Starting with Java 9, the content is modeled as byte[] and evaluated according to an encoding. Strings can be created either by a constructor call of the class string or as a quoted string, as shown by the following two lines:

```
final String stringObject = new String("New String Object");
final String stringLiteral = "Stringliteral";
```

Methods Relevant to Practice

The following methods are especially important for practice and exercises:

- length() gets the length of the string.

- isEmpty() checks whether the string is empty.

- trim() removes whitespace at the beginning and end of the text.

- toUpperCase()/toLowerCase() creates a new string consisting of uppercase and lowercase letters only.

- charAt(index) provides index-based access to individual characters.

- toCharArray() creates a corresponding char[] based on the string.

- chars() creates an IntStream based on the string. After that the rich capabilities of the stream API are available.

- `substring(startIndexIncl)` extracts a part into a new string consisting of the letters of the original from the given start index to the end of the original string.

- `substring(startIndexIncl, endIndexExcl)` extracts a new substring consisting of the letters of the original from the given start index to the end index (exclusive).

- `indexOf(String)` checks whether the supplied substring is contained in the main string and returns the position (or -1 if no occurrence is found).

Java 11 provides other interesting methods that, for example, repeat a string n times (`repeat(n)`), as well as Unicode-based tests for whitespace (`isBlank()`) and also methods for removing whitespace (`strip()`, `stripLeading()`, and `stripTrailing()`).

4.1.3 The Classes StringBuffer and StringBuilder

Often, when processing textual information, modifications are required to existing strings. However, for instances of the `String` class, this is only possible by tricks such as constructing new objects due to their immutability. Alternatively, the `StringBuffer` and `StringBuilder` classes can be used for string manipulations. Both have an identical API with the difference that the methods of the `StringBuffer` class are synchronized. This is not the case for the methods of the `StringBuilder` class, which does not matter as long as only one thread works on it.

ATTENTION: STRING CONCATENATIONS AND PERFORMANCE

A common tip is to use `StringBuffer` and `StringBuilder` instead of the + operator when preparing large text output. Since both the Java compiler and the JVM perform various optimizations automatically, you should favor the readability of[1] Simple string concatenations using the + operator. For example,

```
String example = "text start" + "XXX" + "text end";
```

---

[1] For more detailed treatment, I refer you to my book *Der Weg zum JavaProfi* [Ind20a].

is much easier to read than constructs like

```
final String example = new StringBuilder().append("text start").
                                            append("XXX").
                                            append("text end").toString();
```

Therefore, only for really performance-critical sections, it is recommended to implement string concatenations using a StringBuilder object. For this book, I prefer readability and comprehensibility and therefore work with StringBuilder rather rarely, only when special functionalities not offered in String are of interest.

Additional Functionality and Comparison with the Class String

Conveniently, both StringBuffer and StringBuilder classes have delete operations. Via the methods deleteCharAt() and delete(), characters can be removed from a string representation. An analogous method named insert() allows you to insert characters.

However, both the StringBuilder and the StringBuffer have certain disadvantages. They lack various methods, such as toLowerCase() and toUpperCase(). Instead they provide the (less frequently needed) reverse() method, which returns the content in reversed order. Table 4-1 shows some important methods of the String class and a mapping to those of the StringBuffer or StringBuilder.

Table 4-1. *Mapping of Important String Methods*

String1	StringBuffer/StringBuilder
+, +=, concat()	append()
replace(), subString()	replace(), subString()
indexOf(), startsWith()	indexOf()
endsWith()	lastIndexOf()
- no method available! -	reverse()
- no method available! -	insert()
- no method available! -	delete(), deleteCharAt()
toUpperCase()/toLowerCase()	*- no method available! -*

4.1.4 The Class Character

The Character class abstracts a single character and can provide certain information via various helper methods, such as whether it is a letter or whitespace:

- isLetter() checks whether the character represents a letter.

- isDigit() checks whether the character corresponds to a decimal digit.

- isUpperCase()/isLowerCase() checks if the character represents an uppercase or lowercase letter.

- toUpperCase()/toLowerCase() converts the given character to an uppercase or lowercase letter.

- isWhiteSpace() checks if the character is interpreted as whitespace (i.e. space, tab, etc.).

- getNumericValue() gets the numeric value. This is quite handy for digits, but also for hexadecimal numbers.

Example

Let's look at a small example:

```
System.out.println(Character.getNumericValue('0'));
System.out.println(Character.getNumericValue('7'));
System.out.println(Character.getNumericValue('9'));

System.out.println(Character.getNumericValue('A'));
System.out.println(Character.getNumericValue('a'));
System.out.println(Character.getNumericValue('F'));
System.out.println(Character.getNumericValue('f'));

System.out.println(Character.getNumericValue('Z'));
System.out.println(Character.getNumericValue('z'));
```

The lines above provide the following outputs:

```
0
7
9
10
10
15
15
35
35
```

As you can easily see, the getNumericValue() method is quite useful if you have to perform conversions between different number systems or if you want to get the numeric value for a letter.

4.1.5 Examples Related to Character and String

To conclude the introduction, let's look at two examples of using the Character and String classes.

Homemade Conversions with Character

Using the Character class, you can perform conversions from textual digits to their numeric value. For decimal digits, the following conversion is common. Something similar can be used for the letters in the alphabet.

```
int digitValue = digitAsChar - '0';
int posOfChar = currentChar - 'A';
```

For hexadecimal numbers, further distinctions are then required. Let's illustrate the advantages of getNumericValue() with the example of converting hexadecimal numbers to decimal numbers. Below I show which steps are necessary—first using the method getNumericValue() and second using the custom creation hexDigitToDecimal(). Please note that the custom variant does not support lowercase hexadecimal numbers!

```java
static int convertToDecimal(final String hexDigits)
{
    int valueOldStyle = 0;
    int valueNewStyle = 0;

    for (int i = 0; i < hexDigits.length(); i++)
    {
        final char currentChar = hexDigits.charAt(i);

        // OLD and cumbersome: invoking own method
        int digitValueOld = hexDigitToDecimal(currentChar);
        valueOldStyle = valueOldStyle * 16 + digitValueOld;
        // NEW and short and crisp: JDK Method
        int digitValue = Character.getNumericValue(currentChar);
        valueNewStyle = valueNewStyle * 16 + digitValue;
    }
    return valueNewStyle;
}

// OLD and cumbersome: Implementation of own method
static int hexDigitToDecimal(final char currentChar)
{
    if (Character.isDigit(currentChar))
        return currentChar - '0';

    // "Optimistische" Annahme: A ... F
    return currentChar - 'A' + 10;
}
```

The homemade conversion is fragile and relies especially on correct characters—so ideally, you should do a validity check beforehand.

Possible readable alternative   To convert a character of a hexadecimal number to the decimal value, it is possible to use indexOf() to determine the position in the predefined value set. However, the previously mentioned weakness of lowercase letters as digits is still present.

```java
static int hexDigitToDecimalAlternative(final char hexDigit)
{
    final int position = "0123456789ABCDEF".indexOf(hexDigit);
    if (position < 0)
        throw new IllegalArgumentException("invalid char: " + hexDigit);

    return position;
}
```

Other special features   Quite often, we only think of the normal characters and maybe umlauts. Thus intuitively, one could assume that isDigit() only checks the ASCII characters as the digits 0 to 9. But this is not the case! There are other (fancier) digits that are converted correctly. Here the advantage of getNumericValue() is evident:

```java
System.out.println("\u0669");
System.out.println(Character.isDigit('\u0669'));
System.out.println(Character.getNumericValue('\u0669'));
System.out.println(hexDigitToDecimal('\u0669'));
```

This leads to the output shown in Figure 4-1.

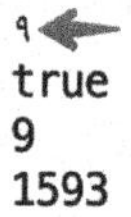

```
٩ ⬅
true
9
1593
```

Figure 4-1. *Special representation of digits*

Example: String Processing

As an example for class String, you want to count the number of occurrences of each of the letters, treating lowercase and uppercase letters equally. For the text "Otto", you expect 2 x t and 2 x o by its conversion to lowercase letters. Such processing is also called a *histogram*. A histogram is a representation of the distribution of objects, and often these are numerical values. It is known from photography for the brightness distribution of an image. In the following it concerns the distribution and/or determination of the frequencies of letters for a text:

```
static Map<Character, Integer> generateCharacterHistogram(final String word)
{
    final Map<Character, Integer> charCountMap = new TreeMap<>();

    final char[] chars = word.toLowerCase().toCharArray();
    for (char currentChar : chars)
    {
        if (Character.isLetter(currentChar))
        {
            // Trick, but attention to the order!
            charCountMap.putIfAbsent(currentChar,  0);
            charCountMap.computeIfPresent(currentChar,
                                      (key, value) -> value + 1);

            // Alternative
            // final int count = charCountMap.getOrDefault(currentChar, 0);
            // charCountMap.put(currentChar, count + 1);
        }
    }
    return charCountMap;
}
```

Let's try the whole thing out in the JShell:

```
jshell> generateCharacterHistogram("Otto")
$9 ==> {o=2, t=2}

jshell> generateCharacterHistogram("Hello Michael")
$10 ==> {a=1, c=1, e=2, h=2, i=1, l=3, m=1, o=1}

jshell> generateCharacterHistogram("Java Challenge, Your Java-Training")
$11 ==> {a=6, c=1, e=2, g=2, h=1, i=2, j=2, l=2, n=3, o=1, r=2, t=1, u=1,
v=2, y=1}
```

NOTE: ASSISTANCE IN JAVA 8

As an aside, in Java 8, several helpful methods have been added to the `Map<K,V>` interface, namely, among others:

- `putIfAbsent()`

- `computeIfPresent()`

They often permit algorithms to be written more easily. Please keep in mind that the order of the calls matters.

4.2 Exercises

4.2.1 Exercise 1: Number Conversions (★★☆☆☆)

Based on a string, implement validation for binary numbers, conversion for them, and also for hexadecimal numbers.

> **Note**   The conversion can be solved with `Integer.parseInt(value, radix)` and base 2 for binary numbers and base 16 for hexadecimal numbers. Do not use these explicitly, but implement it yourself.

Examples

Input	Method	Result
"10101"	isBinaryNumber()	true
"111"	binaryToDecimal()	7
"AB"	hexToDecimal()	171

Exercise 1a (★☆☆☆☆)

Write method boolean `isBinaryNumber(String)` that checks that a given string consists only of the characters 0 and 1 (i.e., represents a binary number).

Exercise 1b (★★☆☆☆)

Write method `int binaryToDecimal(String)` that converts a (valid) binary number represented as a string to the corresponding decimal number.

Exercise 1c (★★☆☆☆)

Write the entire conversion again, but this time for hexadecimal numbers.

4.2.2 Exercise 2: Joiner (★☆☆☆☆)

Exercise 2a (★☆☆☆☆)

Write method `String join(List<String>, String)` that joins a list of strings with the specified separator string and returns it as one string. Implement this by yourself initially without using any special JDK functionality.

Exercise 2b (★☆☆☆☆)

Implement string concatenation using appropriate methods from the Stream API in method `String joinStrings(List<String>, String)`.

Examples

Input	Separator	Result
["hello", "world", "message"]	" +++ "	"hello +++ world +++ message"
["Micha", "Zurich"]	" likes "	"Micha likes Zurich"

4.2.3 Exercise 3: Reverse String (★★☆☆☆)

Write method `String reverse(String)` that reverses the letters in a string and returns it as a result. Implement this yourself without using any special JDK functionality, such as the `reverse()` method from the `StringBuilder` class.

Examples

Input	Result
"ABCD"	"DCBA"
"OTTO"	"OTTO"
"PETER	"RETEP"

4.2.4 Exercise 4: Palindrome (★★★☆☆)

Exercise 4a (★★☆☆☆)

Write method boolean isPalindrome(String) that checks whether a given string is a palindrome regardless of case. A palindrome is a word that reads the same from the front and the back.

Note   You can easily solve the verification with StringBuilder.reverse(). Explicitly do not use JDK components, but implement the functionality yourself.

Examples

Input	Result
"Otto"	true
"ABCBX"	false
"ABCXcba"	true

Exercise 4b (★★★☆☆)

Write an extension that also does not consider spaces and punctuation as relevant, allowing whole sentences to be checked, such as this one:

```
Was it a car or a cat I saw?
```

4.2.5 Exercise 5: No Duplicate Chars (★★★☆☆)

Determine if a given string does not contain duplicate letters. Uppercase and lowercase letters should not make any difference. Write method `boolean checkNoDuplicateChars (String)` for this purpose.

Examples

Input	Result
"Otto"	false
"Adrian"	false
"Micha"	true
"ABCDEFG"	true

4.2.6 Exercise 6: Remove Duplicate Letters (★★★☆☆)

Write method `String removeDuplicates(String)` that keeps each letter only once in a given text, thus deleting all subsequent duplicates regardless of case. However, the original order of the letters should be preserved.

Examples

Input	Result
"bananas"	"bans"
"lalalamama"	"lam"
"MICHAEL"	"MICHAEL"

4.2.7 Exercise 7: Capitalize (★★☆☆☆)

Exercise 7a (★★☆☆☆)

Write method `String capitalize(String)` that converts a given text into an English title format where each word starts with a capital letter.

Examples

Input	Result
"this is a very special title"	"This Is A Very Special Title"
"effective java is great"	"Effective Java Is Great"

Exercise 7b: Modification (★★☆☆☆)

Assume now that the input is a list of strings and that a list of strings should be returned, with the individual words then starting with a capital letter. Use the following signature as a starting point:

```
List<String> capitalize(List<String> words)
```

Exercise 7c: Special Treatment (★★☆☆☆)

In headings, it is common to encounter special treatment of words like "is" or "a" that are not capitalized. Implement this as method `List<String>` `capitalizeSpecial(List<String>, List<String>)`, which gets the words to be excluded from the conversion as the second parameter.

Example

Input	Exceptions	Result
["this", "is", "a", "title"]	["is", "a"]	["This", "is", "a", "Title"]

4.2.8 Exercise 8: Rotation (★★☆☆☆)

Consider two strings, `str1` and `str2`, where the first string is supposed to be longer than the second. Figure out if the first one contains the other one. In doing so, the characters within the first string may also be rotated. Characters can be moved from the beginning or the end to the opposite position (even repeatedly). To do this, create method `boolean containsRotation(String, String)`, which is case-insensitive during the check.

Examples

Input 1	Input 2	Result
"ABCD"	"ABC"	True
"ABCDEF	"EFAB"	true ("ABCDEF" ↞ x 2 ⇒ "CDEFAB" contains "EFAB")
"BCDE"	"EC"	False
"Challenge"	"GECH"	True

4.2.9 Exercise 9: Well-Formed Braces (★★☆☆☆)

Write method boolean checkBraces(String) which checks whether the sequence of round braces passed as string contains matching (properly nested) pairs of braces.

Examples

Input	Result	Comment
"(())"	true	
"()()"	true	
"(())((())"	false	Although the same amount of opening and closing braces, they're not properly nested
"((()"	false	No suitable bracing

4.2.10 Exercise 10: Anagram (★★☆☆☆)

The term *anagram* is used to describe two strings that contain the same letters in the same frequency. Here, uppercase and lowercase should not make any difference. Write method boolean isAnagram(String, String).

Examples

Input 1	Input 2	Result
"Otto"	"Toto"	true
"Mary	"Army"	true
"Ananas"	"Bananas"	false

4.2.11 Exercise 11: Morse Code (★★☆☆☆)

Write method `String toMorseCode(String)` that is capable of translating a given text into Morse code characters. They consist of sequences of one to four short and long tones per letter, symbolized by a period (.) or hyphen (-). It is desirable for easier distinguishability to place a space between each tone and three spaces between each sequence of letter tones. Otherwise, S (...) and EEE (...) would not be distinguishable from each other.

For simplicity, limit yourself to the letters E, O, S, T, and W with the following encoding:

Letter	Morse Code
E	.
O	- - -
S	...
T	-
W	. - -

Examples

Input	Result
SOS	... - - - ...
TWEET	- . - - . . -
WEST	. - - . ... -

Bonus   Try to find out the corresponding Morse code for all letters of the alphabet, (e.g., to convert your name). You can find the necessary hints for this at `https://en.wikipedia.org/wiki/Morse_code`.

4.2.12 Exercise 12: Pattern Checker (★★★☆☆)

Write method `boolean matchesPattern(String, String)` that examines a space-separated string (second parameter) against the structure of a pattern passed in the form of individual characters as the first parameter.

Examples

Input pattern	Input text	Result
"xyyx"	"tim mike mike tim"	true
"xyyx"	"tim mike tom tim"	false
"xyxx"	"tim mike mike tim"	false
"xxxx"	"tim tim tim tim"	true

4.2.13 Exercise 13: Tennis Score (★★★☆☆)

Write method `String tennisScore(String, String, String)` that makes an announcement in a familiar style such as *Fifteen Love*, *Deuce*, or *Advantage Player X* based on a textual score for two players, PL1 and PL2. Thereby their score is given in the format <PL1 points>:<PL2 points>.

The following counting rules apply to a game in tennis:

- A game is won (Game <PlayerX>) when a player reaches 4 or more points and is ahead by at least 2 points.

- Points from 0 to 3 are named Love, Fifteen, Thirty, and Forty.

- In case of at least 3 points and a tie, this is called Deuce.

- With at least 3 points and one point difference, this is called Advantage <PlayerX> for the one who has one more point.

Examples

Input	Score
"1:0", "Micha", "Tim"	"Fifteen Love"
"2:2", "Micha", "Tim"	"Thirty Thirty"
"2:3", "Micha", "Tim"	"Thirty Forty"
"3:3", "Micha", "Tim"	"Deuce"
"4:3", "Micha", "Tim"	"Advantage Micha"
"4:4", "Micha", "Tim"	"Deuce"
"5:4", "Micha", "Tim"	"Advantage Micha"
"6:4", "Micha", "Tim"	"Game Micha"

4.2.14 Exercise 14: Version Numbers (★★☆☆☆)

Write method `int compareVersions(String, String)` that permits you to compare version numbers in the format *MAJOR.MINOR.PATCH* with each other— thereby the specification of *PATCH* is optional. In particular, the return value should be compatible with the `int compare(T, T)` method from the `Comparator<T>` interface.

Examples

Version 1	Version 2	Result
1.11.17	2.3.5	<
2.1	2.1.3	<
2.3.5	2.4	<
3.1	2.4	>
3.3	3.2.9	>
7.2.71	7.2.71	=

Bonus   Implement the functionality using the interface `Comparator<T>`.

4.2.15 Exercise 15: Conversion strToLong (★★☆☆☆)

Convert a string into a `long`. Write method `long strToLong(String)` on your own.

Note   The conversion can be easily achieved with `long.parseLong(value)`. Do not use this explicitly, but implement the entire conversion yourself.

Examples

Input	Result
"+123"	123
"-123"	-123
"7271"	7271
"ABC"	`IllegalArgumentException`
"0123"	83 (for bonus task)
"-0123"	-83 (for bonus task)
"0128"	`IllegalArgumentException` (for bonus task)

Bonus Enable the parsing of octal numbers.

4.2.16 Exercise 16: Print Tower (★★★☆☆)

Write method `void printTower(int)` that represents a tower of *n* slices stacked on top of each other as ASCII graphics, symbolized by the character #, and draw a lower boundary line.

Example A tower of height 3 should look something like this:

```
    |
  # | #
 ## | ##
### | ###
---------
```

4.3 Solutions

4.3.1 Solution 1: Number Conversions (★★☆☆☆)

Based on a string, implement validation for binary numbers, conversion for them, and also for hexadecimal numbers.

Note   The conversion can be solved with `Integer.parseInt(value, radix)` and base 2 for binary numbers and base 16 for hexadecimal numbers. Do not use these explicitly, but implement them yourself.

Examples

Input	Method	Result
"10101"	isBinaryNumber()	true
"111"	binaryToDecimal()	7
"AB"	hexToDecimal()	171

Solution 1a (★☆☆☆☆)

Write method `boolean isBinaryNumber(String)` that checks that a given string consists only of the characters 0 and 1 (i.e., represents a binary number).

Algorithm   The implementation in Java iterates through the string character by character from the beginning to the end, checking whether the current character is 0 or 1. If another character is detected, the loop terminates, and then `false` is returned:

```java
public static boolean isBinaryNumber(final String number)
{
    boolean isBinary = true;

    int i = 0;
    while (i < number.length() && isBinary)
    {
```

```
        final char currentChar = number.charAt(i);
        isBinary = (currentChar == '0' || currentChar == '1');

        i++;
    }

    return isBinary;
}
```

Solution 1b (★★☆☆☆)

Write method int binaryToDecimal(String) that converts a (valid) binary number represented as a string to the corresponding decimal number.

Algorithm   You traverse the string character by character from left to right and process each character as a binary digit. The current character is used to calculate the value by multiplying the previously converted value by 2 and adding the current value. The latter is determined by a subtraction number.charAt(i) - '0', as you learned in the introductory section for decimal numbers. It is possible to formulate the algorithm more clearly, meaning without special treatments, because a valid input is ensured by the previously implemented method isBinaryNumber().

```
public static int binaryToDecimal(final String number)
{
    if (!isBinaryNumber(number))
        throw new IllegalArgumentException(number + " is not a binary number");

    int decimalValue = 0;
    for (int i = 0; i < number.length(); i++)
    {
        final int current = number.charAt(i) - '0';
        decimalValue = decimalValue * 2 + current;
    }

    return decimalValue;
}
```

Solution 1c (★★☆☆☆)

Write the entire conversion again, but this time for hexadecimal numbers.

Algorithm   For hexadecimal numbers, the factor has to be changed to 16. Additionally, getNumericValue() is suitable for determining the value.

```
public static int hexToDecimal(final String number)
{
    if (!isHexNumber(number))
        throw new IllegalArgumentException(number + " is not a hex number");

    int decimalValue = 0;
    for (int i = 0; i < number.length(); i++)
    {
        final char currentChar = number.charAt(i);
        final int value = Character.getNumericValue(currentChar);
        decimalValue = decimalValue * 16 + value;
    }

    return decimalValue;
}
```

The check for valid hexadecimal numbers uses the isDigit() method presented in the introductory section for decimal numbers and checks the letters from A to F manually:

```
public static boolean isHexNumber(final String number)
{
    boolean isHex = true;

    final String upperCaseNumber = number.toUpperCase();

    int i = 0;
    while (i < upperCaseNumber.length() && isHex)
    {
        final char currentChar = upperCaseNumber.charAt(i);
        isHex = Character.isDigit(currentChar) ||
                currentChar >= 'A' && currentChar <= 'F';
```

```
      i++;
   }

   return isHex;
}
```

This challenge is a search problem. You search for the first occurrence of a letter in the string which is not 0 or 1 for binary numbers and not in the range 0 to F for hexadecimal numbers. Search problems like this are also solvable using a while loop—then i >= length() || !condition applies.

```
int i = 0;
while (i < input.length() && condition)
{
    // teste Bedingung
    i++;
    }
```

HINT: POSSIBLE ALTERNATIVES AND OPTIMIZATIONS

Although the implementations shown are fairly straightforward, there are some amazingly elegant alternatives that are also easy to read and understand, namely to check the sequence of letters A through F to see if the character is contained:

```
isHex = Character.isDigit(currentChar) || "ABEDEF".contains(currentChar);
```

Actually, the complete process can be shortened based on the last idea:

```
isHex = "0123456789ABCDEF".indexOf(currentChar) >= 0;
```

Alternatively, even the entire inspection may be made significantly shorter by using a regular expression:

```
static boolean isHexNumber(final String number)
{
    return number.matches("^[0-9a-fA-F]+$");
}
```

Verification

For testing, use the following inputs, which show the correct operation:

```java
@ParameterizedTest(name = "isBinaryNumber({0}) => {1}")
@CsvSource({ "10101, true", "222, false", "12345, false" })
public void isBinaryNumber(String value, boolean expected)
{
    boolean result = Ex01_BasicNumberChecks.isBinaryNumber(value);

    assertEquals(expected, result);
}

@ParameterizedTest(name = "binaryToDecimal({0}) => {1}")
@CsvSource({ "111, 7", "1010, 10", "1111, 15", "10000, 16" })
public void binaryToDecimal(String value, int expected)
{
    int result = Ex01_BasicNumberChecks.binaryToDecimal(value);

    assertEquals(expected, result);
}

@ParameterizedTest(name = "hexToDecimal({0}) => {1}")
@CsvSource({ "7, 7", "A, 10", "F, 15", "10, 16" })
public void hexToDecimal(String value, int expected)
{
    int result = Ex01_BasicNumberChecks.hexToDecimal(value);

    assertEquals(expected, result);
}
```

4.3.2 Solution 2: Joiner (★☆☆☆☆)

Solution 2a (★☆☆☆☆)

Write method String join(List<String>, String) that joins a list of strings with the specified separator string and returns it as one string. Implement this by yourself initially without using any special JDK functionality.

Examples

Input	Separator	Result
["hello", "world", "message"]	" +++ "	"hello +++ world +++ message"
["Micha", "Zurich"]	" likes "	"Micha likes Zurich"

Algorithm   Iterate through the list of values from front to back. In each case, insert the text into a `StringBuilder`, add the separator string, and repeat this until the last value. As a special treatment, do not add a separator string after this last one.

```java
static String join(final List<String> values, final String delimiter)
{
    var sb = new StringBuilder();
    for (int i = 0; i < values.size(); i++)
    {
        sb.append(values.get(i));

        // No separator after last occurrence
        if (i < values.size() - 1)
        {
            sb.append(delimiter);
        }
    }
    return sb.toString();
}
```

Solution 2b (★☆☆☆☆)

Implement string concatenation using appropriate methods from the Stream API in method `String joinStrings(List<String>, String)`.

Algorithm   By using the Stream API, the challenge can be nicely expressed in a compact and understandable way, without any special treatment, as follows:

```java
static String joinStrings(final List<String> values, final String delimiter)
{
    return values.stream().collect(Collectors.joining(delimiter));
}
```

Verification

For testing, use the following inputs, which show the correct operation:

```
@Test
public void testJoinLowLevel()
{
    var result = Ex02_StringJoiner.join(List.of("hello", "world",
                                "message"))," +++ ");

    assertEquals("hello +++ world +++ message", result);
}

@Test
public void testJoinStringsWithStream()
{
    var result = Ex02_StringJoiner.joinStrings(List.of("Micha", "Zurich"),
                                " likes ");

    assertEquals("Micha likes Zurich", result);
}
```

4.3.3 Solution 3: Reverse String (★★☆☆☆)

Write method String reverse(String) that reverses the letters in a string and returns it as a result. Implement this yourself, without using any special JDK functionality, such as the reverse() method from the StringBuilder class.

Examples

Input	Result
"ABCD"	"DCBA"
"OTTO"	"OTTO"
"PETER	"RETEP"

Algorithm   Initially, an idea could be to traverse the original string character by character from the end and add the respective character to the result:

```
static String reverse(final String original)
{
    String reversed = "";

    for (int i = original.length() - 1; i >= 0; i--)
    {
        char currentChar = original.charAt(i);
        reversed += currentChar;
    }

    return reversed;
}
```

However, a small problem exists: the string concatenations with += are potentially *expensive* because thereby new string objects are created. For this reason, it may be better to work with an instance of a `StringBuilder` for more elaborate actions. I will discuss further possibilities in the second part of the solution.

Optimized algorithm   Ask yourself briefly: How could it be more memory-efficient, for example, if very long strings are to be reversed extremely frequently?

The idea is to convert the string to a `char[]` using `toCharArray()` and work directly on the `char[]`. In addition, two position pointers named *left* and *right* are used, which initially point to the first and last character. Now you swap the corresponding letters and the position pointers move inwards. Repeat the whole process as long as *left* < *right* is valid; if *left* >= *right* the process is aborted. Let's illustrate the procedure for the text ABCD, where l stands for *left* and r for *right*:

```
A B C D
l     r

D B C A
  l r

D C B A
  r l      => end
```

You implement the described procedure as follows:

```java
static String reverseInplace(final String original)
{
    final char[] originalChars = original.toCharArray();

    int left = 0;
    int right = originalChars.length - 1;

    while (left < right)
    {
        final char leftChar = originalChars[left];
        final char rightChar = originalChars[right];

        // swap
        originalChars[left] = rightChar;
        originalChars[right] = leftChar;

        left++;
        right--;
    }

    return String.valueOf(originalChars);
}
```

Verification

Let's write a unit test to verify the desired functionality:

```java
@ParameterizedTest(name = "reverse({0}) => {1}")
@CsvSource({ "ABCD, DCBA", "OTTO, OTTO", "PETER, RETEP" })
void testReverse(final String input, final String expectedOutput)
{
    final String result = Ex03_ReverseString.reverse(input);

    assertEquals(expectedOutput, result);
}
```

You could do something similar for the inplace version, but here you just use two calls in the JShell:

```
jshell> reverseInplace("ABCD")
$29 ==> "DCBA"

jshell> reverseInplace("PETER")
$30 ==> "RETEP"
```

4.3.4 Solution 4: Palindrome (★★★☆☆)

Solution 4a (★★☆☆☆)

Write method `boolean isPalindrome(String)` that checks whether a given string is a palindrome regardless of case. A palindrome is a word that reads the same from the front and the back.

Note   You can easily solve the verification with `StringBuilder.reverse()`. Explicitly do not use JDK components, but implement the functionality yourself.

Examples

Input	Result
"Otto"	true
"ABCBX"	false
"ABCXcba"	true

JOB INTERVIEW TIPS

As an example of a job interview, I once again list possible questions you may ask to clarify the scope of the assignment:

- Should it be case-sensitive? ANSWER: No, any

- Are spaces relevant? ANSWER: First yes, later no, then to be ignored

---

Algorithm   As in Exercise 3 Reverse String, the string is represented as char[ ], and you advance one position inward from the left and one position from the right, as long as the characters match, and as long as the left position is still smaller than the right position:

```java
static boolean isPalindrome(final String input)
{
    final char[] chars = input.toLowerCase().toCharArray();

    int left = 0;
    int right = chars.length-1;

    boolean isSameChar = true;
    while (left < right && isSameChar)
    {
        isSameChar = (chars[left] == chars[right]);

        left++;
        right--;
    }

    return isSameChar;
}
```

Algorithm with recursion: How can you solve the palindrome problem recursively and without using char[ ] as an auxiliary data structure? After reading Chapter 3 and working through some of the recursion exercise problems given there, you should be able to implement this easily. With the strategy or the idiom of the helper method in mind, the following recursive implementation emerges, which, starting from the outside, always checks two characters. This is continued inward as long as the characters match, and the left position is smaller than the right one.

```java
public static boolean isPalindromeRec(final String input)
{
    return isPalindromeRec(input.toLowerCase(), 0, input.length() - 1);
}
static boolean isPalindromeRec(final String input,
                                final int left, final int right)
```

```
{
    if (left >= right)
        return true;

    if (input.charAt(left) == input.charAt(right))
    {
        return isPalindromeRec(input, left + 1, right - 1);
    }

    return false;
}
```

An alternative way is always to shorten the string by the characters. Why is this logical solution not so good practically? The answer is obvious: This causes many temporary string objects to be created. Besides, a large number of copy actions would have to take place.

Solution 4b (★★★☆☆)

Write an extension that also does not consider spaces and punctuation as relevant, allowing whole sentences to be checked, such as this one:

```
Was it a car or a cat I saw?
```

Algorithm   You can incorporate special checks for whitespace into the algorithm. Still, it is easier to create a version of the method and replace all unwanted punctuation and whitespace there in advance before calling the original method:

```
public static boolean isPalindrome(final String input,
                                    final boolean ignoreSpacesAndPunctuation)
{
    String adjustedInput = input.toLowerCase();
    if (ignoreSpacesAndPunctuation)
        adjustedInput = input.replaceAll(" |!|\\.", "");

    return isPalindromeRec(adjustedInput);
}
```

Please note that a regular expression is used in `replaceAll()` to remove the characters, namely spaces, exclamation marks, and periods, from the text to be checked. The dot must be masked specifically since it stands for any character in a regular expression.

Verification

For verification, you again write a unit test with the following inputs that show the correct operation:

```
@ParameterizedTest(name = "isPalindromeRec({0} => {1}")
@CsvSource({ "Otto, true",
             "ABCBX, false",
             "ABCXcba, true" })
void isPalindromeRec(String value, boolean expected)
{
    boolean result = Ex04_Palindrome.isPalindromeRec(value);

    assertEquals(expected, result);
}

@ParameterizedTest(name = "''{0}'' should be {1}")
@CsvSource( { "Dreh mal am Herd., true",
              "Das ist kein Palindrom!, false"} )
void isPalindrome(String value, boolean expected)
{
    boolean result = Ex04_Palindrome.isPalindrome(value, true);

    assertEquals(expected, result);
}
```

FINDINGS: PAY ATTENTION TO COMPREHENSIBILITY

It is absolutely natural for strings to choose an iterative solution due to their API and position/index-based access. This would no longer be convenient if one had to determine the palindrome property for the digits of a number. This can be done with recursion and some consideration even without the detour via conversion shown as a solution to exercise 10 in section 3.3.10. Having developed the functionality `reverse()` in the previous exercise, you can profitably use it here as follows:

```
static boolean isPalindrome(final String input)
{
    final String upperInput = input.toUpperCase();
```

```
    return upperInput.equals(reverse(upperInput));
}
```

This demonstrates that problem- and context-aware programming enables the creation of comprehensible and maintainable solutions. The understandable, maintainable, and changeable properties are of high importance in practice since source code is usually modified far more frequently due to changing or new requirements than created completely from scratch.

4.3.5 Solution 5: No Duplicate Chars (★★★☆☆)

Determine if a given string does not contain duplicate letters. Uppercase and lowercase letters should not make any difference. Write method boolean checkNoDuplicateChars (String) for this purpose.

Examples

Input	Result
"Otto"	false
"Adrian"	false
"Micha"	true
"ABCDEFG"	true

Algorithm   While solving the exercise, you might get the idea to store the individual characters in a Set<E>. You traverse the input one character at a time from front to back. For each character, you check to see if it already exists in the Set<E>. If so, you have encountered a duplicate character and abort processing. Otherwise, you insert the character into the Set<E> and continue with the next character.

```
static boolean checkNoDuplicateChars(final String input)
{
    final char[] allCharsOfInput = input.toLowerCase().toCharArray();

    final Set<Character> containedChars = new HashSet<>();
    for (char currentChar : allCharsOfInput)
```

173

```
    {
        if (containedChars.contains(currentChar))
            return false;

        containedChars.add(currentChar);
    }
    return true;
}
```

HINT: POSSIBLE ALTERNATIVES AND OPTIMIZATIONS

Although the implementation shown is quite clear, it is possible to find other even more compact alternatives by taking advantage of the fact that any string can be converted to an IntStream using the chars() method. Trying to keep the logic fairly close to the actual algorithm results maybe in the following—wherein you need boxed() to convert the values of int into a Integer. This is the only method to insert the values into a Set<Integer> and remove duplicates this way. If no duplicates exist, the count of the Set<Integer> must be equal to the length of the string.

```
static boolean checkNoDuplicateCharsStreamV1(final String input)
{
    return input.toLowerCase().chars().
                            boxed().
                            collect(Collectors.toSet()).
                            size() == input.length();
}
```

This is more compact but may not be quite as comprehensible as the classic version. But there is an adequate alternative: You can use distinct() to remove all duplicates and count() to get the number of elements in the stream. If no duplicates exist, the count must be equal to the length of the string. Many words, but few instructions ... the whole thing can be formulated with a one-liner as follows:

```
boolean checkNoDuplicateCharsWithStreamOpt(final String input)
{
    return input.toLowerCase().chars().distinct().count() == input.length();
}
```

Verification

You again use a unit test to verify the desired functionality:

```
@ParameterizedTest(name = "checkNoDuplicateChars({0}) => {1}")
@CsvSource({ "Otto, false", "Adrian, false", "Micha, true", "ABCDEFG, true" })
void checkNoDuplicateChars(final String input, final boolean expected)
{
    var result = Ex05_CheckNoDuplicateChars.checkNoDuplicateChars(input);

    assertEquals(expected, result);
}
```

4.3.6 Solution 6: Remove Duplicate Letters (★★★☆☆)

Write method String removeDuplicates(String) that keeps each letter only once in a given text, thus deleting all subsequent duplicates regardless of case. However, the original order of the letters should be preserved.

Examples

Input	Result
"bananas"	"bans"
"lalalamama"	"lam"
"MICHAEL	"MICHAEL"

Algorithm   Again, you traverse the string character by character and store the corresponding characters in a Set<E> named alreadySeen. If the current character is not yet included there, it is added to both the Set<E> and the result text. However, if such a character already exists, you continue with the next character in the input.

```
static String removeDuplicates(final String input)
{
    var result = new StringBuilder();
    var alreadySeen = new HashSet<>();
```

```
    for (int i = 0; i < input.length(); i++)
    {
        final char currentChar = input.charAt(i);
        if (!alreadySeen.contains(currentChar))
        {
            alreadySeen.add(currentChar);
            result.append(currentChar);
        }
    }

    return result.toString();
}
```

Optimized algorithm   The entire exercise can be solved even more elegantly using Java 8 on-board tools. You benefit from the possibility of converting strings into an IntStream using the chars() method. The stream API allows you to remove duplicates simply by using distinct(). After that, you convert the numeric values back to the char type and finally to short single-character strings. These, in turn, are combined to a result with joining().

```
static String removeDuplicatesImproved(final String input)
{
    return input.chars().distinct().
                    mapToObj(i -> (char) i + "").
                    collect(Collectors.joining());
}
```

Verification

You check the removal of duplicate letters using the following unit test:

```
@ParameterizedTest(name = "removeDuplicates({0}) => {1}")
@CsvSource({ "bananas, bans", "lalalamama, lam", "MICHAEL, MICHAEL" })
void testRemoveDuplicates(final String input, final String expected)
{
    var result = Ex06_DuplicateCharsRemoval.removeDuplicates(input);

    assertEquals(expected, result);
}
```

This is done in the same way for the optimized version.

4.3.7 Solution 7: Capitalize (★★☆☆☆)

Solution 7a (★★☆☆☆)

Write method `String capitalize(String)` that converts a given text into an English title format where each word starts with a capital letter.

Examples

Input	Result
"this is a very special title"	"This Is A Very Special Title"
"effective java is great"	"Effective Java Is Great"

Algorithm   Because strings are immutable, initially you copy the contents into an `char[]` upon which you make the modifications. You traverse this array from front to back, looking for the beginning of a new word. As an indicator, you use a `boolean` flag `capitalizeNextChar`. This indicates that the first letter of the next word has to be capitalized. Initially, this flag is `true`, so the current (first) character is converted into a capital letter. This happens only for letters, not for numbers. After the conversion, the flag gets reset, and letters are skipped until a space is found. You then reset the flag to `true`. This procedure gets repeated until the end of the array is reached. Finally, a new string is created from the array containing the modifications.

```
static String capitalize(final String input)
{
    final char[] inputChars = input.toCharArray();

    boolean capitalizeNextChar = true;
    for (int i = 0; i < inputChars.length; i++)
    {
        var currentChar = inputChars[i];
        if (Character.isWhitespace(currentChar))
        {
            capitalizeNextChar = true;
        }
```

```
        else
        {
            if (capitalizeNextChar && Character.isLetter(currentChar))
            {
                inputChars[i] = Character.toUpperCase(currentChar);
                capitalizeNextChar = false;
            }
        }
    }

    return new String(inputChars);
}
```

Let's try the whole thing in the JShell:

```
jshell> capitalize("everything seems fine")
$14 ==> "Everything Seems Fine"
```

Now, however, you may wonder about the behavior that is supposed to occur for letters after digits or other non-letters:

```
jshell> capitalize("what happens to -a +b 1c")
$15 ==> "What Happens To -A +B 1C"
```

HINT: SPECIAL TREATMENT VARIANT

A moment ago, I brought up another special case. It is a matter of definition how to deal with it. If letters after special characters should not be converted to uppercase, this can be achieved easily. The difference compared to before is subtle: You remove the isLetter() check and call toUpperCase() in every case. This is possible because the method can handle not only letters but also other characters.

```
static String capitalize(final String input)
{
    // ...
        if (Character.isWhitespace(currentChar))
        {
            capitalizeNextChar = true;
        }
```

```
    else
    {
        if (capitalizeNextChar)
        {
            // convert to uppercase
            inputChars[i] = Character.toUpperCase(currentChar);
            capitalizeNextChar = false;
        }
    }
    // ...
}
```

You then obtain the following outputs:

```
jshell> capitalize("what happens to -a +b 1c")
$16 ==> "What Happens To -a +b 1c"
```

Solution 7b: Modification (★★☆☆☆)

Assume now that the input is a list of strings and that a list of strings should be returned, with the individual words then starting with a capital letter. Use the following signature as a starting point:

```
List<String> capitalize(List<String> words)
```

Algorithm   First, create a list to store the converted words. Then iterate through all the passed list elements and process each by calling the `capitalizeWord()` method. To convert the first character to an uppercase letter, separate it with `substring(0, 1)`. The remaining characters are returned by `substring(1)`. A new word is built from both and then inserted into the result. For fault-tolerance, the `capitalizeWord()` method handles an empty input with a sanity check to avoid a `StringIndexOutOfBoundsException` on the following call to `substring()`.

```
static List<String> capitalize(final List<String> words)
{
    final List<String> capitalizedWords = new ArrayList<>();

    for (final String word: words)
        capitalizedWords.add(capitalizeWord(word));
```

179

```
    return capitalizedWords;
}

static String capitalizeWord(final String word)
{
    if (word.isEmpty())
        return "";

    final String upperCaseFirstChar = word.substring(0, 1).toUpperCase();
    final String remainingChars = word.substring(1);

    return upperCaseFirstChar + remainingChars;
}
```

You can alternatively express the functionality using the stream API instead of a classic for loop. Sometimes this increases the readability of the source code. To achieve this, I prefer the *pipeline* layout, where the stream methods are written one below the other to reflect the processing steps in streams:

```
static List<String> capitalizeWithStream(final List<String> words)
{
    return words.stream().map(word -> capitalizeWord(word)).
                        collect(Collectors.toList());
}
```

Solution 7c: Special Treatment (★★☆☆☆)

In headings, it is common to encounter special treatment of words like "is" or "a" that are not capitalized. Implement this as a method List<String> capitalizeSpecial(List<String>, List<String>), which gets the words to be excluded from the conversion as the second parameter.

Example

Input	Exceptions	Result
["this", "is", "a", "title"]	["is", "a"]	["This", "is", "a", "Title"]

Algorithm   The previously developed functionality is extended by a list of words that should not be converted. When traversing, you check if the current word is one from the negative list. If so, it is added to the result without modification. Otherwise, you perform the actions as before.

```java
static List<String> capitalizeSpecial(final List<String> words,
                                      final List<String> ignorableWords)
{
    final List<String> capitalizedWords = new ArrayList<>();

    for (final String word : words)
    {
        if (word.length() > 0)
        {
            if (ignorableWords.contains(word))
                capitalizedWords.add(word);
            else
                capitalizedWords.add(capitalizeWord(word));
        }
    }
    return capitalizedWords;
}
```

Verification

For testing, you use the following inputs, which show the correct operation:

```java
@ParameterizedTest(name = "capitalize({0}) => {1}")
@CsvSource({ "this is a very special title, This Is A Very Special Title",
            "effective java is great, Effective Java Is Great" })
void capitalize(String input, String expected)
{
    var result = Ex07_Capitalize.capitalize(input);

    assertEquals(expected, result);
}
```

```
@Test
void capitalizeWithList()
{
    List<String> input = List.of("this", "is", "a", "special", "title");
    var result = Ex07_Capitalize.capitalize(input);

    assertEquals(List.of("This", "Is", "A", "Special", "Title"), result);
}

@Test
void capitalizeSpecial()
{
    List<String> input = List.of("this", "is", "a", "special", "title");
    var result = Ex07_Capitalize.capitalizeSpecial(input, List.of("is", "a"));

    assertEquals(List.of("This", "is", "a", "Special", "Title"), result);
}
```

4.3.8 Solution 8: Rotation (★★☆☆☆)

Consider two strings, str1 and str2, where the first string is supposed to be longer than the second. Figure out if the first one contains the other one. In doing so, the characters within the first string may also be rotated; characters can be moved from the beginning or the end to the opposite position (even repeatedly). To do this, create method boolean containsRotation(String, String), which is case-insensitive during the check.

Examples

Input 1	Input 2	Result
"ABCD"	"ABC"	True
"ABCDEF	"EFAB"	true ("ABCDEF" ↞ x 2 ⇒ "CDEFAB" contains "EFAB")
"BCDE"	"EC"	False
"Challenge"	"GECH"	True

```
JOB INTERVIEW TIPS: POSSIBLE QUESTIONS AND SOLUTION IDEAS
```

As an example of a job interview, here again, I mention possible questions you may ask to clarify the assignment:

- Is the direction of the rotation known ←/→? Answer: No, arbitrary

- Should the rotation check be case-sensitive? Answer: No, treat as same

Idea 1: Brute force: As a first idea, you could try all combinations. Start without rotation. Then rotate string str1 to the left and check if this rotated string is contained in str2. In the worst case, this procedure is repeated up to n times. This is extremely inefficient.

Idea 2: First check if rotation makes sense: Another idea for solving this is to collect all characters in a Set<E> per string in advance and then use containsAll() to check if all needed letters are included. But even this is laborious and does not really reflect well the problem to be solved.

Idea 3: Procedure in reality: Think for a while and consider how you might solve the problem on a piece of paper. At some point, you have the idea to write the word twice in a sequence:

```
ABCDEF          EFAB
ABCDEFABCDEF EFAB
```

Algorithm   Checking whether one string can be present in the other if rotated can be solved very elegantly with the simple trick of writing the longer string behind the other. In the combination, you check whether the string to be searched for is contained there. With this approach, the solution is both surprisingly short and extremely simple:

```java
static boolean containsRotation(final String str1, final String str2)
{
    final String newDoubledStr1 = (str1 + str1).toLowerCase();

    return newDoubledStr1.indexOf(str2.toLowerCase()) != -1;
}
```

Verification

For testing, use the following inputs, which show the correct operation:

```
@ParameterizedTest(name = "{1} in {0}{0} => {2}")
@CsvSource({ "ABCD, ABC, true", "ABCDEF, EFAB, true", "BCDE, EC, false",
            "Challenge, GECH, true"})
void containsRotation(String value, String rotatedSub, boolean expected)
{
    boolean result = Ex08_RotationV2.containsRotation(value, rotatedSub);

    assertEquals(expected, result);
}
```

4.3.9 Solution 9: Well-Formed Braces (★★☆☆☆)

Write method boolean checkBraces(String) which checks whether the sequence of round braces passed as string contains matching (properly nested) pairs of braces.

Examples

Input	Result	Comment
"(())"	true	
"()()"	true	
"(()))((())"	false	Although the same amount of opening and closing braces, they're not properly nested
"((()"	false	No suitable bracing

Algorithm   Without much consideration, one might be tempted to try all possible combinations. After some thinking, you probably come to the following optimization: You only count the number of opening braces and compare it suitably with the number of closing braces. You have to consider the detail of a closing brace before an opening one. Proceed as follows: Traverse the string from front to back. If the current character is an opening brace, increase the counter for opening braces by one. If it is a closing brace, reduce the counter by one. If the counter falls below 0, you encounter a closing brace without a corresponding opening brace. In the end, the counter must be equal to 0, so that it represents a correct bracing.

```java
static boolean checkBraces(final String input)
{
    int openingCount = 0;

    for (int i = 0; i < input.length(); i++)
    {
        final char ch = input.charAt(i);

        if (ch == '(')
        {
            openingCount++;
        }
        else if (ch == ')')
        {
            openingCount--;
            if (openingCount < 0)
                return false;
        }
    }

    return openingCount == 0;
}
```

Verification

Test your newly developed check for correct bracing with the following inputs for a parameterized test—using an additional hint parameter as a trick, which is not used for testing, but only for preparing an informative JUnit output:

```java
@ParameterizedTest(name = "checkBraces(''{0}'') -- hint: {2}")
@CsvSource({ "(()), true, ok",
             "()(), true, ok",
             "(()))((()), false, not properly nested",
             "((), false, no suitable bracing" })
```

```
void checkBraces(String input, boolean expected, String hint)
{
    boolean result = Ex09_SimpleBracesChecker.checkBraces(input);

    assertEquals(expected, result);
}
```

4.3.10 Solution 10: Anagram (★★☆☆☆)

The term *anagram* is used to describe two strings that contain the same letters in the same frequency. Here, the uppercase and lowercase should not make any difference. Write method boolean isAnagram(String, String).

Examples

Input 1	Input 2	Result
"Otto"	"Toto"	true
"Mary	"Army"	true
"Ananas"	"Bananas"	false

Algorithm   The description of the exercise already provides clues as to how you can proceed. First of all, you transform the words with a method calcCharFrequencies (String) into a histogram. Here, you traverse the corresponding word character by character and fill a Map<K,V>. This is done for both words. Afterwards, you can easily compare the two maps:

```
static boolean isAnagram(final String str1, final String str2)
{
    final Map<Character, Integer> charCounts1 = calcCharFrequencies(str1);
    final Map<Character, Integer> charCounts2 = calcCharFrequencies(str2);

    return charCounts1.equals(charCounts2);
}
```

```
static Map<Character, Integer> calcCharFrequencies(final String input)
{
    final Map<Character, Integer> charCounts = new TreeMap<>();

    for (char currentChar : input.toUpperCase().toCharArray())
    {
        charCounts.putIfAbsent(currentChar, 0);
        charCounts.computeIfPresent(currentChar, (key, value) -> value + 1);
    }

    return charCounts;
}
```

Verification

For testing, use the following inputs, which show the correct functionality:

```
@ParameterizedTest(name = "isAnagram({0}, {1}) => {2}")
@CsvSource({ "Otto, Toto, true", "Mary, Army, true",
            "Ananas, Bananas, false" })
void testIsAnagram(String value1, String value2, boolean expected)
{
    boolean result = Ex10_AnagramChecker.isAnagram(value1, value2);

    assertEquals(expected, result);
}
```

4.3.11 Solution 11: Morse Code (★★☆☆☆)

Write method String toMorseCode(String) that is capable of translating a given text into Morse code characters. They consist of sequences of one to four short and long tones per letter, symbolized by a period (.) or hyphen (-). It is desirable for easier distinguishability to place a space between each tone and three spaces between each sequence of letter tones. Otherwise, S (...) and EEE (...) would not be distinguishable from each other.

For simplicity, limit yourself to the letters E, O, S, T, and W with the following encoding:

Letter	Morse code
E	.
O	- - -
S	...
T	-
W	. - -

Examples

Input	Result
SOS	... - - - ...
TWEET	- . - - . . -
WEST	. - - . ... -

Algorithm   The string is traversed character by character and the current character is mapped to the corresponding Morse code. The method convertToMorseCode(char) performs this task:

```java
static String toMorseCode(final String input)
{
    final StringBuilder convertedMsg = new StringBuilder();

    final String upperCaseInput = input.toUpperCase();
    for (int i = 0; i < upperCaseInput.length(); i++)
    {
        var currentChar = upperCaseInput.charAt(i);
        var convertedLetter = convertToMorseCode(currentChar);

        convertedMsg.append(convertedLetter);
        convertedMsg.append("   ");
    }
}
```

```
    return convertedMsg.toString().trim();
}
```

To map a single letter, use a `switch`—the syntax newly introduced in Java 14 achieves this more elegantly than before.[2]

```
static String convertToMorseCode(char currentChar)
{
    return switch (currentChar)
    {
        case 'E' -> ".";
        case 'O' -> "- - -";
        case 'S' -> ". . .";
        case 'T' -> "-";
        case 'W' -> ". - -";
        default -> "?";
    };
}
```

Bonus

Try to figure out the corresponding Morse code for all letters of the alphabet, (e.g., to convert your name). You can find the necessary hints for this at `https://en.wikipedia.org/wiki/Morse_code`.

Algorithm   You conveniently replace the `switch` statement with a lookup map and then just access that map instead of using the method `convertToMorseCode()`:

```
static Map<Character, String> lookupMap = new HashMap<>()
{{
    put('A', ". -");
    put('B', "- . . .");
    put('C', "- . - .");
    put('D', "- . .");
    put('E', ".");
    put('F', ". . - .");
```

---

[2] More details can be found in my book *Java – die Neuerungen in Version 9 bis 14: Modularisierung, Syntax- und API-Erweiterungen* [Ind20b].

```
    put('G', "- - .");
    put('H', ". . . .");
    put('I', ". .");
    // ..
    put('R', ". - .");
    put('O', "- - -");
    put('S', ". . .");
    put('T', "-");
    put('W', ". - -");
    // ...
}};

static String convertToMorseCode(char currentChar)
{
    return lookupMap.getOrDefault(currentChar, "?");
}
```

For experimentation, verify your attempts using, for example, the following site on the Internet: https://gc.de/gc/morse/. It allows to you convert both normal plain text to Morse code, but most importantly, to convert Morse code to plaintext (the other way around).

Verification

Let's check using a unit test as follows:

```
@ParameterizedTest(name = "toMorseCode({0}) => ''{1}''")
@CsvSource({ "SOS, . . .   - - -   . . .", "TWEET, -   . - -   .   .   -",
            "OST, - - -   . . .   -", "WEST, . - -   .   . . .   -" })
void testToMorseCode(String input, String expected)
{
    var result = Ex11_MorseCode.toMorseCode(input);

    assertEquals(expected, result);
}
```

4.3.12 Solution 12: Pattern Checker (★★★☆☆)

Write method `boolean matchesPattern(String, String)` that examines a space-separated string (second parameter) against the structure of a pattern passed in the form of individual characters as the first parameter.

Examples

Input pattern	Input text	Result
"xyyx"	"tim mike mike tim"	true
"xyyx"	"tim mike tom tim"	false
"xyxx"	"tim mike mike tim"	false
"xxxx"	"tim tim tim tim"	true

JOB INTERVIEW TIPS: PROBLEM SOLVING STRATEGIES

With exercises like this, you should always ask a few questions to clarify the context and gain a better understanding. For this example, possible questions include the following:

1. Is the pattern limited to the characters x and y? ANSWER: No, but only one letter each as a placeholder

2. Is the pattern always only four characters long? ANSWER: No, arbitrary

3. Does the pattern contain no spaces? ANSWER: Yes, never

4. Is the input always separated with exactly one space? ANSWER: Yes

---

Algorithm   As always, it is important first to understand the problem and identify appropriate data structures. You recognize the pattern specification as a sequence of characters and the input values as space-separated words. These can be transformed into a corresponding array of single values using `split()`. Initially, you check if the length of the pattern and the array of input values match. Only in this case do you traverse the pattern character by character as you have done so many times before. As an auxiliary data structure, you use a `Map<K,V>` which maps individual characters of the pattern to words. Now you check if another word has already been inserted for a pattern character. By using this trick, you can easily detect mapping errors.

```java
static boolean matchesPattern(final String pattern, final String input)
{
    // preparation
    final int patternLength = pattern.length();
    final String[] values = input.split(" ");
    final int valuesLength = values.length;

     if (valuesLength != patternLength ||
        (values.length == 1 && values[0].isEmpty()))
        return false;

    final Map<Character, String> placeholderToValueMap = new HashMap<>();

    // run through all characters of the pattern
    for (int i = 0; i< pattern.length(); i++)
    {
        final char patternChar = pattern.charAt(i);
        final String value = values[i];

        // add, if not already there
        placeholderToValueMap.putIfAbsent(patternChar, value);

        // does stored value match current string?
        final String assignedValue = placeholderToValueMap.get(patternChar);
        if (!assignedValue.equals(value))
            return false;
    }
    return true;
}
```

In the code, before the actual check, you still need to verify the special case of an empty input explicitly, since `" ".split(" ")` results in an array of length 1.

The implementation also permits the following specifications, where different wildcard characters (hereafter y and z) are assigned the same value (black):

matchesPattern("xyzx", "red black black red") => **true**

To handle such special cases correctly, it is recommended to execute the following query after the first check:

```
// test for uniqueness of value
if (placeholderToValueMap.values().stream().
                                filter(str -> str.equals(value)).count() > 1)
    return false;
```

Verification

For testing, you use the following inputs, which show the correct operation:

```
@ParameterizedTest(name = "pattern ''{0}'' matches ''{1}'' => {2}")
@CsvSource( {"xyyx, tim mike mike tim, true",
             "xyyx, time mike tom tim, false",
             "xyxx, tim mike mike tim, false",
             "xxxx, tim tim tim tim, true" })
void testInputMatchesPattern(String pattern, String input, boolean expected)
{
    boolean result = Ex12_PatternChecker.matchesPattern(pattern, input);

    assertEquals(expected, result);
}
```

4.3.13 Solution 13: Tennis Score (★★★☆☆)

Write method String tennisScore(String, String, String) that makes an announcement in a familiar style such as *Fifteen Love, Deuce,* or *Advantage Player X* based on a textual score for two players, PL1 and PL2. Thereby their score is given in the format <PL1 points>:<PL2 points>.

The following counting rules apply to a game in tennis:

- A game is won (Game <PlayerX>) when a player reaches 4 or more points and is ahead by at least 2 points.

- Points from 0 to 3 are named Love, Fifteen, Thirty, and Forty.

- In case of at least 3 points and a tie, this is called Deuce.

- With at least 3 points and one point difference, this is called Advantage <PlayerX> for the one who has one more point.

Examples

Input	Score
"1:0", "Micha", "Tim"	"Fifteen Love"
"2:2", "Micha", "Tim"	"Thirty Thirty"
"2:3", "Micha", "Tim"	"Thirty Forty"
"3:3", "Micha", "Tim"	"Deuce"
"4:3", "Micha", "Tim"	"Advantage Micha"
"4:4", "Micha", "Tim"	"Deuce"
"5:4", "Micha", "Tim"	"Advantage Micha"
"6:4", "Micha", "Tim"	"Game Micha"

Algorithm   In this case, it is a two-step algorithm:

1. First, a score in terms of two `int` values should be obtained from the textual representation.

2. Afterwards, it is your task to generate the corresponding textual score names based on these values.

When parsing the score, you can rely on standard JDK functionality, such as `String.split()` as well as `Integer.parseInt()`. In addition, for reusable functionality, it is reasonable to include certain security checks. First, both values should be positive. After that, the specifics on the scores are to be tested: The player who reaches 4 points first wins the match, but only if he leads at least with 2 points. If both players have 3 or more points, then the point difference must be less than 3. Otherwise, it is not a valid state in tennis. You extract the parsing with the checks into the method `extractPoints(String)`.

```java
private static int[] extractPoints(final String score)
{
    final String[] values = score.trim().split(":");

    if (values.length != 2)
        throw new IllegalArgumentException("illegal format -- score has not
                format <points>:<points>, e.g. 7:6");

    final int score1 = Integer.parseInt(values[0]);
    final int score2 = Integer.parseInt(values[1]);

    // sanity check
    if (score1 < 0 || score2 < 0)
        throw new IllegalArgumentException("points must be > 0");

    // verhindert sowohl z. B. 6:3 aber auch 5:1
    if ((score1 > 4 || score2 > 4) && Math.abs(score1 - score2) > 2)
        throw new IllegalArgumentException("point difference must be < 3, " +
                                            "otherwise invalid score");

    return new int[] { score1, score2 };
}
```

After extracting the two scores separated by a semicolon from the input, you proceed with the conversion. Again, you use a multi-step decision procedure. According to the rules, a simple mapping comes into play for scores below 3. This is perfectly described in terms of a map. Starting from 3 points, a tie, advantage, or game win can occur. It is also possible for one player to win with 4 points if the other scores a maximum of 2 points. For the winning message, it is only necessary to determine which of the two players has more points. The described logic is implemented as follows:

```java
static String calculateScore(final String score,
                             final String player1Name,
                             final String player2Name)
{
    final int[] points = extractPoints(score);

    final int score1 = points[0];
    final int score2 = points[1];
```

```
    if (score1 >= 3 && score2 >= 3)
    {
        return generateInfo(score1, score2, player1Name, player2Name);
    }
    else if (score1 >= 4 || score2 >= 4)
    {
        var playerName = (score1 > score2 ? player1Name : player2Name);
        return "Game " + playerName;
    }
    else
    {
        // special naming
        var pointNames = Map.of(0, "Love", 1, "Fifteen",
                                2, "Thirty", 3, "Forty");

        return pointNames.get(score1) + " " + pointNames.get(score2);
    }
}
```

Only one last detail remains, namely the generation of the hint text for advantage or victory:

```
static String generateInfo(final int score1,
                           final int score2,
                           final String player1Name,
                           final String player2Name)
{
    final int scoreDifference = Math.abs(score1 - score2);

    final String playerName = (score1 > score2 ? player1Name :
    player2Name);

    if (score1 == score2)
        return "Deuce";
    if (scoreDifference == 1)
        return "Advantage " + playerName;
    if (scoreDifference == 2)
        return "Game " + playerName;
```

```
throw new IllegalStateException("Unexpected difference: " +
scoreDifference);
}
```

Verification

Let's test the tennis scoring functionality with an imaginary gameplay:

```
@ParameterizedTest(name = "''{0}'' => ''{1}''")
@CsvSource({ "1:0, Fifteen Love", "2:2, Thirty Thirty", "2:3, Thirty Forty",
            "3:3, Deuce", "4:3, Advantage Micha", "4:4, Deuce",
            "5:4, Advantage Micha", "6:4, Game Micha" }
void calculateScore(String score, String expected)
{
    String result = Ex13_TennisPoints.calculateScore(score, "Micha", "Tim");

    assertEquals(expected, result);
}
```

Figure 4-2 shows the output of the test execution in Eclipse.

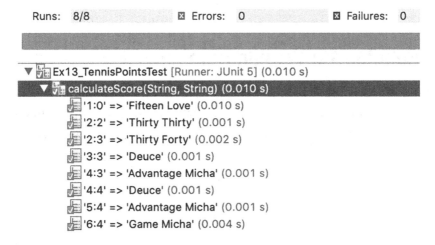

Figure 4-2. *Test execution of the tennis score in Eclipse*

You should add more imaginary game sequences to neatly cover also the edge cases of a close and an unchallenged victory:

```
@ParameterizedTest(name = "''{0}'' => ''{1}''")
@CsvSource({ "1:0, Fifteen Love", "2:2, Thirty Thirty",
            "3:2, Forty Thirty", "4:2, Game Micha" })
void calculateScoreWin(String score, String expected)
{
    String result = Ex13_TennisPoints.calculateScore(score, "Micha", "Tim");

    assertEquals(expected, result);
}

@ParameterizedTest(name = "''{0}'' => ''{1}''")
@CsvSource({ "1:0, Fifteen Love", "2:0, Thirty Love",
            "3:0, Forty Love", "4:0, Game Micha"} )
void calculateScoreStraightWin(String score, String expected)
{
    String result = Ex13_TennisPoints.calculateScore(score, "Micha", "Tim");

    assertEquals(expected, result);
}
```

4.3.14 Solution 14: Version Numbers (★★☆☆☆)

Write method int compareVersions(String, String) that permits you to compare version numbers in the format *MAJOR.MINOR.PATCH* with each other—thereby the specification of *PATCH* is optional. In particular, the return value should be compatible with the int compare(T, T) method from the Comparator<T> interface.

Examples

Version 1	Version 2	Result
1.11.17	2.3.5	<
2.1	2.1.3	<
2.3.5	2.4	<
3.1	2.4	>
3.3	3.2.9	>
7.2.71	7.2.71	=

Algorithm   Subdivide the textual version numbers into a String[] by calling split(). Iterate through the extracted components and convert them to a version number with Integer.valueOf(). Afterwards compare in pairs with Integer.compare() starting at *MAJOR*, then *MINOR*, and *PATCH* if necessary. If one input has more values than the other, then the single last number is not used except when the version number matches up to that component, such as for 3.1 and 3.1.7:

```java
static int compareVersions(final String v1, final String v2)
{
    var v1Numbers = v1.split("\\."); // caution: Reg-Ex, therefore
    var v2Numbers = v2.split("\\."); // would be '.' for each character

    int pos = 0;
    int compareResult = 0;

    while (pos < v1Numbers.length &&
           pos < v2Numbers.length && compareResult == 0)
    {
        final int currentV1 = Integer.valueOf(v1Numbers[pos]);
        final int currentV2 = Integer.valueOf(v2Numbers[pos]);

        compareResult = Integer.compare(currentV1, currentV2);
        pos++;
    }
```

```
if (compareResult == 0) // same beginning for example 3.1 and 3.1.7
    return Integer.compare(v1Numbers.length, v2Numbers.length);

return compareResult;
}
```

```
┌─────────────────────────────────────────────────────────────────────┐
│              PITFALL: REGULAR EXPRESSION IN SPLIT()                   │
└─────────────────────────────────────────────────────────────────────┘
```

Perhaps you also initially fooled yourself when splitting the version numbers into individual components by specifying only a period (.) as a character in `split()`. However, I'm afraid that's not right because the specification expects a regular expression and there the period (.) stands for any character.

Verification

You test the comparison of version numbers with the following inputs for a parameterized test—here again with the trick of an additional hint parameter:

```
@ParameterizedTest(name = "''{0}'' {3} ''{1}''")
@CsvSource({ "1.11.17, 2.3.5, -1, <", "2.3.5, 2.4, -1, <",
            "2.1, 2.1.3, -1, <", "3.1, 2.4, 1, >",
            "3.3, 3.2.9, 1, >", "7.2.71, 7.2.71, 0, =" })
void compareVersions(String v1, String v2, int expected, String hint)
{
    int result = Ex14_VersionNumberComparator.compareVersions(v1, v2);

    assertEquals(expected, result);
}
```

Let's take a look at the easy-to-understand output of the test execution in Eclipse, shown in Figure 4-3.

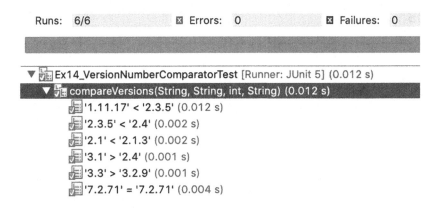

Figure 4-3. *Test execution in Eclipse*

Bonus

Implement the functionality using the Comparator<T> interface.

Algorithm   The comparison functionality can be transformed almost exactly into a comparator with the following one-liner:

```
static Comparator<String> versioNumberComparator =
                    (v1, v2) -> compareVersions(v1, v2);
```

4.3.15 Solution 15: Conversion strToLong (★★☆☆☆)

Convert a string into a long. Write method long strToLong(String) on your own.

> **Note**   The conversion can be easily achieved with long.parseLong(value). Do not use this explicitly, but implement the entire conversion yourself.

Examples

Input	Result
"+123"	123
"-123"	-123
"7271"	7271
"ABC"	IllegalArgumentException
"0123"	83 (for bonus task)
"-0123"	-83 (for bonus task)
"0128"	IllegalArgumentException (for bonus task)

Algorithm   Check if the first character is +/- and set a flag isNegative accordingly. Then iterate through all characters and convert them into digits. The previous value is multiplied by 10 each time, and at the end, the corresponding numeric value is obtained.

```
static long strToLongV1(final String number)
{
    final boolean isNegative = number.charAt(0) == '-';
    long value = 0;

    int pos = startsWithSign(number) ? 1 : 0;

    while (pos < number.length())
    {
        final int digitValue = number.charAt(pos) - '0';
        value = value * 10 + digitValue;

        pos++;
    }

    return isNegative ? -value : value;
}

static boolean startsWithSign(final String number)
{
    return number.charAt(0) == '-' || number.charAt(0) == '+';
}
```

Corrected algorithm   Even without deeper analysis, it is obvious that the above version does not work correctly when mixing letters with digits. In this case, it is reasonable to throw an `IllegalArgumentException` by a check with `isDigit()` as follows:

```
static long strToLongV2(final String number)
{
    final boolean isNegative = number.charAt(0) == '-';
    long value = 0;

    int pos = startsWithSign(number) ? 1 : 0;

    while (pos < number.length())
    {
        if (!Character.isDigit(number.charAt(pos)))
            throw new IllegalArgumentException(number +
                                        " contains not only digits");

        final int digitValue = number.charAt(pos) - '0';
        value = value * 10 + digitValue;

        pos++;
    }

    return isNegative ? -value : value;
}
```

Verification

To test the functionality, you use three numbers, with a positive and a negative sign and without. The positive sign should then just be ignored during the conversion. You check the reaction to input with letters instead of numbers separately and expect an exception.

```
@ParameterizedTest(name = "strToLongV2(\"{0}\") => {1}")
@CsvSource({ "+123, 123", "-123, -123", "123, 123", "7271, 7271" })
void testStrToLongV2(String number, long expected)
{
    long result = Ex15_StrToLong.strToLongV2(number);

    assertEquals(expected, result);
}
```

```java
@Test
void testStrToLongV2Error()
{
    assertThrows(IllegalArgumentException.class,
                () -> Ex15_StrToLong.strToLongV2("ABC"));
}
```

Bonus: Enable the Parsing of Octal Numbers

Octal numbers are marked by a leading zero in Java. As the name suggests, they are of base 8 and not base 10. To support octal numbers, it is necessary first to determine whether a leading zero exists. In this case, the factor for the positions in the number system is changed to 8. Finally, with base 8, of course, the two digits 8 and 9 are no longer allowed. Therefore, you add another check in the loop for processing the values. All in all, the source code is a bit bloated by the special treatments—the complexity is just manageable—especially because problem adapted helper methods with speaking names are used here.

```java
static long strToLongBonus(final String number)
{
    final boolean isNegative = number.charAt(0) == '-';
    final boolean isOctal = number.charAt(0) == '0' ||
                (startsWithSign(number) && number.charAt(1) == '0');

    long value = 0;

    final int factor = isOctal ? 8 : 10;

    int pos = calcStartPos(number, isOctal);

    while (pos < number.length())
    {
        if (!Character.isDigit(number.charAt(pos)))
            throw new IllegalArgumentException(number + " contains not only
                digits");
```

```
        final int digitValue = number.charAt(pos) - '0';
        if (isOctal && digitValue >= 8)
            throw new IllegalArgumentException(number + " found digit >= 8");

        value = value * factor + digitValue;

        pos++;
    }

    return isNegative ? -value : value;
}

private static int calcStartPos(final String number, final boolean isOctal)
{
    int pos = 0;
    if (startsWithSign(number) && isOctal)
    {
        pos = 2;
    }
    else if (startsWithSign(number) || isOctal)
    {
        pos = 1;
    }
    return pos;
}
```

Verification

To test the functionality, use three numbers, with a positive and a negative sign and without. The positive sign should then just be ignored during the conversion. In addition, check a positive and negative octal number. In a separate test, it is ensured that digits greater than or equal to 8 must not occur in octal numbers.

```
@ParameterizedTest(name = "strToLongBonus(\"{0}\") => {1}")
@CsvSource({ "+123, 123", "-123, -123", "123, 123", "7271, 7271",
            "+077, 63", "-077, -63", "077, 63",
            "+0123, 83", "-0123, -83", "0123, 83" })
```

```
void testStrToLongBonus(String number, long expected)
{
    long result = Ex15_StrToLong.strToLongBonus(number);

    assertEquals(expected, result);
}

@Test
void strToLongBonus_should_raise_exception_for_invalid_octal_number()
{
    IllegalArgumentException ex = assertThrows(IllegalArgument
    Exception.class,
                            () -> Ex15_StrToLong.strToLong
                            Bonus("0128"));

    assertTrue(ex.getMessage().contains("found digit >= 8"));
}
```

4.3.16 Solution 16: Print Tower (★★★☆☆)

Write method void printTower(int) that represents a tower of *n* slices stacked on top of each other as ASCII graphics, symbolized by the character #, and also draw a lower boundary line.

Example   A tower of height 3 should look something like this:

```
   |
  #|#
 ##|##
###|###
---------
```

Algorithm   You can divide the drawing into three steps: draw the top bar, draw the slices, and then draw the bottom boundary. Thus, the algorithm can be described using three method calls:

```
static void printTower(final int height)
{
    drawTop(height);
    drawSlices(height);
```

```
    drawBottom(height);
}
```

You implement the drawing of the individual components of this tower in a couple of helper methods, as already indicated:

```
static void drawTop(final int height)
{
    System.out.println(repeatCharSequence(" ", height + 1) + "|");
}
```

```
static void drawBottom(final int height)
{
    System.out.println(repeatCharSequence("-", (height + 1) * 2 + 1));
}
```

In particular, the helper method repeatCharSequence() is used here, which outputs characters repeatedly.

Drawing the slices of the tower is a bit more complex due to their different sizes and the required computation of the free space on the left and right side:

```
static void drawSlices(final int height)
{
    for (int i = height - 1; i >= 0; i--)
    {
        final int value = height - i;
        final int padding = i + 1;

        final String line = repeatCharSequence(" ", padding) +
                            repeatCharSequence("#", value) +
                            "|" +
                            repeatCharSequence("#", value);

        System.out.println(line);
    }
}
```

```
static String repeatCharSequence(final String character, final int length)
{
    String str = "";
    for (int i = 0; i < length; i++)
    {
        str += character;
    }
    return str;
}
```

It is obvious how the problem can be broken down into increasingly smaller subproblems. Each method becomes thereby short for itself and usually also well testable (if no console outputs, but computations with return take place).

With Java 11, instead of using the repeatCharSequence() method above, it is recommended to use the String.repeat() method from the JDK. To change as little as possible, the following procedure is suggested. First, instead of calling your own implementation, simply call the repeat() method inside repeatCharSequence() as follows:

```
static String repeatCharSequence(final String character, final int length)
{
    return character.repeat(length);
}
```

To clean up the unnecessary delegation the refactoring INLINE is helpful. Its usage removes the method repeatCharSequence() and as a consequence repeat() is now called directly in all places.

Verification

To check the functionality, use the JShell one more time—here to print a tower of height 4:

```
jshell> printTower(4)
     |
    #|#
   ##|##
  ###|###
 ####|####
-----------
```

HINT: MODIFICATION WITH RECURSION

Interestingly, the drawing of the individual slices of the tower can also be expressed recursively as follows:

```
private static void drawSlices(final int slice, final int height)
{
    if (slice > 1)
    {
        drawSlices(slice - 1, height);

        System.out.println(repeatCharSequence(" ", height - slice + 1) +
                        repeatCharSequence("#", slice) +
                        "|" +
                        repeatCharSequence("#", slice));
    }
}
```

Then, the call must be minimally modified:

```
static void printTower(final int height)
{
    drawTop(height);
    drawSlices(height, height);
    drawBottom(height);
}
```

CHAPTER 5

Arrays

Arrays are data structures that store either values of a primitive data type or object references in a contiguous storage area. Array creation is shown as follows for numbers of type int and in two variants for names of type String. In the latter case, the shorthand notation and syntactic feature of direct initialization are used, where the size of the array is automatically determined by the compiler by the number of specified elements.

```
int[] numbers = new int[100];                    // definition without data
String[] names1 = new String[] { "Tim", "Mike" }; // standard notation
String[] names2 = { "Tim", "Mike" };             // short form
```

5.1 Introduction

An array only represents a simple data container whose size is specified by the initialization and can be determined via the attribute length. Arrays do not provide any container functionality, so there are neither access methods nor any data encapsulation. These functionalities must be programmed if necessary in a using application. However, indexed access pitfalls lurk straight. If an index from the range 0 to length - 1 is inadvertently not accessed, this then triggers an ArrayIndexOutOfBoundsException.

Despite the limitations mentioned above, arrays are important and common data structures, which can be used profitably in various situations since they are memory-efficient and offer maximum performance with indexed access. Besides, only arrays are capable of storing primitive types directly (without the indirection of auto-boxing).

In this introduction, you will get to know both one-dimensional and multidimensional arrays.

© Michael Inden 2022
M. Inden, *Java Challenges*, https://doi.org/10.1007/978-1-4842-7395-1_5

5.1.1 One-Dimensional Arrays

As an introduction to processing data with arrays and building knowledge of possible interview questions, let's look at some examples.

Textual Output

Arrays do not come with a `toString()` method, which is why you sometimes see strange output like this:

```
jshell> String[] names = { "Tim", "Mike" }

jshell> names.toString()
$40 ==> "[Ljava.lang.String;@53bd815b"
```

As a workaround, the `Arrays.toString(values)` method from the JDK can be beneficial. To get started, however, implement the output of an array yourself:

```
static void printArray(final String[] values)
{
    for (int i = 0; i < values.length; i++)
    {
        final String str = values[i];
        System.out.println(str);
    }
}
```

Both variants provide comprehensible representations:

```
jshell> Arrays.toString(names)
$43 ==> "[Tim, Mike]"

jshell> printArray(names) Tim
Mike
```

Example 1: Swapping Elements

A common functionality is swapping elements at two positions. This can be achieved in a simple and readable way providing method swap(int[], int, int) as follows:

```
public static void swap(final int[] values, final int first, final int second)
{
    final int value1 = values[first];
    final int value2 = values[second];

    values[first] = value2;
    values[second] = value1;
}
```

Of course, you can also solve this with only three assignments and a temporary variable. Still, I think the previous version is a bit more comprehensible.

```
public static void swap(final int[] values, final int first, final int second)
{
    final int tmp = values[first];

    values[first] = values[second];
    values[second] = tmp;
}
```

HINT: PREFER READABILITY AND COMPREHENSIBILITY

Keep in mind that the first version of swap() will probably be optimized after some time anyway by the just-in-time (JIT) compiler built into the JVM. Regardless, readability and understandability are the keys to correctness and maintainability. Besides, this often facilitates testability.

While the helper variable to save one assignment is pretty catchy here, there are definitely more elaborate traceable low-level optimizations in other use cases. They are then usually more difficult to read and less comprehensible.

Example 2: Basic Functionality for Arrays

Now let's write method find(T[], T) to search for a value in an array and return its position or -1 for *not found*:

```
static <T> int find(final T[] values, final T searchFor)
{
    for (int i = 0; i < values.length; i++)
    {
        if (values[i].equals(searchFor))
            return i;
    }
    return -1;
}
```

This can be solved as a typical search problem with a while loop—where the condition is given as a comment at the end of the loop:

```
static <T> int find(final T[] values, final T searchFor)
{
    int pos = 0;
    while (pos < values.length && !values[pos].equals(searchFor))
    {
        pos++;
    }
    // i >= values.length || values[i].equals(searchFor)
    return pos >= values.length ? -1 : pos;
}
```

Example 3: Remove Duplicates

Assuming a sorted array of positive numbers

```
int[] sortedNumbers = { 1, 2, 2, 3, 3, 4, 4, 4 };
```

removing the duplicates should give the following result:

```
[ 1, 2, 3, 4 ]
```

JOB INTERVIEW TIPS: PROBLEM SOLVING STRATEGIES

For assignments like this, you should always ask a few questions to clarify the context and gain a better understanding. For this example, possible questions include the following:

1. Is it necessary to keep the order/sorting of the numbers?

2. May a new array be created or must the actions inplace—within the original array—be done?

3. For inplace, there are further questions:

   a. What exactly should happen when removing/deleting?

   b. What value represents *no entry*?

Solution 1 for example 3: new array and sorted input: Suppose you return a new array as a result when eliminating duplicates. The algorithm then divides into two stages:

1. You start by collecting the numbers in a TreeSet<E>. This way, the duplicates are automatically removed, and also the sorting and the original order are preserved.[1]

2. The second step then involves preparing a new array based on the Set<E>.

This procedure can be implemented fairly directly as follows:

```
static int[] removeDuplicatesNewArray(final int[] sortedNumbers)
{
    final Set<Integer> uniqueValues = collectValues(sortedNumbers);

    return convertSetToArray(uniqueValues);
}
```

---

[1] There are a few things to keep in mind for the TreeSet<E>. First, the values to be collected must be comparable. This means that they must satisfy the Comparable<T> interface, or the TreeSet<E> has to be constructed with a comparator. Second, for unsorted data, their order would become rearranged, but this is not desired. In this example, the TreeSet<E> is applicable because the assignment explicitly talks about sorted values.

The method consists of readable, directly understandable source code that does not show unnecessary details but reflects the concepts.

Now it is time to complete the implementation with the two helper methods called above. When converting the Set<Integer> to an int[] you just have to trick it a little, because a Set<E> does not provide indexed access.

```java
static Set<Integer> collectValues(final int[] sortedNumbers)
{
    final Set<Integer> uniqueValues = new TreeSet<>();
    for (int i = 0; i < sortedNumbers.length; i++)
    {
        uniqueValues.add(sortedNumbers[i]);
    }
    return uniqueValues;
}

static int[] convertSetToArray(final Set<Integer> values)
{
    return values.stream().mapToInt(n -> n).toArray();
}
```

Here you see another difficulty that occurs from time to time in practice. Although there is an automatic conversion between primitive types and their corresponding wrapper classes in Java with auto-boxing/unboxing, this does not work for arrays. Therefore you cannot convert an int[] into an Integer[] or vice versa. This is the reason why you implement the convertSetToArray() method and do not use the predefined toArray() method of the Set<E>, which in your case would return an Object[] or a Integer[] depending on the call.

You cleverly solved this problem with the Stream API and the methods mapToInt() as well as toArray(). An alternative is discussed in the following practical note.

NOTE: OLD SCHOOL

To build up a good understanding of algorithms, you can implement the conversion of a
Set<Integer> to a int[] using an Iterator<E> as follows:

```java
static int[] convertSetToArray(final Set<Integer> uniqueValues)
{
    final int size = uniqueValues.size();
    final int[] noDuplicates = new int[size];
    int i = 0;

    // set posseses no index
    final Iterator<Integer> it = uniqueValues.iterator();
    while (it.hasNext())
    {
        noDuplicates[i] = it.next();
        i++;
    }
    return noDuplicates;
}
```

With the for-each loop, you can even write this a bit shorter:

```java
static int[] convertSetToArray(final Set<Integer> uniqueValues)
{
    final int[] noDuplicates = new int[uniqueValues.size()];
    int i = 0;
    for (final Integer value : uniqueValues)
    {
        noDuplicates[i] = value;
        i++;
    }
    return noDuplicates;
}
```

Solution 2 for example 3: variant for unsorted/arbitrary numbers   The previous task of removing duplicates in sorted numbers was still easy to solve with JDK on-board facilities. But how should you proceed with non-sorted data, assuming that the original order has to be maintained? Specifically, the result shown on the right should then result from the left sequence of values:

```
[1, 4, 4, 2, 2, 3, 4, 3, 4] => [1, 4, 2, 3]
```

Interestingly, neither a TreeSet<E> nor a HashSet<E> would make sense as a result data structure in that case because both would mess up the original order. If you think for a moment, ask an experienced colleague, or browse through a book, you might discover the class LinkedHashSet<E>: This has nearly the properties and performance of a HashSet<E>, but can maintain the insertion order.

When using a LinkedHashSet<E>, you don't have to change anything in your basic algorithm. Even better: This variant works just as well with already sorted data. Thus, in the helper method, you only substitute the data structure used, and everything else remains unchanged:

```java
static Set<Integer> collectValues(final int[] numbers)
{
    final Set<Integer> uniqueValues = new LinkedHashSet<>();
    for (int i = 0; i < numbers.length; i++)
    {
        final int value = numbers[i];
        uniqueValues.add(value);
    }
    return uniqueValues;
}
```

This example illustrates the advantages of programming small functionalities that are self-contained and follow the SRP (single-responsibility principle). Even more: Keeping public methods understandable and moving details to (preferably private) helper methods often allows you to keep subsequent changes as local as possible. By the way, I discuss both the LinkedHashSet<E> and the SRP in detail in my book *Der Weg zum Java-Profi* [Ind20a].

Solution 3 for example 3: variant inplace   Given a sorted array of positive numbers again

```java
int[] sortedNumbers = { 1, 2, 2, 3, 3, 3, 4, 4, 4, 4 };
```

all duplicates are to be removed, but this time it is not allowed to create a new array. This implementation is a little bit more difficult. The algorithm is as follows: Run through the array and check for each element, whether it already exists and whether it is a duplicate. This check can be performed by comparing the current element with its predecessor. This simplification is possible because sorting exists—without it, it would be much more complicated to solve. You start the processing at the frontmost position and proceed step by step. Thereby you collect all numbers without duplicates on the left side of the array. To know where to read or write in the array, you use position pointers named readPos and writePos, respectively. If you find a duplicate number, the read pointer moves on; the write pointer stays in place.

```
static void removeDuplicatesFirstTry(final int[] sortedNumbers)
{
    int prevValue = sortedNumbers[0];
    int writePos = 1;
    int readPos = 1;

    while (readPos < sortedNumbers.length)
    {
        int currentValue = sortedNumbers[readPos];
        if (prevValue != currentValue)
        {
            sortedNumbers[writePos] = currentValue;
            writePos++;

            prevValue = currentValue;
        }
        readPos++;
    }
}
```

Although this variant is functionally correct, the result is confusing:

```
[ 1, 2, 3, 4, 3, 3, 4, 4, 4, 4 ]
```

This is because you are working inplace here. There is no hint for how the result can be separated (i.e., up to where the values are valid and where the invalid, *removed* values start). Accordingly, two things are recommended:

1. You should return the length of the valid range.

2. You should delete the following positions with a special value, like -1 for primitive number types or for reference types often null. This value must not be part of the value set. Otherwise, irritations and inconsistencies are inevitable.

The following modification solves both issues and also uses a for loop, which makes everything a bit more elegant and shorter:

```java
int removeDuplicatesImproved(final int[] sortedNumbers)
{
    int writeIndex = 1;

    for (int i = 1; i < sortedNumbers.length; i++)
    {
        final int currentValue = sortedNumbers[i];
        final int prevValue = sortedNumbers[writeIndex - 1];

        if (prevValue != currentValue)
        {
            sortedNumbers[writeIndex] = currentValue;
            writeIndex++;
        }
    }

    // delete the positions that are no longer needed
    for (int i = writeIndex; i < sortedNumbers.length; i++)
    {
        sortedNumbers[i] = -1;
    }

    return writeIndex;
}
```

An invocation of this method returns the length of the valid range (additionally, after the last valid index in the modified array, all values are set to -1):

```
jshell> int[] sortedNumbers = { 1, 2, 2, 3, 3, 3, 4, 4, 4, 4 };

jshell> removeDuplicatesImproved(sortedNumbers)
$4 ==> 3

jshell> Arrays.toString(sortedNumbers)
$5 ==> "[1, 2, 3, 4, -1, -1, -1, -1, -1, -1]"
```

Interim conclusion   The example illustrates several problematic issues. First, that it is often more complex to work inplace—that is, without creating new arrays, but directly within the original array—and second, how to handle changes when values remain in the array but are no longer part of the result. You can either return a counter or erase the values with a neutral, special value. However, it is often more understandable and therefore recommended to use the variants shown, which create a new array.

JOB INTERVIEW TIPS: ALTERNATIVE WAYS OF LOOKING AT THINGS

As simple as the assignment may have sounded at first, it does hold some potential for different approaches and solution strategies. When removing duplicates, you could also come up with the idea of replacing elements by *no entry* for object references the value null:

```
[1,2,2,4,4,3,3,3,2,2,3,1] => [1,2,null,3,null,null,4,null,null,null,null]
```

For a non-sorted array, it is also possible to retain the values in the order of their original occurrence:

```
[1,2,2,4,4,3,3,3,2,2,3,1] => [1,2,4,3]
```

Alternatively, it is possible to remove only consecutive duplicates at a time:

```
[1,2,2,4,4,3,3,3,2,2,3,1] => [1,2,4,3,2,3,1]]
```

As you can see, there is more to consider, even for apparently simple tasks. This is why requirements engineering and the correct coverage of requirements are a real challenge.

Example 4: Rotation by One or More Positions

Let's look at another problem, namely rotating an array by n positions to the left or to the right, where the elements are then to be shifted cyclically at the beginning or the end, respectively, as visualized here, where the middle array is the starting point:

| 2 | 3 | 4 | 1 | $\Leftarrow$ | 1 | 2 | 3 | 4 | $\Rightarrow$ | 4 | 1 | 2 | 3 |

The algorithm for a rotation by one element to the right is simple: Remember the last element and then repeatedly copy the element that is one ahead in the direction of rotation to the one behind it. Finally, the cached last element is inserted at the foremost position.

```java
void rotateRight(final int[] values)
{
    if (values.length < 2)
        return values;

    final int endPos = values.length - 1;
    final int temp = values[endPos];

    for (int i = endPos; i > 0; i--)
        values[i] = values[i - 1];

    values[0] = temp;
}
```

The rotation to the left works analogously:

```java
void rotateLeft(final int[] values)
{
    if (values.length < 2)
        return values;

    final int endPos = values.length - 1;
    final int temp = values[0];

    for (int i = 0; i < endPos; i++)
        values[i] = values[i + 1];

    values[endPos] = temp;
}
```

Let's try the whole thing out in the JShell:

```
jshell> int[] numbers = { 1, 2, 3, 4, 5, 6, 7 };
numbers ==> int[7] { 1, 2, 3, 4, 5, 6, 7 }

jshell> rotateRight(numbers);
$16 ==> int[7] { 7, 1, 2, 3, 4, 5, 6 }

jshell> rotateLeft(numbers);
$17 ==> int[7] { 1, 2, 3, 4, 5, 6, 7 }
```

Rotation around n positions (simple)   An obvious extension is to rotate by a certain number of positions. This can be solved using brute force by calling the just-developed functionality n times:

```
static void rotateRightByN_Simple(final int[] values, final int n)
{
    for (int i = 0; i < n; i++)
        rotateRight(values);
}
```

This solution is acceptable in principle, although not performant due to the frequent copy actions. How can it be more efficient?

HINT: OPTIMIZATION AT LARGE VALUES FOR n

First, there is one more small feature to consider, namely, if n is larger than the length of the array, you don't have to rotate all the time, but you can limit this to what is actually needed by using the modulo operation `i < n % values.length`.

Rotation around n positions (tricky)   Alternatively, imagine that n positions are added to the original array. This is accomplished by using an independent buffer that caches the last n elements. It is implemented in the method `fillTempWithLastN()`. This first creates a suitably sized array and puts the last n values there. Then you copy the values as before, but with an offset of n. Finally, you just need to copy the values back from the buffer using `copyTempBufferToStart()`.

```
static int[] rotateRightByN(final int[] values, final int n)
{
    final int adjustedN = n % values.length;
    final int[] tempBuffer = fillTempWithLastN(values, adjustedN);

    // copy n positions to the right
    for (int i = values.length - 1; i >= adjustedN; i--)
        values[i] = values[i - adjustedN];

    copyTempBufferToStart(tempBuffer, values);

    return values;
}

static int[] fillTempWithLastN(final int[] values, final int n)
{
    final int[] tempBuffer = new int[n];

    for (int i = 0; i < n; i++)
        tempBuffer[i] = values[values.length - n + i];

    return tempBuffer;
}

static void copyTempBufferToStart(final int[] tempBuffer, final int[] values)
{
    for (int i = 0; i < tempBuffer.length; i++)
        values[i] = tempBuffer[i];
}
```

Here's another hint: The method just presented for rotation can be suboptimal in terms of memory, especially if the value n is very large and the array itself is also huge—but for our examples, this does not matter. Interestingly, the simple version would then be better in terms of memory, although probably rather slow due to the frequent copy actions.

5.1.2 Multidimensional Arrays

In this section, I will briefly discuss multidimensional arrays. Because it is more common in practice and easy to imagine visually, I will limit it to two-dimensional arrays. In the following, a rectangular shape is also often assumed. In fact, multidimensional arrays are organized in Java as arrays of arrays. They thus do not necessarily have to be rectangular. If appropriate, some assignments also support non-rectangular arrays, such as filling an area with a pattern.

Using a two-dimensional rectangular array, you can model a playing field, for example, A Sudoku puzzle or a landscape represented by characters. For a better understanding and an introduction, let's consider an example. Suppose # represents a boundary wall, $ stands for an item to be collected, P stands for the player, and X stands for the exit from a level. These characters are used to describe a playing field as follows:

```
################
##  P         ##
####  $ X  ####
###### $  ######
################
```

In Java, a char[][] can be used to model this (executable as TwoDimArrayWorldExample):

```java
public static void main(final String[] args)
{
    final char[][] world = { "################".toCharArray(),
                             "##  P         ##".toCharArray(),
                             "####  $ X  ####".toCharArray(),
                             "###### $  ######".toCharArray(),
                             "################".toCharArray() };

    printArray(world);
}
```

```java
public static void printArray(final char[][] values)
{
    for (int y = 0; y < values.length; y++)
    {
        for (int x = 0; x < values[y].length; x++)
        {
            final char value = getAt(values, x, y);
            System.out.print(value + " ");
        }
        System.out.println();
    }
}
```

There are two variants of how to specify the coordinates when accessing: One is [x][y], and the other is [y][x] if you think more line-oriented. Between different developers, this can lead to misunderstandings and discussions. A small remedy can be achieved if you write access methods like getAt(char[][], int, int) and consider the respective preference there. I will use this access method preferably in the introduction and later switch over to direct array accesses:

```java
static char getAt(final char[][] values, final int x, final int y)
{
    return values[y][x];
}
```

Let's run the TwoDimArrayWorldExample program to see the output functionality in action. In the following, I will refer to similar things from time to time. Besides debugging, the console output is quite helpful, especially for multidimensional arrays.

```
# # # # # # # # # # # # # #
# #     P                 # #
# # # #     $ X   # # # #
# # # # #   $     # # # # #
# # # # # # # # # # # # # #
```

Introductory Example

Your task now is to rotate an array 90 degrees to the left or right. Let's take a look at this for two rotations to the right:

```
1111        4321        4444
2222   =>   4321   =>   3333
3333        4321        2222
4444        4321        1111
```

Let's try to formalize the procedure a bit. The easiest way to implement the rotation is to create a new array and then populate it appropriately. For the determination of the formulas, you use concrete example data, which facilitates the understanding (xn and yn stand for the new coordinates—in the following the rotation to the left and the rotation to the right is shown on the left/right):

```
        x   0123
        y   ----
        0   ABCD
        1   EFGH
```

```
  xn  01                 xn  01
yn    --               yn    --
  0   DH                 0   EA
  1   CG                 1   FB
  2   BF                 2   GC
  3   AE                 3   HD
```

You see that a 4 × 2 array turns into a 2 × 4 array.

The rotation is based on the following calculation rules, where maxX and maxY are the respective maximum coordinates:

```
               Orig    ->    NewX           NewY
------------------------------------------------------
rotateLeft:    (x,y)   ->    y              maxX - x
rotateRight:   (x,y)   ->    maxY - y       x
```

You proceed to the implementation with this knowledge. You first create a suitably large array and traverse the original array line by line and then position by position. Based on the formulas above, the rotation can be implemented as follows:

```
enum RotationDirection { LEFT_90, RIGHT_90 }

public static Object[][] rotate(Object[][] values, RotationDirection dir)
{
    int origLengthX = values[0].length;
    int origLengthY = values.length;

    final Object[][] rotatedArray = new Object[origLengthX][origLengthY];
//    Class<?> plainType = values.getClass().componentType().componentType();
//    T[][] rotatedArray = (T[][])Array.newInstance(plainType,
//                                                  origLengthX, origLengthY);

    for (int y = 0; y < values.length; y++)
    {
        for (int x = 0; x < values[0].length; x++)
        {
            int maxX = values[0].length - 1;
            int maxY = values.length - 1;

            Object origValue = values[y][x];

            if (dir == RotationDirection.LEFT_90)
            {
                int newX = y;
                int newY = maxX - x;

                rotatedArray[newY][newX] = origValue;
            }
            if (dir == RotationDirection.RIGHT_90)
            {
                int newX = maxY - y;
                int newY = x;
```

```
                rotatedArray[newY][newX] = origValue;
            }
        }
    }

    return rotatedArray;
}

static <T> T getAt(final T[][] values, final int x, final int y)
{
    return values[y][x];
}
```

A purely generic implementation is more complicated here since generic arrays, unfortunately, cannot be created with new T[][]. This requires tricks and reflection, as shown commented out. Because a more detailed treatment is beyond this book's scope, I refer you to my book *Der Weg zum Java-Profi* [Ind20a].

Before you take a look at the functionality, let's define a helper method to output two-dimensional arrays of arbitrary types (except primitives):

```
static <T> void printArray(final T[][] values)
{
    for (int y = 0; y < values.length; y++)
    {
        for (int x = 0; x < values[y].length; x++)
        {
            final T value = values[y][x];
            System.out.print(value + " ");
        }
        System.out.println();
    }
}
```

HINT: IMPLEMENTATION VARIANTS

Instead of the classic `for` loop with index variables, the shorter syntax of the `for` loop available since Java 5 often provides more readability, especially for arrays:

```java
static <T> void printArray(final T[][] values)
{
    for (final T[] value : values)
    {
        for (final T v : value)
        {
            System.out.print(v + " ");
        }
        System.out.println();
    }
}
```

A variant is to leave the string formatting to be done by `Arrays.toString()`. This then creates square brackets and a comma-separated representation:

```java
static <T> void printArrayJdk(final T[][] values)
{
    for (int i = 0; i < values.length; i++)
    {
        System.out.println(Arrays.toString(values[i]));
    }
}
```

Let's take a look at the operations in the JShell:

```java
jshell> var inputArray = new String[][]
{
    { "A", "B", "C", "D" },
    { "E", "F", "G", "H" }
}

jshell> printArray(rotate(inputArray, RotationDirection.LEFT_90))
```

D H
C G
B F
A E

Finally, the call to `printArrayJdk()` shows the formatting of the array rotated by 90 degrees to the right mentioned in the practice tip:

```
jshell> printArrayJdk(rotate(inputArray, RotationDirection.RIGHT_90))
[E, A]
[F, B]
[G, C]
[H, D]
```

Modeling Directions

You encounter directions in a variety of use cases. They can, of course, be modeled simply using an enumeration. In the context of two-dimensional arrays, it is extremely convenient and contributes significantly to readability and comprehensibility to define all essential cardinal directions in the enumeration and, moreover, offsets in x- and y-direction. Since the values are constant, I do not include `get()` methods here:

```
public enum Direction
{
    N(0,-1), NE(1,-1),
    E(1,0), SE(1,1),
    S(0,1), SW(-1,1),
    W(-1,0), NW(-1,-1);

    public final int dx;
    public final int dy;

    private Direction(final int dx, final int dy)
    {
        this.dx = dx;
        this.dy = dy;
    }
```

```java
    public static Direction provideRandomDirection()
    {
        final Direction[] directions = values();
        final int randomIndex = (int) (Math.random() * directions.length);

        return directions[randomIndex];
    }
}
```

Example: random traversal   To go a little deeper on processing with directions, let's develop a traversal for a playfield. Whenever you hit array boundaries, you randomly choose a new direction not equal to the old one (executable as RandomTraversalDirectionExample):

```java
public static void main(final String[] args)
{
    final char[][] world = { "ABCDEf".toCharArray(),
                             "GHIJKL".toCharArray(),
                             "MNOPQR".toCharArray(),
                             "abcdef".toCharArray(),
                             "ghijkl".toCharArray() };

    Direction dir = Direction.provideRandomDirection();
    System.out.println("Direction: " + dir);

    int posX = 0;
    int posY = 0;
    int steps = 0;

    while (steps < 25)
    {
        System.out.print(world[posY][posX] + " ");

        if (!isOnBoard(world, posX + dir.dx, posY + dir.dy))
        {
            dir = selectNewDir(world, dir, posX, posY);
            System.out.println("\nNew Direction: " + dir);
        }
```

```
        posX += dir.dx;
        posY += dir.dy;
        steps++;
    }
}

static Direction selectNewDir(final char[][] world, Direction dir,
                                final int posX, final int posY)
{
    Direction oldDir = dir;
    do
    {
        dir = Direction.provideRandomDirection();
    }
    while (oldDir == dir || !isOnBoard(world, posX + dir.dx, posY + dir.dy));

    return dir;
}
```

In this assignment, you immediately get in touch with another useful method named isOnBoard(). Its task is to check whether a passed x-y value is valid for the array— here assuming that the array is rectangular:

```
static boolean isOnBoard(final char[][] values,
                            final int nextPosX, final int nextPosY)
{
    return nextPosX >= 0 && nextPosY >= 0 &&
            nextPosX < values[0].length && nextPosY < values.length;
}
```

If you start the program RandomTraversalDirectionExample, you will get the following output, which shows the direction changes very well. The output is limited by the maximum number of 25 steps. Therefore, only 3 letters are found at the end.

```
Direction: SE
A H O d k
New Direction: N
e Q K E
```

```
New Direction: SW
J O b g
New Direction: N
a M G A
New Direction: E
B C D E f
New Direction: SW
K P c
```

HINT: VARIATION WITH BUFFER FIELDS AT THE BORDER

Especially for two-dimensional arrays and accesses to adjacent cells, it may be useful to add an unused element at each edge to avoid special cases, indicated below with a X:

```
XXXXXXX
X     X
X     X
X     X
X     X
XXXXXXX
```

Using this trick, you always have eight adjacent cells. This helps to avoid special treatments in your programs. This is also true, for example, when walking through the array. Instead of checking for the array boundaries, you can restrict yourself to checking if you reach a boundary field. Sometimes it is handy to use a neutral element, such as the value 0, since this does not affect computations.

5.1.3 Typical Errors

Not only when accessing arrays, but especially there, one finds a multiplicity of potential sources of errors, in particular, the following:

- **Off-by-one**: Sometimes you are off by one element when accessing because, for example, the index calculation contains an error, such as adding or subtracting 1 to correct the index or comparing on positions with <, <=, >, >=.

- **Array bounds**: Similarly, the bounds of the array are sometimes inadvertently disregarded, for example, by incorrect use of <, <= or >, >= when comparing on length or lower or upper bounds.[2]

- **Dimensions**: As mentioned, how x and y are represented depends on the chosen flavor. This quickly causes x and y to be interchanged for two-dimensional arrays.

- **Rectangular property**: Although an n × m array is assumed to be rectangular, this need not be the case in Java. One can specify a different length for each new row—but many of the examples below use rectangular arrays. In job interviews, you should clarify this by asking a question. For assignments where the rectangular property is less important, I also allow non-rectangular arrays, for example, when filling an area with a pattern.

- **Abstraction**: Arrays provide little abstraction. In many cases you encounter that test for conditions, element swapping, etc., they are implemented directly instead of being extracted as helper methods.

- **Neutral element**: What represents *no value*? Is it -1 or null? How do you deal with this if these are possible values?

- **String output**: Arrays do not have an overridden version of the toString() method, so the toString() method inherited from the Object class is used, which outputs the type as well as the object reference quite cryptically. As a result, you can see sometimes outputs like this for arrays:

```
[I@4d591d15
[I@65ae6ba4
```

As a workaround, the following calls can be used:

```
Arrays.toString(mySimpleArray);
Arrays.deepToString(myMultiDimArray);
```

---

[2] Therefore, thorough testing and a good selection of test cases are recommended in both cases. How to achieve this is described in my book *Der Weg zum Java-Profi* [Ind20a].

5.2 Exercises

5.2.1 Exercise 1: Even Before Odd Numbers (★★☆☆☆)

Write method void `orderEvenBeforeOdd(int[])`. This is supposed to rearrange a given array of `int` values so that the even numbers appear first, followed by the odd numbers. The order within the even and odd numbers is not of relevance.

Examples

Input	Result
[1, 2, 3, 4, 5, 6, 7, 8, 9, 10]	[2, 4, 6, 8, 10, 3, 7, 1, 9, 5]
[2, 4, 6, 1, 8]	[2, 4, 6, 8, 1]
[2, 4, 6, 8, 1]	[2, 4, 6, 8, 1]

5.2.2 Exercise 2: Flip (★★☆☆☆)

Write a generic method that flips a two-dimensional array horizontally with void `flipHorizontally(T[][])` and vertically with void `flipVertically(T[][])`. The array should be rectangular, so no line should be longer than another.

Examples

In the following it is illustrated how this functionality should work:

```
flipHorizontally()        flipVertically()
------------------        ----------------
123          321          1144          3366
456    =>    654          2255    =>    2255
789          987          3366          1144
```

5.2.3 Exercise 3: Palindrome (★★☆☆☆)

Write method boolean isPalindrome(String[]) that checks for an array of strings whether its values form a palindrome.

Examples

Input	Result
["Ein", "Test", " – ", "Test", "Ein"]	true
["Max", "Mike", "Mike", "Max"]	true
["Tim", "Tom", "Mike", "Max"]	false

5.2.4 Exercise 4: Inplace Rotate (★★★☆☆)

Exercise 4a: Iterative (★★★☆☆)

In the introductory section, I showed how to rotate arrays. Now, this is supposed to happen inplace (without creating a new array) for a two-dimensional square array by 90 degrees clockwise. Write generic method void rotateInplace(T[][]) that iteratively implements this.

Example

For a 6 × 6 array, this is visualized as follows:

```
1  2  3  4  5  6        F  G  H  I  J  1
J  K  L  M  N  7        E  T  U  V  K  2
I  V  W  X  O  8   =>   D  S  Z  W  L  3
H  U  Z  Y  P  9        C  R  Y  X  M  4
G  T  S  R  Q  0        B  Q  P  O  N  5
F  E  D  C  B  A        A  0  9  8  7  6
```

Exercise 4b: Recursive (★★★☆☆)

Write recursive method void rotateInplaceRecursive(T[][]) that implements the desired 90 degree clockwise rotation.

5.2.5 Exercise 5: Jewels Board Init (★★★☆☆)

Exercise 5a: Initialize (★★★☆☆)

Initialize a two-dimensional rectangular array with random-based numbers representing various types of diamonds or jewels as numerical values. The constraint is that initially there must not be three diamonds of the same type placed horizontally or vertically in direct sequence. Write method `int[][] initJewelsBoard(int, int, int)`, which will generate a valid array of the given size and quantity of different types of diamonds.

Example

A random distribution of diamonds represented by digits may look like this for four different colors and shapes:

```
2 3 3 4 4 3 2
1 3 3 1 3 4 4
4 1 4 3 3 1 3
2 2 1 1 2 3 2
3 2 4 4 3 3 4
```

To illustrate this, Figure 5-1 shows another example.

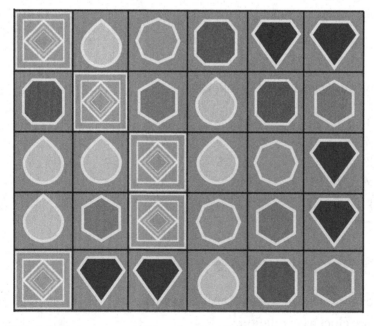

Figure 5-1. *Graphical representation of a Jewels board*

Bonus: Diagonal Check (★★★☆☆)   Add a check for diagonals. This should make the constellation from the example invalid, among other things, because of the diagonals marked in bold with the number 3 at the bottom right.

Exercise 5b: Validity Check (★★★☆☆)

In this subtask, you want to validate an existing playfield. As a challenge, a list of violations found has to be returned. Implement method List<String> checkBoardValidity(int[][]) for a rectangular array.

Example

To try out the validity check, you use the playfield from the introduction— specially marked here:

```
int[][] values = {
                  { 2, 3, 3, 4, 4, 3, 2 },
                  { 1, 3, 3, 1, 3, 4, 4 },
                  { 4, 1, 4, 3, 3, 1, 3 },
                  { 2, 2, 1, 1, 2, 3, 2 },
                  { 3, 2, 4, 4, 3, 3, 4 } };
```

This should produce the following errors due to its diagonals:

```
[Invalid at x=3 y=2 tests: hor=false, ver=false, dia=true,
 Invalid at x=2 y=3 tests: hor=false, ver=false, dia=true,
 Invalid at x=4 y=4 tests: hor=false, ver=false, dia=true]
```

5.2.6 Exercise 6: Jewels Board Erase Diamonds (★★★★☆)

The challenge is to delete all chains of three or more horizontally, vertically, or diagonally connected diamonds from the rectangular playing field and subsequently to fill the resulting empty spaces with the diamonds lying above them (i.e., roughly in the same way as gravity works in nature). The following is an example of how the erasing and then dropping is repeated several times until no more change occurs (spaces are shown as _ for better visibility):

Iteration 1:

```
1 1 1 2 4 4 3   erase    _ _ _ _ 4 4 _   fall down   _ _ _ _ _ _ _
1 2 3 4 2 4 3   =>       1 2 3 4 _ 4 _      =>        1 2 3 4 4 4 _
2 3 3 1 2 2 3            2 3 3 1 2 _ _                2 3 3 1 2 4 _
```

Iteration 2:

```
_ _ _ _ _ _ _   erase    _ _ _ _ _ _ _   fall down   _ _ _ _ _ _ _
1 2 3 4 4 4 _   =>       1 2 3 _ _ _ _      =>        1 2 3 _ _ _ _
2 3 3 1 2 4 _            2 3 3 1 2 4 _                2 3 3 1 2 4 _
```

Exercise 6a: Erase (★★★★☆)

Write method boolean eraseChains(int[][]) that erases all rows of three or more contiguous diamonds in horizontal, vertical, and diagonal orientations from a rectangular playfield array.

Examples

An invocation of the method transforms the output array given on the left into the result shown on the right:

```
All chains without overlap        Special case:  overlaps
1 2 3 3 3 4        0 0 0 0 0 0     1 1 1 2        0 0 0 2
1 3 2 4 2 4        0 3 0 4 2 0     1 1 3 4   =>   0 0 3 4
1 2 4 2 4 4   =>   0 0 4 0 4 0     1 2 1 3        0 2 0 3
1 2 3 5 5 5        0 0 3 0 0 0
1 2 1 3 4 4        0 0 1 3 4 4
```

Exercise 6b: Falling Down (★★★☆☆)

Write method void fallDown(int[][]) working inplace that drops the diamonds from top to bottom, provided there is a space below their position.

Example

An invocation of the method transforms the output array given on the left into the result shown on the right:

```
0 1 3 3 0 0        0 0 0 0 0 0
0 1 0 0 0 0        0 0 0 0 0 0
0 0 3 3 0 0   =>   0 0 3 3 0 0
0 0 0 3 3 4        0 1 3 3 0 0
0 0 3 0 0 0        0 1 3 3 3 4
```

5.2.7 Exercise 7: Spiral Traversal (★★★★☆)

Write generic method List<T> spiralTraversal(T[][]) that traverses a
two-dimensional rectangular array in a spiral and prepares it as a list. The start is in the
upper left corner. First, the outer layer is traversed, and then the next inner layer.

Example

An example is shown in Figure 5-2.

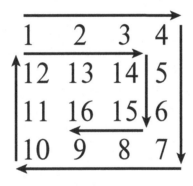

Figure 5-2. *Basic procedure for the spiral traversal*

For the following two arrays, the number or letter sequences listed below should be
the results of a spiral traversal:

```
Integer[][] numbers = { { 1, 2, 3, 4 },
                        { 12, 13, 14, 5 },
                        { 11, 16, 15, 6 },
                        { 10, 9, 8, 7 } };
```

```
String[][] letterPairs = { { "AB", "BC", "CD", "DE" },
                           { "JK", "KL", "LM", "EF" },
                           { "IJ", "HI", "GH", "FG" } };
=>

[1, 2, 3, 4, 5, 6, 7, 8, 9, 10, 11, 12, 13, 14, 15, 16]

[AB, BC, CD, DE, EF, FG, GH, HI, IJ, JK, KL, LM]
```

5.2.8 Exercise 8: Add One to Array as Number (★★☆☆)

Consider an array of numbers representing the digits of a decimal number. Write method int[] addOne(int[]) that performs an addition by the value 1 and is only allowed to use arrays as data structure for the solution.

Examples

Input	Result
[1, 3, 2, 4]	[1, 3, 2, 5]
[1, 4, 8, 9]	[1, 4, 9, 0]
[9, 9, 9, 9]	[1, 0, 0, 0, 0]

5.2.9 Exercise 9: Sudoku Checker (★★★☆☆)

In this challenge, a Sudoku puzzle is examined to see if it is a valid solution. Let's assume a 9 × 9 array with int values. According to the Sudoku rules, each row and each column must contain all numbers from 1 to 9. Besides, all numbers from 1 to 9 must, in turn, occur in each 3 × 3 subarray. Write method boolean isSudokuValid(int[][]) for checking.

Example

A valid solution is shown below.

1	2	3	4	5	6	7	8	9
4	5	6	7	8	9	1	2	3
7	8	9	1	2	3	4	5	6
2	1	4	3	6	5	8	9	7
3	6	5	8	9	7	2	1	4
8	9	7	2	1	4	3	6	5
5	3	1	6	4	2	9	7	8
6	4	2	9	7	8	5	3	1
9	7	8	5	3	1	6	4	2

Bonus   While it is already nice to be able to check a Sudoku board that is completely filled with digits for its validity, it is even better to be able to predict for a board with *gaps* (i.e., still missing digits) whether a valid solution can emerge from it. This is of particular interest if you want to develop an algorithm for solving a Sudoku puzzle.

Example

Based on the example of the valid Sudoku playing field given above, I deleted the digits at random places. This surely results in a valid solution.

1	2		4	5		7	8	9
	5	6	7		9		2	3
7	8		1	2	3	4	5	6
2	1	4		6		8		7
3	6		8		7	2	1	4
	9	7		1	4	3	6	
5	3	1	6		2	9		8
6		2	9	7	8	5	3	1
9	7			3	1	6	4	2

5.2.10 Exercise 10: Flood Fill (★★☆☆☆)

Exercise 10a (★★☆☆☆)

Write method void floodFill(char[], int, int) that fills all free fields in an array with a specified value.

Example

The following shows the filling process for the character *. The filling starts at a given position, such as the upper left corner. It then continues in all four compass directions until the boundaries of the array or a boundary represented by another character are found.

```
"   #  "       "***#  "       "   #      #"       "  #******#"
"     #"       "****#"        "    #      #"       "   #*******#"
"#    #"  =>   "#***#"        "#   #      #"  =>   "#  #******#"
" # # "        " #*# "        " # #       #"       " # #******#"
"  #  "        "  #  "        "  #        #"       "  #******#"
```

Exercise 10b (★★☆☆☆)

Extend the method to fill any pattern passed as a rectangular array. However, spaces are not allowed in the pattern specification.

Example

Below you see how a flood fill with a pattern could look like. The pattern consists of several lines with characters:

```
.|.
_*_
.|.
```

If you start the filling at the bottom center, you get the following result:

```
      x                .|..|.x
     #   #             -*--#--#
     ###    #          .|.###.|#
 #   ###    #    =>    #|.###.|#
  #   #   #            #*--#--*#
   # # #               #.#|..#
   #   #               #.|.#
```

5.2.11 Exercise 11: Array Merge (★★☆☆☆)

Assume that there are two arrays of numbers, each sorted in ascending order In this assignment these arrays are to be merged into a single array according to the respective values' order. Write method int[] merge(int[], int[]).

Examples

Input 1	Input 2	Result
[1, 4, 7, 12, 20]	[10, 15, 17, 33]	[1, 4, 7, 10, 12, 15, 17, 20, 33]
[2, 3, 5, 7]	[11, 13, 17]	[2, 3, 5, 7, 11, 13, 17]
[2, 3, 5, 7, 11]	[7, 11, 13, 17]	[2, 3, 5, 7, 7, 11 11, 13, 17]
[1, 2, 3]	∅ = []	[1, 2, 3]

5.2.12 Exercise 12: Array Min and Max (★★☆☆☆)

Exercise 12a: Min and Max (★☆☆☆☆)

Write two methods int findMin(int[]) and int findMax(int[]) that will find the minimum and maximum, respectively, of a given non-empty array using a self-implemented search—thus eliminating the usage of Math.min(), Arrays.sort(), and Arrays.stream().min() etc :-)

Example

Input	Minimum	Maximum
[2, 3, 4, 5, 6, 7, 8, 9, 1, 10]	1	10

Exercise 12b: Min and Max Pos (★★☆☆☆)

Implement two helper methods int findMinPos(int[], int, int) and int findMaxPos(int[], int, int) that seek and return the position of the minimum and maximum, respectively, for a given non-empty array as well as an index range given as left and right boundaries. In the case of several identical values for minimum or maximum, the first occurrence should be returned. To find minimum and maximum respectively, write two methods int findMinByPos(int[], int, int) and int findMaxByPos(int[], int, int) that use the helper methods.

Examples

Method	Input	Range	Result	Position
findMinXyz()	[5, 3, 4, 2, 6, 7, 8, 9, 1, 10]	0, 10	1	8
findMinXyz()	[5, 3, 4, 2, 6, 7, 8, 9, 1, 10]	0, 7	2	3
findMinXyz()	[5, 3, 4, 2, 6, 7, 8, 9, 1, 10]	2, 7	2	3
findMaxXyz()	[1, 22, 3, 4, 5, 10, 7, 8, 9, 49]	0, 10	49	9
findMaxXyz()	[1, 22, 3, 4, 5, 10, 7, 8, 9, 49]	0, 7	22	1
findMaxXyz()	[1, 22, 3, 4, 5, 10, 7, 8, 9, 49]	2, 7	10	5

5.2.13 Exercise 13: Array Split (★★★☆☆)

Consider an array of arbitrary integers. As a result, the array is to be reordered so that all values less than a special reference value are placed on the left. All values greater than or equal to the reference value are placed on the right. The ordering within the subranges is not relevant and may vary.

Examples

Input	Reference element	Sample result
[4, 7, 1, 20]	9	[1, 4, 7, **9**, 20]
[3, 5, 2]	7	[2, 3, 5, **7**]
[2, 14, 10, 1, 11, 12, 3, 4]	7	[2, 1, 3, 4, **7**, 14, 10, 11, 12]
[3, 5, 7, 1, 11, 13, 17, 19]	11	[1, 3, 5, 7, **11**, 11, 13, 17, 19]

Exercise 13a: Array Split (★★☆☆☆)

Write method int[] arraySplit(int[], int) to implement the functionality. It is allowed to create new data structures, such as lists.

Exercise 13b: Array Split Inplace (★★★☆☆)

Write method int[] arraySplitInplace(int[], int) that implements the described functionality inside the source array (i.e., inplace). It is explicitly not desirable to create new data structures. To be able to include the reference element in the result, the creation of an array is allowed once. Because this has to be returned, it is exceptionally permitted to return a value for an *inplace* method—indeed, it operates only partially inplace here.

Exercise 13c: Array Split Quick Sort Partition (★★★☆☆)

For sorting, according to Quick Sort, you need a partitioning functionality similar to the one just developed. However, often the foremost element of the array is used as the reference element.

Based on the two previously developed implementations using an explicit reference element, now create corresponding alternatives such as the methods int[] arraySplit(int[]) and int[] arraySplitInplace(int[]).

Examples

Input	Reference element	Sample result
[**9**, 4, 7, 1, 20]	9	[1, 4, 7, **9**, 20]
[**7**, 3, 5, 2]	7	[2, 3, 5, **7**]
[**7**, 2, 14, 10, 1, 11, 12, 3, 4]	7	[2, 1, 3, 4, **7**, 14, 10, 11, 12]
[**11**, 3, 5, 7, 1, 11, 13, 17, 19]	11	[1, 3, 5, 7, **11**, 11, 13, 17, 19]

5.2.14 Exercise 14: Minesweeper Board (★★★☆☆)

The chances are high that you've played Minesweeper in the past. To remind you, it's a nice little quiz game with a bit of puzzling. What is it about? Bombs are placed face down on a playing field. The player can choose any field on the board. If a field is uncovered, it shows a number. This indicates how many bombs are hidden in the neighboring fields. However, if you are unlucky, you hit a bomb field, and the game is lost. This task is about initializing such a field and preparing it for a subsequent game.

Exercise 14a (★★☆☆☆)

Write method `boolean[][] placeBombsRandomly(int, int, double)` that creates a playing field as `boolean[][]` specified in size via the first two parameters, randomly filled with *bombs*, respecting the probability from 0.0 to 1.0 passed as `double`.

Example

A playing field of size 16 × 7 is shown here, with bombs placed randomly. Bombs are represented by * and spaces with . as you can see.

```
* * * . * * . * . * * . * . . .
. * * . * . . * . * * . . . . .
. . * . . . . . . . . * * * *
. . . * . * * . * * . * * . . .
* * . . . . * . * . . * . . . *
. . * . . * . * * . . * . * * *
. * . * * . * . * * * . . * * .
```

Exercise 14b (★★★☆☆)

Write method int[][] calcBombCount(boolean[][]) that, based on the bomb fields passed as boolean[][], computes the number of adjacent fields with bombs and returns a corresponding array.

Examples

A calculation for playing fields of size 3 × 3 as well as size 5 × 5, including randomly distributed bombs results in the following:

```
*  .  .           B  2  1          .  *  *  .  .            2  B  B  3  1
.  .  *    =>     1  3  B          *  .  *  *  .            B  6  B  B  1
.  .  *           0  2  B          *  *  .  .  .     =>     B  B  4  3  2
                                  *  .  .  *  .            B  6  4  B  1
                                  *  *  *  .  .            B  B  B  2  1
```

Exercise 14c (★★☆☆☆)

Write method void printBoard(boolean[][], char, int[][]) that allows you to display a board as points and stars as well as numbers and B.

Example

Shown here is the above playing field of size 16 × 7 with all the calculated values for bomb neighbors:

```
B  B  B  4  B  B  3  B  4  B  B  3  B  1  0  0
3  B  B  5  B  3  3  B  4  B  B  4  3  4  3  2
1  3  B  4  3  3  3  3  4  4  4  4  B  B  B  B
2  3  3  B  2  B  B  4  B  B  3  B  B  4  4  3
B  B  3  2  3  4  B  6  B  4  4  B  5  3  4  B
3  4  B  3  3  B  4  B  B  5  4  B  4  B  B  B
1  B  3  B  B  3  B  4  B  B  B  2  3  B  B  3
```

5.3 Solutions

5.3.1 Solution 1: Even Before Odd Numbers (★★☆☆☆)

Write method void orderEvenBeforeOdd(int[]). This is supposed to rearrange a given array of int values so that the even numbers appear first, followed by the odd numbers. The order within the even and odd numbers is not of relevance.

Examples

Input	Result
[1, 2, 3, 4, 5, 6, 7, 8, 9, 10]	[2, 4, 6, 8, 10, 3, 7, 1, 9, 5]
[2, 4, 6, 1, 8]	[2, 4, 6, 8, 1]
[2, 4, 6, 8, 1]	[2, 4, 6, 8, 1]

Algorithm   Traverse the array from the beginning. Skip even numbers. As soon as an odd number is found, search for an even number in the part of the array that follows. If such a number is found, swap it with the current odd number. The procedure is repeated until you reach the end of the array.

```
void orderEvenBeforeOdd(final int[] numbers)
{
    int i = 0;
    while (i < numbers.length)
    {
        int value = numbers[i];
        if (isEven(value))
        {
            // even number, so continue with next number
        }
        else
        {
            // odd number, jump over all odd ones, until the first even
            int j = i + 1;
            while (j < numbers.length && !isEven(numbers[j]))
```

```
        {
            j++;
        }

        if (j < numbers.length)
            swap(numbers, i, j);
        else
            break; // no further numbers
    }
    i++;
    }
}
```

The helper methods for checking and swapping elements have already been implemented in earlier chapters or sections. They are shown here again to make it easier to try out the examples in the JShell.

```
boolean isEven(final int n)
{
    return n % 2 == 0;
}

void swap(final int[] values, final int first, final int second)
{
    final int tmp = values[first];
    values[first] = values[second];
    values[second] = tmp;
}
```

NOTE: VARIATION OF ODD BEFORE EVEN

A variation is to arrange all odd numbers before the even ones. Therefore it is possible to write method void orderOddBeforeEven(int[]), where again the ordering within the odd and even numbers is not important.

The algorithm is identical to that shown except for minimal differences in an inverted test. This modification is so simple that the method is not shown again here.

Optimized Algorithm: Improved Running Time

You recognize that your checks have quadratic running time. Here $O(n \cdot m)$ because two nested loops are used. Although this is not quite so dramatic for pure computations, you should keep in mind to reduce the running time of an algorithm to $O(1)$ in the best case, preferably $O(n)$ or at least $O(n \cdot log(n))$, ideally without reducing readability and comprehensibility. For an introduction to the O-notation, please consult Appendix C.

In this case, reducing the running time to $O(n)$ is actually fairly straightforward. As in many solutions to other problems, two position markers are used, here nextEven and nextOdd. In the beginning, it is assumed that the first element is even and the last odd. Now it is checked if the front number is really even, and the position is shifted to the right. If the first odd number is encountered, it is swapped with the last element. Even if the last element were odd, it would be swapped again in the next step.

In contrast to the previous solution, this solution does not preserve the order of the even numbers; it also potentially shuffles the odd numbers to a greater extent.

```java
void orderEvenBeforeOddOptimized(final int[] numbers)
{
    int nextEven = 0;
    int nextOdd = numbers.length - 1;

    while (nextEven < nextOdd)
    {
        final int currentValue = numbers[nextEven];
        if (isEven(currentValue))
        {
            nextEven++;
        }
        else
        {
            swap(numbers, nextEven, nextOdd);

            nextOdd--;
        }
    }
}
```

Let's take a look at the methods for the unsorted numbers (2, 4, 3, 6, 1). Below e and o represent the position pointers for `nextEven` and `nextOdd`, respectively.

```
2 4 3 6 1
^       ^

e       o
  ^     ^

  e     o
    ^   ^

    e   o
--------- swap
    1 6 3
    ^ ^

    e o
--------- swap
    6 1 3
    ^

    eo
```

Finally, let's have a look at what happens for already sorted numbers (1, 2, 3, 4):

```
1 2 3 4
^     ^

e     o
-------- swap
4 2 3 1
^   ^

e   o
  ^ ^

  e o
    ^

    eo
```

Optimized Algorithm: Less Copying

The previous optimization can be taken a little further. Instead of just skipping the even numbers from the left until you encounter an odd number, you can skip values starting from both sides as long as they are even in the front and odd in the back. This requires two additional `while` loops. However, you are still preserving a $O(n)$ running time since you are traversing the same elements and not performing steps more than once (this insight requires some experience).

The following implementation applies what has been said and swaps elements only when it is indispensable:

```
void orderEvenBeforeOddOptimizedV2(final int[] numbers)
{
    int left = 0;
    int right = numbers.length - 1;
    while (left < right)
    {
        // run to the first odd number or to the end of the array
        while (left < numbers.length && numbers[left] % 2 == 0)
            left++;
        // run to the first even number or to the beginning of the array
        while (right >= 0 && numbers[right] % 2 != 0)
            right--;

        if (left < right)
        {
            swap(numbers, left, right);
            left++;
            right--;
        }
    }
}
```

Verification

To try it out, you use the following inputs that show how it works:

```
jshell> var values1 = new int[]{ 1, 2, 3, 4, 5, 6, 7 }

jshell> var values2 = new int[]{ 1, 2, 3, 4, 5, 6, 7 }

jshell> var values3 = new int[]{ 1, 2, 3, 4, 5, 6, 7 }

jshell> orderEvenBeforeOdd(values1)

jshell> orderEvenBeforeOddOptimized(values2)

jshell> orderEvenBeforeOddOptimizedV2(values3)

jshell> values1
values1 ==> int[7] { 2, 4, 6, 1, 5, 3, 7 }

jshell> values2
values2 ==> int[7] { 6, 2, 4, 5, 3, 7, 1 }

jshell> values3
values3 ==> int[7] { 6, 2, 4, 3, 5, 1, 7 }
```

5.3.2 Solution 2: Flip (★★☆☆☆)

Write generic method that flips a two-dimensional array horizontally with void
flipHorizontally(T[][]) and vertically with void flipVertically(T[][]). The array
should be rectangular, so no line should be longer than another.

Examples

In the following it is illustrated how this functionality should work:

```
flipHorizontally()      flipVertically()
----------------        ----------------
123        321          1144        3366
456  =>    654          2255  =>    2255
789        987          3366        1144
```

Horizontal flipping algorithm   Traverse inwards from the left and right side of the array. To do this, use two position markers named *leftIdx* and *rightIdx*. At each step, swap the values referenced by these positions and move inward until the positions overlap. The termination occurs at *leftIdx* >= *rightIdx*. Repeat the procedure for all lines.The following sequence shows the described actions for one line, where l represents *leftIdx* and r represents *rightIdx*:

```
Step    Array values
--------------------
1           1 2 3 4
            ^     ^
            l     r

2           4 2 3 1
              ^ ^
              l r

3           4 3 2 1
              ^ ^
              r l
```

Algorithm for vertical flipping   Move from the top and bottom towards the center until both positions overlap. Swap the values and repeat this for all columns. The implementation traverses the array in the x-direction and operates with two position markers on the vertical. After each swap, these position markers are moved towards each other until they cross. You then proceed with the next x-position.The implementation uses two position pointers and swaps the respective values until the position pointers cross:

```
static <T> void flipHorizontally(final T[][] values)
{
    for (int y = 0; y < values.length; y++)
    {
        final int endPos = values[y].length;

        int leftIdx = 0;
        int rightIdx = endPos - 1;
```

```
        while (leftIdx < rightIdx)
        {
            final T leftValue = values[y][leftIdx];
            final T rightValue = values[y][rightIdx];

            // swap
            values[y][leftIdx] = rightValue;
            values[y][rightIdx] = leftValue;

            leftIdx++;
            rightIdx--;
        }
    }
}
```

Let's now take a look at the corresponding implementation of vertical flipping:

```
static <T> void flipVertically(final T[][] values)
{
    for (int x = 0; x < values[0].length; x++)
    {
        final int endPos = values.length;

        int topIdx = 0;
        int bottomIdx = endPos - 1;

        while (topIdx < bottomIdx)
        {
            final T topValue = values[topIdx][x];
            final T bottomValue = values[bottomIdx][x];

            // swap
            values[topIdx][x] = bottomValue;
            values[bottomIdx][x] = topValue;

            topIdx++;
            bottomIdx--;
        }
    }
}
```

Modified algorithm   In fact, the implementation for flipping may be simplified a little bit. The number of steps can be directly computed in both cases: it is width/2 or height/2. For odd lengths, the middle element is not taken into account. However, resulting in a correct flip.

With these preliminary considerations, the implementation for horizontal flipping with a `for` loop is illustrated as follows:

```java
static <T> void flipHorizontallyV2(final T[][] values)
{
    for (int y = 0; y < values.length; y++)
    {
        final T[] row = values[y];
        final int rowLength = row.length;

        for (int x = 0; x < rowLength / 2; x++)
        {
            ArrayUtils.swap(row, x, rowLength - x - 1);
        }
    }
}
```

Optimized algorithm   While the solutions shown so far have each made the swaps at the level of individual elements, you can benefit from reassigning entire lines for vertical flipping. This is significantly simpler both in terms of complexity and effort as well as in terms of the amount of source code, and it also increases comprehensibility enormously.

```java
static <T> void flipVerticallySimplified(final T[][] values)
{
    for (int y = 0; y < values.length / 2; y++)
    {
        // swap line based
        ArrayUtils.swap(values, y, values.length - y - 1);
    }
}
```

Verification

To test the functionality, you use the inputs from the introductory example, which show the correct operation:

```
@Test
void flipHorizontally()
{
    final Integer[][] horiNumbers = { { 1, 2, 3 },
                                      { 4, 5, 6 },
                                      { 7, 8, 9 }};

    final Integer[][] expected = { { 3, 2, 1 },
                                   { 6, 5, 4 },
                                   { 9, 8, 7 } };

    Ex02_Flip.flipHorizontally(horiNumbers);

    assertArrayEquals(expected, horiNumbers);
}

@Test
void flipVertically()
{
    final Integer[][] vertNumbers = { { 1, 1, 4, 4 },
                                      { 2, 2, 5, 5 },
                                      { 3, 3, 6, 6 } };

    final Integer[][] expected = { { 3, 3, 6, 6 },
                                   { 2, 2, 5, 5 },
                                   { 1, 1, 4, 4 } };

    Ex02_Flip.flipVertically(vertNumbers);

    assertArrayEquals(expected, vertNumbers);
}
```

Both other methods are tested in exactly the same way as the previous ones. That is why the associated test methods are not shown here again.

5.3.3 Solution 3: Palindrome (★★☆☆☆)

Write method boolean isPalindrome(String[]) that checks for an array of strings whether its values form a palindrome.

Examples

Input	Result
["Ein", "Test", " – ", "Test", "Ein"]	True
["Max", "Mike", "Mike", "Max"]	True
["Tim", "Tom", "Mike", "Max"]	False

Algorithm The palindrome check can easily be expressed recursively. Again, two position pointers are used, which are initially located at the beginning and end of the array. It is checked whether the two values referenced by them are the same. If so, you continue to check recursively and move one position further to the middle on both sides with each recursion step until the positions overlap.

```
static boolean isPalindromeRec(final String[] values)
{
    return isPalindromeRec(values, 0, values.length - 1);
}

static boolean isPalindromeRec(final String[] values,
                               final int left,
                               final int right)
{
    // recursive termination
    if (left >= right)
        return true;

    // check if left == right
    if (values[left].equals(values[right]))
    {
```

```
    // recursive descent
    return isPalindromeRec(values, left + 1, right - 1);
  }

  return false;
}
```

PITFALL: POST-INCREMENT AND POST-DECREMENT IN METHOD CALLS

Once again, I would like to explicitly point out a *popular* careless mistake with recursive descent. Potentially, a post-increment or post-decrement could be more readable when calling the method. However, this is semantically incorrect! Why? The two operations are performed after the call so that the values are not increased or decreased. Please have another look at the chapter on recursion. In that chapter, I explain this problem in a bit more detail in section 3.1.4.

Optimized algorithm   Based on the recursive solution, the palindrome test can easily be transformed into an iterative version:

```
static boolean isPalindromeIterative(final String[] values)
{
    int left = 0;
    int right = values.length - 1;

    boolean sameValue = true;
    while (left < right && sameValue)
    {
        // check left == right and repeat until difference occurs
        sameValue = values[left].equals(values[right]);

        left++;
        right--;
    }
    return sameValue;
}
```

Besides this variant, you can also take advantage of the fact that the maximum number of steps is known. This allows you to directly abort the loop in case of a violation of the palindrome property:

```
static boolean isPalindromeShort(final String[] values)
{
    for (int i = 0; i < values.length / 2; i++)
    {
        if (!values[i].equals(values[values.length - 1 - i]))
            return false;
    }
    return true;
}
```

Verification

For unit testing (again, shown only in excerpts for the recursive variant), you use the inputs from the example above:

```
@ParameterizedTest(name="isPalindromeRec({0}) => {1}")
@MethodSource("createInputArraysAndExpected")
void isPalindromeRec(String[] values, boolean expected)
{
    boolean result = Ex03_Palindrome.isPalindromeRec(values);

    assertEquals(expected, result);
}

private static Stream<Arguments> createInputArraysAndExpected()
{
    String[] inputsOk1 = { "Ein", "Test", " -- ", "Test", "Ein" };
    String[] inputsOk2 = { "Max", "Mike", "Mike", "Max" };
    String[] inputsWrong = { "Tim", "Tom", "Mike", "Max" };

    return Stream.of(Arguments.of(inputsOk1, true),
                     Arguments.of(inputsOk2, true),
                     Arguments.of(inputsWrong, false));
}
```

5.3.4 Solution 4: Inplace Rotate (★★★☆☆)

Solution 4a: Iterative (★★★☆☆)

In the introductory section, I showed how to rotate arrays. Now, this is supposed to happen inplace (i.e., without creating a new array) for a two-dimensional square array by 90 degrees clockwise. Write generic method `void rotateInplace(T[][])` that iteratively implements this.

Example

For a 6 × 6 array, this is visualized as follows:

```
1  2  3  4  5  6        F  G  H  I  J  1
J  K  L  M  N  7        E  T  U  V  K  2
I  V  W  X  O  8   =>   D  S  Z  W  L  3
H  U  Z  Y  P  9        C  R  Y  X  M  4
G  T  S  R  Q  0        B  Q  P  O  N  5
F  E  D  C  B  A        A  0  9  8  7  6
```

Algorithm   Define four corner positions called TL, TR, BL, and BR corresponding to the respective corners. Move from left to right and from top to bottom and copy logically as shown in Figure 5-3.

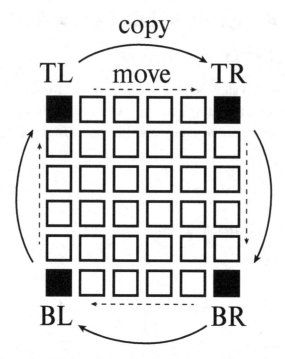

Figure 5-3. *Procedure for inplace rotating*

Repeat the procedure layer by layer for all neighbors of TL until TR is reached (analogously for the neighbors of the other corners). Then move one position inwards at a time until BL and BR intersect. Let's clarify the procedure again step by step.

Starting point   Given the following array:

```
1   2   3   4   5   6
J   K   L   M   N   7
I   V   W   X   O   8
H   U   Z   Y   P   9
G   T   S   R   Q   0
F   E   D   C   B   A
```

Step 1: First, the outer layer is rotated by copying all values to the respective target position as shown in the figure:

```
F   G   H   I   J   1
E   K   L   M   N   2
D   V   W   X   O   3
C   U   Z   Y   P   4
B   T   S   R   Q   5
A   0   9   8   7   6
```

Step 2: Continue with one layer further inwards:

```
F   G   H   I   J   1
E   T   U   V   K   2
D   S   W   X   L   3
C   R   Z   Y   M   4
B   Q   P   O   N   5
A   0   9   8   7   6
```

Step 3: This continues until the innermost level is reached:

```
F   G   H   I   J   1
E   T   U   V   K   2
D   S   Z   W   L   3
C   R   Y   X   M   4
B   Q   P   O   N   5
A   0   9   8   7   6
```

For the processing steps shown, a variable offset determines which *layer* one is in—width/2 steps are required. Based on the layer, the number of positions to copy is obtained, for which an inner loop is used. The corresponding positions in the array are calculated based on their location, as indicated in the figure. Copying is also made easy by the use of helper variables.

```
static <T> void rotateInplace(final T[][] values)
{
    final int height = values.length - 1;
    final int width = values[0].length - 1;
```

```java
    int offset = 0;
    while (offset <= width / 2)
    {
        final int currentWidth = width - offset * 2;
        for (int idx = 0; idx < currentWidth; idx++)
        {
            final int tlX = offset + idx;
            final int tlY = offset;

            final int trX = width - offset;
            final int trY = offset + idx;

            final int blX = offset;
            final int blY = height - offset - idx;

            final int brX = width - offset - idx;
            final int brY = height - offset;

            final T tl = values[tlY][tlX];
            final T tr = values[trY][trX];
            final T bl = values[blY][blX];
            final T br = values[brY][brX];

            // copy around
            values[trY][trX] = tl;
            values[brY][brX] = tr;
            values[blY][blX] = br;
            values[tlY][tlX] = bl;
        }

        offset++;
    }
}
```

Alternatively, you can omit helper variables and only cache the value of the upper left position. However, copying then becomes somewhat tricky because the order in the implementation must be exactly the other way around. This variant of the ring-shaped swap is implemented by the method rotateElements(). To my taste, the previous variant is more understandable.

```
static <T> void rotateInplaceV2(final T[][] values)
{
    int sideLength = values.length;
    int start = 0;
    while (sideLength > 0)
    {
        for (int i = 0; i < sideLength - 1; i++)
        {
            rotateElements(values, start, sideLength, i);
        }
        sideLength = sideLength - 2;
        start++;
    }
}

static <T> void rotateElements(final T[][] array,
                               final int start, final int len, final int i)
{
    final int end = start + len - 1;
    final T tmp = array[start][start + i];

    array[start][start + i] = array[end - i][start];
    array[end - i][start] = array[end][end - i];
    array[end][end - i] = array[start + i][end];
    array[start + i][end] = tmp;
}
```

Solution 4b: Recursive (★★★☆☆)

Write recursive method void rotateInplaceRecursive(T[][]) that implements the desired 90 degree clockwise rotation.

Algorithm   You have already seen that you must rotate layer by layer, going from the outer layer further to the inner layer. This screams for a recursive solution whose ingredient *layer copy* remains the same as before. Only the while loop is replaced by recursive calls.

```
static <T> void rotateInplaceRecursive(final T[][] values)
{
    rotateInplaceRecursive(values, 0, values.length - 1);
}

static <T> void rotateInplaceRecursive(final T[][] values,
                                    final int left, final int right)
{
    if (left >= right)
        return;

    final int rotCount = right - left;
    for (int i = 0; i < rotCount; i++)
    {
        final T tl = values[left + i][left];
        final T tr = values[right][left + i];
        final T bl = values[left][right - i];
        final T br = values[right - i][right];

        values[left + i][left] = tr;
        values[right][left + i] = br;
        values[right - i][right] = bl;
        values[left][right - i] = tl;
    }
    rotateInplaceRecursive(values, left + 1, right - 1);
}
```

Verification

You define the two-dimensional array shown at the beginning. Then you perform the rotation and compare the result with the expectation.

```
@Test
void rotateInplace()
{
    final Character[][] board = { {'1', '2', '3', '4', '5', '6' },
                                  {'J', 'K', 'L', 'M', 'N', '7'},
                                  {'I', 'V', 'W', 'X', 'O', '8'},
                                  {'H', 'U', 'Z', 'Y', 'P', '9'},
                                  {'G', 'T', 'S', 'R', 'Q', '0'},
                                  {'F', 'E', 'D', 'C', 'B', 'A'} };

    Ex04_Rotate_Inplace.rotateInplace(board);

    final Character[][] expectedBoard = { { 'F','G','H','I','J','1'},
                                          { 'E','T','U','V','K','2'},
                                          { 'D','S','Z','W','L','3'},
                                          { 'C','R','Y','X','M','4'},
                                          { 'B','Q','P','O','N','5'},
                                          { 'A','0','9','8','7','6'}};

    assertArrayEquals(expectedBoard, board);
}
```

5.3.5 Solution 5: Jewels Board Init (★★★☆☆)

Solution 5a: Initialize (★★★☆☆)

Initialize a two-dimensional rectangular array with random-based numbers representing various types of diamonds or jewels as numerical values. The constraint is that initially there must not be three diamonds of the same type placed horizontally or vertically in direct sequence. Write method `int[][] initJewelsBoard(int, int, int)`, which will generate a valid array of the given size and quantity of different types of diamonds.

Example

A random distribution of diamonds represented by digits may look like this for four different colors and shapes:

```
2 3 3 4 4 3 2
1 3 3 1 3 4 4
4 1 4 3 3 1 3
2 2 1 1 2 3 2
3 2 4 4 3 3 4
```

To illustrate this, Figure 5-4 shows another example.

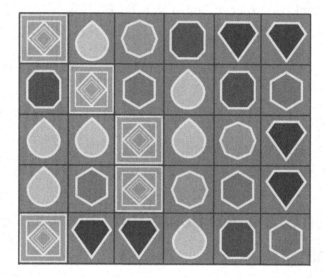

Figure 5-4. *Graphical representation of a Jewels board*

Algorithm   First, you create a suitably sized array. Then you fill it row by row and position by position with random-based values, using method `int selectValidJewel()` which returns the numerical value for the type of diamond. In this method, you have to make sure that the random number just selected does not create a row of three horizontally or vertically.

```java
int[][] initJewelsBoard(final int width, final int height,
                        final int numOfColors)
{
    final int[][] board = new int[height][width];

    for (int y = 0; y < height; y++)
    {
        for (int x = 0; x < width; x++)
        {
            board[y][x] = selectValidJewel(board, x, y, numOfColors);
        }
    }

    return board;
}

int selectValidJewel(final int[][] board, final int x, final int y,
                     final int numOfColors)
{
    int nextJewelNr = -1;

    boolean isValid = false;

    while (!isValid)
    {
        nextJewelNr = 1 + (int) (Math.random() * numOfColors);

        isValid = !checkHorizontally(board, x, y, nextJewelNr) &&
                  !checkVertically(board, x, y, nextJewelNr);
    }

    return nextJewelNr;
}
```

HINT: RANDOM NUMBERS

To obtain a random number greater than or equal to 0.0 and less than 1.0, you use the call `Math.random()`. For example, if you want to simulate the numbers of a dice, you can implement this as follows:

```
int diceEyes = (int)((Math.random()) * 6 + 1);
```

Alternatively, the class `Random()` exists. This can be used, among other things, to generate random numbers in the value range 0 up to a certain maximum value (exclusive) for the type `int`. For the other primitive number types, there is only the variant `nextXyz()`, which returns a random number from the respective entire range of values.

```
Random random = new Random();

// integer random number between 0 (inclusive) and 10 (exclusive)
int zufallsZahl = random.nextInt(10);

// random number in the range Double.MIN_VALUE to Double.MAX_VALUE
double randomNumber = random.nextDouble();
```

ATTENTION: THINGS TO KNOW ABOUT INITIALIZATION

The `selectValidJewel()` method should still be optimized. At the moment, you could not determine that no valid number can be found for a position, for example, for the following constellation with only two types and the position *, for which neither 1 nor 2 is valid as a value, because both would lead to a row of three:

1221
2122
11*

However, the fact that a valid distribution is also available even for only two values gets obvious by the alternating distribution of the white and black squares of a chessboard. One way to fix the just mentioned weakness is to choose a more powerful algorithm, such as one that uses backtracking.

There is another weak point: The generation of random numbers out of a small range of values often produces the same number several times, but this number has probably already been checked. This has to be avoided. For this purpose, all previously selected random numbers can be stored in a set. Besides, you would have to check whether all expected and possible numbers have already been tried. This short list shows that it is much more complex than you might initially expect.

Now let's move on to checking the horizontal and vertical. At first, you could assume that starting from the current position, you would have to check to the left and right as well as up and down. However, if you reread the assignment more carefully, it requires that no chains of length three or longer are allowed. Because you fill the playing field from top to bottom and from left to right, no diamonds to be checked can exist on the right and below the current position. Thus, you can limit yourself to checking to the left and to the top. Furthermore, you do not need to check for longer chains since they cannot occur if you have identified a chain of three.

With these preliminary considerations, you can use the two helper methods to check the respective neighboring fields horizontally and vertically by simply verifying that all of them have the same value as the initial field:

```
boolean checkHorizontally(final int[][] board, final int x, final int y,
                          final int jewelNr)
{
    final int top1 = getAt(board, x, y - 1);
    final int top2 = getAt(board, x, y - 2);

    return top1 == jewelNr && top2 == jewelNr;
}

boolean checkVertically(final int[][] board, final int x, final int y,
                        final int jewelNr)
{
    final int left1 = getAt(board, x - 1, y);
    final int left2 = getAt(board, x - 2, y);

    return left1 == jewelNr && left2 == jewelNr;
}
```

When accessing the array, the negative offsets may result in invalid array indices. Therefore, you implement method getAt(), which is mainly responsible for checking the boundaries and returns the value -1 for *no longer being on the playing field*. This value can never occur on the playing field, and thus it is counted as no chain when comparing.

```java
int getAt(final int[][] board, final int x, final int y)
{
    if (x < 0 || x >= board[0].length || y < 0 || y >= board.length)
        return -1;

    return board[y][x];
}
```

ATTENTION: LITTLE SOURCE CODE VS. SMALL BUT MANY METHODS

In this example, I also follow the strategy of defining small helper methods, which increases the amount of source code. Mostly, however, functionalities can be described and tested very well in isolation. Moreover, this approach often allows expressing the source code on a comprehensible and conceptual level. In many cases, this allows extensions to be easily integrated. As compact as the following solution is, what do you do if a diagonal test is now required?

```java
static int[][] initJewelsBoardCompact(final int width, final int height,
                                      final int numbers)
{
    final Random r = new Random();
    final int[][] board = new int[height][width];
    for (int y = 0; y < height; y++)
    {
        for (int x = 0; x < width; x++)
        {
            do
            {
                board[y][x] = r.nextInt(numbers);
            }
```

```
        while (x >= 2 && board[y][x] == board[y][x - 1] &&
                         board[y][x] == board[y][x - 2]
               || y >= 2 && board[y][x] == board[y - 1][x] &&
                         board[y][x] == board[y - 2][x]);
        }
    }
    return board;
}
```

Solution to the Bonus Task: Diagonal Check (★★★☆☆)

Add a check for diagonals. This should make the constellation from the example invalid, among other things, because of the diagonals marked in bold with the number 3 at the bottom right.

Algorithm   Checking the four diagonals from one position seems much more time-consuming than checking the horizontal and the vertical. Theoretically, there would be four directions for each position. As almost always, it is a good idea to think about a problem a little longer. If you follow this advice, you may come to the solution that in this case, starting from one position, it is sufficient to check only diagonally to the top left and right, because, from the point of view of the positions above, this one corresponds to a check diagonally left and right below, as indicated in the following:

```
X       X
 X     X
  X   X
```

Thus the diagonal check with two helper variables each for the positions of the compass directions northwest and northeast can be implemented as follows and invoked in the method selectValidJewel():

```
boolean checkDiagonally(final int[][] board, final int x, final int y,
                        final int jewelNr)
{
    final int nw1 = getAt(board, x - 1, y - 1);
    final int nw2 = getAt(board, x - 2, y - 2);
```

```
    final int ne1 = getAt(board, x + 1, y - 1);
    final int ne2 = getAt(board, x + 2 , y - 2);

    return (nw1 == jewelNr && nw2 == jewelNr) ||
           (ne1 == jewelNr && ne2 == jewelNr);
}
```

Verification

To verify that correct playing fields are being created now, let's generate and output one of size 5 × 3 with four types of diamonds as follows:

```
jshell> var board = initJewelsBoard(5, 3, 4)

jshell> printArray(board) 1 2 1 1 2
2 4 2 1 2
3 3 2 4 4
```

Here you use the method printArray(int[][]) already presented, but shown again for easier testing:

```
private static void printArray(final int[][] values)
{
    for (int y = 0; y < values.length; y++)
    {
        for (int x = 0; x < values[y].length; x++)
        {
            final int value = values[y][x];
            System.out.print(value + " ");
        }
        System.out.println();
    }
}
```

As a quick reminder, I'll show a more compact implementation again:

```java
private static void printArrayJdk(final int[][] values)
{
    for (int i = 0; i < values.length; i++)
    {
        System.out.println(Arrays.toString(values[i]));
    }
}
```

This produces the following result:

```
[1, 2, 1, 1, 2]
[2, 4, 2, 1, 2]
[3, 3, 2, 4, 4]
```

Solution 5b: Validity Check (★★★☆☆)

In this subtask, you want to validate an existing playfield. As a challenge, a list of violations found has to be returned. Implement method List<String> checkBoardValidity(int[][]) for a rectangular array.

Example

To try out the validity check, you use the playfield from the introduction— specially marked here:

```java
int[][] values = {
                  { 2, 3, 3, 4, 4, 3, 2 },
                  { 1, 3, 3, 1, 3, 4, 4 },
                  { 4, 1, 4, 3, 3, 1, 3 },
                  { 2, 2, 1, 1, 2, 3, 2 },
                  { 3, 2, 4, 4, 3, 3, 4 } };
```

This should produce the following errors due to its diagonals:

```
[Invalid at x=3 y=2 tests: hor=false, ver=false, dia=true,
 Invalid at x=2 y=3 tests: hor=false, ver=false, dia=true,
 Invalid at x=4 y=4 tests: hor=false, ver=false, dia=true]
```

Algorithm   The validity check can be easily developed based on your previously implemented methods. You check for horizontal, vertical, and diagonal rows of three for each playing field position. If such a violation is found, you generate an appropriate error message.

```java
List<String> checkBoardValidity(final int[][] board)
{
    final List<String> errors = new ArrayList<>();

    for (int y = 0; y < board.length; y++)
    {
        for (int x = 0; x < board[0].length; x++)
        {
            final int currentJewel = board[y][x];

            boolean invalidHor = checkHorizontally(board, x, y, currentJewel);
            boolean invalidVer = checkVertically(board, x, y, currentJewel);
            boolean invalidDia = checkDiagonally(board, x, y, currentJewel);

            if (invalidHor || invalidVer || invalidDia)
            {
                errors.add(String.format("Invalid at x=%d y=%d " +
                                "tests: hor=%b, ver=%b, dia=%b\n",
                                x, y, invalidHor, invalidVer, invalidDia));
            }
        }
    }
    return errors;
}
```

Verification

To test out the validity check, you first use the playfield from the introduction, which should produce the following errors due to its diagonals:

```
jshell> int[][] values = { { 2, 3, 3, 4, 4, 3, 2 },
                           { 1, 3, 3, 1, 3, 4, 4 },
                           { 4, 1, 4, 3, 3, 1, 3 },
                           { 2, 2, 1, 1, 2, 3, 2 },
                           { 3, 2, 4, 4, 3, 3, 4 } };
```

```
jshell> checkBoardValidity(values)
$37 ==> [Invalid at x=3 y=2 hor=false, ver=false, dia=true
, Invalid at x=2 y=3 hor=false, ver=false, dia=true
, Invalid at x=4 y=4 hor=false, ver=false, dia=true]
```

Subsequently, you replace the problematic digits with a yet unused digit, such as number 5, and retest the method, expecting no conflicts:

```
jshell> int[][] values2 = { { 2, 3, 3, 4, 4, 3, 2 },
                            { 1, 3, 3, 1, 3, 4, 4 },
                            { 4, 1, 4, 5, 3, 1, 3 },
                            { 2, 2, 5, 1, 2, 3, 2 },
                            { 3, 2, 4, 4, 5, 3, 4 } };

jshell> checkBoardValidity(values2)
$44 ==> []
```

5.3.6 Solution 6: Jewels Board Erase Diamonds (★★★★☆)

The challenge is to delete all chains of three or more horizontally, vertically, or diagonally connected diamonds from the rectangular playing field and subsequently to fill the resulting empty spaces with the diamonds lying above them (i.e., roughly in the same way as gravity works in nature). The following is an example of how the erasing and then dropping is repeated several times until no more change occurs (spaces are shown as _ for better visibility):

Iteration 1:

```
1 1 1 2 4 4 3   erase    _ _ _ _ 4 4 _  fall down  _ _ _ _ _ _ _
1 2 3 4 2 4 3    =>       1 2 3 4 _ 4 _     =>      1 2 3 4 4 4 _
2 3 3 1 2 2 3             2 3 3 1 2 _ _               2 3 3 1 2 4 _
```

Iteration 2:

```
_ _ _ _ _ _ _   erase    _ _ _ _ _ _ _  fall down  _ _ _ _ _ _ _
1 2 3 4 4 4 _    =>       1 2 3 _ _ _ _     =>      1 2 3 _ _ _ _
2 3 3 1 2 4 _             2 3 3 1 2 4 _               2 3 3 1 2 4 _
```

Solution 6a: Erase (★★★★☆)

Write method `boolean eraseChains(int[][])` that erases all rows of three or more contiguous diamonds in horizontal, vertical, and diagonal orientations from a rectangular playfield array.

Examples

An invocation of the method transforms the output array given on the left into the result shown on the right:

```
All chains without overlap           Special case:    overlaps
1 2 3 3 3 4        0 0 0 0 0 0        1 1 1 2          0 0 0 2
1 3 2 4 2 4        0 3 0 4 2 0        1 1 3 4   =>     0 0 3 4
1 2 4 2 4 4   =>   0 0 4 0 4 0        1 2 1 3          0 2 0 3
1 2 3 5 5 5        0 0 3 0 0 0
1 2 1 3 4 4        0 0 1 3 4 4
```

Algorithm: Preliminary considerations   As a first brute force variant, you could erase the values directly when finding. In this case, you search for a chain of length 3 or more and then directly erase these fields. However, this has a crucial weakness: Single diamonds can be part of several chains, as shown in the example above. If you delete immediately, not all occurrences can be found. Depending on which of the checks is done first, the other two fail in the following constellation:

```
XXX
XX
X X
```

A second idea is to modify the algorithm minimally by choosing an intermediate representation that symbolizes the deletion request, such as negative numbers, instead of deletion. After all entries in the array have been processed, the deletion takes place in a separate pass. Specifically, you remove all negative values from the array by replacing them with the numerical value 0.

Algorithm   The implementation of idea 2 starts with marking all the fields to be deleted using the `markElementsForRemoval(int[][])` method. Then they are deleted using the method `eraseAllMarked(int[][])`. For both methods you work position by position. First you have to detect chains of length 3 or more. The method

List<Direction> findChains(int[][], int, int) is responsible for this. Once a chain has been found, it is marked by calling void markDirectionsForRemoval(int[][], int, int, List<Direction>). The next action is to determine whether each field is marked for deletion. In this case, the stored value is replaced with the value 0.

```java
public static boolean eraseChains(final int[][] values)
{
    markElementsForRemoval(values);

    return eraseAllMarked(values);
}

static void markElementsForRemoval(final int[][] values)
{
    for (int y = 0; y < values.length; y++)
    {
        for (int x = 0; x < values[y].length; x++)
            markDirectionsForRemoval(values, x, y, findChains(values, x, y));
    }
}

static boolean eraseAllMarked(final int[][] values)
{
    boolean erasedSomething = false;

    for (int y = 0; y < values.length; y++)
    {
        for (int x = 0; x < values[y].length; x++)
        {
            if (isMarkedForRemoval(values[y][x]))
            {
                values[y][x] = 0;
                erasedSomething = true;
            }
        }
    }
    return erasedSomething;
}
```

```java
static boolean isMarkedForRemoval(final int value)
{
    return value < 0;
}
```

Now let's move on to the two trickier implementations and start picking up and recognizing chains of three or more similar diamonds. For this, you check for all relevant directions if there is a chain (again with the optimization, this time that you have to check diagonally only to the lower right and left). For this, you traverse the fields, count the similar elements, and stop at a deviation. If you find three or more equal values, then that direction is included in the List<Direction> dirsWithChains. As a special feature, you check at the beginning of the method if the current field is empty—you don't want to collect chains of blanks.

```java
static List<Direction> findChains(final int[][] values,
                                   final int startX, final int startY)
{
    final int origValue = values[startY][startX];
    if (origValue == 0) // ATTENTION: consider such special cases
        return Collections.emptyList();

    final List<Direction> dirsWithChains = new ArrayList<>();

    var relevantDirs = EnumSet.of(Direction.S, Direction.SW,
                                   Direction.E, Direction.SE);

    for (Direction currentDir : relevantDirs)
    {
        int nextPosX = startX + currentDir.dx;
        int nextPosY = startY + currentDir.dy;

        int length = 1;

        while (isOnBoard(values, nextPosX, nextPosY) &&
                isSame(origValue, values[nextPosY][nextPosX]))
        {
            nextPosX += currentDir.dx;
            nextPosY += currentDir.dy;
```

```
            length++;
        }

        if (length >= 3)
        {
            dirsWithChains.add(currentDir);
            break;
        }
    }
    return dirsWithChains;
}

static boolean isOnBoard(final int[][] values,
                         final int nextPosX, final int nextPosY)
{
    return nextPosX >= 0 && nextPosY >= 0 &&
           nextPosX < values[0].length && nextPosY < values.length;
}

static boolean isSame(final int val1, final int val2)
{
    return Math.abs(val1) == Math.abs(val2);
}
```

In fact, you are almost there. The only thing missing is the method for marking for deletion. Would you have thought at the beginning that the assignment is that complex? Probably not :-) Let's get to work. You now traverse all chains and convert the original value into one marked for deletion. To accomplish this, you rely on helper method int markForRemoval(int), which for the sake of simplicity converts the value to a negative value (with type char, for example, you can use a conversion to lowercase).

```
static void markDirectionsForRemoval(final int[][] values,
                                     final int startX, final int startY,
                                     final List<Direction> dirsWithChains)
{
    final int origValue = values[startY][startX];
```

```
for (final Direction currentDir : dirsWithChains)
{
    int nextPosX = startX;
    int nextPosY = startY;

    while (isOnBoard(values, nextPosX, nextPosY) &&
            isSame(origValue, values[nextPosY][nextPosX]))
    {
        values[nextPosY][nextPosX] = markForRemoval(origValue);

        nextPosX += currentDir.dx;
        nextPosY += currentDir.dy;
    }
}
}

static int markForRemoval(final int value)
{
    return value > 0 ? -value : value;
}
```

I want to point out that the functionalities are solved using side effects. Here, you are operating directly on the passed data, so this is not bad because the data is not passed further out. Instead, it is all internal functionalities.

Verification

After this exhausting implementation, let's test the deletion as well:

```
@Test
void eraseChains()
{
    int[][] board = { { 1, 1, 1, 2, 4, 4, 3 },
                      { 1, 1, 3, 4, 2, 4, 3 },
                      { 1, 3, 1, 1, 2, 2, 3 } };
```

```
    boolean deleted = EX06_JewelsEraseDiamonds.eraseChains(board);

    int[][] expectedBoard = { { 0, 0, 0, 0, 4, 4, 0 },
                              { 0, 0, 3, 4, 0, 4, 0 },
                              { 0, 3, 0, 1, 2, 0, 0 } };

    assertTrue(deleted);
    assertArrayEquals(expectedBoard, board);
}

@Test
void eraseChainsOtherBoard()
{
    int[][] board = { { 1, 1, 3, 3, 4, 5 },
                      { 1, 1, 0, 0, 4, 5 },
                      { 1, 2, 3, 3, 4, 5 },
                      { 1, 2, 0, 3, 3, 4 },
                      { 1, 2, 3, 4, 4, 4 } };

    boolean deleted = EX06_JewelsEraseDiamonds.eraseChains(board);

    int[][] expectedBoard = { { 0, 1, 3, 3, 0, 0 },
                              { 0, 1, 0, 0, 0, 0 },
                              { 0, 0, 3, 3, 0, 0 },
                              { 0, 0, 0, 3, 3, 4 },
                              { 0, 0, 3, 0, 0, 0 } };

    assertTrue(deleted);
    assertArrayEquals(expectedBoard, board);
}
```

Solution 6b: Falling Down (★★★☆☆)

Write method void fallDown(int[][]) working inplace that drops the diamonds from top to bottom, provided there is a space below their position.

285

Example

An invocation of the method transforms the output array given on the left into the result shown on the right:

```
0 1 3 3 0 0          0 0 0 0 0 0
0 1 0 0 0 0          0 0 0 0 0 0
0 0 3 3 0 0   =>     0 0 3 3 0 0
0 0 0 3 3 4          0 1 3 3 0 0
0 0 3 0 0 0          0 1 3 3 3 4
```

Algorithm   At first, the task seems to be relatively easy to solve. However, the complexity increases due to a few special characteristics.

Let's look at one possible implementation. Let's start with a brute force solution. From left to right, the following is checked for all x-positions in the vertical: Starting from the lowest row to the second highest one, you test whether they represent a blank in each case. If this is the case, the value from the line above is used. In this case, the value from the line above is exchanged with the blank (symbolized here as _, represented in the model with the value 0):

```
1          1          _
2    =>     _    =>   1
_          2          2
```

The procedure can be implemented as follows:

```
static void fallDownFirstTry(final int[][] values)
{
    for (int x = 0; x < values[0].length; x++)
    {
        for (int y = values.length - 1; y > 0; y--)
        {
            final int value = values[y][x];
            if (isBlank(value))
            {
```

```
            // fall down
            values[y][x] = values[y - 1][x];
            values[y - 1][x] = 0;
        }
      }
   }
}

static boolean isBlank(final int value)
{
   return value == 0;
}
```

This works pretty passably, but unfortunately not quite for the following special case:

```
1
           _
_   =>   1

_          _
```

You can see that the propagation is missing.

As a next idea, you could start falling from the top, but this doesn't work in every case either! While with this procedure the previously problematic case

```
1
           _
_   =>   _
_          1
```

is solved, problems occur now for the first constellation. These problems do not occur with the variant before:

```
1          1
2   =>   _
_          2
```

You have had to recognize that both of the variants discussed do not yet work quite correctly. Moreover, it was crucial to use the right set of test data to uncover just these specific problems.

To correct this, you need to implement continuous falling of stones to always move all values per column. The while loop is used for this:

```
static void fallDown(final int[][] values)
{
    for (int x = 0; x < values[0].length; x++)
    {
        for (int y = values.length - 1; y > 0; y--)
        {
            int currentY = y;

            // fall down until there is no more empty space under it
            while (currentY < values.length && isBlank(values[currentY][x]))
            {
                // runterfallen
                values[currentY][x] = values[currentY - 1][x];
                values[currentY - 1][x] = 0;

                currentY++;
            }
        }
    }
}
```

Verification

Let's now take the previously obtained result of the deletion as the starting point for the falling:

```
@Test
void fallDown()
{
    int[][] board = { { 0, 1, 3, 3, 0, 0 },
                      { 0, 1, 0, 0, 0, 0 },
                      { 0, 0, 3, 3, 0, 0 },
                      { 0, 0, 0, 3, 3, 4 },
                      { 0, 0, 3, 0, 0, 0 } };
```

```
EX06_JewelsEraseDiamonds.fallDown(board);

int[][] expectedBoard = { { 0, 0, 0, 0, 0, 0 },
                          { 0, 0, 0, 0, 0, 0 },
                          { 0, 0, 3, 3, 0, 0 },
                          { 0, 1, 3, 3, 0, 0 },
                          { 0, 1, 3, 3, 3, 4 } };

assertArrayEquals(expectedBoard, board);
}
```

Overall Verification

To see your methods in action, you use a prepared char[][] in addition to the example from the introduction, from which you can follow various deletions and iterations very nicely. You will, however, have to rewrite some of the methods for the type char respectively char[][] (see the following practical tip):

```
jshell> int[][] exampleBoard = { { 1, 1, 1, 2, 4, 4, 3 },
   ...>                           { 1, 2, 3, 4, 2, 4, 3 },
   ...>                           { 2, 3, 3, 1, 2, 2, 3 } };
   ...>
   ...> printArray(exampleBoard);
   ...> while (eraseChains(exampleBoard))
   ...> {
   ...>     System.out.println("----------------------------------");
   ...>     fallDown(exampleBoard);
   ...>     printArray(exampleBoard);
   ...> }
1 1 1 2 4 4 3
1 2 3 4 2 4 3
2 3 3 1 2 2 3
----------------------------------
0 0 0 0 0 0 0
1 2 3 4 4 4 0
2 3 3 1 2 4 0
----------------------------------
```

```
0 0 0 0 0 0
1 2 3 0 0 0
2 3 3 1 2 4 0

jshell> char[][] jewelsTestDeletion = { "AACCDE".toCharArray(),
   ...>                                  "AA  DE".toCharArray(),
   ...>                                  "ABCCDE".toCharArray(),
   ...>                                  "AB CCD".toCharArray(),
   ...>                                  "ABCDDD".toCharArray(), };
   ...>
   ...> printArray(jewelsTestDeletion);
   ...>
   ...> while (eraseChains(jewelsTestDeletion))
   ...> {
   ...>     System.out.println("---------------------------------");
   ...>     fallDown(jewelsTestDeletion);
   ...>     printArray(jewelsTestDeletion);
   ...> }
A A C C D E
A A     D E
A B C C D E
A B   C C D
A B C D D D
---------------------------------
    C C
 A C C
 A C C C D
---------------------------------
A
A           D
```

HINT: VARIANTS WITH TYPE CHAR

Some readers may have wondered why I implement different helper methods when they seem very simple. The reason is that this way it becomes possible to use the algorithms almost unchanged for other types instead of `int` just by redefining the corresponding helper methods, for example, these:

```java
static boolean isMarkedForRemoval(final char value)
{
    return Character.isLowerCase(value);
}

static boolean isBlank(final char value)
{
    return value == '_' || value == ' ';
}

static boolean isSame(final char char1, final char char2)
{
    return Character.toLowerCase(char1) == Character.toLowerCase(char2);
}
```

The more conceptual methods for the actions, such as determining the chains to be deleted, the actual deletion, and the dropping of the diamonds, must then be overloaded accordingly and adapted to the desired type. In the following code, this is shown for the method `void fallDown(char[][])` and its alignment to a `char[][]`:

```java
static void fallDown(char[][] values)
{
    for (int y = values.length - 1; y > 0; y--)
    {
        for (int x = 0; x < values[0].length; x++)
        {
            int currentY = y;
            // fall down until there is no more empty space under it
```

```
        while (currentY < values.length && isBlank(values[currentY][x]))
        {
            // runterfallen
            values[currentY][x] = values[currentY - 1][x];
            values[currentY - 1][x] = '_';

            currentY++;
        }
    }
  }
}
```

Without looking very closely, the difference to the method designed at the beginning of the assignment is not noticeable. This is also true for the other methods but is not presented here.

5.3.7 Solution 7: Spiral Traversal (★★★★☆)

Write generic method List<T>spiralTraversal(T[][]) that traverses a two-dimensional rectangular array in a spiral and prepares it as a list. The start is in the upper left corner. First, the outer layer is traversed, and then the next inner layer.

Example

An example is shown in Figure 5-5.

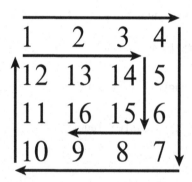

Figure 5-5. *Basic procedure for the spiral traversal*

For the following two arrays, the following number or letter sequences should be the results of a spiral traversal:

```
Integer[][] numbers = { { 1, 2, 3, 4 },
                        { 12, 13, 14, 5 },
                        { 11, 16, 15, 6 },
                        { 10, 9, 8, 7 } };
String[][] letterPairs = { { "AB", "BC", "CD", "DE" },
                           { "JK", "KL", "LM", "EF" },
                           { "IJ", "HI", "GH", "FG" } };
=>

[1, 2, 3, 4, 5, 6, 7, 8, 9, 10, 11, 12, 13, 14, 15, 16]

[AB, BC, CD, DE, EF, FG, GH, HI, IJ, JK, KL, LM]
```

JOB INTERVIEW TIPS: CLARIFY ASSUMPTIONS

Before proceeding with a solution, be sure to clarify any constraints or special requirements by asking questions. In this case, the original data should be a rectangular array. Assume that to be the case here.

Algorithm   Let's start with an idea: For a spiral movement, you must first go to the right until you reach the boundary, change direction downward and advance again until you reach the boundary, then to the left, and finally up to the boundary. For the spiral to narrow, the respective limits must be suitably reduced at each change of direction. Formulating the termination condition correctly is not quite easy when operating only on changes of direction and boundaries. To determine the termination criterion, the following observation helps: The total number of steps is given by *width* $*$ *height* $- 1$, for a 4×3 array thus $4 * 3 - 1 = 12 - 1 = 11$. With these preliminary considerations, you implement the spiral traversal as follows:

```
enum Direction
{
    RIGHT, DOWN, LEFT, UP;
}
```

```java
static <T> List<T> spiralTraversal(final T[][] values)
{
    int posX = 0;
    int posY = 0;

    int minX = 0;
    int maxX = values[0].length;
    int minY = 1;
    int maxY = values.length;

    final List<T> results = new ArrayList<>();

    Direction dir = Direction.RIGHT;
    int steps = 0;

    while (steps < maxX * maxY)
    {
        // perform action
        results.add(values[posY][posX]);

        if (dir == Direction.RIGHT)
        {
            if (posX < maxX - 1)
                posX++;
            else
            {
                dir = Direction.DOWN;
                maxX--;
            }
        }
        if (dir == Direction.DOWN)
        {
            if (posY < maxY - 1)
                posY++;
            else
            {
                dir = Direction.LEFT;
                maxY--;
```

```
            }
        }
        if (dir == Direction.LEFT)
        {
            if (posX > minX)
                posX--;
            else
            {
                dir = Direction.UP;
                minX++;
            }
        }
        if (dir == Direction.UP)
        {
            if (posY > minY)
                posY--;
            else
            {
                dir = Direction.RIGHT;
                minY++;

                // possible mistake: You now have to
                // start at a position further to the right!
                posX++;
            }
        }

        steps++;
    }

    return results;
}
```

After a complete traversal of a *layer*, you have to move the position pointer one position towards the center. This is easily forgotten.

The presented algorithm works, but there are quite a few special treatments. Also, a switch would perhaps be a good choice if the individual action blocks were not so extensive. Look at the image again and then think a bit.

Optimized algorithm   You recognize that initially, the whole array is a valid movement area. At each iteration, the outer layer is processed, and one continues inwards. Now you can specify the valid range by four position markers as before. However, you proceed more cleverly when updating.

You notice that after moving to the right, the top line is completed so that you can increase the counter minY by one. If you move down, then the rightmost side is finished, and the counter maxX is decreased by one. Moving to the left, then the bottom row is processed, and the counter maxY is decreased by one. Finally, when moving upwards, the counter minX is increased by one. To detect when to increment, you implement an utility method isOutside() for range checking.

Additionally, you can still take advantage of defining the direction constants according to the order in the spiral traversal and then implementing method next() in the enum that specifies the subsequent direction in each case. Likewise, you define there the offset values dx and dy.

```
enum Direction
{
    RIGHT(1, 0), DOWN(0, 1), LEFT(-1, 0), UP(0, -1);

    int dx;
    int dy;

    Direction(final int dx, final int dy)
    {
        this.dx = dx;
        this.dy = dy;
    }

    Direction next()
    {
        return values()[(this.ordinal() + 1) % 4];
    }
}
```

With these thoughts and preliminaries, you are then able to write the implementation of the spiral traversal in a readable and understandable way as follows:

```java
static <T> List<T> spiralTraversalOptimized(final T[][] board)
{
    int minX = 0;
    int maxX = board[0].length;
    int minY = 0;
    int maxY = board.length;

    int x = 0;
    int y = 0;
    Direction dir = Direction.RIGHT;

    final List<T> result = new ArrayList<>();

    int steps = 0;
    final int allSteps = maxX * maxY;
    while (steps < allSteps)
    {
        result.add(board[y][x]);

        if (isOutside(x + dir.dx, y + dir.dy, minX, maxX, minY, maxY))
        {
            switch (dir)
            {
                case RIGHT -> minY++;
                case DOWN -> maxX--;
                case LEFT -> maxY--;
                case UP -> minX++;
            }
            dir = dir.next();
        }

        x += dir.dx;
        y += dir.dy;
        steps++;
    }
    return result;
}
```

```
private static boolean isOutside(final int x, final int y,
                                 final int minX, final int maxX,
                                 final int minY, final int maxY)
    {
      return !(x >= minX && x < maxX && y >= minY && y < maxY);
    }
}
```

In the code, you use the new Java 14 syntax at `switch`, making the whole construct even shorter and more elegant.[3]

Verification

Let's check once if your algorithm as well as its optimized variant realize the expected traversal through the array for the inputs from the above example:

```
@ParameterizedTest(name="spiralTraversal({0}) => {1}")
@MethodSource("createArrayAndExpected")
void spiralTraversal(Object[][] values, List<Object> expected)
{
    var result = Ex07_SpiralTraversal.spiralTraversal(values);

    assertEquals(expected, result);
}

@ParameterizedTest(name="spiralTraversalOptimized({0}) => {1}")
@MethodSource("createArrayAndExpected")
void spiralTraversalOptimized(Object[][] values, List<Object> expected)
{
    var result = Ex07_SpiralTraversal.spiralTraversalOptimized(values);

    assertEquals(expected, result);
}
```

---

[3] The new features in Java 14 are covered in detail in my book *Java – die Neuerungen in Version 9 bis 14: Modularisierung, Syntax- und API-Erweiterungen* [Ind20b].

```
private static Stream<Arguments> createArrayAndExpected()
{
    String[][] letters = { { "A", "B", "C", "D" },
                           { "J", "K", "L", "E" },
                           { "I", "H", "G", "F" } };

    Integer[][] numbers = { { 1, 2, 3, 4 },
                            { 12, 13, 14, 5 },
                            { 11, 16, 15, 6 },
                            { 10, 9, 8, 7 } };

    return Stream.of(Arguments.of(letters,
                          List.of("A","B", "C", "D", "E", "F",
                                  "G", "H", "I", "J", "K", "L")),
                     Arguments.of(numbers,
                          List.of(1, 2, 3, 4, 5, 6, 7, 8, 9, 10,
                                  11, 12, 13, 14, 15, 16)));
}
```

5.3.8 Solution 8: Add One to Array as Number (★★☆☆☆)

Consider an array of numbers representing the digits of a decimal number. Write method int[] addOne(int[]) that performs an addition by the value 1 and is only allowed to use arrays as the data structure for the solution.

Examples

Input	Result
[1, 3, 2, 4]	[1, 3, 2, 5]
[1, 4, 8, 9]	[1, 4, 9, 0]
[9, 9, 9, 9]	[1, 0, 0, 0, 0]

Algorithm   You may remember back to your school days and use digit-oriented processing: traversing the array from back to front. Then you add the overflow value of the last addition to the respective digit value. Initially, you start with the assumption that there is an overflow. If the value 10 is reached again, the overflow must be propagated further. In the special case that the overflow propagates to the very front, the array has to be increased by one position to accommodate the new leading 1.

```
static int[] addOne(final int[] values)
{
    if (values.length == 0)
        throw new IllegalArgumentException("must pass a valid
        non empty array");

    final int[] result = Arrays.copyOf(values, values.length);

    boolean overflow = true;
    int pos = values.length - 1;
    while (overflow && pos >= 0)
    {
        int currentValue = result[pos];
        if (overflow)
            currentValue += 1;

        result[pos] = currentValue %  10;

        overflow = currentValue >= 10;

        pos--;
    }

    return handleOverflowAtTop(result, overflow);
}
```

For special handling of the carry at the front, you implement the following method:

```
static int[] handleOverflowAtTop(final int[] result, final boolean overflow)
{
    if (overflow)
    {
        // new array and a 1 at the front
        final int[] newValues = new int[result.length + 1];
        newValues[0] = 1;
        for (int i = 0; i < result.length; i++)
            newValues[1 + i] = result[i];
```

```
        return newValues;
    }

    return result;
}
```

Verification

To check your implementation, you use the three value combinations from the introductory examples—covering the three main cases of *no propagation, propagation by one digit,* and *propagation over all digits*. Additionally, you include the propagation for two digits.

```java
@ParameterizedTest(name = "addOne({0}) => {1}")
@MethodSource("intArrays")
void addOne(int[] input, int[] expected)
{
    int[] result = Ex08_AddOneToAnArrayOfNumbers.addOne(input);

    assertArrayEquals(expected, result);
}

private static Stream<Arguments> intArrays()
{
    int[] values1 = { 1, 3, 2, 4 };
    int[] expected1 = { 1, 3, 2, 5 };

    int[] values2 = { 1, 4, 8, 9 };
    int[] expected2 = { 1, 4, 9, 0 };

    int[] values3 = { 1, 3, 9, 9 };
    int[] expected3 = { 1, 4, 0, 0 };

    int[] values4 = { 9, 9, 9, 9 };
    int[] expected4 = { 1, 0, 0, 0, 0 };

    return Stream.of(Arguments.of(values1, expected1),
                     Arguments.of(values2, expected2),
                     Arguments.of(values3, expected3),
                     Arguments.of(values4, expected4));
}
```

5.3.9 Solution 9: Sudoku Checker (★★★☆☆)

In this challenge, a Sudoku puzzle is examined to see if it is a valid solution. Let's assume a 9 × 9 array with int values. According to the Sudoku rules, each row and each column must contain all numbers from 1 to 9. Besides, all numbers from 1 to 9 must, in turn, occur in each 3x3 subarray. Write method boolean isSudokuValid(int[][]) for checking.

Example

A valid solution is shown here:

1	2	3	4	5	6	7	8	9
4	5	6	7	8	9	1	2	3
7	8	9	1	2	3	4	5	6
2	1	4	3	6	5	8	9	7
3	6	5	8	9	7	2	1	4
8	9	7	2	1	4	3	6	5
5	3	1	6	4	2	9	7	8
6	4	2	9	7	8	5	3	1
9	7	8	5	3	1	6	4	2

Algorithm   In Sudoku, three different types of checks have to be performed. These checks can be very well divided into three corresponding methods. First are checkHorizontally() and checkVertically(), which ensure horizontally and vertically that all digits from 1 to 9 always occur exactly once in a row or column, respectively. To check this, you collect all digits stored in the respective alignment in a list and compare them in the allDesiredNumbers() method to see if they contain the desired numbers:

```
boolean checkHorizontally(final int[][] board)
{
    for (int row = 0; row < 9; row++)
    {
        // collect all values of a row in a list
        final List<Integer> rowValues = new ArrayList<>();
```

```
    for (int x = 0; x < 9; x++)
    {
        rowValues.add(board[row][x]);
    }

    if (!allDesiredNumbers(rowValues))
    {
        return false;
    }
    }
    return true;
}

boolean checkVertically(final int[][] board)
{
    for (int x = 0; x < 9; x++)
    {
        // collect all values of a column in a list
        final List<Integer> columnValues = new ArrayList<>();
        for (int row = 0; row < 9; row++)
        {
            columnValues.add(board[row][x]);
        }

        if (!allDesiredNumbers(columnValues))
        {
            return false;
        }
    }
    return true;
}
```

You might wonder whether it's preferable to collect the values in a Set<E>. Although this is obvious and works well for fully filled Sudoku puzzles, collecting data in a Set<E> complicates subsequent checking, however, if you permit empty fields as well.

Regardless, both checks rely on the following helper method:

```
boolean allDesiredNumbers(final Collection<Integer> values)
{
    if (values.size() != 9)
        throw new IllegalStateException("implementation problem");

    final Set<Integer> oneToNine = Set.of(1, 2, 3, 4, 5, 6, 7, 8, 9);
    final Set<Integer> valuesSet = new TreeSet<>(values);

    return oneToNine.equals(valuesSet);
}
```

I would like to explicitly point out the elegance of the helper method
allDesiredNumbers(). It unifies various things in its brevity: actually, you need to check
that the collected values do not contain duplicates and that there are exactly nine of
them. Due to your implementation, you don't need to check the length. Still, you do it
anyway to guard against carelessness errors with an exception. By converting the values
into a set and comparing it to the set from the expected values, the process is nice and
short.

Next, you need to check each of the 9 subfields of size 3×3. This doesn't sound
easy at first. But let's think a bit: You can use two nested loops to run off the 3×3 boxes.
Two more nested loops run the respective x and y values. Simple multiplications and
additions are used to derive the corresponding index values in the original array. By
following the previously presented idea of collecting the values into a list, which is finally
checked against the expected target set of digits 1 to 9, the implementation loses its
initial horror.

```
public static boolean checkBoxes(final int[][] board)
{
    // 3 x 3-boxes
    for (int yBox = 0; yBox < 3; yBox ++)
    {
        for (int xBox = 0; xBox < 3; xBox ++)
        {
            // values per box
            final List<Integer> boxValues = collectBoxValues(board,
            yBox, xBox);
```

```
        if (!allDesiredNumbers(boxValues))
        {
            return false;
        }
      }
    }
    return true;
}

private static List<Integer> collectBoxValues(final int[][] board,
                                              final int yBox, final int xBox)
{
    final List<Integer> boxValues = new ArrayList<>();

    // innerhalb der Boxen jeweils 3 x 3 Felder
    for (int y=0; y < 3; y++)
    {
        for (int x = 0; x < 3; x++)
        {
            // actual index values
            final int realY = yBox * 3 + y;
            final int realX = xBox * 3 + x;

            boxValues.add(board[realY][realX]);
        }
    }
    return boxValues;
}
```

For a complete Sudoku check, you then need to combine these values all together by AND:

```
boolean isSudokuValid(final int[][] board)
{
    return checkHorizontally(board) &&
           checkVertically(board) &&
           checkBoxes(board);
}
```

Verification

You first define the Sudoku playfield as I showed in the introduction and then you test all three variants:

```
jshell> int[][] board = new int[9][9];
   ...> board[0] = new int[]{ 1, 2, 3, 4, 5, 6, 7, 8, 9 };
   ...> board[1] = new int[]{ 4, 5, 6, 7, 8, 9, 1, 2, 3 };
   ...> board[2] = new int[]{ 7, 8, 9, 1, 2, 3, 4, 5, 6 };
   ...> board[3] = new int[]{ 2, 1, 4, 3, 6, 5, 8, 9, 7 };
   ...> board[4] = new int[]{ 3, 6, 5, 8, 9, 7, 2, 1, 4 };
   ...> board[5] = new int[]{ 8, 9, 7, 2, 1, 4, 3, 6, 5 };
   ...> board[6] = new int[]{ 5, 3, 1, 6, 4, 2, 9, 7, 8 };
   ...> board[7] = new int[]{ 6, 4, 2, 9, 7, 8, 5, 3, 1 };
   ...> board[8] = new int[]{ 9, 7, 8, 5, 3, 1, 6, 4, 2 };

jshell> System.out.println("V: " + checkVertically(board));
   ...> System.out.println("H: " + checkHorizontally(board));
   ...> System.out.println("B: " + checkBoxes(board));
V: true
H: true
B: true

jshell> isSudokuValid(board)
$72 true
```

Bonus

While it is already nice to be able to check a Sudoku board that is completely filled with digits for its validity, it is even better to be able to predict for a board with *gaps* (i.e., still missing digits) whether a valid solution can emerge from it. This is of particular interest if you want to develop an algorithm for solving a Sudoku puzzle.

Example

Based on the example of the valid Sudoku game field given above, I have deleted the digits at random places. This surely results in a valid solution.

1	2		4	5		7	8	9
	5	6	7		9		2	3
7	8		1	2	3	4	5	6
2	1	4		6		8		7
3	6		8		7	2	1	4
	9	7		1	4	3	6	
5	3	1	6		2	9		8
6		2	9	7	8	5	3	1
9	7			3	1	6	4	2

Algorithm   A partially filled playfield can be checked for validity fairly easily if you take the previous implementation as a basis. First, you need modeling for the blank fields. In this case, the value 0 is a good choice. Based on this, you can leave the implementation for collecting the values horizontally, vertically, and in the boxes as it is. You only have to slightly modify the final check whether all values from 1 to 9 are included. First, you remove the value 0 from the collected values if any. Then you make sure that there are no duplicates. Finally, you check whether the collected values are a subset of 1 to 9.

```
static boolean allDesiredNumbers(final Collection<Integer>
allCollectedValues)
{
    // remove irrelevant empty fields
    final List<Integer> relevantValues = new ArrayList<>(allCollectedValues);
    relevantValues.removeIf(val -> val == 0);

    // no duplicates?
    final Set<Integer> valuesSet = new TreeSet<>(relevantValues);
    if (relevantValues.size() != valuesSet.size())
        return false;

    // only 1 to 9?
    final Set<Integer> oneToNine = Set.of(1, 2, 3, 4, 5, 6, 7, 8, 9);

    return oneToNine.containsAll(valuesSet);
}
```

The very best comes at the end: This method works for completely filled Sudoku puzzles and those containing blanks!

NOTE: DELETING ELEMENTS FROM LISTS

Sometimes an assignment sounds much simpler than it actually is. In the example above, all numbers with the value 0 are to be deleted from a List<Integer>. Sometimes one sees attempts like the following two:

```
// ATTENTION: wrong attempts
values.remove(0); // Attention INDEX
values.remove(Integer.valueOf(0)); // ONLY first occurrence
```

Why is the whole thing that tricky? It's because of the API, which gives you position- based access on the one hand and the ability to delete a value on the other. However, if you want to delete several of the same elements, you can use the method removeAll(), but you have to pass a list of values to it—a bit awkward, but with a one-element list, you get there:

```
values.removeAll(List.of(0));
```

In fact, it is possible to achieve this a little bit more elegantly. Since Java 8 you might use the method removeIf() and supply a suitable Predicate<T>. This is the best way to express the algorithm:

```
values.removeIf(value -> value == 0);
```

Verification

Again you define the Sudoku playfield with blanks, as shown before. After that, you check a slightly modified playfield, where in the first line at position 3, a 2 was inserted directly, which makes the playfield invalid.

```
@Test
void isSudokuValid()
{
    final int[][] board = createInitializedBoard();

    final boolean validSudoku = Ex09_SudokuChecker.isSudokuValid(board);

    assertTrue(validSudoku);
}
```

```
@Test
void isSudokuValidForInvalidBoard()
{
    final int[][] board = createInitializedBoard();

    board[0][2] = 2;
    ArrayUtils.printArray(board);

    final boolean validSudoku = Ex09_SudokuChecker.isSudokuValid(board);

    assertFalse(validSudoku);
}

private int[][] createInitializedBoard()
{
    final int[][] board = new int[9][9];
    board[0] = new int[] { 1, 2, 0, 4, 5, 0, 7, 8, 9 };
    board[1] = new int[] { 0, 5, 6, 7, 0, 9, 0, 2, 3 };
    board[2] = new int[] { 7, 8, 0, 1, 2, 3, 4, 5, 6 };
    board[3] = new int[] { 2, 1, 4, 0, 6, 0, 8, 0, 7 };
    board[4] = new int[] { 3, 6, 0, 8, 9, 7, 2, 1, 4 };
    board[5] = new int[] { 0, 9, 7, 0, 1, 4, 3, 6, 0 };
    board[6] = new int[] { 5, 3, 1, 6, 0, 2, 9, 0, 8 };
    board[7] = new int[] { 6, 0, 2, 9, 7, 8, 5, 3, 1 };
    board[8] = new int[] { 9, 7, 0, 0, 3, 1, 6, 4, 2 };

    return board;
}
```

The faulty playfield of the second test case looks like this—the problematic value is marked in bold:

```
1 2 2 4 5 0 7 8 9
0 5 6 7 0 9 0 2 3
7 8 0 1 2 3 4 5 6
2 1 4 0 6 0 8 0 7
3 6 0 8 9 7 2 1 4
0 9 7 0 1 4 3 6 0
5 3 1 6 0 2 9 0 8
6 0 2 9 7 8 5 3 1
9 7 0 0 3 1 6 4 2
```

5.3.10 Solution 10: Flood Fill (★★☆☆☆)

Solution 10a (★★☆☆☆)

Write method void floodFill(char[], int, int) that fills all free fields in an array with a specified value.

Example

The following shows the filling process for the character *. The filling starts at a given position, such as the upper left corner. It then continues in all four compass directions until the boundaries of the array or a boundary represented by another character are found.

```
"    #  "        "***#  "        "   #   #"        "    #******#"
"     #"         "****#"         "   #   #"        "    #******#"
" #   #"   =>    "#***#"         "#   #   #"   =>   "#   #*****#"
" # # "         " #*# "         " # #   #"         " # #******#"
"   #   "        "  #  "         "   #   #"         "   #*****#"
```

Algorithm Recursively check the neighboring cells in the four cardinal directions. If a field is empty, fill it and again check its four neighbors. If you reach the array boundaries or a filled cell, you stop. This can be formulated recursively in a wonderful way:

```java
static void floodFill(final char[][] values, final int x, final int y)
{
    // recursive termination
    if (x < 0 || y < 0 || y >= values.length || x >= values[y].length)
        return;

    if (values[y][x] == ' ')
    {
        values[y][x] = '*';

        // recursive descent: fill in all 4 directions
        floodFill(values, x, y-1);
        floodFill(values, x+1, y);
```

```
        floodFill(values, x, y+1);
        floodFill(values, x-1, y);
    }
}
```

The version shown here can handle non-rectangular arrays by cleverly checking the width per row. It can also deal with non-rectangular arrays and fill them appropriately.

Verification

Now let's define the array shown in the introduction as a starting point and then do a fill with a start in the upper left corner. For verification, the array is printed on the console (exceptionally as a part of the unit test also). In addition, you show a non-rectangular array with a fill starting from the bottom in the middle.

```
@ParameterizedTest(name = "{0}, {4}")
@MethodSource("createWorldAndExpectedFills")
public void testFloodFill2(char[][] world, char[][] expected,
                           int startX, int startY, String hint)
{
    Ex10_FloodFillExample.floodFill(world, startX, startY);
    ArrayUtils.printArray(world);

    assertArrayEquals(expected, world);
}

private static Stream<Arguments> createWorldAndExpectedFills()
{
    return Stream.of(Arguments.of(firstWorld(), firstFilled), 0, 0, "rect"),
                Arguments.of(nonRectWorld(), nonRectFilled(), 4, 4,
                             "no rect"));
}

private static Stream<Arguments> createWorldAndExpectedFills()
{
    return Stream.of(Arguments.of(firstWorld(), firstFilled(), 0, 0, "rect"),
                Arguments.of(nonRectWorld(), nonRectFilled(), 4, 4,
                             "no rect"));
}
```

```java
private static char[][] firstWorld()
{
    return new char[][] { "  #   ".toCharArray(),
                          "     # ".toCharArray(),
                          "#   # ".toCharArray(),
                          " # # ".toCharArray(),
                          "  #   ".toCharArray()};
}

private static char[][] firstFilled()
{
    return new char[][] { "***#  ".toCharArray(),
                          "****# ".toCharArray(),
                          "#***# ".toCharArray(),
                          " #*#  ".toCharArray(),
                          "  #   ".toCharArray()};
}

private static char[][] nonRectWorld()
{
    return new char[][] { "  #       #".toCharArray(),
                          "     #     #".toCharArray(),
                          "#    #     #".toCharArray(),
                          " # #    #".toCharArray(),
                          "  #    #".toCharArray()};
}

private static char[][] nonRectFilled()
{
    return new char[][] { "   #******#".toCharArray(),
                          "    #******#".toCharArray(),
                          "#   #*****#".toCharArray(),
                          " # #*****#".toCharArray(),
                          "  #*****#".toCharArray()};
}
```

Solution 10b (★★☆☆☆)

Extend the method to fill any pattern passed as a rectangular array. However, spaces are not allowed in the pattern specification.

Example

Below you see a flood fill with a pattern. The pattern consists of several lines with characters:

```
.|.
-*-
.|.
```

If you start the filling at the bottom center, you get the following result:

```
      x                  . |..|.x
    #   #               - *--#--#
    ###    #            . |.###.|#
#   ###    #    =>    # |.###.|#
#    #     #          # *--#--*#
  # #     #           #.# |..#
    #     #            #. |.#
```

Algorithm   First of all, you have to pass the desired pattern to the method. Interestingly, the fill algorithm remains almost the same and is only modified concerning the fill character's determination. Instead of a fixed value, helper method findFillChar() is invoked here, which determines the fill character relevant for the position. The recursive descent is formulated elegantly by using an enumeration for the directions as an alternative to the four individual calls.

```
static void floodFill(final char[][] values, final int x, final int y,
                      final char[][] pattern)
{
    // recursive termination
    if (x < 0 || y < 0 || y >= values.length || x >= values[y].length)
        return;
```

313

```
    if (values[y][x] == ' ')
    {
        // determine appropriate fill character
        values[y][x] = findFillChar(x, y, pattern);

        final EnumSet<Direction> directions = EnumSet.of(Direction.N,
                                                         Direction.E,
                                                         Direction.S,
                                                         Direction.W);

        // recursive descent in 4 directions
        for (final Direction dir : directions)
        {
            floodFill(values, x + dir.dx, y + dir.dy, pattern);
        }
    }
}
```

Now let's determine the fill character based on a simple modulo calculation from the current position in relation to the width or the height of the array with the pattern characters:

```
static char findFillChar(final int x, final int y, final char[][] pattern)
{
    final int adjustedX = x % pattern[0].length;
    final int adjustedY = y % pattern.length;

    return pattern[adjustedY][adjustedX];
}
```

Please remember that for the whole thing to work, no spaces have to be specified in the fill pattern.

Verification

Analogous to before, you would like to fill the array with delimiters shown in the introduction with the pattern shown before. Therefore, you first generate the pattern using the following method:

```
private static char[][] generatePattern()
{
    return new char[][] { ".|.".toCharArray(),
                          "-*-".toCharArray(),
                          ".|.".toCharArray()};
}
private static char[][] generatePattern2()
{
    return new char[][] { "---".toCharArray(),
                          "~~~".toCharArray(),
                          "===.".toCharArray()};
}
private static char[][] generateBigWorld()
{
    return new char[][]  {
    "          #  |".toCharArray(),
    "     ##   #  |".toCharArray(),
    "   #####    #  _".toCharArray(),
    "       ###   #    |".toCharArray(),
    " ###   #    #       |".toCharArray(),
    "   #   #    #       |".toCharArray(),
    "    # #    #    --".toCharArray(),
    "     #    #    |".toCharArray()};
}
```

For testing, you generate the initial pattern and fill from the top left with the first
pattern and with the second pattern in the right part:

```
jshell> char[][] bigworld = generateBigWorld()

jshell> floodFill(bigworld,1,1, generatePattern())

jshell> floodFill(bigworld, 14, 4, generatePattern2())
```

For control purposes, you now print out the array. This allows you to examine the filling with the respective pattern:

```
jshell> printArray(bigworld)
.|..|..|..|#---|
-*--*--##-*-#~~~|
.|..#####.|..#===
.|..|..###|..#-----|
-###*--*#-*--#~~~~~~|
.|..#..|#.|..#=====|
.|..|#.#..|.#------
-*--*-#*--*#~~~~|
```

As a reminder, the method for printing a two-dimensional array is shown here once again—in this case with the modification of printing the characters directly next to each other:

```
static void printArray(final char[][] values)
{
    for (int y= 0; y < values.length; y++)
    {
        for (int x = 0; x < values[y].length; x++)
        {
            final char value = values[y][x];
            System.out.print(value + "");
        }
        System.out.println();
    }
}
```

5.3.11 Solution 11: Array Merge (★★☆☆☆)

Assume that there are two arrays of numbers, each sorted in ascending order. In this assignment, these arrays are to be merged into a single array according to the respective values' order. Write method int[] merge(int[], int[]).

Examples

Input 1	Input 2	Result
[1, 4, 7, 12, 20]	[10, 15, 17, 33]	[1, 4, 7, 10, 12, 15, 17, 20, 33]
[2, 3, 5, 7]	[11, 13, 17]	[2, 3, 5, 7, 11, 13, 17]
[2, 3, 5, 7, 11]	[7, 11, 13, 17]	[2, 3, 5, 7, 7, 11 11, 13, 17]
[1, 2, 3]	∅ = []	[1, 2, 3]

Algorithm   First, you create an appropriately sized result array. After that, the two arrays are traversed; thereby the respective values are compared and the smaller element is transferred to the result. For assistance, you use two position pointers that refer to the respective value. If a value from array 1 is transferred to the result, then the position pointer of array 1 is increased, and the same is done for array 2. If the end of one or the other array is reached in the meantime, the remaining values from the other array can be transferred with ease.

```
static int[] merge(final int[] first, final int[] second)
{
    final int length1 = first.length;
    final int length2 = second.length;

    final int[] result = new int[length1 + length2];

    int pos1 = 0;
    int pos2 = 0;
    int idx = 0;

    // iterate as long as the two position pointers are below the
    // length of their arrays
    while (pos1 < length1 && pos2 < length2)
    {
        int value1 = first[pos1];
        int value2 = second[pos2];
```

```
    if (value1 < value2)
    {
        result[idx] = value1;

        idx++;
        pos1++;
    }
    else
    {
        result[idx] = value2;

        idx++;
        pos2++;
    }
}

// collect the remaining elementsf
while (pos1 < length1)
{
    result[idx] = first[pos1];

    idx++;
    pos1++;
}

while (pos2 < length2)
{
    result[idx] = second[pos2];

    idx++;
    pos2++;
}

    return result;
}
```

Mini optimization   As you can see clearly, the source code for adding the remainder from array 1 and array 2 to the result hardly differs. It is a good idea to move this functionality to the following helper method:

```
static void addRemaining(final int[] values, final int[] result,
                          int pos, int idx)
{
    while (pos < values.length)
    {
        result[idx] = values[pos];

        idx++;
        pos++;
    }
}
```

This simplifies the picking up of the elements as follows:

```
// Collect the remaining elements
addRemaining(first, result, pos1, idx);
addRemaining(second, result, pos2, idx);
```

The nice thing about this is that you don't have to distinguish whether you need to append the rest of one array or the other. You just invoke this helper method for both arrays, and the correct actions will happen automatically.

Verification

To check the functionality, you use the inputs from the introduction as usual:

```
@ParameterizedTest(name="{0} + {1} = {2}")
@MethodSource("createInputArraysAndExpected")
public void merge(int[] values1, int[] values2, int[] expected)
{
    int[] result = Ex11_MergeArrays.merge(values1, values2);

    assertArrayEquals(expected, result);
}

private static Stream<Arguments> createArraysAndExpected()
{
    int[] values1a = { 1, 4, 7, 12, 20 };
    int[] values1b = { 10, 15, 17, 33 };
    int[] result1 = { 1, 4, 7, 10, 12, 15, 17, 20, 33 };
```

```java
int[] values2a = { 2, 3, 5, 7 };
int[] values2b = { 11, 13, 17 };
int[] result2 = { 2, 3, 5, 7, 11, 13, 17 };

int[] values3a = { 2, 3, 5, 22 };
int[] values3b = { 7, 11, 13, 17 };
int[] result3 = { 2, 3, 5, 7, 11, 13, 17, 22 };

return Stream.of(Arguments.of(values1a, values1b, result1),
                 Arguments.of(values2a, values2b, result2),
                 Arguments.of(values3a, values3b, result3));
}
```

NOTE: COMPACTNESS VS. COMPREHENSIBILITY

For me, the most important thing in programming is developing small, comprehensible, and reusable building blocks. These blocks are often easy to understand due to their clarity, and therefore the probability for errors is reduced. Even better: Most of the time, these building blocks can also be easily tested by unit tests. However, this is partly at the expense of a compact notation. This is nevertheless quite desirable for frequently used libraries and to facilitate algorithm analyses.

Now let's consider a compact implementation style:

```java
public static int[] mergeCompact(final int[] first, final int[] second)
{
    final int[] result = new int[first.length + second.length];

    int idx1 = 0;
    int idx2 = 0;
    int destIdx = 0;

    while (idx1 < first.length && idx2 < second.length)
    {
        if (first[idx1] < second[idx2])
            result[destIdx++] = first[idx1++];
        else
            result[destIdx++] = second[idx2++];
    }
```

```
    while (idx1 < first.length)
        result[destIdx++] = first[idx1++];

    while (idx2 < second.length)
        result[destIdx++] = second[idx2++];
    return result;
}
```

Wow, that's pretty compact. However, you have to look a little closer at the analysis. With the solution derivation in mind, the whole thing is quite understandable. However, the post increments hidden in the assignments make it difficult to follow. In general, this is rather unattractive for business methods but quite tolerable for algorithms. While unit tests are almost always recommended, this is even more true for such implementations. This should make it easy to detect volatile errors.

5.3.12 Solution 12: Array Min and Max (★★☆☆☆)
Solution 12a: Min and Max (★☆☆☆☆)

Write two methods int findMin(int[]) and int findMax(int[]) that will find the minimum and maximum, respectively, of a given non-empty array using a self-implemented search—thus eliminating the usage of Math.min(), Arrays.sort(), and Arrays.stream().min() etc :-)

Examples

Input	Minimum	Maximum
[2, 3, 4, 5, 6, 7, 8, 9, 1, 10]	1	10

Algorithm   Loop through the array from the beginning. In both cases, assume that the first element is the minimum or maximum. After that, the array is traversed, and when a smaller or larger element is found, the minimum or maximum is reassigned.

```java
public static int findMin(final int[] values)
{
    if (values.length == 0)
        throw new IllegalArgumentException("values must not be empty");

    int min = values[0];
    for (int i = 1; i < values.length; i++)
    {
        if (values[i] < min)
            min = values[i];
    }
    return min;
}

public static int findMax(final int[] values)
{
    if (values.length == 0)
        throw new IllegalArgumentException("values must not be empty");

    int max = values[0];
    for (int i = 1; i < values.length; i++)
    {
        if (values[i] > max)
            max = values[i];
    }
    return max;
}
```

Due to the boundary constraint of a not-empty source array, you can always start with the first element as minimum or maximum.

Solution 12b: Min and Max Pos (★★☆☆)

Implement two helper methods int findMinPos(int[], int, int) and int findMaxPos(int[], int, int) that seek and return the position of the minimum and maximum, respectively, for a given non-empty array as well as an index range given as left and right boundaries. In the case of several identical values for minimum or maximum, the first occurrence should be returned. To find minimum and maximum respectively, write two methods int findMinByPos(int[], int, int) and int findMaxByPos(int[], int, int) that use the helper methods.

Examples

Method	Input	Range	Result	Position
findMinXyz()	[5, 3, 4, 2, 6, 7, 8, 9, 1, 10]	0, 10	1	8
findMinXyz()	[5, 3, 4, 2, 6, 7, 8, 9, 1, 10]	0, 7	2	3
findMinXyz()	[5, 3, 4, 2, 6, 7, 8, 9, 1, 10]	2, 7	2	3
findMaxXyz()	[1, 22, 3, 4, 5, 10, 7, 8, 9, 49]	0, 10	49	9
findMaxXyz()	[1, 22, 3, 4, 5, 10, 7, 8, 9, 49]	0, 7	22	1
findMaxXyz()	[1, 22, 3, 4, 5, 10, 7, 8, 9, 49]	2, 7	10	5

Algorithm   Based on the determined position of the minimum or maximum, the appropriate return of the corresponding element can be implemented trivially:

```
public static int findMinByPos(final int[] values, int start, int end)
{
    final int minPos = findMinPos(values, start, end);

    return values[minPos];
}

public static int findMaxByPos(int[] values, int start, int end)
{
    int maxPos = findMaxPos(values, start, end);

    return values[maxPos];
}
```

To complete the process, you still need to determine the position of the minimum and maximum. For this, you proceed as follows: To find the respective position of minimum and maximum, you go through all elements, compare with the current value for minimum or maximum, and update the position if the value is smaller or larger:

```java
static int findMinPos(final int[] values, final int startPos, final int endPos)
{
    int minPos = startPos;
    for (int i = startPos + 1; i < endPos; i++)
    {
        if (values[i] < values[minPos])
            minPos = i;
    }
    return minPos;
}

static int findMaxPos(final int[] values, final int startPos, final int endPos)
{
    int maxPos = startPos;
    for (int i = startPos + 1; i < endPos; i++)
    {
        if (values[i] > values[maxPos])
            maxPos = i;
    }
    return maxPos;
}
```

Verification

You test the functionality as usual with the inputs from the introduction:

```java
@Test
void findMinAndMax()
{
    final int[] values = { 2, 3, 4, 5, 6, 7, 8, 9, 1, 10 };

    assertAll(() -> assertEquals(1, Ex12_ArraysMinMax.findMin(values)), () ->
                assertEquals(10, Ex12_ArraysMinMax.findMax(values)));
}

@ParameterizedTest(name = "findMinPos([5, 3, 4, 2, 6, 7, 8, 9, 1, 10], " +
                "{0}, {1}) => {1}")
@CsvSource({ "0, 10, 8, 1", "2, 7, 3, 2", "0, 7, 3, 2" })
```

```
void findMinxPos(int lower, int upper, int expectedPos, int expectedValue)
{
    final int[] values = { 5, 3, 4, 2, 6, 7, 8, 9, 1, 10 };

    int resultPos = Ex12_ArraysMinMax.findMinPos(values, lower, upper);

    assertEquals(expectedPos, resultPos);
    assertEquals(expectedValue, values[resultPos]);
}

@ParameterizedTest(name = "findMaxPos([1, 22, 3, 4, 5, 10, 7, 8, 9, 49], " +
                    "{0}, {1}) => {1}")
@CsvSource({ "0, 10, 9, 49", "2, 7, 5, 10", "0, 7, 1, 22" })
void findMaxPos(int lower, int upper, int expectedPos, int expectedValue)
{
    final int[] values = { 1, 22, 3, 4, 5, 10, 7, 8, 9, 49 };

    int resultPos = Ex12_ArraysMinMax.findMaxPos(values, lower, upper);

    assertEquals(expectedPos, resultPos);
    assertEquals(expectedValue, values[resultPos]);
}
```

5.3.13 Solution 13: Array Split (★★★☆☆)

Consider an array of arbitrary integers. As a result, the array is to be reordered so that all values less than a special reference value are placed on the left. All values greater than or equal to the reference value are placed on the right. The ordering within the subranges is not relevant and may vary.

Examples

Input	Reference element	Sample result
[4, 7, 1, 20]	9	[1, 4, 7, **9**, 20]
[3, 5, 2]	7	[2, 3, 5, **7**]
[2, 14, 10, 1, 11, 12, 3, 4]	7	[2, 1, 3, 4, **7**, 14, 10, 11, 12]
[3, 5, 7, 1, 11, 13, 17, 19]	11	[1, 3, 5, 7, **11**, 11, 13, 17, 19]

Solution 13a: Array Split (★★☆☆☆)

Write method int[] arraySplit(int[], int) to implement the functionality. It is allowed to create new data structures, such as lists.

Algorithm   To split an array concerning a reference element into two halves with values less than or greater than or equal to the reference value, define two result lists named lesser and biggerOrEqual. Afterwards, you iterate through the array and populate one of the two lists for each element, depending on the comparison of the current element with the reference element. Finally, you only need to combine the lists and the reference element to one result list and convert it into a int[].

```java
static int[] arraySplit(final int[] values, final int referenceElement)
{
    final List<Integer> lesser = new ArrayList<>();
    final List<Integer> biggerOrEqual = new ArrayList<>();

    for (int i = 0; i < values.length; i++)
    {
        final int current = values[i];
        if (current < referenceElement)
            lesser.add(current);
        else
            biggerOrEqual.add(current);
    }

    final List<Integer> result = new ArrayList<>();
    result.addAll(lesser);
    result.add(referenceElement);
    result.addAll(biggerOrEqual);

    return result.stream().mapToInt(i -> i).toArray();
}
```

Solution 13b: Array Split Inplace (★★★☆☆)

Write method int[] arraySplitInplace(int[], int) that implements the described
functionality inside the source array (i.e., inplace). It is explicitly not desirable to create
new data structures. To be able to include the reference element in the result, the creation
of an array is allowed once. Because this has to be returned, it is exceptionally permitted to
return a value for a *inplace* method—indeed, it operates only partially inplace here.

Algorithm   You have started with the simpler version, which improved your
understanding of the processes, so now dare to try the inplace version. Here you cannot
use auxiliary data structures but rather you must implement the logic by swapping
elements several times. Two position markers indicate which elements are to be
swapped. The first position marker is increased as long as you find smaller values
than the reference element, starting from the beginning. You do the same with the
position marker for the upper part. As long as the values are larger than or equal to the
reference element, you decrease the position. Finally, you swap the two values at the
index positions found, but only if the position markers have not yet crossed. In that case,
you have found no more mismatching elements. The last thing to do is to integrate the
reference element at the correct position based on the newly arranged array.

```
static int[] arraySplitInplace(final int[] values, final int referenceElement)
{
    int low = 0;
    int high = values.length - 1;

    while (low < high)
    {
        while (low < high && values[low] < referenceElement)
            low++;

        while (high > low && values[high] >= referenceElement)
            high--;

        if (low < high)
            swap(values, low, high);
    }

    return integrateReferenceElement(values, high, referenceElement);
}
```

327

To integrate the reference element, it is recommended to write method int[] integrateReferenceElement(int[], int, int). There you first have to create an array that is larger by one element. This is filled from the original array as long as the passed position is not yet reached. The reference element is inserted at the position itself, and then any remaining values are copied from the original array. This results in the following implementation:

```
static int[] integrateReferenceElement(final int[] values,
                                        final int pos, final int
                                        referenceElement)
{
    final int[] result = new int[values.length + 1];

    // copy lower part in
    for (int i = 0; i < pos; i++)
        result[i] = values[i];

    // reference element
    result[pos] = referenceElement;

    // successor element, if available
    for (int i = pos + 1; i < values.length + 1; i++)
        result[i] = values[i - 1];

    return result;
}
```

Solution 13c: Array Split Quick Sort Partition (★★★☆☆)

For sorting, according to Quick Sort, you need a partitioning functionality similar to the one just developed. However, often the foremost element of the array is used as the reference element.

Based on the two previously developed implementations using an explicit reference element, now create corresponding alternatives such as the methods int[] arraySplit(int[]) and int[] arraySplitInplace(int[]).

Examples

Input	Reference element	Sample result
[**9**, 4, 7, 1, 20]	9	[1, 4, 7, **9**, 20]
[**7**, 3, 5, 2]	7	[2, 3, 5, **7**]
[**7**, 2, 14, 10, 1, 11, 12, 3, 4]	7	[2, 1, 3, 4, **7**, 14, 10, 11, 12]
[**11**, 3, 5, 7, 1, 11, 13, 17, 19]	11	[1, 3, 5, 7, **11**, 11, 13, 17, 19]

Algorithm 1   As a modification, the only thing that has to be taken into account in the implementation with two result lists is that the reference element is stored at position 0. Thus the processing starts at index 1.

```java
static int[] arraySplit(final int[] values)
{
    final List<Integer> lesser = new ArrayList<>();
    final List<Integer> biggerOrEqual = new ArrayList<>();

    final int referenceValue = values[0];
    for (int i = 1; i < values.length; i++)
    {
        final int current = values[i];
        if (current < referenceValue)
            lesser.add(current);
        else
            biggerOrEqual.add(current);
    }

    final List<Integer> result = new ArrayList<>();
    result.addAll(lesser);
    result.add(referenceValue);
    result.addAll(biggerOrEqual);

    return result.stream().mapToInt(i -> i).toArray();
}
```

Algorithm 2   The inplace variant also works with two position markers as before and swapping elements several times if necessary. This is repeated as long as the position markers have not yet crossed. In this particular situation, you no longer find any unsuitable elements. The last thing to do is to move the reference element from its position 0 to the crossover point (i.e., the matching position).

```
static void arraySplitInplace(final int[] values)
{
    final int referenceValue = values[0];

    int low = 1;
    int high = values.length - 1;

    while (low < high)
    {
        while (values[low] < referenceValue && low < high)
            low++;

        while (values[high] >= referenceValue && high >= low)
            high--;

        if (low < high)
            swap(values, low, high);
    }
    // important for 1,2 => then 1 would be pivot, do not swap!
    if (referenceValue > values[high])
        swap(values, 0, high);
}
```

The last special case is still a little disturbing. Sometimes special treatments are an indication that you can do even better. In fact, this is possible as follows:

```
static void arraySplitInplaceShorter(final int[] values)
{
    final int referenceValue = values[0];

    int left = 0;
    int right = values.length - 1;
```

```
    while (left < right)
    {
        while (values[left] < referenceValue && left < right)
                left++;
        while (values[right] > referenceValue && right > left)
                right--;

        swap(values, left, right);
    }
} '
```

The main difference is that the right position marker is moved only in the case of greater than and not in the case of greater than or equal.

Verification

You test the functionality as usual with the inputs from the introduction:

```
jshell> int[] values = {2, 14, 10, 1, 11, 12, 3, 4}

jshell> arraySplit(values, 7)
$56 ==> int[9] { 2, 1, 3, 4, 7, 14, 10, 11, 12 }

jshell> arraySplitInplace(values, 7)
$60 ==> int[9] { 2, 4, 3, 1, 7, 11, 12, 10, 14 }
```

Let's have a look at the Quick Sort variants in action:

```
jshell> int[] values2 = {7, 2, 14, 10, 1, 11, 3, 12, 4}

jshell> arraySplit(values2)
$68 ==> int[9] { 2, 1, 3, 4, 7, 14, 10, 11, 12 }

jshell> arraySplitInplace(values2)

jshell> values2
values2 ==> int[9] { 1, 2, 4, 3, 7, 11, 10, 12, 14 }

jshell> int[] values3 = {7, 2, 14, 10, 1, 11, 3, 12, 4}

jshell> arraySplitInplaceShorter(values3)
```

Due to the slightly different algorithm, the elements in the first variant remain in the order in which they appear in the original array. The inplace variants swap elements, and thus there is a reshuffle. However, all smaller values are still found to the left of the reference element and all larger ones to the right.

5.3.14 Solution 14: Minesweeper Board (★★★☆☆)

The chances are high that you've played Minesweeper in the past. To remind you, it's a nice little quiz game with a bit of puzzling. What is it about? Bombs are placed face down on a playing field. The player can now choose any field on the board. If a field is uncovered, it shows a number. This indicates how many bombs are hidden in the neighboring fields. However, if you are unlucky, you hit a bomb field, and the game is lost. This task is about initializing such a field and preparing it for a subsequent game.

Solution 14a (★★☆☆☆)

Write method `boolean[][] placeBombsRandomly(int, int, double)` that creates a playing field as `boolean[][]` specified in size via the first two parameters, randomly filled with *bombs*, respecting the probability from 0.0 to 1.0 passed as `double`.

Example

A playing field of size 16 × 7 is shown here, with bombs placed randomly. Bombs are represented by * and spaces with . as you can see.

```
* * * . * * . * . * * . * . . .
. * * . * . . * . * * . . . . .
. . * . . . . . . . . . * * * *
. . . * . * * . * * . * * . . .
* * . . . . * . * . . * . . . *
. . * . . * . * * . . * . * * *
. * . * * . * . * * * . . * * .
```

Algorithm   The algorithm for placing randomly distributed bombs in a playing field works as follows: For each position, a random number generated with `Math.random()` and a given probability are used to determine whether a bomb should be placed on the board. As a result, a suitable boolean[][] is generated. Here, the peculiarity is found, namely the playing field extended in all directions by one position each, as it is thematized in the following practical tip.

```java
static boolean[][] placeBombsRandomly(final int width, final int height,
                                      final double probability)
{
    final boolean[][] bombs = new boolean[height + 2][width + 2];

    for (int i = 1; i < bombs.length - 1; i++)
    {
        for (int j = 1; j < bombs[0].length - 1; j++)
        {
            bombs[i][j] = (Math.random() < probability);
        }
    }
    return bombs;
}
```

NOTE: PLAYFIELD WITH BORDER

For many two-dimensional algorithms, it is necessary to perform special checks on the edges. In some cases, it is helpful to place a border of one position around the actual playfield. In particular, this can simplify calculations with neighboring cells in all compass directions, as is the case here with the bombs. But then you have to assign a neutral value to the border cells. Here this is simply the value 0. Sometimes, however, special characters like # can be used with char-based playfields.

Some calculations become easier with this artificial boundary cell. However, you must then note that the bounds range from 1 to length − 1—an additional stumbling block to the treacherous off-by-one errors commonly made with arrays.

Verification

You omit explicit testing and trial and error here because, on the one hand, you are dealing with random numbers, and a unit test does not directly make sense for this. On the other hand, the algorithm is quite simple, and the functionality is tested indirectly later.

Solution 14b (★★★☆☆)

Write method int[][] calcBombCount(boolean[][]) that, based on the bomb fields passed as boolean[][], computes the number of adjacent fields with bombs and returns a corresponding array.

Examples

A calculation for playing fields of size 3×3 as well as size 5×5, including randomly distributed bombs, results in the following:

```
*  .  .           B  2  1       .  *  *  .  .          2  B  B  3  1
.  .  *    =>     1  3  B       *  .  *  *  .          B  6  B  B  1
.  .  *           0  2  B       *  *  .  .  .    =>    B  B  4  3  2
                                *  .  .  *  .          B  6  4  B  1
                                *  *  *  .  .          B  B  B  2  1
```

Algorithm   To calculate the number of neighboring cells with bombs, you again consider each cell in turn. Here you take advantage of the special margin, so you don't have to do range checks or special handling. First, you initialize a int[][] of appropriate size with a value of 0 as an assumption that there are no bombs in the neighborhood. If a cell represents a bomb, you use the value 9 as an indicator. If it does not contain one, you must check all eight neighboring cells to see if they are home to a bomb. In this case, the counter is increased by one. This is facilitated by the use of the already known enumeration for the compass directions and their delta values in x- and y-direction.

```java
static int[][] calcBombCount(final boolean[][] bombs)
{
    final int[][] bombCount = new int[bombs.length][bombs[0].length];

    for (int y = 1; y < bombs.length - 1; y++)
    {
        for (int x = 1; x < bombs[0].length - 1; x++)
        {
            if (!bombs[y][x])
            {
```

```
            for (final Direction currentDir : Direction.values())
            {
                if (bombs[y + currentDir.dy][x + currentDir.dx])
                    bombCount[y][x]++;
            }
        }
        else
            bombCount[y][x] = 9;
        }
    }
    return bombCount;
}
```

For better comprehension, the enum enumeration Direction is shown here again:

```
enum Direction
{
    N(0, -1), NE(1, -1), E(1, 0), SE(1, 1),
    S(0, 1), SW(-1, 1), W(-1, 0), NW(-1, -1);

    int dx;

    int dy;

    private Direction(int dx, int dy)
    {
        this.dx = dx;
        this.dy = dy;
    }
}
```

Verification

To check the implementation, you use the 3×3 distribution, but you have to consider the boundary cells accordingly. However, everything is based on a boolean[][]. Wouldn't it be more practical to work on graphical representations and have them convert appropriately? Let's consider this as a unit test:

```java
@ParameterizedTest
@MethodSource("createBombArrayAndExpected")
public void calcBombCount(boolean[][] bombs, int[][] expected)
{
    int[][] result = Ex14_Minesweeper.calcBombCount(bombs);

    assertArrayEquals(expected, result);
}

private static Stream<Arguments> createBombArrayAndExpected()
{
    String[] bombs1 = { "*..",
                        "..*",
                        "..*" };

    String[] result1 = { "B21",
                         "13B",
                         "02B" };

    String[] bombs2 = { ".**..",
                        "*.**.",
                        "**...",
                        "*..*.",
                        "***.."};

    String[] result2 = { "2BB31",
                         "B6BB1",
                         "BB432",
                         "B64B1",
                         "BBB21"};

    return Stream.of(Arguments.of(toBoolArray(bombs1), toIntArray(result1)),
                     Arguments.of(toBoolArray(bombs2), toIntArray(result2)));
}

// hiding the border field logic and conversion
static boolean[][] toBoolArray(final String[] bombs)
{
    final int width = bombs[0].length();
```

```
    final int height = bombs.length;
    final boolean[][] result = new boolean[height + 2][width + 2];

    for (int y = 0; y < height; y++)
    {
        for (int x = 0; x < width; x ++)
        {
            if (bombs[y].charAt(x) == '*')
                result[y + 1][x + 1] = true;
        }
    }
    return result;
}
```

The helper method toIntArray() looks like this:

```
static int[][] toIntArray(final String[] values)
{
    final int width = values[0].length();
    final int height = values.length;
    final int[][] result = new int[height + 2][width + 2];

    for (int y = 0; y < height; y++)
    {
        for (int x = 0; x < width; x ++)
        {
            final char currentChar = values[y].charAt(x);
            if (currentChar == 'B')
                result[y + 1][x + 1] = 9;
            else
                result[y + 1][x + 1] = Character.
                getNumericValue(currentChar);
        }
    }
    return result;
}
```

Let's look again at the helper methods: First, you have a textual representation of the distribution of bombs, which is converted into the array data structure required by the functionality using toBoolArray(). In doing so, you don't have to worry about generating the boundary fields. The helper method toIntArray() takes it one step further and converts the textual digits into the corresponding int values and takes into account the representation of bombs as B specifically.

HINT: READABILITY AND COMPREHENSIBILITY IN TESTING

These two helper methods enable the creation of test cases to be kept simple and understandable. This makes it more likely that someone will extend the tests. If, on the other hand, writing unit tests is rather tedious or even difficult, hardly anyone will bother to extend them.

Solution 14c (★★☆☆☆)

Write method void printBoard(boolean[][], char, int[][]) that allows you to display a board as points and stars as well as numbers and B.

Example

Shown here is the above playing field of size 16 × 7 with all the calculated values for bomb neighbors:

```
B B B 4 B B 3 B 4 B B 3 B 1 0 0
3 B B 5 B 3 3 B 4 B B 4 3 4 3 2
1 3 B 4 3 3 3 4 4 4 4 B B B B
2 3 3 B 2 B B 4 B B 3 B B 4 4 3
B B 3 2 3 4 B 6 B 4 4 B 5 3 4 B
3 4 B 3 3 B 4 B B 5 4 B 4 B B B
1 B 3 B B 3 B 4 B B B 2 3 B B 3
```

Algorithm   For rendering, you use position-based processing. Since you want to implement both an output based on a boolean[][] and—if passed—the values of the number of bomb neighbors in this method, a few cases have to be provided in addition to the loops nested for the x- and the y-direction:

```
static void printBoard(final boolean[][] bombs,
                       final char bombSymbol,
                       final int[][] solution)
{
    for (int y = 1; y < bombs.length - 1; y++)
    {
        for (int x = 1; x < bombs[0].length - 1; x++)
        {
            if (bombs[y][x])
                System.out.print(bombSymbol + " ");
            else if (solution != null && solution.length != 0)
                System.out.print(solution[y][x] + " ");
            else
                System.out.print(". ");
        }
        System.out.println();
    }
    System.out.println();
}
```

Verification

Combine your three methods to experience the functionality in its entirety:

```
jshell> var bombs = placeBombsRandomly(16, 7, 0.4)

jshell> printBoard(bombs, '*', new int[0][0])
* * * . * * . * . * * . * . . .
. * * . * . . * . * * . . . . .
. . * . . . . . . . . * * * *
. . . * . * * . * * . * * . . .
* * . . . . * . * . . * . . . *
. . * . . * . * * . . * . * * *
. * . * * . * . * * * . . * * .
```

```
jshell> int[][] solution = calcBombCount(bombs)

jshell> printBoard(bombs, 'B', solution)
B B B 4 B B 3 B 4 B B 3 B 1 0 0
3 B B 5 B 3 3 B 4 B B 4 3 4 3 2
1 3 B 4 3 3 3 3 4 4 4 B B B B
2 3 3 B 2 B B 4 B B 3 B B 4 4 3
B B 3 2 3 4 B 6 B 4 4 B 5 3 4 B
3 4 B 3 3 B 4 B B 5 4 B 4 B B B
1 B 3 B B 3 B 4 B B B 2 3 B B 3
```

## CHAPTER 6

Date Processing

With Java 8, the JDK was extended with some functionality for date processing. First, the rather unintuitive machine time exists, which proceeds linearly and is represented by the class `java.time.Instant`. However, various classes are better suited to human ways of thinking. For example, the classes `LocalDate`, `LocalTime`, and `LocalDateTime` from the package `java.time` represent date values without time zones in the form of a date, a time, and a combination thereof.

6.1 Introduction

In the following, I will describe some enumerations, classes, and interfaces from different packages under `java.time` before moving on to the exercises.

6.1.1 The Enumerations DayOfWeek and Month

Using the enumerations `java.time.DayOfWeek` and `java.time.Month` provides good readability and avoids errors because you can use type-safe constants instead of magic numbers. In addition, calculations are possible with these enumeration types. I will demonstrate this in the `MonthAndDayOfTheWeekExample` as follows by adding 5 days to a Sunday and 13 months to February by calling `plus()`:

```
public static void main(final String[] args)
{
    final DayOfWeek sunday = DayOfWeek.SUNDAY;
    final Month february = Month.FEBRUARY;

    System.out.println(sunday.plus(5));
    System.out.println(february.plus(13));
}
```

© Michael Inden 2022
M. Inden, *Java Challenges*, https://doi.org/10.1007/978-1-4842-7395-1_6

As expected, you will end up on a Friday or in March, if you execute the program:

```
FRIDAY
MARCH
```

6.1.2 The Classes LocalDate, LocalTime, and LocalDateTime

As mentioned, the representation of time information in milliseconds, which is helpful for computer processing, has very little to do with the human way of thinking and their orientation in the time system. Humans prefer to think in terms of time periods or recurring dates, for example, 12/24 for Christmas Eve, 12/31 for New Year's Eve, etc. (i.e., dates without time and year). Sometimes you need *incomplete time information*, like times without reference to a date, such as 6:00 after work, or as a combination, like Tuesdays and Thursdays 7 p.m. Karate training.[1] Expressing something similar with the API that existed before Java 8 was quite difficult. Let's now take a look at the possibilities since JDK 8.

The class LocalDate represents a piece of date information consisting only of year, month, and day without time information. The class LocalTime models a time without date information (e.g. 6:00). The class LocalDateTime is a combination of both. The LocalDateAndTimeExample program shows the usage of these classes and how easy and meaningful date arithmetic can be implemented. You see the query of a weekday as well as that of the day in the month or in the year, which have expressive method names in each case:

```
public static void main(final String[] args)
{
    final LocalDate michasBirthday = LocalDate.of(1971, Month.FEBRUARY, 7);
    final LocalDate barbarasBirthday = michasBirthday.plusYears(2).
                                       plusMonths(1).
                                       plusDays(17);
    final LocalDate lastDayInFebruary = michasBirthday.with(TemporalAdjusters.
                                       lastDayOfMonth());
```

---

[1] In particular, you are usually not interested in the time zone in which the appointments take place— except for telephone appointments with overseas business partners, for example.

```
System.out.println("michasBirthday:    " + michasBirthday);
System.out.println("barbarasBirthday:  " + barbarasBirthday);
System.out.println("lastDayInFebruary: " + lastDayInFebruary);

final LocalTime atTen = LocalTime.of(10,00,00);
final LocalTime tenFifteen = atTen.plusMinutes(15);
final LocalTime breakfastTime = tenFifteen.minusHours(2);

System.out.println("\natTen:        " + atTen);
System.out.println("tenFifteen:      " + tenFifteen);
System.out.println("breakfastTime: " + breakfastTime);

System.out.println("\nDay Of Week: " + michasBirthday.getDayOfWeek());
System.out.println("Day Of Month:  " + michasBirthday.getDayOfMonth());
System.out.println("Day Of Year:   " + michasBirthday.getDayOfYear());
}
```

The code shows several calculations using the plusXyz() and minusXyz() methods. You also use the utility class TemporalAdjusters, in which various utility methods are defined. This is, for example, the method lastDayOfMonth() to determine the last day of the month, here to calculate the last day of February in 1971. Executing the program produces the following output:

```
michasBirthday:    1971-02-07
barbarasBirthday:  1973-03-24
lastDayInFebruary: 1971-02-28

atTen:             10:00
tenFifteen:        10:15
breakfastTime:     08:15

Day Of Week:    SUNDAY
Day Of Month:   7
Day Of Year:    38
```

Extensions in the LocalDate Class with Java 9

With JDK 9, the class LocalDate got an overloaded method called datesUntil(). It creates a Stream<LocalDate> between two LocalDate instances and allows you to optionally specify a step size.

The DatesUntilExample uses the author's birthday and Christmas Eve of the same year to demonstrate calculations with the datesUntil() method:

```
public static void main(final String[] args)
{
    final LocalDate myBirthday = LocalDate.of(1971, Month.FEBRUARY, 7);
    final LocalDate christmas = LocalDate.of(1971, Month.DECEMBER, 24);

    System.out.println("Day-Stream");
    final Stream<LocalDate> daysUntil = myBirthday.datesUntil(christmas);
    daysUntil.skip(150).limit(4).forEach(System.out::println);

    System.out.println("\n3-Month-Stream");
    final Stream<LocalDate> monthsUntil =
                    myBirthday.datesUntil(christmas, Period.ofMonths(3));
    monthsUntil.limit(3).forEach(System.out::println);
}
```

If you execute the program, it jumps 150 days into the future, starting from February 7, which brings us to July 7. Then you get four values from a stream of days:

```
Day-Stream
1971-07-07
1971-07-08
1971-07-09
1971-07-10
```

On top of that, the second output shows the default of an increment, here three months. Starting from February 7, two more dates into the future are listed in addition to this date:

```
3-Month-Stream
1971-02-07
1971-05-07
1971-08-07
```

6.1.3 The Class ZonedDateTime

In addition to the class LocalDateTime for representing date and time without time zone reference, there is a class called java.time.ZonedDateTime. It includes a time zone, and calculations take into account not only the time zone but also the effects of summer and winter time.

The ZonedDateTimeExample program shows several examples of calculations with the class ZonedDateTime, in particular also a change of year, month, and day in two variants as well as with a different time zone:

```
public static void main(final String[] args)
{
    // determine current time as ZonedDateTime object
    final ZonedDateTime someDay = ZonedDateTime.of(LocalDate.
                                    parse("2020-02-07"),
                                    LocalTime.parse("17:30:15"),
                                    ZoneId.of("Europe/Zurich"));

    // modify the time and save it in a new object
    final ZonedDateTime someDayChangedTime = someDay.withHour(11).
    withMinute(44);

    // create new object with completely changed date
    final ZonedDateTime dateAndTime = someDayChangedTime.withYear(2008).
                                            withMonth(9).
                                            withDayOfMonth(29);

    // using a month constant and changing the time zone
    final ZonedDateTime dateAndTime2 = someDayChangedTime.withYear(2008).
                                withMonth(Month.SEPTEMBER.getValue()).
                                withDayOfMonth(29).
                                withZoneSameInstant(ZoneId.of("GMT"));

    System.out.println("someDay:        " + someDay);
    System.out.println("-> 11:44:       " + someDayChangedTime);
    System.out.println("-> 29.9.2008:   " + dateAndTime);
    System.out.println("-> 29.9.2008:   " + dateAndTime2);
}
```

Running the program will initially start in the year 2020 but then change to the year 2008, which results in the following outputs. They especially show the influence of summer and winter time, whereby in September 2008, the deviation of +02:00 is indicated. What this refers to can then be spotted by changing the time zone to GMT.

```
someDay:       2020-02-07T17:30:15+01:00[Europe/Zurich]
-> 11:44:      2020-02-07T11:44:15+01:00[Europe/Zurich]
-> 29.9.2008:  2008-09-29T11:44:15+02:00[Europe/Zurich]
-> 29.9.2008:  2008-09-29T09:44:15Z[GMT]
```

6.1.4 The class ZoneId

Now let's learn about time zone processing through an example. First, based on some textual time zone identifiers, you determine the corresponding ZoneId instance by calling ZoneId.of(String) and constructing a ZonedDateTime object out of each. Then you call ZoneId.getAvailableZoneIds() to retrieve all available time zones. Using streams and the two methods filter() and limit() you get three candidates from Europe:

```
public static void main(final String[] args)
{
    final Stream<String> zoneIdNames = Stream.of("Africa/Nairobi",
                                                 "Europe/Zurich",
                                                 "America/Los_Angeles");

    zoneIdNames.forEach(zoneIdName ->
    {
        final ZoneId zoneId = ZoneId.of(zoneIdName);
        var someDay = ZonedDateTime.of(LocalDate.parse("2020-04-05"),
                                       LocalTime.parse("17:30:15"),
                                       zoneId);

        System.out.println(zoneIdName + ": " + someDay);
    });

    final Set<String> allZones = ZoneId.getAvailableZoneIds();
    final Predicate<String> inEurope = name -> name.startsWith("Europe/");
```

```
final List<String> threeFromEurope = allZones.stream().
                                  filter(inEurope).limit(3).
                                  collect(Collectors.toList());

System.out.println("\nSome timezones in europe:");
threeFromEurope.forEach(System.out::println);
}
```

The program, ZoneIdExample, produces the following output:

```
Africa/Nairobi: 2020-04-05T17:30:15+03:00[Africa/Nairobi] Europe/
Zurich: 2020-04-05T17:30:15+02:00[Europe/Zurich] America/Los_Angeles:
2020-04-05T17:30:15-07:00[America/Los_Angeles]

Some timezones in europe:
Europe/London
Europe/Brussels
Europe/Warsaw
```

6.1.5 The Class Duration

The class java.time.Duration allows for specifying a duration in nanoseconds. Instances of the class Duration can be constructed by calling various methods (e.g., from values of different time units[2]) as follows:

```
public static void main(final String[] args)
{
    // creation with ofXyz() methods
    final Duration durationFromNanos = Duration.ofNanos(3);
    final Duration durationFromMillis = Duration.ofMillis(7);
    final Duration durationFromSeconds = Duration.ofSeconds(15);
    final Duration durationFromMinutes = Duration.ofMinutes(30);
    final Duration durationFromHours = Duration.ofHours(45);
    final Duration durationFromDays = Duration.ofDays(60);
```

---

[2]Variable length time units, such as months, are not supported.

```
    System.out.println("From Nanos:    " + durationFromNanos);
    System.out.println("From Millis:   " + durationFromMillis);;
    System.out.println("From Seconds:  " + durationFromSeconds);
    System.out.println("From Minutes:  " + durationFromMinutes);
    System.out.println("From Hours:    " + durationFromHours);
    System.out.println("From Days:     " + durationFromDays);
}
```

If you run this program, `DurationExample`, you get the output shown below, wherein particular the following things are of interest: Time differences are apparently represented at a minimum in the time unit of seconds and maximum in the time unit of hours, resulting in the value of 1440 hours for 60 days:

```
From Nanos:     PT0.000000003S
From Millis:    PT0.007S
From Secs:      PT15S
From Minutes:   PT30M
From Hours:     PT45H
From Days:      PT1440H
```

When looking at this output, you might be irritated by the string representation of `Duration`. This may seem a bit unusual at first. However, it follows the ISO 8601 standard. The output always starts with the abbreviation PT.[3] After that, there are sections for hours (H), minutes (M), and seconds (S). If necessary, milliseconds or even nanoseconds are displayed as decimal numbers.

In addition, simple calculations can be performed with the `between()` method, which calculates a `Duration` from the difference of two `Instant` objects. As another special feature, there are `with()` methods that return a new instance of a `Duration`, with suitably modified timings. In contrast, while multiple cascading calls to `ofXyz()` are possible, they result in the last *winning*, so only that one is decisive. See the following section for more on this.

---

[3] See http://en.wikipedia.org/wiki/ISO_8601#Durations; this results from the historical naming Period, so P, and the T stands for Time.

6.1.6 The Class Period

Similar to the class Duration the class java.time.Period models a period of time, but with a longer duration. Examples are *2 months* or *3 days*. Let's construct a few instances of Period:

```java
public static void main(final String[] args)
{
    // create a Period with 1 year, 6 months and 3 days
    final Period oneYear_sixMonths_ThreeDays = Period.ofYears(1).withMonths(6).
                                                            withDays(3);

    // chaining of() works differently than you might expect!
    // results in a Period with 3 days instead of 2 months, 1 week and 3 days
    final Period twoMonths_OneWeek_ThreeDays = Period.ofMonths(2).ofWeeks(1).
                                                            ofDays(3);

    final Period twoMonths_TenDays = Period.ofMonths(2).withDays(10);
    final Period sevenWeeks = Period.ofWeeks(7);
    final Period threeDays = Period.ofDays(3);

    System.out.println("1 year 6 months ...:    " + oneYear_sixMonths_
                                                ThreeDays);
    System.out.println("Surprise just 3 days:   " + twoMonths_OneWeek_
                                                ThreeDays);
    System.out.println("2 months 10 days:       " + twoMonths_TenDays);
    System.out.println("sevenWeeks:             " + sevenWeeks);
    System.out.println("threeDays:              " + threeDays);
}
```

If you run this program, PeriodExample, the output is as follows:

```
1 year 6 months ...:  P1Y6M3D
Surprise just 3 days: P3D
2 months 10 days:     P2M10D
sevenWeeks:           P49D
threeDays:            P3D
```

From the example and its output, you learn a few things about the class `Period`. First, there is the somewhat cryptic string representation once again, which follows ISO 8601. Here P is the start abbreviation (for Period) and then Y stands for years, M for months, and D for days. As a special feature, there is also the conversion for weeks: P14D stands for 2 weeks. It could be generated by `Period.ofWeeks(2)` for example. Furthermore, negative offsets are also allowed, for example, P-2M4D.

Besides these details of the output, you see that calls to `ofXyz()` can be executed consecutively—but the last invoked one wins, which is logical if you know that `ofXyz()` are static methods. Therefore, you cannot combine time periods in this way; instead, you specify an initial time period. If you want to add more time periods, you have to use different `withXyz()` methods. This reveals an implementation detail. The class `Period` manages three single values, namely for years, months, and days, but not for weeks. Thus there is no method `withWeeks()`, only an `ofWeeks()`, which internally performs a conversion to days.

6.1.7 Date Arithmetic

To complete your knowledge, you will get in touch with more complex calculations, such as jumping to the beginning of the month or a few days or even months into the future or the past. Conveniently, various useful operations of date arithmetic are bundled in the utility class `TemporalAdjusters` from the package `java.time.temporal`. The example for the classes `LocalDate`, `LocalTime`, and `LocalDateTime` delivered a first impression of the possibilities. Now you want to expand this knowledge.

Predefined TemporalAdjusters

The utility class `TemporalAdjusters` provides a set of common date arithmetic operations. Some examples are as follows:

- `firstDayOfMonth()`, `firstDayOfNextMonth()`, and `lastDayOfMonth()` calculate the first or last day in the (next) month.

- `firstDayOfYear()`, `firstDayOfNextYear()`, and `lastDayOfYear()` determine the first or last day in the (next) year.

- `firstInMonth(DayOfWeek)` and `lastInMonth(DayOfWeek)` jump to the first or last day of the week in the month.

- next(DayOfWeek), nextOrSame(DayOfWeek), previous(DayOfWeek), and previousOrSame(DayOfWeek) calculate the next or previous day of the week, such as the next Friday. They may also take into account whether you are already on that day of the week. In this case, of course, no adjustment takes place.

More Specific Predefined TemporalAdjusters

The previously mentioned TemporalAdjusters are sufficient for many use cases. If you need more flexibility, there are two more methods:

- dayOfWeekInMonth(int, DayOfWeek) calculates the nth day of the week in the month. Thereby it also jumps over month boundaries, for example, if an attempt was made to determine the (non-existent) 7th Tuesday of a month. Besides, negative values are allowed, whereby the values 0 and -1 carry special meanings. 0 determines the last desired weekday in the previous month and -1 the last desired weekday in this month. The negative values move back by the given number of weeks starting from the month's last weekday.

- ofDateAdjuster(UnaryOperator<LocalDate>) creates TemporalAdjusters. The desired calculations are described using a UnaryOperator<LocalDate>. This allows many calculations, for example, using the lambda date -> date.plusDays(5) jumps five days into the future.

Example

For clarification, let's look at one more example. Here you perform some time jumps to the beginning and the end of the month, as well as to different days of the week:

```
public static void main(final String[] args)
{
    final LocalDate michasBirthday = LocalDate.of(1971, Month.FEBRUARY, 7);

    var firstDayInFebruary =
        michasBirthday.with(TemporalAdjusters.firstDayOfMonth());
    var lastDayInFebruary =
        michasBirthday.with(TemporalAdjusters.lastDayOfMonth());
```

```
var previousMonday =
    michasBirthday.with(TemporalAdjusters.previous(DayOfWeek.MONDAY));
var nextFriday =
    michasBirthday.with(TemporalAdjusters.next(DayOfWeek.FRIDAY));

System.out.println("michasBirthday:     " + michasBirthday);
System.out.println("firstDayInFebruary: " + firstDayInFebruary);
System.out.println("lastDayInFebruary:  " + lastDayInFebruary);
System.out.println("previousMonday:     " + previousMonday);
System.out.println("nextFriday:         " + nextFriday);
}
```

In the code you see various calculations using `TemporalAdjusters`, such as invoking the method `lastDayOfMonth()` to determine the last day in the month, here to determine the last day of February in 1971. These calculations are applied calling `with()` on the respective `LocalDate`.

Running the `TemporalAdjustersExample` program produces the following output:

```
michasBirthday:     1971-02-07
firstDayInFebruary: 1971-02-01
lastDayInFebruary:  1971-02-28
previousMonday:     1971-02-01
nextFriday:         1971-02-12
```

Example: Define TemporalAdjuster Yourself

Indeed, the possibilities of the predefined `TemporalAdjusters` are already impressive and should be sufficient for various use cases. Nevertheless, sometimes you may want to create your own variants. Let's have a look at the example `FridayAfterMidOfMonth`. Here, starting from a `LocalDate`, you want to jump to the Friday after the middle of the month. For this, the method `Temporal adjustInto(Temporal)` has to be implemented suitably. The only hurdle is to get a `LocalDate` from the passed `Temporal`. This can be achieved by invoking `LocalDate.from()`. After that, you have to jump to the 15th day of the month (or the 14th for February), which is easily done by calling `withDayOfMonth()`. Finally, you apply one of the predefined adjusters with `nextOrSame(DayOfWeek)`.

```java
public class FridayAfterMidOfMonth implements TemporalAdjuster
{
    @Override
    public Temporal adjustInto(final Temporal temporal)
    {
        final LocalDate startday = LocalDate.from(temporal);

        final int dayOfMonth = startday.getMonth() == Month.FEBRUARY ? 14 : 15;

        return startday.withDayOfMonth(dayOfMonth).
                        with(TemporalAdjusters.nextOrSame(DayOfWeek.FRIDAY));
    }
}
```

It's pretty remarkable how easy it is to implement functionality if you use the appropriate APIs.

To try it out in the JShell you need the following imports:

```
jshell> import java.time.*
```

```
jshell> import java.time.temporal.*
```

Now you can define the above class there and call it, for example, as follows:

```
jshell> LocalDate feb7 = LocalDate.of(2020, 2, 7) feb7 ==> 2020-02-07
```

```
jshell> var adjustedDay = feb7.with(new FridayAfterMidOfMonth())
adjustedDay ==> 2020-02-14
```

```
jshell> adjustedDay.getDayOfWeek()
$17 ==> FRIDAY
```

```
jshell> LocalDate mar24 = LocalDate.of(2020, 3, 24)
mar24 ==> 2020-03-24
```

```
jshell> var adjustedDay2 = mar24.with(new FridayAfterMidOfMonth())
adjustedDay2 ==> 2020-03-20
```

```
jshell> adjustedDay2.getDayOfWeek()
$22 ==> FRIDAY
```

6.1.8 Formatting and Parsing

The class java.time.format.DateTimeFormatter is useful for formatted output and parsing of date values. In addition to various predefined formats, you can also provide a wide variety of your own variants. This is made possible by invoking the methods ofPattern() as well as ofLocalizedDate() and parse() with the specification of a format. Here, it is conveniently possible to specify a more complex pattern for formatting and even use it for parsing. This is demonstrated in the following code, executable as FormattingAndParsingExample. Various other possibilities exist but cannot be presented here. Therefore it is recommended to take a look at the detailed documentation of the JDK.

```java
public static void main(final String[] args)
{
    // definition of some special formatters
    final DateTimeFormatter ddMMyyyyFormat = ofPattern("dd.MM.yyyy");
    final DateTimeFormatter italiandMMMMy = ofPattern("d.MMMM y",
                                                   Locale.ITALIAN);
    final DateTimeFormatter shortGerman =
                    DateTimeFormatter.ofLocalizedDate(FormatStyle.SHORT).
                    withLocale(Locale.GERMAN);

    // attention: the textual parts are to be enclosed in quotation marks
    final String customPattern = "'Der 'dd'. Tag im 'MMMM' im Jahr 'yy'.'";
    final DateTimeFormatter customFormat = ofPattern(customPattern);

    System.out.println("Formatting:\n");
    final LocalDate february7th = LocalDate.of(1971, 2, 7);

    System.out.println("ddMMyyyyFormat: " + ddMMyyyyFormat.format(february7th));
    System.out.println("italiandMMMMy:  " + italiandMMMMy.format(february7th));
    System.out.println("shortGerman:    " + shortGerman.format(february7th));
    System.out.println("customFormat:   " + customFormat.format(february7th));
```

```
    // Parsing date values
    System.out.println("\nParsing:\n");

    final LocalDate fromIsoDate = LocalDate.parse("1971-02-07");
    final LocalDate fromddMMyyyyFormat = LocalDate.parse("18.03.2014",
                                                  ddMMyyyyFormat);
    final LocalDate fromShortGerman = LocalDate.parse("18.03.14",
                                                  shortGerman);
    final LocalDate fromCustomFormat =
                    LocalDate.parse("Der 31. Tag im Dezember im Jahr 19.",
                                customFormat);

    System.out.println("From ISO Date:         " + fromIsoDate);
    System.out.println("From ddMMyyyyFormat:   " + fromddMMyyyyFormat);
    System.out.println("From short german:     " + fromShortGerman);
    System.out.println("From custom format:    " + fromCustomFormat);
}
```

This program produces the following output, which provides an initial grasp of formatting and parsing:

```
Formatting:

ddMMyyyyFormat:  07.02.1971
italian_dMMMMy:  7.febbraio 1971
shortGerman:     07.02.71
customFormat:    Der 07. Tag im Februar im Jahr 71.

Parsing:

From ISO Date:          1971-02-07
From ddMMyyyyFormat:    2014-03-18
From short german:      2014-03-18
From custom format:     2019-12-31
```

6.2 Exercises

6.2.1 Exercise 1: Leap Years (★☆☆☆☆)

While in our calendar the year is usually divided into 365 days, this is not quite correct astronomically. The year has a length of about 365.25 days. Due to this, a correction is necessary almost every 4 years by using a leap year with 366 days. There are two special aspects to be considered:

- Years divisible by 100 are called secular years and are not leap years.

- However, secular years that are also divisible by 400 are leap years after all.

For details, see `https://en.wikipedia.org/wiki/Leap_year`. Write method `boolean isLeap(int)`—without using `java.time.Year.isLeap()`, of course.

Examples

Input	Rule	Result
1900	Secular year	No leap year
2000	Secular years, but divisible by 400	Leap year
2020	Divisible by 4	Leap year

6.2.2 Exercise 2: Basic Knowledge Date-API (★★☆☆☆)

Exercise 2a: Creation (★☆☆☆☆)

Represent your birthday as `LocalDate`, the end of work 5:30pm as `LocalTime` and now as `LocalDateTime`. Further, model a time span of 1 year, 10 months, and 20 days, and a duration of 7 hours and 15 minutes.

Exercise 2b: Time Durations (★★☆☆☆)

Calculate the duration of time between today and your birthday and vice versa.

6.2.3 Exercise 3: Length of Month (★★☆☆☆)

Exercise 3a: Calculations (★☆☆☆☆)

Jump starting from 2/2/2012 and from 2/2/2014, as well as from 4/4/2014 and 5/5/2014 with the method plusMonths() of the class LocalDate one month into the future and output the date in each case.

Exercise 3b: Length of Month (★★☆☆☆)

For the calculations, what happens if instead of using plusMonths() you use the method plusDays()? What corresponds to a month: 28, 29, 30, or 31 days? How do you to determine the correct length of a month?

6.2.4 Exercise 4: Time Zones (★★☆☆☆)

Get all time zones starting with America/L or Europe/S and fill a sorted set accordingly. For this purpose, write method Set<String> selectedAmericanAndEuropeanTimeZones().

Example

The computed set should contain the following values:

[America/La_Paz, America/Lima, America/Los_Angeles, America/Louisville, America/Lower_Princes, Europe/Samara, Europe/San_Marino, Europe/Sarajevo, Europe/Saratov, Europe/Simferopol, Europe/Skopje, Europe/Sofia, Europe/Stockholm]

Tip   Use the class ZoneId and its method getAvailableZoneIds(). Utilize streams and the filter-map-reduce framework to find the time zone IDs matching the previously specified prefixes.

6.2.5 Exercise 5: Time Zone Calculation (★★☆☆☆)

If a flight from Zurich to San Francisco takes 11 hours and 50 minutes and departs at 1:10 p.m. on 9/15/2019, what local time does it arrive in San Francisco? What time does that correspond to at the departure point?

Example

The following arrival times should be determined for this flight:

```
2019-09-16T01:00+02:00[Europe/Zurich]
2019-09-15T16:00-07:00[America/Los_Angeles]
```

Tip   Use the class `Duration` to model the flight time. The time zone in San Francisco is `America/Los_Angeles`. Use the `withZoneSameInstant()` method from the class `ZonedDateTime`.

6.2.6 Exercise 6: Calculations with LocalDate

Exercise 6a: Friday the 13th (★★☆☆☆)

Compute all occurrences of Friday the 13th for a range defined by two `LocalDates`. Write general-purpose method `List<LocalDate> allFriday13th(LocalDate, LocalDate)`, specifying the start date inclusive and end date exclusive.

Example

For this period of 1/1/2013 to 12/31/2015 inclusive, the following date values should be determined:

Period	Result
2013 – 2015	[2013-09-13, 2013-12-13, 2014-06-13, 2015-02-13, 2015-03-13, 2015-11-13]

Exercise 6b: Several Occurrences of Friday the 13th (★★☆☆☆)

In which years there were several occurrences of Friday the 13th? To answer this question, compute a map in which the corresponding Fridays are associated with each year. Write the method `Map<Integer, List<LocalDate>> friday13thGrouped(LocalDate, LocalDate)` for this purpose.

Examples

Year	Result
2013	[2013-09-13, 2013-12-13]
2014	[2014-06-13]
2015	[2015-02-13, 2015-03-13, 2015-11-13]

6.2.7 Exercise 7: Calendar Output (★★★☆☆)

Write method void printCalendar(Month, int), which, for a given month and year, prints a calendar page to the console.

Example

For April 2020, you expect the following output:

```
Mon Tue Wed Thu Fri Sat Sun
..  ..  01  02  03  04  05
06  07  08  09  10  11  12
13  14  15  16  17  18  19
20  21  22  23  24  25  26
27  28  29  30  --  --  --
```

For an example ending on a Sunday, you can pick May 2020. To verify a start on a Monday, use June 2020.

6.2.8 Exercise 8: Weekdays (★☆☆☆☆)

Exercise 8a: Weekdays (★☆☆☆☆)

What day of the week was Christmas Eve 2019 (December 24, 2019)? What days of the week were the first and last days of December 2019?

Examples

The following days of the week should be the result:

Input	Result
December 24, 2019	Tuesday
December 01, 2019	Sunday
December 31, 2019	Tuesday

Exercise 8b: Date (★☆☆☆☆)

Calculate the respective dates of the first and last Friday and Sunday in March 2019 by writing method `Map<String, LocalDate> firstAndLastFridayAndSunday(YearMonth)`. Along the way, learn about the `YearMonth` class for modeling a year and month.

Example

The computed map should contain the following values and be sorted by key:

```
{firstFriday=2019-03-01, firstSunday=2019-03-03,
 lastFriday=2019-03-29, lastSunday=2019-03-31}
```

Exercise 8c: Day in Month or Year (★☆☆☆☆)

In exercise part 8b, you identified four dates in March 2019. Which day in March was that in each case? And which day of the year?

Examples

Input	Day in month	Day in year
firstFriday=2019-03-01	1	60
firstSunday=2019-03-03	3	62
lastFriday=2019-03-29	29	88
lastSunday=2019-03-31	31	90

6.2.9 Exercise 9: Sundays and Leap Years (★★☆☆☆)

Exercise 9a: Sundays

Count the Sundays in a range given by two `LocalDate`s. To do this, write method `Stream<LocalDate> allSundaysBetween(LocalDate, LocalDate)`, wherein the start date is inclusive and the end date is exclusive.

Examples

Period	Result
1.1.2017 – 1.1.2018	53
1.1.2019 – 7.2.2019	5

Exercise 9b: Leap Years

Count the number of leap years in a range given by `Year` instances. For this, write method `long countLeapYears(Year, Year)`, where the start year is inclusive and the end year is exclusive.

Examples

Period	Result
2010 – 2019	2
2000 – 2019	5

6.2.10 Exercise 10: TemporalAdjuster (★★★☆☆)

Write a `TemporalAdjuster` that moves a date value to the beginning of each quarter, such as from February 7 to January 1.

Examples

Input	Result
LocalDate.of(2014, 3, 15)	2014-01-01
LocalDate.of(2014, 6, 15)	2014-04-01
LocalDate.of(2014, 9, 15)	2014-07-01
LocalDate.of(2014, 11, 15)	2014-10-01

Tip   Look around a bit in the `Month` and `IsoFields` classes.

6.2.11 Exercise 11: NthWeekdayAdjuster (★★★☆☆)

Write class `NthWeekdayAdjuster` that jumps to the nth day of the week, such as the third Friday. This should start from the beginning of the month given by a `LocalDate`. For larger values of *n,* it should jump to the succeeding months.

Examples

Verify this class using the following time jumps with a start date of 08/15/2015:

Start date	Jump target	Result
2015-08-15 (2015-08-15)	Second Friday	2015-08-14
2015-08-15 (2015-08-15)	Third Sunday	2015-08-16
2015-08-15 (2015-08-15)	Fourth Tuesday	2015-08-25

6.2.12 Exercise 12: Payday TemporalAdjuster (★★★☆☆)

Implement class `Ex12_NextPaydayAdjuster` that computes the typical payday in Switzerland. This is often the 25th of the month. If this day falls on a weekend, the Friday before is taken as the payday. If you are after the day of payment, then this is considered to be in the following month. As a freestyle, you still have to implement a special rule for the salary payment in December, when the payment should be made in the middle of the month. If necessary, the payment is moved to the following Monday if the payday is on a weekend.

Example

Validate this class based on the following date values:

Input	Result	Rule
2019-07-21	2019-07-25	Normal adjustment
2019-06-27	2019-07-25	Normal adjustment, next month
2019-08-21	2019-08-23	Friday, if 25th on weekend
2019-12-06	2019-12-16	December: mid of month, Monday after weekend
2019-12-23	2020-01-24	Next month and Friday if 25th on weekend

6.2.13 Exercise 13: Formatting and Parsing (★★☆☆☆)

Create a LocalDateTime object and print it in various formats. Format and parse from these formats: dd.MM.yyyy HH, dd.MM.yy HH:mm, ISO_LOCAL_DATE_TIME, SHORT, and the US locale.

Examples

For 07/27/2017 at 13:14:15 h the output should be as follows:

Formatted	Parsed	Format
27 07 2017 13	2017-07-27T13:00	dd MM yyyy HH
27.07.17 13:14	2017-07-27T13:14	dd.MM.yy HH:mm
2017-07-27T13:14:15	2017-07-27T13:14:15	ISO_LOCAL_DATE_TIME
7/27/17, 1:14 PM	2017-07-27T13:14	SHORT + Locale.US

Tip Use the DateTimeFormatter class and its constants as well as its methods like ofPattern() and ofLocalizedDateTime().

6.2.14 Exercise 14: Fault-Tolerant Parsing (★★☆☆☆)

Error tolerance is often important when evaluating user input. Your task is to create method `Optional<LocalDate> faultTolerantParse(String, Set<DateTimeFormatter>)` that allows you to parse the following date formats: `dd.MM.yy`, `dd.MM.yyy`, `MM/dd/yyyy`, and `yyyy-MM-dd`.

Examples

The following table shows the expected results of parsing different inputs. Be sure to notice that with two-digit years in the pattern, sometimes it doesn't generate the correct or expected date!

Input	Result
"07.02.71"	2071-02-07
"07.02.1971"	1971-02-07
"02/07/1971"	1971-02-07
"1971-02-07"	1971-02-07

6.3 Solutions

6.3.1 Solution 1: Leap Years (★☆☆☆☆)

While in our calendar the year is usually divided into 365 days, this is not quite correct astronomically. The year has a length of about 365.25 days. Due to this, a correction is necessary almost every 4 years by using a leap year with 366 days. There are two special aspects to be considered:

- Years divisible by 100 are called secular years and are not leap years.

- However, secular years that are also divisible by 400 are leap years after all.

For details, see `https://en.wikipedia.org/wiki/Leap_year`. Write method `boolean isLeap(int)`—without using `java.time.Year.isLeap()`, of course.

Examples

Input	Rule	Result
1900	Secular year	No leap year
2000	Secular years, but divisible by 400	Leap year
2020	Divisible by 4	Leap year

Algorithm   Compute the conditions each with modulo operations and combine them appropriately:

```
static boolean isLeap(final int year)
{
    final boolean everyFourthYear = year % 4 == 0;
    final boolean isSecular = year % 100 ==  0;
    final boolean isSecularSpecial = year % 400 == 0;

    return everyFourthYear && (!isSecular || isSecularSpecial)
}
```

As already indicated, the Year class already has a predefined check for leap years:

```
static boolean isLeap_Jdk8(final int year)
{
    return Year.of(year).isLeap();
}
```

Verification

Let's try this out as a unit test:

```
@ParameterizedTest(name = "isLeap({0} => {2}, Hinweis: {1}")
@CsvSource({ "1900, Secular, false",
            "2000, Secular (but rule of 400), true",
            "2020, Every 4th year, true" })
```

```
void testIsLeap(int year, String hint, boolean expected)
{
    boolean result = Ex01_LeapYear.isLeap(year);

    assertEquals(expected, result);
}
```

6.3.2 Solution 2: Basic Knowledge Date-API (★★☆☆☆)

Solution 2a: Creation (★☆☆☆☆)

Represent your birthday as LocalDate, the end of work 5:30pm as LocalTime and now as LocalDateTime. Further, model a time span of 1 year, 10 months, and 20 days, and a duration of 7 hours and 15 minutes.

Algorithm   Use the API appropriately:

```
final LocalDate myBirthday = LocalDate.of(1971, 2, 7);
final LocalTime time = LocalTime.of(17, 30);
final LocalDateTime now = LocalDateTime.now();

final Period oneYear10Month20Days = Period.of(1, 10, 20);
final Duration sevenHours15Minutes = Duration.ofHours(7).plusMinutes(15);
```

Solution 2b: Time Durations (★★☆☆☆)

Calculate the duration of time between today and your birthday and vice versa.

Algorithm   Use the API and especially the until() and between() methods appropriately:

```
final LocalDate now = LocalDate.now();
final LocalDate birthday = LocalDate.of(1971, 2, 7);

System.out.println("Using until()");
System.out.println("now -> birthday: " + now.until(birthday));
System.out.println("birthday -> now: " + birthday.until(now));
System.out.println("\nUsing Period.between()");
System.out.println("now -> birthday: " + Period.between(now, birthday));
System.out.println("birthday -> now: " + Period.between(birthday, now));
```

6.3.3 Solution 3: Length of Month (★★☆☆☆)

Solution 3a: Calculations (★☆☆☆☆)

Jump starting from 2/2/2012 and from 2/2/2014, as well as from 4/4/2014 and 5/5/2014 with the method plusMonths() of the class LocalDate one month into the future and output the date in each case.

Algorithm   Call the mentioned method suitably:

```
final LocalDate february_2_2012 = LocalDate.of(2012, 2, 2);
final LocalDate february_2_2014 = LocalDate.of(2014, 2, 2);
final LocalDate april_4_2014 = LocalDate.of(2014, 4, 4);
final LocalDate may_5_2014 = LocalDate.of(2014, 5, 5);

System.out.println("2/2/2012 + 1 month = " + february_2_2012.plusMonths(1));
System.out.println("2/2/2014 + 1 month = " + february_2_2014.plusMonths(1));
System.out.println("4/4/2014 + 1 month = " + april_4_2014.plusMonths(1));
System.out.println("5/5/2014 + 1 month = " + may_5_2014.plusMonths(1));
```

Solution 3b: Length of Month (★★☆☆☆)

For the calculations, what happens if instead of using plusMonths() you use the method plusDays()? What corresponds to a month: 28, 29, 30, or 31 days? How do you to determine the correct length of a month?

Algorithm   Let's invoke plusDays() for different values:

```
System.out.println("2/2/2012 + 28 days = " + february_2_2012.plusDays(28));
System.out.println("2/2/2014 + 28 days = " + february_2_2014.plusDays(28));
System.out.println("4/4/2014 + 30 days = " + april_4_2014.plusDays(30));
System.out.println("5/5/2014 + 31 days = " + may_5_2014.plusDays(31));
```

Verification

With plusMonths() the correct length of the respective month is always added (also considering a potential leap year). However, this does not apply to the plusDays() method. This adds the specified number of days, forcing you to always pass this value correctly. For this purpose, the `Month` class provides the `length(boolean)` method. Alternatively, there is the method `LocalDate.lengthOfMonth()`. Let's have a look at the program output:

```
2/2/2012 + 1 month = 2012-03-02
2/2/2014 + 1 month = 2014-03-02
4/4/2014 + 1 month = 2014-05-04
5/5/2014 + 1 month = 2014-06-05
2/2/2012 + 28 days = 2012-03-01
2/2/2014 + 28 days = 2014-03-02
4/4/2014 + 30 days = 2014-05-04
5/5/2014 + 31 days = 2014-06-05
```

6.3.4 Solution 4: Time Zones (★★☆☆☆)

Get all time zones starting with `America/L` or `Europe/S` and fill a sorted set accordingly. For this purpose write method `Set<String> selectedAmericanAndEuropeanTimeZones()`.

Example

The computed set should contain the following values:

```
[America/La_Paz, America/Lima, America/Los_Angeles, America/Louisville,
 America/Lower_Princes, Europe/Samara, Europe/San_Marino,
 Europe/Sarajevo, Europe/Saratov, Europe/Simferopol,
 Europe/Skopje, Europe/Sofia, Europe/Stockholm]
```

Tip Use the class `ZoneId` and its method `getAvailableZoneIds()`. Utilize streams and the filter-map-reduce framework to find the time zone IDs matching the previously specified prefixes.

Algorithm   First, you determine all time zone IDs. Then you define two filter conditions and finally a combination of them. This allows you to use basic functionalities of the Stream API:

```
static Set<String> selectedAmericanAndEuropeanTimeZones()
{
    final Set<String> allZones = ZoneId.getAvailableZoneIds();

    final Predicate<String> inEuropeS = name -> name.startsWith("Europe/S");
    final Predicate<String> inAmericaL = name -> name.startsWith("America/L");
    final Predicate<String> europeOrAmerica = inEuropeS.or(inAmericaL);

    return allZones.stream().
                    filter(europeOrAmerica).
                    collect(Collectors.toCollection(TreeSet::new));
}
```

Verification

To verify, run the following unit test:

```
@Test
public void selectedAmericanAndEuropeanTimeZones()
{
    var expected = Set.of("America/La_Paz", "America/Lima",
                    "America/Los_Angeles", "America/Louisville",
                    "America/Lower_Princes", "Europe/Samara",
                    "Europe/San_Marino", "Europe/Sarajevo",
                    "Europe/Saratov", "Europe/Simferopol",
                    "Europe/Skopje", "Europe/Sofia",
                    "Europe/Stockholm");

    Set<String> result = Ex04_ZoneIds.selectedAmericanAndEuropeanTimeZones();

    assertEquals(expected, result);
}
```

6.3.5 Solution 5: Time Zone Calculation (★★☆☆☆)

If a flight from Zurich to San Francisco takes 11 hours and 50 minutes and departs at 1:10 p.m. on 9/15/2019, what local time does it arrive in San Francisco? What time does that correspond to at the departure point?

Example

The following arrival times should be determined for this flight:

```
2019-09-16T01:00+02:00[Europe/Zurich]
2019-09-15T16:00-07:00[America/Los_Angeles]
```

Tip   Use the class Duration to model the flight time. The time zone in San Francisco is America/Los_Angeles. Use the withZoneSameInstant() method from the class ZonedDateTime.

Algorithm   First, you construct objects for the departure day and time as well as the time zone to create a corresponding ZonedDateTime object. Then you define the flight time in terms of a Duration. By simply adding this time difference, you get the arrival time as it would be in Europe. Using withZoneSameInstant() and the time zone America/Los_Angeles you finally get the arrival time related to the American time zone:

```java
public static void main(final String[] args)
{
    final LocalDate departureDate = LocalDate.of(2019, 9, 15);
    final LocalTime departureTime = LocalTime.of(13, 10);
    final ZoneId zoneEurope = ZoneId.of("Europe/Zurich");

    // departure time
    final ZonedDateTime departure = ZonedDateTime.of(departureDate,
                                        departureTime, zoneEurope);

    // flight duration
    final Duration flightDuration = Duration.ofHours(11).plusMinutes(50);

    // arrival time based on flight duration (and time zone)
    final ZonedDateTime arrival1 = departure.plus(flightDuration);
    final ZoneId zoneAmerica = ZoneId.of("America/Los_Angeles");
    final ZonedDateTime arrival2 = arrival1.withZoneSameInstant(zoneAmerica);

    System.out.println(arrival1);
    System.out.println(arrival2);
}
```

Verification

Let's check the calculation by a simple program run—and the author remembers the flight again :-)

```
2019-09-16T01:00+02:00[Europe/Zurich]
2019-09-15T16:00-07:00[America/Los_Angeles]
```

6.3.6 Solution 6: Calculations With LocalDate

Exercise 6a: Friday the 13th (★★☆☆☆)

Compute all occurrences of Friday the 13th for a range defined by two LocalDates. Write general-purpose method List<LocalDate> allFriday13th(LocalDate, LocalDate), specifying the start date inclusive and end date exclusive.

Example

For this period from 1/1/2013 to 12/31/2015 inclusive, the following date values should be determined:

Period	Result
2013 – 2015	[2013-09-13, 2013-12-13, 2014-06-13, 2015-02-13, 2015-03-13, 2015-11-13]

Algorithm   In this exercise, you use two predicates to test for both Friday and the 13th. To provide the corresponding days to be tested, the datesUntil() method introduced with Java 9 helps you. The filtering is then performed using the standard methods from the Stream API.

```java
static List<LocalDate> allFriday13th(final LocalDate start,
                                     final LocalDate end)
{
    final Predicate<LocalDate> isFriday = day -> day.getDayOfWeek() ==
                                    DayOfWeek.FRIDAY;

    final Predicate<LocalDate> is13th = day -> day.getDayOfMonth() == 13;
```

```
final List<LocalDate> allFriday13th = start.datesUntil(end).
                                       filter(isFriday).
                                       filter(is13th).
                                       collect(Collectors.toList());
    return allFriday13th;
}
```

Alternatively, you could start with a Friday and then call `datesUntil(end, period)` with a period of 7 days. This might be a bit more efficient.

Let's execute the above lines in the JShell or in a `main()` method with appropriate date values as follows:

```
var allFriday13th = allFriday13th(LocalDate.of(2013, 1, 1),
                         LocalDate.of(2016, 1, 1));

System.out.println("allFriday13th: " + allFriday13th);
```

This provides the following output (formatted a bit nicer here):

```
allFriday13th: [2013-09-13, 2013-12-13, 2014-06-13, 2015-02-13, 2015-03-13,
               2015-11-13]
```

Solution 6b: Several Occurrences of Friday the 13th (★★☆☆☆)

In which years there were several occurrences of Friday the 13th? To answer this question, compute a map in which the corresponding Fridays are associated with each year. Write the method `Map<Integer, List<LocalDate>>` `friday13thGrouped(LocalDate, LocalDate)` for this purpose.

Examples

Year	Result
2013	[2013-09-13, 2013-12-13]
2014	[2014-06-13]
2015	[2015-02-13, 2015-03-13, 2015-11-13]

Algorithm   Based on the previously defined method, you can again use the Stream API for grouping by years using the method groupingBy(). Finally, you want to arrange the years in a sorted way, which is why you transfer the result into a TreeMap<K,V>.

```
static Map<Integer, List<LocalDate>> friday13thGrouped(final LocalDate start,
                                                       final LocalDate end)
{
    return new TreeMap<>(allFriday13th(start, end).stream().
                      collect(Collectors.groupingBy(LocalDate::getYear)));
}
```

Verification

Let's take a quick look at what an associated unit test might look like:

```
@Test
void testAllFriday13th()
{
    final LocalDate start = LocalDate.of(2013, 1, 1);
    final LocalDate end = LocalDate.of(2016, 1, 1);

    var result = Ex06_Friday13thExample.allFriday13th(start, end);

    // trick: Use Stream.of() and map() to have less typing work
    var expected = Stream.of("2013-09-13", "2013-12-13", "2014-06-13",
                        "2015-02-13", "2015-03-13", "2015-11-13").
                   map(str -> LocalDate.parse(str)).
                   collect(Collectors.toList());

    assertEquals(expected, result);
}
```

You test the grouping as follows:

```
@Test
void testFriday13thGrouped()
{
    final LocalDate start = LocalDate.of(2013, 1, 1);
    final LocalDate end = LocalDate.of(2016, 1, 1);
```

```
var result = Ex06_Friday13thExample.friday13thGrouped(start, end);

var expected = Map.of(2013, List.of(LocalDate.parse("2013-09-13"),
                                     LocalDate.parse("2013-12-13")),
                      2014,  List.of(LocalDate.parse("2014-06-13")),
                      2015,  List.of(LocalDate.parse("2015-02-13"),
                                     LocalDate.parse("2015-03-13"),
                                     LocalDate.parse("2015-11-13")));

    assertEquals(expected, result);
}
```

6.3.7 Solution 7: Calendar Output (★★★☆☆)

Write method void printCalendar(Month, int), which, for a given month and year, prints a calendar page to the console.

Example

For April 2020, you expect the following output:

```
Mon Tue Wed Thu Fri Sat Sun
..  ..  01  02  03  04  05
06  07  08  09  10  11  12
13  14  15  16  17  18  19
20  21  22  23  24  25  26
27  28  29  30  --  --  --
```

For an example ending on a Sunday, you can pick May 2020. To verify a start on a Monday, use June 2020.

Preliminary considerations for the algorithm: From the calendar page for April 2020, you can already see a few special aspects and challenges that await you:

- Potentially incomplete first and last week

- There is always a linebreak on Sunday.

- How do you relate weekdays and the number of days?

Algorithm   At the beginning, you display a header line with the weekdays. After that, you determine the weekday the month starts with and then skip some weekdays with skipTillFirstDayOfMonth() if necessary. To output the individual days, you need to specify the month length based on the leap year's information with length(). Next comes the part with a few tricks. You iterate through all the date values and print the number in a formatted way. When you reach a Sunday, you continue in the next line. To move the day of the week, you use helper method calcNextWeekDay(). Finally, all days that no longer belong to the month should be marked with the --. This is the task of the fillFromMonthEndToSunday() method.

```java
static void printCalendar(final Month month, final int year)
{
    System.out.println("Mon Tue Wed Thu Fri Sat Sun");

    LocalDate cur = LocalDate.of(year, month, 1);
    DayOfWeek firstInMonth = cur.getDayOfWeek();

    skipTillFirstDayOfMonth(firstInMonth);

    DayOfWeek currentWeekDay = firstInMonth;
    int lengthOfMonth = month.length(Year.of(year).isLeap());
    for (int i = 1; i <= lengthOfMonth; i++)
    {
        System.out.print(String.format("%03d", i) + " ");
        if (currentWeekDay == DayOfWeek.SUNDAY)
            System.out.println();

        currentWeekDay = nextWeekDay(currentWeekDay);
    }

    fillFromMonthEndToSunday(currentWeekDay);

    // last day not Sunday, then pagination
    if (currentWeekDay != DayOfWeek.MONDAY)
        System.out.println();
}
```

Now you come to the helper method for moving one day of the week to the next and cyclically from Sunday to Monday. This can be implemented based on the enumeration DayOfWeek and a modulo operation. It is even easier to use the method plus() which realizes this special handling automatically.

```
static DayOfWeek calcNextWeekDay(final DayOfWeek nextWeekDay)
{
    return nextWeekDay.plus(1);
}
```

The methods for printing the first and last days of the week that are not part of the month remain. For the former, you proceed from a Monday to the weekday of the first day of the month, using the helper method shown:

```
static void skipTillFirstDayOfMonth(final DayOfWeek firstInMonth)
{
    DayOfWeek currentWeekDay = DayOfWeek.MONDAY;
    while (currentWeekDay != firstInMonth)
    {
        System.out.print(".. ");
        currentWeekDay = nextWeekDay(currentWeekDay);
    }
}
```

Finally, to finish the output of the calendar, you fill up with -- until you arrive at a Sunday, starting from the last day of the week of the month:

```
static void fillFromMonthEndToSunday(final DayOfWeek currentWeekDay)
{
    DayOfWeek nextWeekDay = currentWeekDay;
    while (nextWeekDay != DayOfWeek.MONDAY)
    {
        System.out.print("-- ");
        nextWeekDay = nextWeekDay(nextWeekDay);
    }
}
```

HINT: HELPER METHODS AND PROPER STRUCTURING

As demonstrated a couple of times, creating appropriate helper methods simplifies problem solving (often significantly). This allows you to stay more at the logical level in the implementation of the algorithm and to avoid getting distracted with implementation details.

Verification

Copy the methods into the JShell and remember to import `import java.time.*`. After that, you can then just walk through the three exemplary cases once:

```
jshell> printCalendar(Month.APRIL, 2020)
Mon Tue Wed Thu Fri Sat Sun
..  ..  01  02  03  04  05
06  07  08  09  10  11  12
13  14  15  16  17  18  19
20  21  22  23  24  25  26
27  28  29  30  --  --  --

jshell> printCalendar(Month.MAY, 2020)
Mon Tue Wed Thu Fri Sat Sun
..  ..  ..  ..  01  02  03
04  05  06  07  08  09  10
11  12  13  14  15  16  17
18  19  20  21  22  23  24
25  26  27  28  29  30  31

jshell> printCalendar(Month.JUNE, 2020)
Mon Tue Wed Thu Fri Sat Sun
01  02  03  04  05  06  07
08  09  10  11  12  13  14
15  16  17  18  19  20  21
22  23  24  25  26  27  28
29  30  --  --  --  --  --
```

6.3.8 Solution 8: Weekdays (★☆☆☆☆)

Solution 8a: Weekdays (★☆☆☆☆)

What day of the week was Christmas Eve 2019 (December 24, 2019)? What days of the week were the first and last days of December 2019?

Examples

The following days of the week should be the result:

Input	Result
December 24, 2019	Tuesday
December 01, 2019	Sunday
December 31, 2019	Tuesday

Algorithm   You create a LocalDate object and use the method getDayOfWeek() or DayOfWeek.from() to determine the corresponding weekday. After jumping to the first or last day of December using a matching TemporalAdjuster, you repeat this.

```
LocalDate christmasEve = LocalDate.of(2019, 12, 24); System.out.
println("Dec. 24, 2019 = " + christmasEve.getDayOfWeek());
System.out.println("Dec. 24, 2019 = " + DayOfWeek.from(christmasEve));

var decemberFirst = christmasEve.with(TemporalAdjusters.firstDayOfMonth());
System.out.println("Dec. 01, 2019 = " + ecemberFirst.getDayOfWeek());

var decemberLast = christmasEve.with(TemporalAdjusters.lastDayOfMonth());
System.out.println("Dec. 31, 2019 = " + decemberLast.getDayOfWeek());
```

Verification

The above lines output the following:

```
Dec. 24, 2019 = TUESDAY
Dec. 24, 2019 = TUESDAY
Dec. 01, 2019 = SUNDAY
Dec. 31, 2019 = TUESDAY
```

Please do not forget to perform the following import for execution in the JShell:

```
jshell> import java.time.temporal.*
```

Solution 8b: Date (★☆☆☆☆)

Calculate the respective dates of the first and last Friday and Sunday in March 2019 by writing method Map<String, LocalDate> firstAndLastFridayAndSunday(YearMonth). Along the way, learn about the YearMonth class for modeling a year and month.

Example

The computed map should contain the following values and be sorted by key:

```
{firstFriday=2019-03-01, firstSunday=2019-03-03, lastFriday=2019-03-29,
 lastSunday=2019-03-31}
```

Algorithm   With suitably chosen methods of the utility class TemporalAdjusters you can easily define appropriate time jumps by specifying the desired weekdays:

```
static Map<String, LocalDate>
       firstAndLastFridayAndSunday(final YearMonth yearMonth)
{
    var toFirstFriday = TemporalAdjusters.firstInMonth(DayOfWeek.FRIDAY);
    var toFirstSunday = TemporalAdjusters.firstInMonth(DayOfWeek.SUNDAY);
    var toLastFriday = TemporalAdjusters.lastInMonth(DayOfWeek.FRIDAY);
    var toLastSunday = TemporalAdjusters.lastInMonth(DayOfWeek.SUNDAY);

    var day = LocalDate.of(yearMonth.getYear(), yearMonth.getMonth(), 15);

    return new TreeMap<>(Map.of("firstFriday", day.with(toFirstFriday),
                               "firstSunday", day.with(toFirstSunday),
                               "lastFriday", day.with(toLastFriday),
                               "lastSunday", day.with(toLastSunday)));
}
```

Verification

Let's create a unit test for verification:

```
@Test
void testFirstAndLastFridayAndSunday()
{
    final YearMonth march2019 = YearMonth.of(2019, Month.MARCH);

    var expected = Map.of("firstFriday", LocalDate.of(2019, 3, 1),
                          "firstSunday", LocalDate.of(2019, 3, 3),
                          "lastFriday",  LocalDate.of(2019, 3, 29),
                          "lastSunday",  LocalDate.of(2019, 3, 31));

    var result = Ex08_WeekDays.firstAndLastFridayAndSunday(march2019);

    assertEquals(expected, result);
}
```

Solution 8c: Day in Month or Year (★☆☆☆☆)

In exercise part 8b, you identified four dates in March 2019. Which day in March was that in each case? And which day of the year?

Examples

Input	Day in month	Day in year
firstFriday=2019-03-01	1	60
firstSunday=2019-03-03	3	62
lastFriday=2019-03-29	29	88
lastSunday=2019-03-31	31	90

Algorithm   The assignment is easy to implement with suitable calls. To achieve an appealing output, you further use `String.format()` with appropriate format specifications:

```
static void dayOfMonthAndDayInYear(final Map<String, LocalDate> days)
{
    System.out.println("Day            Of Month / Of Year");

    for (final String key : List.of("firstFriday", "firstSunday",
                                     "lastFriday", "lastSunday"))
    {
        final LocalDate day = days.getOrDefault(key, LocalDate.now());

        System.out.println(String.format("%-12s %9d %9d",
                                          key,
                                          day.getDayOfMonth(),
                                          day.getDayOfYear()));
    }
}
```

Verification

The above lines output the following when invoked with the map computed in exercise part 8b as input:

```
Day          Of Month / Of Year
firstFriday         1        60
firstSunday         3        62
lastFriday         29        88
lastSunday         31        90
```

6.3.9 Solution 9: Sundays and Leap Years (★★☆☆☆)

Solution 9a: Sundays

Count the Sundays in a range given by two LocalDates. To do this, write method Stream<LocalDate> allSundaysBetween(LocalDate, LocalDate), wherein the start date is inclusive and the end date is exclusive.

Examples

Period	Result
1.1.2017 – 1.1.2018	53
1.1.2019 – 7.2.2019	5

Algorithm   Based on the Stream API, the assignment can be realized quite easily:

```
static Stream<LocalDate> allSundaysBetween(final LocalDate start,
                                           final LocalDate end)
{
    final Predicate<LocalDate> isSunday =
                        day -> day.getDayOfWeek() == DayOfWeek.SUNDAY;

    return start.datesUntil(end).filter(isSunday);
}
```

Verification

For the year 2017, 53 Sundays are determined. From 1/1/2019 to 7/2/2019, the number is 5, according to expectations. The following unit test ensures both:

```
@ParameterizedTest(name = "allSundaysBetween({0}, {1}) => {2}")
@CsvSource({ "2017-01-01, 2018-01-01, 53", "2019-01-01, 2019-02-07, 5" })
void allSundaysBetween(LocalDate start, LocalDate end, int expected)
{
    var result = Ex09_CountSundays.allSundaysBetween(start, end);

    assertEquals(expected, result.count());
}
```

Once again, you can see how helpful the argument converters integrated into JUnit 5 are. With them, dates are automatically converted into a LocalDate. This results in very readable and understandable tests.

Solution 9b: Leap Years

Count the number of leap years in a range given by Year instances. For this, write method long countLeapYears(Year, Year), where the start year is inclusive and the end year is exclusive.

Examples

Period	Result
2010 – 2019	2
2000 – 2019	5

Algorithm   While with some thought and trickery you could fall back to the datesUntil() method, here you want to take a different approach. With the Stream API and the method range() it is possible to create numerical values as a stream. Now you filter all leap years. After that, you only need to call count() to count the remaining years from the Stream API.

```
static long countLeapYears(final Year start, final Year end)
{
    return IntStream.range(start.getValue(), end.getValue()).
                    filter(Year::isLeap).
                    count();
}
```

Verification

If you check the functionality for the period from 2010 to 2019, you should get two leap years as a result. In the period from 2000 to 2019, there are five.

```
@ParameterizedTest(name = "countLeepYears({0}, {1}) => {2}")
@CsvSource({ "2010, 2019, 2", "2000, 2019, 5" })
public void countLeapYears(Year start, Year end, int expected)
{
    long result = Ex09_CountSundays.countLeapYears(start, end);

    assertEquals(expected, result);
}
```

Again, JUnit 5's built-in argument processing automation helps you convert numbers into objects of type Year. This keeps this test nice and short, concise, and precise.

6.3.10 Solution 10: TemporalAdjuster (★★★☆☆)

Write a TemporalAdjuster that moves a date value to the beginning of each quarter, such as from February 7 to January 1.

Examples

Input	Result
LocalDate.of(2014, 3, 15)	2014-01-01
LocalDate.of(2014, 6, 15)	2014-04-01
LocalDate.of(2014, 9, 15)	2014-07-01
LocalDate.of(2014, 11, 15)	2014-10-01

Tip   Look around a bit in the Month and IsoFields classes.

Algorithm   If you explore the Date and Time API a bit, you might discover that there is a method getLong(TemporalField) in the Month class that can be used to get the quarter for a month. Now, based on that, you can determine the appropriate starting month for the quarter in an array.

```java
public class Ex10_FirstDayOfQuarter implements TemporalAdjuster
{
    private static final Month[] startMonthOfQuarter = { Month.JANUARY,
                                                         Month.APRIL,
                                                         Month.JULY,
                                                         Month.OCTOBER };

    @Override
    public Temporal adjustInto(final Temporal temporal)
    {
        final int currentQuarter = getQuarter(temporal);

        final Month startMonth = startMonthOfQuarter[currentQuarter - 1];
```

```
        return LocalDate.from(temporal).
                        withMonth(startMonth.getValue()).
                        with(firstDayOfMonth());
    }

    private int getQuarter(final Temporal temporal)
    {
        return (int)Month.from(temporal).
                        getLong(IsoFields.QUARTER_OF_YEAR);
    }
}
```

Optimized algorithm   The solution just shown is universal and can be adapted to other requirements. Further experimentation with the Date and Time API brings us to an exquisitely short and equally eloquent solution:

```
public class Ex10_FirstDayOfQuarterOptimized implements TemporalAdjuster
{
    @Override
    public Temporal adjustInto(final Temporal temporal)
    {
        return LocalDate.from(temporal).with(IsoFields.DAY_OF_QUARTER, 1);
    }
}
```

Verification

A unit test that uses the two variants looks like this:

```
@ParameterizedTest(name = "move {0} to first of quarter: {1}")
@CsvSource({ "2014-03-15, 2014-01-01", "2014-06-16, 2014-04-01",
            "2014-09-15, 2014-07-01", "2014-11-15, 2014-10-01" })
void adjustToFirstDayOfQuarter(LocalDate startDate, LocalDate expected)
{
    var result = new Ex10_FirstDayOfQuarter().adjustInto(startDate);

    assertEquals(expected, result);
}
```

```
@ParameterizedTest(name = "move {0} to first of quarter: {1}")
@CsvSource({ "2014-03-15, 2014-01-01", "2014-06-16, 2014-04-01",
            "2014-09-15, 2014-07-01", "2014-11-15, 2014-10-01" })
void adjustToFirstDayOfQuarterOptimized(LocalDate startDate, LocalDate
expected)
{
    var result = new Ex10_FirstDayOfQuarterOptimized().adjustInto(startDate);

    assertEquals(expected, result);
}
```

6.3.11 Solution 11: NthWeekdayAdjuster (★★★☆☆)

Write class NthWeekdayAdjuster that jumps to the nth day of the week, such as the third Friday. This should start from the beginning of the month given by a LocalDate. For larger values of n, it should jump to the succeeding months.

Examples

Verify this class using the following time jumps with a start date of 08/15/2015:

Start date	Jump target	Result
2015-08-15 (2015-08-15)	Second Friday	2015-08-14
2015-08-15 (2015-08-15)	Third Sunday	2015-08-16
2015-08-15 (2015-08-15)	Fourth Tuesday	2015-08-25

Algorithm   You define class Ex11_NthWeekdayAdjuster, to which you pass both the desired day of the week and its number to adjust to the nth weekday. By calling the from(TemporalAccessor) method from the LocalDate class, you create a LocalDate instance that corresponds to the Temporal object passed in, which you move to the first desired day of the week using its firstInMonth(DayOfWeek) method. After that, you use the next(DayOfWeek) method, which advances you to the next specified weekday. For counting, you have to keep in mind that you are talking about the fourth Sunday, but of course, the count starts at 1.

```java
public class Ex11_NthWeekdayAdjuster implements TemporalAdjuster
{
    private final DayOfWeek dayToAdjust;
    private final int count;

    public Ex11_NthWeekdayAdjuster(final DayOfWeek dayToAdjust, final int
    count)
    {
        this.dayToAdjust = dayToAdjust;
        this.count = count;
    }

    public Temporal adjustInto(final Temporal input)
    {
        final LocalDate startday = LocalDate.from(input);

        LocalDate adjustedDay =
                    startday.with(TemporalAdjusters.firstInMonth(dayToAdjust));

        for (int i = 1; i < count; i++)
        {
            adjustedDay = adjustedDay.with(TemporalAdjusters.next(dayToAdjust));
        }

        return input.with(adjustedDay);
    }
}
```

Remember to start at the value 1 when implementing to move to the nth day of the week, since the human mindset is (usually) not 0-based!

Verification

Let's verify your solution using the following unit test:

```java
@ParameterizedTest(name = "adjusting {0} to {1}. {2} => {3}")
@CsvSource({ "2015-08-15, 2, FRIDAY, 2015-08-14",
            "2015-08-15, 3, SUNDAY, 2015-08-16",
            "2015-08-15, 4, TUESDAY, 2015-08-25" })
```

```
void adjustToFirstDayOfQuarter(LocalDate startDay, int count,
                               DayOfWeek dayOfWeek, LocalDate expected)
{
    var nthWeekdayAdjuster = new Ex11_NthWeekdayAdjuster(dayOfWeek, count);

    var result = nthWeekdayAdjuster.adjustInto(startDay);

    assertEquals(expected, result);
}
```

6.3.12 Solution 12: Payday TemporalAdjuster (★★★☆☆)

Implement class Ex12_NextPaydayAdjuster that computes the typical payday in
Switzerland. This is often the 25th of the month. If this day falls on a weekend, the Friday
before is taken as the payday. If you are after the day of payment, then this is considered
to be in the following month. As a freestyle, you still have to implement a special rule for
the salary payment in December. Here, the payment should be made in the middle of the
month. If necessary, the payment is moved to the following Monday if the payday is on a
weekend.

Example

Validate this class based on the following date values:

Input	Result	Rule
2019-07-21	2019-07-25	Normal adjustment
2019-06-27	2019-07-25	Normal adjustment, next month
2019-08-21	2019-08-23	Friday, if 25th on weekend
2019-12-06	2019-12-16	December: mid of month, Monday after weekend
2019-12-23	2020-01-24	Next month and Friday if 25th on weekend

Algorithm   Let's try to develop the requirements step by step. Start by adjusting an
arbitrary date to the 25th day of the month.

Calculating the 25th of a month   To implement the desired adjustment of the weekday, you rely on the interface TemporalAdjuster and specifically the method adjustInto(Temporal). First, by calling the method from(TemporalAccessor) from the class LocalDate, you determine a LocalDate instance corresponding to the passed Temporal object. To move this to the 25th, you use the method withDayOfMonth(int) of codeLocalDate:

```
class Ex12_NextPaydayAdjuster implements TemporalAdjuster
{
    @Override
    public Temporal adjustInto(final Temporal temporal)
    {
        LocalDate date = LocalDate.from(temporal);

        date = date.withDayOfMonth(25);

        return temporal.with(date);
    }
}
```

Let's try this out in the JShell:

```
jshell> import java.time.*
jshell> import java.time.temporal.*

jshell> var jan31 = LocalDate.of(2015, Month.JANUARY, 31)

jshell> jan31.with(new Ex12_NextPaydayAdjuster())
$24 ==> 2015-01-25

jshell> var feb7 = LocalDate.of(2015, Month.FEBRUARY, 7);

jshell> feb7.with(new Ex12_NextPaydayAdjuster())
$26 ==> 2015-02-25
```

As shown here, the adjustment already works pretty well. However, one small thing has to be considered: on days after the 25th, the next payday will not be in the same month. The days from the 26th to the end of the month are counted towards the next month. Thus, you adjust the calculation as follows:

```java
@Override
public Temporal adjustInto(final Temporal temporal)
{
    LocalDate date = LocalDate.from(temporal);

    if (date.getDayOfMonth() > 25)
    {
        date = date.plusMonths(1);
    }
    date = date.withDayOfMonth(25);

    return temporal.with(date);
}
```

This is a good step. You're still missing is the consideration of weekends.

Special correction for weekends   If a payday occurs on a weekend, choose the Friday before it. This results in the addition marked in bold:

```java
@Override
public Temporal adjustInto(final Temporal temporal)
{
    LocalDate date = LocalDate.from(temporal);

    if (date.getDayOfMonth() > 25)
    {
        date = date.plusMonths(1);
    }
    date = date.withDayOfMonth(25);

    if (date.getDayOfWeek() == SATURDAY ||
        date.getDayOfWeek() == SUNDAY)
    {
        date = date.with(TemporalAdjusters.previous(FRIDAY));
    }

    return temporal.with(date);
}
```

You can see how the originally straightforward method gets a bit complicated by integrating the real-world requirements. Nevertheless, it remains quite readable thanks to the Date and Time API!

Special treatment for December   You now integrate the special treatment for December. There, the salary payment is made in the middle of the month or, if the 15th falls on a weekend, on the following Monday.

When reflecting a bit on the problem and the solution, the predefined TemporalAdjuster classes may come to mind. Here the methods nextOrSame(DayOfWeek) and previousOrSame(DayOfWeek) and the matching TemporalAdjuster instances can be used as follows:

```
if (isDecember)
{
    date = date.with(TemporalAdjusters.nextOrSame(MONDAY));
}
else
{
    date = date.with(TemporalAdjusters.previousOrSame(FRIDAY));
}
```

Complete implementation   After these individual steps, let's take a look at the resulting complete implementation for a better understanding:

```
public class Ex12_NextPaydayAdjuster implements TemporalAdjuster
{
    @Override
    public Temporal adjustInto(final Temporal temporal)
    {
        LocalDate date = LocalDate.from(temporal);

        boolean isDecember = date.getMonth() == Month.DECEMBER;
        int paymentDay = isDecember ? 15 : 25;

        if (date.getDayOfMonth() > paymentDay)
        {
            date = date.plusMonths(1);
```

```
    // queries necessary again, as possibly postponed by one month
    isDecember = date.getMonth().equals(Month.DECEMBER);
    paymentDay = isDecember ? 15 : 25;
}

date = date.withDayOfMonth(paymentDay);

if (date.getDayOfWeek() == DayOfWeek.SATURDAY ||
    date.getDayOfWeek() == DayOfWeek.SUNDAY)
{
    if (isDecember)
      date = date.with(TemporalAdjusters.nextOrSame(DayOfWeek.
      MONDAY));
    else
      date = date.with(TemporalAdjusters.previousOrSame(DayOfWeek.
      FRIDAY));
}
return temporal.with(date);
    }
}
```

Verification

Because this implementation is already quite complex, a thorough unit test with a few test cases is strongly recommended. Below you will learn how to create significant tests using JUnit 5. To do this, you will use the following tricks:

- You include an additional parameter not used for the test case, which provides info about the test case.

- So far, you have used @CsvSource to specify comma-separated values. This is not easily possible here since commas are used in the hint texts. As a workaround, @CsvSource allows specifying the desired delimiter by providing delimiter.

```
@ParameterizedTest(name="adjustToPayday({0}) => {1}, {2}")
@CsvSource(value= { "2019-07-21; 2019-07-25; nnormal adjustment",
        "2019-06-27; 2019-07-25; normal adjustment, next month",
        "2019-08-21; 2019-08-23; Friday, if 25th in weekend",
        "2019-12-06; 2019-12-16; December: mid of month, Monday after weekend",
        "2019-12-23; 2020-01-24; next month and Friday if 25th on weekend" }},
        delimiterString=";")
public void adjustInto(LocalDate startDay, LocalDate expected, String info)
{
    final TemporalAdjuster paydayAdjuster = new Ex12_NextPaydayAdjuster();

    final Temporal result = paydayAdjuster.adjustInto(startDay);

    assertEquals(expected, result);
}
```

Because the whole thing should really convince even the last test muffle, I still want to map the informative output in Eclipse (see Figure 6-1).

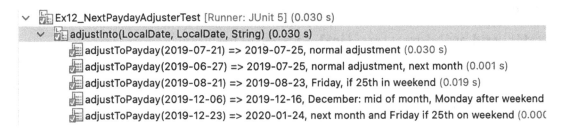

Figure 6-1. *Ouput of the unit test for Ex12_NextPaydayAdjuster*

6.3.13 Solution 13: Formatting and Parsing (★★☆☆☆)

Create a LocalDateTime object and print it in various formats. Format and parse from these formats: dd.MM.yyy HH, dd.MM.yy HH:mm, ISO_LOCAL_DATE_TIME, SHORT, and the US locale.

393

Examples

For 07/27/2017 at 13:14:15 h the output should be as follows:

Formatted	Parsed	Format
27 07 2017 13	2017-07-27T13:00	dd MM yyyy HH
27.07.17 13:14	2017-07-27T13:14	dd.MM.yy HH:mm
2017-07-27T13:14:15	2017-07-27T13:14:15	ISO_LOCAL_DATE_TIME
7/27/17, 1:14 PM	2017-07-27T13:14	SHORT + Locale.US

Tip   Use the `DateTimeFormatter` class and its constants as well as its methods like `ofPattern()` and `ofLocalizedDateTime()`.

Algorithm   For formatting and parsing, the class `DateTimeFormatter` and its various utility methods are used. A utility method that first converts to the desired format and then parses from it is implemented as follows:

```
static void applyFormatters(final LocalDateTime base,
                            final List<DateTimeFormatter> formatters)
{
    formatters.forEach((formatter) -> {

        final String formatted = base.format(formatter);

        try
        {
            // attention: pitfall
            // TemporalAccessor parsed = formatter.parse(formatted);

            LocalDateTime parsed = LocalDateTime.parse(formatted, formatter);

            System.out.println("Formatted: " + formatted + " / " +
                            "Parsed: " + parsed);
        }
```

```
      catch (DateTimeParseException ignore)
      {

      }
   });
}
```

Thereby you see as a hint a pitfall that people like to fall for. The formatter provides a method `parse()` for parsing, but this returns a generic `TemporalAccessor` object and not the required specialization.

Verification

To try it out in JShell, another import is needed in addition to the well-known first one:

```
import java.time.*
import java.time.format.*
```

Then you can type the following lines and comprehend the different formatting:

```
jshell> var someday = LocalDateTime.of(2017, 7, 27, 13, 14, 15)
   ...>
   ...> var format1 = DateTimeFormatter.ofPattern("dd.MM.yyyy HH")
   ...> var format2 = DateTimeFormatter.ofPattern("dd.MM.yy HH:mm")
   ...> var format3 = DateTimeFormatter.ISO_LOCAL_DATE_TIME
   ...> var format4 = DateTimeFormatter.ofLocalizedDateTime(FormatStyle.SHORT,
   ...>                                         FormatStyle.SHORT)
   ...>             .withLocale(Locale.US);
   ...>
   ...> applyFormatters(someday, List.of(format1, format2,
   ...>                          format3, format4));

Formatted: 27.07.2017 13 / Parsed: 2017-07-27T13:00
Formatted: 27.07.17 13:14 / Parsed: 2017-07-27T13:14
Formatted: 2017-07-27T13:14:15 / Parsed: 2017-07-27T13:14:15
Formatted: 7/27/17, 1:14 PM / Parsed: 2017-07-27T13:14
```

6.3.14 Solution 14: Fault-Tolerant Parsing (★★☆☆☆)

Error tolerance is often important when evaluating user input. Your task is to create method `Optional<LocalDate> faultTolerantParse(String, Set<DateTimeFormatter>)` that allows you to parse the following date formats: `dd.MM.yy`, `dd.MM.yyy`, `MM/dd/yyyy`, and `yyyy-MM-dd`.

Examples

The following table shows the expected results of parsing different inputs. Be sure to notice that with two-digit years in the pattern, sometimes it doesn't generate the correct or expected date!

Input	Result
"07.02.71"	2071-02-07
"07.02.1971"	1971-02-07
"02/07/1971"	1971-02-07
"1971-02-07"	1971-02-07

Algorithm   The fault-tolerant parsing involves trying the parsing for a set of supplied `DateTimeFormatters` at a time. If an exception occurs, the format is not suitable, and the next formatter is tried, as long as there are more available. The formatter needed for the task is created in a separate method:

```
static Optional<LocalDate> faultTolerantParse(final CharSequence input,
                                              final Set<DateTimeFormatter>
                                                  formatters)
{
    LocalDate result = null;

    var it = formatters.iterator();
    while (result == null && it.hasNext())
    {
        var entry = it.next();
```

```
    try
    {
        result = LocalDate.parse(input, entry);
    }
    catch (DateTimeParseException ignore)
    {
        // try next
    }
    }

    return Optional.ofNullable(result);
}

static Set<DateTimeFormatter> populateFormatters()
{
    final Set<DateTimeFormatter> formatters = new LinkedHashSet<>();
    formatters.add(DateTimeFormatter.ofPattern("dd.MM.yy"));
    formatters.add(DateTimeFormatter.ofPattern("dd.MM.yyyy"));
    formatters.add(DateTimeFormatter.ofPattern("MM/dd/yyyy"));
    formatters.add(DateTimeFormatter.ofPattern("yyyy-MM-dd"));
    return formatters;
}
```

Verification

You define four different date formats to be supported and then some date notations corresponding to the formats. The test shows that inputs in each of the four formats are successfully recognized and parsed:

```
@ParameterizedTest(name = "faultTolerantParse({0}) expected date {1}")
@CsvSource({ "07.02.71, 2071-02-07", "07.02.1971, 1971-02-07",
            "02/07/1971, 1971-02-07", "1971-02-07, 1971-02-07" })
void faultTolerantParse(String dateAsString, LocalDate expected)
{
    var formatters = Ex14_FaultTolerantParser.populateFormatters();
```

```
var optParsedLocalDate =
    Ex14_FaultTolerantParser.faultTolerantParse(dateAsString,
    formatters);

assertTrue(optParsedLocalDate.isPresent());
assertEquals(expected, optParsedLocalDate.get());
}
```

Finally, let's look at how fault-tolerant parsing behaves for two divergent formats. You expect that due to mismatching formats, you can't supply a LocalDate:

```
@ParameterizedTest(name = "faultTolerantParse({0}) expected empty")
@CsvSource({ "31-01-1940", "1940/01/31" })
void faultTolerantParseInvalidFormats(String dateAsString)
{
    var formatters = Ex14_FaultTolerantParser.populateFormatters();

    var optParsedLocalDate =
        Ex14_FaultTolerantParser.faultTolerantParse(dateAsString,
        formatters);

    assertTrue(optParsedLocalDate.isEmpty());
}
```

## CHAPTER 7

Basic Data Structures: Lists, Sets, and Maps

In the Collections framework, lists, sets, and maps as key-value stores are implemented by so-called *container classes*. They manage objects of other classes. The interfaces List<E>, Set<E>, and Map<K,V> from the package java.util serve as the basis for the container classes. They store object references. Thus, processing primitive types is only possible if they are converted to a wrapper object (such as Byte, Integer, or Double). This is done automatically by the auto-boxing/unboxing implicit since Java 5.

7.1 Introduction

7.1.1 The Interface Collection

The interface java.util.Collection<E> defines the basis for various container classes that implement the interface List<E> respectively Set<E>. The interface Collection<E> provides the following methods, but *no* indexed access:

- int size() gets the number of elements stored in the collection.
- boolean isEmpty() checks if elements are present.
- boolean add(E element) adds an element to the collection.
- boolean addAll(Collection<? extends E> collection) is *a bulk operation*, which adds all passed elements to the collection.
- boolean remove(Object object) removes an element from the collection.
- boolean removeAll(Collection<?> collection) removes from the collection all passed elements, if any.

© Michael Inden 2022
M. Inden, *Java Challenges*, https://doi.org/10.1007/978-1-4842-7395-1_7

- `boolean contains(Object object)` checks if the element is contained in the collection.

- `boolean containsAll(Collection<?> collection)` checks if all specified elements are contained in the collection.

- `boolean retainAll(Collection<?> collection)` retains all elements of the collection that are contained in the given collection.

The modification methods like `add()` and `remove()` return the value `true` if the collection has changed, otherwise `false`. This is especially important for sets.

HINT: SIGNATURE OF CONTAINS(), CONTAINSALL(), AND OTHERS

One small note: Why do the methods `contains()`, `containsAll()`, and `retainAll()` and also `remove()` as well as `removeAll()` not use the generic type E but `Object`? According to the method contract, `equals(Object)` compares the input object with the elements of the collection, but the type is only indirectly relevant through the implementation of `equals(Object)`.

7.1.2 Lists and the Interface List<E>

A list is a sequence of elements ordered by their position. Duplicates are also allowed. The Collections framework defines the interface `List<E>` to describe lists. This allows indexed access and, among other things, the addition and removal of elements. Known implementations are the classes `ArrayList<E>` and `LinkedList<E>`.

The Interface List<E>

The interface `List<E>` forms the basis for all lists and provides *additional* to the methods of the interface `Collection<E>` the following indexed, 0-based accesses:

- `E get(int index)` gets the element at position `index`.

- `void add(int index, E element)` adds the element `element` at position index.

- `E set(int index, E element)` replaces the element at position
  index with the passed element `element` and returns the element
  previously stored at this position.

- `E remove(int index)` removes the element at the `index` position of
  the list and returns the deleted element.

- `int indexOf(Object object)` and `lastIndexOf(Object)` return
  the position of a searched element. The equality between the search
  element and the individual elements of the list is checked with the
  method `equals(Object)`. The search starts either at the beginning
  (`indexOf(Object)`) or at the end of the list (`lastIndexOf(Object)`).

7.1.3 Sets and the Interface Set

In the following sections, you proceed to sets and the interface `Set<E>`. The
mathematical concept of sets states that they do not contain duplicates.

The Interface Set<E>

The interface `Set<E>` is based on the interface `Collection<E>`. In contrast to the
interface `List<E>`, there are no additional methods to those of the `Collection<E>`
interface in the interface `Set<E>`. However, the behavior for the `add(E)` and
`addAll(Collection<? extends E>)` methods is specified such that duplicates are not
possible. This is necessary to guarantee that it is duplicate-free, even if the same object is
added to the set multiple times.

7.1.4 Key-Value Mappings and the Interface Map

Let's now consider the interface `Map<K,V>`. Implementations of it realize mappings from
keys to values. Often maps are also called *dictionaries* or *lookup tables*. The underlying
idea is to assign a unique key to each stored value. An intuitive example is a telephone
directory, where names are mapped to telephone numbers. A search over a name (key)
usually returns a phone number (value) quite quickly. If there is no mapping from phone
number to name, finding a name to a phone number becomes quite time-consuming.

The Interface Map<K,V>

Maps store data as key-value pairs. Each entry is represented by the inner interface Map. Entry<K,V>, which implements the mapping between keys (type parameter K) and values (type parameter V). The methods in the Map<K,V> interface are therefore designed for this particular way of storing key-value mappings. Still, they are similar to those in the Collection<E> interface. However, Collection<E> does not serve as the basis of Map<K,V>, which is rather an independent base type.

The interface Map<K,V> provides the following methods, among others:

- V put(K key, V value) adds a mapping (from key to value) to this map as an entry. If a value is already stored for the key passed, it will be overwritten with the new value. The method returns the value previously associated with this key if there was such an entry; otherwise, it returns null.

- void putAll(Map<? extends K, ? extends V> map) inserts all entries from the passed map into this map. Values of already existing entries are overwritten, analogous to the operation of the method put(K,V).

- V remove(Object key) deletes an entry (key and associated value) from the map. The return value is the value associated with the key key or null if no entry was stored for this key.

- V get(Object key) gets the associated value for a key key. If no entry exists for the key, null is returned.

- boolean containsKey(Object key) checks if the key key is stored in the map and returns true if it is.

- boolean containsValue(Object value) checks if the value value is stored in the map and returns true if it is.

- void clear() deletes all entries of the map.

- int size() gets the number of entries stored in the map.

- boolean isEmpty() checks whether the map is empty.

In addition to the methods just presented, there are also the following methods that provide access to stored keys, values, and entries:

- `Set<K> keySet()` returns a set with all keys.

- `Collection<V> values()` returns the values as a collection.

- `Set<Map.Entry<K,V>> entrySet()` returns the set of all entries. This gives access to both the keys and the values.

These three methods each provide views of the data. If changes are made in the underlying map, they are reflected in the views. ***Please note that changes in the respective view are also transferred to the map***.

Briefly I would like to discuss the different return types of `keySet()` and `values()`. The `keySet()` method returns a `Set<K>` because the keys in the map must be unique. The values may occur multiple times, so `values()` returns a `Collection<V>`.

7.1.5 The Stack as a LIFO Data Structure

The Stack data structure is implemented in the JDK by the class `java.util.Stack<E>`.

A stack is similar to a stack of paper or a desk tray. You put things on top and you can only take things from the top. In addition, a view of the top element is possible. Beyond that, there exists size information or at least a check whether elements are present. This results in the following methods that form the API:

- `void push(E)` adds an element on top.

- `E pop()` takes the element from the top.

- `E peek()` takes a look at the top element.

- `boolean isEmpty()` checks if the stack is empty.

These four methods are sufficient to use stacks profitably for various tasks in practice and for algorithms, for example, when sequences have to be reversed. This property is described in computer science by the term LIFO for Last In, First Out.

Example

For example, you can put some elements on the stack, look at the top element, take elements from the top, and finally, check if the stack is empty according to expectations:

```
final Stack<String> stack = new Stack<>();
stack.push("first");
stack.push("second");
```

```
System.out.println("PEEK: " + stack.peek());
System.out.println("POP: " + stack.pop());
System.out.println("POP: " + stack.pop());
System.out.println("ISEMPTY: " + stack.isEmpty());
```

This provides the following output:

```
PEEK: second
POP: second
POP: first
ISEMPTY: true
```

7.1.6 The Queue as a FIFO Data Structure

To conclude this introduction into important data structures, I would like to mention the data structure queue, which is modeled in the JDK by the interface `java.util.Queue<E>`. A queue is similar to a queue at a cash register. People queue up, and whoever came first is served first, known in computer science as FIFO for First In, First Out.

Unfortunately, the `Queue<E>` interface in the JDK is quite cluttered since it is derived from `Collection<E>`—a similar design flaw to the JDK's stack. In both cases, the API is polluted with many irrelevant methods, which means that misuse is inevitable.[1]

Normally, only a few actions, such as adding and removing elements, are needed to benefit from a queue. In addition, a look at the element at the beginning is possible. Beyond that, it still offers size information or at least a check whether elements are present. This results in the following methods that form the API:

- `void offer(E)` adds an element to the end of the queue.

- `E poll()` takes a look at the element at the beginning of the queue.

- `E peek()` takes a look at the element at the beginning of the queue.

- `boolean isEmpty()` checks if the queue is empty.

---

[1] Please note that `java.util.Stack` was created long before the Collections Framework existed and is based on `java.util.Vector`. The class `Stack` was later refactored so that it could be integrated into the Collection framework. But, even in the beginning, it should not have to be derived from `Vector`. Instead, delegation would have been appropriate.

These four methods are sufficient to create queues for various tasks in practice and for algorithms, such as if you intend to transform recursive algorithms into iterative ones.

A small side note is still the following: The method names for insertion and removal are borrowed from the Java API. If you were to develop the data container yourself, void enqueue(E) for insertion and E dequeue() for removal would certainly be better names, as they reflect the concept more clearly.

Example

For example, you can add some elements to the queue and then process them as long as there are elements. To show special handling, reprocessing is targeted for the entry *Michael*. Similar idioms exist in various algorithms that use queues as a data structure.

```java
public static void main(final String[] args)
{
    final Queue<String> waitingPersons = new LinkedList<>();

    waitingPersons.offer("Marcello");
    waitingPersons.offer("Michael");
    waitingPersons.offer("Karthi");

    while (!waitingPersons.isEmpty())
    {
        if (waitingPersons.peek().equals("Michael"))
        {
            // At the end " queue again" and process
            waitingPersons.offer("Michael again");
            waitingPersons.offer("Last Man");
        }
        final String nextPerson = waitingPersons.poll();
        System.out.println("Processing " + nextPerson);
    }
}
```

The small sample program provides the following output:

```
Processing Marcello
Processing Michael
Processing Karthi
Processing Michael again
Processing Last Man
```

7.2 Exercises

7.2.1 Exercise 1: Set Operations (★★☆☆☆)

Exercise 1a: Common Elements (★★☆☆☆)

Find the common elements of two collections *A* and *B*, both with and without using matching methods of the Collections framework. Write method Set<T> findCommon(Collection<T>, Collection<T>).

Examples

Input A	Input B	Result
[1, 2, 4, 7, 8]	[2, 3, 7, 9]	[2, 7]
[1, 2, 7, 4, 7, 8]	[7, 7, 3, 2, 9]	[2, 7]
[2, 4, 6, 8]	[1, 3, 5, 7, 9]	Ø = []

Exercise 1b: Set Operations (★★☆☆☆)

Given the two sets *A* and *B*, compute the difference sets *A* − *B* and *B* − *A*, the union set *A* ∪ *B*, and the intersection set *A* ∩ *B*, respectively.

Examples

Input A	Input B	A - B	B - A	A ∪ B	A ∩ B
[1, 2, 3, 4, 5]	[2, 4, 6, 7]	[1, 3, 5]	[6, 7]	[1, 2, 3, 4, 5, 6, 7]	[2, 4]
[2, 4, 6]	[1, 3, 5, 7]	[2, 4, 6]	[1, 3, 5, 7]	[1, 2, 3, 4, 5, 6, 7]	Ø = []

7.2.2 Exercise 2: List Reverse (★★☆☆☆)

Exercise 2a: List Reverse (★★☆☆☆)

Write method `List<T> reverse(List<T>)` that creates a result list and returns the elements of the original list in reverse order.

Examples

Input	Result
[1, 2, 3, 4]	[4, 3, 2, 1]
["A", "BB", "CCC", "DDDD"]	["DDDD", "CCC", "BB", "A"]

Exercise 2b: List Reverse Inplace (★★☆☆☆)

What is different if you want to implement reversing the order inplace to be memory-optimal for very large datasets? What should be given then?

Exercise 2c: List Reverse Without Performant Index Access (★★☆☆☆)

Now let's assume that no performant random index access is available. What happens if you want to reverse the order of a `LinkedList<E>`? There, any position-based access will result in a list traversal to the desired element. How do you avoid this?

Tip   Use a stack.

7.2.3 Exercise 3: Remove Duplicates (★★☆☆☆)

You are supposed to remove duplicate entries from a list. The constraint is that the original order should be preserved. Therefore write method `List<T> removeDuplicates(List<T>)`.

Examples

Input	Result
[1, 1, 2, 3, 4, 1, 2, 3]	[1, 2, 3, 4]
[7, 5, 3, 5, 1]	[7, 5, 3, 1]
[1, 1, 1, 1]	[1]

7.2.4 Exercise 4: Maximum Profit (★★★☆☆)

Let's imagine you have a sequence of prices ordered in time and you want to calculate the maximum profit. The challenge is to determine at what time (or value, in this case) it would be ideal to buy and sell. Write method int maxRevenue(List<Integer>) for this purpose, where the temporal order is expressed by the index in the list.

Examples

Input	Result
[250, 270, 230, 240, 222, 260, 294, 210]	72
[0, 10, 20, 30, 40, 50, 60, 70]	70
[70, 60, 50, 40, 30, 20, 10, 0]	0
[]	0

7.2.5 Exercise 5: Longest Sequence (★★★☆☆)

Suppose you are modeling stock prices or altitudes of a track by a list of numbers. Find the longest sequence of numbers whose values ascend or at least stay the same. Write method List<Integer> findLongestGrowingSequence(List<Integer>).

Examples

Input	Result
[7, 2, 7, 1, 2, 5, 7, 1]	[1, 2, 5, 7]
[7, 2, 7, 1, 2, 3, 8, 1, 2, 3, 4, 5]	[1, 2, 3, 4, 5]
[1, 1, 2, 2, 2, 3, 3, 3, 3]	[1, 1, 2, 2, 2, 3, 3, 3, 3]

7.2.6 Exercise 6: Own Stack (★★☆☆☆)

Consider the class java.util.Stack<E> from the JDK. Perform a design analysis and identify possible vulnerabilities. Define the basic requirements for a stack and, based on them, implement class Ex06_Stack<E> using a List<E>.

7.2.7 Exercise 7: Well-Formed Braces (★★☆☆☆)

Write method boolean checkParentheses(String) that checks whether a sequence of braces is neatly nested in each case. This should accept round, square, and curly braces but no other characters.

Examples

Input	Result	Comment
"(())"	true	
"([[]])"	true	
"((())"	false	Odd number of braces
"((a)"	false	Wrong character, no braces
"(([)"	false	No matching braces

Bonus   Extend the solution to provide a clear mapping of error causes. Start with the following enum enumeration:

```
static enum CheckResult
{
    OK, ODD_LENGTH, CLOSING_BEFORE_OPENING, MISMATCHING, INVALID_CHAR,
    REMAINING_OPENING
}
```

7.2.8 Exercise 8: Check a Magic Triangle (★★★☆☆)

Write method boolean isMagicTriangle(List<Integer>) that checks whether a sequence of numbers forms a magic triangle. Such a triangle is defined as one where the respective sums of the three sides' values must all be equal.

Examples

The following shows this for one triangle each of side length 3 and side length 4:

```
  1           2
 6 5         8 5
2 4 3       4   9
           3 7 6 1
```

This results in the following sides and sums:

Input	Values 1	Values 2
side 1	1 + 5 + 3 = 9	2 + 5 + 9 + 1 = 17
side 2	3 + 4 + 2 = 9	1 + 6 + 7 + 3 = 17
side 3	2 + 6 + 1 = 9	3 + 4 + 8 + 2 = 17

Tip   Represent the individual sides of the triangle as sublists and use the List<E> subList(int startInclusive, int endExclusive) method to extract the respective sides.

7.2.9 Exercise 9: Pascal's Triangle (★★★☆☆)

Write method List<List<Integer>> pascal(int) that computes Pascal's triangle in terms of nested lists. As you know, each new line results from the previous one. If there are more than two elements in it, two values are added, and the sums build the values of the new line. In each case, a 1 is appended to the front and back.

Example

For the value 5, the desired representation is as follows:

```
[1]
[1, 1]
[1, 2, 1]
[1, 3, 3, 1]
[1, 4, 6, 4, 1]
```

7.2.10 Exercise 10: Most Frequent Elements (★★☆☆☆)

Write method Map<Integer, long> valueCount(List<Integer>) that computes a histogram, that is, the distribution of the frequencies of the numbers in the passed list. Also, write method Map<Integer, Long> sortByValue(Map<Integer, Long>) that sorts the map by its values instead of by keys. A descending sort has to be implemented, whereby the highest values are listed at the beginning.

Examples

Input	Result	Most frequent(s)
[1, 2, 3, 4, 4, 4, 3, 3, 2, 4]	{1=1, 2=2, 3=3, 4=4}	4=4
[1, 1, 1, 2, 2, 2, 3, 3, 3]	{1=3, 2=3, 3=3}	Depending on query, logically all

7.2.11 Exercise 11: Addition of Digits (★★★☆☆)

Consider two decimal numbers that are to be added. Sounds simple, but for this assignment, the numbers are interestingly represented as a list of digits. Write method List<Integer> listAdd(List<Integer>, List<Integer>). Also, consider the special case where there is an overflow.

Exercise 11a: Addition (★★★☆☆)

In the first part of the task, the digits are to be stored in the order of their occurrence in the list.

Examples

Input 1	Input 2	Result
123 = [1, 2, 3]	456 = [4, 5, 6]	579 = [5, 7, 9]
927 = [9, 2, 7]	135 = [1, 3, 5]	1062 = [1, 0, 6, 2]

Exercise 11b: Addition Inverse (★★★☆☆)

What changes if the digits are stored in reverse order in the list?

Examples

Input 1	Input 2	Result
123 = [3, 2, 1]	456 = [6, 5, 4]	579 = [9, 7, 5]
927 = [7, 2, 9]	135 = [5, 3, 1]	1062 = [2, 6, 0, 1]

7.2.12 Exercise 12: Compound Key (★★☆☆☆)

Imagine that you want to use two or more values as a key in a map. That is, you want to use a so-called *compound key*. For example, such a key consists of two int values or of one String and one int. How can this be achieved?

Examples

Compound key (name, age)	Hobbies
(Peter, 22)	TV
(Mike, 48)	Java, Cycling, Movies

Compound key (month, year)	Conferences
(September, 2019)	ch open Zurich, Oracle Code One SF
(October, 2019)	JAX London
(November, 2019)	W-JAX Munich

7.2.13 Exercise 13: List Merge (★★☆☆☆)

Given two lists of numbers, each sorted in ascending order, merge them into a result list according to their order. Write method List<Integer> merge(List<Integer>, List<Integer>).

Examples

Input 1	Input 2	Result
1, 4, 7, 12, 20	10, 15, 17, 33	1, 4, 7, 10, 12, 15, 17, 20, 33
2, 3, 5, 7	11, 13, 17	2, 3, 5, 7, 11, 13, 17
2, 3, 5, 7, 11	7, 11, 13, 17	2, 3, 5, 7, 7, 11, 11, 13, 17
[1, 2, 3]	∅ = []	[1, 2, 3]

7.2.14 Exercise 14: Excel Magic Select (★★☆☆☆)

If you have worked a little with Excel, then you have probably used the so-called Magic Selection. It continuously populates a selected area with values based on the previous values. This works for numbers, weekdays, or dates, for example. To achieve something similar on your own, write method List<Integer> generateFollowingValues(int, int), that implements this for numbers. Create a variation of this suitable for weekdays and with the following signature: List<DayOfWeek> generateFollowingValues(DayOfWeek, int)

Examples

Initial value	Count	Result
1	7	[1, 2, 3, 4, 5, 6, 7]
5	4	[5, 6, 7, 8]
FRIDAY	8	[FRIDAY, SATURDAY, SUNDAY, MONDAY, TUESDAY, WEDNESDAY, THURSDAY, FRIDAY]

7.3 Solutions

7.3.1 Solution 1: Set Operations (★★☆☆☆)

Solution 1a: Common Elements (★★☆☆☆)

Find the common elements of two collections *A* and *B*, both with and without using matching methods of the Collections framework. Write method Set<T> findCommon(Collection<T>, Collection<T>).

Examples

Input A	Input B	Result
[1, 2, 4, 7, 8]	[2, 3, 7, 9]	[2, 7]
[1, 2, 7, 4, 7, 8]	[7, 7, 3, 2, 9]	[2, 7]
[2, 4, 6, 8]	[1, 3, 5, 7, 9]	∅ = []

Algorithm   The Collections framework provides the `retainAll()` method to determine common elements. This requires a new `Set<E>` to be created for the result so that no modification occurs in the original collections:

```
static <T> Set<T> findCommon(final Collection<T> collection1,
                             final Collection<T> collection2)
{
    final Set<T> results = new HashSet<>(collection1);
    results.retainAll(collection2);

    return results;
}
```

Instead of using JDK methods, you now use maps. You maintain a counter for being contained in Collection 1 or 2. To fill them appropriately, you first iterate through all elements from Collection 1 and enter the value 1 in the map. Now you traverse all elements of the second collection. With `computeIfPresent()` you increase the counter if there is already an entry in the map for the value. Thus, all elements in both Collections receive the value 2 and with multiple occurrences a higher value. On the other hand, elements exclusively from Collection 2 are never stored. Finally, you keep only those entries whose number is greater than or equal to 2.

```
static <T> Set<T> findCommonNoJdk(final Collection<T> collection1,
                                  final Collection<T> collection2)
{
    final Map<T, Long> results = new HashMap<>();
    populateFromCollection1(collection1, results);
    markIfAlsoInSecond(collection2, results);

    return removeAllJustInOneCollection(results);
}

static <T> void populateFromCollection1(final Collection<T> collection1,
                                        final Map<T, Long> results)
{
    for (T elem1 : collection1)
    {
        results.put(elem1, 1L);
    }
}
```

```java
static <T> void markIfAlsoInSecond(final Collection<T> collection2,
                                   final Map<T, Long> results)
{
    for (T elem2 : collection2)
    {
        results.computeIfPresent(elem2, (key, value) -> value + 1);
    }
}

static <T> Set<T> removeAllJustInOneCollection(final Map<T, Long> results)
{
    return results.entrySet().stream().filter(entry -> entry.getValue() >= 2).
                              map(entry -> entry.getKey()).
                              collect(Collectors.toSet());
}
```

Looking at it, it clearly seems too complicated. So how do you do it better?

Optimized algorithm   In fact, the problem can be solved in a much more compact and understandable way by checking for all elements from the first collection, whether it is contained in the second one, and then including this value in the result set for the case:

```java
static <T> Set<T> findCommonTwoLoops(final Collection<T> collection1,
                                     final Collection<T> collection2)
{
    final Set<T> results = new HashSet<>();

    for (T elem1 : collection1)
    {
        for (T elem2 : collection2)
        {
            if (elem1.equals(elem2))
                results.add(elem1);
        }
    }
    return results;
}
```

Verification

You check the implementation by the following unit tests—here only shown in excerpts for the most complex variant:

```
@ParameterizedTest(name = "findCommonNoJdk({0}, {1}) = {2}")
@MethodSource("createCollectionsAndExpected")
void testFindCommonNoJdk(Collection<Integer>  col1,
                         Collection<Integer> col2, Set<Integer> expected)
{
    final Set<Integer> result = Ex01_SetOperations.findCommonNoJdk(col1, col2);

    assertEquals(expected, result);
}

private static Stream<Arguments> createCollectionsAndExpected()
{
    return Stream.of(Arguments.of(List.of(1, 2, 4, 7, 8),
                                  List.of(2, 3, 7, 9), Set.of(2, 7)),
                     Arguments.of(List.of(1, 2, 7, 4, 7, 8),
                                  List.of(7, 7, 3, 2, 9), Set.of(2, 7)),
                     Arguments.of(List.of(2, 4, 6, 8),
                                  List.of(1, 3, 5, 7, 9), Set.of()));
}
```

Solution 1b: Set Operations (★★☆☆☆)

Given the two sets A and B, compute the difference sets $A - B$ and $B - A$, the union set $A \cup B$, and the intersection set $A \cap B$, respectively.

Examples

Input A	Input B	A - B	B - A	A ∪ B	A ∩ B
[1, 2, 3, 4, 5]	[2, 4, 6, 7]	[1, 3, 5]	[6, 7]	[1, 2, 3, 4, 5, 6, 7]	[2, 4]
[2, 4, 6]	[1, 3, 5, 7]	[2, 4, 6]	[1, 3, 5, 7]	[1, 2, 3, 4, 5, 6, 7]	$\emptyset = []$

Algorithm   You already learned that the methods of the Collections framework are capable of determining the intersection set, for example. Further is possible: With the help of removeAll() and addAll() difference sets and union sets can be determined.

These methods have to be called appropriately to implement the assignment. As a starting point, you fill a HashSet<E> with the values of the first collection. After that, you execute the desired action so that elements are removed or added. Your methods are named difference(), union(), and intersection() so that their uses should be intuitive.

```
static <T> Set<T> difference(final Collection<T> collection1,
                             final Collection<T> collection2)
{
    final Set<T> results = new HashSet<>(collection1);
    results.removeAll(collection2);
    return results;
}

static <T> Set<T> union(final Collection<T> collection1,
                        final Collection<T> collection2)
{
    final Set<T> results = new HashSet<>(collection1);
    results.addAll(collection2);
    return results;
}

static <T>  Set<T> intersection(final Collection<T> collection1,
                                final Collection<T> collection2)
{
    final Set<T> results = new HashSet<>(collection1);
    results.retainAll(collection2);
    return results;
}
```

Optimized algorithm   Although the implementation shown is quite understandable as well as nice and short, you may still be bothered by one detail: You always have to create a new result collection to avoid changes in the original collection.

Let's look at alternatives with the Stream API. While difference() and intersection() are pretty obvious with filter(), union() implements the probably seldom used and rather less known method concat() from the Stream API to concatenate two streams. The resulting stream will contain all elements of the first stream and then all elements of the second stream.

```
static <T> Set<T> differenceV2(final Collection<T> collection1,
                               final Collection<T> collection2)
{
    return collection1.stream().
                   filter(element -> !collection2.contains(element)).
                   collect(Collectors.toSet());
}

static <T> Set<T> unionV2(final Collection<T> collection1,
                          final Collection<T> collection2)
{
    return Stream.concat(collection1.stream(), collection2.stream()).
              collect(Collectors.toSet());
}

static <T> Set<T> intersectionV2(final Collection<T> collection1,
                                 final Collection<T> collection2)
{
    return collection1.stream().
                   filter(element -> collection2.contains(element)).
                   collect(Collectors.toSet());
}
```

Verification

To comprehend the set operations, you define two lists each with the values from the introduction, and then call the method performSetOperations(), which performs the four set operations:

```
jshell> performSetOperations(List.of(1, 2, 3, 4, 5), List.of(2, 4, 6, 7, 8))
A: [1, 2, 3, 4, 5]
B: [2, 4, 6, 7, 8]
```

```
dif A-B: [1, 3, 5]
dif B-A: [6, 7, 8]
uni A+B: [1, 2, 3, 4, 5, 6, 7, 8]
sec A+B: [2, 4]

jshell> performSetOperations(List.of(2, 4, 6, 8), List.of(1, 3, 5, 7))
A: [2, 4, 6, 8]
B: [1, 3, 5, 7]
dif A-B: [2, 4, 6, 8]
dif B-A: [1, 3, 5, 7]
uni A+B: [1, 2, 3, 4, 5, 6, 7, 8]
sec A+B: []
```

You implement the helper method as follows:

```
static void performSetOperations(final Collection<Integer> colA,
                                 final Collection<Integer> colB)
{
    System.out.println("A: " + colA);
    System.out.println("B: " + colB);
    System.out.println("dif A-B: " + difference(colA, colB));
    System.out.println("dif B-A: " + difference(colB, colA));
    System.out.println("uni A+B: " + union(colA, colB));
    System.out.println("sec A+B: " + intersection(colA, colB));
    System.out.println();
}
```

Let's take a look at a test case for the union set as an example—the other tests are implemented analogously:

```
@ParameterizedTest(name = "unionV2({0}, {1}) = {2}")
@MethodSource("createCollectionsAndUnionExpected")
void testUnionV2(Set<Integer> colA, Set<Integer> colB,
                Set<Integer> expectedUnion)
{
    final Set<Integer> result = Ex01_SetOperations.unionV2(colA, colB);

    assertEquals(expectedUnion, result);
}
```

```
private static Stream<Arguments> createCollectionsAndUnionExpected()
{
    return Stream.of(Arguments.of(Set.of(1, 2, 3, 4, 5), Set.of(2, 4, 6, 7, 8),
                                Set.of(1, 2, 3, 4, 5, 6, 7, 8)),
                    Arguments.of(Set.of(2, 4, 6), Set.of(1, 3, 5, 7),
                                Set.of(1, 2, 3, 4, 5, 6, 7)));
}
```

7.3.2 Solution 2: List Reverse (★★☆☆☆)

Solution 2a: List Reverse (★★☆☆☆)

Write method List<T> reverse(List<T>) that creates a result list and returns the elements of the original list in reverse order.

Examples

Input	Result
[1, 2, 3, 4]	[4, 3, 2, 1]
["A", "BB", "CCC", "DDDD"]	["DDDD", "CCC", "BB", "A"]

Algorithm   A simple solution is to traverse a list from back to front, and for each position, add the current element to a result list. This can be implemented index-based as follows:

```
static <T> List<T> reverse(final List<T> values)
{
    final List<T> result = new ArrayList<>();

    for (int i = values.size() - 1; i >= 0; i--)
    {
        result.add(values.get(i));
    }
    return result;
}
```

Here, an index-based access is performed with get(i) in each case. Such an access is performant for ArrayList<E> with $O(1)$, but significantly worse for LinkedList<E> with $O(n)$. A more elegant way to do this is to use a ListIterator<T>. On the one hand, the running time is independent of the list implementation because depending on the concrete type, either ArrayList<E> navigates via the index or LinkedList<E> via its nodes. On the other hand, ListIterator<T> allows specifying the start position via a parameter. Subsequently, this position is placed after the last element for the traversal from the end. Finally, in addition to the normal Iterator<T>, the methods hasPrevious() and previous() can be used to navigate backwards.

```
static <T> List<T> listReverseWithListIterator(final List<T> values)
{
    final List<T> result = new ArrayList<>();

    final ListIterator<T> it = values.listIterator(values.size());
    while (it.hasPrevious())
    {
        result.add(it.previous());
    }
    return result;
}
```

Solution 2b: List Reverse Inplace (★★☆☆☆)

What is different if you want to implement reversing the order inplace to be memory-optimal for enormous datasets? What should be given then?

Algorithm   Based on indexed access, you proceed inwards from the beginning and the end, swapping the elements:

```
// only performant with indexed access with O(1)
static <T> void listReverseInplace(final List<T> inputs)
{
    // run from the left and right, swap the elements based on their positions
    int left = 0;
    int right = inputs.size() - 1;
```

```
    while (left < right)
    {
        final T leftValue = inputs.get(left);
        final T rightValue = inputs.get(right);

        inputs.set(left, rightValue);
        inputs.set(right, leftValue);

        left++;
        right--;
    }
}
```

However, this is only performant as long as index-based access with a running time $O(1)$ is given. For a LinkedList<E> this does not apply. Therefore the shown solution would not be very performant and consequently not well suited. Moreover, the passed list must be mutable. Otherwise, the elements cannot be changed by calls to set().

Solution 2c: List Reverse Without Performant Index Access (★★☆☆)

Now let's assume that no performant random index access is available. What happens if you want to reverse the order of a LinkedList<E>? There, any position- based access will result in a list traversal to the desired element. How do you avoid this?

Tip   Use a stack.

Algorithm   In the case that no performant indexed-based access is available and you still have to reverse the order with running time complexity of $O(n)$, a stack comes into play—just as for various other algorithms, including this one. You traverse the list from front to back and put the current element on the stack each time. Afterwards, you iteratively remove the top element from the stack and add it to a result list until the stack is empty.

```
static <T> List<T> listReverseWithStack(final List<T> inputs)
{
    // idea: Run through the list from front to back (performant) and
    // fill a stack
```

```
    final Stack<T> allValues = new Stack<>();
    final Iterator<T> it = inputs.iterator();
    while (it.hasNext())
    {
        allValues.push(it.next());
    }

    // empty the stack and fill a result list
    final List<T> result = new ArrayList<>();
    while (!allValues.isEmpty())
    {
        result.add(allValues.pop());
    }

    return result;
}
```

This solution requires two passes and additional memory. Still, it is much more efficient than the version with calls to the index-based method get() in a loop. Why? When using a LinkedList<E>, it iterates through its elements to the desired position for each index access, resulting in $O(n^2)$.

Verification

Let's experiment with the input values from the example and invoke the methods you created earlier:

```
@ParameterizedTest(name = "listReverse({0}) = {1}")
@MethodSource("listInputsAndExpected")
<T> void listReverse(List<T> inputs, List<T> expected)
{
    final List<T> result = Ex02_ListReverse.listReverse(inputs);

    assertEquals(expected, result);
}

@ParameterizedTest(name = "listReverseInplace({0}) = {1}")
@MethodSource("listInputsAndExpected")
<T> void listReverseInplace(List<T> inputs, List<T> expected)
```

```
{
    // allow modification of the list by wrapping
    final List<T> modifiableInputs = new ArrayList<>(inputs);
    Ex02_ListReverse.listReverseInplace(modifiableInputs);

    assertEquals(expected, modifiableInputs);
}

static Stream<Arguments> listInputsAndExpected()
{
    return Stream.of(Arguments.of(List.of(1, 2, 3, 4),
                                  List.of(4, 3, 2, 1)),
                     Arguments.of(List.of("A", "BB", "CCC", "DDDD"),
                                  List.of("DDDD", "CCC", "BB", "A")));
}
```

7.3.3 Solution 3: Remove Duplicates (★★☆☆☆)

You are supposed to remove duplicate entries from a list. The constraint is that the original order should be preserved. Therefore write method List<T> removeDuplicates(List<T>).

Examples

Input	Result
[1, 1, 2, 3, 4, 1, 2, 3]	[1, 2, 3, 4]
[7, 5, 3, 5, 1]	[7, 5, 3, 1]
[1, 1, 1, 1]	[1]

Algorithm   First, copy the input to allow modifications. Then traverse the list from front to back and successively fill a set with the entries contained in the list. For each element of the list, check whether it is already contained in the set of entries found. If a duplicate is identified, use the remove() method of the Iterator to remove it from the result list.

```java
static <T> List<T> removeDuplicates(final List<T> inputs)
{
    final List<T> result = new ArrayList<>(inputs);
    final Set<T> numbers = new HashSet<>();

    final Iterator<T> it = result.iterator();
    while (it.hasNext())
    {
        final T elem = it.next();

        if (numbers.contains(elem))
            it.remove(); // remove duplicate
        else
            numbers.add(elem);
    }

    return result;
}
```

Optimized algorithm   While implementing it, you might already get the idea of deleting the duplicates simply by refilling them into a set. This works, but both HashSet<E> and TreeSet<E> would potentially mix up the order of the elements. The recommended workaround uses the LinkedHashSet<E> class, which preserves the insertion order. This makes the duplicate removal implementation a snap.

```java
static List<Integer> removeDuplicatesV2(final List<Integer> inputs)
{
    return new ArrayList<>(new LinkedHashSet<>(inputs));
}
```

As almost always, there are alternatives. I would like to present one using the Stream API. In this implementation, you take advantage of the fact that the Stream API provides the distinct() method, which removes duplicates. After that, you only need to convert the result into a list.

```java
static List<Integer> removeDuplicatesV3(final List<Integer> inputs)
{
    return inputs.stream().distinct().collect(Collectors.toList());
}
```

Verification

Again, you use the introductory example's values to verify the implementation. The tests for the two optimized versions are not shown below because they are—apart from the method call—identical.

```
@ParameterizedTest(name = "removeDuplicates({0}) = {1}")
@MethodSource("listInputsAndExpected")
void removeDuplicates(List<Integer> inputs, List<Integer> expected)
{
    List<Integer> result = Ex03_ListRemove.removeDuplicates(inputs);

    assertEquals(expected, result);
}

private static Stream<Arguments> listInputsAndExpected()
{
    return Stream.of(Arguments.of(List.of(1, 1, 2, 3, 4, 1, 2, 3),
                                  List.of(1, 2, 3, 4)),
                    Arguments.of(List.of(7, 5, 3, 5, 1),
                                  List.of(7, 5, 3, 1)),
                    Arguments.of(List.of(1, 1, 1, 1), List.of(1)));
}
```

7.3.4 Solution 4: Maximum Profit (★★★☆☆)

Let's imagine you have a sequence of prices ordered in time and you want to calculate the maximum profit. The challenge is to determine at which time (or value in this case) it's ideal to buy and sell. Write method int maxRevenue(List<Integer>) for this purpose, where the temporal order is expressed by the index in the list.

Examples

Input	Result
[250, 270, 230, 240, 222, 260, 294, 210]	72
[0, 10, 20, 30, 40, 50, 60, 70]	70
[70, 60, 50, 40, 30, 20, 10, 0]	0
[]	0

Algorithm   Initially, you may be tempted to determine the minimum and the maximum and simply return their difference. After a short reflection, it becomes clear that a time dimension has to be considered in this case. First, a purchase and then a sale at a higher price must take place to realize a profit.

The next idea is to run through the list twice. First, all minimum values are determined by looking to see if the current value is less than the current minimum. This is then added to the list of minimum values valid for the time. In the second run, you determine the largest difference by comparing element by element. If the current value is greater than the currently valid minimum value, then the profit thus obtained is the difference between the current value and the minimum value determined at the position. Finally, the maximum profit is calculated from the maximum of the current maximum and the current profit. For example 1, the result is as follows:

value	250	270	230	240	222	260	294	210
minimum	250	250	230	230	222	222	222	210
difference	0	20	0	10	0	38	72	0
max. difference	0	20	20	20	20	38	72	72

Based on this idea, you implement it in Java as follows:

```java
static int maxRevenue(final List<Integer> prices)
{
    final List<Integer> relevantMins = calcRelevantMins(prices);
    return calcMaxRevenue(prices, relevantMins);
}

static List<Integer> calcRelevantMins(final List<Integer> prices)
{
    final List<Integer> relevantMins = new ArrayList<>();

    int currentMin = Integer.MAX_VALUE;
    for (int currentPrice : prices)
    {
        currentMin = Math.min(currentMin, currentPrice);
        relevantMins.add(currentMin);
    }
```

```
        return relevantMins;
}

static int calcMaxRevenue(final List<Integer> prices,
                          final List<Integer> relevantMins)
{
    int maxRevenue = 0;
    for (int i = 0; i < prices.size(); i++)
    {
        if (prices.get(i) > relevantMins.get(i))
        {
            final int currentRevenue = prices.get(i) - relevantMins.get(i);
            maxRevenue = Math.max(maxRevenue, currentRevenue);
        }
    }
    return maxRevenue;
}
```

Optimized algorithm   The variation just shown requires two passes. As long as the accesses are made in memory, this hardly plays a crucial role in the performance. The situation is somewhat different if the data is determined each time, for example, via a REST call or from a database.

In fact, the number of necessary calls and loop iterations can be reduced. However, this optimization can probably only be achieved if the previous implementation has been completed first.

```
static int maxRevenueV2(final List<Integer> prices)
{
    int currentMin = Integer.MAX_VALUE;
    int maxRevenue = 0;

    for (int currentPrice : prices)
    {
        currentMin = Math.min(currentMin, currentPrice);
        final int currentRevenue = currentPrice - currentMin;
```

```
        maxRevenue = Math.max(maxRevenue, currentRevenue);
    }
    return maxRevenue;
}
```

The statements in the loop could even be optimized a bit. If a call to min() would be costly, then this step might be worthwhile. As optimization, either the minimum (then maxRevenue cannot change) or the profit must be adjusted, provided that the minimum does not change.

```
if (currentPrice < currentMin)
    currentMin = currentPrice;
else
    maxRevenue = Math.max(maxRevenue, currentPrice - currentMin);
```

Verification

For testing, you again use the values from the introductory example:

```
@ParameterizedTest(name = "maxRevenue({0}) = {1}")
@MethodSource("listInputsAndExpected")
void maxRevenue(List<Integer> inputs, int expected)
{
    int result = Ex04_FindMaxRevenue.maxRevenue(inputs);

    assertEquals(expected, result);
}

private static Stream<Arguments> listInputsAndExpected()
{
    return Stream.of(Arguments.of(List.of(250, 270, 230, 240,
                                        222, 260, 294, 210), 72),
                Arguments.of(List.of(0, 10, 20, 30, 40, 50, 60, 70), 70),
                Arguments.of(List.of(70, 60, 50, 40, 30, 20, 10, 0), 0),
                Arguments.of(List.of(), 0));
}
```

7.3.5 Solution 5: Longest Sequence (★★★☆☆)

Suppose you are modeling stock prices or altitudes of a track by a list of numbers. Find the longest sequence of numbers whose values ascend or at least stay the same. Write method List<Integer> findLongestGrowingSequence(List<Integer>).

Examples

Input	Result
[7, 2, 7, 1, 2, 5, 7, 1]	[1, 2, 5, 7]
[7, 2, 7, 1, 2, 3, 8, 1, 2, 3, 4, 5]	[1, 2, 3, 4, 5]
[1, 1, 2, 2, 2, 3, 3, 3, 3]	[1, 1, 2, 2, 2, 3, 3, 3, 3]

Algorithm   Here a so-called *greedy* algorithm is used. The idea is to collect the subsequent elements starting from one element until the next element is smaller than the current one. A temporary list and a result list are used for this purpose. Both are initially empty and are successively filled: the temporary list at each element read that is greater than or equal to the predecessor and the result list whenever a smaller successor value is found. If a value is smaller, the temporary list is cleared and starts as a one-element list with the current value. If the result list at a flank change is shorter than the temporary list with the previously collected elements, then the temporary list becomes the new result list. This procedure is repeated until you reach the end of the initial list.

Let's look at a procedure for the input 1272134572:

Input	Current character	Temporary list	Result list
1272134572	1	1	
1272134572	2	12	
1272134572	7	127	
1272134572	2	2	127
1272134572	1	1	127
1272134572	3	13	127
1272134572	4	134	127

(*continued*)

Input	Current character	Temporary list	Result list
1272134572	5	1345	127
1272134577	7	13457	127
1272134572	2	2	13457

```java
static List<Integer> findLongestGrowingSequence(final List<Integer> values)
{
    List<Integer> longestSubsequence = List.of();
    List<Integer> currentSubsequence = new ArrayList<>();

    int lastValue = Integer.MIN_VALUE;

    for (int currentValue : values)
    {
        if (currentValue >= lastValue)
        {
            lastValue = currentValue;
            currentSubsequence.add(currentValue);
        }
        else
        {
            // end of this sequence, start new sequence
            if (currentSubsequence.size() >= longestSubsequence.size())
            {
                longestSubsequence = currentSubsequence;
            }
            currentSubsequence = new ArrayList<>();
            lastValue = currentValue;
            currentSubsequence.add(currentValue);
        }
    }
```

```
        // important, because otherwise the last sequence might not be considered
        if (currentSubsequence.size() >= longestSubsequence.size())
        {
            longestSubsequence = currentSubsequence;
        }
        return longestSubsequence;
}
```

Be sure to note the additional check after the for loop—otherwise, a final sequence will not be correctly returned as a result.

Mini optimization   The check should be optimized a bit further. As you can see, assigning the value and adding it to the current temporary list happens in every case. Thus, these actions can be separated from the condition and written as follows:

```
for (int currentValue : values)
{
    if (currentValue < lastValue)
    {
        // end of this sequence, start new sequence
        // check the length, possibly new longest sequence
        if (currentSubsequence.size() >= longestSubsequence.size())
        {
            longestSubsequence = currentSubsequence;
        }
        currentSubsequence = new ArrayList<>();
    }

    lastValue = currentValue;
    currentSubsequence.add(currentValue);
}
```

Procedure for sections of equal length   When checking for the longest sequence, you can either compare with > or >=. If there are two or more sequences of the same length, in the first case with > the first one is taken as a result, with >= always the last one.

Alternative and optimized algorithm   Sometimes creating temporary data structures can be rather undesirable, for example, when the subsections can become huge. In such a case, it offers itself to determine only the respective index borders. As a final step, you extract the appropriate part. Even here, you can do without creating a new list when using subList(). In the following code, you represent the index range for the longest section using the language feature record of modern Java:

```java
static record StartEndPair(int start, int end)
{
    int length()
    {
        return end - start;
    }
}

static List<Integer> findLongestGrowingSequenceOptimized(List<Integer> values)
{
    if (values.isEmpty())
        return values;

    StartEndPair longest = new StartEndPair(0, 0);
    int startCurrent = 0;
    int endCurrent;

    for (endCurrent = 1; endCurrent < values.size(); endCurrent++)
    {
        if (values.get(endCurrent) < values.get(endCurrent - 1))
        {
            if (endCurrent - startCurrent > longest.length())
            {
                longest = new StartEndPair(startCurrent, endCurrent);
            }
            startCurrent = endCurrent;
        }
    }
```

```java
    if (endCurrent - startCurrent > longest.length())
    {
        longest = new StartEndPair(startCurrent, endCurrent);
    }

    return values.subList(longest.start, longest.end);
}
```

Verification

Use the sequences of values from the introduction to compare the computed results with
your expectations:

```java
@ParameterizedTest(name = "findLongestGrowingSequence({0}) = {1}")
@MethodSource("listInputsAndExpected")
void findLongestGrowingSequence(List<Integer> inputs,
                                List<Integer> expected)
{
    List<Integer> result =
                Ex05_Sequence.findLongestGrowingSequence(inputs);

    assertEquals(expected, result);
}

private static Stream<Arguments> listInputsAndExpected()
{
    return Stream.of(Arguments.of(List.of(7, 2, 7, 1, 2, 5, 7, 1),
                            List.of(1, 2, 5, 7)),
                    Arguments.of(List.of(7, 2, 7, 1, 2, 3, 8, 1, 2, 3, 4, 5),
                            List.of(1, 2, 3, 4, 5)),
                    Arguments.of(List.of(1, 1, 2, 2, 2, 3, 3, 3, 3),
                            List.of(1, 1, 2, 2, 2, 3, 3, 3, 3)));
}
```

7.3.6 Solution 6: Own Stack (★★☆☆☆)

Consider the class java.util.Stack<E> from the JDK. Perform a design analysis and identify possible vulnerabilities. Define the basic requirements for a stack and, based on that, implement class Ex06_Stack<E> using a List<E>.

Design review   The class Stack<E> is derived from the class Vector<E>. This unfortunately allows method calls for the Stack<E> class that contradict the way a stack works, such as methods get(int), indexOf(Object), or even those with modifying accesses, such as add(int, E) or remove(int). Furthermore, several methods with slightly different names exist that do the same thing, for example empty() and isEmpty(). These examples should make you aware of the problem of implementation inheritance.

The resulting pitfalls become clearly visible when using both methods of the base class Vector<E> and those of the class Stack<E>. Suppose some elements were added instead of by calling push(E) by calling the method add(E). Intuitively, one expects an insertion at the last position. In fact, the topmost element of a stack corresponds to the last element of the underlying base class Vector<E>.

Such non-intuitive APIs complicate programming and distract from the task at hand. Thereby a correct implementation would have been easily possible by using a reference to the class Vector<E> (or any list) and delegation. This is shown next.

Algorithm   It is possible to implement a stack yourself, using a list as data storage but not providing direct access to it externally. Users just have access through the following methods typical of a stack:

- void push(E) adds an element on top.

- E pop() takes the element from the top.

- E peek() takes a look at the top element.

- boolean isEmpty() checks if the stack is empty.

Each call to push() adds an element at the beginning of the list. This way, you simulate the stack. When accessing the top element, it is checked in each case whether the stack is empty, in which case an Ex06_StackIsEmptyException is thrown. Otherwise, the top element is returned.

```
public class Ex06_Stack<E>
{
    private final List<E> values = new LinkedList<>();
```

```java
    public void push(final E elem)
    {
        values.add(0, elem);
    }

    public E pop()
    {
        if (isEmpty())
            throw new Ex06_StackIsEmptyException();

        return values.remove(0);
    }

    public E peek()
    {
        if (isEmpty())
            throw new Ex06_StackIsEmptyException();

        return values.get(0);
    }

    public boolean isEmpty()
    {
        return values.isEmpty();
    }

    static class Ex06_StackIsEmptyException extends RuntimeException
    {
    }
}
```

Unlike the Stack<E> class from the JDK, your implementation is not thread-safe. One way to achieve this is to add synchronized for each method.

Please also note that this implementation relies on a LinkedList<E> which allows performant insertions and removals at the front. For ArrayList<E> this would not be an adequate solution. Then it would be best if you used the last position to insert and remove, but this requires some index math.

Verification

You verify the correct working of the stack you just implemented using a predefined flow. First, you insert two elements. Then you look at the top one with peek(). After that you remove elements twice with pop(). They should be supplied in reverse order of insertion. Finally, you check to see if the stack is empty. Because this is the case, a subsequent inspection of the topmost element should throw an Ex06_StackIsEmptyException.

```
Ex06_Stack<String> stack = new Ex06_Stack<>();
stack.push("first");
stack.push("second");

System.out.println("PEEK: " + stack.peek());
System.out.println("POP: " + stack.pop());
System.out.println("POP: " + stack.pop());
System.out.println("ISEMPTY: " + stack.isEmpty());
System.out.println("POP: " + stack.pop());
```

This results in the following output:

```
PEEK: second
POP: second
POP:    first
ISEMPTY: true
|  Exception REPL.$JShell$11$Ex06_Stack$StackIsEmptyException
|       at Ex06_Stack.pop (#1:21)
```

7.3.7 Solution 7: Well-Formed Braces (★★☆☆☆)

Write method boolean checkParentheses(String) that checks whether a sequence of braces is neatly nested in each case. This should accept round, square, and curly braces but no other characters.

Examples

Input	Result	Comment
"(())"	true	
"({[]})"	true	
"((())"	false	Odd number of braces
"((a)"	false	Wrong character, no braces
"(()"	false	No matching braces

Algorithm   Traverse the string from front to back. If the current character is an opening bracket—that is, one of the characters (, [, or {—store it in a stack. If it is a closing brace, try to match it with the last opening brace. If there is no opening brace yet, or if the brace types do not match, `false` is returned. If they match, the next character is read. If it is an opening parenthesis, proceed as before. If it is a closing brace, get the top element from the stack and compare it to the character just read. Check for matching the type of parenthesis: (and), [and], and { and }. Let's look at a flow for the input (()].

Input	Current character	Stack	Comment
(()]			Start
(()]	(	(	Store
(()]	(	((	Store
(()]	)	(	Match
(()]	]	(	Mismatch

The implementation uses a stack and performs the checks and actions described above:

```
static boolean checkParentheses(final String input)
{
    // odd length cannot be a well-formed bracing
    if (input.length() % 2 != 0)
        return false;

    final Stack<Character> openingParentheses = new Stack<>();
```

```java
    for (int i = 0; i < input.length(); i++)
    {
        final char currentChar = input.charAt(i);
        if (isOpeningParenthesis(currentChar))
        {
            openingParentheses.push(currentChar);
        }
        else if (isClosingParenthesis(currentChar))
        {
            if (openingParentheses.isEmpty())
            {
                // closing before opening brace
                return false;
            }

            final char lastOpeningParens = openingParentheses.pop();
            if (!isMatchingParenthesisPair(lastOpeningParens, currentChar))
            {
                // different pairs of braces
                return false;
            }
        }
        else
        {
            // invalid character
            return false;
        }
    }

    return openingParentheses.isEmpty();
}
```

Once again, it is recommended to extract helper methods such as isOpeningParenthesis(char) to be able to implement the actual algorithm at a higher level of abstraction and thus more clearly. Finally, let's take an examining look at the three helper methods:

```
static boolean isOpeningParenthesis(final char ch)
{
    return ch == '(' || ch == '[' || ch == '{';
}

static boolean isClosingParenthesis(final char ch)
{
    return ch == ')' || ch == ']' || ch == '}';
}

static boolean isMatchingParenthesisPair(final char opening, final char
closing)
{
    return (opening == '(' && closing == ')') ||
           (opening == '[' && closing == ']') ||
           (opening == '{' && closing == '}');
}
```

Let's come back to the implementation and how the return values are provided. Several comments appear there as to why true or false is returned. Wouldn't it be much more intuitive to express this with an appropriate enum as the return? You'll take a look at this in the bonus.

Verification

You use the values from the introduction to see your just-implemented functionality in action:

```
@ParameterizedTest(name = "checkParentheses(''{0}'') should be valid")
@CsvSource({ "()", "()[]{}", "[((()[]{}))]" })
void checkParentheses_ValidInput_Success(String input)
{
    boolean result = Ex07_ParenthesisExample.checkParentheses(input);

    assertTrue(result);
}
```

```
@ParameterizedTest(name = "checkParentheses(''{0}'') should be invalid")
@CsvSource({ "(()", "((})", "(()}", ")()(", "()((", "()A(" })
void checkParentheses_InvalidInputs_Should_Fail(String input)
{
    boolean result = Ex07_ParenthesisExample.checkParentheses(input);

    assertFalse(result);
}
```

Bonus

Extend the solution to provide a clear mapping of error causes. Start with the following enum:

```
static enum CheckResult
{
    OK,
    ODD_LENGTH,
    CLOSING_BEFORE_OPENING,
    MISMATCHING_PARENTHESIS,
    INVALID_CHAR,
    REMAINING_OPENING
}
```

By using the enumeration, possible error causes may be communicated more clearly. Besides, you can omit the comments on the return values in the source code since the enumeration values adequately describe them.

```
static CheckResult checkParenthesesV2(final String input)
{
    if (input.length() % 2 != 0)
        return CheckResult.ODD_LENGTH;

    final Stack<Character> openingParens = new Stack<>();

    for (int i = 0; i < input.length(); i++)
    {
        final char currentChar = input.charAt(i);
```

```
    if (isOpeningParenthesis(currentChar))
    {
        openingParens.push(currentChar);
    }
    else if (isClosingParenthesis(currentChar))
    {
        if (openingParens.isEmpty())
            return CheckResult.CLOSING_BEFORE_OPENING;

        final char lastOpeningParens = openingParens.pop();
        if (!isMatchingParenthesisPair(lastOpeningParens, currentChar))
            return CheckResult.MISMATCHING_PARENTHESIS;
    }
    else
        return CheckResult.INVALID_CHAR;
  }

  if (openingParens.isEmpty())
      return CheckResult.OK;

  return CheckResult.REMAINING_OPENING_PARENS;
}
```

TRICK: ENUM WITH VARIABLE CONTENT

Almost all Java developers know the simple form of enums. It's quite common to define one or more attributes in enum. These are almost always `final` and are assigned once.

As seen, the enum as a return is already an improvement. Sometimes you want to report some more information about the cause of the error to the caller. For this purpose, I'll show you a rather unknown trick that allows assigning dynamic information to static enum values at runtime. However, this is only safe for local returns and without the influence of multithreading, since otherwise values can be changed accidentally.

```
static enum CheckResultV2
{
    ODD_LENGTH, CLOSING_BEFORE_OPENING, MISMATCHING,
    INVALID_CHAR, OK, REMAINING_OPENING;
```

```java
    private String additionalInfo;

    public CheckResultV2 withInfo(String info)
    {
        this.additionalInfo = info;
        return this;
    }

    @Override
    public String toString()
    {
        return super.toString() + " / Additional Info: " + additionalInfo;
    }
}
```

Now you come to the result enum. First, various results are defined as constants. The trick is to provide an additional attribute and a corresponding modification method to change dynamic state information runtime. With this extension, it is possible to make the following calls at the respective position:

```java
return CheckResultV2.CLOSING_BEFORE_OPENING.withInfo("" + currentChar);
```

```java
return CheckResultV2.MISMATCHING_PARENTHESIS.withInfo("" +
                    lastOpeningParens + " <> " + currentChar);
```

```java
return CheckResultV2.INVALID_CHAR.withInfo("" + currentChar);
```

Please note both the limitations of use and the merits. As already indicated, there are potential difficulties using multithreading or caching results. Therefore, this technique is mainly useful for local result returns.

7.3.8 Solution 8: Check a Magic Triangle (★★★☆☆)

Write method boolean isMagicTriangle(List<Integer>) that checks whether a sequence of numbers forms a magic triangle. Such a triangle is defined as one where the respective sums of the three sides' values must all be equal.

Examples

The following shows this for one triangle each of side length 3 and side length 4:

```
1                   2
 6 5                 8 5
2 4 3               4   9
                   3 7 6 1
```

This results in the following sides and sums:

Input	Values 1	Values 2
side 1	1 + 5 + 3 = 9	2 + 5 + 9 + 1 = 17
side 2	3 + 4 + 2 = 9	1 + 6 + 7 + 3 = 17
side 3	2 + 6 + 1 = 9	3 + 4 + 8 + 2 = 17

Tip   Represent the individual sides of the triangle as sublists and use the `List<E> subList(int startInclusive, int endExclusive)` method to extract the respective sides.

HINT: PROBLEM SOLVING STRATEGIES FOR THE JOB INTERVIEW

If the problem is initially unclear, it is advisable to reduce the problem to one or two concrete value assignments and to find the appropriate abstractions based on them.

Using the triangle of side length 3 as an example, you can build the sides shown above. If you think for a while, you will find out that the sides can be expressed as sublists using the method `subList()`. However, the last side requires special treatment. For closing the figure again, the value of position 0 has to be taken into account. Still, it is not part of the sublist. Here two alternative tricks offer themselves. The first one is to duplicate the list and extend it by the 0th element:

```
final List<Integer> valuesWithLoop = new ArrayList<>(values);
// close the triangle
valuesWithLoop.add(values.get(0));

List<Integer> side1 = valuesWithLoop.subList(0, 3);
List<Integer> side2 = valuesWithLoop.subList(2, 5);
List<Integer> side3 = valuesWithLoop.subList(4, 7));
```

In the second trick, you add the third side appropriately—but keep in mind for this case that the subList() method returns an immutable view, so you have to do a wrapping to be able to add an element:

```
List<Integer> side1 = values.subList(0, 3);
List<Integer> side2 = values.subList(2, 5);
List<Integer> side3 = new ArrayList<>(values.subList(4, 6)); // immutable
side3.add(side1.get(0)); // error, if only subList()
```

Algorithm: For triangles with side length 3   With the previous knowledge gathered, you start implementing the check for the special case of a triangle of side length 3. Therefore you first determine the sides and then build and compare the partial sums of the numbers contained there:

```
static boolean isMagic6(final List<Integer> values)
{
    final List<Integer> valuesWithLoop = new ArrayList<>(values);
    // close the triangle
    valuesWithLoop.add(values.get(0));

    final List<Integer> side1 = valuesWithLoop.subList(0, 3);
    final List<Integer> side2 = valuesWithLoop.subList(2, 5);
    final List<Integer> side3 = valuesWithLoop.subList(4, 7);

    return compareSumOfSides(side1, side2, side3);
}
```

You have extracted the summing of the values of the sides as well as their comparison to the method compareSumOfSides():

```
static boolean compareSumOfSides(final List<Integer> side1,
                                 final List<Integer> side2,
                                 final List<Integer> side3)
```

```
{
    final int sum1 = sum(side1);
    final int sum2 = sum(side2);
    final int sum3 = sum(side3);

    return sum1 == sum2 && sum2 == sum3;
}
```

You still need a helper method to compute the sum of the elements of a list. The easiest way to solve this is by using the Stream API as follows:

```
static int sum(final List<Integer> values)
{
    return values.stream().mapToInt(n -> n).sum();
}
```

Intermediate inspection   Now you should at least check the implementation with some values before you move on to the generalization:

```
jshell> isMagic6(List.of(1, 5, 3, 4, 2, 6))
$55 ==> true

jshell> isMagic6(List.of(1, 2, 3, 4, 5, 6))
$56 ==> false
```

Algorithm: General variant   With the knowledge gained from the concrete example, a general variant can be created. The variance resides in calculating the indices for the sides of the triangle. Additionally, you add a sanity check at the beginning of the method. This prevents you from working on potentially invalid data constellations.

```
static boolean isMagic(final List<Integer> values)
{
    if (values.size() % 3 != 0)
        throw new IllegalArgumentException("Not a triangle: " +
        values.size());

    final int sideLength = 1 + values.size() / 3;

    final List<Integer> valuesWithLoop = new ArrayList<>(values);
    // close the triangle
    valuesWithLoop.add(values.get(0));
```

```java
    final List<Integer> side1 = valuesWithLoop.subList(0, sideLength);
    final List<Integer> side2 = valuesWithLoop.subList(sideLength - 1,
                                                sideLength * 2 - 1);
    final List<Integer> side3 = valuesWithLoop.subList((sideLength - 1) * 2,
                                                sideLength * 3 - 2);

    return compareSumOfSides(side1, side2, side3);
}
```

Verification

Let's check the implementation with the following unit test:

```java
@ParameterizedTest(name = "isMagic({0})? {1}")
@MethodSource("listInputsAndExpected")
void isMagic(List<Integer> inputs, boolean expected)
{
    boolean result = Ex08_MagicTriangle.isMagic(inputs);

    assertEquals(expected, result);
}

private static Stream<Arguments> listInputsAndExpected()
{
    return Stream.of(Arguments.of(List.of(1, 5, 3, 4, 2, 6), true),
                     Arguments.of(List.of(1, 2, 3, 4, 5, 6), false),
                     Arguments.of(List.of(2, 5, 9, 1, 6, 7, 3, 4, 8), true),
                     Arguments.of(List.of(1, 2, 3, 4, 5, 6, 7, 8, 9), false));
}
```

Alternative algorithm   Based on the generalization already done, you can go one step further and omit the extraction of the sublists.

This algorithm once again uses the idea of a position counter and traverses the original list in two loops. The outer loop represents the current side; in an inner loop, the respective position is handled. Thereby two tricks are used:

1. The variable pos models the current position within the list. The new position is determined by adding 1. However, you need to reaccess the list's first value at the end of the list, so a modulo operation is used here.

2. After adding up the values for one side, you have to go back by one
    position since the end value of one side of the triangle is also the
    start value of the next side.

As usual, you add a sanity check at the beginning of the method. This will prevent
you from potentially invalid data constellations.

```java
static boolean isMagicV2(final List<Integer> values)
{
    if (values.size() % 3 != 0)
        throw new IllegalArgumentException("Not a triangle: " + values.size());

    final int[] sumOfSides = new int[3];

    final int sideLength = values.size() / 3 + 1;
    int pos = 0;
    for (int currentSide = 0; currentSide < 3; currentSide++)
    {
        for (int i = 0; i < sideLength; i++)
        {
            sumOfSides[currentSide] += values.get(pos);

            // trick 1: with modulo => no special treatment
            // for last value needed
            pos = (pos + 1) % values.size();
        }

        // trick 2: The sides overlap, end field = next start field
        pos--;
    }

    return sumOfSides[0] == sumOfSides[1] && sumOfSides[1] == sumOfSides[2];
}
```

Verification

The test is performed with a unit test analogous to the previous one and is therefore not
shown again.

7.3.9 Solution 9: Pascal's Triangle (★★★☆☆)

Write method List<List<Integer>> pascal(int) that computes Pascal's triangle in terms of nested lists. As you already know, each new line results from the previous one. If there are more than two elements in it, two values are added, and the sums build the values of the new line. In each case, a 1 is appended to the front and back.

Example

For the value 5, the desired representation is as follows:

```
[1] .
[1, 1]
[1, 2, 1]
[1, 3, 3, 1]
[1, 4, 6, 4, 1]
```

Algorithm   The determination of the individual lines is done recursively. For the first line, a one-element list with the value 1 is generated. For all others, you calculate the values by invoking helper method calcLine(List<Integer>) based on the predecessor line and then adding the intermediate result to your overall result. It might be a bit irritating that the call is 1-based, but the list index is, of course, 0-based.

```
static List<List<Integer>> pascal(final int n)
{
    final List<List<Integer>> result = new ArrayList<>();
    pascal(n, result);
    return result;
}

static List<Integer> pascal(final int n, final List<List<Integer>> results)
{
    // recursive termination
    if (n == 1)
    {
        results.add(List.of(1));
    }
```

```
    else
    {
        // recursive descent: compute based on predecessor line
        final List<Integer> previousLine = pascal(n - 1, results);

        final List<Integer> currentLine = calcLine(previousLine);

        results.add(currentLine);
    }

    return results.get(n - 1);
}
```

Computing a row's values based on the predecessor row is performed for all rows with $n \geq 2$ as follows: If there is more than one value stored in the predecessor row list, iterate through it and sum each. To complete the computation, the value 1 is appended at the front and the back.

Somewhat more formally it can be written it as follows, whereby the index of the rows and columns starts from 1 and not as in Java from 0:

$$pascal(row, col) = \begin{cases} 1 & row = 1 \text{ and } col = 1 \,(\text{top}) \\ 1 & \forall row\, \{1, n\} \text{ and } col = 1 \\ 1 & \forall row\, \{1, n\} \text{ and } col = row \\ pascal(row - 1, col) + \\ pascal(row - 1, col - 1) & \text{otherwise}\,(\text{based on predecessors}) \end{cases}$$

The implementation is done directly and is much more understandable than the purely recursive definition for each value already presented in section 3.3.9:

```
// each row is calculated from the values of the row above it,
// flanked in each case by a 1
static List<Integer> calcLine(final List<Integer> previousLine)
{
    final List<Integer> currentLine = new ArrayList<>();
    currentLine.add(1);
```

```java
for (int i = 0; i < previousLine.size() - 1; i++)
{
    final int newValue = previousLine.get(i) + previousLine.get(i + 1);
    currentLine.add(newValue);
}

currentLine.add(1);
return currentLine;
}
```

Verification

To test the implementation, you compute Pascal's triangle for the value 5 and then print it appropriately:

```
jshell> pascal(5).forEach(System.out::println) [1]
[1, 1]
[1, 2, 1]
[1, 3, 3, 1]
[1, 4, 6, 4, 1]
```

If you like it a bit more formal, a matching unit test is provided in the sample project.

7.3.10 Solution 10: Most Frequent Elements (★★☆☆☆)

Write method Map<Integer, long> valueCount(List<Integer>) that computes a histogram, that is, the distribution of the frequencies of the numbers in the passed list. Also, write method Map<Integer, Long> sortByValue(Map<Integer, Long>) that sorts the map by its values instead of by keys. A descending sort has to be implemented, whereby the highest values are listed at the beginning.

Examples

Input	Result	Most frequent(s)
[1, 2, 3, 4, 4, 4, 3, 3, 2, 4]	{1=1, 2=2, 3=3, 4=4}	4=4
[1, 1, 1, 2, 2, 2, 3, 3, 3]	{1=3, 2=3, 3=3}	Depending on query, logically all

Algorithm   Based on the input values, you compute a histogram as a map with frequency values:

```
static Map<Integer, Long> valueCount(final List<Integer> values)
{
    final Map<Integer,Long> valueToCount = new TreeMap<>();

    values.forEach(value ->
    {
        valueToCount.putIfAbsent(value, 0L);
        valueToCount.computeIfPresent(value, (orig, count) -> ++count);
    });

    return valueToCount;
}
```

Alternatively, you can also take advantage of the Stream API for simplification, though with the problem that the chosen identity mapping (n -> n) unfortunately does not allow the compiler to determine the type of the key correctly, and so Object is used here unattractively:

```
static Map<Object, Long> valueCountWrong(final List<Integer> values)
{
    return values.stream().
                collect(Collectors.groupingBy(n -> n, Collectors.counting()));
}
```

You achieve an improvement by using Integer.valueOf(int). It gets more readable by statically importing the collectors as well as using a method reference (most of this can be conveniently achieved using the IDE's quick fixes):

```
static Map<Integer, Long> valueCountV2(final List<Integer> values)
{
    return values.stream().collect(groupingBy(Integer::valueOf, counting()));
}
```

The last step is to sort the resulting map by value. Conveniently, since Java 8, this is easily possible with a predefined comparator:

```java
static Map<Integer, Long> sortByValue(final Map<Integer, Long> counts)
{
    return counts.entrySet().stream().
            sorted(Map.Entry.<Integer, Long>comparingByValue().reversed())
            collect(Collectors.toMap(Map.Entry::getKey,
                                    Map.Entry::getValue,
                                    (e1, e2) -> e1, LinkedHashMap::new));
}
```

Verification

As usual, you use the values from the introduction to check your just implemented functionality with unit tests:

```java
@ParameterizedTest(name = "valueCountV2({0}) = {1}")
@MethodSource("listInputsAndExpected")
void valueCountV2(List<Integer> inputs, Map<Integer, Long> expected)
{
    Map<Integer, Long> result = Ex10_HaeufigstesElement.valueCountV2(inputs);

    assertEquals(expected, result);
}

private static Stream<Arguments> listInputsAndExpected()
{
    return Stream.of(Arguments.of(List.of(1, 2, 3, 4, 4, 4, 3, 3, 2, 4),
                                Map.of(1, 1L, 2, 2L, 3, 3L, 4, 4L)),
                    Arguments.of(List.of(1, 1, 1, 2, 2, 2, 3, 3, 3),
                                Map.of(1, 3L, 2, 3L, 3, 3L)));
}
```

```
@Test
public void sortByValue()
{
    Map<Integer, Long> counts = Map.of(1, 1L, 2, 2L, 3, 3L, 4, 4L);
    Map<Integer, Long> expected = new LinkedHashMap<>();
    expected.put(4, 4L);
    expected.put(3, 3L);
    expected.put(2, 2L);
    expected.put(1, 1L);

    Map<Integer, Long> result = Ex10_HaeufigstesElement.sortByValue(counts);

    assertIterableEquals(expected.entrySet(),  result.entrySet());
}
```

To test sorting by value, you have to do a little trickery. Comparing the maps via assertEquals() always returns true if the same entries are there, but here you are concerned with the order. At first, you get the idea of running through the respective entrySet()s with two iterators. But there is a better way, namely with assertIterableEquals(). As shown, it is not only nice and short but also quite elegant.

7.3.11 Solution 11: Addition of Digits (★★★☆☆)

Consider two decimal numbers that are to be added. Sounds simple, but for this assignment, the numbers are interestingly represented as a list of digits. Write method List<Integer> listAdd(List<Integer>, List<Integer>). Also, consider the special case where there is an overflow.

Solution 11a: Addition (★★★☆☆)

In the first part of the task, the digits are to be stored in the order of their occurrence in the list.

Examples

Input 1	Input 2	Result
123 = [1, 2, 3]	456 = [4, 5, 6]	579 = [5, 7, 9]
927 = [9, 2, 7]	135 = [1, 3, 5]	1062 = [1, 0, 6, 2]

Algorithm   You start with a simplification, namely that the numbers have the same amount of digits. Analogous to adding on the blackboard, you go from back to front from position to position and add the digits in each case. There may be a carry, which you have to take into account in the following addition. If there is also a carry at the end of the processing (so for you at the front most position), you must add the value 1 to the result at the front position. See Figure 7-1.

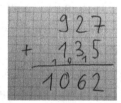

Figure 7-1. *Example of an addition with carries*

You apply this procedure to two lists of digits and traverse them from back to front—at the beginning still simplifying lists of equal length, which avoids special treatments:

```
static List<Integer> listAdd(final List<Integer> values1,
                             final List<Integer> values2)
{
    final List<Integer> result = new ArrayList<>();

    int carry = 0;
    for (int i = values1.size() - 1; i >= 0; i--)
    {
        final int value1 = values1.get(i);
        final int value2 = values2.get(i);
        final int sum = value1 + value2 + carry;
        result.add(0, sum % 10);
```

```
        carry = sum >= 10 ? 1 : 0;
    }

    // add a 1 at the front of a carryover
    if (carry == 1)
        result.add(0, 1);

    return result;
}
```

Improved algorithm   If you want to provide a generally valid addition, you have to add the digits again starting from the back. However, with unequal length, it is then at some point no longer possible to access any digits because one number has fewer digits than the other. The auxiliary method safeGetAt() helps to handle a potentially failing access and provides a fallback of 0 in this case.

```
static List<Integer> listAddImproved(final List<Integer> inputs1,
                                     final List<Integer> inputs2)
{
    final List<Integer> result = new ArrayList<>();

    int carry = 0;
    int idx1 = values1.size() - 1;
    int idx2 = values2.size() - 1;

    while (idx1 >= 0 || idx2 >= 0)
    {
        final int value1 = safeGetAt(values1, idx1);
        final int value2 = safeGetAt(values2, idx2);
        final int sum = value1 + value2 + carry;
        result.add(0, sum % 10);

        carry = sum >= 10 ? 1 : 0;

        idx1--;
        idx2--;
    }
```

```
    // add a 1 at the front of a carryover
    if (carry == 1)
        result.add(0, 1);

    return result;
}
```

Let's take a quick look at the implementation of the safe indexed access, which maps accesses outside the allowed index range to the value 0:

```
static int safeGetAt(final List<Integer> inputs, final int pos)
{
    if (pos >=0 && pos < inputs.size())
        return inputs.get(pos);

    return 0;
}
```

Verification

You use unit tests to verify that the implementation produces the desired result for a given sequence of numbers:

```
@Test
void listAdd_for_Values1()
{
    List<Integer> result = Ex11_ListAdder.listAddImproved(List.of(1, 2, 3),
                                                           List.of(4, 5, 6));

    assertEquals(List.of(5, 7, 9), result);
}

@Test
void listAdd_for_Values2()
{
    List<Integer> result = Ex11_ListAdder.listAddImproved(List.of(9, 2, 7),
                                                           List.of(1, 3, 5));

    assertEquals(List.of(1, 0, 6, 2), result);
}
```

Let's also consider the special case of unequal lengths of numbers for both implementations. Only the second improved variant handles this correctly:

```
jshell> var result3 = listAdd(List.of(7,2,1), List.of(1,2,7,0,0,0)) result3
==> [8, 4, 8]
```

```
jshell> var result4 = listAddImproved(List.of(7,2,1), List.of(1,2,7,0,0,0))
result4 ==> [1, 2, 7, 7, 2, 1]
```

Solution 11b: Addition Inverse (★★★☆☆)

What changes if the digits are stored in reverse order in the list?

Examples

Input 1	Input 2	Result
123 = [3, 2, 1]	456 = [6, 5, 4]	579 = [9, 7, 5]
927 = [7, 2, 9]	135 = [5, 3, 1]	1062 = [2, 6, 0, 1]

Algorithm If the order of the digits in the list is reversed to that within the number, things get simpler. You can then add directly, and the handling of numbers with unequal amounts of digits becomes easier. Again, you use the safeGetAt() method. Moreover, in case of an overflow, it is only necessary to add in the natural direction.

```
static List<Integer> listAddV2(final List<Integer> inputs1,
                               final List<Integer> inputs2)
{
    final List<Integer> result = new ArrayList<>();

    int carry = 0;
    for (int i = 0; i < inputs1.size() || i < inputs2.size(); i++)
    {
        final int value1 = safeGetAt(inputs1, i);
        final int value2 = safeGetAt(inputs2, i);
        final int sum = value1 + value2 + carry; result.add(sum % 10);

        carry = sum >= 10 ? 1 : 0;
    }
```

```
    // add a 1 to a carry "front"
    if (carry == 1)
        result.add(1);

    return result;
}
```

Verification

Consider two numbers in the form of lists with single digits. The values are written the other way around than in the number. In particular, this variant allows the addition of numbers of different lengths without having to deal with two index values.

```
@ParameterizedTest(name = "listAddImproved({0} + {1}) = {2}")
@MethodSource("reverseOrderInputs")
void listAddImproved(List<Integer> inputs1, List<Integer> inputs2,
                     List<Integer> expected)
{
    List<Integer> result = Ex11_ListAdder.listAddImproved(inputs1, inputs2);

    assertEquals(expected, result);
}

private static Stream<Arguments> reverseOrderInputs()
{
    return Stream.of(Arguments.of(List.of(3, 2, 1), List.of(6, 5, 4),
                              List.of(9, 7, 5)),
                  Arguments.of(List.of(7, 2, 9), List.of(5, 3, 1),
                              List.of(2, 6, 0, 1)),
                  Arguments.of(List.of(5, 3, 1),
                              List.of(0, 0, 0, 1, 3, 5),
                              List.of(5, 3, 1, 1, 3, 5)));
}
```

7.3.12 Solution 12: Compound Key (★★☆☆☆)

Imagine that you want to use two or more values as a key in a map. That is, you want to use a so-called *compound key*. For example, such a key consists of two int values or of one String and one int. How can this be achieved?

Examples

Compound key (name, age)	Hobbies
(Peter, 22)	TV
(Mike, 48)	Java, Cycling, Movies

Compound key (month, year)	Conferences
(September, 2019)	ch open Zurich, Oracle Code One SF
(October, 2019)	JAX London
(November, 2019)	W-JAX Munich

Algorithm   Define a suitable class XyKey such as for a String and a int as the class StringIntKey. Especially important are the methods boolean equals(Object) and int hashCode(), whose contract-compliant implementation ensures correct functionality.[2] So that you get a readable representation later when debugging or outputting, you let the IDE generate the method String toString() and modify it slightly. This results in the following implementation:

```
static class StringIntKey
{
    public final String strValue;
    public final int intValue;

    public static StringIntKey of(final String strValue, final int intValue)
    {
        return new StringIntKey(strValue, intValue);
    }

    private StringIntKey(final String strValue, final int intValue)
    {
        this.strValue = strValue;
        this.intValue = intValue;
    }
```

---

[2] For details, see my book *Der Weg zum Java-Profi* [Ind20a].

```java
@Override
public int hashCode()
{
    return Objects.hash(intValue,  strValue);
}

@Override
public boolean equals(Object obj)
{
    if (this == obj)
        return true;
    if (obj == null)
        return false;
    if (getClass() != obj.getClass())
        return false;

    StringIntKey other = (StringIntKey) obj;
    return intValue == other.intValue &&
            Objects.equals(strValue, other.strValue);
}

@Override
public String toString()
{
    return "StringIntKey [" + strValue + " / " + intValue + "]";
}
}
```

With modern Java, so-called records were introduced. This is an excellent way to implement compound keys shortly and concisely:[3]

---

[3] Records are treated in greater in detail in my book *Java – die Neuerungen in Version 9 bis 14: Modularisierung, Syntax- und API-Erweiterungen* [Ind20b].

```
record StringIntKey(String strValue, int intValue)
{
    public static StringIntKey of(final String strValue, final int intValue)
    {
        return new StringIntKey(strValue, intValue);
    }
}
```

Verification

First, you define a few composite keys consisting of people's names and ages, and then use them for mapping to a list of hobbies:

```
public static void main(final String[] args)
{
    // definition of the keys
    final StringIntKey key1 = new StringIntKey("Peter", 22);
    final StringIntKey key2 = new StringIntKey("Mike", 48);
    final StringIntKey key3 = new StringIntKey("Tom", 33);

    // alternative definition
    final StringIntKey mike48 = StringIntKey.of("Mike", 48);
    final StringIntKey tom33 = StringIntKey.of("Tom", 33);
    final StringIntKey michael48 = StringIntKey.of("Michael", 48);

    // usage in the map
    final Map<StringIntKey, List<String>> personToHobbies = new HashMap<>();
    personToHobbies.put(key1, List.of("TV"));
    personToHobbies.put(key2, List.of("Java", "Cycling", "Movies"));
    personToHobbies.put(michael48, List.of("Java", "Cycling"));
    personToHobbies.put(tom33, List.of("Running", "Movies"));

    // access
    System.out.println(mike48 + " => " + personToHobbies.get(mike48));
    final StringIntKey newTom33 = StringIntKey.of("Tom", 33);
    System.out.println(newTom33 + " => " + personToHobbies.get(newTom33));
}
```

Because the equals() and hashCode() methods are defined in accordance with the contract, you can use them when accessing new key objects:

```
StringIntKey [Mike / 48] => [Java, Cycling, Movies]
StringIntKey [Tom / 33] => [Running, Movies]
```

7.3.13 Solution 13: List Merge (★★☆☆☆)

Given two lists of numbers, each sorted in ascending order, merge them into a result list according to their order. Write method List<Integer> merge(List<Integer>, List<Integer>).

Examples

Input 1	Input 2	Result
1, 4, 7, 12, 20	10, 15, 17, 33	1, 4, 7, 10, 12, 15, 17, 20, 33
2, 3, 5, 7	11, 13, 17	2, 3, 5, 7, 11, 13, 17
2, 3, 5, 7, 11	7, 11, 13, 17	2, 3, 5, 7, 7, 11, 11, 13, 17
[1, 2, 3]	Ø = []	[1, 2, 3]

Algorithm At first, the problem seems quite easy to solve. You start at the beginning of both lists. Then you compare the respective position's values, insert the smaller one into the result, and increase the position in the list from which the element originates. This looks like the following:

```
static List<Integer> mergeFirstTry(final List<Integer> values1,
                                    final List<Integer> values2)
{
    final List<Integer> result = new ArrayList<>();

    int idx1 = 0;
    int idx2 = 0;

    while (idx1 < values1.size() || idx2 < values2.size())
    {
        final int value1 = values1.get(idx1);
        final int value2 = values2.get(idx2);
```

```
        if (value1 < value2)
        {
            result.add(value1);
            idx1++;
        }
        else
        {
            result.add(value2);
            idx2++;
        }
    }
    return result;
}
```

Although this solution seems to be intuitive and good, it still contains problems. To identify them, let's try the method once for the second combination of values:

```
jshell> mergeFirstTry(List.of(2, 3, 5, 7), List.of(11, 13, 17))
| Exception java.lang.ArrayIndexOutOfBoundsException: Index 4 out of bounds
    for length 4
```

As a quick fix, you could replace the OR (||) with an AND (&&), which eliminates problems with exception. But this leads to another problem: Not all of the elements of both lists are processed any longer, usually depending on the value distribution even different numbers. So this is not a universal solution, but still a good start. You only have to cover the special needs of the elements remaining in a list appropriately. They are added to the result for this purpose:

```
static List<Integer> merge(final List<Integer> values1,
                           final List<Integer> values2)
{
    final List<Integer> result = new ArrayList<>();

    int idx1 = 0;
    int idx2 = 0;
```

```
    while (idx1 < values1.size() && idx2 < values2.size())
    {
        final int value1 = values1.get(idx1);
        final int value2 = values2.get(idx2);

        if (value1 < value2)
        {
            result.add(value1);
            idx1++;
        }
        else
        {
            result.add(value2);
            idx2++;
        }
    }

    addRemaining(result, values1, idx1);
    addRemaining(result, values2, idx2);

    return result;
}
```

You move the functionality of appending the remaining elements into method addRemaining(). Interestingly, no special checks are required before calling it. This is indirectly given by supplying the respective index as well as the termination condition in the for loop:

```
static void addRemaining(final List<Integer> result,
                         final List<Integer> values, final int idx)
{
    for (int i = idx; i < values.size(); i++)
    {
        result.add(values.get(i));
    }
}
```

Verification

To check functionality, you use the value combinations from the introduction as usual:

```
@ParameterizedTest(name = "merge({0}, {1}) = {2}")
@MethodSource("listInputsAndExpected")
void listMerge(List<Integer> inputs1, List<Integer> inputs2,
               List<Integer> expected)
{
    List<Integer> result = Ex13_ListMerger.merge(inputs1, inputs2);

    assertEquals(expected, result);
}

private static Stream<Arguments> listInputsAndExpected()
{
    return Stream.of(Arguments.of(List.of(1, 4, 7, 12, 20),
                                  List.of(10, 15, 17, 33),
                                  List.of(1, 4, 7, 10, 12, 15, 17, 20, 33)),
                     Arguments.of(List.of(2, 3, 5, 7), List.of(11, 13, 17),
                                  List.of(2, 3, 5, 7, 11, 13, 17)),
                     Arguments.of(List.of( 1, 2, 3), List.of(),
                                  List.of( 1, 2, 3)));
}
```

7.3.14 Solution 14: Excel Magic Select (★★☆☆☆)

If you have worked a little with Excel, then you have probably used the so-called Magic Selection. It continuously populates a selected area with values based on the previous values. This works for numbers, weekdays, or dates, for example. To achieve something similar on your own, write method List<Integer> generateFollowingValues(int, int), that implements this for numbers. Create a variation of this suitable for weekdays and with the following signature: List<DayOfWeek> generateFollowingValues(DayOfWeek, int).

Examples

Initial value	Count	Result
1	7	[1, 2, 3, 4, 5, 6, 7]
5	4	[5, 6, 7, 8]
FRIDAY	8	[FRIDAY, SATURDAY, SUNDAY, MONDAY, TUESDAY, WEDNESDAY, THURSDAY, FRIDAY]

Algorithm   At first, you might think that this is based on something very sophisticated. But when thinking a second time about the algorithm, you quickly realize that all you need is a list as the result data structure and a loop to populate it:

```
static List<Integer> generateFollowingValues(int currentValue,
                                              int sequenceLength)
{
    final List<Integer> result = new ArrayList<>();

    while (sequenceLength-- > 0)
    {
        result.add(currentValue);
        currentValue++;
    }
    return result;
}
```

It is similarly easy to populate with weekdays, which, unlike numeric values, always repeat after 7 values. Two things are helpful for this:

1. All enumerations (enum) return an array representation when invoking their values() method.

2. Finding a value (see the introduction of Chapter 5) as well as cyclically traversing arrays, which you extracted to helper method nextCyclic().

With this knowledge, you minimally modify the previously used algorithm:

```
static List<DayOfWeek> generateFollowingValues(final DayOfWeek startDay,
                                                int sequenceLength)
{
    final DayOfWeek[] allWeekDays = DayOfWeek.values();
    int currentPos = find(allWeekDays, startDay);

    final List<DayOfWeek> result = new ArrayList<>();

    DayOfWeek nextDay = startDay;
    while (sequenceLength-- > 0)
    {
        result.add(nextDay);
        nextDay = nextCyclic(allWeekDays, currentPos);
        currentPos++;
    }
    return result;
}
```

Your implementation uses search as an array base functionality:

```
static <T> int find(final T[] values, final T searchFor)
{
    for (int i = 0; i < values.length; i++)
    {
        if (values[i].equals(searchFor))
            return i;
    }
    return -1;
}
```

However, because you are operating on a fixed range of values of an enumeration here, you can abbreviate it as follows instead of the above method:

```
int currentPos = startDay.getValue() - 1;
```

The second method is intended to allow cyclic traversal of an array in the forward direction by starting again at the beginning after passing the last element:

```java
static <T> T nextCyclic(final T[] values, final int currentPos)
{
    final int nextPos = (currentPos + 1) % values.length;

    return values[nextPos];
}
```

Simplification   Since DayOfWeek is an enumeration that provides this functionality natively, you can write the method as follows:

```java
static List<DayOfWeek> generateFollowingValuesSimpler(final DayOfWeek
                                                      startDay, int
                                                      sequenceLength)
{
    final List<DayOfWeek> result = new ArrayList<>();

    DayOfWeek nextDay = startDay;
    while (sequenceLength > 0)
    {
        result.add(nextDay);
        nextDay = day.plus(1);
        sequenceLength--;
    }

    return result;
}
```

Verification

To track the functionality of the magic completion just implemented, you again define parameterized tests, for example, one starting on a Friday and then generating eight values:

```java
@ParameterizedTest(name = "generateFollowingValues({0}, {1}) = {2}")
@MethodSource("simpleInputs")
void generateFollowingValues(int startValue, int sequenceLength,
                             List<Integer> expected)
```

```java
{
    var result =
        Ex14_ExcelMagicSelection.generateFollowingValues(startValue,
                                                sequenceLength);

    assertEquals(expected, result);
}

@ParameterizedTest(name = "generateFollowingValues({0}, {1}) = {2}")
@MethodSource("enumInputs")
void generateFollowingValues(DayOfWeek startValue, int sequenceLength,
                        List<DayOfWeek> expected)
{
    var result =
    Ex14_ExcelMagicSelection.generateFollowingValues(startValue,
                                                sequenceLength);

assertEquals(expected, result);
}

private static Stream<Arguments> simpleInputs()
{
    return Stream.of(Arguments.of(1, 7, List.of(1, 2, 3, 4, 5, 6, 7)),
                    Arguments.of(5, 4, List.of(5, 6, 7, 8)));
}

private static Stream<Arguments> enumInputs()
{
    return Stream.of(Arguments.of(DayOfWeek.MONDAY, 3,
                    List.of(DayOfWeek.MONDAY, DayOfWeek.TUESDAY,
                        DayOfWeek.WEDNESDAY)),
                    Arguments.of(DayOfWeek.FRIDAY, 8,
                    List.of(DayOfWeek.FRIDAY, DayOfWeek.SATURDAY,
                        DayOfWeek.SUNDAY, DayOfWeek.MONDAY,
                        DayOfWeek.TUESDAY, DayOfWeek.WEDNESDAY,
                        DayOfWeek.THURSDAY, DayOfWeek.FRIDAY)));
}
```

HINT: FREESTYLE WITH THE STREAM API

You've just seen that there's not that much behind the magic. In fact, you can write this much more elegantly by using the Stream API and specifically the `iterate()` method, which creates an infinite stream based on a calculation rule. To limit the stream to the desired number of values, `limit()` helps you. In the first case, you use an `IntStream` that operates on the type `int`. Therefore, `boxed()` must be called to convert the int value to a corresponding `Integer`, which then allows the conversion to a List<Integer>.

```
static List<Integer> generateFollowingValues(final int startValue,
                                              final int sequenceLength)
{
    return IntStream.iterate(startValue, n -> n + 1).
                    limit(sequenceLength).boxed().
                    collect(Collectors.toList());
}

static List<DayOfWeek> generateFollowingValues(final DayOfWeek startDay,
                                               final int sequenceLength)
{
    return Stream.iterate(startDay, day -> day.plus(1)).
                limit(sequenceLength).
                collect(Collectors.toList());
}

static List<LocalDate> generateFollowingValues(final LocalDate startValue,
                                               final int sequenceLength)
{
    return Stream.iterate(startValue, day -> day.plusDays(1)).
                limit(sequenceLength).
                collect(Collectors.toList());
}
```

The associated JUnit tests are analogous to the previous ones, except for the method invoked. For the method with LocalDate as a parameter, you slightly modify the testing as follows:

```
@ParameterizedTest(name = "generateFollowingValuesLocalDate({0}, {1}) " +
                          "last day should be {2}")
@CsvSource({ "2020-03-13, 8, 2020-03-20", "2010-02-07, 366, 2011-02-07" })
void generateFollowingValuesLocalDate(LocalDate startValue,
                                      int sequenceLength,
                                      LocalDate expectedEndDate)
{
    var expected =
        startValue.datesUntil(startValue.plusDays(sequenceLength)).
                collect(Collectors.toList());

    var result =
        Ex14_ExcelMagicSelection.generateFollowingValues(startValue,
                                                          sequenceLength);

    assertAll(() -> assertEquals(expected, result),
            () -> assertEquals(expectedEndDate,
                            result.get(result.size() - 1)));
}
```

PART II

More Advanced and Tricky Topics

CHAPTER 8

Recursion Advanced

In this chapter, you explore some more advanced aspects around recursion. You start with the optimization technique called *memoization*. After that, you look at backtracking as a problem-solving strategy that relies on trial and error and tries out possible solutions. Although this is not optimal in terms of performance, it can keep various implementations comprehensible.

8.1 Memoization

In Chapter 3, you learned that recursion is feasible for describing many algorithms and calculations in an understandable and, at the same time, elegant way. However, you also noticed that recursion sometimes leads to many self-calls, which can harm performance. This applies, for example, to the calculation of Fibonacci numbers or Pascal's triangle. How can this problem be overcome?

For this purpose, there is a useful technique called memoization. It follows the same ideas as the caching or buffering of previously calculated values. It avoids multiple executions by reusing already calculated results for subsequent actions.

8.1.1 Memoization for Fibonacci Numbers

Conveniently, memoization can often be easily added to an existing algorithm and only requires minimal modification. Let's replicate this for the calculation of Fibonacci numbers.

Let's briefly repeat the recursive definition of Fibonacci numbers:

$$fib(n) = \begin{cases} 1, & n = 1 \\ 1, & n = 2 \\ fib(n-1) + fib(n-2), & \forall n > 2 \end{cases}$$

© Michael Inden 2022
M. Inden, *Java Challenges*, https://doi.org/10.1007/978-1-4842-7395-1_8

The recursive implementation in Java follows the mathematical definition exactly:

```java
static long fibRec(final int n)
{
    if (n <= 0)
        throw new IllegalArgumentException("n must be > 0");

    // recursive termination
    if (n == 1 || n == 2)
        return 1;

    // recursive descent
    return fibRec(n - 1) + fibRec(n - 2);
}
```

So how do you add memoization? In fact, this is not too difficult. You need a helper method that calls the actual calculation method, and most importantly, a data structure to store intermediate results. In this case, you use a map that is passed to the computation method:

```java
static long fibonacciOptimized(final int n)
{
    return fibonacciMemo(n, new HashMap<>());
}
```

In the original method, you surround the actual computation with the actions for memoization. For every computation step, you first look in the map to see if a result already exists and return it if it does. Otherwise, you execute the algorithm as before, with the minimal modification that you store the computation result in a variable, to be able to deposit it at the end suitably in the lookup map:

```java
static long fibonacciMemo(final int n, final Map<Integer, Long> lookupMap)
{
    if (n <= 0)
        throw new IllegalArgumentException("n must be > 0");

    // MEMOIZATION: check if precalculated result exists
    if (lookupMap.containsKey(n))
        return lookupMap.get(n);
```

```
// normal algorithm with auxiliary variable for result
long result = 0;
// recursive termination
if (n == 1 || n == 2)
    result = 1;
// recursive descent
else
    result = fibonacciMemo(n - 1, lookUpMap) +
             fibonacciMemo(n - 2, lookUpMap);

// MEMOIZATION: save calculated result
lookupMap.put(n, result);
return result;
}
```

Performance comparison   If you run the two variants for the 47th Fibonacci number, the purely recursive variant on my iMac 4 GHz returns a result after about 7 seconds, while the other with memoization returns a result after a few milliseconds.

Notes It should be noted that there is a variant of the Fibonacci calculation that starts at the value 0. Then $fib(0) = 0$ holds as well as $fib(1) = 1$ and afterwards recursively $fib(n) = fib(n-1) + fib(n-2)$. This produces the same sequence of numbers as the initial definition, only with the value for 0 added.

Furthermore, there are the following points to consider:

- **Data type**: The calculated Fibonacci numbers can get huge quite quickly, so even the value range of a long is not sufficient, and a BigInteger is a good choice as the type for the return and lookup map.

- **Recursive termination**: For implementation purposes, it's worth considering the recursive termination before processing with memoization. This would probably be minimally more performant, but then the algorithm can't be reformulated that clearly from the existing one. Especially if you are not familiar with memoization yet, the shown variant seems a bit catchier.

8.1.2 Memoization for Pascal's Triangle

Pascal's triangle is defined recursively, as are the Fibonacci numbers:

$$pascal(row, col) = \begin{cases} 1, & row = 1 \text{ and } col = 1 \text{ (top)} \\ 1, & \forall row \{1, n\} \text{ and } col = 1 \\ 1, & \forall row \{1, n\} \text{ and } col = row \\ pascal(row-1, col) + \\ pascal(row-1, col-1), & \text{otherwise (all other positions)} \end{cases}$$

Let's first look at the purely recursive implementation again:

```
static int pascalRec(final int row, final int col)
{
    // recursive termination: top
    if (col == 1 && row == 1)
        return 1;

    // recursive termination: borders
    if (col == 1 || col == row)
        return 1;

    // recursive descent
    return pascalRec(row - 1, col) + pascalRec(row - 1, col - 1);
}
```

Even for the computation of Pascal's triangle by using memoization, the original algorithm hardly changes. You merely surround it with the accesses to the lookup map and the storage:

```
static int pascalOptimized(final int row, final int col)
{
    return calcPascalMemo(row, col, new HashMap<>());
}

static int calcPascalMemo(final int row, final int col,
                          final Map<IntIntKey, Integer> lookupMap)
{
```

```
// MEMOIZATION
final IntIntKey key = new IntIntKey(row, col);
if (lookupMap.containsKey(key))
    return lookupMap.get(key);

int result;
// recursive termination:  top
if (col == 1 && row == 1)
    result = 1;
// recursive termination:  borders
else if (col == 1 || col == row)
    result = 1;
else
    // recursive descent
    result = calcPascalMemo(row - 1, col, lookupMap) +
            calcPascalMemo(row - 1, col - 1, lookupMap);

// MEMOIZATION
lookupMap.put(key, result);
return result;
}
```

A closer look reveals that you cannot use a standard type for the key but rather need a more special variant consisting of a row and a column due to the two-dimensional layout. For this purpose, you define the following record named IntIntKey. Modern Java 17 makes it feasible to define simple data container classes using the record keyword as follows:

```
static record IntIntKey(int value1, int value2)
{
}
```

Performance comparison   To compare the performance, you choose a call with the parameters for line 42 and column 15. The purely recursive variant requires a rather long running time of about 80 seconds for the selected values on an iMac with 4 GHz. The optimized variant completes after a few milliseconds.

Conclusion

For the two examples presented here, the purely recursive definition results in many self-calls. Without memoization, they cause the same intermediate results to be calculated and discarded over and over again. This is unnecessary and costs performance.

Memoization is a remedy that is as simple as it is ingenious and efficient. Additionally, many problems may still be solved elegantly with the help of a recursive algorithm, but without the need to accept the disadvantages in terms of performance. All in all, memoization can often reduce the running time (very) significantly.

NOTE: BACKGROUND KNOWLEDGE ON MEMOIZATION

The term memoization, which seems a bit strange, goes back to Donald Michie (`https://en.wikipedia.org/wiki/Memoization`). As described earlier, it is a technique to optimize the processing of computations by caching partial results. In such a way, nested calls with the same input can be accelerated significantly. However, for memoization to be used, the wrapped recursive functions must be so-called *pure functions*. This means that such a stable function returns the same value if it is called with a particular input. In addition, these functions must be free of any side effects.

8.2 Backtracking

Backtracking is a problem-solving strategy based on trial and error and it investigates all possible solutions. When detecting an error, previous steps are reset, hence the name ***backtracking***. The goal is to reach a solution step by step. When an error occurs, you try another path to the solution. Thus potentially all possible (and therefore perhaps also a lot of) ways are followed. However, this also has a disadvantage, namely a rather long running time until the problem is solved.

To keep the implementation manageable, backtracking is often used in combination with recursion for the following problems:

- Solving the n-Queens Problem

- Finding a solution to a Sudoku puzzle

- Finding a way out of a maze given as a 2D array

8.2.1 n-Queens Problem

The n-Queens Problem is a puzzle to be solved on an n x n board. Queens (from the chess game) have to be placed so that no two queens can beat each other according to the chess rules. Thus, other queens may neither be placed on the same row, column, nor in the diagonals. As an example, here is the solution for a 4 × 4 board, where the queens are symbolized by a Q (for queen):

```
- - - - - - - - -
|  |Q|  |  |
- - - - - - - - -
|  |  |  |Q|
- - - - - - - - -
|Q|  |  |  |
- - - - - - - - -
|  |  |Q|  |
- - - - - - - - -
```

Algorithm

You start with a queen in row 0 and position 0 (upper left corner). After each placement, a check is made to ensure that there are no collisions in the vertical and diagonal left and right directions upwards with already placed queens. A check downwards is not necessary because no queens can be placed there yet since the filling is done from top to bottom. This is also the reason why a check in the horizontal direction is not necessary.

Provided the position is valid, you move to the next row, trying all positions from 0 to $n - 1$. This procedure is repeated until you have finally placed the queen in the last row. If there is a problem in positioning a queen, you use backtracking. You remove the last placed queen and try again at the next possible position. If the end of the row is reached without a solution, this is an invalid constellation, and the preceding queen must also be placed again. You can observe that backtracking sometimes goes back up one row and in extreme cases up to the first row.

Backtracking by example: Let's look at the steps to the solution, where on the horizontal level, some intermediate steps are partly omitted, and invalid positions are marked with x:

```
-----------------            -----------------            -----------------
 Q |   |   |                  Q |   |   |                  Q |   |   |
-----------------            -----------------            -----------------
   |   |   |                  x | x | Q |                    |   | Q |
-----------------     =>     -----------------     =>     -----------------
   |   |   |                    |   |   |                  x | x | x | x
-----------------            -----------------            -----------------
   |   |   |                    |   |   |                    |   |   |
-----------------            -----------------            -----------------
```

=> **Backtracking**

Because no valid placement exists for a queen in the second row, you continue to find a solution at the next position in the first row as follows:

```
-----------------            -----------------            -----------------
 Q |   |   |                  Q |   |   |                  Q |   |   |
-----------------            -----------------            -----------------
 x | x | x | Q                  |   |   | Q                  |   |   | Q
-----------------     =>     -----------------     =>     -----------------
   |   |   |                  x | Q |   |                    | Q |   |
-----------------            -----------------            -----------------
   |   |   |                    |   |   |                  x | x | x | x
-----------------            -----------------            -----------------
```

=> **Backtracking**

Even with the queen in the third position in the first row, no valid position for a queen in the second row exists in the constellation. So you have to go back not only one row but two rows and start the search again with the queen in row zero in position one:

```
---------------          ---------------          ---------------          ---------------
 | Q |   |                | Q |   |                | Q |   |                | Q |   |
---------------          ---------------          ---------------          ---------------
 x | x | x | Q            |   |   | Q            |   |   | Q            |   |   | Q
---------------    =>    ---------------    =>    ---------------    =>    ---------------
 |   |   |                |   |   |              Q |   |   |              Q |   |   |
---------------          ---------------          ---------------          ---------------
 |   |   |                |   |   |                |   |   |                x | x | Q |
---------------          ---------------          ---------------          ---------------
```

=> **Solution found**

You see that by taking a few trial-and-error steps, you arrive at a solution.

Implementation of backtracking   You again subdivide the previously described algorithm for solving the n-Queens Problem into a couple of methods to solve one subproblem at a time.

First you think about how you want to model the playfield. A char[][] is a good choice. A Q represents a queen and a blank represents an empty field. To initially create an empty board, you write method initializeBoard(). Then you call the actual recursive, backtracking method solveNQueens(), which determines the solution inplace on the char[][]. If one is found, the helper method returns the value true, otherwise false. To allow callers to easily evaluate, you wrap this in an Optional<T> if there is a solution. Otherwise you return an empty optional.

```
static Optional<char[][]> solveNQueens(final int size)
{
    final char[][] board = initializeBoard(size);

    // start the recursive solution discovery process
    if (solveNQueens(board, 0))
        return Optional.of(board);

    return Optional.empty();
}
```

Now let's get back to the main task, finding a solution using recursion and backtracking. As described, the algorithm proceeds row by row and then tries the respective columns:

```java
static boolean solveNQueens(final char[][] board, final int row)
{
    final int maxRow = board.length;
    final int maxCol = board[0].length;

    // recursive termination
    if (row >= maxRow)
        return true;

    boolean solved = false;
    int col = 0;
    while (!solved && col < maxCol)
    {
        if (isValidPosition(board, col, row))
        {
            placeQueen(board, col, row);

            // recursive descent
            solved = solveNQueens(board, row + 1);

            // backtracking, if no solution
            if (!solved)
                removeQueen(board, col, row);
        }
        col++;
    }
    return solved;
}
```

To keep the algorithm as free of details and array accesses as possible as well as thereby understandable, you define two helper methods named placeQueen() and removeQueen():

```java
static void placeQueen(final char[][] board, final int col, final int row)
{
    board[row][col] = 'Q';
}
```

```java
static void removeQueen(final char[][] board, final int col, final int row)
{
    board[row][col] = ' ';
}
```

Additionally, I want to mention how to process modifications in algorithms with backtracking. In one variation, used here, modifications made before the recursion steps are reverted. As a second variation, you can pass copies during the recursion step and perform the modification in the copy. Then no undo or *delete* is necessary anymore.

For the sake of completeness, the implementation of the initialization of the playfield is as follows:

```java
private static char[][] initializeBoard(final int size)
{
    final char[][] board = new char[size][size];

    for (int row = 0; row < size; row++)
    {
        for (int col = 0; col < size; col++)
        {
            board[row][col] = ' ';
        }
    }
    return board;
}
```

What Is Still Missing in the Implementation? What is the Next Step?

As an exercise in section 8.3.9 you are left with the task of implementing the isValidposition(char[][], int, int) method. This is to check whether a playfield is valid. Due to the chosen algorithm of the line-by-line approach and because only one queen can be placed per line, collisions have to be excluded only vertically and diagonally.

8.3 Exercises

8.3.1 Exercise 1: Towers of Hanoi (★★★☆☆)

In the Towers of Hanoi problem, there are three towers or sticks named A, B, and C. At the beginning, several perforated discs are placed on stick A in order of size, with the largest at the bottom. The goal is now to move the entire stack (i.e. all the discs) from A to C. The discs must be placed on the top of the stack. The goal is to move one disk at a time and never place a smaller disc below a larger one. That's why you need the helper stick B. Write method void solveTowersOfHanoi(int) that prints the solution on the console in the form of the movements to be executed.

Example

The whole thing looks something like Figure 8-1.

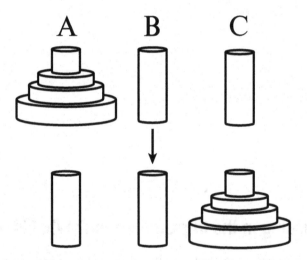

Figure 8-1. *Task definition for the Towers of Hanoi problem*

The following solution should be provided for three slices:

```
Tower Of Hanoi 3
A -> C
A -> B
C -> B
A -> C
B -> A
B -> C
A -> C
```

Bonus   Create a console-based graphical format. For two slices, it would look something like this:

```
Tower Of Hanoi 2
   A           B           C
   |           |           |
  #|#          |           |
 ##|##         |           |
-------     -------     -------
Moving slice 1: Tower [A] -> Tower [B]
   A           B           C
   |           |           |
   |           |           |
 ##|##        #|#          |
-------     -------     -------

Moving slice 2: Tower [A] -> Tower [C]
   A           B           C
   |           |           |
   |           |           |
   |          #|#        ##|##
-------     -------     -------
Moving slice 1: Tower [B] -> Tower [C]
   A           B           C
   |           |           |
   |           |          #|#
   |           |         ##|##
-------     -------     -------
```

8.3.2 Exercise 2: Edit Distance (★★★★☆)

For two strings, compute how many changes they are, case-insensitive, apart. That is, find out how to transition one string to the other by applying any of the following actions one or more times:

- Add a character (+).

- Delete a character (−).

- Change a character (↝).

Write method `int editDistance(String, String)` that tries the three actions character by character and checks the other part recursively.

Examples

The following modifications are required for the inputs shown:

Input 1	Input 2	Result	Actions
"Micha"	"Michael"	2	Micha →(+e) Michae →(+l) Michael
"rapple"	"tables"	4	rapple →(+s) rapples →(p↝b) rapbles →(−p) rables →(r↝t) tables

Bonus (★★★☆☆)   Optimize edit distance with memoization

8.3.3 Exercise 3: Longest Common Subsequence (★★★☆☆)

The previous exercise was about how many changes are needed to transform two given strings into each other. Another interesting problem is to find the longest common but not necessarily contiguous sequence of letters in two strings that occurs in two strings in the same sequence. Write method `String lcs(String, String)`, which recursively processes the strings from the back, and in case of two parts of the same length, it uses the second one.

Examples

Input 1	Input 2	Result
"ABCE"	"ZACEF"	"ACE"
"ABCXY"	"XYACB"	"AB"
"ABCMIXCHXAEL"	"MICHAEL"	"MICHAEL"
"sunday-Morning"	"saturday-Night-Party"	"suday-ig"

Bonus   Use memoization for the longest common subsequence

8.3.4 Exercise 4: Way Out of a Labyrinth (★★★☆☆)

In this assignment, you are asked to find the way out of a maze. Assume a maze is given as a two-dimensional array with walls symbolized by # and target positions (exits) symbolized by X. From any position, a path to all exits is supposed to be determined. If there are two exits in a row, only the first of the two has to be supplied. You are only allowed to move in the four compass directions, but not diagonally. Write method `boolean findWayOut(char[][], int, int)` that logs each found exit with FOUND EXIT at ....

Example

A larger playfield with four target fields is shown below. The bottom figure shows each of the paths indicated by a dot (.). In between you see the logging of the found positions of the exits. For this example, the search starts from the upper left corner with coordinates x=1, y=1.

```
#################################
# #         #    #    #  #   X#X#
#  ##### #### ##   ##  #  # ###  #
#  ##  #    #  ## ##  # #     # #
#    #  ###  # ## ##   #   ### # #
# #   ####      ##  ##    ###  # #
####   #      ####    #  # ####  #
######    #########   ##   # ###  #
##    #   X X####X #  #  # ### ##
#################################
```

```
FOUND EXIT: x: 30, y: 1
FOUND EXIT: x: 17, y: 8
FOUND EXIT: x: 10, y: 8
##################################
#.#         #....#.....#  #...X#X#
#..##### ####.##...##..#  #.### #
# .## #    #..## ## .# #..   # #
# ...# ###..#.## ## ..#...### # #
# # ..####.....## ##.... ### # #
#### ..#... #### ....# # #### #
#####...#########...##   # ### #
##      #..X X####X.# # # ### ##
##################################
```

Based on the outputs, it is also clear that two of the target fields marked with X are not detected from the start position. One is the X at the very top right corner, which cannot be reached due to a missing link. The other is the lower middle X, which is behind another exit.

8.3.5 Exercise 5: Sudoku Solver (★★★★☆)

Write method boolean solveSudoku(int[][]) that determines a valid solution, if any, for a partially initialized playfield passed as a parameter.

Example

A valid playfield with some blanks is as follows:

1	2		4	5		7	8	9
	5	6	7		9		2	3
7	8		1	2	3	4	5	6
2	1	4		6		8		7
3	6		8		7	2	1	4
	9	7		1	4	3	6	
5	3	1	6		2	9		8
6		2	9	7	8	5	3	1
9	7			3	1	6	4	2

It should be completed to the following solution:

1	2	3	4	5	6	7	8	9
4	5	6	7	8	9	1	2	3
7	8	9	1	2	3	4	5	6
2	1	4	3	6	5	8	9	7
3	6	5	8	9	7	2	1	4
8	9	7	2	1	4	3	6	5
5	3	1	6	4	2	9	7	8
6	4	2	9	7	8	5	3	1
9	7	8	5	3	1	6	4	2

8.3.6 Exercise 6: Math Operator Checker (★★★★☆)

This assignment is about a mathematically inclined puzzle. For a set of digits and another set of possible operators, you want to find all combinations that result in the desired value. The order of the digits may not be changed. Still, it is possible to insert any operator from the possible operators between the digits, except before the first digit. Write method Set<String> allCombinationsWithValue(List<Integer>, int) that determines all combinations that result in the value passed as a parameter. Check for the digits 1 to 9 and the operations + and − and also *combine the digits*. Start with method Map<String, Long> allCombinations(List<Integer>), which is passed the corresponding digits.

Examples

Let's consider two combinations only for the digits 1, 2, and 3:

$$1 + 2 + 3 \quad = \quad 6$$
$$1 + 23 \quad = \quad 24$$

In total, these digits allow the following different combinations to be formed:

Input	Result (allCombinations())
[1, 2, 3]	{12-3=9, 123=123, 1+2+3=6, 1+2-3=0, 1-2+3=2, 1-23=-22, 1-2-3=-4, 1+23=24, 12+3=15}

Suppose you want to generate the value 100 from the given digits 1 to 9 and the set of available operators (+, −, and *combine the digits*). This is possible, for example, as follows:

$$1 + 2 + 3 - 4 + 5 + 6 + 78 + 9 = 100$$

In total, the following variants should be determined:

Input	Result (allCombinationsWithValue())
100	[1+23-4+5+6+78-9, 123+4-5+67-89, 123-45-67+89, 12+3-4+5+67+8+9, 1+23-4+56+7+8+9, 12-3-4+5-6+7+89, 123-4-5-6-7+8-9, 1+2+34-5+67-8+9, 12+3+4+5-6-7+89, 123+45-67+8-9, 1+2+3-4+5+6+78+9]

Tip In Java, you can perform dynamic calculations at runtime only with some tricks. However, if you use Java's built-in JavaScript engine, it is fairly easy to evaluate expressions:

```
jshell> import javax.script.*

jshell> ScriptEngineManager manager = new ScriptEngineManager()

jshell> ScriptEngine jsEngine = manager.getEngineByName("js")

jshell> jsEngine.eval("7+2")
$63 ==> 9
```

Write method int evaluate(String) to evaluate an expression with digits and the operators + and −.

8.3.7 Exercise 7: Water Jug Problem (★★★ ☆ ☆)

Consider two jugs with capacities of m and n liters. Unfortunately, these jugs have no markings or indications of their fill level. The challenge is to measure x liters, where x is less than m or n. At the end of the procedure, one jug should contain x liters, and the other should be empty. Write method `boolean solveWaterJugs(int, int, int)` that displays the solution on the console and, if successful, returns `true`, otherwise `false`.

Examples

For two jugs, one with a capacity of 4 liters and one with a capacity of 3 liters, you can measure 2 liters in the following way:

State	Action
Jug 1: 0/Jug 2: 0	Both jugs initial empty
Jug 1: 4/Jug 2: 0	Fill jug 1 (unnecessary, but due to the algorithm)
Jug 1: 4/Jug 2: 3	Fill jug 2
Jug 1: 0/Jug 2: 3	Empty jug 1
Jug 1: 3/Jug 2: 0	Pour jug 2 into jug 1
Jug 1: 3/Jug 2: 3	Fill jug 2
Jug 1: 4/Jug 2: 2	Pour jug 2 in jug 1
Jug 1: 0/Jug 2: 2	Empty jug 1
Solved	

On the other hand, measuring 2 liters is impossible with two jugs of 4 liters capacity each.

8.3.8 Exercise 8: All Palindrome Substrings (★★★★☆)

In this assignment, given a word, you want to determine whether it contains palindromes and, if so, which ones. Write recursive method Set<String> allPalindromePartsRec(String) that determines all palindromes with at least two letters in the passed string and returns them sorted alphabetically.[1]

Examples

Input	Result
"BCDEDCB"	["BCDEDCB", "CDEDC", "DED"]
"ABALOTTOLL"	["ABA", "LL", "LOTTOL", "OTTO", "TT"]
"racecar"	["aceca", "cec", "racecar"]

Bonus   Find the longest of all palindrome substrings
This time there is no requirement for maximum performance.

8.3.9 Exercise 9: n-Queens Problem (★★★☆☆)

In the n-Queens Problem, n queens are to be placed on an n x n board in such a way that no two queens can beat each other according to chess rules. Thus, other queens must not be placed on the same row, column, or diagonals. To do this, extend the solution shown in section 8.2.1 and implement the method boolean isValidPosition(char[][], int, int). Also write method void printBoard(char[][]) to display the board as well as output the solution to the console.

---

[1] Of course, you are not interested in empty strings and single characters in this assignment although, strictly speaking, they are also palindromes by definition.

Example

For a 4 × 4 playfield, there is the following solution, with the queens symbolized by a Q.

```
- - - - - - - - -
|  |Q|  |  |
- - - - - - - - -
|  |  |  |Q|
- - - - - - - - -
|Q|  |  |  |
- - - - - - - - -
|  |  |Q|  |
- - - - - - - - -
```

8.4 Solutions

8.4.1 Solution 1: Towers of Hanoi (★★★☆☆)

In the Towers of Hanoi problem, there are three towers or sticks named A, B, and C. At the beginning, several perforated discs are placed on stick A in order of size, with the largest at the bottom. The goal is now to move the entire stack (i.e. all the discs) from A to C. The discs must be placed on the top of the stack. The goal is to move one disk at a time and never place a smaller disc below a larger one. That's why you need the helper stick B. Write method `void solveTowersOfHanoi(int)` that prints the solution on the console in the form of the movements to be executed.

Example

The whole thing looks something like Figure 8-2.

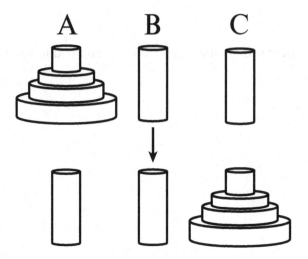

Figure 8-2. *Task definition for the Towers of Hanoi problem*

The following solution should be provided for three slices:

```
Tower Of Hanoi 3
A -> C
A -> B
C -> B
A -> C
B -> A
B -> C
A -> C
```

Algorithm   The movement of the disks is implemented in method `void moveTower(int, char, char, char)`, which gets the number of slices to be moved, the initial source stick, the auxiliary stick, and the target stick. Initially you use n and 'A', 'B', and 'C' as initial parameters. The `moveTower()` method splits the problem into three smaller problems:

1. First, the tower, which is smaller by one slice, is transported from the source to the auxiliary stick.

2. Then, the last and largest slice is moved from the source to the target stick.

3.   Finally, the remaining tower must be moved from the auxiliary to
the target stick.

The action *move source to target* serves as a recursive termination when the height
is 1. It gets a little tricky when swapping the source, target, and auxiliary stick during the
actions.

```
void moveTower(final int n, final char source,
               final char helper, final char destination)
{
    if (n == 1)
        System.out.println(source + " -> " + destination);
    else
    {
        // move all but last slice from source to auxiliary stick
        // destination thus becomes the new auxiliary stick
        moveTower(n - 1, source, destination, helper);

        // move the largest slice from source to target
        moveTower(1, source, helper, destination);

        // from auxiliary stick to targetl
        moveTower(n - 1, helper, source, destination);
    }
}
```

To show fewer details, it is useful to define the following method:

```
void solveTowersOfHanoi(final int n)
{
    System.out.println("Tower Of Hanoi " + n);
    moveTower(n, 'A', 'B', 'C');
}
```

To solve the problem, the method must be invoked with the desired number of slices, something like the following:

```
jshell> solveTowersOfHanoi(3)
Tower Of Hanoi 3
A -> C
A -> B
C -> B
A -> C
B -> A
B -> C
A -> C
```

HINT: RECURSION AS A TOOL

Although the problem sounds rather tricky at first, it can be solved quite easily with recursion. This assignment shows again that recursion is useful to reduce the difficulty by decomposing a problem into several smaller subproblems that are not so difficult to solve.

Bonus: Create a Console-Based Graphical Format

For two slices, this would look something like this:

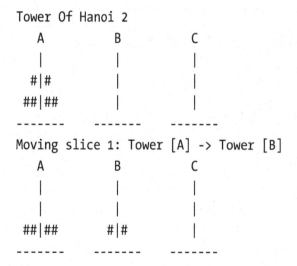

```
Tower Of Hanoi 2
   A          B          C
   |          |          |
  #|#         |          |
 ##|##        |          |
-------    -------    -------
Moving slice 1: Tower [A] -> Tower [B]
   A          B          C
   |          |          |
   |          |          |
 ##|##       #|#         |
-------    -------    -------
```

```
Moving slice 2: Tower [A] -> Tower [C]
   A           B            C
   |           |            |
   |           |            |
   |          #|#         ##|##
------- ------- -------
Moving slice 1: Tower [B] -> Tower [C]
   A           B            C
   |           |            |
   |           |          #|#
   |           |         ##|##
------- ------- -------
```

First, let's look at how the graphical output algorithm changes. This part for finding solutions remains absolutely the same. You just add the class Tower to your implementation and an action that you pass as a lambda expression when solving. You modify the method solveTowersOfHanoi(int) in such a way that three Tower objects are created there, and the desired number of disks is placed on the output tower accordingly.

```java
void solveTowersOfHanoi(final int n)
{
    System.out.println("Tower Of Hanoi " + n);

    final Tower source = new Tower("A");
    final Tower helper = new Tower("B");
    final Tower destination = new Tower("C");

    // Attention: reverse order: largest slice first
    for (int i = n; i > 0; i--)
        source.push(i);

    final Runnable action =
                () -> printTowers(n + 1, source, helper, destination);
    action.run();

    moveTower(n, source, helper, destination, action);
}
```

The implementation of moveTower() receives a Runnable as additional parameter, which allows an action to be executed at the recursive end:

```
void moveTower(final int n, final Tower source, final Tower helper,
               final Tower destination, final Runnable action)
{
    if (n == 1)
    {
        final Integer elemToMove = source.pop();
        destination.push(elemToMove);

        System.out.println("Moving slice " + elementToMove +
                        ": " + source + " -> " + destination);
        action.run();
    }
    else
    {
        moveTower(n - 1, source, destination, helper, action);
        moveTower(1, source, helper, destination, action);
        moveTower(n - 1, helper, source, destination, action);
    }
}
```

The class Tower: The Tower class uses a string for identification and a Stack<E> to store the slices:

```
class Tower
{
    private final String name;
    private final Stack<Integer> values = new Stack<>();

    public Tower(final String name)
    {
        this.name = name;
    }
```

```java
@Override
public String toString()
{
    return "Tower [" + name + "]";
}

public void push(final Integer item)
{
    values.push(item);
}

public Integer pop()
{
    return values.pop();
}

...
```

Console output of towers   In Chapter 4 on strings, you learned about a first variant for drawing towers in section 4.2.16 in exercise 16. Taking advantage of the knowledge gained there, you modify the implementation appropriately. First, you draw the top part of the tower with drawTop(). Then you draw the slices with drawSlices() and finally a bottom boundary line with drawBottom():

```java
static List<String> printTower(final int maxHeight)
{
    final int height = values.size() - 1;

    final List<String> visual = new ArrayList<>();

    visual.addAll(drawTop(maxHeight, height));
    visual.addAll(drawSlices(maxHeight, height));
    visual.add(drawBottom(maxHeight));

    return visual;
}
```

```java
private List<String> drawTop(final int maxHeight, final int height)
{
    final List<String> visual = new ArrayList<>();
    final String nameLine = repeatCharSequence(" ", maxHeight) + name +
                            repeatCharSequence(" ", maxHeight);
    visual.add(nameLine);

    for (int i = maxHeight - height - 1; i > 0; i--)
    {
        final String line = repeatCharSequence(" ", maxHeight) + "|" +
                            repeatCharSequence(" ", maxHeight);
        visual.add(line);
    }
    return visual;
}

static List<String> drawSlices(final int maxHeight, final int height)
{
    final List<String> visual = new ArrayList<>();

    for (int i = height; i >= 0; i--)
    {
        final int value = values.get(i);
        final int padding = maxHeight - value;

        final String line = repeatCharSequence(" ", padding) +
                            repeatCharSequence("#", value) + "|" +
                            repeatCharSequence("#", value);
        visual.add(line);
    }

    return visual;
}

static String drawBottom(final int height)
{
    return repeatCharSequence("-", height * 2 + 1);
}
```

As already demonstrated in other exercises, it is often beneficial to move functionality to separate helper methods, here for repeating a character. In Java 11 and later, it is possible to use the method repeat() provided by the String class. Otherwise you write a helper method like repeatCharSequence() (see section 2.3.7).

Output all towers   Finally, you combine the output functionality in the following method to print the towers represented as three lists side by side:

```java
static void printTowers(final int maxHeight,
                        final Tower source,
                        final Tower helper,
                        final Tower destination)
{
    final List<String> tower1 = source.printTower(maxHeight);
    final List<String> tower2 = helper.printTower(maxHeight);
    final List<String> tower3 = destination.printTower(maxHeight);

    for (int i = 0; i < tower1.size(); i++)
    {
        final String line = tower1.get(i) + "   " +
                            tower2.get(i) + "   " +
                            tower3.get(i);

        System.out.println(line);
    }
}
```

Verification

For testing, you invoke the method, and the output shows the correct operation:

```
jshell> solveHanoi(2)
Tower Of Hanoi 2
    A           B           C
    |           |           |
   #|#          |           |
  ##|##         |           |
 -------     -------     -------
```

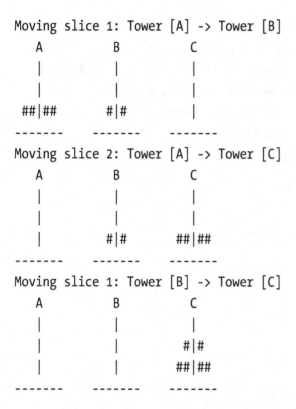

```
Moving slice 1: Tower [A] -> Tower [B]
    A           B           C
    |           |           |
    |           |           |
  ##|##        #|#          |
 -------     -------     -------
Moving slice 2: Tower [A] -> Tower [C]
    A           B           C
    |           |           |
    |           |           |
    |          #|#        ##|##
 -------     -------     -------
Moving slice 1: Tower [B] -> Tower [C]
    A           B           C
    |           |           |
    |           |          #|#
    |           |         ##|##
 -------     -------     -------
```

8.4.2 Solution 2: Edit Distance (★★★★☆)

For two strings, compute how many changes they are, case-insensitive, apart. That is, how do you to transition one string to the other by applying any of the following actions one or more times:

- Add a character (+).

- Delete a character (−).

- Change a character (↝).

Write method int editDistance(String, String) that tries the three actions character by character and checks the other part recursively.

Examples

The following modifications are required for the inputs shown:

Input 1	Input 2	Result	Actions
"Micha"	"Michael"	2	Micha $\rightarrow$ Michae $\rightarrow$ Michael $\quad\ \ +e\quad\quad\ +l$
"rapple"	"tables"	4	rapple $\rightarrow$ rapples $\rightarrow$ rapbles $\rightarrow$ rables $\rightarrow$ tables $\quad\ \ +s\quad\quad\ p\rightsquigarrow b\quad\quad -p\quad\quad r\rightsquigarrow t$

Algorithm   Let's start to consider how you can proceed here. If both strings match, then the edit distance is 0. If one of the two strings contains no (more) characters, then the distance to the other is the number of characters remaining in the other string. This would mean inserting the corresponding characters several times. This defines the recursive termination.

Otherwise, you check both strings from their beginning and compare them character by character. If they are the same, you go one position further towards the end of the string. If they are different, you check three different modifications:

1. **Insert**: Recursive call for the next characters

2. **Remove**: Recursive call for the next characters

3. **Replace**: Recursive call for the next characters

```
static int editDistance(final String str1, final String str2)
{
    return editDistanceRec(str1.toLowerCase(), str2.toLowerCase());
}

static int editDistanceRec(final String str1, final String str2)
{
    // recursive termination
    // both match
    if (str1.equals(str2))
        return 0;
```

```
    // if one of the strings is at the beginning and the other is
    // not yet, then take the length of the remaining string
    if (str1.length() == 0)
        return str2.length();
    if (str2.length() == 0)
        return str1.length();

    // check if the characters match and then advance to the next one
    if (str1.charAt(0) == str2.charAt(0))
    {
        // recursive descent
        return editDistance(str1.substring(1), str2.substring(1));
    }
    else
    {
        // recursive descent: check for insert, delete, change
        final int insertInFirst = editDistanceRec(str1.substring(1), str2);
        final int deleteInFirst = editDistanceRec(str1, str2.substring(1));
        final int change = editDistanceRec(str1.substring(1), str2.substring(1));

        // minimum from all three variants + 1
        return 1 + minOf3(insertInFirst, deleteInFirst, change);
    }
}

static int minOf3(final int x, final int y, final int z)
{
    return Math.min(x, Math.min(y, z));
}
```

The implementation shown is quite comprehensible, which is an advantage in itself. However, the calls to substring() create quite a few substrings temporarily. How can you do it better?

Before you think about optimizations and start making changes in the source code, you should first measure whether it is necessary at all. Besides, it makes a lot of sense to create unit tests that, on the one hand, initially check whether your implementation works as desired and, on the other hand, can form a safety net during the optimizations and show whether you have introduced any errors by mistake.

Verification

To follow up, you invoke the method you just created for some input values in a unit test:

```
@ParameterizedTest(name = "edit distance between {0} and {1} is {2}")
@CsvSource({ "Micha, Michael, 2", "rapple, tables, 4" })
void editDistance(String input1, String input2, int expected)
{
    var result = Ex02_EditDistance.editDistance(input1, input2);

    assertEquals(expected, result);
}
```

Also, let's have a look at the performance. Since only a rough classification is important, the accuracy of currentTimeMillis(() is absolutely sufficient here:

```
public static void main(final String args[])
{
    final String[][] inputs_tuples = { { "Micha", "Michael"},
                                       { "sunday-Morning",
                                         "saturday-Night" },
                                       { "sunday-Morning-Breakfast",
                                         "saturday-Night-Party" } };

    for (final String[] inputs : inputs_tuples)
    {
        final long start = System.currentTimeMillis();
        System.out.println(inputs[0] + " -> " + inputs[1] +
                        " edits: " + editDistance(inputs[0], inputs[1]));
        final long end = System.currentTimeMillis();
        System.out.println("editDist took " + (end - start) + " ms");
    }
}
```

When executing the above lines, with (a lot of) patience, you get approximately the following output (in fact, I stopped the last computation after a few minutes, so it is not shown here):

```
Micha -> Michael edits: 2
editDist took 0 ms
sunday-Morning -> saturday-Night
edits: 9 editDist took 6445 ms
```

The running times increase significantly the more the two inputs differ. Already at the third comparison of still quite short strings, you have about 6 seconds running time.

Let's take a two-step approach to improve this. First, look at how to avoid the many temporary strings and the impact this has. Finally, memoization is always a good way to optimize. The solution of the bonus task shows how this works.

Optimized algorithm   To achieve optimization for avoiding the creation of many String objects, consider using position pointers, in this case *pos1* and *pos2*. As a small modification of the algorithm, the comparisons start from the end of the strings. Thus you compare character by character from the end and work your way towards the string's beginning. The following applies:

1. **Insert**: Recursive call for the next characters, that is *pos*1 and *pos*2 − 1

2. **Remove**: Recursive call for the next characters, that is *pos*1 − 1 and *pos*2

3. **Replace**: Recursive call for the next characters, that is *pos*1 − 1 and *pos*2 − 1

This leads to the following implementation:

```
static int editDistance(final String str1, final String str2)
{
    return editDistance(str1.toLowerCase(), str2.toLowerCase(),
                        str1.length() - 1, str2.length() - 1);
}
```

```
static int editDistance(final String str1, final String str2,
                        final int pos1, final int pos2)
{
    // recursive termination
    // if one of the strings is at the beginning and the other one
    // not yet, then take the length of the remaining string (which is pos + 1)
    if (pos1 < 0)
        return pos2 + 1;

    if (pos2 < 0)
        return pos1 + 1;

    // check if the characters match and then advance to the next one
    if (str1.charAt(pos1) == str2.charAt(pos2))
    {
        // recursive descent
        return editDistance(str1, str2, pos1 - 1, pos2 - 1);
    }
    else
    {
        // recursive descent: check for insert, delete, change
        final int insertInFirst = editDistance(str1, str2, pos1, pos2 - 1);
        final int deleteInFirst = editDistance(str1, str2, pos1 - 1, pos2);
        final int change = editDistance(str1, str2, pos1 - 1, pos2 - 1);

        // minimum from all three variants + 1
        return 1 + minOf3(insertInFirst, deleteInFirst, change);
    }
}
```

Verification

The source code has become a bit more complicated. Again, you create a unit test that looks the same as before. Its execution shows that the above implementation continues to produce the expected results.

Let's now see if there is an improvement in the running time, using the program framework shown initially. This yields the following running times:

```
Micha -> Michael edits: 2
editDist took 0 ms
sunday-Morning -> saturday-Night edits: 9
editDist took 634 ms
```

In fact, it is significantly faster for the third case. However, I also stopped the computation for the fourth pair of values after a few minutes.

You can see that micro-optimizations may lead to improvements, but they do not result in a significant change. I discuss this extensively in my book *Der Weg zum Java-Profi* [Ind20a]. In it I also show that optimizations on higher levels (i.e., algorithms, design, and architecture) should be preferred. Here now, memoization offers itself as an improvement in the algorithm.

Bonus: Optimize Edit Distance with Memoization (★★★☆☆)

In the introduction, I described memoization as a technique and mentioned that a map is often used as a cache. Because you have already learned about this, I would like to show a variant of memoization after a short solution sketch, whose concrete implementation you can find in the companion project's sources.

For the first variant, you can use memoization with a map, but then you need a compound key of two strings as key, which leads to some source code until Java 14. With Java 14, you use a record:

```java
record StringPair(String frist, String second)
{
}
```

In the source code, this looks exemplary, as follows:

```java
// MEMOIZATION
final StringPair key = new StringPair(str1, str2);
if (memodata.containsKey(key))
    return memodata.get(key);
```

What is the effect now? By using memoization, you get an extreme improvement in terms of running time:

```
Micha -> Michael edits: 2
editDist took 3 ms
sunday-Morning -> saturday-Night edits: 9
editDist took 4 ms
sunday-Morning-Breakfast -> saturday-Night-Party edits: 16
editDist took 4 ms
```

Please keep in mind that `currentTimeMillis()` is slightly inaccurate. That's why the output can be 17 ms on one run and 5 ms on another. The important thing is the magnitude, which you have significantly improved here.

Variant for the second implementation: For the already optimized implementation that works with positions, a `int[][]` is more suitable for data storage of the memoization. Note that you preinitialize the array with -1. Otherwise, you would not be able to recognize an edit distance of 0 for two positions.

```java
static int editDistanceOptimized(final String str1, final String str2)
{
    final int length1 = str1.length();
    final int length2 = str2.length();

    var memodata = new int[length1][length2];
    for (int i = 0; i < length1; i++)
        for (int j = 0; j < length2; j++)
            memodata[i][j] = -1;

    return editDistanceWithMemo(str1.toLowerCase(), str2.toLowerCase(),
                                length1 - 1, length2 - 1, memodata);
}

static int editDistanceWithMemo(final String str1, final String str2,
                                final int pos1, final int pos2,
                                final int[][] values)
```

```
{
    // recursive termination
    // if one of the strings is at the beginning and the other one
    // not yet, then take the length of the remaining string (which is pos + 1)
    if (pos1 < 0)
        return pos2 + 1;

    if (pos2 < 0)
        return pos1 + 1;

    // MEMOIZATION
    if (memodata[pos1][pos2] != -1)
        return memodata[pos1][pos2];

    int result = 0;
    // check if the characters match and then advance to the next one
    if (str1.charAt(pos1) == str2.charAt(pos2))
    {
        // recursive descent
        result = editDistanceWithMemo(str1, str2, pos1 - 1, pos2 - 1, values);
    }
    else
    {
        // recursive descent: check for insert, delete, change
        final int insertInFirst =
                editDistanceWithMemo(str1, str2, pos1, pos2 - 1, values);
        final int deleteInFirst =
                editDistanceWithMemo(str1, str2, pos1 - 1, pos2, values);
        final int change =
                editDistanceWithMemo(str1, str2, pos1 - 1, pos2 - 1, values);

        // minimum from all three variants + 1
        result = 1 + minOf3(insertInFirst, deleteInFirst, change);
    }
    // MEMOIZATION
    memodata[pos1][pos2] = result;

    return result;
}
```

If you run the same checks as before, this is slightly faster than the first variant with memorization, even the last computation of the Edit Distance of 16, resulting in a running time of just one millisecond.

```
Micha -> Michael edits: 2
editDist took 0 ms
sunday-Morning -> saturday-Night edits: 9
editDist took 0 ms
sunday-Morning-Breakfast -> saturday-Night-Party edits: 16
editDist took 1 ms
```

8.4.3 Solution 3: Longest Common Subsequence (★★★☆☆)

The previous exercise was about how many changes are needed to transform two given strings into each other. Another interesting problem is to find the longest common but not necessarily contiguous sequence of letters that occurs in two strings. Write method `String lcs(String, String)`, which recursively processes the strings from the back, and in case of two parts of the same length, it uses the second one.

Examples

Input 1	Input 2	Result
"ABCE"	"ZACEF"	"ACE"
"ABCXY"	"XYACB"	"AB"
"ABCMIXCHXAEL"	"MICHAEL"	"MICHAEL"
"sunday-Morning"	"saturday-Night-Party"	"suday-ig"

Algorithm   You move from the back to the front. If the characters match, the character is included in the result. If the characters differ, the check has to be repeated recursively for the strings shortened by one character.

```java
static String lcs(final String str1, final String str2)
{
    return lcs(str1, str2, str1.length() - 1, str2.length() - 1);
}

static String lcs(final String str1, final String str2,
                  final int pos1, final int pos2)
{
    // recursive termination
    if (pos1 < 0 || pos2 < 0)
        return "";

    // are the characters the same?
    if (str1.charAt(pos1) == str2.charAt(pos2))
    {
        // recursive descent
        return lcs(str1, str2, pos1 - 1, pos2 - 1) + str1.charAt(pos1);
    }
    else
    {
        // otherwise take away one of both letters and try it
        // again, but neither letter belongs in the result
        final String lcs1 = lcs(str1, str2, pos1, pos2 - 1);
        final String lcs2 = lcs(str1, str2, pos1 - 1, pos2);

        if (lcs1.length() > lcs2.length())
            return lcs1;

        return lcs2;
    }
}
```

Verification

For testing, you use the following inputs, which show the correct operation:

```
@ParameterizedTest(name = "lcs({0}, {1}) = {2}")
@CsvSource({ "ABCE, ZACEF, ACE",
             "ABCXY, XYACB, AB",
             "ABCMIXCHXAEL, MICHAEL, MICHAEL" })
void lcs(String input1, String input2, String expected)
{
    var result = Ex03_LCS.lcs(input1, input2);

    assertEquals(expected, result);
}
```

Again, you want to examine the performance. It also applies here that currentTimeMillis() is sufficient for classification:

```
public static void main(final String args[])
{
    final String[][] inputs_tuples = { { "ABCMIXCHXAEL", "MICHAEL"},
                                        { "sunday-Morning",
                                          "saturday-Night-Party" },
                                        { "sunday-Morning-Wakeup",
                                          "saturday-Night" } }; };

    for (String[] inputs : inputs_tuples)
    {
        final long start = System.currentTimeMillis();
        System.out.println(inputs[0] + " -> " + inputs[1] +
                            " lcs: " + lcs(inputs[0], inputs[1]));
        final long end = System.currentTimeMillis();
        System.out.println("lcs took " + (end - start) + " ms");
    }
}
```

You measure the following execution times (they will vary slightly for you):

```
ABCMIXCHXAEL -> MICHAEL lcs: MICHAEL
lcs took 1 ms
sunday-Morning -> saturday-Night-Party lcs: suday-ig
lcs took 3318 ms
sunday-Morning-Wakeup -> saturday-Night lcs: suday-ig
lcs took 6151 ms
```

Bonus: Use Memoization for Longest Common Subsequence

When calculating LCS you notice the following: The larger the differences in the two inputs, the higher the resulting running times since there are so many possible subsequences. Therefore, pure recursion is not really performant. So how do you do it better? Again, you use memoization for performance optimization. This time you use a String[][] for data storage:

```java
static String lcsOptimized(final String str1, final String str2)
{
    return lcsWithMemo(str1, str2, str1.length() - 1, str2.length() - 1,
                    new String[str1.length() - 1][str2.length() - 1]);
}
```

The actual implementation uses memoization as follows:

```java
static String lcsWithMemo(final String str1, final String str2,
                        final int pos1, final int pos2,
                        final String[][] values)
{
    // recursive termination
    if (pos1 < 0 || pos2 < 0)
        return "";

    // MEMOIZATION
    if (values[pos1][pos2] != null)
        return values[pos1][pos2];

    String lcs;
```

```
// are the characters the same?
if (str1.charAt(pos1) == str2.charAt(pos2))
{
    // recursive descent
    final char sameChar = str1.charAt(pos1);
    lcs = lcsWithMemo(str1, str2, pos1 - 1, pos2 - 1, values) + sameChar;
}
else
{
    // otherwise take away one of both letters and try it
    // again, but neither letter belongs in the result
    final String lcs1 = lcsWithMemo(str1, str2, pos1, pos2 - 1, values);
    final String lcs2 = lcsWithMemo(str1, str2, pos1 - 1, pos2, values);

    if (lcs1.length() > lcs2.length())
        lcs = lcs1;
    else
        lcs = lcs2;
}

// MEMOIZATION
values[pos1][pos2] = lcs;

return lcs;
}
```

With this optimization, the execution time gets down to a few milliseconds. Start the program EX03_LCSWithMemo for evaluation.

8.4.4 Solution 4: Way Out of a Labyrinth (★★★☆☆)

In this assignment, you are asked to find the way out of a maze. Assume a maze is given as a two-dimensional array with walls symbolized by # and target positions (exits) symbolized by X. From any position, a path to all exits is supposed to be determined. If there are two exits in a row, only the first of the two has to be supplied. You can only move in the four compass directions, but not diagonally. Write method boolean findWayOut(char[][], int, int) that logs each found exit with FOUND EXIT at ....

Example

A larger playfield with four target fields is shown next. The bottom figure shows each of the paths indicated by a dot (.). In between you see the logging of the found positions of the exits. For this example, the search starts from the upper left corner with coordinates x=1, y=1.

```
##################################
# #           #     #     #  #   X#X#
#  ##### #### ##    ##  #  # ###  #
#  ## #     #  ## ## # #       # #
#    #  ###  # ## ##   #   ### # #
# #   ####     ## ##      ###  # #
#### #    #  ####    #  # #### #
######    #########   ##  # ### #
##      #  X X####X # #  # ###  ##
##################################
FOUND EXIT: x: 30, y: 1
FOUND EXIT: x: 17, y: 8
FOUND EXIT: x: 10, y: 8
##################################
#.#         #....#.....#  #...X#X#
#..##### ####.##...##..#  #.###  #
#  .## #    #..## ## .#  #..    # #
#  ...#  ###..#.## ## ..#...### # #
# #  ..####.....## ##.... ###  # #
#### ..#...  ####  ....#  # #### #
######...#########...##   # ### #
##      #..X X####X.# #  # ### ##
##################################
```

Based on the outputs, it is also clear that two of the target fields marked with X are not detected from the start position. One is the X at the very top right corner, which cannot be reached due to a missing link. The other is the lower middle X, which is behind another exit.

Algorithm   The algorithm for finding a way out of a labyrinth checks whether there is a way in the four compass directions, starting from the current position. To do this, neighboring fields that have already been visited are marked with the dot (.) character, just as you would do in reality with small stones, for example. The trial and error continues until you come to an X as a solution, a wall in the form of a #, or an already visited field (marked by a dot). If there is no possible direction left for a position, you use backtracking, resume the last chosen path, and try the remaining paths from there. This is implemented as follows:

```
static boolean findWayOut(final char[][] values, final int x, final int y)
{
    if (x < 0 || y < 0 || x > values[0].length || y >= values.length)
        return false;

    // recursive termination
    if (values[y][x] == 'X')
    {
        System.out.println(String.format("FOUND EXIT: x: %d, y: %d", x, y));
        return true;
    }
    // wall or already visited?
    if (values[y][x] == '#' || values[y][x] == '.')
        return false;

    // recursive descent
    if (values[y][x] == ' ')
    {
        // mark as visited
        values[y][x] = '.';

        // try all 4 cardinal directions
        final boolean up = findWayOut(values, x, y - 1);
        final boolean left = findWayOut(values, x + 1, y);
        final boolean down = findWayOut(values, x, y + 1);
        final boolean right = findWayOut(values, x - 1, y);
```

```
    // backtracking because no valid solution
    final boolean foundAWay = up || left || down || right;
    if (!foundAWay)
    {
        // wrong path, thus delete field marker
        values[y][x] = ' ';
    }
    return foundAWay;
}
throw new IllegalStateException("wrong char in labyrinth");
}
```

Note that you use the natural alignment of x and y coordinates in the methods. Still, when accessing the array, the order is [y][x] because you are working in rows, as I discussed in the introductory section of the chapter on arrays in section 5.1.2.

Verification

For testing, you define the maze from the introduction. Next, you call the findWayOut() method, which then logs the previously shown exits from the maze and finally visualizes the paths with the dots (.):

```
char[][] world_big = { "#################################".toCharArray(),
                       "# #          #    #     #  #   X#X#".toCharArray(),
                       "# ##### #### ##   ##  #  # ###  #".toCharArray(),
                       "# ## #   #  ## ## # #     # #".toCharArray(),
                       "#   #  ### # ## ##   #   ### # #".toCharArray(),
                       "# #   ####     ## ##    ### # #".toCharArray(),
                       "####   #      ####    #  # ####  #".toCharArray(),
                       "######   #########   ##  # ###  #".toCharArray(),
                       "##      #  X X####X # #  # ### ##".toCharArray(),
                       "#################################".toCharArray() };
printArray(world_big);
if (findWayOut(world_big, 1, 1))
    printArray(world_big);
```

Alternative

The implementation shown quite nicely prepares the paths to the target fields graphically. However, it has two minor disadvantages. On the one hand, it breaks off directly when an exit is encountered and thus does not find an exit behind it. On the other hand, if there are several paths to a target field, the program also logs the finding of an exit several times. The latter could be solved quite easily by collecting all solution paths in a set. You can find this as an implementation in the companion resources as method findWayOutWithResultSet().

If you want to find all reachable exits, it is possible to modify the method shown before so that visited fields are marked with a #. However, this way, the field is quite filled up at the end and does not show the way anymore, which was an advantage of the initial variant.

```
static boolean findWayOutV2(final char[][] board,
                            final int x, final int y)
{
    if (board[y][x] == '#')
        return false;

    boolean found = board[y][x] == 'X';
    if (found)
        System.out.printf("FOUND EXIT: x: %d, y: %d%n", x, y);

    board[y][x] = '#';
    found = found | findWayOutV2(board, x + 1, y);
    found = found | findWayOutV2(board, x - 1, y);
    found = found | findWayOutV2(board, x, y + 1);
    found = found | findWayOutV2(board, x, y - 1);
    return found;
}
```

8.4.5 Solution 5: Sudoku Solver (★★★★☆)

Write method boolean solveSudoku(int[][]) that determines a valid solution, if any, for a partially initialized playfield passed as a parameter.

Example

A valid playfield with some blanks is shown here:

1	2		4	5		7	8	9
	5	6	7		9		2	3
7	8		1	2	3	4	5	6
2	1	4		6		8		7
3	6		8		7	2	1	4
	9	7		1	4	3	6	
5	3	1	6		2	9		8
6		2	9	7	8	5	3	1
9	7			3	1	6	4	2

It should be completed to the following solution:

1	2	3	4	5	6	7	8	9
4	5	6	7	8	9	1	2	3
7	8	9	1	2	3	4	5	6
2	1	4	3	6	5	8	9	7
3	6	5	8	9	7	2	1	4
8	9	7	2	1	4	3	6	5
5	3	1	6	4	2	9	7	8
6	4	2	9	7	8	5	3	1
9	7	8	5	3	1	6	4	2

Algorithm   To solve Sudoku, you use backtracking. As with other backtracking problems, Sudoku can be solved by step-by-step trial and error. In this case, that means trying different numbers for each of the empty squares. According to the Sudoku rules, the current digit must not already exist horizontally, vertically, or in a 3 × 3 block.

If you find a valid value assignment, you can continue recursively at the next position to test whether you arrive at a solution. If none is found, then you try the procedure with the next digit. However, if none of the digits from 1 to 9 lead to a solution, you need backtracking to examine other possible paths to the solution.

You proceed as follows in the implementation:

1. Find the next empty field. To do this, skip all fields that are already filled. This can also change lines.

2. If no more empty fields exist until the last row, you have found the solution.

3. Otherwise you try out the digits from 1 to 9:

   a. Is there a conflict? Then you have to try the next digit.

   b. The digit is a possible candidate. You call your method recursively for the following position (next column or even next row).

   c. If the recursion returns **false**, this digit does not lead to a solution and you use backtracking.

```
static boolean solveSudoku(final int[][] board)
{
    return solveSudoku(board, 0, 0);
}

static boolean solveSudoku(final int[][] board,
                           final int startRow, final int startCol)
{
    int row = startRow;
    int col = startCol;

    // 1) skip fields with numbers until you reach the next empty field
    while (row < 9 && board[row][col] != 0)
    {
        col++;
        if (col > 8)
        {
```

```
            col = 0;
            row++;
        }
    }

    // 2) already processed all lines?
    if (row > 8)
        return true;

    // 3) try for the current field all digits from 1 to 9 through
    for (int num = 1; num <= 9; num++)
    {
        // set digit tentatively in the field
        board[row][col] = num;

        // 3a) check if the whole field with the digit is still valid
        if (isValidPosition(board))
        {
            // 3b) recursive descent for the following field
            boolean solved = false;

            if (col < 8)
                solved = solveSudoku(board, row, col + 1);
            else
                solved = solveSudoku(board, row + 1, 0);

            // 3c) backtracking if recursion is not successful
            if (!solved)
                board[row][col] = 0;
            else
                return true;
        }
        else
        {
            // try next digit
            board[row][col] = 0;
        }
```

```
    }
    return false;
}

static boolean isValidPosition(final int[][] board)
{
    return checkHorizontally(board) &&
           checkVertically(board) &&
           checkBoxes(board);
}
```

Looking at this implementation, you might already doubt whether this variant is really optimal, even without knowing the details of the helper methods shown in the following. Why? You keep checking the entire playfield for validity at every step, and even worse, doing that in combination with backtracking! I'll go into this in more detail later.

Let's first consider the three methods checkHorizontally(int[][]), checkVertically(int[][]), and checkBoxes(int[][]). You implemented them in exercise 9 in section 5.3.9. They are shown again here for completeness:

```
static boolean checkHorizontally(final int[][] board)
{
    for (int row = 0; row < 9; row++)
    {
        final List<Integer> rowValues = new ArrayList<>();
        for (int x = 0; x < 9; x++)
            rowValues.add(board[row][x]);

        if (!allDesiredNumbers(rowValues))
            return false;
    }
    return true;
}

static boolean checkVertically(final int[][] board)
{
    for (int x = 0; x < 9; x++)
    {
        final List<Integer> columnValues = new ArrayList<>();
```

```java
        for (int row = 0; row < 9; row++)
            columnValues.add(board[row][x]);

        if (!allDesiredNumbers(columnValues))
            return false;
    }
    return true;
}

static boolean checkBoxes(final int[][] board)
{
    // 3 x 3-Boxes
    for (int yBox = 0; yBox < 3; yBox++)
    {
        for (int xBox = 0; xBox < 3; xBox++)
        {
            final List<Integer> boxValues = collectBoxValues(board, yBox, xBox);

            if (!allDesiredNumbers(boxValues))
                return false;
        }
    }
    return true;
}

static List<Integer> collectBoxValues(final int[][] board,
                                      final int yBox, final int xBox)
{
    final List<Integer> boxValues = new ArrayList<>();
    // inside the boxes each 3 x 3 fields
    for (int y = 0; y < 3; y++)
    {
        for (int x = 0; x < 3; x++)
        {
            boxValues.add(board[yBox * 3 + y][xBox * 3 + x]);
```

```
        }
    }
    return boxValues;
}

static boolean allDesiredNumbers(final List<Integer> allCollectedValues)
{
    final List<Integer> relevantValues = new ArrayList<>(allCollectedValues);
    relevantValues.removeIf(val -> val == 0);

    // no duplicates?
    final Set<Integer> valuesSet = new TreeSet<>(relevantValues);
    if (relevantValues.size() != valuesSet.size())
        return false;

    // just 1 to 9?
    final Set<Integer> oneToNine = Set.of(1, 2, 3, 4, 5, 6, 7, 8, 9);

    return oneToNine.containsAll(valuesSet);
}

static void printArray(final int[][] values)
{
    for (int y = 0; y < values.length; y++)
    {
        for (int x = 0; x < values[y].length; x++)
        {
            final int value = values[y][x];
            System.out.print(value + " ");
        }
        System.out.println();
    }
}
```

Verification

You test this implementation with the example from the introduction:

```
jshell> int[][] boardExample = new int[][] {
              { 1, 2, 0, 4, 5, 0, 7, 8, 9 },
              { 0, 5, 6, 7, 0, 9, 0, 2, 3 },
              { 7, 8, 0, 1, 2, 3, 4, 5, 6 },
              { 2, 1, 4, 0, 6, 0, 8, 0, 7 },
              { 3, 6, 0, 8, 9, 7, 2, 1, 4 },
              { 0, 9, 7, 0, 1, 4, 3, 6, 0 },
              { 5, 3, 1, 6, 0, 2, 9, 0, 8 },
              { 6, 0, 2, 9, 7, 8, 5, 3, 1 },
              { 9, 7, 0, 0, 3, 1, 6, 4, 2 } }

jshell> if (solveSudoku(boardExample))
   ...> {
   ...>     System.out.println("Solved: ");
   ...>     printArray(boardExample);
   ...> }
Solved:
1 2 3 4 5 6 7 8 9
4 5 6 7 8 9 1 2 3
7 8 9 1 2 3 4 5 6
2 1 4 3 6 5 8 9 7
3 6 5 8 9 7 2 1 4
8 9 7 2 1 4 3 6 5
5 3 1 6 4 2 9 7 8
6 4 2 9 7 8 5 3 1
9 7 8 5 3 1 6 4 2
```

The solution is displayed within a few fractions of a second. So far, everything has worked really well. But what happens if the given playfield contains hardly any digits but lots of empty fields?

Playfields with more blanks   When you tackle the challenge of trying to solve playfields with only a few given digits, there are many variations to be tried, and a lot of backtracking comes into play. Suppose you want to solve something like the following playfield:

```
final int[][] board2 = { { 6, 0, 2, 0, 5, 0, 0, 0, 0 },
                         { 0, 0, 0, 0, 0, 4, 0, 3, 0 },
                         { 0, 0, 0, 0, 0, 0, 0, 0, 0 },
                         { 4, 3, 0, 0, 0, 8, 0, 0, 0 },
                         { 0, 1, 0, 0, 0, 0, 2, 0, 0 },
                         { 0, 0, 0, 0, 0, 0, 7, 0, 0 },
                         { 5, 0, 0, 2, 7, 0, 0, 0, 0 },
                         { 0, 0, 0, 0, 0, 0, 0, 8, 1 },
                         { 0, 0, 0, 6, 0, 0, 0, 0, 0 } };
```

In principle, this is already possible with your algorithm, but it takes several minutes. Although this is quite long, you probably still couldn't solve difficult puzzles by hand in this time span, but with the computer, it should be even faster. So what can you improve?

Reasonable Optimizations

Idea 1: Optimization of the check: Checking the entire playfield for validity in every step is neither useful, necessary, nor performant. As an optimization, you modify the check so that only a single column, row, and the relevant box are checked at a time. To do this, first modify the method isValidPosition() slightly so that it receives column and row as parameters:

```
static boolean isValidPosition(final int[][] board,
                               final int row, final int col)
{
    return checkSingleHorizontally(board, row) &&
           checkSingleVertically(board, col) &&
           checkSingleBox(board, row, col);
}
```

Besides, you then create specific test methods such as the following:

```
static boolean checkSingleHorizontally(final int[][] board, final int row)
{
    final List<Integer> columnValues = new ArrayList<>();

    for (int x = 0; x < 9; x++)
    {
        columnValues.add(board[row][x]);
    }

    return allDesiredNumbers(columnValues);
}
```

This optimization results in running times in the range of a few seconds (between 20 and 50 seconds for complicated playfields). That is already much better, but it can still be much more performant.

Idea 2: More clever testing: If you look at the processes, you notice that you try all digits. This violates a bit of common sense. Wouldn't it make more sense only to use potentially valid paths, and to do so, check in advance whether the current digit is even usable in the context? You can then directly exclude all those digits that already exist in a row, column, or box. To do this, you need to modify the check as follows and pass the potential digit as a parameter:

```
private static boolean isValidPosition(final int[][] board,
                                       final int row, final int col,
                                       final int num)
{
    return checkNumNotInColumn(board, col, num) &&
           checkNumNotInRow(board, row, num) &&
           checkNumNotInBox(board, row, col, num);
}

static boolean checkNumNotInRow(final int[][] board,
                                final int row, final int num)
{
    for (int col = 0; col < 9; col++)
    {
```

```
        if (board[row][col] == num)
            return false;
    }

    return true;
}

static boolean checkNumNotInColumn(final int[][] board,
                                   final int col, final int num)
{
    for (int row = 0; row < 9; row++)
    {
        if (board[row][col] == num)
            return false;
    }

    return true;
}

static boolean checkNumNotInBox(final int[][] board,
                                final int row, final int col, final int num)
{
    final int adjustedRow = (row / 3) * 3;
    final int adjustedCol = (col / 3) * 3;

    for (int y = 0; y < 3; y++)
    {
        for (int x = 0; x < 3; x++)
        {
            if (board[adjustedRow + y][adjustedCol + x] == num)
                return false;
        }
    }

    return true;
}
```

Idea 3: Optimized sequence of setting and checking   Finally, you modify the trial and error so that only after determining that the digit is valid is it also placed on the playfield. So far, in the solveSudoku() method as step 3, you have tried all the digits as follows:

```
def solveSudokuHelper(board, startRow, startCol):

    // ...

    solved = False

    # 3) for the current field, try all digits from 1 to 9
    for num in range(1, 10):
        board[row][col] = num

        # 3a) check if the whole playfield containing the digit is still valid
        if isValidPosition(board, row, col, num):
```

...

You optimize this test twice. First, you change the method to isValidPosition(board, row, col) so that it also gets the row and column. As a further improvement, you pass the number to be checked isValidPosition(board, row, col, num).

Now you go one step further and change the order of inserting the value and checking. Therefore you switch only two lines, namely the assignment and the if with the call of the optimized variant of the validity check:

```
    # 3) for the current field, try all digits from 1 to 9
    for num in range(1, 10):
        # board[row][col] = num

        # 3a) check if the whole playfield containing the digit is still valid
        if isValidPosition(board, row, col, num):
            board[row][col] = num
```

Results of the optimizations made   Your optimizations (which, by the way, do not lead to any limitations in readability or comprehensibility) also save you from having to try very many solutions that never lead to the goal. Even for more complex playfields, the solutions are always determined in under 1 second on my iMac (i7 4 GHz).

8.4.6 Solution 6: Math Operator Checker (★★★★☆)

This assignment is about a mathematically inclined puzzle. For a set of digits and another set of possible operators, you want to find all combinations that result in the desired value. The order of the digits cannot be changed. Still, it is possible to insert any operator from the possible operators between the digits, except before the first digit. Write method `Set<String> allCombinationsWithValue(List<Integer>, int)` that determines all combinations that result in the value passed as a parameter. Check this for the digits 1 to 9 and the operations + and − and also *combine the digits*. Start with method `Map<String, Long> allCombinations(List<Integer>)`, which is passed the corresponding digits.

Examples

Let's consider two combinations only for the digits 1, 2 and 3:

$$1 + 2 + 3 \;=\; 6$$
$$1 + 23 \;=\; 24$$

In total, these digits allow the following different combinations to be formed with:

Input	Result (`allCombinations()`)
[1, 2, 3]	{12-3=9, 123=123, 1+2+3=6, 1+2-3=0, 1-2+3=2, 1-23=-22, 1-2-3=-4, 1+23=24, 12+3=15}

Suppose you want to generate the value 100 from the given digits 1 to 9 and the set of available operators (+, −, and *combine the digits*). Then this is possible, for example, as follows:

$$1 + 2 + 3 - 4 + 5 + 6 + 78 + 9 = 100$$

In total, the following variants should be determined:

Input	Result (`allCombinationsWithValue()`)
100	[1+23-4+5+6+78-9, 123+4-5+67-89, 123-45-67+89, 12+3-4+5+67+8+9, 1+23-4+56+7+8+9, 12-3-4+5-6+7+89, 123-4-5-6-7+8-9, 1+2+34-5+67-8+9, 12+3+4+5-6-7+89, 123+45-67+8-9, 1+2+3-4+5+6+78+9]

Tip   In Java, you can perform dynamic calculations at runtime only with some tricks. However, if you use Java's built-in JavaScript engine, it is fairly easy to evaluate expressions:

```
jshell> import javax.script.*

jshell> ScriptEngineManager manager = new ScriptEngineManager()

jshell> ScriptEngine jsEngine = manager.getEngineByName("js")

jshell> jsEngine.eval("7+2")
$63 ==> 9
```

Write method int evaluate(String) to evaluate an expression with digits and the operators + and −.

Algorithm   First, you subdivide the problem at the high level by computing all possible combinations by calling the allCombinations() method, and then using findByValue() to search for those combinations whose evaluation yields the default value. This can be easily expressed using the Stream API and a suitable filter condition:

```
static Set<String> allCombinationsWithValue(final List<Integer> baseValues,
                                             final int desiredValue)
{
    final Map<String, Long> allCombinations = allCombinations(baseValues);

    return findByValue(allCombinations, desiredValue);
}

static Set<String> findByValue(final Map<String, Long> results,
                               final int desiredValue)
{
    return results.entrySet().stream().
                        filter(entry -> entry.getValue() ==
                        desiredValue).
                        map(entry -> entry.getKey()).
                        collect(Collectors.toSet());
}
```

In fact, you can simplify things considerably again by using the removeIf() method introduced with Java 8:

```java
static Set<String> allCombinationsWithValueShort(final List<Integer> baseValues,
                                                  final int desiredValue)
{
    final Map<String, Long> allCombinations = allCombinations(baseValues);

    allCombinations.entrySet().
                    removeIf(entry -> entry.getValue() != desiredValue);

    return allCombinations.keySet();
}
```

The method findByValue() is useful for experiments when you want to compute the combinations only once. You will now look at this computation.

To calculate the combinations, the input is split into a left and a right part. This results in three subproblems to be solved, namely $l+r$, $l-r$, and lr, where l and r stand for the left and right parts of the input. You compute their result with the method evaluate(). If there is only one digit left, this is the result and constitutes the recursive termination:

```java
static Map<String, Long> allCombinations(final List<Integer> digits)
{
    return allCombinations(digits, 0);
}

static Map<String, Long> allCombinations(final List<Integer> digits,
                                          final int pos)
{
    // recursive termination
    if (pos >= digits.size() - 1)
    {
        final long lastDigit = digits.get(digits.size() - 1);
        return Map.of("" + lastDigit, lastDigit);
    }
```

```java
    // recursive descent
    final Map<String, Long> results = allCombinations(digits, pos + 1);

    // check combinations
    final Map<String, Long> solutions = new HashMap<>();
    results.forEach((key, value) ->
    {
        final long currentDigit = digits.get(pos);

        solutions.put(currentDigit + "+" + key,
                    evaluate("" + currentDigit + "+" + key));
        solutions.put(currentDigit + "-" + key,
                    evaluate("" + currentDigit + "-" + key));
        solutions.put(currentDigit + key,
                    evaluate("" + currentDigit + key));
    });

    return solutions;
}
```

You implement the execution using JavaScript as follows:

```java
static long evaluate(final String expression)
{
    try
    {
        return (long) jsEngine.eval(expression);
    }
    catch (final ScriptException e)
    {
        throw new RuntimeException("unprocessable expression " + expression);
    }
}
```

Thereby the variable jsEngine must be defined either in the JShell as shown in the introduction or in a Java program, for example, as a static variable. Please think of import javax.script.* in the JShell.

Variant with Streams

Often there are many possible solutions. The assignment is also solvable very nicely with the help of the Stream API. The actions are analogous to those of the previously shown variant, but this time you work your way through the numbers from front to back. As a special feature, you have to create the streams three times to compute the results. For merging them concat() is a good choice:

```
static Map<String, Long> allCombinationsWithStreams(final List<Integer> digits)
{
    return allExpressions(digits).collect(Collectors.toMap(Function.identity(),
                                        Ex06_MathOperationChecker::evaluate));
}

private static Stream<String> allExpressions(final List<Integer> digits)
{
    if (digits.size() == 1)
        return Stream.of("" + digits.get(0));

    final long first = digits.get(0);

    final List<Integer> remainingDigits = digits.subList(1, digits.size());

    var resultCombine =
        allExpressions(remainingDigits).map(expr -> first + expr);
    var resultAdd =
        allExpressions(remainingDigits).map(expr -> first + "+" + expr);
    var resultMinus =
        allExpressions(remainingDigits).map(expr -> first + "-" + expr);

    return Stream.concat(resultCombine, Stream.concat(resultAdd, resultMinus));
}
```

Variant as of Java 15

As of Java 15, support for the JavaScript engine is removed from the JDK, so you have to write your own evaluation. Since, fortunately, only addition and subtraction have to be calculated here, you can solve it with a little knowledge about regular expressions as follows:

```java
static long evaluate(final String expression)
{
    final String[] values = expression.split("\\+|-");

    // use numbers as separators
    final String[] tmpoperators = expression.split("\\d+");

    // filter out empty elements, limit to the real operators
    final String[] operators = Arrays.stream(tmpoperators).
                                    filter(str -> !str.isEmpty()).
                                    toArray(String[]::new);

    long result = Long.parseLong(values[0]);
    for (int i = 1; i < values.length; i++)
    {
        final String nextOp = operators[i - 1];
        final long nextValue = Long.parseLong(values[i]);
        if (nextOp.equals("+"))
            result = result + nextValue;
        else if (nextOp.equals("-"))
            result = result - nextValue;
        else
            throw new IllegalStateException("unsupported operator " + nextOp);
    }
    return result;
}
```

Verification

First, you write a unit test that checks for inputs 1 to 3, which combinations can be built. Additionally, you want to verify the functionality for the result value 100.

```
@ParameterizedTest(name = "allCombinations({0}) = {1}")
@MethodSource("digitsAndCombinations")
void allCombinations(List<Integer> digits, Map<String, Integer> expected)
{
    var result = Ex06_MathOperationChecker.allCombinations(digits);

    assertEquals(expected, result);
}

private static Stream<Arguments> digitsAndCombinations()
{
    var results = Map.ofEntries(Map.entry("12-3", 9L), Map.entry("123", 123L),
                                Map.entry("1+2+3", 6L), Map.entry("1+2-3", 0L),
                                Map.entry("1-2+3", 2L), Map.entry("1-23", -22L),
                                Map.entry("1-2-3", -4L), Map.entry("1+23", 24L),
                                Map.entry("12+3", 15L));

    return Stream.of(Arguments.of(List.of(1, 2, 3), results));
}

@ParameterizedTest(name = "allCombinationsWithValue({0}, {1}) = {2}")
@MethodSource("digitsAndCombinationsWithResult100")
void allCombinationsWithValue(List<Integer> numbers, int desiredValue,
                              Set<String> expected)
{
    var result =
        Ex06_MathOperationChecker.allCombinationsWithValue(numbers,
                                                           desiredValue);

    assertEquals(expected, result);
}
```

```java
private static Stream<Arguments> digitsAndCombinationsWithResult100()
{
    var results = Set.of("1+23-4+5+6+78-9", "12+3+4+5-6-7+89", "123-45-67+89",
                         "123+4-5+67-89", "123-4-5-6-7+8-9", "123+45-67+8-9",
                         "1+2+3-4+5+6+78+9", "12+3-4+5+67+8+9",
                         "1+23-4+56+7+8+9", "1+2+34-5+67-8+9",
                         "12-3-4+5-6+7+89");

    return Stream.of(Arguments.of(List.of(1, 2, 3, 4, 5, 6, 7, 8, 9), 100,
                                  results));
}
```

8.4.7 Solution 7: Water Jug Problem (★★★☆☆)

Consider two jugs with capacities of *m* and *n* liters. Unfortunately, these jugs have no markings or indications of their fill level. The challenge is to measure *x* liters, where *x* is less than *m* or *n*. At the end of the procedure, one jug should contain *x* liters, and the other should be empty. Write method boolean solveWaterJugs(int, int, int), which displays the solution on the console and, if successful, returns true, otherwise false.

Examples

For two jugs, one with a capacity of 4 liters and one with a capacity of 3 liters, you can measure 2 liters in the following way:

State	Action
Jug 1: 0/Jug 2: 0	Both jugs initial empty
Jug 1: 4/Jug 2: 0	Fill jug 1 (unnecessary, but due to the algorithm)
Jug 1: 4/Jug 2: 3	Fill jug 2
Jug 1: 0/Jug 2: 3	Empty jug 1
Jug 1: 3/Jug 2: 0	Pour jug 2 into jug 1
Jug 1: 3/Jug 2: 3	Fill jug 2
Jug 1: 4/Jug 2: 2	Pour jug 2 in jug 1
Jug 1: 0/Jug 2: 2	Empty jug 1
Solved	

On the other hand, measuring 2 liters is impossible with two jugs of 4 liters capacity each.

Algorithm   To solve the water jug problem, you use recursion with a greedy algorithm. Here, at each time point, you have the following next actions as possibilities:

- Empty jug 1 completely.

- Empty jug 2 completely.

- Fill jug 1 completely.

- Fill jug 2 completely.

- Fill jug 1 from jug 2 until the source jug is empty or the jug to be filled is full.

- Fill jug 2 from jug 1 until the source jug is empty or the jug to be filled is full.

You try these six variants step by step until one of them succeeds. To do this, you need to test each time whether there is the desired number of liters in one of the jugs and whether the other is empty.

```
static boolean isSolved(final int currentJug1, final int currentJug2,
                        final int desiredLiters)
{
    return (currentJug1 == desiredLiters && currentJug2 == 0) ||
           (currentJug2 == desiredLiters && currentJug1 == 0);
}
```

Because trying out many solutions can be quite time-consuming, you use the already known technique of memoization for optimization. In this case, it prevents cycles (i.e., the same actions being executed repeatedly). The already calculated levels are modeled in the form of a compound key. Here you use class IntIntKey (see section 8.1.2). To find the solution, you start with two empty jugs:

```
static boolean solveWaterJugs(final int size1, final int size2,
                              final int desiredLiters)
{
    return solveWaterJugsRec(size1, size2, desiredLiters, 0, 0,
                             new HashMap<>());
}
```

```java
static boolean solveWaterJugsRec(final int size1, final int size2,
                                 final int desiredLiters,
                                 final int currentJug1, final int currentJug2,
                                 final Map<IntIntKey, Boolean> alreadyTried)
{
    if (isSolved(currentJug1, currentJug2, desiredLiters))
    {
        System.out.println("Solved Jug 1: " + currentJug1 +
                           " / Jug 2: " + currentJug2);;
        return true;
    }

    final IntIntKey key = new IntIntKey(currentJug1, currentJug2);
    if (!alreadyTried.containsKey(key))
    {
        alreadyTried.put(key, true);

        // Try all 6 variants
        System.out.println("Jug 1: " + currentJug1 + " / Jug 2: " +
                           currentJug2);

        final int min_2_1 = Math.min(currentJug2, (size1 - currentJug1));
        final int min_1_2 = Math.min(currentJug1, (size2 - currentJug2));
        boolean result = solveWaterJugsRec(size1, size2, desiredLiters,
                                  0, currentJug2, alreadyTried) ||
                     solveWaterJugsRec(size1, size2, desiredLiters,
                                  currentJug1, 0, alreadyTried) ||
                     solveWaterJugsRec(size1, size2, desiredLiters,
                                  size1, currentJug2, alreadyTried) ||
                     solveWaterJugsRec(size1, size2, desiredLiters,
                                  currentJug1, size2, alreadyTried) ||
                     solveWaterJugsRec(size1, size2, desiredLiters,
                                  currentJug1 + min_2_1,
                                  currentJug2 - min_2_1,
                                  alreadyTried) ||
                     solveWaterJugsRec(size1, size2, desiredLiters,
                                  currentJug1 - min_1_2,
```

```
                                    currentJug2 + min_1_2,
                                    alreadyTried);

    alreadyTried.put(key, result);
    return result;
  }

  return false;
}
```

ATTENTION: POSSIBLE PITFALL

When implementing this, you might get the idea of simply examining all six variants independently, as one would do to determine all exits from a maze, for example. However, I'm afraid that's not right because it would allow multiple actions in one step. Therefore only one step has to be examined at a time. Only in case of a failure do you proceed with another one. Thus, the variant shown below is not correct. It detects the solution, but additional, partly confusing steps are executed:

```
// Intuitive, BUT WRONG, because 2 or more steps possible
boolean actionEmpty1 = solveWaterJugsRec(size1, size2, desiredLiters,
                                  0, currentJug2, alreadyTried);
boolean actionEmpty2 = solveWaterJugsRec(size1, size2, desiredLiters,
                                  currentJug1, 0, alreadyTried);
boolean actionFill1 = solveWaterJugsRec(size1, size2, desiredLiters,
                                  size1, currentJug2, alreadyTried);
boolean actionFill2 = solveWaterJugsRec(size1, size2, desiredLiters,
                                  currentJug1, size2, alreadyTried);

int min_2_1 = Math.min(currentJug2, (size1 - currentJug1));
boolean actionFillUp1From2 = solveWaterJugsRec(size1, size2, desiredLiters,
                                  currentJug1 + min_2_1),
                                  currentJug2 - min_2_1);
int min_1_2 = Math.min(currentJug1, (size2 - currentJug2));
boolean actionFillUp2From1 = solveWaterJugsRec(size1, size2, desiredLiters,
                                  currentJug1 - min_1_2),
                                  currentJug2 + min_1_2);
```

Verification

Let's determine the solution in the JShell for the combination from the example:

```
jshell> solveWaterJugs(4, 3, 2)
Jug 1: 0 / Jug 2: 0
Jug 1: 4 / Jug 2: 0
Jug 1: 4 / Jug 2: 3
Jug 1: 0 / Jug 2: 3
Jug 1: 3 / Jug 2: 0
Jug 1: 3 / Jug 2: 3
Jug 1: 4 / Jug 2: 2
Solved Jug 1: 0 / Jug 2: 2
$5 ==> true
```

8.4.8 Solution 8: All Palindrome Substrings (★★★★☆)

In this assignment, given a word, you want to determine whether it contains palindromes and, if so, which ones. Write recursive method `Set<String> allPalind romePartsRec(String)` that determines all palindromes with at least two letters in the passed string and returns them sorted alphabetically.[2]

Examples

Input	Result
"BCDEDCB"	["BCDEDCB", "CDEDC", "DED"]
"ABALOTTOLL"	["ABA", "LL", "LOTTOL", "OTTO", "TT"]
"racecar"	["aceca", "cec", "racecar"]

---

[2] Of course, you are not interested in empty strings and single characters in this assignment although, strictly speaking, they are also palindromes by definition.

Algorithm   This problem is broken down into three subproblems for texts of at least length 2:

1. Is the entire text a palindrome?

2. Is the part shortened on the left a palindrome? (for all positions from the right)

3. Is the right-shortened part a palindrome? (for all positions from the left)

For a better understanding, look at the procedure for the initial value LOTTOL:

```
1) LOTTOL
2) OTTOL, TTOL, TOL, OL
3) LOTTO, LOTT, LOT, LO
```

After that, you move both left and right inwards by one character and repeat the checks and this procedure until the positions overlap. For the example, the checks would then continue as follows:

```
1) OTTO
2) TTO, TO
3) OTT, OT
```

And finally, in the last step, only one check remains because the other substrings consist of only one character:

```
1) TT
2) T
3) T
```

As previously applied several times, a two-step variant is used here again. Here, the first method primarily initializes the result object and then starts the recursive call appropriately.

Based on this step-by-step procedure, let's implement the check for palindrome substrings as follows:

```java
static Set<String> allPalindromeParts(final String input)
{
    final Set<String> allPalindromsParts = new TreeSet<>();
    allPalindromePartsRec(input, 0, input.length() - 1, allPalindromsParts);

    return allPalindromsParts;
}

static void allPalindromePartsRec(final String input,
                                  final int left, final int right,
                                  final Set<String> results)
{
    // recursive termination
    if (left >= right)
        return;

    // 1) check if the whole string is a palindrome
    final boolean completeIsPalindrome = isPalindromeRec(input, left, right);
    if (completeIsPalindrome)
    {
        final String newCandidate = input.substring(left, right + 1);
        results.add(newCandidate);
    }

    // 2) check text shortened from left
    for (int i = left + 1; i < right; i++)
    {
        final boolean leftPartIsPalindrome = isPalindromeRec(input, i, right);
        if (leftIsPalindrome)
        {
            final String newCandidate = input.substring(i, right + 1);
            results.add(newCandidate);
        }
    }
}
```

```
// 3) check text shortened from right
for (int i = right - 1; i > left; i--)
{
    final boolean rightPartIsPalindrome = isPalindromeRec(input, left, i);
    if (rightIsPalindrome)
    {
        final String newCandidate = input.substring(left, i + 1);
        results.add(newCandidate);
    }
}

// recursive descent
allPalindromePartsRec(input, left + 1, right - 1, results);
}
```

Here you use the method boolean isPalindromeRec(String, int, int) already created in section 4.2.4 in exercise 4 to check for palindromes on ranges of a string. This is shown again here for completeness:

```
static boolean isPalindromeRec(final String input,
                               final int left, final int right)
{
    // recursive termination
    if (left >= right)
        return true;

    if (input.charAt(left) == input.charAt(right))
    {
        // recursive descent
        return isPalindromeRec(input, left + 1, right - 1);
    }
    return false;
}
```

Although the algorithm shown is quite comprehensible, it seems rather awkward with all the loops and index accesses. In fact, an exquisite solution exists.

Optimized algorithm   Instead of painstakingly trying through all the shortened substrings, you can do much better by recursively invoking your method for a shortened part:

```
static void allPalindromePartsRecOpt(final String input, final int left,
                                     final int right, final Set<String> results)
{
    // recursive termination
    if (left >= right)
        return;

    // 1) check if the whole string is a palindrome
    if (isPalindromeRec(input, left, right))
        results.add(input.substring(left, right + 1;);

    // recursive descent: 2) + 3) test from left / right
    allPalindromePartsRecOpt(input, left + 1, right, results);
    allPalindromePartsRecOpt(input, left, right - 1, results);
}
```

This can be made a bit more readable, but the performance is (slightly) worse due to the creation of substrings:

```
static void allPalindromePartsRecV3(final String input,
                                    final Set<String> result)
{
    // recursive termination
    if (input.length() < 2)
        return;

    // 1) check if the whole string is a palindrome
    if (isPalindromeRec(input))
        result.add(input);

    // recursive descent:  2) + 3) test from left / right
    allPalindromePartsRecV3(input.substring(1), result);
    allPalindromePartsRecV3(input.substring(0, input.length() - 1), result);
}
```

Bonus: Find the Longest of All Palindrome Substrings

This time there is no requirement for maximum performance.

   Algorithm   After computing all the palindrome substrings, finding the longest one is just a matter of defining the appropriate comparator and then applying the stream API and its max(Comparator<T>) method:

```java
static Optional<String> longestPalindromePart(final String input)
{
    final Set<String> allPalindromeParts = allPalindromePartsRec(input);
    final Comparator<String> byLength = Comparator.comparing(String::length);

    return allPalindromeParts.stream().max(byLength);
}
```

Verification

For testing, you use the following inputs, which show the correct operation:

```java
@ParameterizedTest(name = "allPalindromeParts({0}) = {1}")
@MethodSource("inputAndPalindromeParts")
void allPalindromePartsRec(String input, List<String> expected)
{
    Set<String> result = Ex08_AllPalindromeParts.allPalindromeParts(input);

    assertIterableEquals(expected, result);
}

@ParameterizedTest(name = "allPalindromePartsOpt({0}) = {1}")
@MethodSource("inputAndPalindromeParts")
void allPalindromePartsOpt(final String input, final List<String> expected)
{
    Set<String> result = Ex08_AllPalindromeParts.allPalindromePartsOpt(input);

    assertIterableEquals(expected, result);
}
```

```
private static Stream<Arguments> inputAndPalindromeParts()
{
    return Stream.of(Arguments.of("BCDEDCB",
                                  List.of("BCDEDCB", "CDEDC", "DED")),
                     Arguments.of("ABALOTTOLL",
                                  List.of("ABA", "LL", "LOTTOL", "OTTO", "TT")),
                     Arguments.of("racecar",
                                  List.of("aceca", "cec", "racecar")));
}
```

Two things are worth mentioning here: First, it is important to test for a sorted result. To achieve this, you would either need a TreeSet<E> or to switch to a List<E> since you want to simplify the test design. Moreover, after this modification you also need to check with assertIterableEquals() so that the elements' order is taken into account.

8.4.9 Solution 9: n-Queens Problem (★★★☆☆)

In the n-Queens Problem, n queens are to be placed on an n x n board in such a way that no two queens can beat each other according to chess rules. Thus, other queens must not be placed on the same row, column, or diagonals. To do this, extend the solution shown in section 8.2.1 and implement the method boolean isValidPosition(char[][], int, int). Also write method void printBoard(char[][]) to display the board as well as output the solution to the console.

Example

For a 4 × 4 playfield, there is the following solution, with the queens symbolized by a Q:

```
---------
| |Q| | |
---------
| | | |Q|
---------
|Q| | | |
---------
| | |Q| |
---------
```

Algorithm   You attempt to place the queens one after the other at different positions. You start with a queen in row 0 and position 0 (upper left corner). After each placement, a check is made to ensure that there are no collisions in the vertical and diagonal left and right directions upwards with queens that have already been placed. A check downwards is logically not necessary in any case because no queens can be placed there yet. After all, the filling is done from top to bottom. Since you also proceed line by line, a check in the horizontal direction is unnecessary.

Provided the position is valid, move to the next row, trying all positions from 0 to $n - 1$. This procedure is repeated until you have finally placed the queen in the last row. If there is a problem positioning a queen, use backtracking. Remove the last placed queen and try again at the next possible position. If the end of the row is reached without a solution, this is an invalid constellation, and the previous queen must also be placed again. You can see that backtracking sometimes goes back up one row, and in extreme cases to the first row.

Let's start with the easy part, namely recapping the introduction and creating the playfield, and invoking the method to solve it:

```
static Optional<char[][]> solveNQueens(final int size)
{
    final char[][] board = initializeBoard(size);

    if (solveNQueens(board, 0))
        return Optional.of(board);

    return Optional.empty();
}

private static char[][] initializeBoard(final int size)
{
    final char[][] board = new char[size][size];

    for (int row = 0; row < size; row++)
    {
        for (int col = 0; col < size; col++)
        {
```

```
            board[row][col] = ' ';
        }
    }
    return board;
}
```

To model the playfield you use a char[][]. A Q represents a queen and a space represents a free field. To keep the algorithm understandable, you extract the two methods shown next, placeQueen() and removeQueen(), for placing and deleting the queens:

```
static boolean solveNQueens(final char[][] board, final int row)
{
    final int maxRow = board.length;
    final int maxCol = board[0].length;

    // recursive termination
    if (row >= maxRow)
        return true;

    boolean solved = false;
    int col = 0;
    while (!solved && col < maxCol)
    {
        if (isValidPosition(board, col, row))
        {
            placeQueen(board, col, row);

            // recursive descent
            solved = solveNQueens(board, row + 1);

            // backtracking, if no solution
            if (!solved)
                removeQueen(board, col, row);
        }
        col++;
    }
    return solved;

}
```

The extraction of the following two methods leads to a better readability:

```java
static void placeQueen(final char[][] board, final int col, final int row)
{
    board[row][col] = 'Q';
}

static void removeQueen(final char[][] board, final int col, final int row)
{
    board[row][col] = ' ';
}
```

Let's now get down to implementing the helper methods. First, the one that checks whether a constellation is valid:

```java
static boolean isValidPosition(final char[][] board,
                               final int col, final int row)
{
    final int maxRow = board.length;
    final int maxCol = board[0].length;

    return checkHorizontally(board, row, maxCol) &&
           checkVertically(board, col, maxRow) &&
           checkDiagonallyLeftUp(board, col, row) &&
           checkDiagonallyRightUp(board, col, row, maxCol);
}
```

Actually, the horizontal check is superfluous since you are just checking a new row where no other queen can be placed yet. For the sake of illustration, you implement and call the method anyway.

In the implementation, you use the following helper methods to check in the x and y directions:

```java
static boolean checkHorizontally(final char[][] board,
                                 final int row, final int maxX)
{
    boolean xfree = true;
```

```
    for (int x = 0; x < maxX; x++)
        xfree = xfree && board[row][x] == ' ';

    return xfree;
}
```

This implementation leaves room for improvement. In fact, the check does not have to scan all fields. You can stop already when an occupied field is found:

```
static boolean checkHorizontally(final char[][] board,
                                 final int row, final int maxX)
{
    int x = 0;

    while (x < maxX && board[row][x] == ' ')
        x++;

    return x >= maxX;
}

static boolean checkVertically(final char[][] board,
                               final int col, final int maxY)
{
    int y = 0;

    while (y < maxY && board[y][col] == ' ')
        y++;

    return y >= maxY;
}
```

For the diagonals, it is also possible to optimize. You don't have to check downward. Since you fill the board from top to bottom, no queen can be placed under the current position yet. Thus, you limit yourself to the relevant diagonals to the top left and right:

```
static boolean checkDiagonallyRightUp(final char[][] board, final int col,
                                      final int row, final int maxX)
{
    int x = col;
    int y = row;
```

```
    boolean diagRUfree = true;
    while (diagRUfree && x < maxX && y >= 0)
    {
        diagRUfree = board[y][x] == ' ';
        y--;
        x++;
    }

    return diagRUfree;
}
```

For the second diagonal check, I would like to demonstrate a syntactic variation for the loop. The variant just shown is straightforward to understand, but it is a little long. The for loop allows you to define multiple loop variables, check them, and change them. This allows diagonal traversal to be written compactly as follows:

```
static boolean checkDiagonallyLeftUp(final char[][] board,
                                     final int col, final int row)
{
    boolean diagLUfree = true;

    for (int y = row, x = col; y >= 0 && x >= 0; y--, x--)
        diagLUfree = diagLUfree && board[y][x] == ' ';

    return diagLUfree;
}
```

By directly aborting the loop when you detect an occupied field this can also be optimized minimally. Then it is even possible to compress the for loop further, but at the expense of readability and therefore it is not shown here.

In my opinion, the most comprehensible construct is the one already shown with a while loop.

You implement the output of the stylized chessboard with n × n squares as follows, only the computation of the grids and the cross lines is a bit more special here:

```
static void printBoard(final char[][] values)
{
    final String line = "-".repeat(values[0].length * 2 + 1);
    System.out.println(line);
```

```java
    for (int y = 0; y < values.length; y++)
    {
        System.out.print("|");
        for (int x = 0; x < values[y].length; x++)
        {
            final Object value = values[y][x];
            System.out.print(value + "|");
        }
        System.out.println();
        System.out.println(line);
    }
}
```

Verification

For two different sized playfields, you compute the solution to the n-Queens Problem using solveNQueens(). Finally, you display the playfield determined as the solution in each case on the console.

```java
public static void main(final String[] args)
{
    solveAndPrint(4);
    solveAndPrint(8);
}

private static void solveAndPrint(final int size)
{
    final Optional<char[][]> optBoards = solveNQueens(size);

    optBoards.ifPresentOrElse(board -> printBoard(board),
                        () -> System.out.println("No Solution!"));
}
```

Only the output for the 4 × 4 size field is shown below:

```
- - - - - - - - -
|  |Q|  |  |
- - - - - - - - -
|  |  |  |Q|
- - - - - - - - -
|Q|  |  |  |
- - - - - - - - -
|  |  |Q|  |
- - - - - - - - -
```

Alternative Solution Approach

Although the previously chosen representation as a two-dimensional array is absolutely catchy, there is an optimization. Because only one queen may be placed per row, it is possible to use a list for modeling the playfield and the queens' positioning, which simplifies a lot. Sounds strange at first. How is it supposed to work?

For the solution of the n-Queens Problem, you need in each case x and y coordinates. You reconstruct them by the following trick. The y-coordinate results from the position in the list. For the x-coordinate, you store a corresponding numerical value in the list. The presence of a queen, previously indicated by the character Q, can now be determined indirectly. If the list contains a numerical value greater than or equal to 0 at the position of the y-coordinate, then a queen is present.

With this knowledge, you can adjust the implementation of the algorithm in the appropriate places. In fact, the basic logic does not change, but the method signatures and position processing do. Conveniently, you also no longer need to generate char[][] in advance. But let's look at the actual algorithm first:

```java
static List<Integer> solveNQueens(final int size)
{
    final List<Integer> board = new ArrayList<>();

    if (solveNQueens(board, 0, size))
        return board;

    return List.of();
}
```

```java
static boolean solveNQueens(final List<Integer> board,
                            final int row, final int size)
{
    // recursive termination
    if (row >= size)
        return true;

    boolean solved = false;
    int col = 0;
    while (!solved && col < size)
    {
        if (isValidPosition(board, col, row, size))
        {
            placeQueen(board, col, row);

            // recursive descent
            solved = solveNQueens(board, row + 1, size);

            // backtracking, if no solution
            if (!solved)
                removeQueen(board, col, row);
        }
        col++;
    }
    return solved;
}
```

For better readability, you modify the following methods appropriately:

```java
static void placeQueen(final List<Integer> board, final int col, final int row)
{
    board.add(col);
}

static void removeQueen(final List<Integer> board, final int col, final int row)
{
    board.remove(row);
}
```

The implementation of the check whether a constellation is valid becomes enormously simplified. For the vertical, it is checked whether the list already contains the same column. Only the check of the diagonals is still done in a separate helper method.

```
static boolean isValidPosition(final List<Integer> board,
                               final int col, final int row, final int size)
{
    final boolean yfree = !board.contains(col);

    return yfree && checkDiagonally(board, col, row, size);
}
```

Again, with the diagonals, you can apply the following trick: The difference in the x direction must correspond to the difference in the y direction for the queens being located on a diagonal. For this, starting from the current position, only the coordinates have to be computed and compared.

```
(x - 2, y - 2)  X        X  (x + 2, y - 2)
                  \    /
(x - 1, y - 1)    X  X    (x + 1, y - 1)
                   \ /
                    X
                  (x,y)
```

You implement this as follows:

```
static boolean checkDiagonally(final List<Integer> board,
                               final int col, final int row,
                               final int size)
{
    boolean diagLUfree = true;
    boolean diagRUfree = true;

    for (int y = 0; y < row; y++)
    {
        int xPosLU = col - (row - y);
        int xPosRU = col + (row - y);
```

```
        if (xPosLU >= 0)
            diagLUfree = diagLUfree && board.get(y) != xPosLU;

        if (xPosRU < size)
            diagRUfree = diagRUfree && board.get(y) != xPosRU;
    }

    return diagRUfree && diagLUfree;
}
```

The output of the stylized chessboard with n × n squares is minimally adapted to the new data structure:

```java
static void printBoard(final List<Integer> board, final int size)
{
    final String line = "-".repeat(size * 2 + 1);
    System.out.println(line);
    for (int y = 0; y < size; y++)
    {
        System.out.print("|");
        for (int x = 0; x < size; x++)
        {
            Object value = ' ';
            if (x == board.get(y))
                value = 'Q';

            System.out.print(value + "|");
        }
        System.out.println("\n" + line);
    }
}
```

Verification

Again, for two playfields, you compute the solution to the n-Queens Problem using solveNQueens(). The solution is supplied here as a list. This time, wrapping with an Optional<T> is omitted because the existence of a solution can also be cleverly encoded using the list. If it is empty, there is no solution; otherwise, the list contains the solution. The solution is then printed on the console.

```java
public static void main(final String[] args)
{
    solveAndPrint(4);
    solveAndPrint(8);
}

private static void solveAndPrint(final int size)
{
    final List<Integer> board = solveNQueens(size);
    if (board.isEmpty())
        System.out.println("No Solution!");
    else
        printBoard(board, size);
}
```

The results are identical to the previous ones and are therefore not shown again.

CHAPTER 9

Binary Trees

While the Collections framework provides a rich variety of real-world data structures, it unfortunately does not include trees for direct use.[1] However, trees are helpful for various use cases and therefore desirable. Because the topic of trees is quite extensive, and not to go beyond the scope of this book, you will deal mainly with binary trees and binary search trees (BSTs) as special cases.

Before you look at trees in more detail, I would like to mention some fields of usage:

- A file system is hierarchically structured and can be modeled as a tree. Here the nodes correspond to the directories and the leaves to the files.

- Mathematical calculations can be represented by trees. You will see this in an exercise later.

- In the area of databases, so-called B-trees are used for efficient storage and search.

- In compiler construction, one uses a so-called Abstract Syntax Tree (AST) to represent the source code.[2]

9.1 Introduction

In this introduction, you first learn some terminology before briefly exploring the binary tree and the binary search tree. After that, I discuss traversal and some properties of trees. Finally, I introduce three trees that are used repeatedly in the text and the assignments.

---

[1] The class `TreeMap<K,V>` is implemented using a so-called red-black tree.

[2] To be more precise, actually it's used to represent the abstract syntax structure of the source code—not the source code itself.

© Michael Inden 2022
M. Inden, *Java Challenges*, https://doi.org/10.1007/978-1-4842-7395-1_9

9.1.1 Structure, Terminology, and Examples of Use

Trees allow both structured storage and efficient access to data managed there. For this purpose, *trees* are strictly hierarchical and, as in real trees, no branch grows back into the trunk. A branching point is called *node* and stores a value. A node at the end of a branch is called *leaf* and values are also found there. The connecting branch pieces are called *edges*. Figure 9-1 gives a first impression.

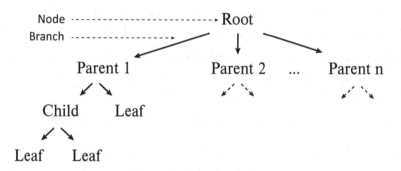

Figure 9-1. *Tree with some nodes and leaves*

Figure 9-1 illustrates that trees consist of hierarchically organized nodes. They start from a root (which, interestingly enough, is located at the top in computer science) and branch out into several children, which in turn can have any number of child nodes. Thus they are parents and represent the roots of subtrees. Each node is referenced by exactly one other node.

9.1.2 Binary Trees

A binary tree is a special tree in which each node stores one value, and each node possesses at most two successors, often called left and right. This restriction makes it easier to express many algorithms. As a result, the binary tree is widely used in computer science.

Binary tree in homebrew   A binary tree needs just a little effort to be implemented (by the class BinaryTreeNode<T> itself) here even simplifying more without data encapsulation (information hiding):

```
public class BinaryTreeNode<T>
{
    public final T item;
```

```java
public BinaryTreeNode<T> left;
public BinaryTreeNode<T> right;

public BinaryTreeNode(final T item)
{
    this.item = item;
}

@Override
public String toString()
{
    return String.format("BinaryTreeNode [item=%s, left=%s, right=%s]",
                    item, left, right);
}

public boolean isLeaf()
{
    return left == null && right == null;
}

// other methods like equals(), hashCode(), ...
}
```

For the examples in this book, you do not need to provide a binary tree model as a standalone class, but you always use a special node as the root. However, to simplify the handling in your own and especially more complex business applications, the definition of a separate class called BinaryTree<T> is a good idea. This allows you to provide various useful functionalities there as well.

9.1.3 Binary Trees with Order: Binary Search Trees

Sometimes the terms *binary tree* and *binary search tree* are used interchangeably, but this is not correct. A binary search tree is indeed a binary tree, but one with the additional property that the nodes are arranged according to their values. The constraint is that the root's value is greater than that of the left successor and less than that of the right successor. This constraint applies recursively to all subtrees, as illustrated by Figure 9-2. Consequently, a BST does not contain any value more than once.

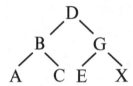

Figure 9-2. *Example of a binary search tree with letters*

Search in a BST   A search in a BST can be performed in logarithmic time due to the ordering of the values. You implement the method `BinaryTreeNode<T>` `find(BinaryTreeNode<T>, T)` for this purpose. Depending on the comparison of the value with the current node's value, the search continues in the appropriate part of the tree until the value is found. If it is not found, `null` is returned:

```
<T extends Comparable<T>> BinaryTreeNode<T> find(BinaryTreeNode<T> startNode,
                                                 T searchFor)
{
    // recursive termination
    if (startNode == null)
        return null;

    // recursive descent to the left or right depending on the comparison
    final int compareResult = startNode.item.compareTo(searchFor);
    if (compareResult < 0)
        return find(startNode.right, searchFor);
    if (compareResult > 0)
        return find(startNode.left, searchFor);

    return startNode;
}
```

Insertion into a BST   The insertion into a BST may be expressed recursively as well. The insertion has to start at the root so that the ordering of values within the BST can be ensured:

```
static <T extends Comparable<T>> BinaryTreeNode<T>
    insert(final BinaryTreeNode<T> root, final T value)
{
    // recursive termination
```

```
if (root == null)
    return new BinaryTreeNode<>(value);

// recursive descent: to the left or right depending on the comparison
final int compareResult = root.item.compareTo(value);
if (compareResult > 0)
    root.left = insert(root.left, value);
else if (compareResult < 0)
    root.right = insert(root.right, value);

return root;
}
```

Example of a BST   The methods shown earlier are also part of the utility class for this chapter called TreeUtils. With this class, BSTs can then be constructed quite easily and readably. In the following, you use the trick *underscore as a prefix* to keep the names of the nodes as self-explanatory as possible. Besides, you only need the assignment to a variable if you want to continue working with the node. In particular, however, the root is always returned.

```
final BinaryTreeNode<Integer> _3 = new BinaryTreeNode<>(3);
TreeUtils.insert(_3, 1).
TreeUtils.insert(_3, 2);
TreeUtils.insert(_3, 4);

TreeUtils.nicePrint(_3);
System.out.println("tree contains 2? " + find(_3, 2));
System.out.println("tree contains 13? " + find(_3, 13));
```

This generates the following output:

```
        3
  |-----+-----|
  1           4
  |--|
     2
tree contains 2?  BinaryTreeNode [item=2, left=null, right=null]
tree contains 13? null
```

Problematic insertion order   Please note that the sequence in which elements are added can greatly impact the performance of subsequent actions such as searches. I cover this briefly in section 9.1.5. The following example demonstrates how quickly a tree degenerates into a list:

```
final BinaryTreeNode<Integer> _4 = new BinaryTreeNode<>(4);
BinaryTreeNode.insert(_4, 3);
BinaryTreeNode.insert(_4, 2);
BinaryTreeNode.insert(_4, 1);
TreeUtils.nicePrint(_4);
```

This generates the following output:

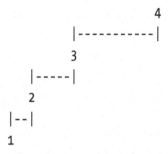

HINT: ASCII OUTPUT OF TREES

For the output of trees in the examples and exercises, the method `nicePrint()` is invoked. Its implementation is not shown further here for now. Still, it is to be implemented as Exercise 13. The related solution is developed step by step starting on page 657.

9.1.4 Traversals

When traversing a tree, a distinction is made between depth-first and breadth-first searches. Figure 9-3 illustrates both.

Depth-First Search

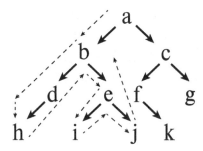

Breadth-First Search

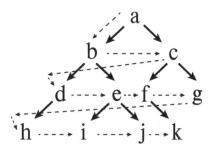

Figure 9-3. *Procedure for a depth-first search and a breadth-first search*

In a depth-first search, you traverse the tree as deeply as possible. With the breadth-first search, you move from the root level by level through the tree. This is why it is also called level-order or breadth-first.

Breadth-First/Level-Order

The following sequence results then for the tree from the example when traversing the levels from the root downwards. The implementation is the subject of Exercise 5.

```
a b c d e f g h i j k
```

Conversion from tree to list   A great advantage of the level-order traversal is its good traceability and comprehensibility. If you have a tree in mind, you can easily predict this traversal and its result. This is an important and useful feature, especially when testing.

Let's assume that you have already solved Exercise 5 and thus have access to the implementation of the method levelorder(BinaryTreeNode<T>, Consumer<T>). Based on it, you can convert a tree into a list as follows:

```java
static List<String> convertToList(final BinaryTreeNode<String> node)
{
    final List<String> result = new ArrayList<>();

    levelorder(node, result::add);

    return result;
}
```

Depth-First Searches

The three known depth-first search methods are preorder, inorder, and postorder. Preorder first processes the node itself and then those from the left and then the right subtrees. For inorder, the processing order is first the left subtree, then the node itself, and then the right subtree. Postorder processes first the subtree on the left, then on the right, and finally the node itself. The three depth-first search methods pass through the previously shown values as follows:

```
Preorder:     a b d h e i j c f k g
Inorder:      h d b i e j a f k c g
Postorder:    h d i j e b k f g c a
```

The output is not quite as intuitive. In the case of a BST, the inorder traversal returns the nodes' values according to the order of their values. This yields 1 2 3 4 5 6 7 for the following tree:

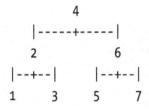

Recursive implementations of depth-first searches   Interestingly, these traversals can be easily implemented recursively. The action is highlighted in bold in each case:

```java
static <T> void preorder(final BinaryTreeNode<T> currentNode)
{
    if (currentNode != null)
    {
        System.out.println(currentNode.item);
        preorder(currentNode.left);
        preorder(currentNode.right);
    }
}
```

```java
static <T> void inorder(final BinaryTreeNode<T> currentNode)
{
    if (currentNode != null)
    {
        inorder(currentNode.left);
        System.out.println(currentNode.item);
        inorder(currentNode.right);
    }
}

static <T> void postorder(final BinaryTreeNode<T> currentNode)
{
    if (currentNode != null)
    {
        postorder(currentNode.left);
        postorder(currentNode.right);
        System.out.println(currentNode.item);
    }
}
```

NOTE: PRACTICAL RELEVANCE OF POSTORDERS

Postorder is an important type of tree traversal, among others, for the following use cases:

- **Delete:** When deleting a root node of a subtree, you must always ensure that the child nodes are also deleted correctly. A postorder traversal is a good way to do this.

- **Mathematical expressions:** To evaluate mathematical expressions in the so-called reverse Polish notation (RPN)[a] a postorder traversal is an appropriate choice.

- **Calculations of sizes:** To determine the size of a directory or a hierarchical project's duration, postorder is best suited.

[a] *An example is the expression (5 + 2) * 6, which in RPN is 5 2 + 6 *. Interestingly, in RPN, parenthesis can be omitted, since those elements up to the next operator are always suitably concatenated. However, the RPN is quite poorly readable for more complex expressions.*

9.1.5 Balanced Trees and Other Properties

One speaks of *balanced trees* if in a binary tree the heights of the two subtrees differ by at most 1 (sometimes by some other constant value). The opposite is a *degenerate tree*, which arises, among other things, from inserting data in ways that are awkward for the tree, specifically when numbers are added in an ordered fashion into a binary search tree. This causes the tree to degenerate into a linear list, as you saw in an example in section 9.1.3.

Sometimes one or more rotation(s) restores the balance. For the tree from the introduction, a rotation to the left and one to the right is visualized. In the middle, you can see the balanced starting position. See Figure 9-4.

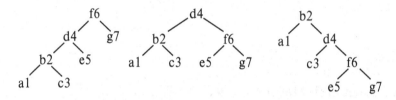

Figure 9-4. *Rotation to the left, original, rotation to the right*

The Properties Level and Height

As indicated in the introduction, trees are hierarchically structured and consist of nodes, which optionally have child nodes and may be nested arbitrarily deep. To describe this, the two terms *level* and *height* exist. The level is usually counted from 0 and starts at the root and then goes down to the lowest leaf. For height, the following applies: For a single node, it is 1. It is determined by the number of nodes on the way down to the lowest leaf for a subtree. This is visualized in Figure 9-5 where some nodes labeled as a child are, in fact, also the parent of others.

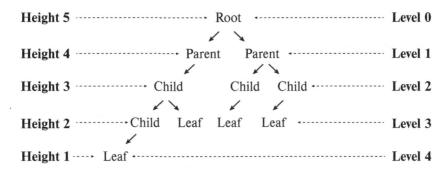

Figure 9-5. *Level and height of a tree*

The Properties Completeness and Perfectness

A complete binary tree is characterized by the fact that all levels must be completely filled, except for the last level. Moreover, all nodes have to be as far to the left as possible in the last level, so there are no gaps, or all nodes are present.

In a *complete binary tree* values may be missing on the right side (in algorithmics this is also called *left-full*):

```
    4
   / \
  2   6
 / \ /
1  3 5
```

If all positions are occupied, then this is called a *perfect tree*.

```
    4
   / \
  2   6
 / \ / \
1  3 5  7
```

The following constellation (here the missing 5 from the upper tree) is not allowed in a binary tree in the context of completeness (because the tree is then not *left-full*):

```
    4
   / \
  2   6
 / \   \
1  3    7
```

575

Let's try something more formal:

- A *perfect binary tree* is one in which all leaves are on the same level and all nodes have two successors each.

- A *complete binary tree* is one in which all levels are completely filled, except for the last one, where nodes may be missing, but only as far to the right as possible.

- Then you have the definition of a *full binary tree*, which means that each node has either no children or two children, as shown in the following diagram:

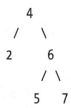

```
    4
  /   \
 2     6
      / \
     5   7
```

This is from the weakest requirement. A graphical illustration can be found online at www.programiz.com/dsa/complete-binary-tree.

9.1.6 Trees for the Examples and Exercises

Because you will repeatedly refer to some typical tree structures in the following, you implement three creation methods in the utility class ExampleTrees.

Tree with Letters and Numbers

To try out tree traversal and other actions, you construct a tree of seven nodes. Therefore you define objects of type BinaryTreeNode<T>, which still have to be connected appropriately after their creation. For simplicity, the examples here are implemented without information hiding. Consequently, you directly access the attributes left and right.

```
static BinaryTreeNode<String> createExampleTree()
{
    final BinaryTreeNode<String> a1 = new BinaryTreeNode<>("a1");
    final BinaryTreeNode<String> b2 = new BinaryTreeNode<>("b2");
```

```
final BinaryTreeNode<String> c3 = new BinaryTreeNode<>("c3");
final BinaryTreeNode<String> d4 = new BinaryTreeNode<>("d4");
final BinaryTreeNode<String> e5 = new BinaryTreeNode<>("e5");
final BinaryTreeNode<String> f6 = new BinaryTreeNode<>("f6");
final BinaryTreeNode<String> g7 = new BinaryTreeNode<>("g7");

d4.left = b2;
d4.right = f6;
b2.left = a1;
b2.right = c3;
f6.left = e5;
f6.right = g7;

return d4;
}
```

This results in the following tree with root d4:

```
        d4
     |-----+-----|
    b2          f6
  |--+--|     |--+--|
 a1    c3    e5    g7
```

You may be surprised about the combination of letters and numbers. I chose this intentionally because it allows understanding some algorithms a bit easier—for example, to check traversals' order.

Trees with Textual and Real Digits

For some exercises, you also need a tree where the nodes' values consist only of digits (but textually as string). Because it is impossible to name the variables for the individual nodes with digits, you again use the trick of starting the variable name with an underscore.

To construct the tree, you utilize the method insert(), which puts the value to be inserted in the appropriate place for it. This is only possible if you work with a BST and its order. As you can easily see, this will be much easier than the manual linking shown before.

```
static BinaryTreeNode<String> createNumberTree()
{
    final BinaryTreeNode<String> _4 = new BinaryTreeNode<>("4");
    TreeUtils.insert(_4, "2");
    TreeUtils.insert(_4, "1");
    TreeUtils.insert(_4, "3");
    TreeUtils.insert(_4, "6");
    TreeUtils.insert(_4, "5");
    TreeUtils.insert(_4, "7");

    return _4;
}
```

This results in the following tree:

```
          4
    |-----+-----|
    2           6
 |--+--|     |--+--|
 1     3     5     7
```

Variant with integers: The tree shown is generated as a variant for integers as follows:

```
static BinaryTreeNode<Integer> createIntegerNumberTree()
{
    final BinaryTreeNode<Integer> _4 = new BinaryTreeNode<>(4);
    TreeUtils.insert(_4, 2);
    TreeUtils.insert(_4, 1);
    TreeUtils.insert(_4, 3);
    TreeUtils.insert(_4, 6);
    TreeUtils.insert(_4, 5);
    TreeUtils.insert(_4, 7);

    return _4;
}
```

9.2 Exercises

9.2.1 Exercise 1: Tree Traversal (★★☆☆☆)

Extend the tree traversal methods presented in the introduction to perform an action on the current node while traversing. Add `Consumer<T>` to the respective method signature, such as for inorder: `void inorder(BinaryTreeNode<T>, Consumer<T>)`.

Bonus: Fill up a tree into a list   Populate a list with the values of the nodes. Therefor write method `List<T> toList(BinaryTreeNode<T>)` for an inorder traversal. In addition, the methods `List<T> toListPreorder(BinaryTreeNode<T>)` and `List<T> toListPostorder(BinaryTreeNode<T>)` are based on a preorder and postorder traversal, respectively.

9.2.2 Exercise 2: Preorder, Inorder, and Postorder Iteratives (★★★★☆)

In the introduction, you learned about preorder, inorder, and postorder as recursive variants. Now implement these types of traversals iteratively.

Example

Use the following tree:

```
        d4
    |-----+-----|
   b2          f6
 |--+--|     |--+--|
a1     c3   e5     g7
```

The three depth-first search methods traverse this tree as follows:

```
Preorder:    d4 b2 a1 c3 f6 e5 g7
Inorder:     a1 b2 c3 d4 e5 f6 g7
Postorder:   a1 c3 b2 e5 g7 f6 d4
```

9.2.3 Exercise 3: Tree Height (★★☆☆☆)

Implement method int getHeight(BinaryTreeNode<T>) to determine the height for both a tree and for subtrees with a single node as root.

Example

The following tree of height 4 is used as a starting point:

```
                    E
        |-----------+-----------|
        C                       G
     |-----|                 |-----+-----|
     A                       F           H
                                      |--|
                                       I
```

9.2.4 Exercise 4: Lowest Common Ancestor (★★★☆☆)

Compute the lowest common ancestor (LCA) for two nodes, A and B, hosted in an arbitrary binary search tree. The LCA denotes the node that is the ancestor of both A and B and is located as deep as possible in the tree (the root is always the ancestor of both A and B). Write method BinaryTreeNode<Integer> findLCA(BinaryTreeNode<Integer>, int, int), which, in addition to the start node of the search (usually the root) also receives lower and upper limits, which indirectly describe the nodes that are closest to these values. If the values for the limits are outside the range of values, then there is no LCA, and it is supposed to be returned null.

Example

A binary tree is shown below. If the least common ancestor is determined for the nodes with the values 1 and 5, this is the node with the value 4. In the tree, the respective nodes are circled, and the ancestor is additionally marked in bold.

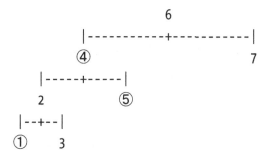

9.2.5 Exercise 5: Breadth-First (★★★☆☆)

In this exercise, you are supposed to implement the breadth-first search, also called level-order, using the method `void levelorder(BinaryTreeNode<T>, Consumer<T>)`. The breadth-first search starts at the given node (usually the root) and then works its way through the tree level by level.

Note   Use a `Queue<E>` to store data on the nodes yet to be visited. The iterative variant is a bit easier than the recursive one.

Examples

For the following two trees, the sequence 1 2 3 4 5 6 7 (for the left) and M I C H A E L (for the right) are to be determined as the result.

```
            1                           M
    |-----+-----|               |-----+-----|
    2           3               I           C
  |--+--|     |--+--|         |--+--|     |--+--|
  4     5     6     7         H     A     E     L
```

9.2.6 Exercise 6: Level Sum (★★★★☆)

In the previous exercise, you implemented the breadth-first search. Now you want to sum up the values per level of a tree. For this purpose, let's assume that the values are of type `Integer`. Write method `Map<Integer, Integer> levelSum(BinaryTreeNode <Integer>)`.

Example

For the tree shown, the sums of the values of the nodes per level should be calculated and return the following result: {0=4, 1=8, 2=17, 3=16}.

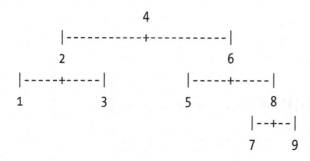

Level	Value(s)	Result
0	4	4
1	2, 6	8
2	1, 3, 5, 8	17
3	7, 9	16

9.2.7 Exercise 7: Tree Rotate (★★★☆☆)

Binary trees, especially binary search trees, may degenerate into lists if values are inserted only in ascending or descending order. A dysbalance can be addressed by rotating parts of the tree. Write the methods `BinaryTreeNode<T> rotateLeft(BinaryTreeNode<T>)` and `BinaryTreeNode<T> rotateRight(BinaryTreeNode<T>)`, which will rotate the tree around the node passed as parameter to the left or right, respectively.

Example

Figure 9-6 visualizes a rotation to the left and a rotation to the right with the balanced starting position in the middle.

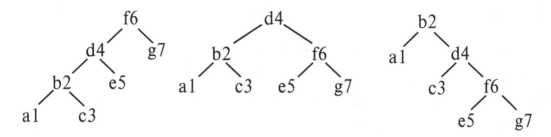

Figure 9-6. *Rotation to the left, original, rotation to the right*

9.2.8 Exercise 8: Reconstruction (★★★☆☆)

Exercise 8a: Reconstruction from an Array (★★☆☆☆)

In this exercise, you want to reconstruct a binary search tree that is as balanced as possible from an ascending sorted int[].

Example

Given the int values of

final int[] values = { 1, 2, 3, 4, 5, 6, 7 };

then the following tree should be reconstructed from it:

```
            4
     |-----+-----|
     2           6
  |--+--|     |--+--|
  1     3     5     7
```

Exercise 8b: Reconstruction from Preorder/Inorder (★★★☆☆)

Suppose you have the sequence of values in preorder and inorder, each prepared as a list. This information about an arbitrary binary tree should be used to reconstruct the corresponding tree therefrom. Write method BinaryTreeNode<T> reconstruct(List<T>, List<T>).

Example

Two sequences of values of the traversals are given below. Based on these values, you should reconstruct the tree shown in the previous part of the exercise.

```
var preorderValues = List.of(4, 2, 1, 3, 6, 5, 7);
var inorderValues = List.of(1, 2, 3, 4, 5, 6, 7);
```

9.2.9 Exercise 9: Math Evaluation (★★☆☆☆)

Consider using a tree to model mathematical expressions with the four operators $+$, $-$, $/$, and $*$. It is your task to compute the value of individual nodes, including, in particular, the value of the root node. For this purpose, write method int evaluate(BinaryTree Node<String>).

Example

Represent the expression $3 + 7 * (7 - 1)$ by the following tree to compute the value 45 for the root node:

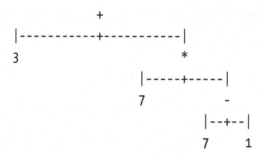

9.2.10 Exercise 10: Symmetry (★★☆☆☆)

Check if an arbitrary binary tree is symmetric in its structure. Therefore write method boolean isSymmetric(BinaryTreeNode<T>). In addition to the structural examination, you can also check for equality of values.

Examples

To check for symmetry, you use a binary tree that is symmetric in structure (left) and a binary tree that is also symmetric concerning values (right).

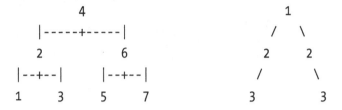

```
          4                                 1
   |-----+-----|                          /   \
   2           6                         2     2
|--+--|     |--+--|                      /       \
1     3     5     7                     3         3
```

NOTE: THE SYMMETRY PROPERTY

In a symmetric binary tree, the left and right subtrees are mirrored through the root along an imaginary vertical line (indicated by |):

```
    1
  / | \
 2  |  2
 /  |   \
3   |    3
```

Depending on the definition, a comparison of the values can be omitted for the symmetry. In this case, only the structural organization can be counted as relevant.

Bonus: Mirror tree   In the hint box, I indicated a mirror axis through the root. Create method `BinaryTreeNode<T> invert(BinaryTreeNode<T>)` that mirrors the nodes of a tree at this implied line through the root.

Example

A mirroring looks like this:

```
          4                                      4
   |-----+-----|                          |-----+-----|
   2           6        =>                6           2
|--+--|     |--+--|                    |--+--|     |--+--|
1     3     5     7                    7     5     3     1
```

9.2.11 Exercise 11: Check Binary Search Tree (★★☆☆☆)

In this exercise, you are to check whether an arbitrary binary tree fulfills the property of a binary search tree (i.e., the values in the left subtree are smaller than the root node's value and those in the right subtree are larger—and this holds for each subtree starting from the root). For simplification you assume int values. Write method boolean isBST(BinaryTreeNode<Integer>).

Example

Use the following binary tree, which is also a binary search tree. For example, if you replace the number 1 with a larger number on the left side, it's no longer a binary search tree. However, the right subtree under the 6 is still a binary search tree.

```
            4
     |-----+-----|
     2           6
  |--+--|     |--+--|
  1     3     5     7
```

9.2.12 Exercise 12: Completeness (★★★★★)

In this exercise, you are asked to check the completeness of a tree. To do this, you initially solve the basics in the first two parts of the exercise and then proceed to the trickier completeness check.

Exercise 12a: Number of Nodes (★☆☆☆☆)

Count how many nodes are contained in any binary tree. To do this, write method int nodeCount(BinaryTreeNode<T>).

Example

For the binary tree shown, the value 7 should be determined. If you remove the right subtree, the tree consists of only 4 nodes.

```
            4
    |-----+-----|
    2           6
 |--+--|      |--+--|
 1     3      5     7
```

Exercise 12b: Check for Full / Perfect (★★☆☆☆)

For an arbitrary binary tree, check if all nodes have two successors or leaves each, and thus the tree is full. For perfection, all leaves must be at the same height. Write the methods boolean isFull(BinaryTreeNode<T>) and boolean isPerfect(BinaryTreeNode<T>).

Example

The binary tree shown is both perfect and full. If you remove the two leaves below the 2, it is no longer perfect but still full.

```
   Full and perfect          Full but not perfect
          4                          4
   |-----+-----|              |-----+-----|
   2           6              2           6
|--+--|     |--+--|                    |--+--|
1     3     5     7                    5     7
```

Exercise 12c: Completeness (★★★★☆)

In this subtask, you are asked to check if a tree is complete as defined in the introduction (i.e., a binary tree with all levels fully filled, with the allowed exception on the last level where nodes may be missing, but only with gaps as far to the right as possible).

Example

In addition to the perfect tree used so far, the following tree is also complete by definition. However, if you remove the children from node H, the tree is no longer complete.

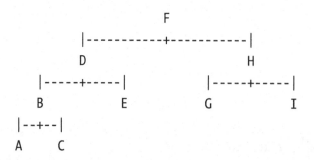

```
                      F
      |------------+-----------|
         D                    H
      |-----+-----|        |-----+-----|
      B         E          G           I
   |--+--|
   A     C
```

Exercise 12d: Completeness Recursive (★★★★★)

In this last subtask, the following challenge remains to be mastered as a special treat: The check is to be solved without additional data structures and purely recursively. At first, this sounds hardly feasible, so I'll give a hint.

Tip   Develop the solution step by step. Create a `boolean[]` as an auxiliary data structure that models whether or not a node exists for a certain position. Then traverse the tree and mark the positions appropriately. Convert this implementation to a purely recursive one without the `boolean[]`.

Example

As before, the following tree is complete by definition:

```
                      F
      |------------+-----------|
         D                    H
      |-----+-----|        |-----+-----|
       B         E         G           I
   |--+--|
   A     C
```

9.2.13 Exercise 13: Tree Printer (★★★★★)

In this exercise, you are to implement a binary tree's graphical output, as you have seen before in the examples.

Therefore, you initially solve the basics in the first three parts of the assignment and then proceed to the trickier graphical presentation of trees.

Tip   Use a fixed grid of blocks of width 3. This significantly contributes to a balanced representation and reduces complexity.

Example

The following tree should cover various special cases:

```
                          F
          |-----------+-----------|
          D                       H
      |-----+                 +-----|
        B                           I
    |--+--|
    A     C
```

Exercise 13a: Width of a Subtree (★★☆☆☆)

In this part of the exercise, you are asked to find the maximum width of a subtree of a given height using the method `int subtreeWidth(int)`. For simplicity, you assume that a maximum of three characters represents the nodes. Besides, there is a distance of at least three characters between them. This is true for the leaves when the tree is full. On higher levels, there is naturally more space between the nodes of two subtrees.

Examples

On the left, you see a tree of height 2, and on the right, a tree of height 3. Based on the grid of three, you get 9 and 21 as widths. See Figure 9-7.

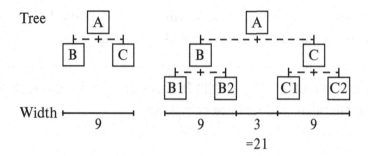

Figure 9-7. *Tree width*

Height	Total width	Width of subtree
1	3	0 (no subtree existing)
2	9	3
3	21	9
4	45	21

Exercise 13b: Draw Node (★★☆☆☆)

Write method `String drawNode(BinaryTreeNode<T>, int)` that creates a graphical output of a node, generating the given set of spaces appropriately. The node value should have a maximum of three digits and be placed in the middle.

Tip   Remember that if the current node has a left successor, the representation of the layer below starts on the left with the string ' |-'.

Example

The example in Figure 9-8 shows a single node with a spacing of 5 characters. Besides, the node value is center-aligned in a three-character box.

drawNode ("A", 5)

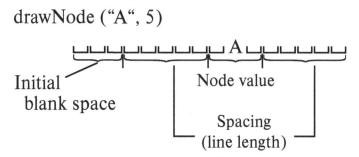

Figure 9-8. *Dimensions when drawing nodes*

Exercise 13c: Draw Connection Lines (★★☆☆☆)

Write method String drawConnections(BinaryTreeNode<T>, int) to build a
graphical output of the connection lines of a node to its two successors. Missing
successors have to be handled correctly.

Tip   The line length refers to the characters between the node representations.
The parts representing ends are still to be appended appropriately in each case, as
well as the middle connector.

Example

The following figure visualizes all cases relevant in drawing, such as with none, one, and
two successor(s).

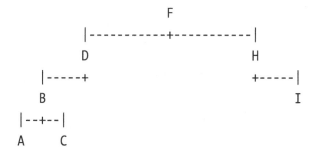

A schematic representation is shown in Figure 9-9.

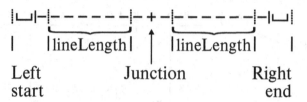

drawConnections (node, lineLength)

Figure 9-9. *Schematic representation of the connecting lines*

Exercise 13d: Tree Representation (★★★★★)

Combine all solutions of the parts of the exercise and complete the necessary steps to be able to print an arbitrary binary tree suitably on the console. To do this, write method `ni cePrint(BinaryTreeNode<T>)`.

Example

The output of the tree shown in the introductory example should also look something like this through `nicePrint()`:

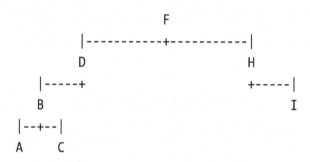

Also, check your algorithm with a real monster of a tree that you can find in the sources. Here is a much slimmed down representative:

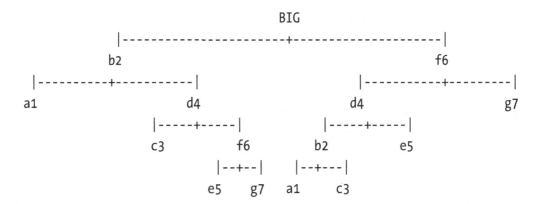

9.3 Solutions

9.3.1 Solution 1: Tree Traversal (★★☆☆☆)

Extend the tree traversal methods presented in the introduction to performing an action on the current node while traversing. Add Consumer<T> to the respective method signature, such as for inorder: void inorder(BinaryTreeNode<T>, Consumer<T>).

Algorithm   With this extension, each method for traversing the tree receives an additional parameter of type Consumer<T>. Then the method accept(T) is called at the appropriate place instead of the console output.

```
static <T> void inorder(final BinaryTreeNode<T> node,
                        final Consumer<T> action)
{
    if (node == null)
        return;

    inorder(node.left, action);
    action.accept(node.item);
    inorder(node.right, action);
}

static <T> void preorder(final BinaryTreeNode<T> node,
                        final Consumer<T> action)
{
    if (node == null)
        return;
```

```
    action.accept(node.item);
    preorder(node.left, action);
    preorder(node.right, action);
}

static <T> void postorder(final BinaryTreeNode<T> node,
                          final Consumer<T> action)
{
    if (node == null)
        return;

    postorder(node.left, action);
    postorder(node.right, action);
    action.accept(node.item);
}
```

Bonus: Fill Up a Tree into a List

Populate a list with the values of the nodes. Therefor write method List<T>
toList(BinaryTreeNode<T>) for an inorder traversal. In addition, the methods List<T>
toListPreorder(BinaryTreeNode<T>) and List<T> toListPostorder(BinaryTreeNode
<T>) are based on a preorder and postorder traversal, respectively.

Algorithm   Instead of the console output used so far as an action, the current value
is added depending on the chosen traversal strategy. For the recursive descent, you then
use addAll() to add the partial results and the method add() from List<E> for the value
of the current node.

```
static <T> List<T> toList(final BinaryTreeNode<T> startNode)
{
    if (startNode == null)
        return List.of();

    final List<T> result = new ArrayList<>();
    result.addAll(toList(startNode.left));
    result.add(startNode.item);
    result.addAll(toList(startNode.right));

    return result;
}
```

```
static <T> List<T> toListPreorder(final BinaryTreeNode<T> startNode)
{
    final List<T> result = new ArrayList<>();
    preorder(startNode, result::add);
    return result;
}

static <T> List<T> toListPostorder(final BinaryTreeNode<T> startNode)
{
    final List<T> result = new ArrayList<>();
    postorder(startNode, result::add);
    return result;
}
```

You use the previously implemented traversals (for preorder and postorder) with a Consumer<T> to appropriately populate a list. However, please keep in mind that usually you should avoid state changes within lambdas or method references because this contradicts the functional way of thinking. In this local context, and especially without multithreading, it is acceptable to make an exception here.

Verification

At first, you define a tree, then perform an inorder traversal with the Consumer<T> passed, and finally populate two more lists from the tree:

```
public static void main(final String[] args)
{
    final BinaryTreeNode<String> root = ExampleTrees.createExampleTree();
    TreeUtils.nicePrint(root);

    System.out.println("\nInorder with consumer: ");
    inorder(root, str -> System.out.print(str + " "));
    System.out.println();

    System.out.println("\ntpList: " + toList(root));
    System.out.println("toListPreorder: " + toListPreorder(root));
}
```

If you execute this `main()` method, you get the following output, which shows that your implementation works as expected:

```
          d4
     |-----+-----|
    b2            f6
 |--+--|        |--+--|
 a1    c3      e5    g7
```

```
Inorder with consumer:
a1 b2 c3 d4 e5 f6 g7
```

```
toList: [a1, b2, c3, d4, e5, f6, g7]
toListPreorder: [d4, b2, a1, c3, f6, e5, g7]
```

9.3.2 Solution 2: Preorder, Inorder, and Postorder Iteratives (★★★★☆)

In the introduction, you learned about preorder, inorder, and postorder as recursive variants. Now implement these types of traversals iteratively.

Example

Use the following tree:

```
          d4
     |-----+-----|
    b2            f6
 |--+--|        |--+--|
 a1    c3      e5    g7
```

The three depth-first search methods traverse this tree as follows:

```
Preorder:    d4 b2 a1 c3 f6 e5 g7
Inorder:     a1 b2 c3 d4 e5 f6 g7
Postorder:   a1 c3 b2 e5 g7 f6 d4
```

Preliminary considerations for the algorithms   For each of the iterative implementations, you need an auxiliary data structure. This is what I will now discuss in detail for the three variants.

596

Algorithm for Preorder (★★☆☆☆)   Interestingly, preorder is quite simple because the root of a subtree is always processed first. Then the left and right subtrees are processed. For this, you use a stack, which you fill initially with the current node. As long as the stack is not empty, you determine the top element and execute the desired action. Then you place the left and right successor nodes on the stack if they exist. It is important to note that the order of adding is opposite to that of reading. For the left subtree to be processed first, you must put the right node on the stack before the left one. This is repeated until the stack is empty. The following sequence results for the tree of the example:

currentNode	Stack	Action(s)
	[d4]	Start: push d4
d4	[b2, f6]	Pop + action d4, push f6, push b2
b2	[a1, c3, f6]	Pop + action b2, push c3, push a1
a1	[c3, f6]	Pop + action a1
c3	[f6]	Pop + action c3
f6	[e5, g7]	Pop + action f6, push g7, push e5
e5	[g7]	Pop + action e5
g7	[]	Pop + action g7
null	[]	End

This results in the following iterative preorder implementation, which is structurally very similar to the recursive variant:

```java
static <T> void preorderIterative(final BinaryTreeNode<T> startNode,
                                  final Consumer<T> action)
{
    if (startNode == null)
        return;

    final Stack<BinaryTreeNode<T>> nodesToProcess = new Stack<>();
    nodesToProcess.push(startNode);

    while (!nodesToProcess.isEmpty())
    {
        final BinaryTreeNode<T> currentNode = nodesToProcess.pop();
        if (currentNode != null)
```

```
        {
            action.accept(currentNode.item);

            // so that left is processed first, here order reversed
            nodesToProcess.push(currentNode.right);
            nodesToProcess.push(currentNode.left);
        }
    }
}
```

To keep the analogy as strong as possible, it is helpful that collections can also store null values. This allows you to perform the null check once when extracting from the stack and otherwise keep the source code free of special handling.

Algorithm for Inorder (★★★☆☆)   When implementing an inorder traversal, you use a stack to temporarily store nodes that have to be processed later and variable currentNode to store the current node. The basic idea is to start from the root, move to the bottom left of the tree, and put the current node on the stack until no successor is left. Then you take the uppermost node from the stack and process it (by the Consumer<T>). Now you continue with the right successor. Again: If there is no successor, process the top node from the stack.

The following sequence results for the tree of the example:

currentNode	Stack	Action(s)	Direction of descent
d4	[]	Push d4	↙
b2	[d4]	Push b2	↙
a1	[b2, d4]	Push a1	↙
Null	[a1, b2, d4]	Pop + action a1	↘
Null	[b2, d4]	Pop + action b2	↘
c3	[d4]	Push c3	↙
null	[c3, d4]	Pop + action c3	↘
null	[d4]	Pop + action d4	↘
f6	[]	Push f6	↙
e5	[f6]	Push e5	↙
null	[e5, f6]	Pop + action e5	↘

(*continued*)

currentNode	Stack	Action(s)	Direction of descent
null	[f6]	Pop + action f6	↘
g7	[]	Push g7	↗
null	[g7]	Pop + action g7	↘
null	[]	End	

Based on this, the iterative implementation of inorder looks like this:

```java
static <T> void inorderIterative(final BinaryTreeNode<T> startNode,
                                 final Consumer<T> action)
{
    if (startNode == null)
        return;

    final Stack<BinaryTreeNode<T>> nodesToProcess = new Stack<>();
    BinaryTreeNode<T> currentNode = startNode;

    // are there still nodes on the stack or is the current node not null?
    while (!nodesToProcess.isEmpty() || currentNode != null)
    {
        if (currentNode != null)
        {
            // descent to the left
            nodesToProcess.push(currentNode);
            currentNode = currentNode.left;
        }
        else
        {
            // no left successor, then process current node
            currentNode = nodesToProcess.pop();
            action.accept(currentNode.item);

            // continue with right successor
            currentNode = currentNode.right;
        }
    }
}
```

Algorithm for Postorder (★★★★☆)   With postorder, you also use a stack for the intermediate storage of the nodes to be processed later. Of the three, however, this algorithm is the one with the greatest challenges and it is tricky to implement. Since with postorder, although the traversal starts at the root, the action has to be executed after visiting the left and right subtrees. Therefore you have an interesting change compared to the previous two algorithms. In those algorithms' if an element was taken from the stack, then it was processed and *not touched again*. With the postorder implementation, an element is potentially inspected twice or more with peek() and later on removed only after that.

This time, you'll look at the source code first, and then I'll give further explanations:

```java
static <T> void postorderIterative(final BinaryTreeNode<T> startNode,
                                   final Consumer<T> action)
{
    if (startNode == null)
        return;

    final Stack<BinaryTreeNode<T>> nodesToProcess = new Stack<>();
    BinaryTreeNode<T> currentNode = startNode;
    BinaryTreeNode<T> lastNodeVisited = null;

    while (!nodesToProcess.isEmpty() || currentNode != null)
    {
        if (currentNode != null)
        {
            // descent to the left
            nodesToProcess.push(currentNode);
            currentNode = currentNode.left;
        }
        else
        {
            final BinaryTreeNode<T> peekNode = nodesToProcess.peek();
            if (peekNode.right != null && lastNodeVisited != peekNode.right)
            {
```

```
        // descent to the right
        currentNode = peekNode.right;
    }
    else
    {
        // sub root or leaf processing
        lastNodeVisited = nodesToProcess.pop();
        action.accept(lastNodeVisited.item);
    }
  }
 }
}
```

This is how the process works: You start with the root node, put it on the stack, and continue in the left subtree. You repeat this until you no longer find a left successor. Now you have to move to the right successor. Only after that may the root be processed. Since you have saved all nodes on the stack, you now inspect the node from the stack. If this one has no right children and you have not just visited it, then you execute the passed action and remember this node as the last visited. For the other case, that there is a right subtree, you also traverse it as just described. This procedure is repeated until the stack is empty.

currentNode	Stack	peekNode	Action
d4	[d4]		Push d4
b2	[b2, d4]		Push b2
a1	[a1, b2, d4]		Push a1
null	[a1, b2, d4]	a1	Action a1
null	[b2, d4]	b2	Peek + right
c3	[c3, b2, d4]		Push c3
null	[c3, b2, d4]	c3	Action c3
null	[b2, d4]	b2	Action b2
f6	[f6, d4]		Push f6
e5	[e5, f6, d4]		Push e5

(continued)

currentNode	Stack	peekNode	Action
null	[f6, d4]	e5	Action e5
null	[f6, d4]	f6	Peek + right
g7	[g7, f6, d4]		Push g7
null	[g7, f6, d4]	g7	Action g7
null	[f6, d4]	f6	Action f6
null	[d4]	d4	Action d4
null	[]		

NOTE: ITERATIVE IMPLEMENTATION OF POSTORDER

While the implementations of the three traversals' recursive variants are all equally easy, and each is not very complex, this does not apply to the iterative implementations in any way. Preorder and inorder can still be implemented with a little thinking without major difficulties. With postorder, however, you really have to fight. Therefore, it is no shame to need a couple of attempts there and to have to apply error corrections.

Don't worry. It's not always that tricky. Even the breadth-first traversal discussed later, which traverses level by level, is in my estimation much less complex to implement than the iterative postorder.

In some cases, recursion is the key to simplicity. However, for many problems, there are very understandable iterative variants.

Verification

You define the tree from the introductory example and then traverse it each time using the desired procedure:

```
public static void main(final String[] args)
{
    final BinaryTreeNode<String> d4 = ExampleTrees.createExampleTree();
    TreeUtils.nicePrint(d4);
```

```
        System.out.println("\ninorder iterative");
        inorderIterative(d4, str -> System.out.print(str + " "));

        System.out.println("\npreorder iterative");
        preorderIterative(d4, str -> System.out.print(str + " "));

        System.out.println("\npostorder iterative");
        postorderIterative(d4, str -> System.out.print(str + " "));
}
```

If you execute the main() method, you get the following output, which shows that your implementation works as expected:

```
          d4
     |-----+-----|
    b2          f6
  |--+--|     |--+--|
  a1     c3   e5     g7

inorder iterative
a1 b2 c3 d4 e5 f6 g7
preorder iterative
d4 b2 a1 c3 f6 e5 g7
postorder iterative
a1 c3 b2 e5 g7 f6 d4
```

Verification with unit test   As a unit test, I start showing how to the test an inorder traversal. For this purpose, the current value is filled into a list during the traversal, and this is then checked against the expected values:

```
@Test
void testInorderIterative()
{
    var root = ExampleTrees.createExampleTree();
    var expected = List.of("a1", "b2", "c3", "d4", "e5", "f6", "g7");
```

```
    final List<String> result = new ArrayList<>();
    Ex02_IterativeTreeTraversals.inorderIterative(root, result::add);

    assertEquals(expected, result);
}
```

For the sake of completeness, I'll show the two tests for preorder and postorder. Especially the latter traversal should be examined more closely since the implementation has already demanded a lot from you.

```
@Test
void testPreorderIterative()
{
    var root = ExampleTrees.createExampleTree();
    var expected = List.of("d4", "b2", "a1", "c3", "f6", "e5", "g7");

    final List<String> result = new ArrayList<>();
    Ex02_IterativeTreeTraversals.preorderIterative(root, result::add);

    assertEquals(expected, result);
}

@Test
void testPostOrderIterative() throws Exception
{
    var root = ExampleTrees.createExampleTree();
    var expected = List.of("a1", "c3", "b2", "e5", "g7", "f6", "d4");

    final List<String> result = new ArrayList<>();
    Ex02_IterativeTreeTraversals.postorderIterative(root, result::add);

    assertEquals(expected, result);
}
```

It is a question of style whether the creation of the tree is done in each test method or whether this is moved to a @Before-annotated setup method. With the above variant, you always have everything in view. With the variant with @Before, the initialization is moved out into a test fixture. It would have to be adjusted only once if necessary.

Surprise Algorithm

While preorder was quite easy to design iteratively, it became a bit more difficult with inorder and even really tricky with postorder.

But then I got a tip from Prof. Dr. Dominik Gruntz on how to simplify the entire process iteratively. Many thanks to Dominik for this great algorithm suggestion. This is because you keep the sequences analogous to the recursive ones, however, in reverse order, since you work with a stack. Besides, you integrate artificial new tree nodes.

```java
static <T> void inorder(final BinaryTreeNode<T> root)
{
    final Stack<BinaryTreeNode<T>> stack = new Stack<>();
    stack.push(root);

    while (!stack.isEmpty())
    {
        final BinaryTreeNode<T> currentNode = stack.pop();
        if (currentNode != null)
        {
            if (currentNode.isLeaf())
                System.out.print(currentNode.item + " ");
            else
            {
                stack.push(currentNode.right);
                stack.push(new BinaryTreeNode<T>(currentNode.item));
                stack.push(currentNode.left);
            }
        }
    }
    System.out.println();
}
```

And better yet, you can turn it into a general-purpose method that allows all three traversal variations. To do this, you first define an enumeration and then the method `traverse()` that creates an artificial entry with a tree node at each appropriate point in the sequence. As mentioned, these special nodes ensure that the processing occurs at the right place.

```
enum Order {
    PREORDER, INORDER, POSTORDER
}

static <T> void traverse(final BinaryTreeNode<T> root, final Order order)
{
    final Stack<BinaryTreeNode<T>> stack = new Stack<>();
    stack.push(root);

    while (!stack.isEmpty())
    {
        final BinaryTreeNode<T> currentNode = stack.pop();
        if (currentNode != null)
        {
            if (currentNode.isLeaf())
                System.out.print(currentNode.item + " ");
            else
            {
                if (order == Order.POSTORDER)
                    stack.push(new BinaryTreeNode<T>(currentNode.item));

                stack.push(currentNode.right);

                if (order == Order.INORDER)
                    stack.push(new BinaryTreeNode<T>(currentNode.item));

                stack.push(currentNode.left);

                if (order == Order.PREORDER)
                    stack.push(new BinaryTreeNode<T>(currentNode.item));
            }
        }
    }
    System.out.println();
}
```

HINT: INSIGHT

With the help of this example, it is easy to grasp that thorough thinking about a problem can lead to a simpler, more comprehensible, and less complex source code. Besides, it is always good to get a second or third opinion if a solution is more complex than desired.

9.3.3 Solution 3: Tree Height (★★☆☆☆)

Implement method int getHeight(BinaryTreeNode<T>) to determine the height for both a tree and for subtrees with a single node as root.

Example

The following tree of height 4 is used as a starting point:

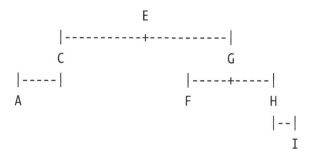

Algorithm   The tree height calculation uses a recursive algorithm that determines the height of the left and the right subtree. Finally, you must compute the maximum from this and then add the value 1 for the current level.

```
static <T> int getHeight(final BinaryTreeNode<T> node)
{
    // recursive termination
    if (node == null)
        return 0;
```

```
    // recursive descent
    final int leftHeight = getHeight(node.left);
    final int rightHeight = getHeight(node.right);

    return 1 + Math.max(leftHeight, rightHeight);
}
```

Verification

You construct the tree from the example and then have the heights computed for some selected nodes:

```
public static void main(final String[] args)
{
    final BinaryTreeNode<String> e = createHeightExampleTree();
    TreeUtils.nicePrint(e);

    printInfo(e.left, e, e.right, e.right.right.right);
}

protected static BinaryTreeNode<String> createHeightExampleTree()
{
    final BinaryTreeNode<String> e = new BinaryTreeNode<>("E");
    TreeUtils.insert(e, "C");
    TreeUtils.insert(e, "A");
    TreeUtils.insert(e, "G");
    TreeUtils.insert(e, "F");
    TreeUtils.insert(e, "H");
    TreeUtils.insert(e, "I");
    return e;
}

private static void printInfos(final BinaryTreeNode<String> c,
                               final BinaryTreeNode<String> e,
                               final BinaryTreeNode<String> g,
                               final BinaryTreeNode<String> i)
{
```

```
    System.out.println("\nHeight of root E: " + getHeight(e));
    System.out.println("Height from leftParent C:  " + getHeight(c));
    System.out.println("Height from rightParent G: " + getHeight(g));
    System.out.println("Height from rightChild I:  " + getHeight(i));
}
```

The following output occurs:

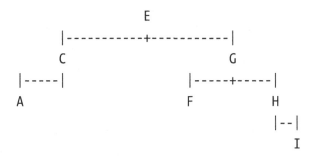

```
Height of root E: 4
Height from leftParent C:  2
Height from rightParent G: 3
Height from rightChild I:  1
```

9.3.4 Solution 4: Lowest Common Ancestor (★★★☆☆)

Compute the lowest common ancestor (LCA) for two nodes, A and B, hosted in an arbitrary binary search tree. The LCA denotes the node that is the ancestor of both A and B and is located as deep as possible in the tree (the root is always the ancestor of both A and B). Write method BinaryTreeNode<Integer> findLCA(BinaryTreeNode<Integer>, int, int), which, in addition to the start node of the search (usually the root), also receives lower and upper limits, which indirectly describe the nodes that are closest to these values. If the values for the limits are outside the range of values, then there is no LCA, and it is supposed to be returned null.

Example

A binary tree is shown below. If the least common ancestor is determined for the nodes with the values 1 and 5, this is the node with the value 4. The respective nodes are circled, and the ancestor is additionally marked in bold.

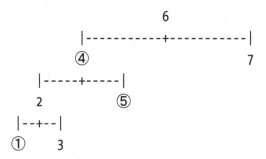

Algorithm   Intuitively, you are tempted to go up from the two nodes until the paths cross. However, this is impossible whenever no backward direction exists in the node to the parent, like here.

But there is a straightforward implementation starting from the root. From there, you proceed as follows: Let currentValue be the value of the current node. In addition, let value1 and value2 be the passed node values (i.e. those of the two nodes of the potential successors). If value1 and value2 are smaller than currentValue, then due to the sorting property within the binary search tree, both have to be located in the left subtree so continue searching there. If both value1 and value2 are greater than currentValue, then continue searching on the right. Otherwise for the cases value1 < currentValue < value2 or value2 < currentValue < value1, you have found the LCA; it is the current node.

```
static BinaryTreeNode<Integer> findLCA(final BinaryTreeNode<Integer>
                                       startNode,
                            final int value1, final int value2)
{
    // recursive termination
    if (startNode == null)
        return null;

    final int currentValue = startNode.item;

    // recursive descent
    if (value1 < currentValue && value2 < currentValue)
        return lca(startNode.left, value1, value2);

    if (value1 > currentValue && value2 > currentValue)
        return lca(startNode.right, value1, value2);
```

```
    // recursive termination
    // value1 < currentValue && currentValue < value2  bzw.
    // value2 < currentValue && currentValue < value1
    return startNode;
}
```

Verification

You construct the tree shown in the example and invoke your method:

```
@ParameterizedTest(name = "findLCA({0}, {1}) = {2}")
@CsvSource({ "1, 3, 2", "1, 5, 4", "2, 5, 4",
             "3, 5, 4", "1, 7, 6" })
void findLCA(int value1, int value2, int expected)
{
    var root = createLcaExampleTree();

    var result = Ex04_LowestCommonAncestor.findLCA(root, value1, value2);

    assertEquals(expected, result.item);
}

@Test
void findLCASpecial()
{
    var root = createLcaExampleTree();

    var result = Ex04_LowestCommonAncestor.findLCA(root, 1, 2);

    assertEquals(2, result.item);
}
```

If you only check the quite obvious cases, everything works fine. If you consider checking two nodes in a parent-child relationship, namely the nodes with the values 1 and 2, you will intuitively expect the node with the value 4. However, the node with the value 2 is calculated. According to the definition (among others in Wikipedia), each node is also considered a successor of itself. Thus the node with the value 2 is indeed the LCA in this case.

For the sake of completeness, the construction of the tree is shown:

```
static BinaryTreeNode<Integer> createLcaExampleTree()
{
    final BinaryTreeNode<Integer> _6 = new BinaryTreeNode<>(6);
    TreeUtils.insert(_6, 7);
    TreeUtils.insert(_6, 4);
    TreeUtils.insert(_6, 5);
    TreeUtils.insert(_6, 2);
    TreeUtils.insert(_6, 1);
    TreeUtils.insert(_6, 3);

    return _6;
}
```

HINT: MODIFICATION FOR ANY COMPARABLE TYPES

The algorithm shown is a bit tricky, but it is quite easy to understand with some thinking. It's a shame that I am limited to a concrete type here. It would be nicer to be generally applicable.

Practically, this requires only a few changes. First of all, you define the method `findLCA()` generically and require the types to satisfy `Comparable<T>`. If this is given, instead of using `<` and `>` for numbers, you have to compare the values here with `compareTo(T)`.

```
static <T extends Comparable<T>> BinaryTreeNode<T>
                        findLCA(final BinaryTreeNode<T> startNode,
                                final T value1, final T value2)
{
    if (startNode == null)
        return null;

    final T currentValue = startNode.item;

    if (value1.compareTo(currentValue) < 0 &&
        value2.compareTo(currentValue) < 0)
    {
        return findLCA(startNode.left, value1, value2);
    }
```

```java
if (value1.compareTo(currentValue) > 0 &&
    value2.compareTo(currentValue) > 0)
{
    return findLCA(startNode.right, value1, value2);
}

return startNode;
}
```

This can be easily understood by rotating the now well-known example tree to the left, which results in this tree as the base:

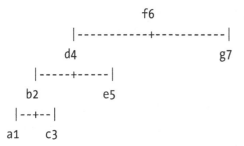

The rotation and a few checks are implemented as follows:

```java
final BinaryTreeNode<String> root = ExampleTrees.createExampleTree();
final BinaryTreeNode<String> rotatedRoot = TreeUtils.rotateLeft(root);
TreeUtils.nicePrint(rotatedRoot);

System.out.println("LCA(a, c) = " + findLCA(rotatedRoot, "a", "c")); // b2
System.out.println("LCA(a, e) = " + findLCA(rotatedRoot, "a", "e")); // d4
System.out.println("LCA(b, e) = " + findLCA(rotatedRoot, "b", "e")); // d4
System.out.println("LCA(a, g) = " + findLCA(rotatedRoot, "a", "g")); // f6
```

9.3.5 Solution 5: Breadth-First (★★★☆☆)

In this exercise, you are supposed to implement the breadth-first search, also called level-order, using the method void levelorder(BinaryTreeNode<T>, Consumer<T>). The breadth-first search starts at the given node, usually the root, and then works its way through the tree level by level.

Note   Use a Queue<E> to store data on the nodes yet to be visited. The iterative variant is a bit easier than the recursive one.

Examples

For the following two trees, the sequence 1 2 3 4 5 6 7 (for the left) and M I C H A E L (for the right) are to be determined as the result.

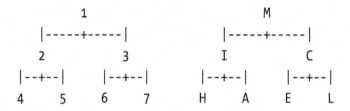

Algorithm   For the breadth-first search, you use a queue as a cache for nodes to be processed later. First, you insert the root into the queue. Then you process elements as long as there are elements in the queue. This is divided into these steps: First, perform the desired action for each element. Then put the left and right successor nodes into the queue if such a node exists.

```java
static <T> void levelorder(final BinaryTreeNode<T> startNode,
                           final Consumer<T> action)
{
    if (startNode == null)
        return;

    final Queue<BinaryTreeNode<T>> toProcess = new LinkedList<>();
    toProcess.offer(startNode);

    while (!toProcess.isEmpty())
    {
        final BinaryTreeNode<T> currentNode = toProcess.poll();
        if (currentNode != null)
        {
            action.accept(currentNode.item);
```

```
            toProcess.offer(currentNode.left);
            toProcess.offer(currentNode.right);
        }
    }
}
```

To minimize special treatments and avoid null checks, it is helpful that collections can also store null values. This allows you to perform the null check once when removing values from the stack and not have to check it when adding the child nodes.

Instead of the while loop, you can also solve this by using recursive calls. If you are interested, study the source code in the companion project.

Let's clarify the processes in detail.

Queue	Action
[1]	1
[3, 2]	2
[5, 4, 3]	3
[7, 6, 5, 4]	4
[7, 6, 5]	5
[7, 6]	6
[7]	7
[]	End

Verification

You construct the tree and invoke the method you just created:

```
public static void main(final String[] args)
{
    final BinaryTreeNode<String> _1 = createExampleLevelorderTree();
    TreeUtils.nicePrint(_1);

    System.out.print("\nLevelorder: ");
    levelorder(_1, str -> System.out.print(str + " "));
}
```

615

```java
static BinaryTreeNode<String> createExampleLevelorderTree()
{
    final BinaryTreeNode<String> _1 = new BinaryTreeNode<>("1");
    final BinaryTreeNode<String> _2 = new BinaryTreeNode<>("2");
    final BinaryTreeNode<String> _3 = new BinaryTreeNode<>("3");
    final BinaryTreeNode<String> _4 = new BinaryTreeNode<>("4");
    final BinaryTreeNode<String> _5 = new BinaryTreeNode<>("5");
    final BinaryTreeNode<String> _6 = new BinaryTreeNode<>("6");
    final BinaryTreeNode<String> _7 = new BinaryTreeNode<>("7");

    _1.left = _2;
    _1.right = _3;
    _2.left = _4;
    _2.right = _5;
    _3.left = _6;
    _3.right = _7;

    return _1;
}
```

The following output occurs:

```
            1
    |-----+-----|
    2           3
|--+--|     |--+--|
4     5     6     7
```

Levelorder: 1 2 3 4 5 6 7

Verification with unit test   The current value is filled into a list and checked against the expected values as a unit test:

```java
@Test
void testLevelorder()
{
    var root = Ex05_BreadthFirst.createExampleLevelorderTree();
    var expected = List.of("1", "2", "3", "4", "5", "6", "7");
```

```
final List<String> result = new ArrayList<>();
Ex05_BreadthFirst.levelorder(root, result::add);

assertEquals(expected, result);
}
```

9.3.6 Solution 6: Level Sum (★★★★☆)

In the previous exercise, you implemented the breadth-first search. Now you want to sum up the values per level of a tree. For this purpose, let's assume that the values are of type `Integer`. Write method `Map<Integer, Integer> levelSum(BinaryTreeNode<Integer>)`.

Example

For the tree shown, the sums of the values of the nodes per level should be calculated and return the following result: {0=4, 1=8, 2=17, 3=16}.

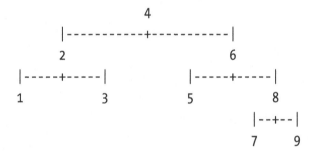

Level	Value(s)	Result
0	4	4
1	2, 6	8
2	1, 3, 5, 8	17
3	7, 9	16

Algorithm   The breadth-first search provides a good basis. You are still missing a suitable data structure and a way to determine the current level to complete the solution. With a bit of thought, you come up with using a map as the result data structure. The current level serves as the key. The value is represented by the class (or to be precise, the record) `Pair<BinaryTreeNode<Integer>, Integer>` shown below. You traverse the

617

tree as you did with level-order. To determine the levels, you cheat. Since you start from the root (of a subtree), you can assume level 0. Each change to a lower level increases the value. For this you use the second value from Pair<BinaryTreeNode<Integer>, Integer>. This way, you always know on which level the currently processed node is located. With the two methods putIfAbsent() and computeIfPresent() located in the interface Map<K,V> the summation can be formulated easily.

```java
static Map<Integer, Integer> levelSum(final BinaryTreeNode<Integer>
startNode)
{
    if (startNode == null)
        return Map.of();

    final Map<Integer, Integer> result = new TreeMap<>();

    final Queue<TreeNodeLevelPair> toProcess = new LinkedList<>();
    toProcess.offer(new TreeNodeLevelPair(startNode, 0));

    while (!toProcess.isEmpty())
    {
        final TreeNodeLevelPair current = toProcess.poll();

        final BinaryTreeNode<Integer> currentNode = current.first;
        final int nodeValue = currentNode.item;
        final int level = current.second;

        result.putIfAbsent(level, 0);
        result.computeIfPresent(level, (key, value) -> value + nodeValue);

        if (currentNode.left != null)
            toProcess.offer(new TreeNodeLevelPair(currentNode.left,
                level + 1));

        if (currentNode.right != null)
            toProcess.offer(new TreeNodeLevelPair(currentNode.right,
                level + 1));
    }

    return result;
}
```

As an auxiliary data structure, you define yourself a pair of values minimalistically as follows, using records as a language feature of modern Java:

```java
record TreeNodeLevelPair(BinaryTreeNode<Integer> first, Integer second)
{
}
```

Algorithm with depth-first search   Interestingly, the same can be easily implemented using a depth-first search, regardless of the type of traversal. In the following, it is implemented with inorder, and the variants for preorder and postorder are indicated as comments:

```java
static Map<Integer, Integer>
    levelSumDepthFirst(final BinaryTreeNode<Integer> root)
{
    final Map<Integer, Integer> result = new TreeMap<>();

    traverseDepthFirst(root, 0, result);

    return result;
}

static void traverseDepthFirst(final BinaryTreeNode<Integer> currentNode,
                               final int level,
                               final Map<Integer, Integer> result)
{
    if (currentNode != null)
    {
        // PREORDER
        //result.put(level, result.getOrDefault(level, 0) +
          currentNode.item);
        traverseDepthFirst(currentNode.left, level + 1, result);

        // INORDER
        result.put(level, result.getOrDefault(level, 0) + currentNode.item);

        traverseDepthFirst(currentNode.right, level + 1, result);
```

```
    // POSTORDER
    //map.result(level, result.getOrDefault(level, 0) +
        currentNode.item);
  }
}
```

As a data structure, you use a map whose key is the level. If there is already an entry for the level, the value of the current node is added. Otherwise by using getOrDefault() you are able to provide a start value of 0.

Verification

Let's construct the tree from the example as usual and invoke the method you just implemented:

```
public static void main(final String[] args)
{
    final BinaryTreeNode<Integer> root = createExampleLevelSumTree();
    TreeUtils.nicePrint(root);

    final Map<Integer, Integer> result = levelSum(root);
    System.out.println("\nlevelSum: " + result);
}

static BinaryTreeNode<Integer> createExampleLevelSumTree()
{
    final BinaryTreeNode<Integer> _4 = new BinaryTreeNode<>(4);
    TreeUtils.insert(_4, 2);
    TreeUtils.insert(_4, 1);
    TreeUtils.insert(_4, 3);
    TreeUtils.insert(_4, 6);
    TreeUtils.insert(_4, 5);
    TreeUtils.insert(_4, 8);
    TreeUtils.insert(_4, 7);
    TreeUtils.insert(_4, 9);
    return _4;
}
```

Then you get the following output:

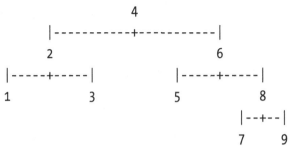

```
levelSum: {0=4, 1=8, 2=17, 3=16}
```

Verification with unit test   This can also be expressed quite simply as a unit test. Here you use the collection factory method `Map.ofEntries()` because this eases the distinction between keys and values:

```
@Test
public void testLevelSum()
{
    var root = Ex06_LevelSum.createExampleLevelSumTree();
    var expected = Map.ofEntries(Map.entry(0, 4), Map.entry(1, 8),
                                 Map.entry(2, 17), Map.entry(3, 16));

    var resultBreadthFirst = Ex06_LevelSum.levelSum(root);
    var resultDepthFirst = Ex06_LevelSum.levelSumDepthFirst(root);

    assertAll(() -> assertEquals(expected, resultBreadthFirst),
            () -> assertEquals(expected, resultDepthFirst));
}
```

9.3.7 Solution 7: Tree Rotate (★★★☆☆)

Binary trees, especially binary search trees, may degenerate into lists if values are inserted only in ascending or descending order. A dysbalance can be addressed by rotating parts of the tree. Write the methods `BinaryTreeNode<T> rotateLeft(BinaryTreeNode<T>)` and `BinaryTreeNode<T> rotateRight(BinaryTreeNode<T>)` which will rotate the tree around the node passed as parameter to the left or right, respectively.

Example

Figure 9-10 visualizes a rotation to the left and a rotation to the right with the balanced starting position in the middle.

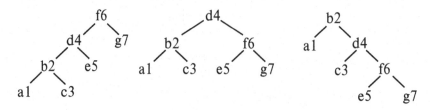

***Figure 9-10.** Rotation to the left, original, rotation to the right*

Algorithm At first, you might be frightened by the expected, but in fact only supposed, complexity of the undertaking. In general, it is a good idea to mentally go through the process using a simple example, such as the one above. Quite quickly, you will realize that far fewer nodes are involved and fewer actions are necessary than probably expected. To execute the respective rotation, you actually only have to consider the root and the left or right neighbor as well as a node from the level below, as shown in Figure 9-11.

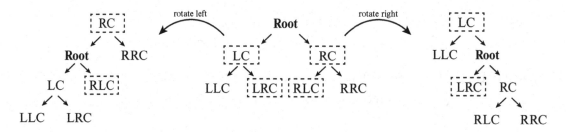

***Figure 9-11.** Affected nodes for rotations*

This diagram illustrates that you just need to reassign two links in the tree to complete the rotation. To gain a better understanding of this, the relevant nodes are named accordingly. In Figure 9-11, LC and RC stand for Left Child and Right Child, LLC and LRC for Left Left Child and Left Right Child, and RLC and RRC for Right Left Child and Right Right Child.

With these preliminary considerations, the implementation of the rotations follows exactly the sequence illustrated in the diagrams:

```
static <T> BinaryTreeNode<T> rotateLeft(final BinaryTreeNode<T> rootNode)
{
    if (rootNode.right == null)
        throw new IllegalStateException("can't rotate left, no valid root");

    final BinaryTreeNode<T> rc = rootNode.right;
    final BinaryTreeNode<T> rlc = rootNode.right.left;
    rootNode.right = rlc;
    rc.left = rootNode;

    return rc;
}

static <T> BinaryTreeNode<T> rotateRight(final BinaryTreeNode<T> rootNode)
{
    if (rootNode.left == null)
        throw new IllegalStateException("can't rotate right, no valid root");

    final BinaryTreeNode<T> lc = rootNode.left;
    final BinaryTreeNode<T> lrc = rootNode.left.right;
    rootNode.left = lrc;
    lc.right = rootNode;

    return lc;
}
```

Please keep in mind that these methods change the subtrees' references and thus may affect previously cached nodes. The root is then suddenly no longer the root but located one level below.

Verification

First, you define the tree in the middle like in the example. Then you rotate it first to the left and then twice to the right, which should correspond to a simple rotation to the right starting from the tree in the middle.

```
public static void main(final String[] args)
{
    final BinaryTreeNode<String> root = ExampleTrees.createExampleTree();
    TreeUtils.nicePrint(root);
```

```
        System.out.println("\nRotate left");
        var leftRotatedRoot = rotateLeft(root);
        TreeUtils.nicePrint(leftRotatedRoot);

        System.out.println("\nRotate right");
        var rightRotatedRoot = rotateRight(rotateRight(leftRotatedRoot));
        TreeUtils.nicePrint(rightRotatedRoot);
}
```

First, the tree is displayed unrotated:

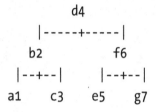

```
            d4
     |-----+-----|
    b2           f6
  |--+--|       |--+--|
 a1     c3     e5     g7
```

After that, the rotations are performed and produce the following output:

Rotate left

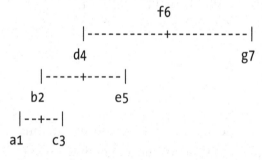

```
                    f6
         |-----------+-----------|
        d4                       g7
     |-----+-----|
    b2           e5
  |--+--|
 a1     c3
```

Rotate right

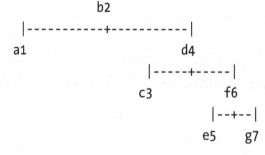

```
                    b2
         |-----------+-----------|
        a1                       d4
                           |-----+-----|
                          c3           f6
                                     |--+--|
                                    e5     g7
```

Verification with unit test   Let's consider how you could test this using unit tests. Again, it depends on the appropriate idea and data structure. It would be difficult and costly to check the resulting trees for consistency structurally. It is much easier if you compare the result of a traversal with the expected values. But pay attention. When doing this, you have to avoid using the inorder traversal since it always produces the same node order for an arbitrary binary search tree, regardless of the tree's structure! Here either a preorder or a postorder or, better still, a level-order pass is suitable. The latter has the great advantage that the order can be easily derived from a graphical representation of the tree and is, therefore, best suited for the unit test because this remains comprehensible and understandable. You already implemented the conversion at the beginning in section 9.1.4 as method convertToList().

```
@Test
void testRotateLeft()
{
    final BinaryTreeNode<String> root = ExampleTrees.createExampleTree();
    var expected = List.of("f6", "d4", "g7", "b2", "e5", "a1", "c3");

    var leftRotatedRoot = Ex07_RotateBinaryTree.rotateLeft(root);
    final List<String> result = convertToList(leftRotatedRoot);

    assertEquals(expected, result);
}

@Test
void testRotateRight()
{
    final BinaryTreeNode<String> root = ExampleTrees.createExampleTree();
    var expected = List.of("b2", "a1", "d4", "c3", "f6", "e5", "g7");

    var rightRotatedRoot = Ex07_RotateBinaryTree.rotateRight(root);
    final List<String> result = convertToList(rightRotatedRoot);

    assertEquals(expected, result);
}
```

9.3.8 Solution 8: Reconstruction (★★★☆☆)

Solution 8a: Reconstruction from an Array (★★☆☆☆)

In this exercise, you want to reconstruct a binary search tree that is as balanced as possible from an ascending sorted int[].

Example

Given the int values of

final int[] values = { 1, 2, 3, 4, 5, 6, 7 };

then the following tree should be reconstructed from them:

```
          4
    |-----+-----|
    2           6
 |--+--|     |--+--|
 1     3     5     7
```

Algorithm   Reconstructing a binary search tree from a sorted array in ascending order is not that difficult. Due to the sorting, you can split the array in half and use the value in the middle as the base for the new node. You construct the left and right subtree recursively from the array's left and right parts, respectively. You continue the bisection until the subarray has only the size 0 or 1.

```
static BinaryTreeNode<Integer> reconstruct(final int[] values)
{
    // recursive termination
    if (values.length == 0)
        return null;

    final int midIdx = values.length / 2;

    final int midValue = values[midIdx];
    final BinaryTreeNode<Integer> newNode = new BinaryTreeNode<>(midValue);

    // recursive termination
    if (values.length == 1)
        return newNode;
```

```
// recursive descent
final int[] leftPart = Arrays.copyOfRange(values, 0, midIdx);
final int[] rightPart = Arrays.copyOfRange(values, midIdx + 1,
                                             values.length);

newNode.left = reconstruct(leftPart);
newNode.right = reconstruct(rightPart);

return newNode;
}
```

You could omit the query on length 1 in the middle of the method without changing the functionality. The method would then simply be called twice for an empty array and thus terminate directly. For me, this special treatment was a bit more understandable, but that's a matter of taste.

Verification

Let's see your implementation in action and supply an arbitrary but suitably sorted array of int values. With this, you invoke your method, which returns the root of the tree as a result. Finally, you verify that the tree is indeed correctly reconstructed by printing various information to the console.

```
public static void main(final String[] args)
{
    final int[][] inputs = { { 1, 2, 3, 4, 5, 6, 7 },
                             { 1, 2, 3, 4, 5, 6, 7, 8 } };

    for (int[] values : inputs)
    {
        final BinaryTreeNode<Integer> root = reconstruct(values);
        printInfo(root);
    }
}
```

The output method is simple to implement:

```
private static void printInfo(final BinaryTreeNode<Integer> root)
{
    TreeUtils.nicePrint(root);

    System.out.println("Root:  " + root);
    System.out.println("Left:  " + root.left);
    System.out.println("Right: " + root.right);
    System.out.println();
}
```

The following abbreviated output shows that the two trees were correctly reconstructed:

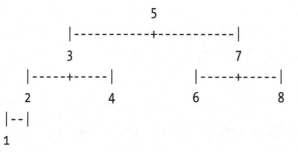

```
            4
    |-----+-----|
    2           6
 |--+--|     |--+--|
 1     3     5     7
Root:  BinaryTreeNode [item=4, left=BinaryTreeNode [item=2, ..
Left:  BinaryTreeNode [item=2, left=BinaryTreeNode [item=1, ...
Right: BinaryTreeNode [item=6, left=BinaryTreeNode [item=5, ...


              5
    |-----------+-----------|
    3                       7
 |-----+-----|           |-----+-----|
 2           4           6           8
 |--|
 1
Root:  BinaryTreeNode [item=5, left=BinaryTreeNode [item=3, ...
Left:  BinaryTreeNode [item=3, left=BinaryTreeNode [item=2, ...
Right: BinaryTreeNode [item=7, left=BinaryTreeNode [item=6, ...
```

Verification with unit test   Once again you use a level-order traversal for the unit test to verify the reconstruction:

```
@Test
void testReconstructFromIntArray()
{
    final int[] inputs = { 1, 2, 3, 4, 5, 6, 7 };

    var expected = List.of(4, 2, 6, 1, 3, 5, 7);

    var resultRoot = Ex08_ReconstructTree.reconstruct(inputs);
    var result = convertToList(resultRoot);

    assertEquals(expected, result);
}
```

The conversion of a tree into a list was already implemented in section 9.1.4 and is shown again here for easy comprehension:

```
private List<String> convertToList(final BinaryTreeNode<String> node)
{
    final List<String> result = new ArrayList<>();
    Ex05_BreadthFirst.levelorder(node, result::add);
    return result;
}
```

Solution 8b: Reconstruction from Preorder/Inorder (★★★☆☆)

Suppose you have the sequence of values in preorder and inorder, each prepared as a list. This information about an arbitrary binary tree should be used to reconstruct the corresponding tree therefrom. Write method `BinaryTreeNode<T>` `reconstruct(List<T>, List<T>)`.

Example

Two sequences of values of the traversals are given below. Based on those values, you should reconstruct the tree shown in the previous part of the exercise.

```
var preorderValues = List.of(4, 2, 1, 3, 6, 5, 7);
var inorderValues = List.of(1, 2, 3, 4, 5, 6, 7);
```

It is shown here again:

```
              4
      |-----+-----|
      2           6
    |--+--|     |--+--|
    1     3     5     7
```

Algorithm   For a better understanding of the need for two inputs and the algorithm, let's take another look at the values of a preorder and inorder traversal with the value of the root highlighted in bold as an example:

```
Preorder    4 2 1 3 6 5 7
Inorder     1 2 3 4 5 6 7
```

The preorder traversal always starts with the root, so based on the first value, you can create the root first. By searching for the value of the root in the value sequence of the inorder traversal, you determine how the values are divided into left and right subtrees. Everything in the inorder to the left of the value of the root represents the values of the left subtree. Analogously, this applies to the values to the right of it and the right subtree. This results in the following sublists:

```
Left:    1 2 3
Right:   5 6 7
```

To call your method recursively, you need to find the corresponding value sequences for preorder. How do you do this?

Let's take a detailed look at the values of a preorder and an inorder pass. By looking closely, you can see the following pattern:

$$\begin{array}{cccc} & \overbrace{\text{root}} & \overbrace{\text{left}} & \overbrace{\text{right}} \\ \textit{Preorder} & 4 & 213 & 657 \\ \textit{Inorder} & 123 & 4 & 567 \\ & \underbrace{}_{\text{left}} & \underbrace{}_{\text{root}} & \underbrace{}_{\text{right}} \end{array}$$

With this knowledge, the algorithm can be implemented as follows, taking advantage of the `List.subList()` method to generate the appropriate subparts from the original and use them for the recursive descent:

```
static <T> BinaryTreeNode<T> reconstruct(final List<T> preorderValues,
                                          final List<T> inorderValues)
{
    if (preorderValues.size() != inorderValues.size())
        throw new IllegalStateException("inputs differ in length");

    // recursive termination
    if (preorderValues.size() == 0 || inorderValues.size() == 0)
        return null;

    final T rootValue = preorderValues.get(0);
    final BinaryTreeNode<T> root = new BinaryTreeNode<>(rootValue);

    // recursive termination
    if (preorderValues.size() == 1 && inorderValues.size() == 1)
        return root;

    // recursive descent
    final int index = inorderValues.indexOf(rootValue);

    // left and right part for preorder
    root.left = reconstruct(preorderValues.subList(1, index + 1),
                            inorderValues.subList(0, index));
    root.right = reconstruct(preorderValues.subList(index + 1,
                                                    preorderValues.size()),
                             inorderValues.subList(index + 1,
                                                   inorderValues.size()));

    return root;
}
```

Again, the query could be omitted on length 1 in the middle of the method without changing the functionality. The method would then simply be called twice for an empty array and thus terminate directly. For me, this special treatment was a bit more understandable, but that's a matter of taste.

Verification

To trace the reconstruction, you provide the matching sequences of values as three nested lists in a Stream<Arguments>. As usual, JUnit automatically extracts the preorder and inorder values from each of these inputs. The result is passed in as level-order traversal. I have mentioned that this way offers good traceability based on the graphical representation. Therefore, print the trees in the unit test on the console as well.

```
@ParameterizedTest(name = "reconstruct(pre={0}, in={2}) => levelorder: {2}")
@MethodSource("preInorderAndResult")
void testReconstructFromLists(List<Integer> preorderValues,
                              List<Integer> inorderValues,
                              List<Integer> expectedLevelorder)
{
    var resultRoot = Ex08_ReconstructTree2.reconstruct(preorderValues,
                                                       inorderValues);

    TreeUtils.nicePrint(resultRoot);

    var result = convertToList(resultRoot);

    assertEquals(expectedLevelorder, result);
}

private static Stream<Arguments> preInorderAndResult()
{
    return Stream.of(Arguments.of(List.of(4, 2, 1, 3, 6, 5, 7),
                                  List.of(1, 2, 3, 4, 5, 6, 7),
                                  List.of(4, 2, 6, 1, 3, 5, 7)),
                     Arguments.of(List.of(5, 4, 2, 1, 3, 7, 6, 8),
                                  List.of(1, 2, 3, 4, 5, 6, 7, 8),
                                  List.of(5, 4, 7, 2, 6, 8, 1, 3)));
}
```

Thus, during the execution of the unit test, the following output of the respective generated tree occurs, which underpins the correct reconstruction:

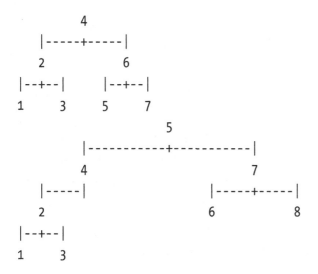

HINT: THINGS TO KNOW ABOUT RECONSTRUCTION

Interestingly, using the algorithm shown, any binary tree can be reconstructed, regardless of whether it is also a binary search tree (for which its nodes follow an order). But it gets even more remarkable: In the case that the values of the preorder traversal originate from a binary search tree, it is possible to reconstruct it based only on that, as follows:

```
static <T extends Comparable<T>>
    BinaryTreeNode<T> reconstruct(final List<T> preorderValues)
{
    // recursive termination
    if (preorderValues.isEmpty())
        return null;

    final T rootValue = preorderValues.get(0);
    final BinaryTreeNode<T> root = new BinaryTreeNode<>(rootValue);

    // filtering
    final List<T> leftValues = new ArrayList<>(preorderValues);
    leftValues.removeIf(value -> value.compareTo(rootValue) >= 0);
```

```
    final List<T> rightValues = new ArrayList<>(preorderValues);
    rightValues.removeIf(value -> value.compareTo(rootValue) <= 0);

    // recursive descent
    root.left = reconstruct(leftValues);
    root.right = reconstruct(rightValues);

    return root;
}
```

This is possible since, in a binary search tree, the values of the preorder traversal are first the value of the root, then the values smaller than the root, and finally the values of the right subtree, which are also larger than the value of the root. This condition also applies recursively. With the help of two filter conditions, all left and right subtree values can be easily extracted— as shown above—and used as input for the recursive call.

Why don't you try the reconstruction with the following `main()` method:

```
public static void main(final String[] args)
{
    var root1 = reconstruct(List.of(4, 2, 1, 3, 6, 5, 7));
    TreeUtils.nicePrint(root1);

    var root2 = reconstruct(List.of(5, 4, 2, 1, 3, 7, 6, 8));
    TreeUtils.nicePrint(root2);
}
```

You will then get the output of the trees already shown in the unit test.

9.3.9 Solution 9: Math Evaluation (★★☆☆☆)

Consider using a tree to model mathematical expressions with the four operators +, −, /, and ∗. It is your task to compute the value of individual nodes, including, in particular, the value of the root node. For this purpose, write method int evaluate(BinaryTreeNode<String>).

Example

Represent the expression $3 + 7 * (7 - 1)$ by the following tree to compute the value 45 for the root node:

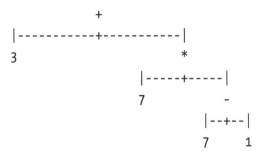

Algorithm   Interestingly, the assignment can be solved very easily and clearly with the syntax enhancement at switch final in Java 14 by a recursive call in connection with the appropriate operators as follows:

```
static int evaluate(final BinaryTreeNode<String> node)
{
    final String value = node.item;

    return switch (value) {
    case "+" -> evaluate(node.left) + evaluate(node.right);
    case "-" -> evaluate(node.left) - evaluate(node.right);
    case "*" -> evaluate(node.left) * evaluate(node.right);
    case "/" -> evaluate(node.left) / evaluate(node.right);
    default -> Integer.valueOf(value);
    };
}
```

Verification

Let's construct the tree from the example and invoke the above method:

```
public static void main(final String[] args)
{
    final BinaryTreeNode<String> plus = new BinaryTreeNode<>("+");
    final BinaryTreeNode<String> _3 = new BinaryTreeNode<>("3");
    final BinaryTreeNode<String> mult = new BinaryTreeNode<>("*");
```

```
final BinaryTreeNode<String> _7 = new BinaryTreeNode<>("7");
final BinaryTreeNode<String> minus = new BinaryTreeNode<>("-");
final BinaryTreeNode<String> _1 = new BinaryTreeNode<>("1");

plus.left = _3;
plus.right = mult;
mult.left = _7;
mult.right = minus;
minus.left = _7;
minus.right = _1;

TreeUtils.nicePrint(plus);
System.out.println("+: " + evaluate(plus));
System.out.println("*: " + evaluate(mult));
System.out.println("-: " + evaluate(minus));
}
```

If you execute this main() method, you get on the one hand the output of the tree as well as the results of the selected individual nodes:

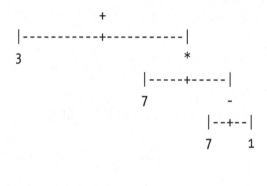

```
+: 45
*: 42
-: 6
```

9.3.10 Solution 10: Symmetry (★★☆☆☆)

Check if an arbitrary binary tree is symmetric in its structure. Therefore write method boolean isSymmetric(BinaryTreeNode<T>). In addition to the structural examination, you can also check for equality of values.

636

Examples

To check for symmetry, you use a binary tree that is symmetric in structure (left) and a binary tree that is also symmetric concerning values (right):

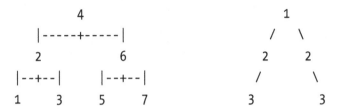

```
          4                                    1
     |-----+-----|                            /   \
     2           6                          2       2
  |--+--|     |--+--|                      /         \
  1     3     5     7                    3             3
```

NOTE: THE SYMMETRY PROPERTY

In a symmetric binary tree, the left and right subtrees are mirrored through the root along an imaginary vertical line (indicated by |):

```
    1
  / | \
 2  |  2
 /  |   \
3   |    3
```

Depending on the definition, a comparison of the values can be omitted for the symmetry. In this case, only the structural organization can be counted as relevant.

Algorithm   Once again, you benefit from a good basic knowledge of recursion. A node with no successor node is always symmetric. If a node has only one successor, the tree cannot be symmetric. Accordingly, only the case for two successor nodes has to be considered. Thereby the left and right subtrees must be mirror-inverted. To do this, you check recursively whether the right subtree of the left and the left subtree of the right node structurally match each other, as well as the left subtree of the right and the right subtree of the left node:

```java
static <T> boolean isSymmetric(final BinaryTreeNode<T> parent)
{
    if (parent == null)
        return true;
```

```
    return isSymmetric(parent.left, parent.right);
}

static <T> boolean isSymmetric(final BinaryTreeNode<T> left,
                               final BinaryTreeNode<T> right)
{
    if (left == null && right == null)
        return true;
    if (left == null || right == null)
            return false;

    // descend both subtrees
    return isSymmetric(left.right, right.left) &&
           isSymmetric(left.left, right.right);
}
```

Advanced algorithm: Value symmetry   In fact, the extension to value checking is simple if you have implemented the previous exercise correctly. Only a boolean parameter checkValue has to be added to the signature and evaluated at the appropriate place before the recursive descent:

```
static <T> boolean isSymmetric(final BinaryTreeNode<T> left,
                               final BinaryTreeNode<T> right,
                               final boolean checkValue)
{
    if (left == null && right == null)
        return true;
    if (left == null || right == null)
            return false;

    // check the values
    if (checkValue && !left.item.equals(right.item))
        return false;

    return isSymmetric(left.right, right.left, checkValue) &&
           isSymmetric(left.left, right.right, checkValue);
}
```

Verification

You construct the two trees from the introduction and invoke the method you just created. The first tree is an already known representative. The other one is explicitly created for this example with createSymmetricNumberTree(). You create a root and then the symmetric structure with nodes with the values 2 and 3. After that, you add the node with the value 4, which then breaks the symmetry.

```
public static void main(final String[] args)
{
    final BinaryTreeNode<String> root = ExampleTrees.createNumberTree();
    TreeUtils.nicePrint(root);
    System.out.println("symmetric: " + isSymmetric(root));

    final BinaryTreeNode<String> root2 = createSymmetricNumberTree();
    TreeUtils.nicePrint(root2);
    System.out.println("symmetric: " + isSymmetric(root2));

    // Modifizierter Baum: Füge eine 4 hinzu
    root2.right.left = new BinaryTreeNode<>("4");
    TreeUtils.nicePrint(root2);
    System.out.println("symmetric: " + isSymmetric(root2));
}

static BinaryTreeNode<String> createSymmetricNumberTree()
{
    final BinaryTreeNode<String> root = new BinaryTreeNode<>("1");
    root.left = new BinaryTreeNode<>("2");
    root.right = new BinaryTreeNode<>("2");
    root.left.left = new BinaryTreeNode<>("3");
    root.right.right = new BinaryTreeNode<>("3");
    return root;
}
```

If you execute this `main()` method, you get the expected results:

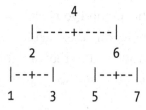

```
symmetric: true
```

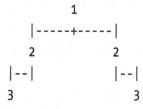

```
symmetric: true
```

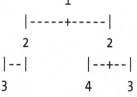

```
symmetric: false
```

Bonus: Mirror Tree

In the hint box, I indicated a mirror axis through the root. Create method `BinaryTreeNode<T> invert(BinaryTreeNode<T>)` that mirrors the nodes of a tree at this implied line through the root.

Example

A mirroring looks like this:

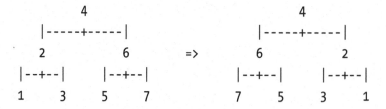

Algorithm   At first, you might once again assume that the challenge is difficult to solve. But in fact, it is much easier to implement with the help of recursion than one initially thinks.

The algorithm proceeds from the root downwards and swaps the left and right subtrees. To do this, you store these subtrees in temporary variables and then assign them to the other side. That's really all there is to it!

```
static <T> BinaryTreeNode<T> invert(final BinaryTreeNode<T> startNode)
{
    if (startNode == null)
        return null;

    final BinaryTreeNode<T> invertedRight = invert(startNode.right);
    final BinaryTreeNode<T> invertedLeft = invert(startNode.left);

    startNode.left = invertedRight;
    startNode.right = invertedLeft;

    return startNode;
}
```

Verification

You construct the left tree from the introduction and invoke the method you just created.

```
public static void main(final String[] args)
{
    final BinaryTreeNode<String> root = ExampleTrees.createNumberTree();
    final BinaryTreeNode<String> newRoot = invert(root);
    TreeUtils.nicePrint(newRoot);
}
```

If you execute this main() method, you get the expected mirroring:

```
          4
   |-----+-----|
   6           2
|--+--|     |--+--|
7     5     3     1
```

9.3.11 Solution 11: Check Binary Search Tree (★★☆☆☆)

In this exercise, you are to check whether an arbitrary binary tree fulfills the property of a binary search tree (i. e., the values in the left subtree are smaller than the root node's value and those in the right subtree are larger—and this holds for each subtree starting from the root). For simplification you assume int values. Write method boolean isBST(BinaryTreeNode<Integer>).

Example

Use the following binary tree, which is also a binary search tree. For example, if you were to replace the number 1 with a larger number on the left side, it would no longer be a binary search tree. However, the right subtree under the 6 is still a binary search tree.

```
            4
      |-----+-----|
      2           6
   |--+--|     |--+--|
   1     3     5     7
```

Algorithm   From the assignment, you recognize a recursive design. A tree with only one node is always a binary search tree. If there is a left or right successor or even both, you check the values of them for compliance with the value relation and perform this recursively for their successors, if they exist.

```
static boolean isBST(final BinaryTreeNode<Integer> node)
{
    // recursive termination
    if (node == null)
        return true;

    if (node.isLeaf())
        return true;

    // recursive descent
    boolean isLeftBST = true;
    boolean isRightBST = true;
    if (node.left != null)
        isLeftBST = node.left.item < node.item && isBST(node.left);
```

```
    if (node.right != null)
        isRightBST = node.right.item > node.item && isBST(node.right);

    return isLeftBST && isRightBST;
}
```

NOTE: COMPARE OTHER TYPES

To support this for a generic type T, it had to satisfy Comparable<T> and you call the compareTo(T) method for comparison instead of using > and <.

Verification

You construct the tree from the example and invoke the method you just created. You also apply two modifications and check again.

```
public static void main(final String[] args)
{
    final BinaryTreeNode<Integer> _4 = ExampleTrees.createInteger
    NumberTree();
    TreeUtils.nicePrint(_4);

    final BinaryTreeNode<Integer> _2 = _4.left;
    final BinaryTreeNode<Integer> _6 = _4.right;

    // change the tree on the left in a wrong way
    // and on the right in a correct way
    _2.left = new BinaryTreeNode<>(13);
    _6.right = null;

    TreeUtils.nicePrint(_4);
    System.out.println("isBST(_4): " + isBST(_4));
    System.out.println("isBST(_2): " + isBST(_2));
    System.out.println("isBST(_6): " + isBST(_6));
}
```

If you execute this `main()` method, you get both the output of the tree and the results for selected individual nodes, whether these nodes themselves represent a binary search tree.

However, if you carelessly store a larger value in the left subtree (e.g., 13), neither the whole tree nor the part with node 2 as root is a BST. For the right subtree, if you delete the node with the value 7, the right subtree with the node with the value 6 remains a BST.

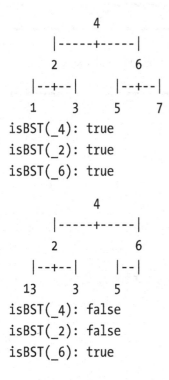

```
          4
    |-----+-----|
    2           6
 |--+--|     |--+--|
 1     3     5     7
isBST(_4): true
isBST(_2): true
isBST(_6): true

          4
    |-----+-----|
    2           6
 |--+--|     |--|
 13    3     5
isBST(_4): false
isBST(_2): false
isBST(_6): true
```

9.3.12 Solution 12: Completeness (★★★★★)

In this exercise, you are asked to check the completeness of a tree. To do this, you initially solve some basics in the first two parts of the exercise and then proceed to the trickier completeness check.

Solution 12a: Number of Nodes (★☆☆☆☆)

Count how many nodes are contained in any binary tree. To do this, write method `int nodeCount(BinaryTreeNode<T>)`.

Example

For the binary tree shown, the value 7 should be determined. If you remove the right subtree, the tree consists of only 4 nodes.

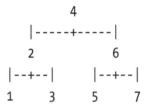

Algorithm   The algorithm is really extremely straightforward if you express it recursively. Each node counts 1. Then you continue counting in both its left and right subtrees and add their results until you hit a leaf:

```java
static <T> int nodeCount(final BinaryTreeNode<T> startNode)
{
    if (startNode == null)
        return 0;

    return 1 + nodeCount(startNode.left) + nodeCount(startNode.right);
}
```

Solution 12b: Check for Full/Perfect (★★☆☆☆)

For an arbitrary binary tree, check if all nodes have two successors or leaves each, and thus the tree is full. For perfection, all leaves must be at the same height. Write the methods `boolean isFull(BinaryTreeNode<T>)` and `boolean isPerfect(BinaryTreeNode<T>)`.

Example

The binary tree shown is both perfect and full. If you remove the two leaves below the 2, it is no longer perfect but still full.

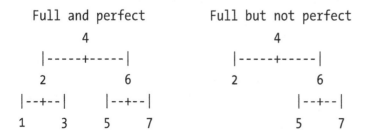

Algorithm   The check whether a tree is full is not that difficult if it is implemented recursively. For each node, you check whether it has no or two successors. Otherwise, it cannot be a full tree.

```
static <T> boolean isFull(final BinaryTreeNode<T> currentNode)
{
    if (currentNode == null)
        return true;

    return isFull(currentNode.left, currentNode.right);
}

static <T> boolean isFull(final BinaryTreeNode<T> leftNode,
                          final BinaryTreeNode<T> rightNode)
{
    if (leftNode == null && rightNode == null)
        return true;

    if (leftNode != null && rightNode != null)
        return isFull(leftNode) && isFull(rightNode);

    return false;
}
```

This is already a good start. Based on this, you need some smaller extensions to be able to check the perfectness. First, you have to determine the height of the whole tree, starting from the root. After that, you proceed quite similar to isFull(), but now every node must have two successors. On the level of the leaves, you additionally have to check if they are at the correct level. Thereby you stumble over the fact that the height of a leaf is 1. Therefore you still need the level on which they are located. For this, you cheat with an additional parameter currentLevel in your method. This results in the following implementation:

```
static <T> boolean isPerfect(final BinaryTreeNode<T> parent)
{
    if (parent == null)
        return true;
```

```java
    final int height = Ex03_TreeHeight.getHeight(parent);

    return isPerfect(parent.left, parent.right, height, 1);
}

static <T> boolean isPerfect(final BinaryTreeNode<T> leftNode,
                             final BinaryTreeNode<T> rightNode,
                             final int height, final int currentLevel)
{
    if (leftNode == null || rightNode == null)
        return false;

    if (leftNode.isLeaf() && rightNode.isLeaf())
        return onSameHeight(leftNode, rightNode, height, currentLevel);

    return isPerfect(leftNode.left, leftNode.right, height,
            currentLevel + 1) && isPerfect(rightNode.left,
            rightNode.right, height, currentLevel + 1);
}

static <T> boolean onSameHeight(final BinaryTreeNode<T> leftNode,
                                final BinaryTreeNode<T> rightNode,
                                final int height, final int currentLevel)
{
    return Ex03_TreeHeight.getHeight(leftNode) + currentLevel == height &&
            Ex03_TreeHeight.getHeight(rightNode) + currentLevel == height;
}
```

Verification

You construct the tree with numbers from the introduction and invoke the methods you just created. In addition, you modify the tree by deleting the reference to the right subtree. Then you invoke the methods again.

```java
public static void main(final String[] args)
{
    final BinaryTreeNode<String> _4 = ExampleTrees.createNumberTree();
    printInfo(_4);
```

```
    // modify the tree
    _4.left.left = null;
    _4.left.right = null;
    printInfo(_4);
}

protected static void printInfo(final BinaryTreeNode<String> root)
{
    TreeUtils.nicePrint(root);
    System.out.println("#nodes:   " + nodeCount(root));
    System.out.println("isFull?: " + isFull(root));
    System.out.println("isPerfect?: " + isPerfect(root));
    System.out.println();
}
```

If you execute this main() method, you get the expected results:

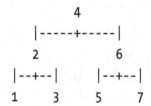

```
#nodes:  7
isFull?: true
isPerfect?: true
```

```
                4
        |-----+-----|
        2           6
                 |--+--|
                 5     7
```

```
#nodes:  5
isFull?: true
isPerfect?: false
```

Solution 12c: Completeness (★★★★☆)

In this subtask, you are asked to check if a tree is complete as defined in the introduction (i.e., a binary tree with all levels fully filled, with the allowed exception on the last level where nodes may be missing, but only with gaps as far to the right as possible).

Example

In addition to the perfect tree used so far, the following tree is also complete by definition. However, if you remove the children from node H, the tree is no longer complete.

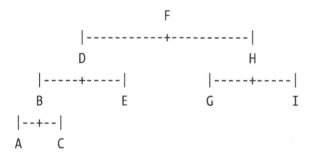

Algorithm   At first, this seems to be a rather tricky task, in any case much more complicated than the *checks* shown before. If you study the definition again, the tree is supposed to contain successors in pairs. Moreover, there must be no gaps in the tree (i.e., no node with a missing left successor but with a right successor). If the tree is not fully filled, then only leaves from the right may be missing. On closer visual inspection, it is noticeable that you could traverse level by level, but only in the last level nodes may be missing.

Now the level-order pass comes to mind. You use it here and just add a few checks. For each node there must be no right successor without a left one. Besides, you check whether you have discovered a missing node in the meantime. How can this happen? This is possible whenever you want to add a node's successors to the queue, but there is only one left or right successor. This is expressed by the flag missingNode. So if a missing successor has been detected, then the nodes processed afterwards must be leaves only.

```
static <T> boolean levelorderIsComplete(final BinaryTreeNode<T> startNode)
{
    if (startNode == null)
        return false;
```

```
    final Queue<BinaryTreeNode<T>> toProcess = new LinkedList<>();
    toProcess.offer(startNode);

    // indicator that a node does not have two successors
    boolean missingNode = false;

    while (!toProcess.isEmpty())
    {
        final BinaryTreeNode<T> current = toProcess.poll();

        // only descendants on the right side
        if (current.left == null && current.right != null)
            return false;

        // if a missing node was previously detected,
        // then the next may be only a leaf
        if (missingNode && !current.isLeaf())
            return false;

        // include sub-elements, mark if not complete
        if (current.left != null)
            toProcess.offer(current.left);
        else
            missingNode = true;

        if (current.right != null)
            toProcess.offer(current.right);
        else
            missingNode = true;
    }

    // all nodes successfully tested
    return true;
}
```

Verification

You construct the tree from the example and invoke the method you just created. In addition, you modify the tree by removing the leaves below the H node. Then you check again.

650

```
public static void main(final String[] args)
{
    final BinaryTreeNode<String> F = createCompletenessExampleTree();
    TreeUtils.nicePrint(F);
    System.out.println("levelorderIsComplete? " + levelorderIsComplete(F));

    // modification: remove leaves under H
    F.right.left = null;
    F.right.right = null;
    TreeUtils.nicePrint(F);
    System.out.println("levelorderIsComplete? " + levelorderIsComplete(F));
}

protected static BinaryTreeNode<String> createCompletenessExampleTree()
{
    final BinaryTreeNode<String> F = new BinaryTreeNode<>("F");
    TreeUtils.insert(F, "D");
    TreeUtils.insert(F, "H");
    TreeUtils.insert(F, "B");
    TreeUtils.insert(F, "E");
    TreeUtils.insert(F, "A");
    TreeUtils.insert(F, "C");
    TreeUtils.insert(F, "G");
    TreeUtils.insert(F, "I");
    return F;
}
```

If you execute this main() method, you get the expected results:

```
                    F
        |-----------+-----------|
        D                       H
    |-----+-----|           |-----+-----|
    B           E           G           I
  |--+--|
  A     C
```

```
levelorderIsComplete? true
```

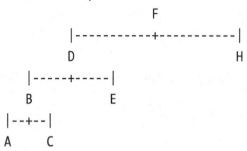

```
levelorderIsComplete? false
```

Solution 12d: Completeness Recursive (★★★★★)

In this last subtask, the following challenge remains to be mastered as a special treat: The check is to be solved without additional data structures and purely recursively. At first, this sounds hardly feasible, so I'll give a hint.

Tip   Develop the solution step by step. Create a boolean[ ] as an auxiliary data structure that models whether or not a node exists for a certain position. Then traverse the tree and mark the positions appropriately. Convert this implementation to a purely recursive one without the boolean[ ].

Example

As before, the following tree is complete by definition:

```
                       F
          |-----------+-----------|
          D                       H
     |-----+-----|           |-----+-----|
     B           E           G           I
 |--+--|
 A     C
```

Algorithm   In fact, the assignment sounds hardly manageable, but that is why it is a tough challenge. As it is so often, it is worthwhile to start by developing a version that does not yet meet all the required properties and gradually refine it. You start with the ideas from the tip.

The idea is this: You traverse the tree, and for each node that exists, you mark exactly that in a boolean[]. When doing so, you number the positions according to level-order from left to right and top to bottom. To determine the position of the current node in the array, you perform the following computation: For position i, the left successor has position $i * 2 + 1$ and the right successor has position $i * 2 + 2$.[3] Figure 9-12 illustrates this.

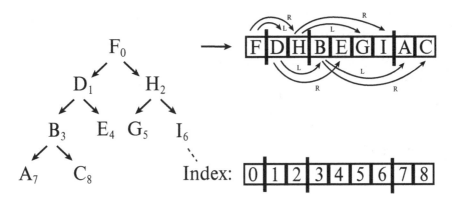

Figure 9-12. *Mapping a tree to an array*

Now you still need to know how large the array needs to be. Theoretically, at most, it can contain 2^{height} elements. However, for very deep and thus expanding trees, many leaves might not exist at all. To optimize the memory, you count the number of nodes to determine the actual size needed. This is where Exercise 12a helps you. Then you traverse all the tree elements using the traverseAndMark() method. Finally, you summarize the data using allAssigned().

```
static <T> boolean isComplete(final BinaryTreeNode<T> startNode)
{
    final int nodeCount = nodeCount(startNode);

    final boolean[] nodeExists = new boolean[nodeCount];

    // now you traverse the tree from the root downwards
    traverseAndMark(startNode, nodeExists, 0);

    return allAssigned(nodeExists);
}
```

---

[3] The computation gets a little bit easier if you assign the index 1 to the root. Then the children have positions $2i$ and $2i + 1$.

Let's move on to traversing the tree and filling the array. Interestingly, it doesn't matter whether you use preorder, inorder, or postorder here. The only important thing is that the positions are determined according to the mentioned computation rule:

```java
static <T> void traverseAndMark(final BinaryTreeNode<T> startNode,
                                final boolean[] nodeExists, final int pos)
{
    // recursive termination
    if (startNode == null)
        return;
    if (pos >= nodeExists.length)
        return;

    // perform action
    nodeExists[pos] = true;

    // recursive descent
    traverseAndMark(startNode.left, nodeExists, pos * 2 + 1);
    traverseAndMark(startNode.right, nodeExists, pos * 2 + 2);
}
```

Finally, you need to check if there is a position in the array that is not occupied by true. In this case, you detected that the tree is not complete. This is determined by the following method:

```java
private static boolean allAssigned(final boolean[] nodeExists)
{
    for (boolean exists : nodeExists)
        if (!exists)
            return false;

    return true;
}
```

```
HINT: WHY IS ALLASSIGNED() IMPLEMENTED IN SUCH AN OLD SCHOOL WAY?
```

If you take a quick look at the method `allAssigned()`, you may be inclined to replace it by the following much more elegant construct:

```
private static boolean allAssigned(final boolean[] nodeExists)
{
    return Arrays.stream(nodeExists).noneMatch(value -> value == false);
}
```

Unfortunately, as nice as it would be, it does not compile because `Arrays.stream()` is not defined for `boolean[]`.

Phew, that was quite a bit of work so far, and you needed several tricks. On a positive note, this algorithm works. I'll show that later along with the algorithm converted purely to recursive processing based on these ideas.

On the negative side, however, you need quite a bit of additional memory depending on the tree's size. Let's see how you can avoid this by using the purely recursive variant.

Recursive algorithm   Your goal is to eliminate the use of the array and work only recursively. Therefore, the `traverseAndMark()` method is a good starting point. If you are not allowed to use an array as a data store, you need the number of nodes as a parameter. Instead of recursively filling the array each time, the method simply invokes itself:

```
public static <T> boolean isCompleteRec(final BinaryTreeNode<T> startNode)
{
    return isCompleteRec(startNode, 0, nodeCount(startNode));
}

public static <T> boolean isCompleteRec(final BinaryTreeNode<T> startNode,
                                        final int pos, final int nodeCount)
{
    if (startNode == null)
        return true;
    if (pos >= nodeCount)
        return false;
```

```
    if (!isCompleteRec(startNode.left, 2* pos + 1, nodeCount))
        return false;

    if (!isCompleteRec(startNode.right, 2* pos + 2, nodeCount))
        return false;

    return true;
}
```

Without the intermediate steps, it would have been challenging, at least for me, to formulate the task recursively since the trick of the logic in the position calculation can hardly be derived without the array in mind. It is quite impressive what these few lines accomplish.

Verification

Again, you construct the tree and modify it after testing:

```
public static void main(final String[] args)
{
    final BinaryTreeNode<String> F = createCompletenessExampleTree();
    TreeUtils.nicePrint(F);
    System.out.println("isComplete? " + isComplete(F));
    System.out.println("isCompleteRec? " + isCompleteRec(F));

    // modification: remove leaves under H
    F.right.left = null;
    F.right.right = null;
    TreeUtils.nicePrint(F);
    System.out.println("isComplete? " + isComplete(F));
    System.out.println("isCompleteRec? " + isCompleteRec(F));
}

protected static BinaryTreeNode<String> createCompletenessExampleTree()
{
    final BinaryTreeNode<String> F = new BinaryTreeNode<>("F");
    TreeUtils.insert(F, "D");
    TreeUtils.insert(F, "H");
    TreeUtils.insert(F, "B");
```

```
    TreeUtils.insert(F, "E");
    TreeUtils.insert(F, "A");
    TreeUtils.insert(F, "C");
    TreeUtils.insert(F, "G");
    TreeUtils.insert(F, "I");
    return F;
}
```

If you execute this main() method, you get the expected results. Moreover, they are consistent for the method variations.

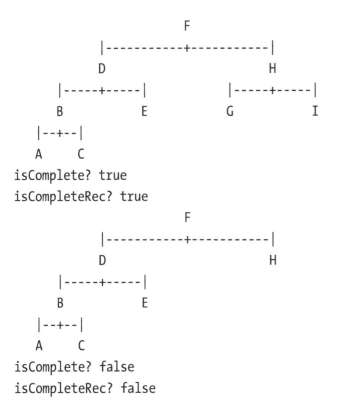

```
                    F
        |-----------+-----------|
        D                       H
    |-----+-----|           |-----+-----|
    B           E           G           I
|--+--|
A     C
isComplete? true
isCompleteRec? true
                    F
        |-----------+-----------|
        D                       H
    |-----+-----|
    B           E
|--+--|
A     C
isComplete? false
isCompleteRec? false
```

9.3.13 Solution 13: Tree Printer (★★★★★)

In this exercise, you are to implement a binary tree's graphical output, as you have seen before in the examples.

Therefore, you initially solve the basics in the first three parts of the assignment and then proceed to the trickier graphical presentation of trees.

657

Tip   Use a fixed grid of blocks of width 3. This significantly contributes to a balanced representation and reduces complexity.

Example

The following tree should cover various special cases:

```
                        F
        |-----------+-----------|
        D                       H
    |-----+                 +-----|
    B                             I
  |--+--|
  A     C
```

Solution 13a: Width of a Subtree (★★☆☆☆)

In this part of the exercise, you are asked to find the maximum width of a subtree of a given height using the method int subtreeWidth(int). For simplicity, you assume that a node is represented by a maximum of three characters. Besides, there is a distance of at least three characters between them. This is true for the leaves when the tree is full. On higher levels, there is naturally more space between the nodes of two subtrees.

Examples

On the left, you see a tree of height 2, and on the right, a tree of height 3. Based on the grid of three, you get 9 and 21 as widths. See Figure 9-13.

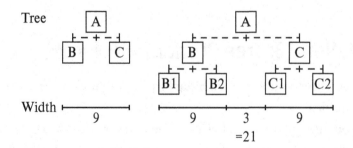

Figure 9-13. Tree width

Height	Total width	Width of subtree
1	3	0 (no subtree existing)
2	9	3
3	21	9
4	45	21

Algorithm   In the diagram, you recognize that the lowest level of a binary tree can contain at most 2^n nodes, with n as the height of the tree. In order not to exceed the scope, you want to ignore variable widths of the nodes. To determine the maximum width for a height, the total width results as follows:

$$maxNumOfLeaves * leafWidth + (maxNumOfLeaves - 1) * spacing$$

This is the basis for the following implementation. Perhaps the last computation is a bit tricky. You have to subtract the spacing and divide by two since you only want to determine the maximum width of a subtree:

```java
static int subtreeWidth(final int height)
{
    if (height <= 0)
        return 0;

    final int leafWidth = 3;
    final int spacing = 3;

    final int maxNumOfLeaves = (int) Math.pow(2, height - 1);
    final int widthOfTree = maxNumOfLeaves * leafWidth +
                            (maxNumOfLeaves - 1) * spacing;
    final int widthOfSubtree = (widthOfTree - spacing) / 2;

    return widthOfSubtree;
}
```

Solution 13b: Draw Node (★★☆☆☆)

Write method `String drawNode(BinaryTreeNode<T>, int)` that creates a graphical output of a node, generating the given set of spaces appropriately. The node value should have a maximum of three digits and be placed in the middle.

Tip   Remember that if the current node has a left successor, the representation of the layer below starts on the left with the string ' |-'.

Example

Figure 9-14 shows a single node with a spacing of 5 characters. Besides, the node value is center-aligned in a three-character box.

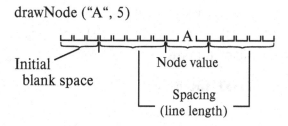

Figure 9-14. *Dimensions when drawing nodes*

Algorithm   As usual, it is a good idea to reduce the complexity by subdividing an assignment into several smaller subtasks. Using method `spacing(int)` you create the required spacing both to the left and right of the node representation. Its preparation first checks for the special cases of no existence or no value in the node. Then this corresponds graphically to a free space of three characters. Otherwise, you pad the value converted to a string with spaces if it is shorter than three characters. If it is longer, you truncate the text to three characters. This is done in the method `String stringifyNod eValue(BinaryTreeNode<T>)`. Because subsequent lines start with the text ' |-' if a left successor exists, you add three more spaces to the front of your string representation.

```
static <T> String drawNode(final BinaryTreeNode<T> currentNode,
                           final int lineLength)
```

```
{
    String strNode = "    ";
    strNode += spacing(lineLength);
    strNode += stringifyNodeValue(currentNode);
    strNode += spacing(lineLength);

    return strNode;
}

static <T> String stringifyNodeValue(final BinaryTreeNode<T> node)
{
    if (node == null || node.item == null)
        return "    ";

    final String nodeValue = "" + node.item;
    if (nodeValue.length() == 1)
        return " " + nodeValue + " ";
    if (nodeValue.length() == 2)
        return nodeValue + " ";

    return nodeValue.substring(0, 3);
}

static String spacing(final int lineLength)
{
    return " ".repeat(lineLength);
}
```

Solution 13c: Draw Connection Lines (★★☆☆☆)

Write method String drawConnections(BinaryTreeNode<T>, int) building a graphical output of the connection lines of a node to its two successors. Missing successors have to be handled correctly.

Tip   The line length refers to the characters between the node representations. The parts representing ends are still to be appended appropriately in each case, as well as the middle connector.

Example

This figure visualizes all cases relevant in drawing, so with none, one, and two successor(s):

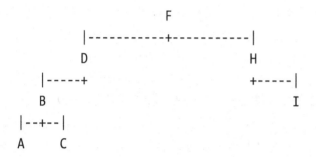

```
                       F
         |-----------+-----------|
         D                       H
      |-----+                 +-----|
        B                         I
      |--+--|
      A     C
```

A schematic representation is shown in Figure 9-15.

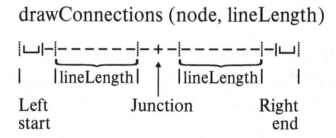

drawConnections (node, lineLength)

Figure 9-15. *Schematic representation of the connecting lines*

Algorithm   When drawing the connecting lines below a node, all three variants with and without left or right successor are to be covered. Even a little more interesting is the fact that a non-existent node must also produce a corresponding output of blanks. This is needed if there are no children on the left side. Otherwise, the nodes on the right side would not be indented correctly.

You divide the drawing into three parts. First, you prepare the left part of the output with drawLeftConnectionPart(). After that, in drawJunction(node) you create the connection point respecting all special cases. Finally, with drawRightConnectionPart() you prepare the right part.

```
static <T> String drawConnections(final BinaryTreeNode<T> currentNode,
                                  final int lineLength)
```

```
{
    if (currentNode == null)
        return " " + spacing(lineLength) + " " + spacing(lineLength) + " ";

    String connection = drawLeftConnectionPart(currentNode, lineLength);
    connection += drawJunction(currentNode);
    connection += drawRightConnectionPart(currentNode, lineLength);
    return connection;
}

static <T> String drawLeftConnectionPart(final BinaryTreeNode<T> currentNode,
                                         final int lineLength)
{
    if (currentNode.left == null)
        return "   " + spacing(lineLength);

    return " |-" + drawLine(lineLength);
}

static <T> String drawJunction(final BinaryTreeNode<T> currentNode)
{
    if(currentNode.left == null && currentNode.right == null)
        return "   ";
    else if (currentNode.left == null)
        return " +-";
    else if (currentNode.right == null)
        return "-+ ";

    return "-+-";
}

static <T> String drawRightConnectionPart(final BinaryTreeNode<T> currentNode,
                                          final int lineLength)
{
    if (currentNode.right == null)
        return spacing(lineLength) + "   ";

    return drawLine(lineLength) + "-| ";
}
```

```
static String drawLine(int lineLength)
{
    return "-".repeat(lineLength);
}
```

Solution 13d: Tree Representation (★★★★★)

Combine all solutions of the parts of the exercise and complete the necessary steps to be able to print an arbitrary binary tree suitably on the console. To do this, write a method nicePrint(BinaryTreeNode<T>).

Example

The output of the tree shown in the introductory example should also look something like this through nicePrint():

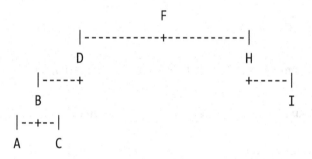

Also, check your algorithm with a real monster of a tree that you can find in the sources. Here is a much slimmed down representative:

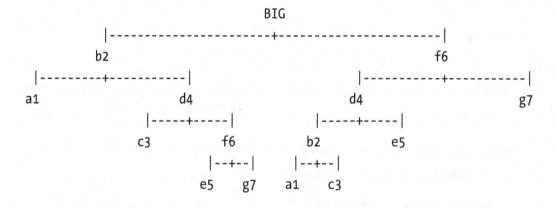

Algorithm   In the previous task, you learned how to map binary trees to arrays. Here, this has to be slightly modified because, in the tree, nodes can be missing at arbitrary places in contrast to completeness. For computing the size of the array, you need the height of the tree. This is also important to compute the corresponding distances and line lengths. In this case, the trick also helps determine the maximum width of a subtree and use it appropriately.

These ideas mentioned earlier may be picked up to create a suitable array in which the nodes are stored in a scattered manner. The following methods will assist you in doing so:

```
static <T> List<BinaryTreeNode<T>>
        fillNodeArray(final BinaryTreeNode<T> startNode)
{
    final int height = Ex03_TreeHeight.getHeight(startNode);
    final int maxNodeCount = (int) Math.pow(2, height);

    final List<BinaryTreeNode<T>> nodes =
        new ArrayList<>(Collections.nCopies(maxNodeCount, null));

    traverseAndMark(startNode, nodes, 0);

    return nodes;
}

static <T> void traverseAndMark(final BinaryTreeNode<T> startNode,
                                final List<BinaryTreeNode<T>> nodes,
                                final int pos)
{
    // recursive termination
    if (startNode == null)
        return;
    if (pos >= nodes.size())
        return;

    // perform action
    nodes.set(pos, startNode);
```

```
// recursive descent
traverseAndMark(startNode.left, nodes, pos * 2 + 1);
traverseAndMark(startNode.right, nodes, pos * 2 + 2);
}
```

For drawing, the tree and the array are traversed level by level, and the graphical representation is prepared. However, this has the disadvantage that very extensive trees also require quite a lot of additional memory when drawing since they are kept as an array or list.

There are still a few challenges waiting for you:

- As you start drawing at the top, you need to move the previously prepared lines for each new level by appropriate positions to the right.

- The distances between the nodes and the lengths of the connecting lines have to be computed and kept depending on the total height, the current level, and position. Thereby the lowest level still needs special treatment.

Figure 9-16 illustrates the grid and the different distances between the nodes per level and from one level to the next.

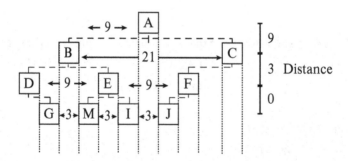

Figure 9-16. *Spacing between nodes*

The associated implementation benefits from the use of the helper methods:

```
static <T> void nicePrintV1(final BinaryTreeNode<T> startNode)
{
    if (startNode == null)
        return;
```

```java
final int treeHeight = Ex03_TreeHeight.getHeight(startNode);
final List<BinaryTreeNode<T>> allNodes = fillNodeArray(startNode);

int offset = 0;
final List<String> lines = new ArrayList<>();
for (int level = 0; level < treeHeight; level++)
{
    final int lineLength = subtreeWidth(treeHeight - 1 - level);

    // indent predecessor lines to the right
    for (int i = 0; i < lines.size(); i++)
    {
        lines.set(i, "   " + spacing(lineLength) + lines.get(i));
    }

    final int nodesPerLevel = (int) Math.pow(2, level);
    String nodeLine = "";
    String connectionLine = "";

    for (int pos = 0; pos < nodesPerLevel; pos++)
    {
        final BinaryTreeNode<T> currentNode = allNodes.get(offset + pos);

        nodeLine += drawNode(currentNode, lineLength);
        nodeLine += spacingBetweenNodes(treeHeight, level);
        connectionLine += drawConnections(currentNode, lineLength);
        connectionLine += spacingBetweenConnections(treeHeight, level);
    }

    lines.add(nodeLine.stripTrailing());
    lines.add(connectionLine.stripTrailing());

    // jump in the array further
    offset += nodesPerLevel;
}

lines.forEach(System.out::println);
}
```

Besides, you still need two methods to provide the distance between the nodes and for the connecting lines, respectively:

```
static String spacingBetweenNodes(final int treeHeight, final int level)
{
    final int spacingLength = subtreeWidth(treeHeight - level);
    String spacing = " ".repeat(spacingLength);
    if (spacingLength > 0)
        spacing += "     ";
    return spacing;
}

static String spacingBetweenConnections(final int treeHeight,
                                        final int level)
{
    final int spacingLength = subtreeWidth(treeHeight - level);
    return " ".repeat(spacingLength);
}
```

Memory-optimized algorithm: In the following, I would like to present a modification, which does not need any additional memory. Instead, it renders the graphical representation of the tree with a level-order traversal. Here you use a list with single lines, wherein those with nodes and connecting lines alternate. In my opinion, the previously shown version is somewhat clearer, especially because the following version needs the special treatment of changing levels, which is performed more naturally in the first version.

Overall, however, it is still a clear level-order traversal, whose action is a bit more extensive in this case.

```
static <T> void nicePrint(final BinaryTreeNode<T> startNode)
{
    if (startNode == null)
        return;

    final int treeHeight = Ex03_TreeHeight.getHeight(startNode);
    final List<String> lines = new ArrayList<>();
```

```
int level = 0;
String nodeLine = "";
String connectionLine = "";

final Queue<Pair<BinaryTreeNode<T>, Integer>> toProcess = new
LinkedList<>(); toProcess.offer(new Pair<>(startNode, 0));

while (!toProcess.isEmpty() && level < treeHeight)
{
    // levelorder
    final Pair<BinaryTreeNode<T>, Integer> current = toProcess.poll();
    final BinaryTreeNode<T> currentNode = current.first;
    final int nodelevel = current.second;

    // perform action
    int lineLength = subtreeWidth(treeHeight - 1 - level);

    // Wechsel in der Ebene
    if (level != nodelevel)
    {
        level = nodelevel;
        lineLength = subtreeWidth(treeHeight - 1 - level);

        lines.add(nodeLine.stripTrailing());
        lines.add(connectionLine.stripTrailing());
        nodeLine = "";
        connectionLine = "";

        // indent predecessor lines to the right
        for (int i = 0; i < lines.size(); i++)
        {
            lines.set(i, "    " + spacing(lineLength) + lines.get(i));
        }
    }

    nodeLine += drawNode(currentNode, lineLength);
    nodeLine += spacingBetweenNodes(treeHeight, level);
    connectionLine += drawConnections(currentNode, lineLength);
    connectionLine += spacingBetweenConnections(treeHeight, level);
```

669

```
        // levelorder
        if (currentNode != null)
        {
            toProcess.offer(new Pair<>(currentNode.left, level + 1));
            toProcess.offer(new Pair<>(currentNode.right, level + 1));
        }
        else
        {
            // artificial placeholders for correct layout
            toProcess.offer(new Pair<>(null, level + 1));
            toProcess.offer(new Pair<>(null, level + 1));
        }
    }

    lines.forEach(System.out::println);
}
```

The omission of the auxiliary data structure leads to a more complex realization. It is necessary to add artificial null-nodes as placeholders so that the trees are drawn correctly if the left node is missing. This would cause the level-order traversal to no longer terminate since new nodes are always being added. To prevent this, not only the queue but also the current level are queried.

Verification

You have developed quite a bit. Now you want to see the fruits of your labor. For this purpose, you use the trees from the introductory example. The first tree shows well the principle way of working. The second is a combination of the previous example trees, but rotated to the left and right and united under a new root with the value BIG.

```
protected static BinaryTreeNode<String> createTreePrintExampleTree()
{
    final BinaryTreeNode<String> F = new BinaryTreeNode<>("F");
    TreeUtils.insert(F, "D");
    TreeUtils.insert(F, "H");
    TreeUtils.insert(F, "B");
```

```
    TreeUtils.insert(F, "A");
    TreeUtils.insert(F, "C");
    TreeUtils.insert(F, "I");
    return F;
}

protected static BinaryTreeNode<String> createBigTree()
{
    var d4a = ExampleTrees.createExampleTree();
    var d4b = ExampleTrees.createExampleTree();
    var BIG = new BinaryTreeNode<>("BIG");
    BIG.left = Ex07_RotateBinaryTree.rotateRight(d4a);
    BIG.right = Ex07_RotateBinaryTree.rotateLeft(d4b);
    return BIG;
}
```

These methods create the following trees:

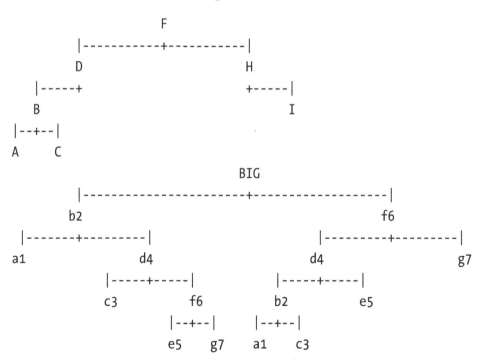

If you want to see how beautifully really expansive trees are rendered, call the method for the following construct:

```
protected static BinaryTreeNode<String> createMonsterTree()
{
    final var mon = new BinaryTreeNode<>("MON");
    mon.left = createBigTree();
    mon.right = createBigTree();
    return mon;
}
```

In the companion project, you will find a double combination of this *monster tree*, which for fun I have named *King Kong*.

CHAPTER 10

Searching and Sorting

Searching and sorting are two elementary topics of computer science in the field of algorithms and data structures. The Collections framework provides efficient implementations for both of them and thus takes a lot of work off your shoulders. However, understanding the underlying algorithms helps in choosing the most suitable variant for a particular use case. I only skim over the topic of searching here so please see my book *Der Weg zum Java-Profi* [Ind20a] for a more detailed treatment.

In this chapter, you primarily dedicate yourself to some essential sorting algorithms because you can learn several algorithmic tricks in the meantime.

10.1 Introduction Search

When managing data, now and then you need to search for items, such as customers with the first name *Carsten* or an invoice with specific order date.

10.1.1 Searching in Collections and Arrays

Conveniently, all container classes have methods to search for elements and check whether elements are in the container.

Searching with contains()

If container classes are accessed via the general type Collection<E>, it is possible to determine whether a desired element is present by calling the method contains(Object). In addition, containsAll(Collection<?>) can be used to check whether a set of elements is contained. The internal implementation iterates over the elements of the collection, and each one is checked for equality with the given element(s) based on equals(Object). For maps, there are corresponding methods containsKey(Object) and containsValue(Object).

© Michael Inden 2022
M. Inden, *Java Challenges*, https://doi.org/10.1007/978-1-4842-7395-1_10

HINT: SIGNATURE OF CONTAINS()

One more note: Why doesn't `contains()` use a generic type, rather than `Object`? According to the method contract, the input object of any type is compared with the collection elements using `equals(Object)`. Due to the signature of `equals(Object)`, the concrete type is only indirectly important through the implementation and its internal type checking.

Searching with indexOf() and lastIndexOf()

For lists, in addition to `contains(Object)`, there are the methods `indexOf(Object)` and `lastIndexOf(Object)` to determine the position of a desired element. The first method starts searching at the beginning of a list and the second starts at its end. In this way, either the first or the last occurrence, if any, can be determined. If no element is found, the return value is -1. Equality is again checked by `equals(Object)`.

Programming Searches in Arrays Yourself

As you just saw, the interfaces `Collection<E>` and `List<E>` provide various kinds of searches, such as by being contained or by index. Unfortunately, there is nothing similar in the auxiliary class `java.util.Arrays`. However, it is fairly easy to implement this functionality for arrays yourself. Because thematically appropriate, I also include the following method for an array in the `ArrayUtils` class developed in Chapter 5.

The implementation for an index-based search returns either the desired element's position or the value -1 for *not found*. You implement the search exemplarily for the type `int[]`. The search is implemented as follows (once starting from the beginning and once from the end of the array):

```java
static int indexOf(final int[] values, final int searchFor)
{
    for (int pos = 0; pos < values.length; pos++)
    {
        if (values[pos] == searchFor)
            return pos;
    }
    return -1;
}
```

```
static int lastIndexOf(final int[] values, final int searchFor)
{
    for (int pos = values.length - 1; pos >= 0; pos--)
    {
        if (values[pos] == searchFor)
            return pos;
    }
    return -1;
}
```

Relying on the previously shown index-based search, method contains(int[], int) for the type int[] can be created very easily by yourself (again analogously to the one for Collection<E>):

```
static boolean contains(final int[] values, final int searchFor)
{
    return indexOf(values, searchFor) != -1;
}
```

10.1.2 Binary Search with binarySearch()

In addition to the search methods just mentioned, which iteratively look at all elements of the data structure until they find what they are looking for, an efficient search, the so-called *binary search*, is provided in the JDK for the data structures array and List<E>. *This requires sorted data*, which is ideally provided by choosing an appropriate data structure such as a TreeSet<E> that always keeps the elements sorted. If you have to sort data explicitly first, then the advantage over a linear search is hardly given, especially with small datasets.

For larger volumes of data, however, the logarithmic running time of a binary search is significantly better than that of a linear search. The low running time is achieved by the algorithm splitting the areas to be processed in half in each case and then continuing the search in the appropriate chunk. The described procedure for a binary search is implemented in the JDK by the overloaded method binarySearch() in the utility classes Arrays and Collections. Figure 10-1 illustrates the principle procedure, with discarded parts marked in gray.

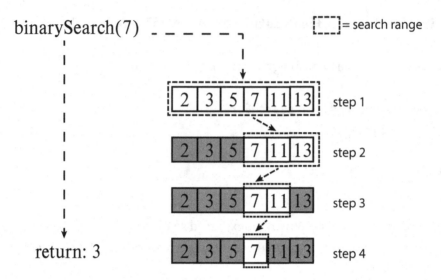

Figure 10-1. *Schematic procedure for a binary search*

In the figure, the arrow points between the elements in the first step. Depending on the implementation of binarySearch(), the left or right element directly adjacent to the center is used for comparison if the number is even.

10.2 Introduction Sort

In this section, I introduce some sorting algorithms that form the basis for the later exercise.

10.2.1 Insertion Sort

Insertion sort is illustrated the best by sorting a deck of cards in your hand in a card game. Typically you start on the left side, take the next card to the right, and insert it appropriately into the already sorted left part, which usually causes some cards to move to the right. With this procedure, you can skip the first card since it is sorted by itself and start with the second card. Let's look at this for the number sequence 4, 2, 7, 9, 1. For this purpose, the respective new element to be sorted in is marked. The already sorted part on the left is separated with ‖ from the unsorted part on the right:

```
4 || ② 7 9 1
2 4 || ⑦ 9 1
2 4 7 || ⑨ 1
2 4 7 9 || ①
1 2 4 7 9
```

In the example, you start with the value 2. For each number, you have to determine the correct insertion position. There are two ways to do this, as described below.

Determine Insertion Position

Starting from the current position, move to the left as long as the compared values are larger. Alternatively, you can also start from the beginning and move one position to the right as long as the compared values are smaller.

```java
static int findInsertPosFromCurrent(final int[] numbers, final int currentPos)
{
    int insertPos = currentPos;
    while (insertPos > 0 && numbers[insertPos - 1] > numbers[currentPos])
        insertPos--;

    return insertPos;
}

static int findInsertPosFromStart(final int[] numbers, final int currentPos)
{
    int insertPos = 0;
    while (insertPos < currentPos &&  numbers[insertPos] < numbers[currentPos])
        insertPos++;

    return insertPos;
}
```

HINT: STABLE SORTING

When sorting elements of the same value, keeping their original order in the collection is referred to as a **_stable sort_**. This is often a preferable behavior because it prevents data associated with the elements from getting out of order.

For the example, `findInsertPosFromCurrent(int[], int)` results in a stable sorting, but the second one does not. However, if you replace the < with <= there, the resulting sorting algorithm also becomes stable:

while (insertPos < currentPos && numbers[insertPos] <= numbers[currentPos])

This is due to the fact that a most recently found element of the same value is always placed behind all elements of the same value.

Implementation of Insertion Sort

After identifying the correct insertion position for a value, all values (up to the currently considered value) have to be shifted by one position to the right. Finally, the value is inserted at the determined position.

```
static void insertionSort(final int[] numbers)
{
    for (int currentPos = 1; currentPos < numbers.length; currentPos++)
    {
        final int currentVal = numbers[currentPos];
        final int insertPos = findInsertPosFromCurrent(numbers, currentPos);

        moveRight(numbers, currentPos, insertPos);

        numbers[insertPos] = currentVal;
    }
}

static void moveRight(final int[] numbers,
                      final int currentPos, final int insertPos)
{
```

```
    int movePos = currentPos;
    while (movePos > insertPos)
    {
        numbers[movePos] = numbers[movePos - 1];
        movePos--;
    }
}
```

The code shows a well-understandable implementation that focuses on comprehensibility and not on speed. In fact, it is possible to combine some actions cleverly and thus avoid multiple runs. Later, in exercise 4, you will deal with exactly this optimization.

10.2.2 Selection Sort

Selection sort is another intuitive method for sorting. It offers two variations, one based on the minimum and the other on the maximum. In the minimum version, the array to be sorted is traversed from front to back. In each step, the minimum is determined from the section that is still unsorted. This is moved forward by swapping it with the current element. This causes the sorted area to grow from the front and the remaining unsorted section to shrink. For the version based on the maximum, the data to be sorted is processed from the back to the front. The respective maximum is placed at the end so that the sorted area grows from the back.

To gain a better understanding, let's reproduce this for a small set of values. For this purpose, the respective current minimum or maximum is specially marked. The sorted part is separated from the unsorted part with ||. You can easily observe how the sorted part grows.

```
    MIN                           MAX
    ->                            <-
    || 4   2   7   9  ①    4   2   7  ⑨   1  ||
1:  1  ||  ②   7   9   4    4   2  ⑦   1   ||  9
2:  1   2  ||  7   9  ④    ④   2   1   ||  7   9
3:  1   2   4  ||  9  ⑦    1  ②  ||  4   7   9
4:  1   2   4   7  ||  9    1  ||  2   4   7   9
```

The implementation of the version concerning the minimum is as follows:

```java
static void selectionSortMin(final int[] values)
{
    for (int i = 0; i < values.length - 1; i++)
    {
        int minIdx = i;

        // find minimum
        for (int j = i + 1; j < values.length; j++)
        {
            if (values[j] < values[minIdx])
                minIdx = j;
        }

        // swap current value with minimum
        int tmp = values[minIdx];
        values[minIdx] = values[i];
        values[i] = tmp;
    }
}
```

If you only look at algorithms at this low level, it is usually difficult to understand and comprehend. Of course, the final algorithms used in frameworks must be as optimal as possible. This requires estimations with the O-notation. This is easier to perform on the low level than on the high level since then all constructs, including invoked methods, must be considered. However, to learn and get started, it is much more suitable to program comprehensively first and then optimize in further steps.

OPINION: START WITH COMPREHENSIBILITY

How can selection sort be described on a higher level of abstraction? To do this, I rely on some auxiliary methods we created for arrays in the corresponding chapter's introduction, such as the method swap() for swapping elements, and additionally the method findMinPos() for finding the position of the smallest element, which was created as the solution for exercise 12 in section 5.3.12. By using these methods, the actual procedure becomes almost immediately apparent. You traverse the array from the beginning and, in each case, find the minimum of the remaining part and swap it with the value of the current position:

```java
static void selectionSortMinReadable(final int[] values)
{
    for (int curIdx = 0; curIdx < values.length - 1; curIdx++)
    {
        final int minIdx = findMinPos(values, curIdx, values.length);

        swap(values, minIdx, curIdx);
    }
}
```

To make experiments within JShell easier, the two helper methods defined in the ArrayUtils class are shown here again:

```java
static int findMinPos(int[] values, int startPos, int endPos)
{
    int minPos = startPos;
    for (int i = startPos + 1; i < endPos; i++)
    {
        if (values[i] < values[minPos])
            minPos = i;
    }
    return minPos;
}

static void swap(final int[] values, final int pos1, final int pos2)
{
    final int temp = values[pos1];
```

681

```
        values[pos1] = values[pos2];
        values[pos2] = temp;
}
```

Let's try this out in JShell:

```
jshell> int[] values = { 4, 2, 7, 9, 1 };

jshell> selectionSortMinReadable(values)

jshell> values
values ==> int[5] { 1, 2, 4, 7, 9 }
```

10.2.3 Merge Sort

Merge sort is based on a divide-and-conquer approach. It recursively splits the array
to be sorted into smaller and smaller subarrays of about half the original size until they
consist of only one or possibly no element. Afterwards, the subarrays are combined
again. In this merging step, the sorting is done by the appropriate merging based on the
respective values. The process is illustrated in Figure 10-2.

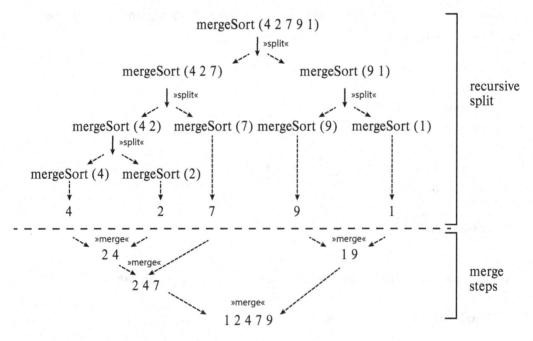

Figure 10-2. Merge sort procedure

The splitting algorithm can be implemented recursively and well comprehensibly, though also somewhat inefficiently, as long as you are allowed to create new arrays. The implementation of the method merge(int[], int[]) was already presented as solution to exercise 11 in section 5.3.11. It is used here:

```
static int[] mergesort(final int[] toSort)
{
    // recursive termination: length 0 (only if initially empty array) or 1
    if (toSort.length <= 1)
        return toSort;

    // recursive descent: divide into two halves
    final int midPos = toSort.length / 2;
    final int[] left = Arrays.copyOfRange(toSort, 0, midPos);
    final int[] resultLeft = mergesort(left);

    final int[] right = Arrays.copyOfRange(toSort, midPos, toSort.length);
    final int[] resultRight = mergesort(right);

    // combine the partial results into larger sorted array
    return merge(resultLeft, resultRight);
}
```

HINT: ANALOGY FROM REAL LIFE LEADS TO OPTIMIZATION

The analogy to sorting a deck of cards is suitable for merge sort as well. If you need to sort a fairly large pile of cards, you can divide it into many, much smaller piles, sort them separately, and then merge them successively. However, instead of reducing the piles down to one card, it is a good idea to sort the smaller piles using another method, often insertion sort, which has a running time of $O(n)$ for small, ideally neatly ordered arrays. This is useful for fine-tuning. Ingeniously, merge sort makes this easy as pie:

```
static int[] mergesortWithInsertionsort(final int[] toSort)
{
    // recursive termination including mini-optimization
    if (toSort.length < 5)
    {
        InsertionSortExample.insertionSort(toSort);
```

```
        return toSort;
    }

    // recursive descent: divide into two halves
    final int midPos = toSort.length / 2;
    final int[] left = Arrays.copyOfRange(toSort, 0, midPos);
    final int[] resultLeft = mergesortWithInsertionsort(left);

    final int[] right = Arrays.copyOfRange(toSort, midPos, toSort.length);
    final int[] resultRight = mergesortWithInsertionsort(right);

    // combine the partial results into larger sorted array
    return merge(resultLeft, resultRight);
}
```

Finally, I would like to point out that the limit at which one should switch to insertion sort has been set here quite arbitrarily to the value 5. Presumably, values between 10 and 20 elements are quite practical. However, it would be best if you rely on the knowledge of algorithm professionals who create mathematically sound estimates for running times.

10.2.4 Quick Sort

Just like merge sort, quick sort is based on a divide-and-conquer approach and splits the array to be sorted into smaller and smaller subarrays. A special element (called a *pivot*) is chosen that determines the grouping or processing. For simplicity, you can choose the first element of the subarray to be sorted as the pivot element, but other ways are conceivable. In quick sort, sorting is done based on this pivot element by arranging all elements of the parts according to their value to the left (less than or equal to) or to the right (greater than) of the pivot. This way, the pivot element is placed in the correct position. The whole process is repeated recursively for the left and right parts until the parts consist of only one element. The process is shown in Figure 10-3.

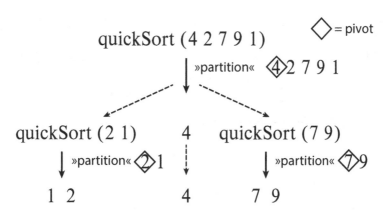

Figure 10-3. *Procedure for quick sort*

Let's start with an implementation for lists since this is more easily accessible and understandable. As a result, breaking down the contents of a list into smaller and larger elements is easy to implement. Later, combining the results of the recursive computations is also straightforward. The whole implementation is intentional. It's not optimized for speed, but for comprehensibility.

For partitioning, you collect all elements that are less than or equal to or greater than the value of the pivot element in one separate result list. To achieve this, you use the Stream API and the following trick: You convert the original list into a Stream<Integer>, skip the first element since it is the pivot element, and then apply appropriate Predicate<Integer>s:

```
static List<Integer> quicksort(final List<Integer> values)
{
    // recursive termination
    if (values.size() <= 1)
        return values;

    // pick up less than or equal to / greater than pivot
    final Integer pivot = values.get(0);
    final List<Integer> belowOrEquals = collectAll(values.stream().skip(1),
                                                   cur -> cur <= pivot);
    final List<Integer> aboves = collectAll(values.stream().skip(1),
                                            cur -> cur > pivot);

    // recursive descent
    final List<Integer> sortedLowersPart = quicksort(belowOrEquals);
```

```
    final List<Integer> sortedUppersPart = quicksort(aboves);

    // assemble
    final List<Integer> result = new ArrayList<>();
    result.addAll(sortedLowersPart); result.add(pivot);
    result.addAll(sortedUppersPart);

    return result;
}
```

Finally, collecting elements and applying the Predicate<Integer>s is implemented by the auxiliary method collectAll() with ease using filter() and collect() from the Stream API as follows:

```
static List<Integer> collectAll(final Stream<Integer> values,
                                final Predicate<Integer> condition)
{
    return values.filter(condition).collect(Collectors.toList());
}
```

The whole thing is quite intuitive for lists and when not optimized for performance. It becomes considerably more awkward if you want to realize the partitioning for arrays inplace (i.e., directly in the original array itself). You can see this for yourself later when solving exercise 6. You will now take a look at the basic procedure.

Inplace Implementation for Arrays

The basic algorithm can be implemented as follows, although the realization of the partitioning, as already mentioned, will be a practice exercise:

```
static void quicksort(final int values[])
{
    quicksort(values, 0, values.length - 1);
}
```

```
public static void quicksort(final int values[], final int begin, final int
end)
{
    // recursive termination
```

```
    if (begin >= end)
        return;

    final int partitionIndex = partition(values, begin, end);

    // recursive descent
    quicksort(values, begin, partitionIndex - 1);
    quicksort(values, partitionIndex + 1, end);
}
```

HINT: AVOIDING SIDE EFFECTS BY COPYING

If the original array should be left unchanged, you can first create a copy of it and then call the inplace method:

```
static int[] quicksortWithCopy(final int[] values)
{
    final int[] copy = Arrays.copyOf(values, values.length);

    quicksort(copy);

    return copy;
}
```

10.2.5 Bucket Sort

Bucket sort is an interesting sorting method whose algorithm is only outlined below since the implementation is the subject of exercise 7.

Bucket sort is a two-step procedure for sorting data. First, the values are collected in special containers (called *buckets*). Then, these values are transferred appropriately into a sorted array. For the algorithm to be feasible, the elements to be sorted must have a limited set of values. For example, this applies to the age information of persons, where you can assume a range of values from 0 to 150.

```
int[] ages = { 10, 50, 22, 7, 42, 111, 50, 7 };
```

This definition of a maximum number of different values means that a corresponding number of containers, the buckets, can store the values or, more precisely, their frequency. One bucket is provided for each possible value.

Step 1: Distribution to buckets   At first, the initial set of data is traversed, and their occurrence is recorded in the buckets. For the age information above, the distribution is as follows:

```
bucket[7] = 2
bucket[10] = 1
bucket[22] = 1
bucket[42] = 1
bucket[50] = 2
bucket[111] = 1
```

All other buckets store the value 0.

Step 2: Preparation of the sorted result   In a final step, the buckets are traversed from the beginning. The respective values are inserted into the result as many times as their number is stored in the bucket. This produces this sorting:

```
int[] result = { 7, 7, 10, 22, 42, 50, 50, 111 };
```

10.2.6 Final Thoughts

Many of the more intuitive algorithms, such as insertion sort and selection sort, possess the disadvantage of having a running time of $O(n^2)$. However, insertion sort has a positive and remarkable feature: As long as the output data is (nearly) sorted, insertion sort becomes extremely performant with $O(n)$.

Quick sort and merge sort are usually very performant with a running time of $O(n \cdot log(n))$. Still, they also have higher complexity of the source code, especially when working inplace. For frameworks and larger datasets, performance is essential. Potentially unfavorable for merge sort, on the other hand, is the creation of many copies of subranges. The same applies to quick sort and its partitioning. For both, however, some variants do this inplace. Interestingly, the respective divisions of the subranges to be sorted are quite easy to express by recursion, but the partitioning or merging part is then more complex and more difficult to implement. This holds, in particular, if you work inplace. For merge sort, you will find an example in the provided Eclipse project. For quick sort, you may try it in exercise 6.

Bucket sort remains. This algorithm sometimes runs even in linear running time. However, in contrast to the other sorting algorithms presented, it is not generally applicable since it has the already mentioned restriction concerning the number of allowed values.

10.3 Exercises

10.3.1 Exercise 1: Contains All (★★☆☆☆)

Analogous to the method `boolean containsAll(Collection<?>)` from the JDK for `Collection<E>`, your task is to implement a `boolean containsAll(int[], int...)` method for arrays. It should check whether all values passed as var args are present in the array.

Examples

Input	Search values	Result
[0, 1, 2, 3, 4, 5, 6, 7, 8, 9]	[7, 2]	True
[0, 1, 2, 3, 4, 5, 6, 7, 8, 9]	[5, 11]	False

10.3.2 Exercise 2: Partitioning (★★★★☆)

The challenge is to suitably sort or arrange a mixed sequence of the letters A and B in a single pass so that all As occur before the Bs. This can also be extended to three letters.

Examples

Input	Result
"ABAABBBAAABBBA"	"AAAAAAABBBBBBB"
"ABACCBBCAACCBBA"	"AAAAABBBBBCCCCC"

Exercise 2a: Partitioning Two Letters (★★★☆☆)

Write method `String partition2(String)` that takes a given sequence built of the two letters A and B given as `String` or `char[]` and turns it into an ordered sequence where all As occur before the Bs.

Exercise 2b: Partitioning Three Letters (★★★★☆)

Write method `String partition3(String)` that partitions a sequence built of the three letters A, B, and C given as `String` into an ordered sequence where all As occur before Bs and they in turn before Cs. Instead of letters, this can be thought of as colors of a flag. Then it is known as the Dutch Flag Problem.

10.3.3 Exercise 3: Binary Search (★★☆☆☆)

Exercise 3a: Binary Search Recursive (★★☆☆☆)

Write recursive method `boolean binarySearch(int[], int)` that performs a search for the desired value in a sorted array.

Examples

Input	Search values	Result
[1, 2, 3, 4, 5, 7, 8, 9]	5	True
[1, 2, 3, 4, 5, 7, 8, 9]	6	False

Exercise 3b: Binary Search Iterative (★★☆☆☆)

Convert the recursive method to an iterative one named `int binarySearchIterative(int[], int)`, with the modification to return the position of the search value or -1 for not found instead of `true` respectively `false`.

Examples

Input	Search values	Result
[1, 2, 3, 4, 5, 7, 8, 9]	5	4
[1, 2, 3, 4, 5, 7, 8, 9]	6	-1

10.3.4 Exercise 4: Insertion Sort (★★☆☆☆)

The introductory section 10.2.1 showed a simplified, easy-to-follow realization of insertion sort. In this exercise, the goal is to optimize the whole thing by now finding the insertion position and performing the necessary swapping and insertion in one go. Write an optimized version of int[] insertionSort(int[]).

Example

Input	Result
[7, 2, 5, 1, 6, 8, 9, 4, 3]	[1, 2, 3, 4, 5, 6, 7, 8, 9]

10.3.5 Exercise 5: Selection Sort (★★☆☆☆)

Write a variation of selection sort that uses the maximum instead of the minimum and that has the following signature: void selectionSortMaxInplace(int[]).

What needs to be modified so that the sort algorithm leaves the original data unchanged and returns a new sorted array? Write method int[] selectionSortMaxCopy(int[]) for this purpose.

Example

Input	Result
[7, 2, 5, 1, 6, 8, 9, 4, 3]	[1, 2, 3, 4, 5, 6, 7, 8, 9]

10.3.6 Exercise 6: Quick Sort (★★★☆☆)

I described quick sort in the introductory section 10.2.4. Whereas the splitting into two ranges with values less than or equal to the pivot elements can be implemented very easily with lists, this is more challenging for arrays. Now the partitioning is to be implemented with the method int partition(int[], int, int). In the following, the already existing source code is shown once again:

```java
static int[] quicksort(final int values[])
{
    quicksort(values, 0, values.length - 1);
    return values;
}

static void quicksort(final int values[], final int begin, final int end)
{
    // recursive termination
    if (begin >= end)
        return;

    final int partitionIndex = partition(values, begin, end);

    // recursive descent
    quicksort(values, begin, partitionIndex - 1);
    quicksort(values, partitionIndex + 1, end);
}
```

Examples

Input	Result
[5, 2, 7, 1, 4, 3, 6, 8]	[1, 2, 3, 4, 5, 6, 7, 8]
[5, 2, 7, 9, 6, 3, 1, 4, 8]	[1, 2, 3, 4, 5, 6, 7, 8, 9]
[5, 2, 7, 9, 6, 3, 1, 4, 2, 3, 8]	[1, 2, 2, 3, 3, 4, 5, 6, 7, 8, 9]

10.3.7 Exercise 7: Bucket Sort (★★☆☆☆)

In the introductory section 10.2.5, bucket sort's algorithm was described. In this exercise, you want to create method `int[] bucketSort(int[], int)` that implements this sorting algorithm for an `int[]` and an expected maximum value.

Example

Input	Maximum value	Result
[10, 50, 22, 7, 42, 111, 50, 7]	150	[7, 7, 10, 22, 42, 50, 50, 111]

10.3.8 Exercise 8: Search in Rotated Data (★★★★☆)

In this exercise, your task is to implement a search in a sorted sequence of integer values. The challenge is that the values are ordered but rotated within themselves. According to that, the smallest element may not be at the front of the data. Additionally, the largest element does often not reside at the end of the data (except in the special case of a rotation by 0 positions).

Tip Be careful also to check the special case of a rotation of 0 or a multiple of the array length, which would again correspond to a rotation for the value 0.

Exercise 8a: Flank Change Efficient (★★★★☆)

Write method `int findFlankPos(int[])` that efficiently finds the position of an flank change in a given sorted sequence of n integer values, say 25, 33, 47, 1, 2, 3, 5, 11, in logarithmic time, that is $O(log(n))$. Write two methods named `int minValue(int[])` and `int maxValue(int[])` based on `int findFlankPos(int[])` that, according to their names, determine the minimum and maximum, respectively, from the given sorted but rotated sequence of values.

Examples

Input	Flank position	Minimum	Maximum
[25, 33, 47, 1, 2, 3, 5, 11]	3	1	47
[5, 11, 17, 25, 1, 2]	4	1	25
[6, 1, 2, 3, 4, 5]	1	1	6
[1, 2, 3, 4, 5, 6]	0 (special case)	1	6

Exercise 8b: Binary Search in Rotated Data (★★★★☆)

Write method int binarySearchRotated(int[], int) that efficiently searches in a sorted sequence of integer values, say the number sequence 25, 33, 47, 1, 2, 3, 5, 11, for a given value and returns its position or -1 if not found.

Examples

Input	Flank position	Search value	Result
[25, 33, 47, 1, 2, 3, 5, 11]	3	47	2
[25, 33, 47, 1, 2, 3, 5, 11]	3	3	5
[25, 33, 47, 1, 2, 3, 5, 11]	3	13	-1
[1, 2, 3, 4, 5, 6, 7]	0 (special case)	5	4
[1, 2, 3, 4, 5, 6, 7]	0 (special case)	13	-1

10.4 Solutions

10.4.1 Solution 1: Contains All (★★☆☆☆)

Analogous to the method boolean containsAll(Collection<?>) from the JDK for Collection<E>, your task is to implement a boolean containsAll(int[], int...) method for arrays. It should check whether all values passed as var args are present in the array.

Examples

Input	Search values	Result
[0, 1, 2, 3, 4, 5, 6, 7, 8, 9]	[7, 2]	True
[0, 1, 2, 3, 4, 5, 6, 7, 8, 9]	[5, 11]	False

Algorithm   In section 10.1.1 the method boolean contains(int[], int) was created. For your implementation, you call it repeatedly for all elements passed in to check for containment:

```java
static boolean containsAll(final int[] values, final int... searchFor)
{
    for (int current : searchFor)
    {
        if (!ArrayUtils.contains(values, current))
            return false;
    }
    return true;
}
```

Verification

Let's define an int[] with the numbers from 0 to 9 and check if the values 7 and 2, as well as 5 and 11, are present there:

```java
@ParameterizedTest(name = "containsAll({0}, {1}) => {2}")
@MethodSource("createInputsAndExpected")
void containsAll(int[] values, int[] searchvalues, boolean expected)
{
    boolean result = Ex01_ContainsAll.containsAll(values, searchvalues);

    assertEquals(expected, result);
}

private static Stream<Arguments> createInputsAndExpected()
{
    final int[] values = { 0, 1, 2, 3, 4, 5, 6, 7, 8, 9 };
```

```
final int[] searchValues1 = { 7, 2 };
final int[] searchValues2 = { 5, 11 };

return Stream.of(Arguments.of(values, searchValues1, true),
                 Arguments.of(values, searchValues2, false));
}
```

10.4.2 Solution 2: Partitioning (★★★☆☆)

The challenge is to suitably sort or arrange a mixed sequence of the letters A and B in a single pass so that all As occur before the Bs. This can also be extended to three letters.

Examples

Input	Result
"ABAABBBAAABBBA"	"AAAAAAABBBBBBB"
"ABACCBBCAACCBBA"	"AAAAABBBBBCCCCC"

Solution 2a: Partitioning Two Letters (★★☆☆☆)

Write method String partition2(String) that takes a given sequence build out of the two letters A and B given as String or char[] and turns it into an ordered sequence where all As occur before the Bs.

Algorithm   Although one is initially tempted to compare all possible positions, an ingenious and performant solution exists, which solves the task in one pass. You work with two position pointers, *low* and *high*, which mark the front and back position, in this case, the valid range given by the rearmost As and the foremost Bs. When an A is found, its position is incremented. When a B is found, it is swapped to the back. Afterwards, the position pointer of the Bs is decreased, expanding the already correctly divided area.

```
static String partition2(final String charValues)
{
    return partition2(charValues.toCharArray());
}
```

```
static String partition2(final char[] charValues)
{
    int low = 0;
    int high = charValues.length - 1;

    while (low <= high)
    {
        if (charValues[low] == 'A')
            low++;
        else
        {
            ArraysUtils.swap(charValues, low, high);

            high--;
        }
    }
    return new String(charValues);
}
```

Because a B may also move to the front when swapping, the lower position pointer must stay unchanged. In one of the next steps, the B will then move to the back again.

This tricky algorithm makes it possible to arrange all As in front of the Bs in a single pass.

Solution 2b: Partitioning Three Letters (★★★☆☆)

Write method `String partition3(String)` that partitions a sequence build of the three letters A, B, and C given as `String` into an ordered sequence where all As occur before Bs and they in turn before Cs. Instead of letters, this can be thought of as colors of a flag. Then it is known as the Dutch Flag Problem.

Algorithm   The extension from two to three letters (or colors) employs similar ideas as before, but with a few more tricks and special treatments. You start again at the beginning of the array but using the three position markers *low*, *mid*, and *high*. Initially, they are located for the first and middle character at position 0; the one for *high* is at the end position. If an A is found, the position for *low* and *mid* shift by one to the right. Before that, the last character from the lower range is swapped with the current (middle) one. If one reads a B, only the middle position is shifted towards the end. If the current character is a C, this is swapped to the back. The position marker for the upper area is then reduced by 1.

```java
static String partition3(final String input)
{
    final char[] charValues = input.toCharArray();
    int low = 0;
    int mid = 0;
    int high = charValues.length - 1;

    while (mid <= high)
    {
        if (charValues[mid] == 'A')
        {
            ArraysUtils.swap(charValues, low, mid);

            low++;
            mid++;
        }
        else if (charValues[mid] == 'B')
            mid++;
        else
        {
            ArraysUtils.swap(charValues, mid, high);

            high--;
            // low, mid must remain unchanged, because also a B or C
            // can be swapped to the front
        }
    }
    return new String(charValues);

}
```

Verification

To check functionality, you use two strings consisting of a shuffled sequence of the letters A and B or A, B, and C, respectively:

```
@Test
public void testPartition2()
{
    final String result = Ex02_FlagPartitioning.partition2("ABAABBBAAABBBA");

    assertEquals("AAAAAAABBBBBBB", result);
}

@Test
public void testPartition3()
{
    final String result = Ex02_FlagPartitioning.partition3("ABACCBBCAACCBBA");

    assertEquals("AAAAABBBBBCCCCC", result);
}
```

10.4.3 Solution 3: Binary Search (★★☆☆☆)

Solution 3a: Binary Search Recursive (★★☆☆☆)

Write recursive method boolean binarySearch(int[], int) that performs a search for the desired value in a sorted array.

Examples

Input	Search values	Result
[1, 2, 3, 4, 5, 7, 8, 9]	5	True
[1, 2, 3, 4, 5, 7, 8, 9]	6	False

Algorithm   Divide the array into two halves. Determine the value in the middle and see if you need to search further in the top or bottom half. This can be easily determined based on the given sort order:

$$value_{center} \quad == searchvalue \quad \rightarrow \quad \text{found, end}$$
$$value_{center} \quad < searchvalue \quad \Rightarrow \quad \text{continue searching at top}$$
$$value_{middle} \quad > searchvalue \quad \Rightarrow \quad \text{continue searching at the bottom}$$

The implementation in Java strictly follows the description. As usual, be especially careful at the boundaries of the array to avoid making careless mistakes.

```
static boolean binarySearch(final int[] sortedValues,
                            final int searchValue)
{
    final int midPos = sortedValues.length / 2;

    // recursive termination
    if (searchValue == sortedValues[midPos])
        return true;

    if (sortedValues.length > 1) // there are still at least 2 numbers
    {
        if (searchValue < sortedValues[midPos])
        {
            // recursive descent: search further in the lower part
            final int[] lowerHalf = Arrays.copyOfRange(sortedValues, 0, midPos);

            return binarySearch(lowerHalf, searchValue);

        }
        if (searchValue > sortedValues[midPos])
        {
            // recursive descent: continue search in the upper part
            final int[] upperHalf = Arrays.copyOfRange(sortedValues,
                                        midPos + 1, sortedValues.length);

            return binarySearch(upperHalf, searchValue);
        }
    }
    return false;
}
```

Optimized algorithm   The solution shown is not really optimal because parts of the original array are permanently copied to perform further searches. The entire process can be done completely without the potentially time-consuming copying of arrays with the help of two index variables. The following solution is certainly preferable:

```java
static boolean binarySearchOptimized(final int[] values, final int searchValue)
{
    return binarySearchOptimized(values, searchValue, 0, values.length - 1);
}

static boolean binarySearchOptimized(final int[] values, final int searchValue,
                                     final int left, final int right)
{
    if (right >= left)
    {
        final int midIdx = (left + right) / 2;

        if (searchValue == values[midIdx])
            return true;

        // recursive descent: search in the lower / upper part further
        if (searchValue < values[midIdx])
            return binarySearchOptimized(values, searchValue,
            left, midIdx - 1);
        else
            return binarySearchOptimized(values, searchValue,
            midIdx + 1, right);
    }
    return false;
}
```

Solution 3b: Binary Search Iterative (★★☆☆☆)

Convert the recursive method to an iterative one named int
binarySearchIterative(int[], int), with the modification to return the position of
the search value or -1 for not found instead of true respectively false.

Examples

Input	Search values	Result
[1, 2, 3, 4, 5, 7, 8, 9]	5	4
[1, 2, 3, 4, 5, 7, 8, 9]	6	-1

Algorithm   Based on the recursive version just shown, the iterative implementation may be derived quite easily. You use two position markers, *left* and *right* for left and right, which initially start at the beginning and end (position 0 and *length* − 1). These two markers determine the respective index boundaries in which further searching is performed. At first, you compare the value in the middle with the searched one. If the values are equal, you return the index. Otherwise, you divide the search area into two parts and continue until either the search is successful or the left and right position markers cross each other.

```
static int binarySearchIterative(final int[] values, final int searchValue)
{
    int left = 0;
    int right = values.length - 1;

    while (right >= left)
    {
        int midIdx = (left + right) / 2;

        if (searchValue == values[midIdx])
            return midIdx;

        if (searchValue < values[midIdx])
            right = midIdx - 1;
        else
            left = midIdx + 1;
    }

    return -1;
}
```

Verification

For testing, you use the following inputs, which show the correct operation:

```
@ParameterizedTest(name = "searching in {0} for {1} => {2}")
@MethodSource("createInputsAndExpected")
void containsAll(int[] values, int searchFor, boolean expected)
{
    boolean result = Ex03_BinarySearch.binarySearch(values, searchFor);

    assertEquals(expected, result);
}

private static Stream<Arguments> createInputsAndExpected()
{
    final int[] values = { 1, 2, 3, 4, 5, 7, 8, 9 };

    return Stream.of(Arguments.of(values, 5, true),
                     Arguments.of(values, 6, false));
}

@Test
void binarySearchIterative_should_return_pos()
{
    final int[] values = { 1, 2, 3, 4, 5, 7, 8, 9 };

    int result = Ex03_BinarySearch.binarySearchIterative(values, 5);

    assertEquals(4, result);
}

@Test
void binarySearchIterative_no_value()
{
    final int[] values = { 1, 2, 3, 4, 5, 7, 8, 9 };

    int result = Ex03_BinarySearch.binarySearchIterative(values, 6);

    assertEquals(-1, result);
}
```

To make things a little more interesting, let's take a look at the unit test and its execution in the IDE. See Figure 10-4.

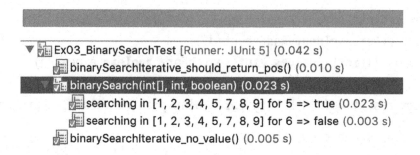

Figure 10-4. *Results of the test execution for binary search*

10.4.4 Solution 4: Insertion Sort (★★☆☆☆)

The introductory section 10.2.1 showed a simplified, easy-to-follow realization of insertion sort. In this exercise, the goal is to optimize the whole thing by now finding the insertion position and performing the necessary swapping and insertion in one go. Write an optimized version of int[] insertionSort(int[]).

Example

Input	Result
[7, 2, 5, 1, 6, 8, 9, 4, 3]	[1, 2, 3, 4, 5, 6, 7, 8, 9]

Algorithm   For all elements, you perform the following procedure, which is described exemplarily for the value sequence **24317**: Let's consider 3 as the value to be sorted in. You have to swap with the left neighbor starting from its position as long as the neighbor's value is greater than the current one. You have not yet reached the very front in the array in this case, so you swap the 3 only with the 4. Next, you need to swap the 1 all the way to the front. Finally, the 7 is already in the right position.

```
static void insertionSort(final int[] values)
{
    for (int i = 1; i < values.length; i++)
    {
```

```
    // check if current element is larger than predecessor
    int currentIdx = i;
    while (currentIdx > 0 && values[currentIdx - 1] > values[currentIdx])
    {
        swap(values, currentIdx - 1, currentIdx); currentIdx--;
    }
    }
}
```

Verification

You verify that the implementation produces the desired result for the given sequence of numbers using a unit test:

```
@Test
void testInsertionSort()
{
    final int[] values = { 7, 2, 5, 1, 6, 8, 9, 4, 3 };
    final int[] expected = { 1, 2, 3, 4, 5, 6, 7, 8, 9 };

    Ex04_InsertionSort.insertionSort(values);

    assertArrayEquals(expected, values);
}
```

10.4.5 Solution 5: Selection Sort (★★☆☆☆)

Write a variation of selection sort that uses the maximum instead of the minimum and that has the following signature: void selectionSortMaxInplace(int[]).

What needs to be modified so that the sort algorithm leaves the original data unchanged and returns a new sorted array? Write method int[] selectionSortMaxCopy(int[]) for this purpose.

Example

Input	Result
[7, 2, 5, 1, 6, 8, 9, 4, 3]	[1, 2, 3, 4, 5, 6, 7, 8, 9]

Algorithm   The array to be sorted is traversed from back to front while the largest element in each case is moved back to the current position. By calling the method findMaxPos(), you determine the position of the maximum from the remaining unsorted subrange. This method was created as a solution to exercise 12 in section 5.3.12. Subsequently, the element is moved to the back accordingly by swapping it with the current element. This reduces the size of the remaining not-yet-sorted part until it consists only of the foremost element.

```
static void selectionSortMaxInplace(final int[] values)
{
    for (int i = values.length - 1; i > 0 ; i--)
    {
        final int maxPos = ArraysUtils.findMaxPos(values, 0, i + 1);

        ArraysUtils.swap(values, maxPos, i);
    }
}
```

The method with the copy functionality is trivial to implement if you have created the previous method:

```
static int[] selectionSortMaxCopy(final int[] values)
{
    final int[] copy = Arrays.copyOf(values, values.length);

    selectionSortMaxInplace(copy);

    return copy;
}
```

Verification

You verify that the implementation produces the desired result for the given sequence of numbers using a unit test:

```
@Test
void selectionSortMaxInplace()
{
    final int[] values = { 7, 2, 5, 1, 6, 8, 9, 4, 3 };
    final int[] expected = { 1, 2, 3, 4, 5, 6, 7, 8, 9 };

    Ex05_SelectionSort.selectionSortMaxInplace(values);

    assertArrayEquals(expected, values);
}
```

10.4.6 Solution 6: Quick Sort (★★★☆☆)

I described quick sort in the introductory section 10.2.4. Whereas the splitting into two ranges with values less than or equal to the pivot elements can be implemented very easily with lists, this is more challenging for arrays. Now the partitioning is to be implemented with the method int partition(int[], int, int). In the following, the already existing source code is shown once again:

```
static void quicksort(final int values[])
{
    quicksort(values, 0, values.length - 1);
}

static void quicksort(final int values[], final int begin, final int end)
{
    // recursive termination
    if (begin >= end)
        return;

    final int partitionIndex = partition(values, begin, end);
```

```
// recursive descent
quicksort(values, begin, partitionIndex - 1);
quicksort(values, partitionIndex + 1, end);
}
```

Examples

Input	Result
[5, 2, 7, 1, 4, 3, 6, 8]	[1, 2, 3, 4, 5, 6, 7, 8]
[5, 2, 7, 9, 6, 3, 1, 4, 8]	[1, 2, 3, 4, 5, 6, 7, 8, 9]
[5, 2, 7, 9, 6, 3, 1, 4, 2, 3, 8]	[1, 2, 2, 3, 3, 4, 5, 6, 7, 8, 9]

Algorithm   Your goal is to subdivide an array (or a range of an array) into two parts by passing the lower start and upper end index and choosing a value at a special position (e.g., the foremost element) as the pivot element. Now the two parts are rearranged. All elements with values smaller than or equal to the pivot element should reside in the lower part. Furthermore, all elements with a value larger than the pivot element should reside in the upper part. Here, the two indices *leftIndex* and *rightIndex* each move inward as long as the conditions *values*[*leftIndex*] <= *pivot* hold for left and *pivot* < *values*[*rightIndex*] for right. If an inappropriately ordered element is found on the left side, the examination starts on the right side. If an inappropriately ordered element is found here as well, the two are swapped. This process is repeated as long as the position markers do not cross each other. Finally, the element from the *rightIndex* position is swapped with the pivot element. There is also the special case that the array has only two elements. In this case, you also have to make sure that the right value is actually larger than that of the pivot.

```
static int partition(final int[] values, final int left, final int right)
{
    final int pivot = values[left];

    int leftIndex = left + 1;
    int rightIndex = right;

    while (leftIndex < rightIndex)
```

```
{
    // move the position leftIndex to the right, as long as value
    // less than or equal to pivot and left limit less than right limit
    while (values[leftIndex] <= pivot && leftIndex < rightIndex)
    {
        leftIndex++;
    }

    // move the position rightIndex to the left, as long as value greater
    // than pivot and right limit greater than or equal to left limit
    while (pivot < values[rightIndex] && rightIndex >= leftIndex)
    {
     rightIndex--;
    }

    if (leftIndex < rightIndex)
        ArrayUtils.swap(values, leftIndex, rightIndex);
}

// special case 2-element array with wrong sorting, but no
// pass (leftIndex == rightIndex) as well as normal case at the very end
if (values[rightIndex] < pivot)
    ArrayUtils.swap(values, left, rightIndex);

return rightIndex;
}
```

Verification

Define the three arrays from the introductory examples and use them to check your implementation of quick sort:

```
@ParameterizedTest(name = "{0} should be sorted to {1}")
@MethodSource("createInputAndExpected")
void testQuicksort(int[] values, int[] expected)
{
    // inplace
    Ex06_Quicksort.quicksort(values);
```

```
        assertArrayEquals(expected, values);
}

private static Stream<Arguments> createInputAndExpected()
{
    return Stream.of(Arguments.of(new int[] { 5, 2, 7, 1, 4, 3, 6, 8 },
                           new int[] { 1, 2, 3, 4, 5, 6, 7, 8 }),
                   Arguments.of(new int[] { 5, 2, 7, 9, 6, 3, 1, 4, 8 },
                           new int[] { 1, 2, 3, 4, 5, 6, 7, 8, 9 }),
                   Arguments.of(new int[] { 5, 2, 7, 9, 6, 3, 1, 4, 2,
                                    3, 8 },
                           new int[] { 1, 2, 2, 3, 3, 4, 5, 6, 7,
                                    8, 9 }));
}
```

10.4.7 Solution 7: Bucket Sort (★★☆☆☆)

In the introductory section 10.2.5, the bucket sort algorithm was described. In this exercise, you want to create method int[] bucketSort(int[], int) that implements this sorting algorithm for an int[] and an expected maximum value.

Example

Input	Maximum value	Result
[10, 50, 22, 7, 42, 111, 50, 7]	150	[7, 7, 10, 22, 42, 50, 50, 111]

Algorithm   Bucket sort is one of the most straightforward sorting algorithms to implement and also one of the fastest with a linear running time, but with the prerequisite of a limited range of values.

First, you create all buckets that store the count of values. Afterwards, bucket sort is implemented in two steps:

1. Traverse all input values and assign them to the corresponding buckets. If there are several of the same elements, you have to increment the counter.

2. The final step is to reconstruct the values based on the counter values.

The described procedure is implemented in Java as follows:

```java
static int[] bucketSort(final int[] values, final int expectedMax)
{
    final int[] buckets = new int[expectedMax + 1];
    collectIntoBuckets(values, buckets);

    final int[] results = new int[values.length];
    fillResultFromBuckets(buckets, results);

    return results;
}
```

The algorithm is thereby described in its basic characteristics. Only the implementation of the two helper methods remains, which is also done straightforwardly. To calculate the count of the respective numbers, you have to iterate through the original array and increment the counter in the bucket corresponding to the current value:

```java
static void collectIntoBuckets(final int[] values, final int[] buckets)
{
    for (int current : values)
    {
        buckets[current]++;
    }
}
```

Based on the quantities in the buckets, the generation of the result is just a little bit more complex. For this purpose, you traverse all buckets. If index i contains a quantity greater than 0, this index value has to be copied to the target as often as specified there. In this case, it's solved by the while loop. You only have to carry the position in the target array separately.

```java
static void fillResultFromBuckets(final int[] buckets, final int[] results)
{
    int resultPos = 0;
    for (int i = 0; i < buckets.length; i++)
    {
        int count = buckets[i];
```

```
    while (count > 0)
    {
        results[resultPos] = i;

        count--;
        resultPos++;
    }
  }
}
```

Verification

You write a short test method to check your implementation of bucket sort with some values:

```
@Test
void testBucketSort()
{
    final int[] values = { 10, 50, 22, 7, 42, 111, 50, 7 };
    final int max = 150;
    final int[] expected = { 7, 7, 10, 22, 42, 50, 50, 111 };

    final int[] result = Ex07_BucketSort.bucketSort(values, max);

    assertArrayEquals(expected, result);
}
```

10.4.8 Solution 8: Search in Rotated Data (★★★★☆)

In this exercise, your task is to implement a search in a sorted sequence of integer values. The challenge is that the values are ordered but rotated within themselves. According to that, the smallest element may not be at the front of the data. Additionally, the largest element does often not reside at the end of the data (except in the special case of a rotation by 0 positions).

Tip   Be careful also to check the special case of a rotation of 0 or a multiple of the array length, which would again correspond to a rotation for the value 0.

Solution 8a: Flank Change Efficient (★★★★☆)

Write method int findFlankPos(int[]) that efficiently finds the position of an flank change in a given sorted sequence of *n* integer values, say 25, 33, 47, 1, 2, 3, 5, 11, in logarithmic time, that is $O(log(n))$. Write two methods named int minValue(int[]) and int maxValue(int[]) based on int findFlankPos(int[]) that, according to their names, determine the minimum and maximum, respectively, from the given sorted but rotated sequence of values.

Examples

Input	Flank position	Minimum	Maximum
[25, 33, 47, 1, 2, 3, 5, 11]	3	1	47
[5, 11, 17, 25, 1, 2]	4	1	25
[6, 1, 2, 3, 4, 5]	1	1	6
[1, 2, 3, 4, 5, 6]	0 (special case)	1	6

Preliminary considerations for the algorithm: Let's start with the brute-force version of linear search to check your optimized version against it later on. For the search, you only need to check each element from front to back to determine if the successor of a value is smaller than the current element:

```
static int findFlankPosSimple(final int[] values)
{
    for (int i = 0; i < values.length; i++)
    {
        final int nextIdx = (i + 1) % values.length;
        if (values[i] > values[nextIdx])
            return nextIdx;
    }
    throw new IllegalStateException("should never reach here!");
}
```

Of course, when traversing, you also have to consider the special case that the flank change takes place at the very end of the array, so then you have a non-rotated array as a base.

Algorithm   So, how can you proceed to achieve a logarithmic running time? In this case, you take advantage of the fact that the value sequence is sorted. The search ranges can always be divided in half, following the idea of binary search. Because there is a rotation, however, you must be careful concerning the indices.

There are three comparisons to be made:

- **Case A: With the predecessor**: If it is larger, you have found the flank change.

- **Case B: With the leftmost element**: If it is larger than the current element, then the flank change must happen somewhere in between. So, you can exclude the right half.

- **Case C: With the rightmost element**: If this is smaller, the flank change must happen on the right side. You can exclude the left half.

At the very beginning, it is crucial to check for the special case of the non-rotated initial dataset. This can be determined by the fact that the far left value is smaller than that on the far right.

With these preliminary considerations, the following implementation emerges:

```
static int findFlankPos(final int[] values)
{
    return findFlankPosRec(values, 0, values.length - 1);
}

static int findFlankPosRec(final int[] values, final int left,
                           final int right)
{
    final int midPos = left + (right - left) / 2;
    final int midValue = values[midPos];

    // special case no rotation
    if (values[left] < values[right])
        return 0;

    // case A: value to the left of this is larger, then you got a flank change
    int prevIndex = midPos - 1;
    if (prevIndex < 0)
        prevIndex = values.length - 1;
```

```
    if (values[prevIndex] > midValue)
        return midPos;

    if (values[left] > midValue)
    {
        // case B: flank change must be on the left, since first value
        // larger than in the middle
        return findFlankPosRec(values, left, midPos + 1);
    }
    if (values[right] < midValue)
    {
        // case C: flank change must be on the right, as last value
        // smaller than in the middle
        return findFlankPosRec(values, midPos + 1, right);
    }
    throw new IllegalStateException("should never reach here!");
}
```

Based on this method, it is possible to write the methods for determining minimum and maximum quite simply as follows with the knowledge that the position of the flank change contains the minimum and the position of the maximum is a position to the left of it. For a rotation of 0, a small correction must still be made.

```
static int minValue(final int[] values)
{
    final int flankpos = findFlankPos(values);
    return values[flankpos];
}

static int maxValue(final int[] values)
{
    int flankpos = findFlankPos(values);
    // for rotation0 move after the end
    if (flankpos == 0)
        flankpos = values.length;
    return values[flankpos - 1];
}
```

Verification

You test the determination of the flank change using the following parameterized test. In particular, the special case of non-rotated input values is also verified. Likewise, you test the two methods for determining the minimum and maximum.

```java
@ParameterizedTest(name = "findFlankPos({0}) => {2}")
@MethodSource("createInputAndExpected")
void findFlankPos(int[] values, int expected)
{
    int flankpos = Ex08_RotatedSearch.findFlankPos(values);

    assertEquals(expected, flankpos);
}

private static Stream<Arguments> createInputAndExpected()
{
    return Stream.of(Arguments.of(new int[] { 25, 33, 47, 1, 2, 3, 5, 11 }, 3),
                     Arguments.of(new int[] { 6, 7, 1, 2, 3, 4, 5 }, 2),
                     Arguments.of(new int[] { 1, 2, 3, 4, 5, 6, 7 }, 0));
}

@ParameterizedTest(name = "minmax({0}) => min: {1} / max: {2}")
@MethodSource("createInputAndExpectedMinAndMax")
void minmax(int[] values, int expectedMin, int expectedMax)
{
    int min = Ex08_RotatedSearch.minValue(values);
    int max = Ex08_RotatedSearch.maxValue(values);

    assertAll(() -> assertEquals(expectedMin, min),
              () -> assertEquals(expectedMax, max));
}

private static Stream<Arguments> createInputAndExpectedMinAndMax()
{
    return Stream.of(Arguments.of(new int[] { 25, 33, 47, 1, 2, 3, 5, 11 },
                                  1, 47),
```

```
Arguments.of(new int[] { 6, 7, 1, 2, 3, 4, 5 }, 1, 7),
Arguments.of(new int[] { 1, 2, 3, 4, 5, 6, 7 }, 1, 7));
}
```

Solution 8b: Binary Search in Rotated Data (★★★★☆)

Write method int binarySearchRotated(int[], int) that efficiently searches in a sorted sequence of integer values, say the number sequence 25, 33, 47, 1, 2, 3, 5, 11, for a given value and returns its position or -1 if not found.

Examples

Input	Flank position	Search value	Result
[25, 33, 47, 1, 2, 3, 5, 11]	3	47	2
[25, 33, 47, 1, 2, 3, 5, 11]	3	3	5
[25, 33, 47, 1, 2, 3, 5, 11]	3	13	-1
[1, 2, 3, 4, 5, 6, 7]	0 (special case)	5	4
[1, 2, 3, 4, 5, 6, 7]	0 (special case)	13	-1

Algorithm   After being able to efficiently determine the flank change in $O(log(n))$, one possibility is to enlarge the array. Thereby one cuts out the front part of the array and appends it at the end (this is feasible for medium-sized arrays). Afterwards, you can invoke a binary search, which was developed in exercise 3.

```
25 | 27 | 33 | 2 | 3 | 5     =>     | 2 | 3 | 5 | 25 | 27 | 33
```

However, this procedure causes quite a bit of effort. So how can you improve it?

For this purpose, you adapt the binary search to specify a lower and upper bound. You pick up the idea of the array expansion but make it virtual. Let's take a look at the example of the search for 47 in the number sequence shown in the exercise; see Figure 10-5.

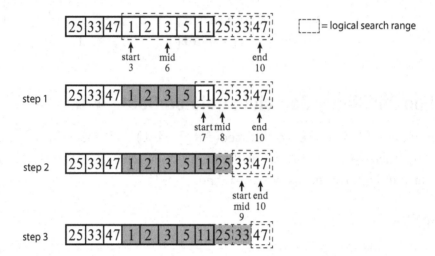

Figure 10-5. *Rotated binary search procedure*

Based on these preliminary ideas, you proceed with the binary search. First, you determine the position of the flank change and use it to specify your search value range. Now you perform a normal binary search, but you use the modulo operator to bring the extended value range back into the array boundaries and determine the comparison value based on this.

```
static int binarySearchRotated(final int[] values, final int searchFor)
{
    final int flankpos = findFlankPos(values);

    return binarySearchRotatedHelper(values, searchFor,
                                     flankpos, flankpos - 1 + values.length);
}

static int binarySearchRotatedHelper(final int[] values, final int searchFor,
                                     final int start, final int end)
{
    if (start > end)
        return -1;

    final int midPos = start + (end - start) / 2;
    final int midValue = values[midPos % values.length];

    if (midValue == searchFor)
        return adjustedMid;
```

```
if (searchFor < midValue)
{
    return binarySearchRotatedHelper(values, searchFor,
                                     start, midPos - 1);
}

if (searchFor > midValue)
{
    return binarySearchRotatedHelper(values, searchFor,
                                     midPos + 1, end);
}
throw new IllegalStateException("should never reach here!");
}
```

Verification

To check the functionality, you use the value combinations from the introductory example:

```
@ParameterizedTest(name = "binarySearchRotated({0}) => {2}")
@MethodSource("createInputsAndExpected")
void binarySearchRotated(int[] values, int searchFor, int expected)
{
    int flankpos = Ex08_RotatedSearch.binarySearchRotated(values, searchFor);

    assertEquals(expected, flankpos);
}

private static Stream<Arguments> createInputsAndExpected()
{
    int[] inputs1 = { 25, 33, 47, 1, 2, 3, 5, 11 };
    int[] inputs2 = { 1, 2, 3, 4, 5, 6, 7 };

    return Stream.of(Arguments.of(inputs1, 47, 2),
                     Arguments.of(inputs1, 3, 5),
                     Arguments.of(inputs1, 13, -1),
                     Arguments.of(inputs2, 5, 4),
                     Arguments.of(inputs2, 13, -1));
}
```

## CHAPTER 11

Conclusion and Supplementary Literature

Now, having reached the end of this exercise book, we conclude. However, I will present two more puzzles before we have a look at the supplementary literature.

11.1 Conclusion

By reading this book, and especially by solving and implementing the exercises, you should have gained plenty of experience. With this knowledge, various tasks from daily practice should now be somewhat easier to complete. Of course, you will profit most if you don't just follow the solutions presented, but also experiment and modify them.

11.1.1 Lessons Learned per Chapter

Let's recap what was taught in each chapter and topic, and what you should have learned.

Mathematical   The chapter on basic mathematical knowledge introduced the modulo operator, which is quite essential, for example, for the extraction of digits and in the calculation of checksums. The exercises on combinatorics have shown how small tricks can easily reduce the running time by order of magnitude. Also, the prime numbers offer some interesting facets, for example, variants to their calculation. In retrospect, this turns out to be much easier than perhaps first thought. In general, for every problem, the algorithm and the approach should be roughly understood because then, for example, even the decomposition into prime factors loses its possible horror.

© Michael Inden 2022
M. Inden, *Java Challenges*, https://doi.org/10.1007/978-1-4842-7395-1_11

Recursion   The introductory chapter on recursion laid the foundations for a good understanding. Many exercises have expanded your knowledge. Additionally, you were able to use the acquired basic knowledge profitably in the following chapters. A prime example is various algorithms on trees, which can often be easily expressed recursively—iteratively, for example, a postorder traversal is already challenging, whereas with recursion, it is effortless.

However, you have also recognized that simple recursion not only has advantages, but also sometimes requires some patience due to long running times. In the advanced chapter on recursion, you significantly expanded your toolbox with memoization and backtracking. This allowed you to increase performance and to solve entertaining and amusing puzzles, such as Sudoku puzzles or the n-Queens problem. It was also possible to find a way out of a maze. All this required a bit more programming effort but could be implemented without too much complexity.

Strings   Strings are an integral part of almost every program. Besides simple tasks for palindrome checking or string reversing, some tasks could be significantly simplified using suitable auxiliary data structures, such as checking for well-formed braces, converting a word into Morse code, and more. In general, it is already noticeable here that solving problems is becoming easier due to the more basic knowledge you have in different areas.

Arrays   Just like strings, arrays are basic building blocks in many programs. In particular, it is important to avoid tricky off-by-one errors. In this chapter, you created small helper methods that, when used appropriately, can make algorithms more understandable. For two-dimensional arrays, you learned, among other things, how to model directions and how this helps filling areas with patterns. More challenging tasks were the spiral traversal as well as the deletion and filling of a Jewels or Minesweeper playfield. Finally, you developed some functionality for merging arrays. This is an elementary component for Merge Sort.

Date processing   While the processing of date values was rather cumbersome before Java 8, the Date and Time API makes it convenient. Besides the basics of the API you learned about calculations, especially the various possibilities with the `TemporalAdjuster`-based *time machines*. Using appropriate helper methods makes it even possible to implement the output of a calendar page comprehensively.

Basic data structures   This chapter deepened your knowledge of basic data structures like lists, sets, and maps. This knowledge is essential in business applications. But not only individually but also in combination, they are useful for solving many tasks, such as the deletion of duplicates from lists. In addition, the task of the magic triangle, for example, trains abstract thinking. A small delicacy was to program the auto-completion of Excel itself. It is quite surprising what an elegant implementation this results in.

Binary trees   Probably the most complex topic in this book is binary trees. Since the Collections framework does not provide them, they are probably not familiar to every Java developer. However, because binary trees are suitable to solve many problems elegantly, this chapter gave an introduction. The exercises helped you to get to know binary trees and their possibilities. Besides straightforward things like rotation, mathematical calculations, for example, can be represented and processed very smartly using binary trees. Something to puzzle over was certainly the determination of the least common ancestor. This is especially true for the check for completeness and the graphical output of a binary tree.

Search and sort   Nowadays, you will hardly program a search or sorting algorithm yourself. Still, it is helpful for the algorithmic understanding to have dealt with it once. While naive implementations often have a running time of $O(n^2)$, this can usually be reduced to $O(n \cdot log(n))$ with Merge Sort and Quick Sort. It is fascinating to see how a fixed range of values can have a significant effect. Bucket Sort with a running time of $O(n)$ plays out its strengths with these constraints.

11.1.2 Noteworthy

When presenting the solutions, I have sometimes deliberately shown a wrong way or a suboptimal brute force variant to demonstrate the learning effect when working on an improvement. In everyday work, too, it is often preferable to proceed iteratively because the requirements may not be 100 % precise, new requests arise, etc. Therefore it is a good idea to start with a comprehensible implementation of the task, which allows it to be modified afterward without any problems. It is often even acceptable to take a not-yet-optimal solution that handles the problem in a conceptually correct way.

Thoughts on Maintainability

One also observes the following: Source code is usually read much more often than it is written. Think about your daily work routine. Usually, you do not start on the greenfield but extend an existing system with some functionality or fix a bug. You will appreciate it if the original program author has chosen comprehensible solutions and program constructs. Ideally, even unit tests exist as a safety net.

Let's get back to development. Make sure that you think about the problem in advance instead of starting directly with the implementation. The more structured and precise you have thought through a problem, the clearer your implementation will be. Once the *penny has dropped*, it is often not too big a step to create or improve an understandable, well-structured solution. However, if you start too early with an implementation simply as source code, this unfortunately too often ends in a disaster and a failure. As a result, some things remain rather half-baked, and it gets harder to add functionality in a meaningful way.

I like to point out that especially traceability and later simplified maintainability are very important in programming. This is achieved generally by small, as-comprehensible-as-practical building blocks. With the potentially (and presumably only) minimally poorer performance as well as the lower compactness, this is often easier to live with than with a fairly certain poor maintainability.

Thoughts on Performance

Keep in mind that in today's world of distributed applications, the impact of individual instructions or unoptimized methods on performance is negligible. By contrast, too frequent or too fine-grained REST calls or database accesses may have a much more serious impact on execution time over an algorithm that has not been optimized down to the last detail. Please note: My statements apply primarily to self-written functionalities in business applications. For frameworks and algorithms that experience millions of calls (or more), however, the inner beauty is potentially less important than their performance. There will probably always be a certain trade-off between the two poles: either compact and performance-optimized or understandable but sometimes a bit slower.

Advantages of Unit Tests

Even when creating only simple programs, one often notices the following fact all over again: If you test implementations of algorithms purely based on console output, errors often remain unnoticed—mainly for special cases, limits, and so on. Moreover, without supporting unit tests, people tend to think less about the interfaces of classes and methods' signatures. But this is exactly what helps to increase manageability for others. Since JUnit 5, writing unit tests has become really fun and smooth. This is mainly due to the pleasant and helpful parameterized tests.

By reading this book and reviewing the solutions, you should have gained a good understanding of unit testing in addition to your skills in the topics covered. Even more, when developing solutions, there is a sense of security when the unit tests pass.

11.2 Puzzles

After you have dealt with a wide variety of programming puzzles, I present two final puzzles to you, which have nothing to do with programming. Still, you can learn a lot about problem-solving strategies by answering them. From time to time, something seems impossible at first, and then there is a straightforward solution. If you like, try your hand at the following puzzles:

- Gold bags: Detect the fake

- Horse race: Determine fastest three horses

11.2.1 Gold Bags: Detect the Fake

This puzzle is about 10 gold bags, each filled with 10 coins, each of which weighs 10g. Thus, each gold bag should weigh 100 g. See Figure 11-1.

Figure 11-1. *Gold bags*

But an impostor has exchanged the gold coins in a bag for fakes, which, at 9g instead of 10g per coin, are somewhat lighter. Find the gold bag containing the fakes with only one weighing. However, you may take different numbers of coins from any bag and weigh them together.

Solution

At first, this task sounds almost impossible since multiple weighings and comparings are not allowed. You might come up with the following trick with a bit of pondering: Line up the bags and number them from 1 to 10. Now work position-based and place as many coins from each corresponding bag as matches its position, and then weigh them all together, as shown in Figure 11-2.

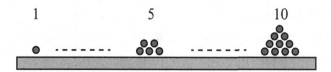

Figure 11-2. *Weighing gold pieces*

Without fakes, the result would be as follows:

$$1 \times 10 + 2 \times 10 + 3 \times 10 + 4 \times 10 + 5 \times 10 + 6 \times 10 + 7 \times 10 + 8 \times 10 + 9 \times 10 + 10 \times 10$$
$$= \quad 10 + 20 + 30 + 40 + 50 + 60 + 70 + 80 + 90 + 100$$
$$= \quad 550$$

Let's assume that bag 5 contains the fakes and look at the result:

$$1 \times 10 + 2 \times 10 + 3 \times 10 + 4 \times 10 + \mathbf{5 \times 9} + 6 \times 10 + 7 \times 10 + 8 \times 10 + 9 \times 10 + 10 \times 10$$
$$= \quad 10 + 20 + 30 + 40 + \mathbf{45} + 60 + 70 + 80 + 90 + 100$$
$$= \quad 545$$

Let's now assume that bag 2 contains the fakes and determine the result:

$$1 \times 10 + \mathbf{2 \times 9} + 3 \times 10 + 4 \times 10 + 5 \times 10 + 6 \times 10 + 7 \times 10 + 8 \times 10 + 9 \times 10 + 10 \times 10$$
$$= \quad 10 + \mathbf{18} + 30 + 40 + 50 + 60 + 70 + 80 + 90 + 100$$
$$= \quad 548$$

According to this, you can identify the corresponding bag based on the difference to 550:

$$550 - weighed\ weight \quad = \quad position$$

11.2.2 Horse Race: Determine Fastest Three Horses

This puzzle is about solving the following: There are 25 racehorses offered for sale, and you want to buy the three fastest. There is a racetrack with space for a maximum of five horses. Still, you have neither a stopwatch nor any other way of measuring time. However, the horses can compete against each other in races, and you may note the order. Under these restrictions, how do you determine the fastest three, and how do you proceed? How many races with which horses do you have to organize at best?

As a simplification, let's assume here that the horses are not exhausted by the races, run exactly the same speed in each race, and also that no two horses are the same speed (just like in a photo finish, there is always an order and a winner).

Solution

Here, too, you have to think quite a bit at first to arrange the right races by a clever exclusion procedure and additionally as few of them as possible. In fact, only seven races are necessary to determine the fastest three horses. How do you go about this?

Step 1   First, you let five horses compete against each other in any five races and thus determine the winners of these races. For better traceability, all horses get a number between 1 and 25, which normally says nothing about the placement. In Figure 11-3 I use the numbers for better distinguishability. It is possible to label the horses just as well with A, B, C, … but then you need further distinctions for the races' winners.

You thus determine the winners from all five races and can directly remove all horses in the respective 4th and 5th places from your selection for the next races by an exclusion procedure.

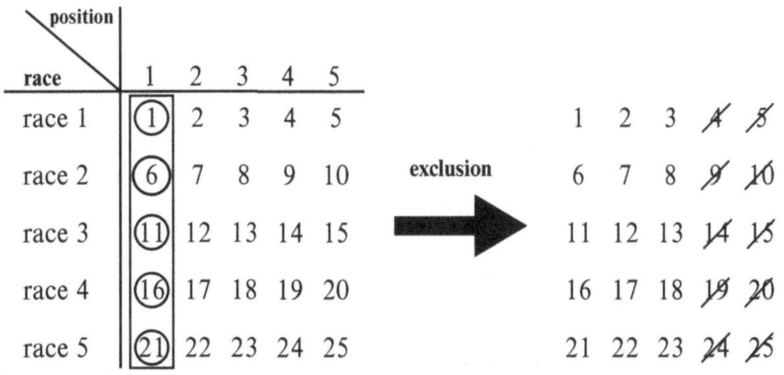

Figure 11-3. *Races 1 to 5*

As a result, 15 horses remain, and if you would like to compare them with each other, at least three races would still be necessary after these five races. According to my statement, however, a total of seven races is enough, so that only two races are still allowed. Consequently, you still have to reduce the number of horses to be compared to suitably.

Step 2   To have significantly less than 15 horses left for further selection, you need to run another race, one with all the winners. Why? So far, you only know something about the horses within the groups themselves, but not between the groups. To get some information about the relative speeds of the winners, you let them race against each other. Again, the last two cannot be among the fastest three horses. See Figure 11-4.

Figure 11-4. *Race of winners*

However, this will automatically eliminate both the horses with numbers 17 and 18 (slower than the horse with number 16) and those with numbers 22 and 23 (slower than the horse with number 21) as candidates.

Step 3   You mark the exclusions in a matrix, and then you combine the gained knowledge to proceed with the next exclusion. To do this, you insert a > notation for "faster than" into the matrix of horses. Because horse 1 also won in the winner's race, you are sure that horse 1 is definitely the fastest. See Figure 11-5.

$$
\begin{array}{l}
\boxed{1} > 2 > 3 \quad \cancel{4} \;\; \cancel{5} \\
\;\;\vee \\
6 > 7 > 8 \quad \cancel{9} \;\; \cancel{10} \\
\;\;\vee \\
11 > 12 > 13 \quad \cancel{14} \;\; \cancel{15} \\
\cancel{16} \;\; \cancel{17} \;\; \cancel{18} \;\; \cancel{19} \;\; 20 \\
\cancel{21} \;\; \cancel{22} \;\; \cancel{23} \;\; \cancel{24} \;\; \cancel{25}
\end{array}
$$

Figure 11-5. *Best 9 at horse racing*

However, there are still nine horses left—actually only eight candidates, since horse 1 is the fastest. That would indicate at least two more races. Let's now consider a bit.

You know the orders by the previous races. Since you want to determine only the fastest three, the horses numbered 8, 12, and 13 are eliminated, and five horses now remain, namely those numbered 2, 3, 6, 7, and 11. See Figure 11-6.

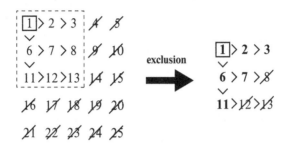

Figure 11-6. *Final exclusion at horse racing*

Thus, you only have to let the other horses (i.e., 2, 3, 6, 7, and 11) compete against each other. The winner and runner-up of this race are the overall second and third horse. This results in the following possible combinations as the final result:

- 1, 2, 3

- 1, 2, 6

- 1, 6, 2

- 1, 6, 7

- 1, 6, 11

11.3 Supplementary Literature

In this book, my main intention was to provide you with a couple of programming exercises and brainteasers and an entertaining time solving them. If the tasks are well solvable for you most of the time, you will find the various books below as supplementary reading.

Interestingly, when dealing with a topic, one always comes across previously unknown literature. Some books inspired me, and I would like to recommend them to you. I grouped the books thematically, and this should serve as a good starting point for further steps.

11.3.1 Introduction to Algorithms and Data Structures

There are various books for getting started with algorithms and data structures. I can recommend the following for completion or a different point of view:

- *Grokking Algorithms* [Bha16] by Aditya Y. Bhargava. A small but fine book, which offers a well readable, comprehensible, and entertaining introduction, and is enriched by many illustrations. The examples, however, are in Python.

- *A Common-Sense Guide to Data Structures and Algorithms* [Wen17] by Jay Wengrow. A wonderful, easy-to-follow book to get started with algorithms and data structures. The extensive illustrations make it easy to follow the steps of the algorithms. Again, the examples are in Python.

- *Problem Solving in Data Structures and Algorithms Using Java* [Jai18] by Hemant Jain. Of the books listed here, this is the most comprehensive and goes far beyond the previous ones in terms of the topics presented. However, it offers fewer explanatory illustrations and is not written as intuitively as the others. This book facilitates the (direct) comprehension of the solutions because Java is used for implementation.

11.3.2 Basic Books

If you like to deep dive more scientifically into the subject of algorithms and data structures as well as learn things from scratch and like it a bit more formal, then take a look at the following books:

- *Algorithms* [Sed11] by Robert Sedgewick. This book provides you with an easy-to-read and comprehensible introduction to the subject. An older edition accompanied me in my university studies back in the 1990s.

- ***Data Structures and Algorithms with Object-Oriented Design Patterns in Java*** [Pre00] by Bruno R. Preiss. This book provides a solid overview of common data structures and shows how to implement them with Java. Because it was written in the year 2000, it does not use generics. Nevertheless, it is my favorite concerning Java and data structures.

- ***Data Structures and Problem Solving Using Java*** [Wei10] by Mark Allen Weiss. This book by Mark Allen Weiss offers a slightly more practical approach than the previous mentioned one. Due to the publication year of 2010, it uses more modern concepts like generics for the implementation of the data structures.

11.3.3 Specializing in Interview Questions

In addition to the basic books mentioned earlier, there are some that focus primarily on interview questions or small programming tasks:

- ***Top 30 Java Interview Coding Tasks*** [Urb18] by Matthew Urban. If you don't have a lot of time and if you are not that interested in background information, this short booklet is definitely something for you. It uses unit tests to check the implementation; unfortunately, it is based on JUnit 4 instead of the newer JUnit 5.

- ***Daily Coding Problem*** [MW19] by Alex Miller and Lawrence Wu. This is another book that provides a lot of information and exercises including solutions on algorithms and data structures. It focuses on small programming tasks for every day and is based on Python.

11.3.4 Supplements for Job Interviews at Top Companies

To prepare for a job interview at one of the top companies, namely Amazon, Apple, Facebook, Google, and Microsoft, I recommend the following books as a supplement to my book. Some of these books go into more depth and offer even trickier tasks or more background knowledge. In addition, all of them describe the interview process itself and how to prepare for it.

- *Cracking the Coding Interview* [McD16] by Gayle Laakmann McDowell. This is a great book by an extremely competent author. However, it is advisable to read a book on algorithms beforehand, so that it is easier for you to follow the explanations. The degree of difficulty of some tasks is challenging in parts.

- *Programming Interviews Exposed* [MKG18] by John Mongan, Noah Kindler, and Eric Giguère. In addition to algorithms and data structures, this book also covers topics such as concurrency, design patterns, and databases. It contains fewer exercises, but very good explanations. The solutions are presented in different programming languages.

- *Elements of Programming Interviews in Java* [ALP15] by Adnan Aziz, Tsung-Hsien Lee, and Amit Prakash. This book covers many different topics, especially data structures and algorithms.

PART III

Appendices

APPENDIX A

Quick Start for JShell

In this book, various examples are tried out directly on the console. This is primarily because Java offers the interactive command line application JShell as a REPL since version 9. In this appendix, you will get to know JShell briefly.

A.1 Java + REPL => `jshell`

The tool `jshell` was integrated in the JDK with Java 9. This tool allows an interactive working style and the execution of small source code snippets, as it is already familiar from various other programming languages. This is also known as REPL (Read-Eval-Print-Loop). Thereby, it becomes possible to write some Java source code and try things out quickly without starting an IDE and creating a project.[1] The magnitude of the benefit is certainly debatable. However, it is convenient that the semicolon requirement is optional for input in the `jshell`. For first experiments and prototyping, it is of even greater advantage that you don't have to worry about handling exceptions, not even Checked Exceptions.[2] You will see this later.

A.1.1 Introductory Example

Let's start the `jshell` and try out some actions and calculations. A variation of a Hello World example serves as a starting point:

```
> jshell
|  Welcome to JShell -- Version 14
|  For an introduction type: /help intro
```

---

[1] Nearly every (professional) developer has his IDE open almost all the time anyway, at least while working. Therefore he could use a `main()` method to do something similar, but with the advantage of direct syntax check and auto-complete.

[2] Exactly: Both apply only to the commands in the `jshell`, but not if you define methods or classes. Then you have to provide a semicolon and handle exceptions.

© Michael Inden 2022
M. Inden, *Java Challenges*, https://doi.org/10.1007/978-1-4842-7395-1_12

```
jshell> System.out.println("Hello JShell")
Hello JShell
```

After that you add two numbers:

```
jshell> 2 + 2
$1 ==> 4
```

Based on the output, you see that the jshell assigns the result of the calculation to a shell variable, which starts with $, here $1.

It is also possible to define your own methods as follows:

```
jshell> int add(int a, int b) {
   ...>      return a + b;
   ...> }
|  created method add(int,int)
```

Conveniently, the jshell recognizes that the statements are not complete and more input is needed in subsequent lines. Only after the completion does the message created method add(int,int) occur.

After the definition is complete, such a method can be invoked as expected. As a special feature, the previously computed result is accessible as follows with $1:

```
jshell> add(3, $1)
$3 ==> 7
```

A.1.2 More Commands and Possibilities

The command /vars lists the currently defined variables:

```
jshell> /vars
|    int $1 = 4
|    int $3 = 7
```

The command /methods displays defined methods, here the just-created method add():

```
jshell> /methods
|    add (int,int)int
```

In addition, the jshell provides a history of commands, which may be useful to execute a previous command repeatedly. To execute the last command again, use /!. When entering /list you get an overview, from where you can execute the <nr>th command with /<nr>:

```
jshell> /list
```

```
  1 : System.out.println("Hello JShell")
  2 : 2+2
  3 :  int add(int a, int b) {
     return a+b;
     }
  4 : add(3, $1)
```

The following keyboard shortcuts simplify editing and navigation in the jshell:

- Ctrl + A/E: Jumps to the beginning/end of a line

- ↑/↓: The cursor keys allow you to navigate through the history of the commands.

- /reset: Clears the command history

You may be not familiar with every possible invocation variant, so the tab completion is quite handy. It presents a set of possible completions similar to an IDE:

```
jshell> String.
CASE_INSENSITIVE_ORDER   class   copyValueOf(   format(   join(   valueOf(

jshell> Class.
class      forName(
```

A.1.3 Using Syntactic Specialties and Modern Java Features

The instruction

```
jshell> Thread.sleep(500)
```

demonstrates two things. On the one hand, you recognize that, as before, it is possible to omit the semicolon for statements in the jshell, and on the other hand, the InterruptedException thrown by Thread.sleep() does not have to be handled.

The definition of lists, sets, and maps is also possible and even quite comfortable with the newer collection factory methods:

```
jshell> List<Integer> numbers = List.of(1,2,3,4,5,6,7)
numbers ==> [1, 2, 3, 4, 5, 6, 7]

jshell> Set<String> names = Set.of("Tim", "Mike", "Max")
names ==> [Tim, Max, Mike]

jshell> Map<String, Integer> nameToAge = Map.of("Tim", 41, "Mike", 42)
nameToAge ==> {Tim=41, Mike=42}
```

After these definitions, let's have a look at the variables again:

```
jshell> /vars
|    int $1 = 4
|    int $3 = 7
|    List<Integer> numbers = [1, 2, 3, 4, 5, 6, 7]
|    Set<String> names = [Tim, Max, Mike]
|    Map<String, Integer> nameToAge = {Tim=41, Mike=42}
```

A.1.4 More Complex Actions

Besides the quite trivial actions shown, the jshell also allows more complex calculations and even the definition of classes.

Including other JDK classes   By default, the jshell can only access types from the module java.base, but this is often enough for several initial experiments. But if you want to use Swing or JavaFX classes, for example, you need an import, like import javax.swing.* for the types like JFrame, etc. Without this import, you get the following error message:

```
jshell> new JFrame("Hello World")
|  Error:
|  cannot find symbol
|    symbol:   class JFrame
|  new JFrame("Hello World")
|      ^----^
```

That is why you now begin with the import:

```
import javax.swing.*
```

```
jshell> new JFrame("Hello World")
$2 ==> javax.swing.JFrame[frame0,0,23,0x0,invalid,hidden,layout=java.awt.
    BorderLayout,title=Hello World,resizable,normal,defaultCloseOperation=
    HIDE_ON_CLOSE,rootPane=javax.swing.JRootPane[,0,0,0x0,invalid,layout=
    javax.swing.JRootPane$RootLayout,alignmentX=0.0,alignmentY=0.0,border=,
    flags=16777673,maximumSize=,minimumSize=,preferredSize=],
    rootPaneCheckingEnabled=true]
```

```
$2.setSize(200, 50)
$2.show()
```

The above command sequence will build and display a window of size 200 x 50. It

Figure A-1. *Simple Swing window started from jshell*

should look something like Figure A-1.

A.1.5 Exiting the JShell

Finally, you can exit the jshell with /exit.

HINT: THE JSHELL AND SOME SPECIAL CHARACTERISTICS

The final keyword is not fully supported by the jshell. This is also true for public and static.

```
jshell> final URI uri = new URI("https://www.oracle.com/index.html");
|  Warning:
|  Modifier 'final' not permitted in top-level declarations, ignored
|  final URI uri = new URI("https://www.oracle.com/index.html");
|  ^---^
uri ==> https://www.oracle.com/index.html
```

Short Introduction to JUnit 5

JUnit is a framework written in Java that supports the creation and automation of test cases. It is easy to learn and takes a lot of work of writing and managing test cases. In particular, only the logic for the test cases themselves needs to be implemented. Thereby the framework supports various methods with which test assertions can be set up and evaluated.

B.1 Writing and Running Tests

B.1.1 Example: A First Unit Test

To test an application class, a corresponding test class is usually written. Often you start to validate the important functionality of your own classes by testing some central methods. It is advisable to extend this step by step. Test cases are expressed as special test methods, which must be marked with the annotation @Test and must not define a return type. Otherwise, they are not considered as a test case by JUnit and will be ignored during test execution.

Let's look at a simple example that merely illustrates what has been said but does not yet test any functionality; rather it just provides a basic framework:

```
import static org.junit.jupiter.api.Assertions.*;

import org.junit.jupiter.api.Test;

class FirstTestWithJUunit5
{
    @Test
    void test()
```

© Michael Inden 2022
M. Inden, *Java Challenges*, https://doi.org/10.1007/978-1-4842-7395-1_13

```
    {
        fail("Not yet implemented");
    }
}
```

The annotation @Test comes from the package org.junit.jupiter.api, and fail() is imported from the class org.junit.jupiter.api.Assertions. The latter are imported statically to allow a shorter notation and better readability when calling the test methods.

B.1.2 Fundamentals of Writing and Running Tests

Now you get to know methods for evaluating conditions. The class Assertions provides a set of test methods, which can be used to express conditions and thus to check assertions about the source code under test:

- The overloaded methods assertTrue() and assertFalse() allow you to check Boolean conditions. The former method assumes that a condition evaluates to true. The opposite is valid for assertFalse().

- Using the overloaded methods assertNull() or assertNotNull() methods, it is possible to check object references for null or not equal to null.

- The overloaded method assertEquals() checks two objects for equality of content (call equals(Object)) or two variables of primitive type for equality. Due to possible rounding inaccuracies in calculations for the float and double types, a maximum deviation from the expected value can be noted.

- Use the overloaded methods assertSame() or assertNotSame() to check object references for equality or inequality according to ==.

- With fail() it is possible to deliberately make a test case fail. This is sometimes useful to be able to react to an unexpected situation.

- JUnit 5 provides a neat way to check if an expected test case fails by using the assertThrows() method.

The following code (JUnit5ExampeTest) shows some of the presented methods in action. Please note that various test methods deliberately provoke errors in this example:

```java
import static org.junit.jupiter.api.Assertions.*;

import org.junit.jupiter.api.Test;

import java.util.List;

public class JUnit5ExampleTest
{
    @Test
    public void testAssertTrue()
    {
        final List<String> names = List.of("Max", "Moritz", "Tom");

        assertTrue(names.size() > 2);
    }

    @Test
    public void testAssertFalse()
    {
        final List<Integer> primes = List.of(2, 3, 5, 7);

        // an error is intentionally provoked here
        assertFalse(primes.isEmpty());
    }

    @Test
    public void testAssertNull()
    {
        assertNull(null);
    }

    @Test
    public void testAssertNotNull()
    {
        // an error is intentionally provoked here
        assertNotNull(null, "Unexpected null value");
    }
```

```java
@Test
public void testAssertEquals()
{
    assertEquals("EXPECTED", "expected".toUpperCase());
}

@Test
public void testAssertEqualsWithPrecision()
{
    assertEquals(2.75, 2.74999, 0.1);
}

@Test
public void testFailWithExceptionJUnit5()
{
    assertThrows(java.lang.NumberFormatException.class, () ->
    {
        // an error is intentionally provoked here
        final int value = Integer.parseInt("Fehler simulieren!");
    });
}
}
```

Testing Multiple Assertions with assertAll()

When formulating test cases, it is often necessary to check multiple conditions, such as the individual parts of an address. With JUnit 5, this semantic bracketing and the execution of all assertions is possible with the method assertAll():

```java
@Test
void assertAachenZipAndCityAndCountry()
{
    final Address address = // ...

    assertAll("Address components",
            () -> assertEquals(52070, address.getZipCode()),
            () -> assertEquals("Aachen", address.getCity()),
            () -> assertEquals("Deutschland", address.getCountry()));
}
```

Test Execution

JUnit is perfectly integrated with popular IDEs. This allows the execution of tests directly from the IDE. To execute tests, you use either the context menu or buttons in the GUI. The output is similar to the one shown in Figure B-1. A red bar indicates errors. Ideally, you will see a *reassuring* green, reporting the successful completion of all test cases.

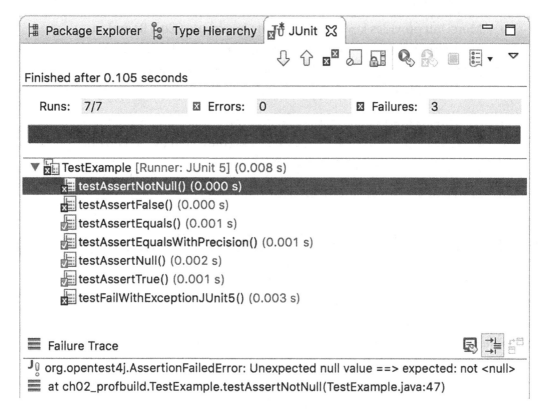

Figure B-1. *Test execution from the GUI of the IDE*

Eclipse plugin MoreUnit

Even if JUnit is well integrated with Eclipse and test cases can not only be executed but even debugged, there is still room for improvement. For example, the keyboard shortcuts for executing unit tests (Alt+Shift+X,T) are rather clumsy. The Eclipse plugin MoreUnit takes care of this and other problems. It is freely available for installation in the Eclipse Marketplace and offers the following features:

- MoreUnit provides keyboard shortcuts to execute (Ctrl+R) and to switch between implementation and unit test of a class (Ctrl+J). If there is no test available, Ctrl+J opens a dialog to create a corresponding unit test.

- An icon decoration is displayed so that you can see directly in the Package Explorer if a test exists for a class (indicated by a green dot).

- During refactoring, classes and corresponding test classes are moved or renamed synchronously to each other.

B.1.3 Handling Expected Exceptions with assertThrows()

Sometimes test cases are supposed to check the raising of exceptions during processing, and an absence would represent an error. An example is the deliberate access to a non-existent element of an array. An `ArrayIndexOutOfBoundsException` should be the result. To handle expected exceptions in the test case so that they represent a test success and not a failure, there are several alternatives.

Since JUnit 5, handling exceptions in test cases got much easier through using the method `assertThrows()`. It fails (produces a test failure) if the executed method does not raise the expected exception. Additionally, the method returns the triggered exception so that further checks can be performed, for example, whether the text of the exception contains the desired and expected information in the text of the exception. The following code is executable as `AssertThrowsTest`:

```java
public class AssertThrowsTest
{
    @Test
    public void arrayIndexOutOfBoundsExceptionExpected()
    {
        var numbers = new int[] { 1, 2, 3, 4, 5, 6, 7 };

        final Executable action = () ->
        {
            numbers[1_000] = 13;
        };

        assertThrows(ArrayIndexOutOfBoundsException.class, action);
    }

    @Test
    public void illegalStateExceptionWithMessageTextExpected()
    {
        final String errorMsg = "XYZ is not initialized";

        final Executable action = () ->
        {
            throw new IllegalStateException(errorMsg,
                                            new IOException("IO"));
        };

        final IllegalStateException exception =
                                assertThrows(IllegalStateException.class,
                                    action);
        assertEquals(errorMsg, exception.getMessage());
        assertEquals(IOException.class, exception.getCause().getClass());
    }
}
```

In this second test case, it gets obvious how easy it is to access the contents of the exceptions (e. g., to check the text or other details).

B.2 Parameterized Tests with JUnit 5

In some cases, you have to test a large number of values. If you had to create a separate test method for each of them, this would make the test class rather bloated and confusing. To solve this more elegantly, there are several variants. All of them have their specific strengths and weaknesses.

In the following, assume that computations use fixed ranges of values or a selected set of inputs.[1]

B.2.1 Introduction to Parameterized Tests with JUnit 5

With JUnit 5, defining parameterized tests is fairly straightforward. Let's start with the scenario where you only want to specify parameters for your test methods and do not want to pass the result. This is handy when only one condition needs to be tested, such as whether a string is non-empty or whether a number is a prime number. You could do both for a small set of given inputs using the annotations @ParameterizedTest and @ValueSource as follows:

```
import org.junit.jupiter.params.ParameterizedTest;
import org.junit.jupiter.params.provider.ValueSource;

// a few errors are produced for demonstration purposest
public class FirstParameterizedTest
{
    @ParameterizedTest(name = "run {index}: ''{0}'' is not empty")
    @ValueSource(strings = { "Tim", "Tom", "", "Mike" })
    void isNotEmpty(String value)
    {
        assertFalse(value.isEmpty());
    }
```

---

[1] For (very) large number of values, it is not a good idea to check all of them. This often significantly increases the unit tests' execution time without providing any (greater) added value. It is especially recommended to use representatives from equivalence classes, which should drastically reduce the number of tests needed. For details, refer to my book *Der Weg zum Java-Profi* [Ind20a].

```java
@ParameterizedTest(name = "run {index}: {0} is a prime")
@ValueSource(ints = { 1, 2, 3, 4, 5, 6, 7 })
void ensureIsPrime(int value)
{
    assertTrue(MathUtils.isPrime(value));
}
}
```

The code shows that each parameterized test must be annotated with @ParameterizedTest. As parameter you can use a string with placeholders in the name attribute. The placeholders have the following meaning: {index} corresponds to the index in the test data, and {0}, {1}, {2}, etc. all reference the parameters and the corresponding data elements, respectively. More often, there will be several inputs, as you will see in the following. Additionally, the test generator needs to know which inputs to test. This information can be specified by @ValueSource, among other things. In the example you use specializations for strings and int values. In addition, there are predefined variants for long and double.

Let's take a quick look at how this all plays out. A separate test case is created and executed for each specified parameter. You get an impression how this will look in Eclipse from Figure B-2. Please keep in mind that a few test bugs have been included for demonstration purposes.

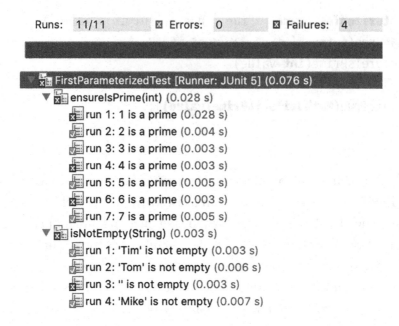

Figure B-2. *Parameterized test cases of the program* `FirstParameterizedTest`

B.2.2 More Practical Parameterized Tests

In practice, however, almost all tests require a tuple of inputs and results. The annotation @CsvSource can help with this. It is possible to create self-contained, comma-separated data for the desired combinations of the respective inputs or parameters for the test method. Reasonably the first or preferably the last parameter represents the expected result. If the last parameter is used, this follows more closely the (European) way of thinking from left to right.

In the following, I show a possible parameterization for reversing a string:

```
@ParameterizedTest(name = "reverse({0}) => {1}")
@CsvSource({ "ABCD, DCBA", "OTTO, OTTO", "PETER, RETEP" })
void testReverse(final String input, final String expectedOutput)
{
    final String result = Ex03_ReverseStringV1.reverse(input);

    assertEquals(expectedOutput, result);
}
```

Another example is the addition of two values, including the expected result. Here you recognize that the textual values are automatically converted to the types used by the parameters:

```
@ParameterizedTest(name = "{index}: {0} + {1} = {2}")
@CsvSource({ "1, 1, 2", "2, -2, 0", "3, 4, 7" })
void testAdd(int first, int second, int expected)
{
    int sum = first + second;

    assertEquals(expected, sum);
}
```

There are predefined conversions ingeniously, for example, for the types from the Date and Time API, and you can write understandable tests with them. In the following code, this is shown for the determination of the first day in the quarter:

```
@ParameterizedTest
@CsvSource({ "2014-03-15, 2014-01-01", "2014-06-16, 2014-04-01",
            "2014-09-15, 2014-07-01", "2014-11-15, 2014-10-01"})
void adjustToFirstDayOfQuarter(LocalDate startDate, LocalDate expected)
{
    final Temporal result = new Ex10_FirstDayOfQuarter().adjustInto(startDate);

    assertEquals(expected, result);
}
```

B.2.3 JUnit Parameterized Tests with @MethodSource

There is one remaining potential difficulty with providing the values. Sometimes the textual specification of the values becomes confusing, or it may not be possible (e.g., for lists). This is shown for a list of input values and an expected result. Therefore there is another way of providing the data as a `Stream<Arguments>`, which is returned by a static method. The method name is specified with `@MethodSource`. Unfortunately, this is only possible textually, but the link is still very intuitive.

```
@ParameterizedTest(name = "removeDuplicates({0}) = {1}")
@MethodSource("listInputsAndExpected")
void removeDuplicates(List<Integer> inputs, List<Integer> expected)
{
    List<Integer> result = Ex02_ListRemove.removeDuplicates(inputs);

    assertEquals(expected, result);
}

static Stream<Arguments> listInputsAndExpected()
{
    return Stream.of(Arguments.of(List.of(1, 1, 2, 3, 4, 1, 2, 3),
                                  List.of(1, 2, 3, 4)),
                     Arguments.of(List.of(1, 3, 5, 7),
                                  List.of(1, 3, 5, 7)),
                     Arguments.of(List.of(1, 1, 1, 1),
                                  List.of(1)));
}
```

APPENDIX C

Quick Start for O-notation

In this book, the so-called O-notation is used to classify the running time of algorithms. This allows a more formal classification of the complexity of algorithms.

C.1 Estimations with O-notation

To estimate and describe the complexity of algorithms and classify their running time behavior, it would be impractical to always take measurements. In addition, measurements only reflect the running time behavior under certain restrictions of the hardware (processor clock, memory, etc.). To be able to classify consequences of design decisions independently of such details and on a more abstract level, computer science uses the so-called *O-notation*, which indicates the upper bound for the complexity of an algorithm. To do so, one would like to be able to answer the following question: *How does a program perform when instead of 1,000 input values, for example, 10,000 or 100,000 input values are processed?* To answer this question, the individual steps of an algorithm must be considered and classified. The aim is to formalize the calculation of complexity to estimate the effects of changes in the number of input data on the program running time.

Consider the following while loop as an introductory example:

```
int i = 0;                  // O(1)
while (i < n)               // O(n)
{
    createPersonInDb(i);    // O(1)
    i++;                    // O(1)
}
```

© Michael Inden 2022
M. Inden, *Java Challenges*, https://doi.org/10.1007/978-1-4842-7395-1_14

Any single instruction is assigned a complexity of $O(1)$. The loop itself is assigned the complexity $O(n)$ due to the n executions of the loop body.[1] Adding these values together, the cost of running the program is thus $O(1) + O(n) * (O(1) + O(1)) = O(1) + O(n)*2$. For an estimation of complexity, constant summands and factors do not matter. Only the highest power of n is of interest. Thus, you get a complexity of $O(n)$ for the program's illustrated piece. This simplification is permissible since, for larger values of n, the influence of factors and smaller complexity classes is insignificant. For the understanding of the considerations in the following sections, this informal definition should be sufficient.

In the following, I would like to quote two sentences by Robert Sedgewick that characterize the O-notation, from his standard work *Algorithms* [Sed92]: "[...] the O-notation is a useful tool for specifying upper bounds on the running time, which are independent of the input data's details and the implementation." It further states "the O-notation proves extremely useful in helping analysts to classify algorithms according to their performance, and by helping algorithms in their search for the *best* algorithms."

C.1.1 Complexity Classes

To be able to compare the running time behavior of different algorithms with each other, seven different complexity classes are usually sufficient. The following list names the respective complexity classes and some examples:

- $O(1)$: The constant complexity results in a complexity that is independent of the number of input data n. This complexity often represents *an instruction* or a simple computation that consists of a few computational steps.

- $O(log(n))$: With logarithmic complexity, the running time doubles when the input data set n is squared. A well-known example of this complexity is *binary search*.

- $O(n)$: In the case of linear complexity, the running time grows proportionally to the number of elements n. This is the case for simple loops and iterations, such as a *search in an array* or a list.

---

[1] The meaning of the notation becomes more understandable on the next page with the presentation of examples for other complexity classes. For a more advanced illustration, see www.linux-related.de/index.html?/coding/o-notation.htm.

- $O(n.log(n))$: This complexity is a combination of linear and logarithmic growth. Some of the fastest *sorting algorithms* (e.g. Mergesort) show this complexity.

- $O(n^2)$: When doubling the amount of input data n, the quadratic complexity leads to a quadrupling of the running time. A tenfold increase in the input data already leads to a hundredfold increase in running time. In practice, this complexity is found with *two nested* for *or* while *loops*. Simple sorting algorithms usually have this complexity.

- $O(n^3)$: With cubic complexity, a doubling of n already leads to an eightfold increase of the running time. The naive *multiplication of matrices* is an example of this complexity class.

- $O(2^n)$: The exponential complexity results for a doubling of n in a squaring of the running time. At first, this does not sound like much. But with a tenfold increase, however, the running time increases by a factor of 20 billion! The exponential complexity occurs frequently with *optimization problems*, for example the so-called *Traveling Salesman Problem*, where the goal is to find the shortest path between different cities while visiting all cities. To cope with the problem of exorbitant running time, the program uses heuristics, which may not find the optimal solution, just an approximation of it, but have much lower complexity and a significantly shorter running time.

Table C-1 shows impressively which effects the mentioned complexity classes have for different sets of input data n.[2]

---

[2] The time complexity $O(2^n)$ is not shown, because its growth is too strong to be expressed meaningfully without the use of powers of 10.

Table C-1. *Effects of Different Time Complexities*

N	O(log(n))	O(n)	O(n.log(n))	O(n²)	O(n³)
10	1	10	10	100	1.000
100	2	100	200	10.000	1.000.000
1.000	3	1.000	3.000	1.000.000	1.000.000.000
10.000	4	10.000	40.000	100.000.000	1.000.000.000.000
100.000	5	100.000	500.000	10.000.000.000	1.000.000.000.000.000
1.000.000	6	1.000.000	6.000.000	1.000.000.000.000	1.000.000.000.000.000.000

Based on the values shown, you get a feeling for the effects of different complexities. Up to about $O(n.log(n))$ the complexity classes are favorable. Optimal and desirable, although not achievable for many algorithms, are the complexities $O(1)$ and $O(log(n))$. Already $O(n^2)$ is usually not favorable for larger input sets, but it can be used for simple computations and smaller values for n without any problems.

NOTE: INFLUENCE OF INPUT DATA

Some algorithms behave differently depending on the input data. For Quick Sort, the average case results in a complexity of $n.log(n)$, but this can increase to n^2 in the extreme case. Since the 0-notation describes the *worst case*, Quick Sort is assigned a complexity of $O(n^2)$.

C.1.2 Complexity and Program Running Time

The numbers calculated by a special O-complexity for a set of input values n may sometimes be daunting. Still, they say nothing about the actual execution time but only about its growth when the input set increases. As already based on the introductory example, the O-notation makes no statement about the duration of individual calculation steps: The increment i++ and the database access createPersonInDb(i) were both rated $O(1)$, even though the database access is several orders of magnitude more expensive than the increment concerning execution time.

For *normal* instructions without accesses to external systems, such as file system, networks, or databases (i.e., additions, assignments, etc.), the impact of n is in many cases not decisive for today's computers for typical business applications with user interactions. The impact on actual runtime hardly really matters for small n (< 1000) at complexities $O(n)$ or $O(n^2)$ and even sometimes at $O(n^3)$ nowadays—but this does not mean that you should not use algorithms that are as optimal as possible. Rather, the reverse is true: You can also start with a first functionally correct implementation and put it into production. The optimized version may be rolled out sometime later.

All in all, I would like to emphasize once again that even multiple nested loops with the complexity $O(n^2)$ or $O(n^3)$ are often executed much faster in absolute terms than some database queries over a network with complexity $O(n)$. The similar is true for a search in an array ($O(n)$) and access to an element of a hash-based data structure ($O(1)$). For small n, the computation of the hash values can take longer than a linear search. However, the larger n gets, the more the impact of the worse complexity class affects the actual running time.

Bibliography

[ALP15] Adnan Aziz, Tsung-Hsien Lee, and Amit Prakash. *Elements of Programming Interviews in Java*. 2015.

[Bha16] Aditya Y. Bhargava. *Grokking Algorithms*. Manning, 2016.

[Ind20a] Michael Inden. *Der Weg zum Java-Profi*. dpunkt.verlag, 5 edition, 2020.

[Ind20b] Michael Inden. *Java - die Neuerungen in Version 9 bis 14: Modularisierung, Syntax- und API-Erweiterungen*. dpunkt.verlag, 2020.

[Jai18] Hemant Jain. *Problem Solving in Data Structures & Algorithms Using Java*. 2nd edition, 2018.

[McD16] Gayle Laakmann McDowell. *Cracking the coding interview*. CareerCup, 6th edition, 2016.

[MKG18] John Mongan, Noah Kindler, and Eric Giguère. *Programming Interviews Exposed*. Wrox, 4th edition, 2018.

[MW19] Alex Miller and Lawrence Wu. *Daily Coding Problem*. 2019.

[Pre00] Bruno R. Preiss. *Data Structures and Algorithms with Object-Oriented Design Patterns in Java*. Wiley, 2000.

[Sed92] Robert Sedgewick. *Algorithmen*. Addison Wesley, 1992.

[Sed11] Robert Sedgewick. *Algorithms*. Addison Wesley, 4th edition, 2011.

[Urb18] Matthew Urban. *Top 30 Java Interview Coding Tasks*. net-boss, 2018.

[Wei10] Mark Allen Weiss. *Data Structures and Problem Solving Using Java*. Pearson, 4th edition, 2010.

[Wen17] Jay Wengrow. *A Common-Sense Guide to Data Structures and Algorithms*. The Pragmatic Programmers, 2017.

© Michael Inden 2022
M. Inden, *Java Challenges*, https://doi.org/10.1007/978-1-4842-7395-1

Index

A

Abstract Syntax Tree (AST), 565
Addition rule, 20, 51
Algorithms, 3, 12, 17, 217, 730
allDesiredNumbers()
     method, 302, 304
Anagram, 155, 186
Arabic numerals, 21
Armstrong numbers, 22, 29, 62
Array min, 110, 111
Arrays, 722
  container functionality, 211
  definition, 211
  flood fill, 244
    algorithm, 310
    example, 310, 313, 314
    verification, 311, 314, 315
  inplace rotate
    iterative, 263–266
    recursive method, 267
    verification, 268
  jewels board erase diamonds
    examples, 280, 282–284
    falling down, 285–287
    type char, 291
    verification, 284, 285, 288–290
  jewels board init
    diagonal check, 275
    initialize, 269–271, 273, 274
    validity check, 277
    verification, 276, 278

merge, 245
Minesweeper board, 248, 249
    example, 332, 333
    verification, 333–336, 338, 339
multidimensional, 225
one-dimensional, 212
solution
    add one array as number, 299–302
    arrays split, 325
    even before odd
      numbers, 250–255
    flip, 255, 256, 258, 259
    merge, 316, 318–320
    min and max, 321–324
    palindrome, 260–262
spiral traversal, 292, 293, 295–298
split
    example, 325, 326, 329, 330
    implace method, 327, 328
    quick sort partition, 328
    verification, 331
Sudu checker
    bonus, 306, 307
    implementation, 304, 305
    verification, 306, 308, 309
typical errors, 234, 235
Write method void
    orderEvenBeforeOdd(int[], 236
Array sum, 108, 109
assertAll() method, 744
assertThrows() method, 746, 747

B

Printed in the United States
by Baker & Taylor Publisher Services